A User's Guide to Data Protection: Law and Pol

Dedication

To Joseph and Frank

A User's Guide to Data Protection: Law and Policy

Fifth edition

Dr Paul Lambert BA, LLB, LLM, TMA, CTMA, PhD

Adjunct Lecturer, Lawyer, Certified Data Protection Officer, Consultant

Visiting Research Fellow, Institute of Advanced Legal Studies, University of London

Bloomsbury Professional

LONDON · DUBLIN · EDINBURGH · NEW YORK · NEW DELHI · SYDNEY

BLOOMSBURY PROFESSIONAL

Bloomsbury Publishing Plc

50 Bedford Square, London, WC1B 3DP, UK

1385 Broadway, New York, NY 10018, USA

29 Earlsfort Terrace, Dublin 2, Ireland

BLOOMSBURY and the Diana logo are trademarks of Bloomsbury Publishing Plc

First published in Great Britain 2023

Copyright © Bloomsbury Professional, 2023

British Library Cataloguing-in-Publication Data

A catalogue record for this book is available from the British Library.

ISBN:	PB:	978 1 52652 728 8
	ePDF:	978 1 52652 730 1
	ePub:	978 1 52652 729 5

Typeset by Compuscript Ltd, Shannon
Printed and bound by CPI Group (UK) Ltd, Croydon, CR0 4YY

To find out more about our authors and books visit
www.bloomsburyprofessional.com. Here you will find extracts, author information,
details of forthcoming events and the option to sign up for our newsletters

Contents

Contents

Contents

Contents

Contents

'Our measures are designed to support businesses in their use of data, and give consumers the confidence that their data is protected and those who misuse it will be held to account.'[1]

'We are pleased the government recognises the importance of data protection, its central role in increasing trust and confidence in the digital economy and the benefits the enhanced protections will bring to the public.'[2]

'[P]ersonal data … are more and more processed and archived.'[3]

The importance of consent[4] cannot be overestimated.

'There is an inherent security issue with many of these online exchanges which if often overlooked. Emails are not particularly secure.'[5]

'A blog [or social networking post] is a bit like a tattoo: a good idea at the time but you might live to regret it.'[6]

[1] Minister of State for Digital, Matt Hancock, referred to in 'Government to Strengthen UK Data Protection Law,' Department for Digital, Culture, Media & Sport and The Rt Hon Matt Hancock MP, 7 August 2017.
[2] Information Commissioner Elizabeth Denham, referred to in 'Government to Strengthen UK Data Protection Law,' Department for Digital, Culture, Media & Sport and The Rt Hon Matt Hancock MP, 7 August 2017.
[3] Davies, C, Editorial, *Communications Law*, (2012)(17), pp 38–39.
[4] Costa, L., and Poullet, Y, 'Privacy and the Regulation of 2012,' *Computer Law & Security Review*, (2012)(28), pp. 254–262, at 256.
[5] Ferretti, F, 'A European Perspective on Data Processing Consent Through the Re-Conceptualisation of European Data Protection's Looking Glass After the Lisbon Treaty: Taking Rights seriously,' *European Review of Private Law*, (2012)(20), pp. 473–506.
[6] Davies, C, Editorial, *Communications Law*, (2012)(17), pp. 38–39.

Abbreviations

These abbreviations shall be used throughout.

Commission:	means the EU Commission;
Controller:	the organisation collecting, processing and holding the personal data (previously called the Data Controller) (see DPD and GDPR detailed definitions below);
Data Subject:	the individual who the personal data relates to (see DPD and GDPR detailed definitions below);
DPA:	Data Protection Act;
DPA 2018:	UK Data Protection Act 2018 (as amended);
DPD:	EU Data Protection Directive 1995 (Directive 95/46/EC of the European Parliament and of the Council of 24 October 1995 on the protection of individuals with regard to the processing of personal data and on the free movement of such data);
DPDI Bill:	Data Protection and Digital Information (No 2) Bill;
DPO:	Data Protection Officer;
EDPB:	European Data Protection Board (pursuant to the GDPR);
EEA:	means the European Economic Area, comprising the EU plus Iceland, Liechtenstein and Norway. (Note, Switzerland has a similar type arrangement with the EU);
ePD:	Directive 2002/58/EC of the European Parliament and of the Council of 12 July 2002 concerning the processing of personal data and the protection of privacy in the electronic communications sector (Directive on privacy and electronic communications). This is also known as the ePrivacy Directive (ePD)(being replaced by the ePrivacy Regulations);
ePR:	the ePrivacy Regulation replacing the ePR (Proposal for a Regulation of the European Parliament and of the Council concerning the respect for private life and the protection of personal data in electronic communications and repealing Directive 2002/58/EC (Regulation on Privacy and Electronic Communications);

Abbreviations

GDPR:	EU General Data Protection Regulation;
	Regulation (EU) 2016/679 of the European Parliament and of the Council of 27 April 2016 on the protection of natural persons with regard to the processing of personal data and on the free movement of such data, and repealing Directive 95/46/EC (General Data Protection Regulation) (Text with EEA relevance) OJ L 119, 4.5.2016, p 1–88; (The GDPR replaces the DPD and is directly effective throughout the EU without the need for separate sets of national implementing legislation);
	There is a two year implementation deadline from the date of official publication, in May 2016;
IC:	Information Commission;
ICO:	Information Commissioner's Office ie the main UK data protection supervisory authority;
ICO:	Information Commission's Office ie the proposed new UK data protection supervisory authority;
Member State:	means a member State of the European Union (EU);
PEC:	Privacy and Electronic Communications
PECR:	Privacy and Electronic Communications (EC Directive) Regulations 2003 (as updated following the ePrivacy Regulation);
PECR Amendment:	Privacy and Electronic Communications (EC Directive) (Amendment) Regulations 2011;
Personal data:	Any data or information identifying or relating to the individual data subject (see DPD and GDPR detailed definitions below);
Processor:	An outsourced third party organisation or related entity carrying out certain defined outsourced activities for and on behalf of the main data controller with the personal data eg outsourced payroll, outsourced direct marketing, etc. (previously called the Data Processor)(see DPD and GDPR detailed definitions below);
UK GDPR:	UK version of the EU General Data Protection Regulations;
WP29:	Article 29 Working Party on Data Protection (replaced by EDPB).

Table of Cases

Table of Cases

Table of Cases

Table of Statutes

Table of Statutes

Table of Statutory Instruments

Table of Statutory Instruments

Table of EU Regulations

Table of EU Regulations

Table of European Directives

Table of Treaties, Conventions and Agreements

Part I
Data Protection

How to Comply with the Data Protection Regime

Chapter 1

Data Protection

What is Data Protection?

1.01 Data protection aims to protect the private personal information of individuals. It provides a regulatory protection regime around personal information, or personal data. Personal data is data or information which relates to or identifies, directly or indirectly, an individual.

The data protection legal regime governs if, when and how organisations may collect, use and process personal data. It also provides for how long they may use such data. The logical conclusion, and which is also specified in the rules, is that data must also be deleted after a certain period.

This applies to all sorts of personal information, from general to highly confidential and sensitive. Examples of the latter include sensitive health data and details of criminal convictions. Indeed, over time more and more forms of personal data have come to exist. It is interesting to note that while the formal data protection regime came about in large part as a result of electronic computing and electronic databases, recent developments in terms of artificial intelligence (AI), AI chatbot ChatGPT, and new forms of data collections may serve to turbo charge consideration of the adequacy of current data protection laws and whether they need to be strengthened. As an indication of these growing concerns the Italian data regulator has banned ChatGDP over data collection, lack of permission, and data breach concerns.[1]

The data protection regime is twofold in the sense of: (a) providing obligations (which are inward-facing and outward-facing, see below) which organisations must comply with; and (b) providing individuals or Data Subjects as they are known, with various data protection rights which they or the Information Commissioner's Office (ICO) (proposed to be replaced with a new Information Commission, hence the Information Commission's Office (ICO)) can invoke or enforce as appropriate. Significantly, recent measures expand the ability to invoke the data protection rights to privacy groups and collective data protection organisations including in group or class type actions (see the EU General Data Protection Regulation (GDPR)). The Data Protection Act 2018 (DPA 2018) and GDPR and UK GDPR brings 'comprehensive reform'[2] to the UK and EU data protection regimes. The previous Data Protection Act 1998 is now repealed.[3] There is also a proposal, in the form of the Data Protection and Digital Information (No 2) Bill, to further amend the DPA 2018 and UK GDPR.

---

1 Milmo, D, 'Italy's Privacy Watchdog Bans ChatGPT Over Data Breach Concerns,' *Guardian*, 1 April 2023.

Certain specific sections of industry and certain specific activities (eg data transfers abroad, direct marketing, cookies and other advertising data collection and profiling technologies), also have additional data protection compliance rules.

In terms of individuals, they can invoke their rights directly with organisations, with the ICO, and also via the courts in legal proceedings. Compensation can also be awarded. In addition, criminal offences can be prosecuted. Data protection compliance is, therefore, very important. From a business perspective, commercial customers increasingly look to the compliance status and past data breach record of the parties that they propose to do business with. Data protection is also an important feature in mergers and acquisitions and asset purchases. Data protection, data mapping and vetting, and due diligence also apply in these situations.

As regards implementing compliance frameworks, an organisation must have defined structures, policies and teams in place to ensure that it knows what personal data it has, for what purposes, ensure that it is held fairly, lawfully and in compliance with the data protection regime, and that it is safely secured against damage, loss and unauthorised access – an increasing problem. All employees must also be aware of their and the company's data protection compliance obligations. The cost of loss, and of data security breach, can be significant both financially and publicly. The IBM Cost of Data Breach Study (2022) puts the average cost at $9.44m (up from $3.92m in 2019). (Interestingly, it also suggests that companies using AI can reduce these costs, and the length of time required in dealing with a data breach. Social media companies also seek to use AI to assist in dealing with certain problem issues.) The UK TalkTalk data breach is estimated at costing £35m. The Target data breach was estimated as costing €162m plus a 5.3 per cent drop in sales. More recent data breaches have led to drops of 40% of share price value and even business closures. Breaches which are criminal offences can be prosecuted. In addition, personal liability can attach to organisational personnel separate and in addition to liability of the organisation itself, in addition to reprimand or even dismissal. It is very important to appreciate, therefore, the wide variety of financial and non-financial costs that can arise from data breaches. (These costs can also arise in other aspects of data law non-compliance apart from data security and data breaches.)

The Importance of Data Protection

1.02 One Editorial notes that the 'waves of [data protection concern are] riding high.'[4] This was even before concerns arising with AI, ChatGPT and new technological forms of data collections. The increasing 'centralisation of information through the computerisation of various records has made the right of [data protection and of] privacy a fundamental concern.'[5] Data protection is important, increasingly topical and an issue of legally required compliance for all organisations. More importantly, it is part of management and organisational best practice. Executives have lost their employment positions relating to data breach and data non-compliance issues. Individuals, employees and customers expect that their personal data will be respected by organisations. They are increasingly aware of their rights, and increasingly they enforce their rights.

---

2   In Brief, *Communications Law* (2012) (17) 3.
3   Data Protection Act 2018, Sch 19, Pt 1, s 43.
4   Editorial, S Saxby, *Computer Law & Security Review* (2012) (28) 251–253, at 251.
5   'Personal Data Protection and Privacy,' Counsel of Europe, at http://www.coe.int/en/.

1.03 The coverage of data protection and data related issues has also increased in the mainstream media. This is due in part to a large number of data loss and data breach incidents. These have involved the personal data of millions of individuals being lost by commercial organisations, but also trusted government entities.

Issues surrounding online abuse, which involves amongst other things privacy and data protection, has also been hitting the headlines. Personal data has become weaponised – and well beyond the fears of the policy makers who foresaw the need to introduce the original data protection laws. Tragically, such online abuse can unfortunately contribute to actual suicide. This is a particular concern in relation to children and teenagers, but it can also affect adults. One would like to think that the vast majority of online content and activity is beneficial and positive, and that small but significant in nature problem areas need remediation. There are some, however, that will suggest the scale of these problem areas are bigger than imagined, and that past and even current remediation efforts are not yet sufficient or proportionate.

Data protection is also in the headlines because of public and official data protection supervisory authority (eg, ICO; Digital, Culture, Media and Sport (DCMS) Committee) concerns with the problem of data misuse and the damage of 'permanent' data online. The CJEU in the light of such concerns issued an important decision in the *Google Spain* case involving the Right to Erasure/Right to be Forgotten (RtbF) directing that certain personal data online had to be deleted, following a complaint, from internet search engine listing results.[6] The High Court also dealt with RtbF in *NC 1* and *NC 2*.[7] Further RtbF cases include *GC and Others*,[8] and *Google v CNIL*,[9] and no doubt more will follow. There is a steady stream of RtbF notices being sent to online entities.

The CJEU also pronounced on the often contentious area of official data retention. This is the obligation placed by countries on (certain) internet service providers (ISPs) to retain certain customer data in relation to telephone calls, internet searches, etc, so that (certain) official agencies can ask to access or obtain copies of such data in the future. Debate frequently surrounds whether this should be permitted at all, if so, when, and under what circumstances, how long ISPs must store such data, the cost of retaining same, etc. The strongest argument for an official data retention regime may relate to the prevention or investigation of terrorism and imminent terrorist attack. Serious crime may come next in terms of priority. There are legitimate concerns that the privacy and data protection costs are such that official data retention, if permitted, should not extend to 'common decent crime' or unlimited access and unlimited retention. The EU Data Retention Directive has held invalid and similar laws in Member States including the UK have also been invalidated, in whole or in part.[10] No doubt

---

6   See Google Spain SL, *Google Inc v Agencia Española de Protección de Datos (AEPD)*, Mario Costeja González, Court of Justice (Grand Chamber), Case C-131/12, 13 May 2014. Also see P Lambert, *The Right to be Forgotten* (Bloomsbury, 2019).

7   *NT 1 & NT 2 v Google LLC* [2018] EWHC 799 (QB).

8   *GC and Others v Commission Nationale de l'Informatique et des Libertés (CNIL) (Déréférencement de données sensibles)*, CJEU [2019] Case C-136/17.

9   *Google LLC, successor in law to Google Inc v Commission Nationale de l'Informatique et des Libertes (CNIL)*, CJEU [2019] Case C-507/17.

10 Judgment in Joined Cases C-293/12 and C-594/12, *Digital Rights Ireland and Seitlinger and Others*, Court of Justice, 8 April 2014. Directive 2006/24/EC of the European Parliament and of the Council of 15 March 2006 on the retention of data generated or processed in connection with the provision of publicly available electronic communications services or of public communications networks and amending Directive 2002/58/EC (OJ 2006 L105, p 54). J Rauhofer and D Mac Sithigh, 'The Data Retention Directive Never Existed,' (2014) (11:1) SCRIPTed 118. The Data Retention and Investigatory Powers Act 2014 (DRIPA 2014) was invalidated after challenge by two MPs. This was brought in

argument, debate and research will ensue in relation to data retention. Some of the concerns are that too much data is held, for too long, and that too many official agencies may seek to access the data once held. The mandated data retention regime will remain, if anything, a contentious area.

While the issues of official mandates data retention are important, it is a separate subject to general data protection. This work focuses specifically on data protection and not data retention.

A further reason as to why data protection is important, and increasingly the focus of press attention, is that organisations are increasingly using data security and respect for data protection as a commercial differentiator in the marketplace. Apple has repeatedly indicated that it does not operate on a user-data-intrusive model collecting user data. In fact, it has even criticised some of its technology competitors. Microsoft has for many years promoted the data protection and privacy friendly policy of Data Protection by Design (DPbD) and by default. Post-Snowden, many US technology companies have been heavily lobbying the US administration for a roll back of certain activities and practices, particularly those felt to be extra-judicial and extra-legal, on the basis that it will disadvantage the US-based cloud industry. Many non-US cloud companies have been highlighting that they are not US-based. There are even calls for more data privacy laws in the US, including adopting parts of the GDPR in the US. Many notable US tech companies have also joined the calls for a comprehensive US federal data privacy law. There is also a developing movement amongst commercial entities around what is referred to as 'data trust' and becoming more data trusted entities – especially in terms of consumer facing issues.

I.04 All organisations collect and process personal data. Whether they are big or new start-ups, they need to comply with the data protection regime. It should also be borne in mind that even a new technology start-up can scale relatively quickly to millions of users. Many issues enhance the importance of getting organisational data protection understanding and compliance right from day one. These include legal obligations, director, board and officer obligations, investigations, data fines, prosecutions, being ordered to *delete* databases, adverse publicity, commercial imperatives and even commercial advantages. There can also be a considerable cost of remediation when problem issues and or non-compliance gap areas are discovered. If one also considers some of the recent large scale data breach incidents, there are examples of chief technology officers as well as managing directors/CEOs, losing their positions as a result of the incident.

Increasingly, data laws seek to place compliance burdens which start well before any personal data may collected in the first instance. This includes data risk assessments and tools such as privacy by design (PbD), data protection by design (DPbD), and data protection by default.

I.05 In addition, organisations often fail to realise that data protection compliance is frequently an issue of dual compliance. They need to be looking both *inward* and *outward*. Internally, they have to be data protection compliant in relation to all of their employees' (and contractors') personal data, which traditionally may have related to HR or personnel files and employee contracts, but now includes issues of electronic

---

after the Directive was invalidated. The second replacement Act (Investigatory Powers Act 2016) was also successfully challenged by Liberty. In relation to data protection as a fundamental right, see, for example S Rodata, 'Data Protection as a Fundamental Right,' in S Gutwirth, Y Poullet, P de Hert, C de Terwangne and S Nouwt, *Reinventing Data Protection?* (Springer, 2009) 77. A case dealing with the issue of how serious the level of crime must be in order for law enforcement authorities to be able to access certain telecoms data is *Ministerio Fiscal*, CJEU [2018] Case C-207/16.

communications, social media, internet usage, filtering, monitoring, abuse, on-site activity, off-site activity, etc.

1.06 Separately, organisations have to be concerned about other sets of personal data, such as those relating to persons outside of the organisation, eg customers, prospects, etc. Comprehensive data protection compliance is also required here. The consequences are significant for non compliance, regardless of whether the data is inward or outward facing, but naturally outward facing breach issues tend to get more attention.

1.07 Substantial fines have been imposed in a number of recent cases, both nationally and internationally. In some instances also, organisations have been ordered to delete their databases. In a new internet or technology start-up situation, this can be the company's most valuable asset. Even in an established organisation, it can be a valuable asset and mandated deletion by a data regulator is a significant event. It can affect the commercial activities of the company, impact sales, and follow through into reduced company value.

1.08 Up until recently the issue of data loss was a small story. More recently, however, the loss of personal data files of tens of millions of individuals in the UK – and from official governmental sources – makes UK data loss a front page issue. There is increased scrutiny from the ICO, and others, and increasing regulation of data security issues, preparedness, and reactivity. In many examples a data breach event can also affect the data of individuals across a number of jurisdictions, and depending on technical architecture, could involve data held in more than one location. Organisations must look at data security issues with increasing rigour. Organisations can face liability issues in breach incidents but also in the aggravating situation where a vulnerability may have already been highlighted internally but not acted upon, thus contributing to the breach incident. As well as an official investigation, data fine and sanction, organisations also face liability issues to users and in some instances potentially to banks and financial intermediaries. Organisations must be proactive and compliant. Being reactive only when a breach event occurs is going to be, in many respects, too late.

1.09 In the UK and elsewhere there are enhanced obligations to report data breaches and data losses; as well as potentially enhanced financial penalties, and in some instances personal director responsibility for data breach and loss. The need for compliance is now a boardroom issue and an important issue of corporate compliance. Proactive and complete data protection compliance is also a matter of good corporate governance, brand loyalty, maintaining firm value, having loan and investment capability, sale value, and a means to ensuring user and customer goodwill (but not necessarily in that order).

1.10 The frequency and scale of breaches of security eg, Uber, Cathay Pacific, Dixons, Morrisons, Yahoo! (500 million users in one breach, and 3 billion in another), 3 UK, CEX, Bupa, TalkTalk, Target, Sony Playstation (70 million individuals' personal data[11] in one instance, and 25 million in another[12]) and Cambridge Analytica make the importance of data security compliance for personal data ever more important.

---

11 See, for example, G Martin, 'Sony Data Loss Biggest Ever,' *Boston Herald*, 27 April 2011.
12 See, for example, C Arthur, 'Sony Suffers Second Data Breach With Theft of 25m More User Details,' *Guardian*, 3 May 2011.

The Revenue and Customs loss of discs with the names, dates of birth, bank and address details involved 25 million UK individuals.[13] The US has also had a number of notable data breach incidents.

1.11 There are many UK cases involving substantial fines for data protection breaches. Brighton and Sussex University Hospitals NHS Trust was fined £325,000 by the ICO.[14] Zurich Insurance was fined £2.3m for losing data in relation to 46,000 customers.[15] Sony was fined £250,000. Facebook was fined £500,000 (re Cambridge Analytica). DSG Retail was fined £500,000 when 14 million customers were affected.[16] Cathay Pacific airlines was also fined £500,000 after data security failings over four years.[17] A pharmacy (Doorstep Dispensaree) was fined £275,000 for failing to secure 500,000 records data.[18] The rideshare company Uber was fined £385,000 by the ICO.[19] Fines also increase under the GDPR and UK GDPR.

Apart from data loss incidents and data security breach incidents, a range of other compliance failings have also been fined. Bounty (UK) was fined £400,000 for illegal sharing and disclosure of personal data.[20] CRDNN was fined £500,000 for 193 million illegal automated marketing calls.[21] The size of the penalty is significant. However, possibly more significant is director liability. Directors and executives can also be fined. Two individual Spam texters were fined a total of £440,000 in respect of their company.[22] They can also be prosecuted, as exemplified when a managing director was prosecuted.[23] The ICO also issued a data fine in relation to breach of the data protection regime by way of incorrect storage and processing when the financial data and files of individual customers were mixed up. Potentially, a customer could have suffered financial loss and adverse consequences.[24] In another case, a health trust was fined £225,000 in relation to third party unauthorised access to files.[25] It is perhaps worrying that a number of health sector related entities have been investigated and fined over data issues. Employees have been prosecuted for unauthorised access to personal records.[26] It is clearly worrying where employees access personal data files that they should not, and worse where these use such data or even disclose such data. It raises data security issues, processes, questions regarding training, and also personal responsibility. The GDPR, UK GDPR, and DPA 2018 vastly increase the potential fines available (up to €20m or 4% of worldwide turnover). We can expect the level of data fines on organisations to increase.

---

13 See, for example, 'Brown Apologises for Record Loss, Prime Minister Gordon Brown has said he "Profoundly Regrets" the Loss of 25 Million Child Benefit Records,' *BBC*, 21 November 2007.

14 See, for example, 'Largest Ever Fine for Data Loss Highlights Need for Audited Data Wiping,' *ReturnOnIt*, at http://www.returnonit.co.uk/largest-ever-fine-for-data-loss-highlights-need-for-audited-data-wiping.php.

15 See, for example, J Oates, 'UK Insurer Hit With Biggest Ever Data Loss Fine,' *The Register*, 24 August 2010. This was imposed by the Financial Services Authority (FSA).

16 *ICO v DSG Retail Limited* [2020] 9/1/2020.

17 *ICO v Cathay Pacific Airways Limited* [2020] 4/3/2020.

18 *ICO v Doorstep Dispensaree* [2019] 20/12/2019.

19 *ICO v Uber* [2018] 26/11/2018.

20 *ICO v Bounty (UK) Limited* 11/4/2019.

21 *ICO v CRDNN* [2010] 2/3/2020.

22 *ICO v Christopher Niebel and Gary McNeish* (2012). ICO, 'Spam Texters Fines Nearly Half a Million Pounds' at https://ico.org.uk. However, note that this was appealed.

23 *ICO v Cullen* [2019] 24/6/2019.

24 Prudential was fined £50,000. *ICO v Prudential* [2012] 6/11/2012.

25 Belfast Health and Social Care (BHSC) Trust. ICO, 'Belfast Trust Fines 22,5000 After Leaving Thousands of Patient Records in Disused Hospital,' at https://ico.org.uk.

26 For example, ICO, 'Bank Employee Fined for Reading Partners Ex Wife Statements' at https://ico.org.uk. Also *ICO v Shaw* [2019] 5/12/2019; *ICO v Shipsey* [2019] 2/12/2019.

1.12   National data protection authorities are increasingly pro-active and undertake audits of data protection compliance frameworks, as well as incidents of breaches.[27] The ICO also investigated some of the personal data issues in the Leveson Inquiry press phone hacking scandal,[28] entitled Operation Motorman.[29] Media phone hacking cases are still ongoing. With the GDPR and UK GDPR, organisations will also have to engage with the ICO where risk related processing operations are envisaged and when data protection impact assessments are carried out – all in advance of any data collections whatsoever having occurred. (Note that there are potential changes and amendments in respect of data risk assessments and if, and when, the ICO must be consulted or notified, per the Data Protection and Digital Information (No 2) Bill.)

The Data Protection Regime

1.13   Personal data protection is enshrined in the DPA 2018 in the UK, and the UK GDPR. (The GDPR is directly effective and applicable in each EU state in addition to national legislation). As a consequence of Brexit occurring (in particular following the EU (Withdrawal Agreement) Act 2020 in January 2020) we might expect further changes, and perhaps even more confusion. Following a recent consultation process, there is a proposal to amend the DPA 2018 and UK GDPR with a new Data Protection and Digital Information (No 2) Bill. It contains a wide variety of additions and changes.

Outward-Facing Data Protection Compliance

1.14   The data protection regime creates legal obligations which organisations must comply with when collecting and processing the personal data of individuals. '[I]f someone can be distinguished from other people, data protection legislation is applicable.'[30] This applies to customers and prospective customers, hence there are outward-facing obligations. It can also apply to non-customers who may be using a particular website but are not a registered customer, if their personal data are being collected. There are certain changes proposed in relation to how personal data or personal information is defined in the Data Protection and Digital Information (No 2) Bill.

Inward-Facing Data Protection Compliance

1.15   The data protection regime also applies to the organisation in its dealings regarding the personal data of its employees. Equally, where the organisation is engaging third party independent contractors but is collecting, processing and using their personal data, the data protection regime will also apply. Hence, the data protection regime in relation to organisations is inward-facing.

1.16   As well as creating legal compliance obligations for organisations, the data protection regime enshrines certain rights or data protection rights for individuals in terms of ensuring their ability to know what personal data are being collected, to

---

27   Facebook was audited by one of the EU data protection authorities. See https://dataprotection.ie. Note also Europe Against Facebook, at http://europe-v-facebook.org/EN/en.html.
28   At https://www.gov.uk/government/organisations/leveson-inquiry.
29   For more details see 'Operation Motorman – Steve Whittamore Notebooks,' ICO website, at https://www.ico.org.uk.
30   L Costa and Y Poullet, 'Privacy and the Regulation of 2012,' *Computer Law & Security Review* (2012) (28) 254 at 256.

consent – or not consent – to the collection of their personal data, and to control the uses to which their personal data may be put. There is also a mechanism through which individuals can complain to Controllers holding their personal data, the ICO, and also via the courts directly.

Information Commissioner/Information Commission

1.17 In order to ensure that the duties are complied with, and the rights of individuals vindicated, there is an official data protection supervisory authority (SA) established to monitor and act as appropriate in relation to compliance with and the efficient operation of the data protection regime. This role is fulfilled in the UK by the Information Commissioner (and the associated Information Commissioner's Office (ICO)). The Data Protection and Digital Information (No 2) Bill proposes to abolish the office of the Information Commissioner – but to replace the office with an Information Commission (see Part 5 of the DPDI Bill, clauses 100–103, and also Schedule 13).

Data Protection Rules

1.18 Why have a data protection regime? We have a data protection regime because of the legal, societal, and political recognition that society respects the personal privacy and informational privacy of individuals. In the context of data protection, that means respect for, control of, and security in relation to informational personal data. The DPA 2018 and UK GDPR protects personal data relating to individuals, which includes employees, contractors, customers and users.

Data protection exists in order to ensure:

- protection and regulation of the collection, use, processing and transfer of personal information;
- protection in relation to personal information;
- the consent of individuals is obtained to collect and process personal data;
- security in respect for the right to privacy and personal information;
- protection against privacy and informational privacy abuse;
- protection against privacy theft and identity theft;
- protection against unsolicited direct marketing (DM);
- remedies are available to individual Data Subjects.

The threats to personal data and informational privacy have increased as the ease with which personal data can be collected and transferred electronically. This has increased further with digital technology, computer processing power increases, Internet 2.0, social media, and now AI and AIs.[31] The threat also increases as new tech advances create more categories of data which can be collected and commercialised (even during a pandemic).

Summary Data Protection Rules

1.19 Controllers must comply with a number of data protection issues, perhaps the foremost of which relate to:

---

31 Note generally, comments of the ICO in relation to Privacy by Design (PbD), and the report *Privacy by Design*, at https://www.ico.org.uk.

- fairness;
- transparency;
- consent;
- accuracy;
- data security;
- proper procedures for processing;
- proportionality of the need and use of personal data;
- risk assessments;
- training.

The collecting, use and onward transfer of personal data must be fair, lawful and transparent.

Transparency (and access to a person's personal data) is increasingly being emphasised in importance in relation to the internet and social media sphere. Recent releases of iterations of AIs will also spur an important delate, and potential data ethics and new data law rules. These issues are arguably only beginning to be examined. Companies and websites need to make improvements, even including the implementation of better privacy policies and statements, reporting mechanisms and procedures. These also need to be assessed at the front and back end. In the earlier *Prudential* case where a fine of £50,000 was issued, there was potential financial loss to the Data Subject. In the *True Visions* case, individuals were filmed in a maternity ward for a TV programme without proper diligence, transparency and consent. This resulted in a fine of £120,000.[32] The practice of selling personal data can also have adverse consequences for individuals. Bounty (UK) was fined for data selling and data brokering, and also questionable data collection practices. The ICO imposed a fine of $400,000.[33] Data regulators in a number of countries are concerned with and considering the data issues involved with so called data broker firms, and even the wider data broker industry.

The personal data must be correct and accurate. The reason is that damage or harm to the individual Data Subject can be a consequence of inaccurately held personal data. For example, a credit rating could be adversely affected through incorrect or wrong personal data records regarding personal payment histories. An as yet underconsidered area is the data protection issues surrounding deep fake videos, particularly those which are of a sexual nature or otherwise seek to abuse or attack an individual. (A separate consideration will be the extent to which the laws of defamation may be applied to sexual and abuse type deep fake videos.)

There is a detailed obligation in terms of safeguarding personal data. Organisations must assess and implement data security measures to protect personal data. Increasingly, this is also being considered in relation to the developing cloud environment and the increasing use of Processors and third parties.[34]

There has been an obligation on Controllers to register or notify the ICO as regards their data processing activities.

If personal data is permitted to be transferred to third countries, it must qualify under a specific exemption, as well as the general security conditions. (Note that the

---

32 *ICO v True Visions Productions* [2019] 10 April 2019.
33 *ICO v Bounty (UK) Limited* [2019] 11 April 2019.
34 In relation to cloud generally, see *W Kuan Hon and Christopher Millard*, 'Data Export Cloud Computing – How Can Personal Data be Transferred Outside the EEA? The Cloud of Unknowing,' SCRIPTed (2012) (9:1); G Singh and S Mishra, 'Cloud Computing Security and Data Protection: A Review,' International Journal of Computers & Technology (2015) (14:7) 5887; F Pfarr, T Buckel and A Winkelmann, 'Cloud Computing Data Protection – A Literature Review and Analysis,' 2014 47th Hawaii International Conference on System Sciences (2014) 5018.

issue of the EU-US data transfers via the Privacy Framework exemption mechanism is of particular import, given that the Court of Justice has invalidated the EU-US Safe Harbour Agreement mechanism[35], and also the later EU-US Privacy Shield. The UK now needs to address how it might legitimately transfer UK and EU data to the US (and elsewhere). This may not be without difficulty, but there are new and developing UK data transfer rules. In addition, the Data Protection and Digital Information (No 2) Bill seeks to make further provision in relation to UK data transfer rules. This is an important but developing area.)

Controllers can have a duty of care to individuals as regards their personal data being processed by the organisation, particularly if loss or damage arises.

Controllers and Processors have obligations in certain circumstances to have legal contracts in place between them. Processors process and deal with personal data for, and on behalf of, a Controller in relation to specific defined tasks, eg activities such as outsourced payroll, Personnel, marketing, market research, customer satisfaction surveys, etc. Additional issues and considerations arise for cloud services and data protection compliance. From an organisational perspective, it is sometimes considered that organisational customers have less opportunity to negotiate clauses in cloud service provider contracts, including Processor and security related contracts. There is, therefore, a greater obligation to be satisfied with the cloud service provider, where data is located and the security measures and security documentation available.

General Criteria for Data Processing

1.20 Generally, in order to lawfully collect and process personal data, a Controller should be aware that:

- the individual Data Subject must consent to the collection and processing of their personal data;
- the Data Subject may say that they object to processing or continued processing;
- legal data protection requirements are complied with;
- the prior information requirements, Principles of data protection, Lawful Processing Conditions, Sensitive/Special Personal Data Lawful Processing Conditions (in the case of sensitive/special personal data), and data security obligations are required to be complied with;
- the rights and interests of the individual Data Subject must be respected and complied with.

The interests of the Controller can sometimes be relevant in particular instances in deciding what data processing is necessary and permitted.

Data Protection Overview

1.21 The DPA 2018 and UK GDPR set out a number of structures, obligations, rights and implementing criteria which are together the basis of the legal data protection regime in the UK.

---

35 *Schrems v Commissioner*, Court of Justice, Case C-362/14, 6 October 2015. The case technically related to Prism and Facebook Europe and transfers to the US. However, the wider import turned out to be the entire EU-US Safe Harbour Agreement and data transfers to the US.

The main criteria and obligations to be respected and complied with in order to be able to legally collect and process personal data include:

- the definitions of personal data and the data protection regime;
- the data Principles of data protection, previously known as the 'data quality principles';
- the Lawful Processing Conditions;
- the requirement that processing of personal data be 'legitimate' under at least one of the Lawful Processing Conditions;
- recognising the two categories of personal data covered by the data protection regime, namely, *sensitive/special* personal data and *non-sensitive/special* general personal data;
- in the case of sensitive/special personal data, complying with the additional Sensitive/Special Personal Data Lawful Processing Conditions;
- ensuring the fair obtaining of all personal data collected and processed;
- taking and ensuring appropriate data security measures in relation to all processing activities;
- implementing formal legal contracts when engaging or dealing with third party Processors (eg outsourcing data processing tasks or activities);
- complying with the separate criteria in relation to *automated decision making processes* or *automated decisions*;
- complying with the legal criteria for direct marketing (DM);
- a duty of care exists in relation to the individual Data Subjects whose personal data the organisation is collecting and processing;
- the jurisdictional transfer of personal data is strictly controlled. Personal data may not be transferred unless specifically permitted under the data protection regime;
- access requests, or requests by individuals for copies of their personal data held by the organisation, must be complied with (with limited exceptions);
- identify processing risk situations in advance;
- implementing internal data protection policies and terms;
- implementing outward facing data protection policies for customers, etc;
- implementing outward facing website privacy statements (generally a data protection policy covers organisation-wide activities, whereas a website privacy statement governs only the online collection and processing of personal data);
- implementing mobile, computer and internet usage policies;
- implementing data loss, data breach, incident handling and incident reporting policies and associated reaction plans;[36]
- keeping abreast of the increasing trend towards sector/issue specific rules eg Spam; direct marketing (DM); industry codes of conduct[37] in relation to personal data, etc;
- complying with new legal developments;
- complying with the new *pre-data* requirements eg risk assessments; data protection by design and default;
- training for employees.

---

36 Note, for example, the ICO PECR security breach notifications – guidance for service providers, at https://www.ico.org.uk.
37 The DPA and the EU data protection regime provide for codes of conduct being agreed with national data protection authorities such as the ICO in relation to specific industry sectors.

Lawful Processing

1.22   There is a prohibition on the collection and processing of personal data and special personal data unless:

- the processing complies with the Principles of data protection; and
- the processing comes within one of a limited number of specified conditions (the Lawful Processing Conditions);
- the processing must also comply with the data security requirements.

Definitions

1.23   The data protection regime contains a number of key definitions. These are central to understanding the data protection regime, and ultimately complying with it. These are essentially the building blocks of the data protection regime. While these can be 'complex concepts,'[38] organisations need to fully understand them. Some examples of the matters defined include:

- Data Subject;
- Controller;
- Processor;
- personal data;
- processing;
- special personal data.

The definitions are found in greater detail in Chapter 3.

---

38   D Hallinan, M Friedewald and P McCarthy, 'Citizens' Perceptions of Data Protection and Privacy in Europe,' *Computer Law & Security Review* (2012) (28) 263.

Chapter 2

Sources of Data Protection Law

Introduction

2.01 Organisations and individuals need to consider a number of sources of the law and policy underpinning the data protection regime. In addition, there are a growing number of sources of interpretation and understanding of data protection law. Reliance on the Data Protection Act 2018 (DPA 2018) and UK GDPR (or the EU General Data Protection Regulation (EU GDPR)) alone can, therefore, be insufficient. Data protection is therefore arguably quite different from many other areas of legal practice. In order to fully understand the data protection regime, one has to look beyond the text, or first principles, of the DPA 2018 and UK GDPR (and as same may be amended by the Data Protection and Digital Information (No 2) Bill once finalised and enacted).

What are the sources of data protection law and policy?

UK DPA 2018

2.02 Primarily, the data protection regime in the UK is governed by the DPA 2018 and the GDPR (and previously EU Data Protection Directive 1995 (DPD 1995)). (Note that Brexit will bring an end to the direct effect of the GDPR in the UK. While this should have ceased from 31 January 2020 given the EU (Withdrawal Agreement) Act 2020 of that date, the intention appears to be that the GDPR will continue during the formal transition period for final negotiations with the EU, which are (currently) scheduled to end on 31 December 2020). In addition, it is also necessary to have regard to a number of other sources of law, policy and the interpretation of the data protection regime, as well as any amendments to same. Ultimately, Brexit will necessitate further data protection regulation in the UK, and this will also be required to be reviewed in addition to the DPA 2018. (See also Chapter 24 below.)

UK GDPR

2.03 The UK GDPR is the second main part of the UK data protection regime. The intention is that it reflects all or most of the same provisions and requirements as are contained in the EU GDPR, but applicable to the UK only. Prior to the Brexit final date, the EU GDPR was directly effective in the UK. Once Brexit occurred, this ceased to be the case. However, for a variety of reasons, one being to demonstrate a high level of equivalence between UK and EU standards of data protection (for data transfer and other purposes), a new UK based measure was needed. This came to be the UK GDPR. The effect is that in order to properly consider UK data protection rules, one must consult both the DPA 2018 and UK GDPR (and subsequent amendments).

The EU data transfer Adequacy Decision can also be considered under this category. This is the instrument by which data transfers from the EU to the UK are now permitted. It is important for a variety of reasons.

DPDI Bill

2.04 The proposed Data Protection and Digital Information (No 2) Bill (DPDI Bill) seeks to amend the UK DPA 2018 and the UK GDPR. It makes amendments and introduces entirely new provisions. It also replaces the Information Commissioner with an Information Commission as the new data regulator. There are 114 clauses and 13 Schedules. These will need careful review as it gets closer to adoption, and ultimate implementation.

UK Secondary Legislation

2.05 In addition to DPA 2018 and UK GDPR, various statutory instruments need to be considered, which include:

- Data Protection (Adequacy) (Republic of Korea) Regulations 2022;
- Protection of Freedoms Act 2012 (Destruction, Retention and Use of Biometric Data) (Transitional, Transitory and Saving Provisions) (Amendment) Order 2022;
- Data Protection Act 2018 (Amendment of Schedule 2 Exemptions) Regulations 2022;
- Data Protection, Privacy and Electronic Communications (Amendments etc) (EU Exit) Regulations 2020;
- Criminal Justice and Data Protection (Protocol No 36) Amendment (Scotland) Regulations 2020;
- Data Protection Act 2018 (Commencement No 3) Regulations 2019;
- Data Protection Act 2018 (Commencement No 2) Regulations 2019;
- Data Protection (Charges and Information) (Amendment) Regulations 2019;
- Data Protection, Privacy and Electronic Communications (Amendments etc) (EU Exit) Regulations 2019;
- Data Protection Act 2018 (Commencement No 1 and Transitional and Saving Provisions) Regulations 2018;
- Data Protection (Charges and Information) Regulations 2018;
- Protection of Freedoms Act 2012 (Destruction, Retention and Use of Biometric Data) (Transitional, Transitory and Saving Provisions) (Amendment) Order 2016;
- Protection of Freedoms Act 2012 (Destruction, Retention and Use of Biometric Data) (Transitional, Transitory and Saving Provisions) (Amendment) Order 2015;
- Data Protection Act 1998 (Commencement No 4) Order 2015;
- Data Protection (Assessment Notices) (Designation of National Health Service Bodies) Order 2014;
- Criminal Justice and Data Protection (Protocol No 36) (Amendment) Regulations 2014;

- Criminal Justice and Data Protection (Protocol No 36) Regulations 2014;
- Protection of Freedoms Act 2012 (Destruction, Retention and Use of Biometric Data) (Transitional, Transitory and Saving Provisions) (Amendment) (No 2) Order 2013;
- Protection of Freedoms Act 2012 (Destruction, Retention and Use of Biometric Data) (Transitional, Transitory and Saving Provisions) (Amendment) Order 2013;
- Protection of Freedoms Act 2012 (Destruction, Retention and Use of Biometric Data) (Transitional, Transitory and Saving Provisions) Order 2013;
- Data Protection (Processing of Sensitive Personal Data) Order 2012;
- Data Protection (Subject Access Modification) (Social Work) (Amendment) Order 2011;
- Etc.

It is also necessary to look out for any repeals, amendments or replacements to the above. In addition, the following need to be considered:

- Data Protection Act 2018 (Commencement No 3) Regulations 2019;
- Data Protection, Privacy and Electronic Communications (Amendments etc) (EU Exit) (No 2) Regulations 2019;
- Data Protection (Charges and Information) (Amendment) Regulations 2019;
- Data Protection, Privacy and Electronic Communications (Amendments etc) (EU Exit) Regulations 2019;
- Protection of Freedoms Act 2012 (Destruction, Retention and Use of Biometric Data) (Transitional, Transitory and Saving Provisions) (Amendment) Order 2018;
- Data Protection Act 2018 (Commencement No 1 and Transitional and Saving Provisions) Regulations 2018;
- Data Protection (Charges and Information) Regulations 2018;
- Protection of Freedoms Act 2012 (Destruction, Retention and Use of Biometric Data) (Transitional, Transitory and Saving Provisions) (Amendment) Order 2016;
- Protection of Freedoms Act 2012 (Destruction, Retention and Use of Biometric Data) (Transitional, Transitory and Saving Provisions) (Amendment) Order 2015.

Notwithstanding that there may be additional primary legislation in order to bring the remainder of the GDPR into UK law after direct effect ceases, and given that the DPA 2018 does not fully incorporate the GDPR, there is wide provision for secondary legislation generally in relation to Brexit issues and it is expected that there will be further data protection specific secondary legislation.

EU Data Protection Law

2.06   The main sources of EU data protection law include:

- GDPR;
- ePR (as enacted)
- Directive 2002/58 on Privacy and Electronic Communications (ePrivacy Directive) amended by Directive 2009/136 (Cookie Regulation Directive);
- Regulation (EC) No 45/2001 on the protection of personal data by EU institutions;[1]

---

1   Regulation (EC) No 45/2001 of the European Parliament and of the Council of 18 December 2000 on the protection of individuals with regard to the processing of personal data by the EU institutions and bodies and on the free movement of such data, Regulation (EC) No 45/2001, OJ L 8, 12.1.2001.

- Regulation (EU) No 910/2014 of the European Parliament and of the Council of 23 July 2014 on electronic identification and trust services for electronic transactions;[2]
- Commission Implementing Regulation (EU) 2018/151 laying down rules for application of Directive (EU) 2016/1148 as regards further specification of the elements to be taken into account by digital service providers for managing the risks posed to the security of network and information systems.[3]

It is also necessary to constantly keep abreast of all amendments to same.

The DPA 2018 and UK GDPR are arguably the most important developments in UK data protection since 1995 (see Part 4). There are significant implications for organisations and data protection practice. Of course, that is not to downplay the significance of Brexit and the changes it brings to the UK data protection regime – and importantly to UK international relationships relating to data protection and data transfers.

Case Law

2.07 Increasingly data protection cases (and cases which involve direct or indirect reference to personal data and information impacting the data protection regime) are coming to be litigated and determined before the courts.

One of the reasons is that individuals are increasingly aware of and concerned about their rights under the data protection regime. A further reason is technological developments have enhanced the potential abuse of personal data, from Spam, unsolicited direct marketing (DM), hacking and data loss, phishing, email and internet scams, online abuse, data transfers, access to personal data, etc, and litigation related to personal data.

The case law which is relevant, whether influential or binding, to applying and interpreting the UK data protection regime include:

- case studies and documentation from the ICO;
- case complaints adjudicated by the ICO and or Tribunal;
- cases in England and Wales;
- cases in Scotland;
- cases in Northern Ireland;
- EU Court of Justice cases (CJEU)(previously ECJ);
- European Court of Human Rights (ECHR) cases;
- relevant cases in other EU states and/or Common Law jurisdictions.

Some of the relevant cases are summarised and referenced herein. The increasing impact of cooperation between data regulators and indeed sometimes joint investigations, should also be considered as they become more influential.

---

2   Regulation (EU) No 910/2014 of the European Parliament and of the Council of 23 July 2014 on electronic identification and trust services for electronic transactions in the internal market and repealing Directive 1999/93/EC.

3   Commission Implementing Regulation (EU) 2018/151 of 30 January 2018 laying down rules for application of Directive (EU) 2016/1148 of the European Parliament and of the Council as regards further specification of the elements to be taken into account by digital service providers for managing the risks posed to the security of network and information systems and of the parameters for determining whether an incident has a substantial impact, C/2018/0471.

Indeed, as data regulator cases elsewhere can also be influential in the subsequent investigation by the ICO of the same issues as they may relate to UK Data Subjects. There are clear examples of corporations being involved in data cases in more than one jurisdiction.

ICO Guides

2.08   The ICO provides a number of guides and interpretations in relation to specific data protection issues and industry sectors. These include guides and guidance for:

- Brexit;
- apps, online and electronic devices;
- audits;
- Big Data;
- Cambridge Analytica;
- CCTV;
- charity;
- child data;
- construction blacklists;
- credit and finance;
- crime mapping;
- criminal, court and police records;
- data processing;
- Data Protection by Design (DPbD);
- data protection by default and by design;
- Data Protection Officers;
- data risk assessment and data protection impact assessments;
- data sharing;
- data subject access;
- data protection – general;
- deletion;
- the new DPA 2018;
- Driver and Vehicle Licensing Agency (DVLA);
- drones;
- education;
- elected officials;
- electoral register;
- electronic communications and marketing;
- employment;
- encryption;
- finance;
- fundraising;
- the GDPR and implications of GDPR for the UK;
- health;
- health records;
- housing;
- identity theft;
- identity scanning;
- international transfer;
- marketing;
- media;

- monetary penalties;
- online;
- online and electronic devices;
- Operation Motorman;
- personal data;
- political campaigning and personal data;
- Principles of data protection;
- privacy and electronic communications – general;
- privacy notice;
- relevant filing system;
- RFID tags;
- Sandbox and research in relation to data protection issues;
- schools, universities and colleges;
- security;
- spam;
- spatial information;
- telecommunications.[4]

These will no doubt continue expand with the increasing importance of respective data protection issues.

ICO Determinations

2.09   In addition, there is a body of decided decisions in relation to complaints filed by individuals with the ICO on various issues. These include the ICO's Office in England and Wales[5] and the ICO's Office in Scotland.[6] They can assist in considering identical and similar situations regarding issues of data protection compliance.[7]

Legal Textbooks

2.10   There are an increasing number of data protection legal textbooks and guides. Frequently also, IT legal textbooks will have chapters or sections dedicated to data protection. Some examples of the former include:

- *Data Protection Law and Practice*, Rosemary Jay (4th edn);
- *Data Protection Law and Practice*, Supplements, Rosemary Jay;
- *The Data Protection Officer, Profession, Rules and Role*, Paul Lambert (2017);
- *Data Protection and Data Transfers Law*, Paul Lambert (2023);
- *Guide to the General Data Protection Regulation: A Companion to Data Protection Law and Practice*, Rosemary Jay, William Malcolm, Ellis Parry, Louise Townsend, and Anita Bapat;
- *Understanding the New European Data Protection Rules*, Paul Lambert (2017);
- *The Right to be Forgotten*, Paul Lambert (2019);
- *Data Protection, Privacy Regulators and Supervisory Authorities*, Paul Lambert (2020);

4   See https://ico.org.uk.
5   At https://ico.org.uk/.
6   At https://ico.org.uk/about_us/our_organisation/scotland.aspx.
7   In relation to the ICO and National Authorities generally regarding data protection not DPD; and also Greenleaf, G, 'Independence of Data Privacy Authorities (Part 1): International Standards,' *Computer Law & Security Review* (2012) (28) 3–13.

- *EU Data Protection Law*, Denis Kelleher and Karen Murray (2017);
- *Transatlantic Data Protection in Practice*, Rolf H. Weber and Dominic Staiger (2017);
- *Emerging Challenges in Privacy Law: Comparative Perspectives*, David Lindsay, Moira Paterson, and Sharon Rodrick (2014);
- *Data Protection: The New Rules*, Ian Long (2016);
- *Data Protection Strategy*, Richard Morgan and Ruth Boardman (2012);
- *Data Protection Law and International Dispute Resolution*, Daniel Cooper and Christopher Kuner (2017);
- *Data Protection Compliance in the UK: A Pocket Guide*, Rosemary Jay and Jenna Clarke (2008);
- *Data Protection: Law and Practice*, Rosemary Jay and Angus Hamilton (2007);
- *Data Protection Law*, David Bainbridge (2005);
- *Data Protection Toolkit*, Alison Matthews (2014);
- *Reforming European Data Protection Law (Law, Governance and Technology Series/Issues in Privacy and Data Protection)*, Serge Gutwirth and Ronald Leenes (2015);
- *Protecting Privacy in Private International and Procedural Law and by Data Protection: European and American Developments*, Burkhard Hess (2015);
- *Market Integration Through Data Protection: An Analysis of the Insurance and Financial Industries in the EU (Law, Governance and Technology Series)*, Mario Viola de Azevedo Cunha (2015);
- *The Foundations of EU Data Protection Law*, Dr Orla Lynskey (2015);
- *Data Protection for Photographers: A Guide to Storing and Protecting Your Valuable Digital Assets*, Patrick H Corrigan (2014);
- *Data Protection on the Move: Current Developments in ICT and Privacy/Data Protection*, Serge Gutwirth and Ronald Leenes (2016);
- *The Emergence of Personal Data Protection as a Fundamental Right of the EU*, Gloria González Fuster (2014);
- *Privacy in the Age of Big Data: Recognizing Threats, Defending Your Rights, and Protecting Your Family*, Hon Howard A Schmidt and Theresa M Payton (2015);
- *Data Protection and the Cloud: Are the Risks Too Great?*, Paul Ticher (2015);
- *Data Protection: A Practical Guide to UK and EU Law*, Peter Carey (2018);
- *Property Rights in Personal Data, A European Perspective*, Nadezhda Purtova (2012);
- *Data Protection: Legal Compliance and Good Practice for Employers*, Lynda AC Macdonald (2008);
- *Data Protection in the Financial Services Industry*, Mandy Webster (2006);
- *Data Protection and Compliance in Context*, Stewart Room (2007);
- *European Data Protection Law: Corporate Compliance and Regulation*, Christopher Kuner (2007);
- *Data Protection for Financial Firms: A Practical Guide to Managing Privacy and Information Risk*, Tim Gough, ed (2009);
- *Data Protection for Voluntary Organisations*, Paul Ticher (2009);
- *Data Protection for Virtual Data Centers*, Jason Buffington (2010);
- *Effective Data Protection: Managing Information in an Era of Change*, Mandy Webster (2011);
- *Data Protection & Privacy: Jurisdictional Comparisons*, Monika Kuschewsky, ed (2012);
- *Implementation of the Data Protection Directive in Relation to Medical Research in Europe*, D Beyleveld *et al* (2005);

- *Research Ethics Committees, Data Protection and Medical Research in European Countries*, D Beyleveld, D Townend and J Wright (2005);
- *Data Protection and Employment Practices*, Susan Singleton (2005);
- *Data Protection: A Practical for Employers*, Engineering Employers' Federation (2005);
- *The New Data Protection Liabilities & Risks for Direct Marketers: Handbook*, Rosemary Smith, and Jenny Moseley (2005);
- *Data Protection in the NHS*, Murray Earle (2003);
- *Data Protection Strategy, Implementing Data Protection Compliance*, Richard Morgan and Ruth Boardman (2012);
- *Data Protection & the Pensions Industry: Implications of the Data Protection Act*, Clare Fawke & Louise Townsend (2002);
- *Data Protection Law: Approaching its Rationale, Logic and Limits*, Lee A Bygrave (2002);
- *Regulating Spam: A European Perspective After the Adoption of the E-Privacy Directive*, L Asscher, and SA Hoogcarspel (2006);
- *Information and Decisional Privacy*, Madeleine Schachter (2003);
- *Privacy on the Line, The Politics of Wiretapping and Encryption*, Whitfield Diffie and Susan Landau (1998);
- *European Data Protection Law: Corporate Regulation and Compliance*, Christopher Kuner (2007);
- *Report on the Implementation of the Data Protection Directive (95/46/EC)* (ie the DPD);
- *Encyclopaedia of Data Protection.*

Some examples of the latter include:

- *Gringras, The Laws of the Internet*, Paul Lambert, editor (2018);
- *Information Technology and Intellectual Property Law*, David Bainbridge (2019);
- *EU Internet Law: Regulation and Enforcement*, Christiana Markou and Thalia Prastitou (2017);
- *New Technology, Big Data and the Law (Perspectives in Law, Business and Innovation)*, Marcelo Corrales and Mark Fenwick (2017);
- *Face Detection and Recognition: Theory and Practice*, Asit Kumar Datta and Madhura Datta (2015);
- *Information Technology Law*, Diane Rowland and Uta Kohl (2016);
- *International Handbook of Social Media Laws*, Paul Lambert (2014);
- *E-Commerce and Convergence: A Guide to the Law of Digital Media*, Mike Butler ed (2012);
- *Information Technology Law*, Ian J Lloyd (2017);
- *Information Technology Law: The Law and Society*, Andrew Murray (2013) (chapters 18 and 19);
- *Concise European IT Law*, Alfred Büllesbach *et al* (2010);
- *Information Technology Law*, Andrew Murray (2016);
- *The EU Regulatory Framework for Electronic Communications Handbook*, Michael Ryan (2010);
- *Law and the Internet*, Lilian Edwards and Charlotte Waelde eds (2009) (chapters 14–21);
- *Introduction to Information Technology Law*, David Bainbridge (2008);
- *Internet Law and Regulation*, Graham JH Smith (2018);
- *Information Technology Law*, Diane Rowland, Elizabeth Macdonald (2005);
- *Computer Law: The Law and Regulation of Information Technology*, Chris Reed and John Angel, eds (2007) (chapters 10 and 11);

- *Outsourcing – The Legal Contract*, Rachel Burnett (2005);
- *Outsourcing IT: The Legal Aspects: Planning, Contracting, Managing and the Law*, Rachel Burnett (2009);
- *A Business Guide to Information Security: How to Protect Your Company's IT Assets, Reduce Risks and Understand the Law*, Alan Calder (2005);
- *The New Legal Framework for E-Commerce in Europe*, L Edwards, ed (2005);
- *Communications Law Handbook*, Mike Conradi, ed (2009);
- *Government and Information: The Law Relating to Access, Disclosure and their Regulation*, Birkinshaw and Varney (2012).

Legal Journals

2.11 There are also relevant learned journals and articles published in relation to data protection compliance and developing data protection issues. Some examples include:

- *Data Protection Law and Practice*;
- *Communications Law*;
- *Journal of Information Law and Technology*;
- *Computers and Law* from the Society of Computers and Law, at www.scl.org;
- *SCRIPTed*;
- *Computer Law and Security Review*;
- *IT Law Today*;
- *International Journal for the Data Protection Officer, Privacy Officer and Privacy Counsel*.

EDPB

2.12 In terms of the interpretation and understanding of the data protection regime in the UK, the European Data Protection Board (EDPB) (established under Article 68 of the GDPR) is also required to be consulted. (Previously this was effectively the WP29).[8] This is an influential body in relation to addressing and interpreting the data protection regime as well as problem areas in data protection practice. It is also influential as it is comprised of members from the respective data protection authorities in the EU, previously including the ICO.

The EDPB is available at https://edpb.europa.eu. It has also issued guidance such as:

- certification mechanisms;
- data transfers;
- deceptive design patterns in social media;
- binding corporate rules;
- personal data breach notification under GDPR;
- facial recognition technology;
- the calculation of administrative fines under the GDPR;
- codes of conduct;
- right of access;

8   WP29 was established under Article 29 of the DPD.

- the concepts of controller and processor in the GDPR;
- virtual voice assistants;
- the legal basis for the storage of credit card data for the sole purpose of facilitating further online transactions;
- the targeting of social media users;
- connected vehicles and mobility related applications;
- data protection by design and by default;
- criteria of the Right to be Forgotten in the search engines cases under the GDPR (Part 1);
- consent;
- scientific research;
- video devices;
- information note on data transfers under the GDPR in the event of a no-deal Brexit;
- information note on BCRs for companies which have ICO as BCR Lead Supervisory Authority;
- Data Protection Officer;
- data protection impact assessments
- high risk processing;
- personal data breach notifications.
- automated decision-making and profiling;
- lead supervisory authority.

Previous WP29 issued working papers, opinions and related documentation, available at:

- http://ec.europa.eu/justice/data-protection/article-29/documentation/opinion-recommendation/index_en.htm.

There are also addition opinions, guidelines, recommendations and best practice documentation – which are very influential as the EDPB is composed of members of the respective data regulators and other officials.

European Data Protection Supervisor

2.13 The European Data Protection Supervisor is also worth consulting and is arguably increasing in prominence and importance. Details are at:

- http://www.edps.europa.eu/EDPSWEB/edps/EDPS.

Council of Europe

2.14 There are various important reference materials in relation to data protection and privacy emanating from the Council of Europe (with over 46 Member States), such as:

- Council of Europe Convention on data protection, No 108 of 1981;
- Convention 108 + Convention for the protection of individuals with regard to the processing of personal data;
- Recommendation R(85) 20 on Direct Marketing;
- Recommendation R(86) 1 on Social Security;
- Recommendation R(97) 1 on the Media;

- Recommendation R(97) 5 on Health Data;
- Recommendation CM/Rec (2014)4 on electronic monitoring;
- Democratic and effective oversight of national security services;
- etc.

These and other documents are available at: http://www.coe.int/t/dghl/standardsetting/dataprotection/Documents_TPD_en.asp.

The Council of Europe Convention on data protection[9] of 1981 predates the DPD and GDPR and is incorporated into the national law of many EU and other states (40 plus) prior to the DPD. The Council of Europe is also reviewed and updating the Convention,[10] now called Convention 108 + (pronounced Convention 108 plus).

Other Data Protection Authorities

2.15 Issues which may not yet be decided or formally reported on in the UK can sometimes have been considered elsewhere. It can, therefore, be useful to consider the decisions and logic behind decisions, reports and opinions of:

- Data protection authorities of other EU and EEA states;
- Data protection authorities of other states eg Canada.

The European Data Protection Supervisor provides links to the data protection authorities in the EU at:

- http://ec.europa.eu/justice/policies/privacy/nationalcomm/index_ en.htm.

Other Official Sources

2.16 Related issues can sometimes arise under freedom of information legislation.

Tribunals can also be relevant, such as the Leveson Inquiry, particularly in terms of protection for personal data, security, deliberate breaches, hacking, etc, and the ICO and Operation Motorman. The report and recommendations of the Leveson Inquiry are of interest from a data protection perspective (see below, Part 4).

Key/Topical Issues

2.17 Some of the key developments and issues which also influence the data protection regime and how it is interpreted include:

- data transfers and data transfer legitimising mechanisms (both UK and EU);
- data security breach incidents;
- data compliance breach incidents;

---

9 Convention for the Protection of Individuals with regard to Automatic Processing of Personal Data, Council of Europe (1982). 'Draft Convention for the Protection of Individuals with Regards to Automatic Processing of Personal Data,' *International Legal Materials* (1980) (19) 284–298.

10 See S Kierkegaard et al, '30 Years On – The Review of the Council of Europe Data Protection Convention 108,' *Computer Law & Security Review* (2011) (27) 223–231; G Greenleaf, 'Modernising Data Protection Convention 108: A Safe Basis for a Global Privacy Treaty,' *Computer Law & Security Review* (2013) (29) 430–436; P de Hert and V Papakonstantinou, 'The Council of Europe Data Protection Convention Reform: Analysis of the New Text and Critical Comment on its Global Ambition,' *Computer Law & Security Review* (2014) (30:6) 633.

- insurance for data breach incidents, which can be a complex and evolving market;
- preparedness and team preparations for incidents arising;
- risk assessments;
- data protection and privacy impact assessments;
- mandated Data Protection Officers (DPOs) in organisations;
- UK changes re mandated Data Protection Officers (DPOs) in organisations;
- deletion, take down, erasure and the Right to be Forgotten;
- security requirements for business;
- employee monitoring and consent;
- spam and direct marketing;
- the relationship between the Controller and the Processor, and which relationship needs to be formalised in contract pursuant to the DPA, UK GDPR, and GDPR;
- disposal of computer hardware. Particular care is needed when considering the disposal of IT hardware, equipment and software. They may still contain personal data files. This can continue to be the case even when it appears that files have been wiped or deleted. There are many examples accessible personal data still being available even after it is believed to have been deleted and the device handed over to a third part, or worse sold on. The new recipient could be able to access the original personal data and records. This could quite easily be a breach of a number of principles in the data protection regime. It is always advised to take professional legal, IT and or forensic advice when considering disposing of computer devices;
- websites and social media compliance with the data protection regime;
- online abuse;
- deep fakes;
- Internet of Things (IoT) and devices;
- location data;
- body data;
- metadata;
- new forms of data and personal data;
- new forms of data collections;
- the ongoing ripples from the Snowden disclosures.

Data Protection Websites and Blogs

2.18   There are number of privacy and data protection websites and blogs, such as Datonomy, available at http://www.datonomy.eu/, the Data Protection Forum at www.dpforum.org.uk and the Society of Computers and Law at www.scl.org.

Other Laws

2.19   Other laws can also be relevant in considering personal data and privacy.[11] Examples include:

- IT law;
- contract law;

---

11   See review of particular laws in R Delfino, 'European Union Legislation and Actions,' *European Review of Contract Law* (2011) (7) 547–551, which includes reference to data protection law.

- consumer law;
- eCommerce law;
- financial services law;
- health and medical law and related obligations;
- computer crime and theft laws;
- abuse and harassment laws;
- insurance law;
- travel, accommodation and hospitality law;
- motoring law;
- vehicle and taxi law;
- succession law;
- developing drone laws, licensing and regulations;
- defamation law;
- family law;
- child law;
- games law;
- software and software development law.

Conferences

2.20   There are a variety of conferences, annual events and training organisations related to data protection. Some will be organised by professional conference firms while others are non-profit technology, legal or related organisations.

Reference

2.21   Useful reference material is available as set out below.

The DPA 2018 at: https://www.legislation.gov.uk/ukpga/2018/12/enacted

The ICO is at: https://ico.org.uk/

The EU Commission is at: https://commission.europa.eu/index_en

The EDPB (and WP29) (https://edpb.europa.eu/edpb_en)

International Journal for the Data Protection Officer, Privacy Officer and Privacy Counsel

The European Court of Justice website is at: https://curia.europa.eu/jcms/jcms/j_6/en/

Court of Justice (previously ECJ and CJEU) cases[12] are at: https://curia.europa.eu/juris/recherche.jsf?%20language=en

The ECHR website is at: https://www.echr.coe.int/home

---

12   M Tzanou, 'Balancing Fundamental Rights, United in Diversity? Some Reflections on the Recent Case Law of the European Court of Justice on Data Protection,' *CYELP* (2010) (6) 53–74.

Chapter 3

Definitions

Introduction

3.01 It is critical to understanding the data protection regime to know and appreciate the definitions of key terms which underpin the legal measures implementing the data protection regime. The definitions are the building blocks for the data protection regime. They are contained in the Data Protection Act 2018 (DPA 2018) and the UK GDPR (and also the EU General Data Protection Regulation (GDPR)). The definitions in the GDPR (the new EU data protection regime) and which the DPA and UK data protection regime should mirror as closely as possible, should be considered in detail. The GDPR will also be the main EU data protection legal measure for many years to come, while some uncertainty appears in the UK with continuing post-Brexit changes.

The main definitions are referred to below.

DPA Definitions

3.02 Section 3 of DPA 2018 sets out the following definitions:

'personal data' means any information relating to an identified or identifiable living individual (subject to s 3(14)(c));

'identifiable living individual' means a living individual who can be identified, directly or indirectly, in particular by reference to:

(a) an identifier such as a name, an identification number, location data or an online identifier; or

(b) one or more factors specific to the physical, physiological, genetic, mental, economic, cultural or social identity of the individual.

'processing' in relation to information, means an operation or set of operations which is performed on information, or on sets of information, such as:

(a) collection, recording, organisation, structure or storage;

(b) adaptation or alteration;

(c) retrieval, consultation or use;

(d) disclosure by transmission, dissemination or otherwise making available;

(e) alignment or combination; or

(f) restriction, erasure or destruction,

(subject to s 3(14)(c) and ss 5(7), 29(2) and 82(3), which make provision about reference to processing in different Parts of the Act);

'data subject'	means the identified or identifiable living individual to whom personal data relates;
'controller' and 'processor'	in relation to the processing of personal data to which Part 2, Part 3 or Part 4 applies, have the same meaning as in that Part (see ss 5, 6, 32 and 83 and see also s 3(14)(d));
'filing system'	means any structured set of personal data which is accessible according to specific criteria, whether held by automated means or manually and whether centralised, decentralised or dispersed on a functional or geographic basis;

'the data protection legislation' means:

    (a) the UK GDPR;

    (b) ...

    (c) this Act;

    (d) Regulations made under this Act; and

    (e) Regulations made under s 2(2) of the European Communities Act 1972 which relate to the EU GDPR or the Law Enforcement Directive;

'biometric data'	means information or personal data resulting from specific technical processing relating to the physical, physiological or behavioural characteristics of an individual, which allows or confirms the unique identification of that individual, such as facial images or dactyloscopic data;
'data concerning health'	means personal data relating to the physical or mental health of an individual, including the provisions of health care services, which reveals information about his or her health status;
'genetic data'	means personal data relating to the inherited or acquired genetic characteristic of an individual which gives unique information about the physiology or the health of the individual and which results, in particular, from an analysis of a biological sample from the individual in question;

'health record' means data record which:

    (a) consists of data concerning health, and

    (b) has been made by or on behalf of a health professional in connection with the diagnosis, care or treatment of the individual to whom the data relates;

'inaccurate'	in relation to personal data, means incorrect or misleading as to any matter of fact;

    [s 205]

Terms used in Part 2 of the 2018 Act (General Processing) have the same meaning in this Part as they have in the UK GDPR.[1]

The definition of 'controller' in Article 4(7) of the UK GDPR has effect subject to:

(a) section 6(2);

(b) section 209; and

(c) section 210.[2]

---

1   Data Protection Act 2018, s 5.

2   Data Protection Act 2018, s 6.

Section 10 of DPA 2018 refers to special categories of personal data, previously known as sensitive personal data. The section refers to various changes and specification in relation to special categories of data and data in relation to criminal conviction as it will apply in the UK. These will need to be considered in detail when appropriate.

Special categories of personal data (previously referred to as sensitive data) contains higher compliance obligations and conditions.

There are also additional definitions for 'health professional' and 'social work professional' in s 204.

GDPR (and UK GDPR) Definitions

3.03   Article 4 of the GDPR sets out the definitions for the new data protection regime as follows:

'personal data'	means any information relating to an identified or identifiable natural person ('Data Subject'); an identifiable natural person is one who can be identified, directly or indirectly, in particular by reference to an identifier such as a name, an identification number, location data, an online identifier or to one or more factors specific to the physical, physiological, genetic, mental, economic, cultural or social identity of that natural person;
'processing'	means any operation or set of operations which is performed on personal data or on sets of personal data, whether or not by automated means, such as collection, recording, organisation, structuring, storage, adaptation or alteration, retrieval, consultation, use, disclosure by transmission, dissemination or otherwise making available, alignment or combination, restriction, erasure or destruction;
'restriction of processing'	means the marking of stored personal data with the aim of limiting their processing in the future;
'profiling'	means any form of automated processing of personal data consisting of the use of the personal data to evaluate certain personal aspects relating to a natural person, in particular to analyse or predict aspects concerning that natural person's performance at work, economic situation, health, personal preferences, interests, reliability, behaviour, location or movements;
'pseudonymisation'	means the processing of personal data in such a manner that the personal data can no longer be attributed to a specific Data Subject without the use of additional information, provided that such additional information is kept separately and is subject to technical and organisational measures to ensure that the personal data are not attributed to an identified or identifiable natural person;
'filing system'	means any structured set of personal data which are accessible according to specific criteria, whether centralised, decentralised or dispersed on a functional or geographical basis;
'Controller'	means the natural or legal person, public authority, agency or any other body which alone or jointly with others determines the purposes and means of the processing of personal data; where the purposes and means of processing are determined by EU law or Member State law, the Controller or the specific criteria for its nomination may be provided for by EU law or Member State law;

'Processor'	means a natural or legal person, public authority, agency or any other body which processes personal data on behalf of the Controller;
'recipient'	means a natural or legal person, public authority, agency or any other body, to which the personal data are disclosed, whether a third party or not. However, public authorities which may receive personal data in the framework of a particular inquiry in accordance with EU or Member State law shall not be regarded as recipients; the processing of those data by those public authorities shall be in compliance with the applicable data protection rules according to the purposes of the processing;
'third party'	means any natural or legal person, public authority, agency or body other than the Data Subject, Controller, Processor and persons who, under the direct authority of the Controller or the Processor, are authorised to process the data;
'the consent'	of the Data Subject means any freely given, specific, informed and unambiguous indication of the Data Subject's wishes by which the Data Subject, by a statement or by a clear affirmative action, signifies agreement to the processing of personal data relating to them;
'personal data breach'	means a breach of security leading to the accidental or unlawful destruction, loss, alteration, unauthorised disclosure of, or access to, personal data transmitted, stored or otherwise processed;
'genetic data'	means all personal data relating to the genetic characteristics of an individual that have been inherited or acquired, which give unique information about the physiology or the health of that individual, resulting in particular from an analysis of a biological sample from the individual in question;
'biometric data'	means any personal data resulting from specific technical processing relating to the physical, physiological or behavioural characteristics of an individual which allows or confirms the unique identification of that individual, such as facial images, or dactyloscopic data;
'data concerning health'	means personal data related to the physical or mental health of an individual, including the provision of health care services, which reveal information about his or her health status;
'main establishment'	means: • as regards a Controller with establishments in more than one Member State, the place of its central administration in the EU, unless the decisions on the purposes and means of the processing of personal data are taken in another establishment of the Controller in the EU and the latter establishment has the power to have such decisions implemented, in this case the establishment having taken such decisions shall be considered as the main establishment; • as regards a Processor with establishments in more than one Member State, the place of its central administration in the EU, and, if the Processor has no central administration in the EU, the establishment of the Processor in the EU where the main processing activities in the context of the activities of an establishment of the Processor take place to the extent that the Processor is subject to specific obligations under this Regulation;

'representative'	means any natural or legal person established in the EU who, designated by the Controller or Processor in writing pursuant to Article 27, represents the Controller or Processor, with regard to their respective obligations under this Regulation;
'enterprise'	means any natural or legal person engaged in an economic activity, irrespective of its legal form, including partnerships or associations regularly engaged in an economic activity;
'group of undertakings'	means a controlling undertaking and its controlled undertakings;
'binding corporate rules'	means personal data protection policies which are adhered to by a Controller or Processor established on the territory of a Member State of the EU for transfers or a set of transfers of personal data to a Controller or Processor in one or more third countries within a group of undertakings or group of enterprises engaged in a joint economic activity;
'supervisory authority'	means an independent public authority which is established by a Member State pursuant to Article 51;
'supervisory authority concerned'	means a supervisory authority which is concerned by the processing, because:

- the Controller or Processor is established on the territory of the Member State of that supervisory authority;
- Data Subjects residing in this Member State are substantially affected or likely to be substantially affected by the processing; or
- a complaint has been lodged to that supervisory authority;

'cross-border processing of personal data'	means either:

- processing which takes place in the context of the activities of establishments in more than one Member State of a Controller or a Processor in the EU and the Controller or Processor is established in more than one Member State; or
- processing which takes place in the context of the activities of a single establishment of a Controller or Processor in the EU but which substantially affects or is likely to substantially affect Data Subjects in more than one Member State;

'relevant and reasoned objection'	means an objection as to whether there is an infringement of this Regulation or not, or, as the case may be, whether the envisaged action in relation to the Controller or Processor is in conformity with the Regulation. The objection shall clearly demonstrate the significance of the risks posed by the draft decision as regards the fundamental rights and freedoms of Data Subjects and where applicable, the free flow of personal data within the EU;
'Information Society service'	means any service as defined in point (b) of Article 1(2) of Directive (EU) 2015/1535 of the European Parliament and of the Council;
'international organisation'	means an organisation and its subordinate bodies governed by public international law or any other body which is set up by, or on the basis of, an agreement between two or more countries.

DPDI Definition Changes

3.04 Organisations also need to be aware of the proposed Data Protection and Digital Information (No 2) Bill (DPDI Bill), as it seeks to make amendments to the definitional building blocks of data protection in the UK. Specifically, it seeks to amend the DPA 2018 and the UK GDPR.

Clauses 1–4 of Part 1 of the DPDI Bill sets out various definitions, namely:

- information relating to an identifiable living person (cl 1);
- meaning of research and statistical purposes (cl 2);
- consent to processing for the purposes of scientific research (cl 3);
- consent to law enforcement processing (cl 4).

Part 3 of the DPDI Bill refers to customer data and business data. Clause 77 refers to definitions and interpretation for this Part 3.

Part 4 of the DPDI Bill refers to other provisions about digital information. Clause 81 refers to definition and meaning of 'direct marketing'.

Part 6 of the DPDI Bill refers to final provisions. Clause 109 refers to interpretational and definitional issues.

The full nature of the definitional changes, and overall changes, will need to be monitored as the DPDI Bill progresses through the legislative process and once finally enacted.

Two Categories of Personal Data

3.05 Organisations need to be familiar with two separate categories of personal data in relation to their data protection actions and compliance obligations. It also affects what personal data they may collect in the first instance.

The first is general personal data. Unless specified otherwise, all personal data falls into this category. The second category is special personal data. The importance of special categories of personal data (previously referred to as sensitive personal data) is that it triggers additional and more onerous obligations of compliance and initial collection conditions.

Why is there a distinction? Certain categories of personal data are more important, personal, special and sensitive to individuals over other categories of personal data. This is recognised in the data protection regime. Additional rules are put in place. First, special categories of personal data is defined differently. Second, in order to collect and process special categories of personal data, an organisation must satisfy additional processing conditions, in addition to the Principles of data protection and the general Lawful Processing Conditions, namely complying with the Special Categories of Personal Data Lawful Processing Conditions.

Special Categories of Personal Data

Special Personal Data under the DPA 2018

3.06 Section 10 of DPA 2018 refers to Special Categories of Personal Data as follows:

'(1) subsections (2) and (3) make provision about the processing of personal data described in Article 9(1) of the UK GDPR (prohibition on processing of special categories of personal data) in reliance on an exception in one of the following points of Article 9(2) –

(a) point (b) (employment, social security and social protection);
(b) point (g) (substantial public interest);
(c) point (h) (health and social care);
(d) point (i) (public health);
(e) point (j) (archiving, research and statistics).

(2) The processing meets the requirement of point (b), (h), (i) or (j) of Article 9(2) of the UK GDPR for authorisation by, or a basis in, the law of the United Kingdom or a part of the United Kingdom only if it meets a condition in Part 1 of Schedule 1.

(3) The processing meets the requirement in point (g) of Article 9(2) of the UK GDPR for a basis in the law of the United Kingdom or a part of the United Kingdom only of it meets a condition in Part 2 of Schedule 1.

(4) Subsection (5) makes provision about the processing of personal data relating to criminal convictions and offences or related security measures that is not carried out under the control of official authority.

(5) The processing meets the requirement in Article 10(1) of the UK GDPR for authorisation by the law of the United Kingdom or a part of the United Kingdom only if it meets a condition in Part 1, 2 or 3 of Schedule 1.

(6) The Secretary of State may by regulations –
(a) amend Schedule 1 –
  (i) by adding or varying conditions or safeguards, and
  (ii) by omitting conditions or safeguards added by regulations under this section, and
(b) consequentially amend this section.'

In addition, s 11 of the DPA 2018 states that:

'(1) For the purposes of Article 9(2)(h) of the UK GDPR (processing for health or social care purposes, etc), the circumstances in which the processing of personal data is carried out subject to the conditions and safeguards referred to in Article 9(3) of the UK GDPR (obligation of secrecy) include circumstances in which it is carried out –
(a) by or under the responsibility of a health professional or a social work professional, or
(b) by another person who in the circumstances owes a duty of confidentiality under an enactment or rule of law.

(2) In Article 10 of the UK GDPR and section 10, references to personal data relating to criminal convictions and offences or related security measures include personal data relating to –
(a) the alleged commission of offences by the data subject, or
(b) proceedings for an offence committed or alleged to have been committed by the data subject or the disposal of such proceedings, including sentencing.'

Special Categories of Personal Data under the GDPR/UK GDPR

3.07 Sensitive personal data are referred to in Recitals 10 and 51 of the new GDPR and special categories of personal data are referred to in Recitals 10, 51, 52, 53, 54, 71, 80, 91 and 97.

Article 9 of the new GDPR refers to processing of special categories of personal data. The processing of personal data revealing racial or ethnic origin, political opinions, religious or philosophical beliefs, trade-union membership, and the processing of genetic data, biometric data in order to uniquely identify a person or data concerning health or sex life and sexual orientation shall be prohibited (Article 9(1)).

The above shall not apply if one of the following applies:

- the Data Subject has given explicit consent to the processing of those personal data for one or more specified purposes, except where EU law or state law provide that the prohibition referred to in paragraph 1 may not be lifted by the Data Subject; or
- processing is necessary for the purposes of carrying out the obligations and exercising specific rights of the Controller or of the Data Subject in the field of employment and social security and social protection law in so far as it is authorised by EU law or state law or a collective agreement pursuant to state law providing for adequate safeguards for the fundamental rights and the interests of the Data Subject; or
- processing is necessary to protect the vital interests of the Data Subject or of another person where the Data Subject is physically or legally incapable of giving consent; or
- processing is carried out in the course of its legitimate activities with appropriate safeguards by a foundation, association or any other non-profit-seeking body with a political, philosophical, religious or trade-union aim and on condition that the processing relates solely to the members or to former members of the body or to persons who have regular contact with it in connection with its purposes and that the data are not disclosed outside that body without the consent of the Data Subjects; or
- the processing relates to personal data which are manifestly made public by the Data Subject; or
- processing is necessary for the establishment, exercise or defence of legal claims or whenever courts are acting in their judicial capacity; or
- processing is necessary for reasons of substantial public interest, on the basis of EU or state law which shall be proportionate to the aim pursued, respect the essence of the right to data protection and provide for suitable and specific measures to safeguard the fundamental rights and the interests of the Data Subject; or
- processing is necessary for the purposes of preventive or occupational medicine, for the assessment of the working capacity of the employee, medical diagnosis, the provision of health or social care or treatment or the management of health or social care systems and services on the basis of EU law or state law or pursuant to contract with a health professional and subject to the conditions and safeguards referred to in Article 9(4); [h] or
- processing is necessary for reasons of public interest in the area of public health, such as protecting against serious cross-border threats to health or ensuring high standards of quality and safety of health care and of medicinal products or medical devices, on the basis of EU law or state law which provides for suitable and specific measures to safeguard the rights and freedoms of the Data Subject, in particular professional secrecy; or
- processing is necessary for archiving purposes in the public interest, or scientific and historical research purposes or statistical purposes in accordance with Article 83(1) based on EU or state law which shall be proportionate to the aim pursued, respect the essence of the right to data protection and provide for suitable and specific measures to safeguard the fundamental rights and the interests of the Data Subject (Article 9(2)).

Personal data referred to in Article 9(1) of the new GDPR may be processed for the purposes referred to in Article 9(2)(h) when those data are processed by or under the responsibility of a professional subject to the obligation of professional secrecy under

EU or state law or rules established by national competent bodies or by another person also subject to an obligation of secrecy under EU or state law or rules established by national competent bodies (Article 9(4)).

States may maintain or introduce further conditions, including limitations, with regard to the processing of genetic data, biometric data or health data (Article 9(5)).

Article 10 of the GDPR refers to processing of data relating to criminal convictions and offences. Processing of personal data relating to criminal convictions and offences or related security measures based on Article 6(1) may only be carried out either under the control of official authority or when the processing is authorised by EU law or state law providing for adequate safeguards for the rights and freedoms of Data Subjects. Any comprehensive register of criminal convictions may be kept only under the control of official authority.

It should be noted that there is a proposal in the Data Protection and Digital Information (No 2) Bill to amend definitions which may impact general personal data and special personal data (eg clauses 1–4). These will need to be examined once enacted.

Conclusion

3.08   It is important for organisations to distinguish, in advance of collecting personal data, whether the proposed data collection relates to general personal data or special personal data. They also need to be able to confirm compliance procedures in advance of collecting and maintaining personal data and particularly sensitive personal data. The organisation could be asked to demonstrate at a future date that it obtained consent, and general compliance. If it cannot, it may have to delete the data, have committed breaches and offences, and potentially face fines and or being sued by the Data Subject. Depending on the circumstances, personal liability can also arise.

Chapter 4

History and Data Protection

Introduction

4.01   The legal discussion in relation to privacy is frequently linked to the Warren and Brandeis's legal article in 1890 entitled 'The Right to Privacy' published in the *Harvard Law Review*.[1] Arguably, data protection is the modern coalface of the debate in relation to privacy and privacy protection.[2] The data protection regime can be considered as setting standards in certain areas of informational privacy protection – which have come to be followed in other jurisdictions internationally beyond the EU.[3] There have also been calls for international level data protection rules.[4] This would add greater certainty for both organisations, industry, and individual Data Subjects. The pressure for better and more international standards and norms is increasing. While privacy discussion has progressed steadily since 1890, this has sped up significantly with the advent of the consumer computer and electronic storage – particularly data protection, and has reached sometimes dizzying speeds with modern internet iterations and associated uses. That was even before the recent release of ChatGPT and other chat AIs such as Jasper, YouChat, and Chatsonic. There is also new art-AIs the most discussed being the one called DALL-E which is sometimes referred to as the art version of ChatGPT. Significant social and legal issues are being raised. Privacy and data protection are certainly some of these issues. Others include employment implications, intellectual property, control, and out of control AIs and robots. There may be parallels between the level of concerns which led to the first generation of data protection laws and current AI and AI-related concerns, and which may lead to policy discussions on the need to enhance modern data protection laws in light of these new concerns.

History of Data Protection

4.02   The growth of the processing of information relating to individuals in electronic computer data format from the 1970s onwards, led to ever increasing concerns

---

1   S Warren and L Brandeis, 'The Right to Privacy,' *Harvard Law Review* (1890) (IV) 193.
2   See JB Rule and G Greenleaf, eds, *Global Privacy Protection – The First Generation* (Cheltenham: Elgar, 2008).
3   See M Birnhack, 'The EU Data Protection Directive: An Engine of a Global Regime,' *Computer Law & Security Report* (2008) (2) 508, at 512.
4   On the topic of international data protection issues, see, for example, P Lambert, *Data Protection and Data Transfers Law* (Bloomsbury, 2023); C de Terwangne, 'Is a Global Data Protection Regulatory Model Possible?' in S Gutwirth, Y Poullet, P de Hert, C de Terwange and S Nouwt, *Reinventing Data Protection?* (Springer, 2009), p 175; and C Kuner, 'Developing an Adequate Legal Framework for International Data transfers,' in S Gutwirth, Y Poullet, P de Hert, C de Terwange and S Nouwt, *Reinventing Data Protection?* (Springer, 2009), p 263.

regarding such processing. Existing laws were 'insufficient to deal with concerns about the amount of information relating to individuals that was held by organisations in electronic form.'[5] The purpose behind the Data Protection Acts generally is largely to promote openness and transparency of information held about individuals, and to protect the privacy and data protection interests and rights of such individuals.[6] In the case of the Data Protection Act 2018 (DPA 2018) there is the added reason of complying with the EU General Data Protection Regulation (GDPR), and with an eye to post-Brexit trade and adequacy.

The main EU data protection instrument was the Data Protection Directive 1995,[7] implemented in the UK by DPA 1998, now replaced across the EU by the GDPR. The new Data Protection Act 2018 (DPA 2018) and UK GDPR seeks to mirror, to some extent, the GDPR.

However, even prior to the 1995 Directive concern for informational privacy in the computer environment was recognised in an early data protection regime. The Council of Europe proposed and enacted the Convention for the Protection of Individuals with Regard to Automatic Processing of Personal Data Done at Strasbourg on the 28 January 1981 (and recently updated with the Convention).[8] The UK implemented the Data Protection Act 1984 (DPA 1984). Ultimately this was replaced with DPA 1998 to implement DPD 1995. It was also implemented in secondary legislation relating to data protection.[9]

There were also a number of official investigations and proposed bills regarding privacy and data protection. The Younger Committee on Privacy[10] proposed ten recommendations and principles regarding personal data. It proposed the following principles:

- information should be regarded as held for a specific purpose and should not be used, without appropriate authorisation, for other purposes;
- access to information should be confined to those authorised to have it for the purpose for which it was supplied;
- the amount of information collected and held should be the minimum necessary for the achievement of a specified purpose;
- in computerised systems handling information for statistical purposes, adequate provision should be made in their design and programs for separating identities from the rest of the data;
- there should be arrangements whereby a subject can be told about the information held concerning them;
- the level of security to be achieved by a system should be specified in advance by the user and should include precautions against the deliberate abuse or misuse of information;

5 P Carey, *Data Protection, A Practical Guide to UK and EU Law* (Oxford: OUP, 2009) 1. Also, Bainbridge, D, *Data Protection* (CLT, 2000) 2.
6 L AC MacDonald, Lynda, *Data Protection: Legal Compliance and Good Practice for Employers* (Tottel, 2008), p 33.
7 RI D'Afflitto, 'European Union Directive on Personal Privacy Rights and Computerised Information,' *Villanova Law Review* (1996) (41) 305–324.
8 Council of Europe Convention for the Protection of Individuals with Regard to Automatic Processing of Personal Data Done at Strasbourg on the 28 January 1981, at https://www.coe.int/en/web/conventions/full-list?module=treaty-detail&treatynum=108. Also, 'Convention for the Protection of Individuals with Regard to Automatic Processing of Personal Data,' *International Legal Materials* (1981) (20) 317–325.
9 See generally P Carey, *Data Protection, A Practical Guide to UK and EU Law* (Oxford, OUP, 2009) chapter 1.
10 Younger Committee on Privacy, Cmnd 5012 (1972).

- a monitoring system should be provided to facilitate the detection of any violation of the security system;
- in the design of information systems, periods should be specified beyond which the information should not be retained;
- data held should be accurate. There should be machinery for the correction of inaccuracy and updating of information;
- care should be taken in coding value judgments.

This was followed by the Lindrop Committee[11] on how best to protect privacy and personal data. The Committee uses the term 'data privacy' to mean the individual Data Subject's right to control the circulation of data about them.[12] While specific recommendations were made, these were not enacted. Ultimately, DPA 1984 was enacted following on from the Council of Europe Convention 1981 relating to data processing. It is entitled 'Convention for the Protection of Individuals with regard to the Automatic Processing of Personal Data.' The Convention sets out the following principles and requirements, namely, that personal data must be:

- obtained and processed fairly and lawfully;
- stored for specified and lawful purposes and not used in a way incompatible with those purposes;
- adequate, relevant and not excessive in relation to the purposes for which they are stored;
- accurate and, where necessary, kept up to date;
- preserved in a form which permits identification of the Data Subjects for no longer than is required for the purpose for which those data are stored.

In addition, the Convention provides that:

- personal data revealing racial origin, political opinions or religious or other beliefs, as well as personal data concerning health or sexual life, may not be processed automatically unless domestic law provides appropriate safeguards. The same shall apply to personal data relating to criminal convictions;
- appropriate security measures shall be taken for the protection of personal data stored in automated data files against accidental or unauthorised destruction or accidental loss as well as against unauthorised access, alteration or dissemination;
- any person shall be enabled,
    - to establish the existence of an automated personal data file, its main purposes, as well as the identity and habitual residence or principal place of business of the Controller of the file;
    - to obtain at reasonable intervals and without excessive delay or expense confirmation of whether personal data relating to them are stored in the automated data file as well as communication to them of such data in an intelligible form;
    - to obtain, as the case may be, rectification or erasure of such data if these have been processed contrary to the provisions of domestic law giving effect to the basic principles set out in Articles 5 and 6 of the Convention;
    - to have a remedy if a request for confirmation or, as the case may be, communication, rectification or erasure are not complied with.[13]

---

11 Lindrop Committee, Cmnd 7341 (1978).
12 Referred to in P Carey, above, at 3.
13 Convention Articles 5–8.

Data Protection Act

4.03   The DPA 1998 implemented the provisions of the EU DPD 1995 on the protection of individuals with regard to the processing of personal data and on the free movement of such data. The GDPR replaces DPD 1995.

The DPA 2018 replaces the DPA 1998 in the UK.[14]

The DPA 2018, and the UK GDPR, have important implications for business and organisations which collect, process and deal in information relating to living individuals, and in particular customers and employees – as does the GDPR. They contain stringent data protection measures to safeguard personal informational privacy and to ensure that personal data is not misused or used for purposes that are incompatible with data protection legislation.

Further legal developments will continue to occur as a result of Brexit, including the referred-to UK GDPR, as rough equivalent version of the GDPR. The DPA and UK GDPR are set to be amended further by the Data Protection and Digital Information (No 2) Bill (DPDI Bill). (See Chapter 24 for further details.)

Legal Instruments

4.04   The introduction or Recitals to the European legal instruments, while not legally binding like the main text of the provisions, are still influential in terms of interpreting the data protection regime, and also highlight some of the history, philosophy and policy behind particular data protections laws and provisions.

GDPR Recitals/ UK GDPR

4.05   The final version of the GDPR was agreed in December 2015 by the tripartite group and passed by the EU Parliament in April 2016. From the date of publication in the Official Journal (4 May 2016) there is a two year implementation period for organisations – and states in terms of any amendments required to national legislation. The Recitals include the following:

DPD Repealed

DPD 1995 is repealed; Commission decisions based on the DPD 1995 remain until replaced (Recital 171); and Directive 2002/58/EC[15] is to be updated following the GDPR (Recital 173).

WP29/EDPB

Establishment of European Data Protection Board (EDPB) which is the effective equivalent of WP29 under the DPD 1995 (Recital 139).

---

14   There was also a previous Data Protection Act in the UK, namely, the Data Protection Act 1984. The DPA of 1998 repealed the DPA of 1984. The DPA was passed into law on 1 March 2000 pursuant to the Data Protection Act (Commencement) Order 2000, SI 2000/183.

15   Directive 2002/58/EC of the European Parliament and of the Council of 12 July 2002 concerning the processing of personal data and the protection of privacy in the electronic communications sector (Directive on privacy and electronic communications).

Background and Rationale

Personal data protection is (now) a fundamental right;[16] Article 8(1) of the Charter of Fundamental Rights of the EU and Article 16(1) of the Treaty (Recital 1); data processing should be designed to serve mankind; balanced with other fundamental rights; principle of proportionality (Recital 4); internal market and cross border transfers (Recital 6); rapid technological developments and challenges (Recital 6); developments require a strong and more coherent data protection framework (Recital 7); the DPD 1995 has not prevented fragmentation in how data protection is implemented (Recital 9); the need to ensure a consistent and high level of protection and to remove obstacles to data flows (Recital 10); the need for a consistent level of protection throughout the EU (Recital 13); the GDPR protects natural persons and their personal data (Recital 12); protections should be technologically neutral (Recital 15).

Obligations

Data processing must be lawful and fair (Recital 39); processing necessary for a contract (Recital 44); processing for a legal obligation (Recital 45); processing necessary to protect life (Recital 46); the legitimate interests of the Controller (Recital 47).

Security

Network and information security, Computer Emergency Response Teams (CERTs) and Computer Security Incident Response Teams (CSIRTs) (Recital 49); appropriate technical and organisational measures (Recitals 81, 87); security and risk evaluation (Recital 90); high risk (Recital 84); impact assessments (Recitals 84, 90, 91, etc); large scale processing operations (Recital 91); consultations (Recital 94); data breach and data breach notification (Recitals 85, 86); and Commission delegated acts.

Processing

Processing; pseudonymised data (Recitals 26, 28, 29); online identifiers (Recital 30); consent (Recitals 32, 38, 40, 42, 43, 44, 50) lawful processing and consent (Recital 40); principle of transparency (Recital 39, 58, 60, 71); children (Recital 38); processing for (additional) other purposes (Recital 50); genetic data (Recital 34); health data (Recital 35); sensitive personal data (Recitals 51, 52, 53, 54); additional identifying information (Recital 57); processing and electoral activities (Recital 56); religious associations (Recital 55); processing and direct marketing (Recital 70); right not to be subject to a decision; automated processing (Recital 68, 71); profiling (Recitals 70, 72); restrictions on principles and rights (Recital 73); responsibility and liability of Controllers (Recital 74); risks (Recitals 75, 76, 83, 84, etc); Processors and Controllers (Recitals 79, 81, 82, etc); Codes of Conduct (Recital 98); transparency and certification mechanisms (Recitals 99, 100); penalties and fines (Recital 148); criminal sanctions (Recital 149); employee data (Recital 155); public authorities; processing in the public interest or official authority; processing and public interest, scientific and historical research purposes, statistical purposes, safeguards; archiving purposes; scientific research purposes; historical research purposes; medical research purposes; statistical purposes; religious organisations.

---

16 In relation to data protection as a fundamental right, see, for example S Rodata, 'Data Protection as a Fundamental Right,' in S Gutwirth, Y Poullet, P de Hert, C de Terwangne and S Nouwt, *Reinventing Data Protection?* (Springer, 2009), p 77. It is necessary to reinforce its protection in order to make it effective and not conditioned by the asymmetries which characterise the relationship between Data Subject and data controllers.

Rights

Data Subject rights (Recital 59); principles of fair and transparent processing (Recital 60); prior information requirements (Recital 61); right of access (Recital 63); right of rectification and right to be forgotten (RtbF) (Recital 65); right to complain (Recital 141); automated processing (Recital 68).

Proceedings

Proceedings against Controllers, Processors and jurisdiction (Recitals 145, 146); damages and compensation (Recital 146); the prevention, investigation, detection or prosecution of offences.

Establishment

Establishment (Recitals 22, 23, 36); groups of undertakings (Recital 37); establishment (Recital 36, etc).

Transfers

Cross border data transfers (Recital 101, etc).

ICO and Supervisory Authorities

Supervisory authorities such as the ICO (SAs) (previously called data protection authorities (DPAs) and the complete independence of SAs (Recitals 117, etc).

New Bodies

Data protection not-for-profit bodies, organisations and associations (Recital 142).

Notification/Registration Replaced

Replacement of 'general' notification/registration requirement (Recital 89).

Exceptions/Exemptions

The GDPR does not address national security (Recital 16); the GDPR should not apply to data processing by a natural person in the course of a purely personal or household activity and thus without a connection with a professional or commercial activity (Recital 18); without prejudice to eCommerce Directive[17] in particular eCommerce defences of Articles 12–15 (Recital 21); the GDPR does not apply to the data of the deceased (Recital 27). (Also fanpage case, ECJ C-210/16, June 2018).

Lawful Processing and Consent

Lawful processing and consent (Recital 40).

Online Identifiers

Online identifiers (Recital 30).

Sensitive Personal Data

Sensitive personal data and special categories of personal data (Recitals 10, 51, 53).

Children and Personal Data

Processing of children's personal data (Recitals 38, 58, 65, 71, 75).

---

17 Directive 2000/31/EC.

Health Data

Health data processing (Recitals 35, 45, 52, 53, 54, 63, 65, 71, 73, 75, 91, 112, 155, 159).

GDPR/UK GDPR

General Provisions

4.06 The initial provisions refer to the context of the GDPR, namely, the subject matter and objectives (Article 1); material scope (Article 2); and territorial scope (Article 3).

The GDPR applies to the processing of personal data wholly or partly by automated means, and to the processing other than by automated means of personal data which form part of a filing system or are intended to form part of a filing system (Article 2(2)). Matters not covered or included are referred to in Article 2(3).

Principles of Data Protection

4.07 Chapter II refers to the Principles of data protection. Article 5 of the new GDPR relates to principles relating to personal data processing.

Personal data must be:

(a) processed lawfully, fairly and in a transparent manner in relation to the Data Subject ('lawfulness, fairness and transparency');

(b) collected for specified, explicit and legitimate purposes and not further processed in a manner that is incompatible with those purposes; further processing for archiving purposes in the public interest, scientific or historical research purposes or statistical purposes shall, in accordance with Article 89(1), not be considered to be incompatible with the initial purposes ('purpose limitation');

(c) adequate, relevant and limited to what is necessary in relation to the purposes for which they are processed ('data minimisation');

(d) accurate and, where necessary, kept up to date; every reasonable step must be taken to ensure that personal data that are inaccurate, having regard to the purposes for which they are processed, are erased or rectified without delay ('accuracy');

(e) kept in a form which permits identification of Data Subjects for no longer than is necessary for the purposes for which the personal data are processed; personal data may be stored for longer periods insofar as the data will be processed solely for archiving purposes in the public interest, scientific or historical research purposes or statistical purposes in accordance with Article 89(1) subject to implementation of the appropriate technical and organisational measures required by the Regulation in order to safeguard the rights and freedoms of the Data Subject ('storage limitation');

(f) processed in a manner that ensures appropriate security of the personal data, including protection against unauthorised or unlawful processing and against accidental loss, destruction or damage, using appropriate technical or organisational measures ('integrity and confidentiality') (Article 5(1)).

The Controller shall be responsible for and be able to demonstrate compliance with Article 5(1) ('accountability' principle) (Article 5(2)).

These can be *summarised* as:

- processed lawfully, fairly and in a transparent manner ('lawfulness, fairness and transparency');
- for specified, explicit and legitimate purposes and not further processed incompatibly with the purpose; (with carveout for archiving purposes in the public interest, scientific or historical research purposes or statistical purposes) ('purpose limitation');
- adequate, relevant and limited to what is necessary for the purposes ('data minimisation');
- accurate and, where necessary, kept up to date; every reasonable step must be taken to ensure that personal data that are inaccurate, having regard to the purposes for which they are processed, are erased or rectified without delay ('accuracy');
- kept in a form which permits identification for no longer than is necessary; (with carveout for archiving purposes in the public interest, or scientific and historical research purposes or statistical purposes subject to appropriate technical and organisational measures) ('storage limitation');
- appropriate security, including protection against unauthorised or unlawful processing and against accidental loss, destruction or damage, using appropriate technical or organisational measures ('integrity and confidentiality').

The Controller must demonstrate compliance ('accountability').

Note that the DPDI Bill proposed amendments in relation to the Principles at clause 5 (lawfulness) and clause 6 (purpose limitation); the duty to keep records (clause 15); Schedule 1 (lawfulness); and Schedule 2 (purpose limitation).

Lawful Processing Conditions

4.08   Article 6 of the new GDPR refers to the lawfulness of processing. Article 6(1) provides that processing of personal data shall be lawful only if and to the extent that at least one of the following applies:

- the Data Subject has given consent to the processing of their personal data for one or more specific purposes;
- processing is necessary for the performance of a contract to which the Data Subject is party or in order to take steps at the request of the Data Subject prior to entering into a contract;
- processing is necessary for compliance with a legal obligation to which the Controller is subject;
- processing is necessary in order to protect the vital interests of the Data Subject or of another natural person;
- processing is necessary for the performance of a task carried out in the public interest or in the exercise of official authority vested in the Controller;
- processing is necessary for the purposes of the legitimate interests pursued by the Controller or by a third party, except where such interests are overridden by the interests or fundamental rights and freedoms of the Data Subject which require protection of personal data, in particular where the Data Subject is a child. This (bullet) shall not apply to processing carried out by public authorities in the performance of their tasks (Article 6(1)).

States may maintain or introduce more specific provisions to adapt the application of the rules of the GDPR with regard to the processing of personal data for compliance with Article 6(1)(c) and (e) by determining more precisely specific requirements for the processing and other measures to ensure lawful and fair processing including for other specific processing situations as provided for in Chapter IX (Article 6(2)).

The basis for the processing referred to in Article 6(1)(c) and (e) of must be laid down by: EU law, or state law to which the Controller is subject.

The purpose of the processing shall be determined on this legal basis, or as regards the processing referred to in Article 6(1)(e), shall be necessary for the performance of a task carried out in the public interest or in the exercise of official authority vested in the Controller. This legal basis may contain specific provisions to adapt the application of rules of the GDPR, *inter alia*, the general conditions governing the lawfulness of data processing by the Controller, the type of data which are subject to the processing, the Data Subjects concerned; the entities to, and the purposes for which the personal data may be disclosed; the purpose limitation; storage periods, and processing operations and processing procedures, including measures to ensure lawful and fair processing, such as those for other specific processing situations as provided for in Chapter IX. EU law or the law of the state must meet an objective of public interest and be proportionate to the legitimate aim pursued (Article 6(3)).

Where the processing for a purpose other than that for which the personal data have been collected is not based on the Data Subject's consent or on an EU or state law which constitutes a necessary and proportionate measure in a democratic society to safeguard the objectives referred to in Article 23(1), the Controller shall, in order to ascertain whether processing for another purpose is compatible with the purpose for which the personal data are initially collected, take into account, *inter alia*:

- any link between the purposes for which the personal data have been collected and the purposes of the intended further processing;
- the context in which the personal data have been collected, in particular regarding the relationship between Data Subjects and the Controller;
- the nature of the personal data, in particular whether special categories of personal data are processed, pursuant to Article 9 or whether data related to criminal convictions and offences are processed, pursuant to Article 10;
- the possible consequences of the intended further processing for Data Subjects;
- the existence of appropriate safeguards, which may include encryption or pseudonymisation (Article 6(4)).

Note that the DPDI Bill proposed amendments in relation to lawfulness at clause 5; the duty to keep records (clause 15); and Schedule 1 (lawfulness of processing: recognised legitimate interest). It also refers to the information that is to be provided to Data Subjects (clauses 9 and 10).

Consent Conditions

4.09 Article 7 of the new GDPR refers to conditions for consent as follows. Where processing is based on consent, the Controller shall be able to demonstrate that the Data Subject has consented to the processing of their personal data (Article 7(1)).

If the Data Subject's consent is given in the context of a written declaration which also concerns other matters, the request for consent must be presented in a manner which is clearly distinguishable from the other matters, in an intelligible and easily accessible form, using clear and plain language. Any part of the declaration which constitutes an infringement of the GDPR shall not be binding (Article 7(2)).

The Data Subject shall have the right to withdraw their consent at any time. The withdrawal of consent shall not affect the lawfulness of processing based on consent before its withdrawal. Prior to giving consent, the Data Subject shall be informed thereof. It must be as easy to withdraw consent as to give consent (Article 7(3)).

When assessing whether consent is freely given, utmost account shall be taken of the fact whether, *inter alia*, the performance of a contract, including the provision of a service, is conditional on consent to the processing of personal data that is not necessary for the performance of that contract (Article 7(4)).

Note that the DPDI Bill proposed amendments in relation to consent eg clause 3 (consent to processing for the purposes of scientific research); and clause 4 (consent to law enforcement processing).

Conclusion

4.10 Privacy and data protection are evolving in terms of how technology is changing how personal data are collected, used and processed. The prior data protection legal regime is perceived as requiring updating. The DPD was enacted in 1995, prior to social media, cloud computing, mass data storage, data mining, electronic profiling, Web 2.0 and the threats to the data security surrounding personal data. This was even before the spotlight centred on abuse issues. Data protection needs to evolve to deal with, or at least more explicitly deal with, these issues. This is partly the reason for the new GDPR. Questions will increasingly arise as to whether the GDPR and GDPR-generation data laws (including the DPA 2018 and UK GDPR) are wholly sufficient for new developments such as AI, AI generated chat, AI generated content, AI data collections, AI data storage, and more.

The GDPR and GDPR-generation data laws are important for the issues they address as well as the current legal provisions they enhance. As a Regulation as opposed to a Directive, it means that it is directly applicable in member states (previously but not currently including the UK) without the need for a Directive or national implementing legislation. However, the UK, as many other states, can also implement national laws. That takes on added resonance given the advent of Brexit and the date when the GDPR is no longer directly effective here in the UK. The law and practice of the UK had changed, as will many of the obligations of organisations. This will also differ more for organisations in particular sectors. These data law changes continue, as evidenced in the DPDI Bill.

There must be better awareness and more hands-on board management responsibility, planning and data protection assessment, and including risk assessment, in advance of product or service launch via the Data Protection by Design (DPbD) concept (see Part 4). For the first time there is explicit recognition of children under the data protection regime. Data protection compliance is now required to be much more considered, organised and planned. The DPDI Bill also proposes changes in relation to digital services, digital verification services, and trust, as well as data protection more generally.

Chapter 5

Principles

Introduction

5.01 All organisations which collect and process personal data must comply with the obligations of the UK data protection regime. It is, therefore, very important to be familiar with the data protection regime. This is set out in the new Data Protection Act 2018 (DPA 2018) and UK GDPR (and the EU General Data Protection Regulation (GDPR)).

When Data Protection Provisions Apply

5.02 The circumstances in which UK data protection provisions apply are important. The data protection regime applies:

- to the processing of personal data where the Controller is established in the UK, whether or not the processing takes place in the UK;
- to the processing of personal data to which Chapter 2 of Part 2 of the Act (ie the UK GDPR) applies where:
  (a) the processing is carried out in the context of the activities of an establishment of a Controller and Processor in a country or territory that is not a member State, whether or not the processing takes place in such a country or territory,
  (b) the personal data relates to a Data Subject who is in the UK when the processing activities take place, and
  (c) the processing activities relate to–
      (i) the offering of goods or services to Data Subjects in the UK, whether or not for payment, or
      (ii) the monitoring of Data Subjects' behaviour in the UK (s 207).

A person established in the UK includes:

- an individual ordinarily resident in the UK;
- a body incorporated under UK law;
- a partnership formed under UK law;
- a person in the above bullets who maintains and carried out activities through an office, branch or agency or other stable arrangements in the UK (s 207(7)).

The Data Protection and Digital Information (No 2) Bill (DPDI Bill) will need to be examined to determine if the final version contains a diminishment or carveouts from when data protection rules apply. Potentially, from an initial review, there appears to be a number of such examples.

Fair Processing Requirements

5.03 The data protection rules provide details as to what constitutes fair processing and identifies the information that must be given to Data Subjects not only where the personal data is obtained directly from the Data Subjects but also when it is obtained indirectly. It also refers to the times at which this information needs to be given.

Organisations cannot collect and process personal data unless they:

- comply with the registration or notification requirements (if still required; note the GDPR removed registration or notification type requirements);
- comply with the Principles of data protection (previously known as the data quality principles);
- ensure the processing is carried out in accordance with the Lawful Processing Conditions (and the Special Personal Data Lawful Processing Conditions in the case of special or sensitive personal data);
- provide specific information to Data Subjects in advance of the collection and processing of personal data, known as the Prior Information Requirements;
- also comply with data security requirements.

These all serve as pre-conditions to lawful data processing of personal data. In addition, the final version of the proposed amendments contained in the DPDI Bill will need careful review.

Principles of Data Protection

5.04 There are seven Principles of data protection to be complied with by all Controllers. It can, therefore, be summarised that all personal data must be:

(1) lawful, fair and transparent processing;
(2) processed for limited purposes;
(3) adequate, relevant and not excessive;
(4) accurate and up to date;
(5) not kept for longer than is necessary;
(6) secure; and
(7) processed in a manner demonstrating compliance with the above.

Section 2(1) of the DPA 2018 (as amended by the Data Protection, Privacy and Electronic Communications (Amendments Etc) (EU Exit) Regulations 2019, SI 2019/419) was drafted to state that:

> 'the UK GDPR and this Act protect individuals with regard to the processing of personal data, in particular by –
>
> (a) requiring personal data to be processed lawfully and fairly, on the basis of the data subject's consent or another specified basis;
> (b) conferring rights on the data subject to obtain information about the processing of personal data and to require inaccurate personal data to be rectified.'

Article 5 of the GDPR sets out these principles as follows. Personal data must be:

- processed lawfully, fairly and in a transparent manner in relation to the Data Subject ('lawfulness, fairness and transparency');
- collected for specified, explicit and legitimate purposes and not further processed in a manner that is incompatible with those purposes; further processing for archiving purposes in the public interest, scientific or historical research purposes

or statistical purposes shall, in accordance with Article 89(1), not be considered to be incompatible with the initial purposes ('purpose limitation');

- adequate, relevant and limited to what is necessary in relation to the purposes for which they are processed ('data minimisation');
- accurate and, where necessary, kept up to date; every reasonable step must be taken to ensure that personal data are inaccurate, having regard to the purposes for which they are processed, are erased or rectified without delay ('accuracy');
- kept in a form which permits identification of Data Subjects for no longer than is necessary for the purposes for which the personal data are processed; personal data may be stored for longer periods insofar as the data will be processed solely for archiving purposes in the public interest, scientific or historical research purposes or statistical purposes in accordance with Article 89(1) subject to implementation of the appropriate technical and organisational measures required by the GDPR in order to safeguard the rights and freedoms of the Data Subject ('storage limitation');
- processed in a manner that ensures appropriate security of the personal data, including protection against unauthorised or unlawful processing and against accidental loss, destruction or damage, using appropriate technical or organisational measures ('integrity and confidentiality').

The Controller must be responsible for and be able to demonstrate compliance with the above ('accountability').

The final version of the proposed amendments relating to the Principles of data protection contained in the DPDI Bill will need careful review, such as clauses 1, 5, 6, 7, 9, 10, 12, 13, 14, 40, 43, 44, 76, 80, 81, 83, and Schedules 1, 2, 3, 4, 8, and 9.

Interpreting the Principles of Data Protection

5.05 The Data Protection Act 1998 (DPA 1998) also contained certain guidance which assisted in interpreting the data protection Principles. These were contained in Schedule 1, Part I. This is not replicated in the DPA 2018.

The final version of the proposed amendments contained in the DPDI Bill will need careful review, as regards how the current rules and Principles of data protection may be affected.

Chapter 6

Ordinary Personal Data Lawful Processing Conditions

Introduction

6.01 Organisations when obtaining and processing personal data must not mislead and must also provide a number of prior information requirements to the individual Data Subjects.

Without these it would be deemed that there is unfair obtaining and processing. In addition, organisations must satisfy and meet one of the Lawful Processing Conditions for lawful processing.

General Lawful Processing Conditions

6.02 The Lawful Processing Conditions are required to be complied with, in addition to the Principles of data protection. Article 4 of the EU General Data Protection Regulation (GDPR), titled lawfulness of processing, contains the general Lawful Processing Conditions (and which are then reflected in the Data Protection Act 2018 (DPA 2018) and UK GDPR). In order to collect and process personal data, in addition to complying with the above data protection Principles, organisations must comply or fall within one of the following general personal data Lawful Processing Conditions.

These conditions might be summarised as follows:

- the Data Subject consent;
- the necessary contract with Data Subject;
- necessary for a legal obligation;
- necessary to protect vital interests;
- necessary for public interest or official task;
- necessary for legitimate interests pursued by Controller except where unwarranted.

Article 7 also specifies requirements in relation to conditions for consent. It states that where processing is based on consent, the Controller must be able to demonstrate that the Data Subject has consented to processing of his or her personal data. If the consent is given in the context of a written declaration which also concerns other matters, the request for consent must be presented in a manner which is clearly distinguishable from the other matters, in an intelligible and easily accessible form, using clear and plain language. Any part of such a declaration which constitutes an infringement of the GDPR shall not be binding. In addition, the Data Subject shall have the right to withdraw his or her consent at any time. The withdrawal of consent shall not affect the lawfulness of processing based on consent before its withdrawal. Prior to giving consent, the Data Subject shall be informed thereof. It shall be as easy to withdraw as to give consent. When assessing whether consent is freely given, utmost account shall be taken of whether, *inter alia*, the performance of a contract, including the provision of a service, is conditional on consent to the processing of personal data that is not necessary for the performance of that contract.

In relation to children, Article 8 refers to conditions applicable to a child's consent in relation to information society services. It provides where Article 6(1)(a) applies, in relation to the offer of information society services directly to a child, the processing of the personal data of a child shall be lawful where the child is at least 16 years old. Where the child is below the age of 16 years, such processing shall be lawful only if and to the extent that consent is given or authorised by the holder of parental responsibility over the child. However, Member States may provide a lower age. The UK has decided to provide the age of 13 in the DPA 2018. It is noted that this is the first time that the data protection regime, at least at the EU data protection regime level, expressly refers to children and child data. Some might suggest that this has been overdue.

Special Personal Data Lawful Processing Conditions

6.03 In the case of special or sensitive personal data, an organisation must, in addition to complying with the Principles of data protection, be able to comply or fall within one of the Special Personal Data Lawful Processing Conditions.

Article 9 of the GDPR sets out the conditions relevant for the purposes of the first data protection Principle in particular in relation to the processing of special personal data. The processing of personal data revealing racial or ethnic origin, political opinions, religious or philosophical beliefs, or trade union membership, and the processing of genetic data, biometric data for the purpose of uniquely identifying a natural person, data concerning health or data concerning a natural person's sex life or sexual orientation shall be prohibited. It sets out the following provisions or exceptions to this restriction, namely:

1   The Data Subject has given explicit consent to the processing of the personal data for one or more specified purpose.
2   The processing is necessary for the purposes of carrying out the obligations and exercising specific rights of the Controller or of the Data Subject in the field of employment and social security and social protection law in so far as it is authorised by Union or Member State law or a collective agreement pursuant to Member State law providing for appropriate safeguards for the fundamental rights and the interests of the data subject.
3   The processing is necessary to protect the vital interests of the Data Subject or of another natural person where the Data Subject is physically or legally incapable of giving consent.
4   The processing is carried out in the course of its legitimate activities with appropriate safeguards by a foundation, association or any other not-for-profit body with a political, philosophical, religious or trade union aim and on condition that the processing relates solely to the members or to former members of the body or to persons who have regular contact with it in connection with its purposes and that the personal data are not disclosed outside that body without the consent of the data subjects.
5   The processing relates to personal data which are manifestly made public by the data subject.

6   The processing is necessary for the establishment, exercise or defence of legal claims or whenever courts are acting in their judicial capacity.

7   The processing is necessary for reasons of substantial public interest, on the basis of Union or Member State law which shall be proportionate to the aim pursued, respect the essence of the right to data protection and provide for suitable and specific measures to safeguard the fundamental rights and the interests of the Data Subject.

8   The processing is necessary for the purposes of preventative or occupational medicine, for the assessment of the working capacity of the employee, medical diagnosis, the provision of health or social care or treatment or the management of health or social care systems and services on the basis of Union or Member State law or pursuant to contract with a health professional and subject to the conditions and safeguards referred to in paragraph 3.

9   The processing is necessary for reasons of public interest in the area of public health, such as protecting against serious cross-border threats to health or ensuring high standards of quality and safety of health care and of medicinal products or medical devices, on the basis of Union or Member State law which provides for suitable and specific measures to safeguard the rights and freedoms of the Data Subject, in particular professional secrecy.

10   The processing is necessary for archiving purposes in the public interest, scientific or historical research purposes or statistical purposes in accordance with Article 89(1) based on Union or Member State law which shall be proportionate to the aim pursued, respect the essence of the right to data protection and provide for suitable and specific measures to safeguard the fundamental rights and the interests of the Data Subject.

These special personal data lawful processing conditions may be summarised as follows:

- explicit consent;
- to comply with employment law;
- to protect vital interests;
- the processing is carried out by a not-for-profit organisation with safeguards;
- the personal data are manifestly made public by the data subject;
- necessary for the establishment, exercise or defence of legal claims;
- necessary for public interest;
- necessary for preventative medicine;
- necessary for public health;
- necessary for archiving purposes in the public interest, scientific or historical research purposes or statistical purposes.

Further rules also set out further obligations in relation to the processing of special personal data.

Note also that the Data Protection and Digital Information (No 2) Bill (DPDI Bill) proposes various amendments to the DPA 2018 and UK GDPR. These include:

- meaning of research and statistical purposes (clause 2);
- consent to processing for the purposes of scientific research (clause 3);
- assessment of high risk processing (clause 17);
- consulting the Commissioner/Commission prior to processing (clause 18);
- amended obligations (clause 20);
- data transfers (various);
- protection of prohibitions, restrictions, and Data Subject's rights (clause 43);
- UK GDPR (clause 44);

- power to make provision in connection with customer data (clause 62);
- power to make provision in connection with business data (clause 64);
- enforcement (clause 67);
- restrictions on powers of investigation (clause 68);
- repeal of provisions relating to supply of customer data (clause 76);
- unreceived communications (clause 80);
- meaning of direct marketing (clause 81);
- email marketing (clause 82);
- power to make consequential amendments (clause 107);
- lawfulness (Schedule 1);
- purpose limitation (Schedule 2);
- automated decisions amendments (Schedule 3);
- obligations amendments (Schedule 4);
- data transfers (Schedule 5); etc.

Chapter 7

Processing Pre-Conditions:
Prior Information Requirements
and Transparency

Introduction

7.01 Organisations, even prior to obtaining and processing personal data, are generally obliged to provide certain information to individual Data Subjects. The data protection regime places great emphasise on the need for transparency. While of course transparency in an ongoing obligation throughout the data lifecycle, there is particular need to achieve transparency through the use of providing specified details and information prior to the initial data collection. This is in order that Data Subjects can be properly informed, and can decide whether to consent or not, to the proposed data collection and data processing. Problems can arise if the Data Subject or a data regulator suggests that there is no valid collection of consent because there was either no prior information provided, or the information provided was incorrect or vague in some way.

Prior Information Requirements under the EU General Data Protection Regulation (GDPR)/UK GDPR

7.02 Articles 12, 13 and 14 of the new GDPR makes provision in relation to information available and provided to the Data Subject, including where personal data are collected, directly or indirectly.

Directly Obtained Data

7.03 Chapter III, Section 2 of the GDPR refers to data access. Article 13 refers to information to be provided where the data are collected from the Data Subject.

Where personal data relating to a Data Subject are collected from the Data Subject, the Controller shall, at the time when personal data are obtained, provide the Data Subject with the following information:

- the identity and the contact details of the Controller and, and where applicable, of the Controller's representative;
- the contact details of the DPO, where applicable;
- the purposes of the processing for which the personal data are intended as well as the legal basis for the processing;
- where the processing is based on Article 6(1)(f), the legitimate interests of the Controller or by a third party;

- the recipients or categories of recipients of the personal data, if any;
- where applicable, that fact that the Controller intends to transfer personal data to a third country or international organisation and the existence or absence of an adequacy decision by the Commission, or in case of transfers referred to in Article 46 or 47, or the second subparagraph of Article 49(1), reference to the appropriate or suitable safeguards and the means to obtain a copy of them or where they have been made available (Article 13(1)).

In addition to the information referred to in Article 13(1), the Controller shall, at the time when personal data are obtained, provide the Data Subject with the following further information necessary to ensure fair and transparent processing:

- the period for which the personal data will be stored, or if this is not possible, the criteria used to determine that period;
- the existence of the right to request from the Controller access to and rectification or erasure of the personal data or restriction of processing concerning the Data Subject or to object to processing as well as the right to data portability;
- where the processing is based on Article 6(1)(a) or Article 9(2)(a), the existence of the right to withdraw consent at any time, without affecting the lawfulness of processing based on consent before its withdrawal;
- the right to lodge a complaint to a supervisory authority;
- whether the provision of personal data is a statutory or contractual requirement, or a requirement necessary to enter into a contract, as well as whether the Data Subject is obliged to provide the data and of the possible consequences of failure to provide such data;
- the existence of automated decision-making including profiling, referred to in Article 22(1) and (4), and at least in those cases, meaningful information about the logic involved, as well as the significance and the envisaged consequences of such processing for the Data Subject (Article 13(2)).

Where the Controller intends to further process the data for a purpose other than that for which the personal data were collected, the Controller shall provide the Data Subject prior to that further processing with information on that other purpose and with any relevant further information as referred to in Article 13(2) (Article 13(3)).

Article 13(1), (2) and (3) shall not apply where and insofar as the Data Subject already has the information (Article 14(5)).

Indirectly Obtained Data

7.04 Article 14 refers to information to be provided where the personal data have not been obtained from the Data Subject.

Where personal data have not been obtained from the Data Subject, the Controller shall provide the Data Subject with the following information:

- the identity and the contact details of the Controller and, where applicable, of the Controller's representative;
- the contact details of the DPO, where applicable;
- the purposes of the processing for which the personal data are intended as well as the legal basis for the processing;
- the categories of personal data concerned;
- the recipients or categories of recipients of the personal data, if any;
- where applicable, that the Controller intends to transfer personal data to a recipient in a third country or international organisation and the existence or absence of an adequacy decision by the Commission, or in case of transfers referred to

in Article 46 or 47, or the second subparagraph of Article 49(1), reference to the appropriate or suitable safeguards and the means to obtain a copy of them or where they have been made available (Article 14(1)).

In addition to the information referred to in Article 14(1), the Controller shall provide the Data Subject with the following information necessary to ensure fair and transparent processing in respect of the Data Subject:

- the period for which the personal data will be stored, or if this is not possible, the criteria used to determine that period;
- where the processing is based on Article 6(1)(f), the legitimate interests pursued by the Controller or by a third party;
- the existence of the right to request from the Controller access to and rectification or erasure of personal data or restriction of processing concerning the Data Subject and to object to the processing as well as the right to data portability;
- where the processing is based on Article 6(1)(a) or Article 9(2)(a), the existence of the right to withdraw consent at any time, without affecting the lawfulness of processing based on consent before its withdrawal;
- the right to lodge a complaint to a supervisory authority;
- from which source the personal data originate, and if applicable, whether it came from publicly accessible sources;
- the existence of automated decision-making, including profiling, referred to in Article 22(1) and (4) and, at least in those cases, meaningful information about the logic involved, as well as the significance and the envisaged consequences of such processing for the Data Subject (Article 14(2)).

The Controller shall provide the information referred to in Article 14(1) and (2):

- within a reasonable period after obtaining the personal data, but at the latest within one month, having regard to the specific circumstances in which the personal data are processed;
- if the personal data are to be used for communication with the Data Subject, at the latest at the time of the first communication to that Data Subject; or
- if a disclosure to another recipient is envisaged, at the latest when the data are first disclosed (Article 14(3)).

Where the Controller intends to further process the personal data for a purpose other than that for which the data were obtained, the Controller shall provide the Data Subject prior to that further processing with information on that other purpose and with any relevant further information as referred to in Article 14(2) (Article 14(4)).

Article 14(1) to (4) shall not apply where and insofar as:

- the Data Subject already has the information; or
- the provision of such information proves impossible or would involve a disproportionate effort, in particular for processing for archiving purposes in the public interest, scientific or historical research purposes or statistical purposes, subject to the conditions and safeguards referred to in Article 89(1) or in so far as the obligation referred to in Article 14(1) is likely to render impossible or seriously impair the achievement of the objectives of that processing. In such cases the Controller shall take appropriate measures to protect the Data Subject's rights and freedoms and legitimate interests, including making the information publicly available;
- obtaining or disclosure is expressly laid down by EU or state law to which the Controller is subject and which provides appropriate measures to protect the Data Subject's legitimate interests; or

- where the data must remain confidential subject to an obligation of professional secrecy regulated by EU or state law, including a statutory obligation of secrecy (Article 14(5)).

Data Protection and Digital Information (No 2) Bill

7.05 The Data Protection and Digital Information (No 2) Bill (DPDI Bill) seeks to make amendments and updates regarding the DPA 2018 and UK GDPR. Clause 1 refers to information relating to an identifiable living individual. Clause 9 refers to information to be provided to data subjects. Clause 10 refers to Data Subject's rights to information and a legal professional privilege exemption. Clause 15 refers to the duty to keep records, and which can include records regarding the information that was provided to Data Subjects. Note also, Schedule 4 referring to obligations and consequential amendments. The DPDI Bill changes will need to monitored, especially the final form as enacted.

Conclusion

7.06 Organisations also need to be aware that if their data processing, data collection, or consent gathering processes are ever challenged in future, they need to be in a position to not only demonstrate a record of the consent, but also a record of all of the information, notices, etc as existed immediately prior to the collection event. This can be difficult as the prior information record is separate to the consent record. In addition, any large organisation will have to maintain these records for thousand or even millions of individuals. In addition, these records and policies will change over time, and so the organisation will need to maintain a record of which version is attached to which consent; when policies or prior information and documentation versions changed, etc. One can appreciate, therefore, that these required tasks are not without a level of complexity. Critical, however, is that if a problem arises with having prior information, or properly recording it, difficult issues arise as to whether any associated consent can be relied upon.

Chapter 8

Exemptions

Introduction

8.01 In considering compliance obligations it is also important to consider the exemptions that may apply. These are important as there are a significant number of adaptations and exemptions from the EU General Data Protection Regulation (GDPR) in the Data Protection Act 2018 (DPA 2018) and UK GDPR.

There is some potential that these may even increase further with primary legislation and potential Ministerial regulations relating to data protection. An example of the former is the Data Protection and Digital Information (No 2) Bill. The final nature of these provisions will need to be carefully assessed. This is also part of the continuing trend for changes and exemptions from the GDPR rules in the post-Brexit UK.

The final suite of UK data protection legislation, including the so-called UK GDPR, will need careful analysis as this may contain further amendments from the GDPR than are set out in the DPA 2018 itself, as well as the important issue of exemptions from the GDPR and or the data protection regime (whether in whole or in part on specific issues). These may also be potentially difficult to track given that already the DPA 2018 is a complex piece of legislation itself, and encompasses not just data protection and aspects of GDPR-data protection, but included other issues in addition.

Separately, the Leveson Report in considering the journalism 'exemption' in the Data Protection Act 1998 (DPA 1998), suggested that it may have been too widely drafted, and also considered the history of the particular section. The Report has suggested that the DPA be amended to ensure a more balanced journalism exemption provision. The interface with the erasure and forgetting right will also be important.

Exemptions under the DPA 2018

8.02 Schedule 2 to the DPA 2018 refers to exemptions from the UK GDPR as follows:

- adaptations and restrictions based on Articles 6(3) and 23(1) (Part 1, Sch 2);
- restrictions based on Article 23(1): restrictions of rules in Articles 13–21 and 34 (Part 2, Sch 2);
- restriction based on Article 23(1): protection of rights of others (Part 3, Sch 2);
- restrictions based in Article 23(1): restrictions of rules in Articles 13–15 (Part 4, Sch 2);
- exemptions, etc, based on Article 85(2) for reasons of freedom of expression and information (Part 5, Sch 2);
- derogations, etc, based on Article 89 for research, statistics and archiving (Part 6, Sch 2).

In addition Schedule 3 of DPA 2018 refers to exemptions from the UK GDPR: health, social work, education and child abuse data, as follows:

- UK GDPR provisions to be restricted (Part 1, Sch 3);
- health data (Part 2, Sch 3);
- social work data (Part 3, Sch 3);
- education data (Part 4, Sch 3);
- child abuse data (Part 5, Sch 3).

Schedule 4 of the DPA 2018 also refers to exemptions from the UK GDPR and specifically disclosure prohibited or restricted by an enactment.

There are also variations made specifically in relation to Part 3 of the DPA 2018 (law enforcement processing) and Part 4 of the DPA 2018 (intelligence services processing).

Further Exemptions by Order

8.03 There is potential for further amendment or exemptions to be made by official Order and or Ministerial regulations.

Exemptions under the GDPR/UK GDPR

8.04 The GDPR does not address national security (Recital 16); the GDPR should not apply to data processing by a natural person in the course of a purely personal or household activity and thus without a connection with a professional or commercial activity (Recital 18); without prejudice to the eCommerce Directive[1] in particular eCommerce defences of Articles 12–15 (Recital 21); the GDPR does not apply to the data of the deceased (Recital 27). Certain states might also seek to apply exemptions in certain respects in relation to parts of the GDPR.

Exemptions under the Data Protection and Digital Information (No 2) Bill

8.05 The Data Protection and Digital Information (No 2) Bill (DPDI Bill) once enacted creates scope under a variety of data issues for further exemptions or similar changes. This is an area requiring ongoing monitoring.

Conclusion

8.06 The exemptions are important when and where applicable. They will often be more relevant to particular sectors. Generally, the exemptions appear to be less litigated than other areas of data protection. The UK's derogations or amendments from aspects of the GDPR also need to be considered by particular organisations and sectors depending on the issue at hand. Organisations need to start with the GDPR, but then check the DPA 2018 and UK GDPR in case there were amendments made which affect the issue.

In addition, depending on when the particular issue under consideration arose or was initiated, it may come to be considered under the DPA 1998 (under transitional

---

1   Directive 2000/31/EC.

provisions) or DPA 2018 and UK GDPR. If certain issues started prior to the DPA 2018, the transitional provisions may mean that the old rules continue to apply for the particular issue, as it is considered as already in process.[2] The DPDI Bill also refers to new sets of transitional provisions that may become relevant.

As with any legislation, it is as important for what it encompasses as well as what it may exclude. The post-Brexit UK data protection regime obviously requires scrutiny of each.

---

2   See Data Protection Act 2018, Sch 20 – Transitional Provisions.

Chapter 9

Individual Data Subject Rights

Introduction

9.01   The data protection regime provides, or enshrines, a number of rights to individuals in relation to their informational data and informational privacy. Transparency and consent are very important aspects of respecting and enabling such fundamental rights to be vindicated, utilised and enforced by Data Subjects. Individual Data Subjects have a right of access to personal data. There are also time limits to be complied with by a Controller in relation to replying to a Data Subject access request (ie a request to access or obtain a copy of their personal data that the organisation holds).

Individuals also have a right to prevent data processing for direct marketing (DM) purposes.

The individual Data Subject has a right to prevent processing likely to cause damage or distress.

A further right relates to automated decision taking, which relates to automated decisions being taken without human oversight or intervention. The traditional example often used is adverse credit decisions being taken automatically. However, it can equally encompass such adverse decisions and activities as so called neutral algorithmic processing and arranging of information and result outputs. Examples could include search rankings and priorities; search suggestions; search prompts; autosuggest; autocomplete; etc. Other examples could arise in relation to profiling and advertising related activities.

Importantly, individual Data Subjects have specific rights in relation to rectification, blocking, erasure and destruction and what is becoming known as the Right to be Forgotten (RtbF). This has added significance and attention following the Court of Justice decision in the RtbF landmark case of *Google Spain*.[1]

Individual Data Subjects are also entitled to compensation and damages, as well as being entitled to complain to the ICO and to the courts to obtain judicial remedies.

The EU General Data Protection Regulation (GDPR) refers to Data Subject rights; principles of fair and transparent processing; prior information requirements; right of access; right of rectification and right to be forgotten (RtbF); right to complain to single supervisory authority; automated processing. The difficulty, however, in dealing with Data Subject rights is that the rights set out in the GDPR have many derogations, amendments and exemptions set out in the Data Protection Act 2018 (DPA 2018) and UK GDPR. These are not always easy to immediately discern given the complexity

---

1   *Google Spain SL, Google Inc v Agencia Española de Protección de Datos (AEPD), Mario Costeja González*, Court of Justice (Grand Chamber), Case C-131/12, 13 May 2014. This relates to outdated search engine result listings. See P Lambert, *The Right to be Forgotten* (Bloomsbury, 2022).

of the DPA 2018, including the extensive materials included in the Schedules to the Act. In addition, the GDPR itself is no longer directly effective in the UK, meaning that readers need to directly consult the DPA 2018 and UK GDPR – and soon the Data Protection and Digital Information (No 2) Bill (DPDI Bill) which seeks to amend both in addition to introducing its own new provisions.

Organisations should note that the new data protection regime is important for creating a number of new rights, and for expanding or strengthening some of the existing rights. In addition, organisations are also required to notify the existence of certain rights to Data Subjects. This can therefore create consequential issues where a required notification has not been provided to the individual. Ultimately, such a failing may feature in complaints with the data regulator or in separate court related litigation.

Principles of Data Protection

9.02 The Principles of data protection require that personal data are:

(1) processed lawfully, fairly and transparently;
(2) purpose limited;
(3) data is minimised;
(4) accurate;
(5) storage limited;
(6) secure; and
(7) accountable.

The GDPR (which the UK GDPR seeks to follow) expresses the Principles as requiring that personal data are:

- processed lawfully, fairly and in a transparent manner in relation to the Data Subject ('lawfulness, fairness and transparency');
- collected for specified, explicit and legitimate purposes and not further processed in a way incompatible with those purposes; further processing for archiving purposes in the public interest, scientific and historical research purposes or statistical purposes shall, in accordance with Article 89(1), not be considered incompatible with the initial purposes ('purpose limitation');
- adequate, relevant and limited to what is necessary in relation to the purposes for which they are processed ('data minimisation');
- accurate and, where necessary, kept up to date; every reasonable step must be taken to ensure that personal data that are inaccurate, having regard to the purposes for which they are processed, are erased or rectified without delay ('accuracy');
- kept in a form which permits identification of Data Subjects for no longer than is necessary for the purposes for which the personal data are processed; personal data may be stored for longer periods insofar as the data will be processed solely for archiving purposes in the public interest, scientific or historical research purposes or statistical purposes in accordance with Article 89(1) subject to implementation of the appropriate technical and organisational measures required by the GDPR in order to safeguard the rights and freedoms of the Data Subject ('storage limitation');
- processed in a manner that ensures appropriate security of the personal data, including protection against unauthorised or unlawful processing and against accidental loss, destruction or damage, using appropriate technical or organisational measures ('integrity and confidentiality').

The Controller must be responsible for and be able to demonstrate compliance ('accountability').

Note that the DPDI Bill seeks to make various amendments, such as in relation to Principles and purpose limitation (see clause 6; and Schedule 2)

Rights for Individual Data Subjects

9.03   The data protection rules contain a number of important rights for individuals in respect of their personal data, such as:

- the prior information that has to be given to them by Controllers;
- access to personal data;
- the right to object to processing;
- not being forced to make an access request as a condition of recruitment, employment or provision of a service;
- not being subjected to 'automated decision making processes'.

The rights are expanding and are becoming more explicit. It is important that organisations keep abreast of the expanding rights and obligations. The data protection rights enshrined in the data protection regime for individuals are set out in the data protection Principles and elsewhere in the data protection rules. They include the following:

- individuals have a right to be informed by organisations as to their identity when they are collecting and processing the individual's personal data;
- the organisation must disclose to the individual the purpose for which it is collecting and processing the individual's personal data;
- if the organisation is forwarding on the personal data to third party recipients, it must disclose this to the individual as well as identify the third party recipients. If it is permitted to transfer the personal data outside of the country, the organisation must then also identify which third party country will be receiving the personal data;
- organisations must answer and comply with requests from the individual in relation to their data protection rights.

This includes requests for access to a copy of the personal data held in relation to the individual. This is known as a personal data access request.

The rights of Data Subjects can be summarised as including:

- right of access;
- right to establish if personal data exists;
- right to be informed of the logic in automatic decision taking;
- right to prevent processing likely to cause damage or distress;
- right to prevent processing for direct marketing;
- right to prevent automated decision taking;
- right to damages and compensation;
- right to rectify inaccurate data;
- right to rectification, blocking, erasure and forgetting, and destruction;
- right to notification of erasure and for getting to third parties, etc;
- right to complain to ICO;
- right to go to court.

As indicated above, there can also be other obligations which may be interpreted in a rights lens, such as the need for individuals to be appraised of certain of their rights.

A Data Subject may wish to complain where they have not been furnished with this information.

The DPDI Bill also refers to rights and changes being made in the UK. Clause 7 refers to vexatious or excessive requests by Data Subjects. Clause 8 refers to time limits for responding to requests by Data Subjects. Clause 9 refers to information to be provided to Data Subjects. Clause 10 refers to Data Subjects rights to information: legal professional privilege exemption. There are also other relevant suggested changes.

Recipients of Right

9.04 The data protection rights apply generally in relation to any individuals whose personal data are being collected and processed. Specifically, it can include:

- employees;
- other workers such as contractors, temps, casual staff;
- agency staff;
- ex-employees and retired employees;
- spouses and family members;
- job applicants, including unsuccessful applicants;
- volunteers;
- apprentices and trainees;
- customers and clients;
- prospective customer and clients;
- suppliers;[2]
- members;
- users;
- any other individuals.

Access Right under the DPA 2018

9.05 An individual is entitled to be informed by a Controller whether personal data of which that individual is the Data Subject are being processed by or on behalf of that Controller and if that is the case, to be given by the Controller a description of:

- the personal data of which that individual is the Data Subject;
- the purposes for which they are being or are to be processed; and
- the recipients or classes of recipients to whom they are or may be disclosed;
- to have communicated to them in an intelligible form, a copy of the personal data; and information as to the source of those data.

Where the processing by automatic means of personal data of which that individual is the Data Subject for the purpose of evaluating matters relating to them such as, for example, performance at work, credit worthiness, reliability or conduct, has constituted or is likely to constitute the sole basis for any decision significantly affecting them, to be informed by the Controller of the logic involved in that decision-taking.

---

2   L AC MacDonald, *Data Protection: Legal Compliance and Good Practice for Employers* (Tottel, 2008) 41.

It is important to consider that being informed only verbally may not always, or at all, be a proper vindication of the Data Subject's access right. This is particularly so where large sets of personal data, or complex details involving personal data, are involved. Generally, personal data is provided in hardcopy. However, in particular circumstances, certain Controllers prefer to furnish personal data in electronic format where large volumes of materials are involved. If a Controller was to refuse to furnish the personal data required, on the basis that it had verbally communicated same, this would jar with the accepted understanding of the data access right. It could also be argued that the Controller was not allowing access to the personal data to be effectively and properly given. Note, however, the case of *Durham County Council v Dunn* [2012] EWCA Civ 1654, which while acknowledging the legitimacy of copies of documents, appears to suggest that other avenues also arise. An organisation should be cautious in embarking in data access disclosures other than in a documented and written manner. It is clearly the case that an organisation has an obligation to be able to demonstrate its compliance with access requests which includes maintaining written procedures and records. Some would also query whether interpreting the data access right as some sort of a *data communicated right* as appears to be suggested in part of *Durham* as compatible with the Data Protection Act 1998 (DPA 1998), the DPA 2018 and now the GDPR (referring to electronic access). Organisations should note that responses to data access request can be responded to electronically. Indeed, under the GDPR there is an enhanced ability for Data Subject to request that the responses be electronic.

Data cases also refer to data access rights issues. In one case a town clerk was prosecuted for frustrating and blocking an access issue, and ultimately facilitating the deletion of records in order that they not be available to be furnished.[3] Hudson Bay Finance was served with an official Enforcement Notice for failing to fulfil the data access right.[4] The London Borough of Lewisham was also issued with an Enforcement Notice over data access right issues.[5]

Note that the DPDI Bill seeks to make changes in relation to certain data rights and including data access rights issues.

Access Right

Access Right under the GDPR

9.06   Article 15 of the GDPR relates to the right of access for the Data Subject.

The Data Subject shall have the right to obtain from the Controller confirmation as to whether or not personal data concerning them are being processed, and where that is the case, access to the personal data and the following information:

- the purposes of the processing;
- the categories of personal data concerned;
- the recipients or categories of recipient to whom the personal data have been or will be disclosed, in particular recipients in third countries or international organisations;

---

3   See *ICO v Young* [2020] 13/3/2020.
4   *ICO v Hudson Bay Finance Limited* [2019] 12/8/2019.
5   *ICO v London Borough of Lewisham* [2018] 6/9/2018.

- where possible, the envisaged period for which the personal data will be stored, or, if not possible, the criteria used to determine that period;
- the existence of the right to request from the Controller rectification or erasure of personal data or restriction of the processing of personal data concerning the Data Subject or to object to such processing;
- the right to lodge a complaint with a supervisory authority;
- where the personal data are not collected from the Data Subject, any available information as to their source;
- the existence of automated decision making including profiling referred to in Article 22(1) and (4) and at least in those cases, meaningful information about the logic involved, as well as the significance and the envisaged consequences of such processing for the Data Subject (Article 15(1)).

Where personal data are transferred to a third country or to an international organisation, the Data Subject shall have the right to be informed of the appropriate safeguards pursuant to Article 46 relating to the transfer (Article 15(2)).

The Controller shall provide a copy of the personal data undergoing processing. For any further copies requested by the Data Subject, the Controller may charge a reasonable fee based on administrative costs. Where the Data Subject makes the request in electronic means, and unless otherwise requested by the Data Subject, the information shall be provided in a commonly used electronic form (Article 15(3)).

The right to obtain a copy referred to in paragraph 3 shall not adversely affect the rights and freedoms of others (Article 15(4)).

The DPDI Bill seeks to make changes in relation to certain data access rights issues.

Dealing with Access Requests

9.07   One commentary[6] refers to the advisability of having a process flow chart in place. The main components referred to include:

- Data Subject calls or asks for personal data;
- Data Subject access request form issued;
- Data Subject access request form returned;
- personal data located, whether by legal department, data protection personnel, etc;
- examining same in relation to whether any third party information; health data, exempt data;
- data reviewed by legal department and DPO;
- personal data copy issues to Data Subject.

The ICO provides the following guidance or checklist:[7]

1   Is this a subject access request?
No – Handle the query as part of the normal course of business.
Yes – Go to 2.

2   Is there enough information to be sure of the requester's identity?
No – If the requester's identity is unclear, ask them to provide evidence to confirm it. For example, one may ask for a piece of information held in your records that the person would be expected to know, such as membership details, or a witnessed copy of their signature. Once satisfied, go to 3.
Yes – Go to 3.

---

6   R Morgan and R Boardman, *Data Protection Strategy* (Sweet & Maxwell, 2003) 252.
7   *Data Protection Good Practice Note, Checklist for Handling Requests for Personal Information* (subject access requests), ICO, at https://ico.org.uk.

3   Is any other information required to find the records they want?
      No – Go to 4.
      Yes – One will need to ask the individual promptly for any other information
      reasonably needed to find the records they want. One might want to ask them to
      narrow down their request. For example, if keeping all customers' information on
      one computer system and suppliers' information on another, one could ask what
      relationship they had with the organisation. Or, one could ask when they had
      dealings with the organisation. However, they do have the right to ask for every-
      thing held about them and this could mean a very wide search. The organisation
      has a timeline to respond to a subject access request after receiving any further
      information one needs. Go to 4.

4   Fee?
      No – Go to 5.
      Yes – Note, that there are restricted circumstances when a fee may be charged.
      Go to 5.

5   Does the organisation hold any information about the person?
      No – If one holds no personal information at all about the individual one must tell
      them this.
      Yes – Go to 6.

6   Will the information be changed between receiving the request and sending the
      response?
      No – Go to 7.
      Yes – One can still make routine amendments and deletions to personal informa-
      tion after receiving a request. However, one must not make any changes to the
      records as a result of receiving the request, even if one finds inaccurate or embar-
      rassing information on the record. Go to 7.

7   Does it include any information about other people?
      No – Go to 8.
      Yes – One will not have to supply the information unless the other people men-
      tioned have given their consent, or it is reasonable to supply the information
      without their consent. Even when the other person's information should not be
      disclosed, one should still supply as much as possible by editing the references to
      other people. Go to 8.

8   Is the organisation obliged to supply the information?
      No – If all the information held about the requester is exempt, then one can reply
      stating that one does not hold any of their personal information required to be
      revealed.
      Yes – Go to 9.

9   Does it include any complex terms or codes?
      No – Go to 10.
      Yes – One must make sure that these are explained so the information can be
      understood. Go to 10.

10   Prepare the response.[8]

Note that data access rights must be fulfilled within a specified timeframe. The ICO
has recently updated its guidance on the operation of the time limit for fulfilling the
data access right. (See Chapter 10 for further details on the time limits, and the ICO's
updated guidance.)

---

8   See above.

GDPR: Rectification and Erasure

9.08   Chapter III, Section 3 of the GDPR refers to rectification and erasure.

Rectification Right

9.09   The GDPR provides that the Data Subject shall have the right to obtain from the Controller without undue delay the rectification of inaccurate personal data concerning them. Taking into account the purposes of the processing, the Data Subject shall have the right to have incomplete personal data completed, including by means of providing a supplementary statement (Article 16).

Erasure and Forgetting Right

9.10   The GDPR provides that the Data Subject shall have the right to obtain from the Controller the erasure of personal data concerning them without undue delay where one of the following grounds applies:

- the data are no longer necessary in relation to the purposes for which they were collected or otherwise processed;
- the Data Subject withdraws consent on which the processing is based according to Article 6(1)(a), or Article 9(2)(a), and where there is no other legal ground for the processing;
- the Data Subject objects to the processing pursuant to Article 21(1) and there are no overriding legitimate grounds for the processing, or the Data Subject objects to the processing pursuant to Article 21(2);
- the personal data have been unlawfully processed;
- the personal data have to be erased for compliance with a legal obligation in EU or state law to which the Controller is subject;
- the data have been collected in relation to the offering of information society services referred to in Article 8(1) (Article 17(1)).[9]

Where the Controller has made the personal data public and is obliged per the above to erase the personal data, the Controller, taking account of available technology and the cost of implementation, shall take reasonable steps, including technical measures, to inform Controllers which are processing the personal data, that the Data Subject has requested the erasure by such Controllers of any links to, or copy or replication of that personal data (Article 17(2)).

Article 17(1) and (2) shall not apply to the extent that processing is necessary:

- for exercising the right of freedom of expression and information;
- for compliance with a legal obligation which requires processing by EU or state law to which the Controller is subject or for the performance of a task carried out in the public interest or in the exercise of official authority vested in the Controller;
- for reasons of public interest in the area of public health in accordance with Article 9(2)(h) and (i) as well as Article 9(3);
- for archiving purposes in the public interest, scientific or historical research purposes or statistical purposes in accordance with Article 89(1) in so far as the right referred to in para 1 is likely to render impossible or seriously impair the achievement of the objectives of that processing;
- for the establishment, exercise or defence of legal claims (Article 17(3)).

9   See P Lambert, *The Right to be Forgotten* (Bloomsbury, 2022).

Synodinou[10] refers to the 'right to oblivion' and notes in relation to her research that media rights are not immune to the right to be forgotten. Examples are given where cases have been successful in preventing particular media stories dragging up past events long after they had occurred, including court cases.[11] Indeed, many countries already obscure party names from decisions and judgments so as to render them anonymous, such as in Germany, Austria, Greece, Finland, Belgium, Hungary, the Netherlands, Poland and Portugal.[12] The right to be forgotten has also been recognised in France and Belgium.[13] UK cases have also granted anonymity to the Plaintiff,[14] as did the Canadian Supreme Court in an online abuse case.[15] To be successful, however, it can be important to change party initials.[16]

Right to Restriction of Processing

9.11 Article 18 of the GDPR refers to the right to restriction of processing. The Data Subject shall have the right to obtain from the Controller the restriction of the processing where one of the following applies:

- the accuracy of the data is contested by the Data Subject, for a period enabling the Controller to verify the accuracy of the personal data;
- the processing is unlawful and the Data Subject opposes the erasure of the personal data and requests the restriction of their use instead;
- the Controller no longer needs the personal data for the purposes of the processing, but they are required by the Data Subject for the establishment, exercise or defence of legal claims;
- the Data Subject has objected to processing pursuant to Article 21(1) pending the verification whether the legitimate grounds of the Controller override those of the Data Subject (Article 18(1)).

Where processing has been restricted under Article 18(1), such personal data shall, with the exception of storage, only be processed with the Data Subject's consent or for the establishment, exercise or defence of legal claims or for the protection of the rights of another natural or legal person or for reasons of important public interest of the EU or of a state (Article 18(2)).

A Data Subject who obtained the restriction of processing pursuant to Article 18(1) shall be informed by the Controller before the restriction of processing is lifted (Article 18(3)).

Notification Obligation re Rectification, Erasure or Restriction

9.12 The GDPR provides that the Controller shall communicate any rectification or erasure of personal data or restriction of processing carried out in accordance with

---

10 Ta-E Synodinou, 'The Media Coverage of Court Proceedings in Europe: Striking a Balance Between Freedom of Expression and Fair Process,' *Computer Law & Security Review* (2012) (28) 208–219, at 217. Also Lambert, above.
11 Above at 218.
12 Above at 218 and fn 106, 218.
13 Above at 208–219, at 217.
14 See *XY v Facebook*, which also said that the website was a publisher. *XY v Facebook*, McCloskey J [2012] NIQB 96, 30 November 2012.
15 *AB v Bragg Communications*, 27 September 2012. At https://scc-csc.lexum.com/scc-csc/scc-csc/en/item/10007/index.do.
16 For example, while the parties and director defendants in a Berlin Facebook data protection case were reduced initials, reducing one party's name to 'MZ' may not have been fully effective. See *The Federal Association of Consumer Organisations and Consumer Groups, Federal Consumer Association, GB v Facebook Ireland Limited, MA, JB, DG, PT and the Chairman* [names redacted], [redacted].

Articles 16, 17(1) and 18 to each recipient to whom the personal data have been disclosed, unless this proves impossible or involves disproportionate effort. The Controller shall inform the Data Subject about those recipients if the Data Subject requests it (Article 19).

Right to Data Portability

9.13   The GDPR provides that the Data Subject shall have the right to receive the personal data concerning them, which they have provided to a Controller, in a structured, commonly used and machine-readable format and have the right to transmit those data to another Controller without hindrance from the Controller to which the personal data have been provided, where:

- the processing is based on consent pursuant to Article 6(1)(a) or Article 9(2)(a) or on a contract pursuant to Article 6(1)(a); and
- the processing is carried out by automated means (Article 20(1)).

In exercising their right to data portability, the Data Subject has the right to have the personal data transmitted directly from Controller to Controller, where technically feasible (Article 20(2)).

The exercise of this right shall be without prejudice to Article 17. That right shall not apply to processing necessary for the performance of a task carried out in the public interest or in the exercise of official authority vested in the Controller (Article 20(3)).

The right referred to in para 1 shall not adversely affect the rights and freedoms of others (Article 20(4)).

The EBPB endorsed the previous WP29 guidelines on data portability, namely,

- Guidelines on the right to data portability under Regulation 2016/679, WP242 rev.01.

The portability right may become increasingly important as users seek to move from one service provider to another, and in order to do so (or to do so in a manner where their data can be easily carried over to the new provider) may have to force the old provider to furnish the required data.

Automated Individual Decision Making Right

9.14   Chapter III, Section 4 of the GDPR refers to the right to object and automated individual decision making.

Right to Object

9.15   The GDPR provides that the Data Subject shall have the right to object, on grounds relating to their particular situation, at any time to the processing of personal data concerning them which is based on Article 6(1)(e) or (f), including profiling based on those provisions. The Controller shall no longer process the personal data unless the Controller demonstrates compelling legitimate grounds for the processing which override the interests, rights and freedoms of the Data Subject or for the establishment, exercise or defence of legal claims (Article 21(1)).

Where personal data are processed for direct marketing purposes, the Data Subject shall have the right to object at any time to the processing of personal data concerning them for such marketing, which includes profiling to the extent that it is related to such direct marketing (Article 21(2)).

Where the Data Subject objects to the processing for direct marketing purposes, the personal data shall no longer be processed for such purposes (Article 21(3)).

At the latest at the time of the first communication with the Data Subject, the right referred to in Article 21(1) and (2) shall be explicitly brought to the attention of the Data Subject and shall be presented clearly and separately from any other information (Article 21(4)).

In the context of the use of information society services, and notwithstanding Directive 2002/58/EC,[17] the Data Subject may exercise their right to object by automated means using technical specifications (Article 21(5)).

Where personal data are processed for scientific and historical research purposes or statistical purposes pursuant to Article 89(1), the Data Subject, on grounds relating to their particular situation, shall have the right to object to processing of personal data concerning them, unless the processing is necessary for the performance of a task carried out for reasons of public interest (Article 21(6)).

The DPDI Bill seeks to make changes in relation to automated decision making, in particular at clause 11. These will need to be considered. It seeks to substitute a new section for Article 22 of the UK GDPR with provisions for automated decisions and significant decisions, and restrictions, safeguards and further provision on both automated decision making, and automated decision making using sensitive personal data. In addition, Schedule 3 refers to automated decision making: consequential amendments.

Automated Individual Decision Making, Including Profiling

9.16 The GDPR provides that Data Subjects shall have the right not to be subject to a decision based solely on automated processing, including profiling, which produces legal effects concerning them or similarly significantly affects them (Article 22(1)).

Article 22(1) shall not apply if the decision:

- is necessary for entering into, or performance of, a contract between the Data Subject and a Controller [a];
- is authorised by EU or state law to which the Controller is subject and which also lays down suitable measures to safeguard the Data Subject's rights and freedoms and legitimate interests; or
- is based on the Data Subject's explicit consent (Article 22(2)) [c].

In cases referred to in Article 22(2) (a) and (c) the Controller shall implement suitable measures to safeguard the Data Subject's rights and freedoms and legitimate interests, at least the right to obtain human intervention on the part of the Controller, to express their point of view and to contest the decision (Article 22(3)).

Decisions referred to in paragraph (2) shall not be based on special categories of personal data referred to in Article 9(1), unless Article 9(2)(a) or (g) apply and suitable measures to safeguard the Data Subject's rights and freedoms and legitimate interests are in place (Article 22(4)).

---

17 Directive 2002/58/EC of the European Parliament and of the Council of 12 July 2002 concerning the processing of personal data and the protection of privacy in the electronic communications sector (Directive on privacy and electronic communications).

The EDPB has adopted and endorsed the following earlier WP29 guidance:

● Guidelines on automated individual decision making and profiling for the purposes of Regulation 2016/679, WP251 rev.01.

Compensation for Data Subjects

9.17 This is an area which will continue to grow in importance. The facts in the *Prudential* case could have resulted in actual financial loss and damage to a Data Subject. While the ICO implemented a fine of £50,000, civil compensation could also have been a possibility.

In another case, a businessman successfully sued a company for spamming.[18] Another victim of spam also sued and received £750 for a single spam message received.[19] Typically, a Spammer sends tens of thousands if not millions of spam messages at a time, so per message fines can add up, even if only a small sample of them result in fines or awards. One of the prominent areas for data regulator investigations, complaints, and data fines is spam and unsolicited marketing and advertising communications.

In the US there have been cases by service providers, in addition to individual recipients of spam. Microsoft successfully sued a spam company in the UK and received £45,000.[20]

The trend in spam laws appears to be to permitting recipients, service providers and a regulator to be able to sue spammers. Indeed, Regulation 30(1) PECR Amendment provides that 'A person who suffers damage by reason of any contravention ... by any other person shall be entitled to bring proceedings for compensation from that person for that damage.'

Injunctions can be possible for spam, as well as other areas involving data protection rights.

The ICO also fined the promoters behind a Spam company a total of £440,000.[21] A managing director has also been personally prosecuted individually – ie separate and apart from the company entity.[22]

The area of compensation and civil litigation in vindication of data protection rights will continue to develop. While the scale of monetary claims, and awards, can differ as between the US and the UK, it is noted that one defendant was happy to settle one such case for approx $20 m.[23]

It is possible that Data Subjects, and indeed Data Subjects who have not suffered financial loss, can still suffer damage and be awarded compensation or damages. Indeed, the Digital, Culture, Media and Sport (DCMS) Committee when considering social media and related issues refers to the existence of 'online harms'.[24]

As data fines will no doubt increase, so too will the level of compensation and damages which may arise for an organisation, albeit that in the context of individual

---

18 H Hart, 'Cutting Down on Spam,' *Solicitors Journal*, 10 March 2005, 290.
19 T Young, 'Courts Put Price on Unsolicited Email,' *Computing*, 15 March 2007, 14.
20 *Microsoft v Paul Martin McDonald* [2006] EWHC 3410 (Ch).
21 *ICO v Niebel, McNeish and Tetrus Telecoms* (2012).
22 See *ICO v Cullen* [2019] 24/6/2019.
23 Facebook was willing to settle a social media privacy and advertising litigation case for approx $20 million. This related to the unlawful use of personal data in relation to the Beacon project.
24 Digital, Culture, Media and Sport (DCMS) Committee, Disinformation and 'Fake News': Final Report (18 February 2019). Available at https://committees.parliament.uk/committee/378/digital-culture-media-and-sport-committee/news/103668/fake-news-report-published-17-19/.

Data Subjects such compensation will likely trail the level of monetary data fines. Arguably levels of compensation and damages have been artificially low. This can partly be explained by a lack of familiarity with the concepts of data protection, and what some may have seen as a certain novelty element. There have also been some robust defence arguments raised on occasion. However, there have also been some untenable defence arguments raised – but which have not always been recognised as such. On the plaintiff side, it sometimes also helps not to appear as the proverbial ambulance chaser. One should also recall that while compensation and damages are provided for, it may not be beneficial to present this as the first remedy being sought. After all, there are many valuable reliefs and remedies available which can be important solutions for individuals. It is appropriate to seek compensation, but it is sometimes wise not to leave this as the only remedy or primary remedy being sought. Overall, however, one can expect the jurisprudence of compensation to develop significantly over the coming years. After all, in many respects the research of the damage that can arise from misuse, loss, and lack of data security is really only now reaching wider understanding.

DPA: Requiring Data Disclosure

9.18   Section 184 of the DPA 2018 provides that it is an offence to require a person to provide or give access to a relevant record (see Sch 18 of the Act) for employment, continued employment or a contract requirement.

Section 185 of the DPA 2018 refers to the need for the avoidance of certain contractual terms relating to health records. The inclusion of such a term is void.

Jurisdiction

9.19   GDPR Recital 22 states that any processing of personal data in the context of the activities of an establishment of a Controller or a Processor in the Union should be carried out in accordance with the GDPR, regardless of whether the processing itself takes place within the EU. Establishment implies the effective and real exercise of activity through stable arrangements. The legal form of such arrangements, whether through a branch or a subsidiary with a legal personality, is not the determining factor in this respect.

GDPR Recital 23 states that in order to ensure that natural persons are not deprived of the protection to which they are entitled under the GDPR, the processing of personal data of Data Subjects who are in the EU by a Controller or a Processor not established in the EU should be subject to the GDPR where the processing activities are related to the offering of goods or services to such Data Subjects irrespective of whether connected to a payment. In order to determine whether such a Controller or Processor is offering goods or services to Data Subjects who are in the EU, it should be ascertained whether it is apparent that the Controller or Processor envisages offering services to Data Subjects in one or more states in the EU. Whereas the mere accessibility of the Controller's, Processor's or an intermediary's website in the Union, of an email address or of other contact details, or the use of a language generally used in the third country where the controller is established, is insufficient to ascertain such intention, factors such as the use of a language or a currency generally used in one or more states with the possibility of ordering goods and services in that other language, or the mentioning of customers or users who are in the EU, may make it apparent that the controller envisages offering goods or services to such Data Subjects in the EU.

Section 180 of the DPA 2018 refers to certain jurisdiction and jurisdiction of court issues. Section 207 refers to the territorial application of the DPA 2018.

Complaints to ICO

9.20 GDPR Recital 141 states that every Data Subject should have the right to lodge a complaint with a single supervisory authority, in particular in the state of their habitual residence, and the right to an effective judicial remedy in accordance with Article 47 of the Charter if the Data Subject considers that their rights under the Regulation are infringed or where the supervisory authority does not act on a complaint, partially or wholly rejects or dismisses a complaint or does not act where such action is necessary to protect the rights of the Data Subject. The investigation following a complaint should be carried out, subject to judicial review, to the extent that is appropriate in the specific case. The supervisory authority should inform the Data Subject of the progress and the outcome of the complaint within a reasonable period. If the case requires further investigation or coordination with another supervisory authority, intermediate information should be given to the Data Subject. In order to facilitate the submission of complaints, each supervisory authority should take measures such as providing a complaint submission form which can also be completed electronically, without excluding other means of communication.

The DPDI Bill replaces the Information Commissioner with an Information Commission. It also makes various amendments and provisions in relation to PECR and electronic advertising and marketing (see DPDI Bill, Part 4). There are also separate provisions in relation to digital verification services (see DPDI Bill, Part 2) and customer data and business data distinctions (see DPDI Bill, Part 3).

Certain of the rules in relation to rights, making complaints, investigations, and consequences are also sought to be altered in the DPDI Bill. Clauses 34–42 refer to enforcement issues. Clause 67 also refers to enforcement. Restrictions on investigations, etc, are referred in clause 68. Data fines are referred to in clause 69 (as financial penalties). Marketing and PECR issues are referred to in Part 4.

Organisational Data Protection Groups

9.21 GDPR Recital 142 states that where a Data Subject considers that their rights under the Regulation are infringed, they should have the right to mandate a not-for-profit body, organisation or association which is constituted according to the law of a state, has statutory objectives which are in the public interest and is active in the field of the protection of personal data to lodge a complaint on their behalf with a supervisory authority, exercise the right to a judicial remedy on behalf of Data Subjects or exercise if provided for in state law exercise the right to receive compensation on behalf of Data Subjects. A state may provide for such a body, organisation or association to have the right to lodge a complaint in that state, independently of a Data Subject's mandate, and the right to an effective judicial remedy where it has reason to consider that the rights of a Data Subject have been infringed as a result of the processing of personal data which infringes the Regulation. That body, organisation or association may not be allowed to claim compensation on a Data Subject's behalf independently of the Data Subject's mandate.

Indeed, there are an increasing number of data protection and privacy groups, both nationally and supra-nationally. Indeed, the Court of Justice case striking down the Data Retention Directive was taken by one such group.[25]

The DPA 2018 at ss 187–190 refers to the representation of Data Subjects, including in 'collective proceedings'.

There have already been a number of cases, including notable cases, where data protection and privacy groups have been involved – if not leading the respective cases and complaints to data regulators. Digital Rights Ireland was instrumental in the decision invalidating the Data Retention Directive.[26] The groundbreaking case where the EU–US Safe Harbours arrangement was invalidated was taken by an individual associated with a European privacy group.[27] The recent challenge to the standard contractual clauses data transfer arrangement (in particular as it relates to certain data transfers from the EU to the US) included submissions from the Electronic Privacy Information Centre (EPIC), the Business Software Alliance (BSA), Digitaleurope, and began with a complaint from Max Schrems (and an associated data protection privacy group).[28]

While there are an increasing number of data protection privacy groups which take or initiate issue specific complaints, they have not generally sought to focus on the compensation and damages potential. In addition, an interesting point will be the extent to which established trade unions or representative bodies may seek to be recognised as an organisation data protection group as envisaged under the GDPR and related legislation such as the UK GDPR.

Court Remedies

9.22 GDPR Recital 143 states that each natural or legal person should have an effective judicial remedy before the competent national court against a decision of a supervisory authority which produces legal effects concerning that person. This is, *inter alia*, distinguished from other matters such as opinions and non legal effects.

Different Supervisory Authorities

9.23 One of the aims of the GDPR was originally to establish a single supervisory authority in respect of which organisations would have to deal with, a so called one-stop-shop, as opposed to dealing with data protection authorities in each state, there is recognition that circumstances can arise for other authorities to become involved.

---

25 Cases C-293/12 and C-594/12, *Digital Rights Ireland and Seitlinger and Others*, Court of Justice, 8 April 2014. Directive 2006/24/EC and amending Directive 2002/58/EC.
26 Directive 2006/24/EC of the European Parliament and of the Council of 15 March 2006 on the retention of data generated or processed in connection with the provision of publicly available electronic communications services or of public communications networks, and amending Directive 2002/58/EC. This was the case of Judgment of the Court (Grand Chamber) of 8 April 2014 (requests for a preliminary ruling from the High Court of Ireland (Ireland) and the *Verfassungsgerichtshof* (Austria)) – *Digital Rights Ireland Ltd (C-293/12) v Minister for Communications, Marine and Natural Resources, Minister for Justice, Equality and Law Reform, The Commissioner of the Garda Síochána, Ireland and the Attorney General, and Kärntner Landesregierung, Michael Seitlinger, Christof Tschohl and Others* (C-594/12), Joined Cases C-293/12 and C-594/12.
27 *Schrems v Data Protection Commissioner*, CJEU [2015] Case C-362/14.
28 *Facebook Ireland and Schrems*, AG Opinion, CJEU [2019] Case C-311/18_O (19 December 2019).

Supervisory authorities may cooperate on specific matters.

GDPR Recital 144 states proceedings may be stayed or declined where there are similar or identical prior proceedings ongoing in another state.

Plaintiff Choice of Jurisdictions and Courts

9.24 GDPR Recital 145 states that for proceedings against a Controller or Processor, the plaintiff should have the choice to bring the action before the courts of the states where the controller or processor has an establishment or where the Data Subject resides, unless the Controller is a public authority of a state acting in the exercise of its public powers.

Compensation

9.25 GDPR Recital 146 states that the Controller or Processor should compensate any damage which a person may suffer as a result of processing that infringes the GDPR. The Controller or Processor should be exempt from liability if it proves that it is not in any way responsible for the damage. The concept of damage should be broadly interpreted in the light of the case law of the Court of Justice in a manner which fully reflects the objectives of the GDPR. This is without prejudice to any claims for damage deriving from the violation of other rules in EU or state law. Processing that infringes the GDPR also includes processing that infringes delegated and implementing acts adopted in accordance with the GDPR and state law specifying rules of the GDPR. Data Subjects should receive full and effective compensation for the damage they have suffered. Where Controllers or Processors are involved in the same processing, each Controller or Processor should be held liable for the entire damage. However, where they are joined to the same judicial proceedings, in accordance with state law, compensation may be apportioned according to the responsibility of each Controller or Processor for the damage caused by the processing, provided that full and effective compensation of the Data Subject who suffered the damage is ensured. Any Controller or Processor which has paid full compensation may subsequently institute recourse proceedings against other Controllers or Processors involved in the same processing. The developing issue of compensation and damages will be one of the more followed areas of the new data protection regime.

Penalties

9.26 GDPR Recital 148 states that in order to strengthen the enforcement of the rules of the GDPR, penalties including administrative fines should be imposed for any infringement of the GDPR, in addition to, or instead of appropriate measures imposed by the supervisory authority pursuant to the GDPR. In a case of a minor infringement or if the fine likely to be imposed would constitute a disproportionate burden to a natural person, a reprimand may be issued instead of a fine. Due regard should be given to the nature, gravity and duration of the infringement, the intentional character of the infringement, actions taken to mitigate the damage suffered, degree of responsibility or any relevant previous infringements, the manner in which the infringement became known to the supervisory authority, compliance with measures ordered against the Controller or Processor, adherence to a code of conduct and any other aggravating or mitigating factor. The imposition of penalties including administrative fines should be subject to appropriate procedural safeguards in accordance with the general principles of EU law and the Charter, including effective judicial protection and due process.

The DPDI Bill refers to data fine and penalty issues at clause 69.

Sanctions

9.27   GDPR Recital 150 states that the in order to strengthen and harmonise administrative penalties for infringements of the GDPR, each supervisory authority should have the power to impose administrative fines. The GDPR should indicate infringements and the upper limit and criteria for setting the related administrative fines, which should be determined by the competent supervisory authority in each individual case, taking into account all relevant circumstances of the specific situation, with due regard in particular to the nature, gravity and duration of the infringement and of its consequences and the measures taken to ensure compliance with the obligations under the GDPR and to prevent or mitigate the consequences of the infringement. Where administrative fines are imposed on an undertaking, an undertaking should be understood to be an undertaking in accordance with Articles 101 and 102 TFEU for those purposes. Where administrative fines are imposed on persons that are not an undertaking, the supervisory authority should take account of the general level of income in the state as well as the economic situation of the person in considering the appropriate amount of the fine. The consistency mechanism may also be used to promote a consistent application of administrative fines. It should be for the states to determine whether and to which extent public authorities should be subject to administrative fines. Imposing an administrative fine or giving a warning does not affect the application of other powers of the supervisory authorities or of other penalties under the GDPR.

The DPDI Bill refers changes to the data regulator and enforcement regime and will need to be carefully considered.

GDPR: Right to Portability

9.28   GDPR Article 20 refers to the right to data portability. The Data Subject shall have the right to receive the personal data concerning them, which they provided to a Controller, in a structured, commonly used and machine-readable format and have the right to transmit those data to another Controller without hindrance from the Controller to which the data have been provided, where:

- the processing is based on consent pursuant to Article 6(1)(a) or Article 9(2)(a) or on a contract pursuant to Article 6(1)(b); and
- the processing is carried out by automated means (Article 20(1)).

In exercising their right to data portability pursuant to para 1, the Data Subject has the right to have the data transmitted directly from Controller to Controller, where technically feasible (Article 20(2)).

The exercise of this right shall be without prejudice to Article 17. That right shall not apply to processing necessary for the performance of a task carried out in the public interest or in the exercise of official authority vested in the Controller (Article 20(3)).

The right referred to in para 1 shall not adversely affect the rights and freedoms of others (Article 20(4)).

GDPR: Right to Object, Automated Decisions and Profiling

9.29   Chapter III, Section 4 of the GDPR refers to the right to object to processing, automated individual decisions and to profiling.

The Data Subject shall have the right to object, on grounds relating to their particular situation, at any time to the processing of personal data concerning them which is based on Article 6(1)(e) or (f), including profiling based on these provisions. The Controller shall no longer process the personal data unless the Controller demonstrates compelling legitimate grounds for the processing which override the interests, rights and freedoms of the Data Subject or for the establishment, exercise or defence of legal claims (Article 21(1)).

Where personal data are processed for direct marketing purposes, the Data Subject shall have the right to object at any time to processing of personal data concerning them for such marketing, which includes profiling to the extent that it is related to such direct marketing (Article 21(2)).

Where the Data Subject objects to processing for direct marketing purposes, the personal data shall no longer be processed for such purposes (Article 21(3)).

At the latest at the time of the first communication with the Data Subject, the right referred to in paras 1 and 2 shall be explicitly brought to the attention of the Data Subject and shall be presented clearly and separately from any other information (Article 21(4)).

In the context of the use of information society services, and notwithstanding Directive 2002/58/EC,[29] the Data Subject may exercise their right to object by automated means using technical specifications (Article 21(5)).

Where personal data are processed for scientific and historical research purposes or statistical purposes pursuant to Article 89(1), the Data Subject, on grounds relating to their particular situation, shall have the right to object to processing of personal data concerning them, unless the processing is necessary for the performance of a task carried out for reasons of public interest (Article 21(6)).

GDPR Automated Individual Decision Making, Including Profiling

9.30   The Data Subject shall have the right not to be subject to a decision based solely on automated processing, including profiling, which produces legal effects concerning them or similarly significantly affects them (see Article 22(1)).

Conclusion

9.31   The rights are very important for organisations to recognise and protect, and reflect in the documented processes, procedures and plans of the organisation. These need to be incorporated from day one, as it may not be possible to retrospectively become compliant if the initial collection and processing was illegitimate. This is increasingly significant as data protection supervisory authorities and Data Subjects become more proactive and as the levels of fines and penalties increase. It is clear that

---

29 Directive 2002/58/EC of the European Parliament and of the Council of 12 July 2002 concerning the processing of personal data and the protection of privacy in the electronic communications sector (Directive on privacy and electronic communications).

the importance attached to data protection has increased significantly, and so too the obligation for organisational compliance.

Cases to Consider

9.32 ICO complaints, cases and case studies which may be useful for organisations to consider include:

- *Chief Constable of the Police Service of Scotland*[30] (re data protection impact assessments and terms and conditions for cloud services);
- *Robert Bartosik For Orders Under Sections 167 and 169 of the Data Protection Act 2018*[31] (seeking erasure of personal data by police);
- *Komisia za zashtita na lichnite danni, Tsentralna izbiratelna komisia v Koalitsia 'Demokratichna Bulgaria – Obedinenie'*[32] (video recording processing of election ballots);
- *Commission v Spain*[33] (failure of a Member State to fulfil obligations re personal data);
- *Norra Stockholm Bygg AB v Per Nycander AB, other party: Entral AB*[34] (proportionality and minimisation of personal data in civil court proceedings and proceedings concerning a request for disclosure of the electronic register of Fastec's staff who had carried out work for Nycander, for determining the amount of work to be paid by the latter);
- *VS, third party: Ministerstvo na vatreshnite raboti, Glavna direktsia za borba s organiziranata prestapnost*[35] (processing of biometric data and genetic data, criminal proceedings, concept of 'strictly necessary');
- *Leistritz v LH*[36] (Data Protection Officer, prohibition of the dismissal, requirement of functional independence);
- *Orange Romania v ANSPDCP*[37] (collection and storage of the copies of identity documents, concept of the data subject, consent);
- *B v Latvijas Republikas Saeima*[38] (concept of 'personal data relating to criminal convictions and offences');
- *VQ v Land Hessen*[39] (data access to committee personal data records);
- *OT v Vyriausioji tarnybinÄ – s etikos komisijam*[40] (personal data, objective of public interest, public disclosures, conflicts of interest);
- *Data Protection Commissioner v Facebook Ireland Ltd, Maximillian Schrems*[41] (data transfers to US);
- *Meta Platforms Ireland Limited, formerly Facebook Ireland Limited v Bundesverband der Verbraucherzentralen und Verbraucherverbände – Verbraucherzentrale*

30 ScotIC 125_2022, 10 November 2022.
31 [2022] ScotCS CSOH_55, 16 August 2022.
32 CJEU, Case C-306/21, 20 October 2022.
33 CJEU, Case C-658/19, 25 February 2021.
34 CJEU, Case C-268/21, 2 March 2023.
35 CJEU, Case C-205/21, 26 January 2023.
36 CJEU, C-534/20, 22 June 2022.
37 CJEU, C-61/19, 11 November 2020.
38 CJEU, Case C-439/19, 22 June 2021.
39 CJEU, Case C-272/19, 9 July 2020.
40 CJEU, Case C-184/20, 1 August 2022.
41 CJEU, Case C-311/18, 16 July 2020.

Bundesverband[42] (protection of personal data, rights of data subject, representative action by a consumer protection association, data protection, consumer law, terms and conditions);

- *Facebook Ireland and Others v Gegevensbeschermingsautoriteit*[43] (protection of personal data, charter, one-stop shop mechanism, cross border processing);
- *TU, RE v Google*[44] (personal data – de-referencing of allegedly false information and removal of preview images (thumbnails), opinion);
- *TU, RE v Google*[45] (removal of search engine results, removal of image results, third parties, delay);
- *BE v Nemzeti Adatvedelmi es Informacioszabadsag Hatosag*[46] (judicial remedies – opinion);
- *Commission v Landesbank Baden-Wurttemberg and SRB*[47] (confidential data);
- *Morrisons* (liable to employees for ex-employee data breach of employees' data) (also described as first data breach class action in UK) (original decision, Court of Appeal, and ultimately the Supreme Court appeal). (The issue was employer responsibility under vicarious liability for a data disclosure by way of upload to the internet by an errant employee. The High Court and Court of Appeal found for the plaintiff victim employees whose data was uploaded. The Supreme Court disagreed. See Chapter 11);[48]
- *ICO v Cathay Pacific*;[49]
- *ICO v CRDNN*;[50]
- *ICO v DSG Retail*;[51]
- *ICO v Cullen*;[52]
- *ICO v Bounty (UK)*;[53]
- *ICO v Grove Pension*;[54]
- *ICO v True Vision*;[55]
- *ICO v IICSA*;[56]
- *NT 1 and NT 2* (Right to Be Forgotten vindicated for businessman);[57]
- *ICO v Yahoo! UK*;[58]

---

42 CJEU, Case C-319/20, 28 April 2022.
43 CJEU, Case C-645/19, 15 June 2021.
44 CJEU, Case C-460/20_O, 7 April 2022.
45 CJEU, Case C-460/20, 8 December 2022.
46 CJEU, Case C-132/21_O, 8 September 2022.
47 CJEU, Case C-584/20P, 15 July 2021.
48 *Various Claimants v Morrison Supermarkets PLC*, High Court [2018] EWHC 1123 (QB), Justice Langstaff, 16 May 2018, The errant ex IT employee, Andrew Skelton, who released the personal data on over 100,000 employees was convicted and imprisoned. That Morrisons was vicariously liable (at trial) opens the possibility of liability to each of the affected employees. The company lost on appeal to the Court of Appeal, but prevailed in the Supreme Court. *Morrison v Various* [2020] UKSC 12 (1 April 2020). A word of caution is still required in relation to over-assuming that a company or employer can never be held vicariously liable for problem data issues. See Chapter 11 for further discussion.
49 *ICO v Cathay Pacific Airways Limited* [2020] 4 March 2020.
50 *ICO v CRDNN Limited* [2020] 2 March 2020.
51 *ICO v DSG Retail Limited* [2020] 9 January 2010.
52 *ICO v Cullen* [2019] 24 June 2019.
53 *ICO v Bounty (UK) Limited* [2019] 11 April 2014.
54 *ICO v Grove Pension Solutions Limited* [2019] 26 March 2019. Refers to use of 'professional' incorrect advices.
55 *ICO v True Visions Productions* [2019] 10 April 2019.
56 *ICO v Independent Inquiry into Child Sexual Abuse (IICSA)* [2017] 18 July 2017.
57 *NT 1 & NT 2 v Google LLC* [2018] EWHC 799 (QB) (13 April 2018). Also see P Lambert, *The Right to be Forgotten* (Bloomsbury, 2019).
58 *ICO v Yahoo! UK*, 21 May 2018. There was a fine of £250,000.

- *ICO v Facebook* (re Cambridge Analytica);[59]
- *ICO v Independent Inquiry into Child Sexual Abuse (IICSA)*;[60]
- *Tele 2 Sverige v Swedish Post and Telecom Authority and Watson v UK*;[61]
- *Nowak v Data Protection Commissioner*[62] (re exam scripts and what is personal data);
- *Valsts policijas Rīgas reģiona pārvaldes Kārtības policijas pārvalde v Rīgas pašvaldības SIA 'Rīgas satiksme'*;[63]
- *Camera di Commercio, Industria, Artigianoto e Agricoltura di Lecce v Salvatore Manni*;[64]
- *Puškár v Finančné riaditeľstvo Slovenskej republiky and Kriminálny úrad finančnej správy*;[65]
- *Breyer v Germany*;[66]
- *VKI v Amazon EU*;[67]
- *ICO v Prudential*;[68]
- *Microsoft v Paul Martin McDonald*;[69]
- *ICO v Niebel, ICO v McNeish*;[70]
- *Rugby Football Union v Viagogo Limited*;[71]
- *Durham County Council v Dunn*;[72]
- *British Gas v Data Protection Registrar*;[73]
- *Brian Reed Beetson Robertson*;[74]
- *Campbell v MGN*;[75]
- *CCN Systems v Data Protection Registrar*;[76]
- *Lindqvist v Kammaraklagaren*;[77]
- *Commission v Bavarian Lager*;[78]
- *Common Services Agency v Scottish Information Commissioner*;[79]
- *Douglas v Hello!*;[80]
- *Halford v UK*;[81]

59 *ICO v Facebook*. The ICO imposed a fine of £500,000. *ICO v Facebook* [2018] 24 October 2018.
60 *ICO v Independent Inquiry into Child Sexual Abuse* (IICSA) [2018] 18 September 2018.
61 *Tele 2 Sverige v Swedish Post and Telecom Authority* and *Watson v UK*, ECJ/CJEU, Joined Cases C-203/15 & C-698/15, 21 December 2016.
62 *Nowak v Data Protection Commissioner*, ECJ/CJEU, Second Chamber, Case C-434/16, 20 December 2017.
63 *Valsts policijas Rīgas reģiona pārvaldes Kārtības policijas pārvalde v Rīgas pašvaldības SIA 'Rīgas satiksme,'* ECJ/CJEU, Second Chamber, Case C-13/16, 4 May 2017.
64 *Camera di Commercio, Industria, Artigianoto e Agricoltura di Lecce v Salvatore Manni*, ECJ/CJEU, Second Chamber, Case C-398/15, 9 March 2017.
65 *Puškár v Finančné riaditeľstvo Slovenskej republiky and Kriminálny úrad finančnej správy*, ECJ/CJEU, Second Chamber, Case C-73/16, 27 September 2017.
66 *Breyer v Germany*, ECJ/CJEU, Case C-582/14, 19 October 2016.
67 *VKI v Amazon EU*, ECJ/CJEU, Case C-191/15, 29 September 2016.
68 *ICO v Prudential*, 'Prudential Fined £50,000 for Customer Account Confusion,' 6 November 2012.
69 [2006] EWHC 3410.
70 28 November 2012.
71 [2012] UKSC 55.
72 [2012] EWCA Civ 1654.
73 [1998] UKIT DA98 – 3/49/2, 4 March 1998.
74 [2001] EWHC Admin 915.
75 [2004] UKHL 22.
76 [1991] UKIT DA90.
77 Case C-101/01, ECR I-12971.
78 Case C-28/08.
79 [2008] UKHL 47.
80 [2005] EWCA Civ 595.
81 [1997] IRLR 47, ECHR.

- *Von Hannover v Germany;*[82]
- *Mosley* (newspaper case);
- *Motion Picture Association v BT;*[83]
- *WP29 (now EDPB) and Data Protection Authorities/Google* (re Google policy change and breaches);
- Barclays/Lara Davies prosecution;[84]
- *ICO v Sony;*[85]
- *Facebook Beacon* case (US);[86]
- *Digital Rights Ireland and Seitlinger and Others;*[87]
- *Schrems v Commissioner;*[88]
- *Tamiz v Google;*[89]
- *Google v Vidal-Hall;*[90]
- *Mosley v Google* (various);
- *Google Spain SL Google Inc v Agencia Española de Protección de Datos, Mario Costeja González;*[91]
- *Weltimmo v Nemzeti Adatvédelmi és Információszabadság Hatóság;*[92]
- *Bărbulescu v Romania;*[93]
- *Bărbulescu v Romania* (this superior ruling overturning the above erroneous (and controversial) decision).[94]
- *Google v Vidal-Hall*[95] (DPA 1998, s 13(2) was declared an invalid implementation of EU law and an impermissive restriction of Data Subject right to sue for damages and compensation, effectively making Data Subject claims easier). (One issue going forward will be any challenges to aspects of the so-called UK GDPR once fully enacted on the basis of being incompatible with the GDPR; and or any challenge to a successful EU adequacy decision in relation to data transfers to the UK on the basis of UK law due to differences directly in UK data protection law or indirectly in relation to wider laws (eg human rights). There have been ongoing comments by politicians that the human rights legislation may be amended after Brexit[96] – notwithstanding that this may have serious adverse complications for an EU data protection adequacy decision for the UK.)

---

82   10 February 2012.
83   28 July 2011.
84   *ICO v Lara Davies*, December 2012.
85   July 2013.
86   *McCall v Facebook*, 20 September 2012.
87   Joined Cases C-293/12 and C-594/12, 8 April 2014.
88   Case C-362/14, 6 October 2015.
89   [2012] EWHC 449 (QB) 3 December 2012.
90   [2014] EWHC 13 (QB).
91   Case C-131/121.
92   Case C-230/14, 1 October 2015.
93   ECHR, Case No 61496/08, 12 January 2016.
94   *Bărbulescu v Romania*, ECtHR (Grand Chamber), Case 61496/08, 5 September 2017.
95   [2015] EWCA Civ 311.
96   One recent example is J Stone, 'Boris Johnson refuses to Commit to Keeping UK in Human Rights Convention' *Independent*, 5 March 2020.

Chapter 10

Time Limits for Compliance

Introduction

10.01   There are various time limits referred to in the data protection regime for the accomplishment of particular tasks. Depending on the task at hand, non-compliance with a time limit could amount to a breach and/or offence.

Time Limits

These are the main time limits and references contained in the GDPR.

Time Limit	Issue	Source
72 hours	*Breach Notification* Controller should notify personal data breach to the supervisory authority without undue delay and, where feasible, not later than 72 hours after having become aware of it	GDPR, Recital 85
72 hours	*Breach Notification* Controller shall without undue delay and, where feasible, not later than 72 hours, notify personal data breach to supervisory authority	GDPR, Article 33
Without undue delay	*Breach Notification* Controller should communicate to data subject a personal data breach, without undue delay. Such communications to data subjects should be made as soon as reasonably feasible	GDPR, Recital 86
Without undue delay	*Breach Notification* Communicate the personal data breach to the data subject without undue delay	GDPR, Article 34
Inform promptly	*Breach Notification* Inform promptly the supervisory authority and the data subject of data breach	GDPR, Recital 7

Time Limit	Issue	Source
One month	*Rights* Data subject rights (*including* access, rectification or erasure and right to object). Controller should respond without undue delay and at the latest within one month	GDPR, Recital 59
One month	*Action taken* Controller shall provide information on action taken on a request under Articles 15–22 to the data subject without undue delay and in any event within one month. Controller shall inform data subject of any extension within one month, with reasons for delay.	GDPR, Article 12(3)
Without undue delay	*Rectification right* Right of rectification without undue delay	GDPR, Article 16
Without undue delay	*Forgetting right* Right to erasure and forgetting without undue delay	GDPR, Article 17
21 days	*Objection right* Right to object to processing. Controller must, before the end of 21 days, give notice to data subject stating that the controller has complied, intends to comply or reasons for not complying	DPA 2018, s 99(3)
Seven days	*Assessment* Assessment notice, before seven days, within seven days	DPA 2018, s 146(8) and (9)

The ICO has updated its guidance in respect of time limits for complying with various obligations under the data regulations. This policy change is on foot of an EU case dealing with time limit issues (albeit in a different subject area). The *Toeters and Verberk* case holds that:

> 'Article 50a of Regulation No 3886/92 laying down detailed rules for the application of the premium schemes ... must be interpreted as meaning that a premium application may be regarded as having been "lodged" in due time only if the competent authority received it prior to the expiry of the time limit. The fact that the competent authority was in a position to transmit certain data to the Commission is irrelevant to the calculation of a time limit, which must be applied uniformly throughout the Community in order, particularly, to maintain equality of treatment between economic operators.'[1]

The ICO advises that:

> 'If you exercise any of your rights under data protection law, the organisation you're dealing with must respond as quickly as possible. This must be no later than one calendar month, starting from the day they receive the request. If the organisation needs something from you to be able to deal with your request (eg ID documents), the time limit will begin once they have received this.

---

1   *Maatschap Toeters and MC Verberk v Productschap Vee en Vlees*, CJEU [2004] Case C-171/03.

If your request is complex or you make more than one, the response time may be a maximum of three calendar months, starting from the day of receipt.'[2]

It also describes what is meant by a calendar month, and states that:

'A calendar month starts on the day the organisation receives the request, even if that day is a weekend or public holiday. It ends on the corresponding calendar date of the next month.

....

However, if the end date falls on a Saturday, Sunday or bank holiday, the calendar month ends on the next working day.

....

Also, if the corresponding calendar date does not exist because the following month has fewer days, it is the last day of the month.'

Conclusion

10.02   When an organisation fails to comply within the required timeframe, this in itself is another breach. It may be taken into consideration by the ICO and/or a court.

Readers should note, however, that there are proposed additional provisions in relation to certain time limit issues contained in the Data Protection and Digital Information (No 2) Bill. Clause 8 refers to time limits for responding to requests by Data Subjects. This seeks to amend Article 12 of the UK GDPR and insert a new Article 12B. These changes once finalised need to be incorporated into these time limit assessments, and also the updating of appropriate corporate rules and policies.

---

2   ICO, 'Time Limits for Responding to Data Protection Rights Requests,' at https://ico.org.uk/for-the public/time-limits-for-responding-to-data-protection-rights-requests/.

Chapter 11

Enforcement and Penalties for Non-Compliance

Introduction

11.01   There are a series of offences set out in the data protection legislation. These are designed to ensure compliance with the data protection regime, from collection to fair use of personal data. Organisations must fully comply with their obligations. In addition to questions arising in relation to their continued use of personal data if it has not been collected fairly, investigations, prosecutions and financial penalties can also arise.

Organisations can be fined up to 20,0000 EUR or 4% of worldwide turnover or equivalent, depending on the breach, or as set out in national legislation as appropriate.

Offences by organisations can also be prosecuted. Individuals can also be fined and prosecuted in addition to the organisation.

Breaches, Offences and Penalties

11.02   The data protection regime sets out the rules with which Controllers must obey. Breaches of these rules sometimes involve offences which are punishable by fines. The offences set out in the data protection regime include the following:

- EU General Data Protection Regulation (GDPR) (see below);
- offence of unlawful obtaining, etc, of personal data (Data Protection Act 2018 (DPA 2018), s 170);
- new offence of re-identification of de-identified personal data (DPA 2018, s 171) (also see s 172 re re-identification effectiveness testing conditions);
- alterations, etc, of personal data to prevent disclosure to Data Subject (DPA 2018, s 173).

In addition, offences are also referred to in the supplementary provisions, as follows:

- penalties for offences (DPA 2018, s 196);
- prosecution (DPA 2018, s 197);
- liability of directors, etc (DPA 2018, s 198);
- recordable offences (DPA 2018, s 199);
- guidance about PACE code of practice (DPA 2018, s 200).

See ICO penalties, fines and prosecutions details below.

Offences also arise under the UK GDPR and GDPR.

Offences can relate to specific breaches of data laws and also non-compliance with data regulator investigations.

Criminal Offences

11.03 The organisation can commit criminal offences in relation to its data processing activities, namely:

- unlawful obtaining or disclosure of personal data;
- selling and offering to sell personal data;
- enforcing individual Data Subject access;
- disclosure of information;
- obstructing or failing to assist in the execution of a warrant;
- processing without a register entry (if still required);
- failing to notify changes regarding registration (if still required);
- carrying on assessable processing;
- failing to make certain particulars available;
- failing to comply with a notice;
- making a false statement in response to a notice.

The Data Protection and Digital Information (No 2) Bill 2023 (DPDI Bill) in the context of enforcement makes new provisions in relation to the power to require documents (clause 34); power to require a report (clause 35); interview notices (clause 36); penalty notices (clause 37); duty to notify unlawful direct marketing (clause 85); PEC enforcement powers (clause 86, and Schedule 10).

Other Consequences of Breach

11.04 Some of the other consequences of a breach of the data protection regime include:

- offences can be committed by the organisation and its officers;
- processing focused offences;
- access related offences;
- offences for non-compliance with ICO and ICO related powers (eg, enforcement notices; assessments; information notices; entry and inspection);
- being sued by individual Data Subjects;
- potentially being sued by rights based organisations (or following complaints by such entities) and or class action type cases (eg Google re Apple; *DRI* case; *Schrems* case) and which cases are likely to increase under the GDPR;
- publicity of an unwanted nature;
- adverse publicity;
- lost or dimished sales and share value;
- reduced sale price (eg as occurred with Yahoo when a massive data breach was disclosed).

Offence Regarding Unlawful Obtaining or Procuring Personal Data

11.05 In one case there were successful convictions regarding blagging and unlawful access to the personal data relating to tenants. The case involved Philip Campbell Smith, Adam Spears, Graham Freeman and Daniel Summers. Amongst other things, the ICO again called for custodial sentences for breach of the data protection regime. This was also a theme in the Leveson recommendations.

The ICO states:

'The Department for Work and Pensions hold important information about each and every one of us. We are very pleased that a DWP staff member was alert to this attempt to blag information and that the call was halted before it was too late. The motive behind Mr Braun's action was financial. He knew that such an underhand method of obtaining the tenant's personal information was illegal but carried on regardless. This case shows that unscrupulous individuals will continue to try and blag peoples' details until a more appropriate range of deterrent punishments is available to the courts. There must be no further delay in introducing tougher powers to enforce the Data Protection Act beyond the current "fine only" regime.'[1]

The ICO also said:

'The scourge of data theft continues to threaten the privacy rights of the UK population. Whilst we welcome today's sentencing of the private investigator, Graham Freeman, and his three accomplices, the outcome of the case underlines the need for a comprehensive approach to deterring information theft. If SOCA had been restricted to pursuing this case solely using their powers under the Data Protection Act then these individuals would have been faced with a small fine and would have been able to continue their activities the very next day. This is not good enough. Unscrupulous individuals will continue to try and obtain peoples' information through deception until there are strong punishments to fit the crime. We must not delay in getting a custodial sentence in place for section 55 offences under the Data Protection Act.'[2]

Offences by Direct Marketers under PECR

11.06   Offences arise in relation to activities referred to under the additional ePrivacy and e-marketing rules, including under the ePrivacy Regulation and amended UK PECR rules (subject to further amendment once the EU ePrivacy Regulation is finalised).

Fines can be significant. Organisations could previously be fined up to £500,000 by the ICO for unwanted marketing phone calls and emails in accordance with the previous PECR rules. Fines increase significantly in potential under the new GDPR and ePrivacy Regulation.

The ICO imposes significant fines in relation to Spamming, including sometimes the promoters and directors of the company engaged in Spamming. Similar examples arise in relation to private investigation firms engaged in breaches. The types of instances where personal liability for breaches arise will continue to increase.

Significant financial penalties also frequently arise for illegal marketing activities. (See examples below in this chapter.)

Note that the DPDI Bill makes various amendments in relation to direct marketing and PEC (eg clause 85; clause 86; Schedule 10).

ICO Monetary Penalties

11.07   The ICO is empowered to impose penalties of a monetary variety. See examples of some of the recent ICO fines and monetary penalties referred to below.

GDPR Changes re Fines and Prosecution

11.08   As noted above, the new GDPR and UK GDPR set out significant amendments to the prosecution and fines regime (see below). This will be further amended with the DPDI Bill once enacted.

1   'Private Detectives Jailed for Blagging: ICO Statement,' ICO, 27 February 2012, at https://ico.org.uk.
2   'Private Detectives Jailed for Blagging: ICO Statement,' ICO, 27 February 2012, at https://ico.org.uk.

Right to Compensation and Liability

11.09   Any person who has suffered material or non-material damage as a result of an infringement of the GDPR shall have the right to receive compensation from the Controller or Processor for the damage suffered (Article 82(1)).

Any Controller involved in processing shall be liable for the damage caused by the processing which infringes the GDPR specifically directed to Processors or where it has acted outside or contrary to lawful instructions of the Controller (Article 82(2)).

A Controller or Processor may be exempted from liability in accordance with Article 78(2) if it proves that it has not in any way responsible for the event giving rise to the damage (Article 82(3)).

Where more than one Controller or Processor, or both a Controller and a Processor are involved in the same processing and where they are, in accordance with Article 82(2) and (3), responsible for any damage caused by the processing, each Controller or Processor shall be held liable for the entire damage in order to ensure effective compensation of the Data Subject (Article 82(4)).

Where a Controller or Processor has, in accordance with Article 82(4), paid full compensation for the damage suffered, that Controller or Processor shall be entitled to claim back from the other Controllers or Processors involved in the same processing that part of the compensation corresponding to their part of responsibility for the damage in accordance with the conditions set out in Article 82(2) (Article 82(5)).

Court proceedings for the right to receive compensation shall be brought before the courts competent under the law of the state referred to in Article 79(2).

Court proceedings against a Controller or Processor can be brought in the state where they are established or in the state where the Data Subject resides (Article 79(2)).

This will increasingly be a potential risk issue for companies.

The issue of compensation, damages, and liability will need to be reviewed after the DPDI Bill is enacted.

General Conditions for Imposing Administrative Fines

11.10   Each supervisory authority shall ensure that the imposition of administrative fines pursuant to this Article in respect of infringements of the GDPR referred to in Article 83(4), (5), (6) shall in each individual case be effective, proportionate and dissuasive (Article 83(1)).

Administrative fines shall, depending on the circumstances of each individual case, be imposed in addition to, or instead of, measures referred to in Article 58(2) (a) to (h) and (j). When deciding whether to impose an administrative fine and deciding on the amount of the administrative fine in each individual case due regard shall be given to the following:

- the nature, gravity and duration of the infringement taking into account the nature, scope or purpose of the processing concerned as well as the number of Data Subjects affected and the level of damage suffered by them;
- the intentional or negligent character of the infringement;
- any action taken by the Controller or Processor to mitigate the damage suffered by Data Subjects;
- the degree of responsibility of the Controller or Processor taking into account technical and organisational measures implemented by them pursuant to Articles 25 and 32;
- any relevant previous infringements by the Controller or Processor;
- the degree of co-operation with the supervisory authority, in order to remedy the infringement and mitigate the possible adverse effects of the infringement;
- the categories of personal data affected by the infringement;

- the manner in which the infringement became known to the supervisory authority, in particular whether, and if so to what extent, the Controller or Processor notified the infringement;
- where measures referred to in Article 58(2), have previously been ordered against the Controller or Processor concerned with regard to the same subject-matter, compliance with these measures;
- adherence to approved codes of conduct pursuant to Article 40 or approved certification mechanisms pursuant to Article 42; and
- any other aggravating or mitigating factor applicable to the circumstances of the case, such as financial benefits gained, or losses avoided, directly or indirectly, from the infringement (Article 83(2)).

If a Controller or Processor intentionally or negligently, for the same or linked processing operations, infringes several provisions of the GDPR, the total amount of the fine shall not exceed the amount specified for the gravest infringement (Article 83(3)).

Infringements of the following provisions shall, in accordance with Article 83(2), be subject to administrative fines up to 10,000,000 EUR, or in case of an undertaking, up to two percent of the total worldwide annual turnover of the preceding financial year, whichever is higher:

- the obligations of the Controller and the Processor pursuant to Articles 8, 11, 25 39, 42 and 43;
- the obligations of the certification body pursuant to Articles 42 and 43;
- the obligations of the monitoring body pursuant to Article 41(4) (Article 83(4)).

Infringements of the following provisions shall, in accordance with Article 83(2), be subject to administrative fines up to 20,000,000 EUR, or in case of an undertaking, up to four percent of the total worldwide annual turnover of the preceding financial year, whichever is higher:

- the basic principles for processing, including conditions for consent, pursuant to Articles 5, 6, 7 and 9;
- the Data Subjects' rights pursuant to Articles 12–22;
- the transfers of personal data to a recipient in a third country or an international organisation pursuant to Articles 44–49;
- any obligations pursuant to state laws adopted under Chapter IX;
- non-compliance with an order or a temporary or definitive limitation on processing or the suspension of data flows by the supervisory authority pursuant to Article 58(2) or failure to provide access in violation of Article 58(1) (Article 83(5)).

Non-compliance with an order by the supervisory authority as referred to in Article 58(2) shall, in accordance with Article 83(2), be subject to administrative fines up to 20,000,000 EUR, or in case of an undertaking, up to 4 percent of the total worldwide annual turnover of the preceding financial year, whichever is higher (Article 83(6)).

Without prejudice to the corrective powers of supervisory authorities pursuant to Article 58(2), each state may lay down the rules on whether and to what extent administrative fines may be imposed on public authorities and bodies established in that state (Article 83(7)).

The exercise by the supervisory authority of its powers under this Article shall be subject to appropriate procedural safeguards in conformity with EU law and state law, including effective judicial remedy and due process (Article 83(8)).

Where the legal system of the state does not provide for administrative fines, Article 83 may be applied in such a manner that the fine is initiated by the competent supervisory authority and imposed by competent national courts, while ensuring that those legal remedies are effective and have an equivalent effect to the administrative fines imposed by supervisory authorities. In any event, the fines imposed shall be effective, proportionate and dissuasive. Those states shall notify to the Commission those provisions of their laws which they adopt pursuant to Article 83 (Article 83(9)).

The issue of data fines and criteria will need to be reviewed after the DPDI Bill is enacted.

Penalties

11.11 States shall lay down the rules on penalties applicable to infringements of the GDPR in particular for infringements which are not subject to administrative fines pursuant to Article 83, and shall take all measures necessary to ensure that they are implemented. Such penalties shall be effective, proportionate and dissuasive (Article 84(1)).

Each state shall notify to the Commission the provisions of its law which it adopts pursuant to Article 84(1), by 25 May 2018 and, without delay, any subsequent amendment affecting them (Article 84(2)).

The issue of data fines and penalties will need to be reviewed after the DPDI Bill is enacted.

Civil Sanctions under the DPA

11.12 This is an area which will continue to expand in future. Individual Data Subjects can also sue for compensation under DPA 2018 (see ss 168, 169). Where a person suffers damage as a result of a failure by a Controller or Processor to meet their data protection obligations, then the Controller or Processor may be subject to civil sanctions by the person affected. Damage suffered by a Data Subject will include damage to reputation, financial loss and mental distress.

Section 168 recognised Article 82 of the GDPR and the right to compensation for material or non-material damage. In addition the section adds that 'non material damage' includes distress. This significantly clarifies and widens the scope for Data Subject actions, compensation and damages.

Compensation and damages can also be made to Data Subject representative bodies (s 168(3)). (Also see representation of Data Subjects in ss 187–190.)

While there are certain conditions, the primary clause refers to 'any contravention' by the organisation. In terms of the defence, in order to be able to avail of it, an organisation will have to establish that it has 'taken such care as in all the circumstances was reasonably required.' This will vary from organisation to organisation, sector to sector, the type of personal data involved, the risks of damage, loss, etc, the nature of the security risks, the security measures and procedures adopted, the history of risk, loss and damage in the organisation and sector.

Certain types of data will convey inherent additional risks over others, such as loss of financial personal data. This can be argued to require higher obligations for the organisation.

One interesting area to consider going forward is online damage, such as viral publication, defamation, bulletin boards, discussion forums and websites (or sections of websites), and social media websites. Where damage occurs as a result of misuse or loss of personal data or results in defamation, abuse and threats, liability could arise for the individual tortfeasors as well as the website.

While there are three eCommerce defences in the eCommerce Directive, one should recall that the data protection regime (and its civil rights, sanctions, duty of care and liability provisions) are separate and stand alone from the eCommerce Directive legal regime. Indeed, even in terms of the eCommerce defences one should also recall that: (a) an organisation must first fall within an eCommerce defence, and not lose that defence, in order to avail of it; and (b) there is no automatic entitlement to an internet service provider (ISP) or website to a global eCommerce defence, as in fact there in not one eCommerce defence but three specific defences relating to specific and technical activities. Not all or every ISP activity will fall into one of these defences. Neither will one activity fall into all three defences.

It is also possible to conceive of a website which has no take down procedures, inadequate take down defences, or non-expeditious take down procedures or remedies, and which will face potential liability under privacy and data protection as well as eCommerce liability. For example, an imposter social media profile which contains personal data and defamatory material could attract liability for the website operator under data protection, and under normal liability if none of the eCommerce defences were available or were lost. The later could occur if, for example, the false impersonating profile was notified to the website (or it was otherwise aware) but it did not do anything.[3]

As indicated above, the issue of civil liability and litigation by Data Subjects to enforce their rights will continue. This will in part be fuelled by increased awareness but also by the increasingly publicised instances of data loss, data breach, damage and instances of abuse which involve personal data. The *Facebook Beacon* settlement, while in the US, for approx. $20 million emphasises the import of individuals seeking to vindicate their privacy and personal data rights. In the UK, while *Prudential* was fined £50,000, it is not inconceivable that loss, damage and financial loss may have ensued. Consider, further that this example appears to have related to a small number of individuals. However, what if thousands of customer suffered financial loss, damage, stress, delay, missed payments, lost flights, lost contracts, etc, as a result of mixing up files, not completing files and transactions. These are all things which can occur, whether through process errors or software glitches. This is not at all far-fetched, as customers of RBS bank will confirm. Google was also sued re Apple breach. Morrisons was sought to be found liable for an errant IT employee related data breach (see further discussion below on the Morrisons case).[4]

While we are well aware of the press phone hacking scandal, the Leveson Inquiry and the ensuing litigation from many victims, as well as there being admissions, interception offences, etc, there are also personal data breach and data protection civil liability issues arising.

These issues will need to be reviewed after the DPDI Bill is enacted.

Morrisons Case

11.13 The *Morrisons* case is a further example of the increasing attention being paid to the important issues of data protection and private personal data. It also exemplifies the earlier discussion referring to data protection as being both inward facing as well as outward facing (and which has also been highlighted from the earliest edition of this publication).

---

3   This is a complex and developing area of law, common law, civil law, Directive, GDPR and case law, both in the UK and internationally. A full detailed analysis is beyond this current work.
4   *Various Claimants v Morrison Supermarkets plc* [2018] EWHC 1123 (QB). The errant ex IT employee, Andrew Skelton, who released the personal data on over 100,000 employees was convicted and imprisoned. That Morrisons was vicariously liable at trial and on appeal in the Court of Appeal opens the possibility of liability to each of the affected employees. The company has indicated that it will appeal. (Notwithstanding that the Supreme Court differed with the two lower courts).

This case is also interesting for many other aspects. Primarily, it is receiving attention because of the claim of vicarious liability as against the employer to other employees resulting from data breach issues. The case involved a large volume of employee records being posted onto the internet. The employee records were also distributed to a number of media outlets – after being further copied or downloaded from the internet.

There are important issues of liability and responsibility – hence the emphasis on the ability of individuals to be compensated when affected by breaches, such as breaches of compliance, rights, data misuse, data loss and data disclosure.

The issues involved are also demonstrated as being important given the extensive jurisprudential record of the case. While the Supreme Court[5] differed somewhat, the affected employees' rights were vindicated as against the employer by the High Court[6] and the Court of Appeal.

The case also demonstrates the difficult and complex nature of many modern data protection cases given the interface of law, rights and technology. Sometimes a detailed appreciation – and even expertise – of IT and computing is required in order to appreciate when and how data protection breaches occur.

I should preface these comments by indicating that this is not a full and detailed examination of all issues discussed and raised in the case, nor indeed a review of all of the evidence, testimony and record available to the respective courts. It focuses mainly on the following issues.

First, there may be an immediate impulse on the part of some to suggest that the case (at least in the Supreme Court) rules out the possibility that employers can be held vicariously liable for errant employees' acts regarding personal data, or wider still that no data protection use or misuse can give rise to liability or vicarious liability. Both suggestions would be incorrect. Indeed, the Supreme Court decision focuses only on an employee's acts (apparently) without knowledge of the employer.

The second point is that the appeal(s) appear focused on issues of vicarious liability alone. Other liability issues can arise and may be contested in other circumstances.

This appears to be because issues of primary liability were discounted by the trail court. (While Morrisons appealed the vicarious liability finding against it, it does not seem that the plaintiffs appealed the lack of primary liability finding). This may well be a live issue in other cases.

While there may or may not be good reasons for the various findings, the record available does raise questions as to whether all appropriate issues referred to were included in the public record. It is unclear whether different outcomes may have been possible with the benefit of further testing of particular issue points in the case – particularly at trial.

The appellate levels appear to have been deprived of the ability to consider legal and factual circumstances and arguments, which may have given rise to primary liability or been relevant to such an issue. The appeals should not be mistaken as deciding and ruling out the potential for primary liability being contested in an appropriate circumstance.

The points of discussion in this analysis focus primarily on some of the questions which arise from the decision records as to whether there were potential gaps or matters not fully available to the court(s) to explore and consider. There may well be additional points.

The trial court seems to have been inclined to discount the primary liability claim(s) on the basis, in part, of testimony on what is and is not relevant accepted industry

---

5   *Morrisons v Various* [2020] UKSC 12 (1 April 2020).
6   *Various v Morrisons (Rev 1)* [2017] EWHC 3133 (QB) (1 December 2017) Langstaff J.

practice in data protection and data security. Some of this discussion as recounted in the trial decision raises some questions as to accuracy and generality. A fuller examination of these issues might potentially have persuaded the judge to a different conclusion on primary liability.

This emphasises the need in certain cases for very careful analysis of forensic and computer technology issues – and up to and including a variety of different experts on each side to present pertinent evidence.

There is great attention paid to the temporality of the upload to the internet by the errant employee, and while some earlier issues of significance are discussed (at trial), these earlier issues do not appear (from the record available) to have received all the attention that they potentially deserve.

The record would arguably have ideally benefitted from a fuller elucidation as to the exact contracts, policies and terms which existed at the time of the incident(s) at issue. These are highly pertinent to cases involving data breach issues with inward facing personal data.

It is not clear to this reader that the firm was not in substantial and material breach of its own policies. Further, there is suggestion even from the record that there were numerous breaches by the firm. In appropriate circumstances these may be very relevant to primary liability issues.

In this context it is necessary to see what all of the relevant policies say – and do not say – and to have appropriate (even expert) explanation as to the significance of these. While the parties' direct evidence can be useful, it can also be appropriate for a court to have the benefit of some less involved (or dare I say, less biased) independent information on policies, procedures and standards.

A firm may have ten policies in place. Yet if one of the important core issues at stake should be addressed in a required policy 11 and is not covered in policies 1–10, that is a potential material failing on the company's part. However, these nuances need to be carefully appraised and considered by the court. It is suggested that the record in this case demonstrated a number of material gaps or failings. It can sometimes be more important for a court to be aware of the gaps in policies than what current policies may say.

It is also noted that in the present case, the company acknowledges that there were policy changes between the date of the events at issues and the trial date. It would be useful to understand the nature of these changes in much greater depth than is presently possible from the current record.

A glaring gap in the record for the court was the exact date and manner of transmission or delivery of the vast payroll documentation to KPMG by the errant employee. The case is also inconclusive on the very important point of *how* delivery was achieved.

One would normally expect that this would be a central and core issue for the employer to have to establish. Perhaps it is, but that is not easily evident.

It is a glaring issue that the firm was not able to establish *when* the documents were given to KPMG. This is a very important and potentially impactful point. The various decisions make clear that it is acknowledged that when the documents were delivered was not established by the firm. This seems an essential issue to have been proven. In fact, the decision seems to suggest that it was left up to the trial judge to try and guess a time period when delivery may have occurred.

This seems somewhat remiss if that is the case (and raised the follow on query as to whether it benefited the company not to have this issue clarified with specificity).

That the firm could not establish a definitive date and time is (very) curious. This in itself demonstrates policy and procedure gaps. Some may call this a policy and evidence failing – or data security failings.

Why were there no documented procedures to safeguard the data when transferring it to a third party and to ensure delivery was guaranteed and recorded? Was there no email before or after delivery to KPMG? Was there no internal email confirming delivery? If delivery was by hand, was there no cover letter? Is it secure and data protection compliant to deliver an electronic storage device with a large set of sensitive data to a third party without cover documentation? Why was the firm not able to establish any company-side policy or delivery recordal?

Why was the firm not able to evidence any correspondence or recordal documentation from KPMG demonstrating when delivery occurred? Why was there no evidence from KMPG indicating when it opened the data delivered?

Some might suggest that these gaps and lack of clarity are a clear demonstration of the firm breaching primary responsibilities.

One would be surprised if there was not some further potential record available in relation to the delivery issue. If so, why was this apparently not available to the court? It seems that there was an element of forensics devoted to other issues regarding the errant employee, but there is apparently no record of forensics available to the court dealing with the delivery issues.

The *when* issue is potentially of large significance to the primary liability issue – and also the vicarious liability issue. The trail judge narrowed the window of delivery (an official task for the employee) to between 15 November to 21 November. The judge also found that the employee also copied or downloaded the data in question to his own USB device (USB2) on 18 November.

So the potentially important question of when delivery occurred comes into play. Did the errant download on 18 December come before delivery to KPMG? Put another way, did the download to USB2 (a personal device) occur *prior to delivery to KPMG* and therefore *during* an official authorised activity?

Note that the firm had (a small number of) official, designated USB devices. Why did data security policy and procedures not pick up and alert management of (a) an unauthorised device access/connection; and (b) an unauthorised and very large download (indeed, so large that it could not be sent by internal email)?

While these are primarily questions which jump out, and certain matters are indeed unclear, it is clear that the respective courts in different circumstances may well have had more to contend with. Indeed, as interesting as the case is already, further factual clarity may have led to the case being of even more importance.

It is also noted that the Supreme Court seems in part concerned primarily to correct misunderstanding or misinterpretation in prior judicial jurisprudence on vicarious liability generally, over the data protection issues arising. Even on the record available from this case, companies should not assume that they are immune from primary liability – nor vicarious liability – in appropriate circumstances. The story of primary or vicarious liability is by no means over.

A separate issue also appears to have been suggested, namely that some distinction needs to be drawn as to when data is copied, and whether the original data remains intact in situ. The suggestion seems to be that there is no liability or responsibility to the employer if the original data has not been deleted. While this aspect of the case requires further review, some might suggest this as being curious to the extent that it may permit all sorts of mischief. If a hacker hacks into a bank and steals data which is then sold to identity thieves, is the hacker immune because the original data remains at the bank? Is there no remedy against a bad actor ransomware attacker because they are not changing or deleting data, but rather locking the firm, hospital, etc out of the ability to access its own data? Is an employee immune for selling the customer database of an employer to a competitor merely because the original data still sits with the employer? Is the company always provided with a blanket defence because an employee or third party attacker copied and did not delete data? Potential unintended mischiefs may occur if data deletion becomes a precondition to other legal consequences arising.

Finally, there appears to be some suggestion in the court records which diverges from established data protection rules and indeed data regulator official guidance. It is not clear if this is the intention or something unintended in the decision, but might need to be explored further.

This is a significant decision, of course, but the stakes at play will mean that this will not be the last contested case dealing with these types of matters.

Director Liability and Offences

11.14 The potential for personal liability (DPA 2018, s 198) is also a significant issue for an organisation and those within positions of authority where the organisation is involved in offences.

Employees and executives can also be liable for offences if they obtain, disclose or procure the personal data in the organisation for their own purposes.

Section 198 of the DPA 2018 refers to liability of directors, etc. Section 198(1) provides that where an offence under the Act has been committed by a body corporate and is proved to have been committed with the consent or connivance of or to be attributable to any neglect on the part of any director, manager, secretary or similar officer of the body corporate or any person who was purporting to act in any such capacity, they as well as the body corporate shall be guilty of that offence and be liable to be proceeded against and punished accordingly.

One interesting case involves using initials in case names.[7] This also occurred in the recent case of *NT1* and *NT2*, both of which related to the erasure and forgetting right.[8] Many cases in European countries have anonymised plaintiffs.

These issues will need to be reviewed after the DPDI Bill is enacted. It is noted that the DPDI Bill refers to a new concept of 'senior responsible individual' in clause 14. This introduces a new provision to the UK GDPR, Article 27A, which refers to the designation of a senior responsible person for certain Controllers. The new Article 27B sets out the tasks of the senior responsible person. There are also provisions in relation to the position of such person (Article 27C). There are also similar provisions in relation to Processors (Articles 58A–58C).

Offences by Processors

11.15 Processors can also commit offences.

Remedies, Liability and Penalties under the GDPR

11.16 Chapter VIII refers to remedies, liability and penalties regarding data protection.

---

7   In a data protection related case in Berlin, not only was the company sued but the directors were also personally named and included in the case. One of the reasons specified was to ensure that the directors made sure that the Board of the company made the appropriate amendments to ensure the breaches were rectified and would not re-occur. A further interesting aspect of the case is that while the directors were included personally, their names were redacted to initials. One such set of initials was 'MZ'. See *The Federal Association of Consumer Organisations and Consumer Groups, Federal Consumer Association, GB v Facebook Ireland Limited, MA, JB, DG, PT and the Chairman MZ,* [names redacted], [redacted] Reach, [redacted] Quay, Dublin, Ireland.

8   *NT 1 & NT 2 v Google LLC* [2018] EWHC 799 (QB).

Right to Lodge Complaint with Supervisory Authority

11.17 Without prejudice to any other administrative or judicial remedy, every Data Subject shall have the right to lodge a complaint with a supervisory authority, in particular in the state their habitual residence, place of work or place of the alleged infringement if the Data Subject considers that the processing of personal data relating to them does not comply with the GDPR (Article 77(1)).

The supervisory authority with which the complaint has been lodged shall inform the complainant on the progress and the outcome of the complaint including the possibility of a judicial remedy pursuant to Article 78 (Article 77(2)).

Right to Judicial Remedy against Supervisory Authority

11.18 Without prejudice to any other administrative or non-judicial remedy, each natural or legal person shall have the right to an effective judicial remedy against a legally binding decision of a supervisory authority concerning them (Article 74(1)).

The supervisory authority with which the complaint has been lodged shall inform the complainant on the progress and the outcome of the complaint including the possibility of a judicial remedy pursuant to Article 78 (Article 77(2)).

Right to an Effective Judicial Remedy Against Controller or Processor

11.19 Without prejudice to any available administrative or non-judicial remedy, including the right to lodge a complaint with a supervisory authority under Article 77, each Data Subject shall have the right to an effective judicial remedy if they consider that their rights under this GDPR have been infringed as a result of the processing of their personal data in non-compliance with the GDPR (Article 79(1)).

Proceedings against a Controller or a Processor shall be brought before the courts of the state where the Controller or Processor has an establishment. Alternatively, such proceedings may be brought before the courts of the state where the Data Subject has his or her habitual residence, unless the Controller or Processor is a public authority of a state acting in the exercise of its public powers (Article 79(2)).

Representation of Data Subjects

11.20 The Data Subject shall have the right to mandate a not-for-profit body, organisation or association, which has been properly constituted according to the law of a state, has statutory objectives are in the public interest, and is active in the field of the protection of Data Subjects' rights and freedoms with regard to the protection of their personal data to lodge the complaint on their behalf, to exercise the rights referred to in Articles 77, 78 and 79 on their behalf and to exercise the right to receive compensation referred to in Article 82 on their behalf where provided for by state law (Article 80(1)).

States may provide that any body, organisation or association referred to in Article 80(1), independently of a Data Subject's mandate, has the right to lodge in that state, a complaint with the supervisory authority competent which is competent pursuant to Article 77 and to exercise the rights referred to in Articles 78 and 79 if it considers that the rights of a Data Subject have been infringed as a result of the processing (Article 80(2)).

There is increasing evidence of more such groups being formed and becoming active in advocacy, filing complaints with data regulators and, one expects, also seeking to develop jurisprudence in relation to compensation and damages. While most of the groups are clearly data protection and privacy focused, it may be possible that new groups are particularly aiming to focus more on compensation issues than advocacy issues. It also remains to be seen if existing bodies seek to cast themselves as partly privacy groups (eg employee' unions).

Suspension of Proceedings

11.21   Where a competent court of a state has information on proceedings, concerning the same subject matter as regards processing by the same Controller or Processor, that are pending in a court in another state, it shall contact that court in the other state to confirm the existence of such proceedings (Article 81(1)).

Where proceedings concerning the same subject matter as regards processing by the same Controller or Processor are pending in a court in another state, any competent court other than the court first seized may suspend its proceedings (Article 81(2)).

Where those proceedings are pending at first instance, any court other than the court first seized may also, on the application of one of the parties, decline jurisdiction if the court first seized has jurisdiction over the actions in question and its law permits the consolidation thereof (Article 81(3)).

Right to Compensation and Liability

11.22   A person who has suffered damage as a result of an infringement of the GDPR shall have the right to receive compensation from the Controller or Processor for the damage suffered (Article 82(1)). (See para **11.09** above for more particular details).

General Conditions for Imposing Administrative Fines

11.23   An organisation can have fines and penalties imposed for non-compliance. The fines regime is significantly updated under the new data protection regime. In particular the level of fines and penalties are increased, and will be updated further with the DPDI Bill. See para **11.10** above for further details.

Penalties

11.24   States shall lay down the rules on penalties applicable to infringements of the GDPR in particular for infringements which are not subject to administrative fines. Further details are referred to in para **11.11** above.

Fines and Remedy Levels

11.25   Article 83 relates to administrative fine sanctions. Each supervisory authority is empowered to impose administrative fines, which are meant to be effective, proportionate and dissuasive, and include reference to the nature, gravity and duration of the breach, amongst other factors.

Certain fines can be up to 10,000,000 EUR (or equivalent), or in case of an enterprise up to two percent of its annual worldwide turnover, whichever is higher. Other fines can amount to 20,000,000 EUR (or equivalent) or four percent of turnover, whichever is higher. Further details are referred to in para **11.10** above.

Powers and Functions of the ICO

11.26   The ICO has a number of promotion, investigation and enforcement powers and functions under the prior DPA 1998. These include:

- to assess whether especially risky or dangerous types of processing are involved;
- to prepare and publish codes of practice for guidance in applying data protection law in particular areas;
- cases;
- investigations;
- complaints;

- audits;
- fines.

Part 6 of the DPA 2018 refers to enforcement issues. This specifies:

- information notices (ss 142–145);
- assessment notices (ss 146–147);
- destroying or falsifying information and documents/information notices and assessment notices and destruction of documents, etc (s 148);
- enforcement notices (ss 149–153);
- powers of entry and inspection (s 154) (also see powers of entry and inspection referred to in Sch 15 of DPA 2018);
- penalties (ss 155–159);
- remedies in court: compliance orders and compensation (ss 167–169);
- dealing with complaints via Data Subjects (s 165);
- orders to progress complaints (via Data Subjects) (s 166).

Note also that the proposed DPDI Bill makes further updates.

Financial Penalties

11.27 The ICO can issue monetary penalty notices or fines. This is where serious breaches occur which are deliberate and with knowledge or where there ought to be knowledge of the breach and of the likely damage. The proposed DPDI Bill makes further updates.

Inspections

11.28 The ICO may also undertake inspections of organisations. This is where the ICO suspects that there may be a breach of the DPA and it obtains a warrant to search the organisational premises. In such an instance the ICO may enter, search, inspect, examine, test equipment, inspect and seize documents, materials, etc. Obstructing such an inspection will be a criminal offence. Legal advices should be immediately sought in relation to such incidents. The proposed DPDI Bill makes further updates.

ICO Data Enforcement, Loss/Data Breaches, Fines and Convictions

11.29

Issue	Date	Party	Breach	Penalty
Data controls, data disclosure breach	31/7/23	NHS Lanarkshire	Breach by sharing patient personal data via unauthorised means and also a disclosure of personal data.	Reprimand
Data security. Data breach	25/7/23	My Media World Limited t/a Brand New Tube	Breach of Arts 32(1) and 32(1)(d) of GDPR. Failed to implement appropriate technical security and organisational measures to properly secure their systems, resulting in unauthorised access and exfiltration of personal data of 345,000 UK Data Subjects.	Reprimand

Issue	Date	Party	Breach	Penalty
Data security	21/7/23	Executive Office	Email newsletter sent with all recipients visible.	Reprimand
Data security	19/7/23	The Patient and Client Council	Breach of Arts 5(1)(f) and 32(1) of UK GDPR with disclosure of special category data in email sent to 15 individuals using carbon copy (CC) rather than blind carbon copy (BCC).	Reprimand
Texts	28/6/23	Fortis Insolvency Limited	Over 500,000 spam texts.	£30,000
Illegal access and collections	21/6/23	Isaacs	Prosecution for illegally obtaining details on customer of RBS bank for bank credit purposes.	Prosecution
TPS calls	8/6/23	Crown Glazing Ltd	Over 500,000 calls to TPS registrants.	£130,000
Calls	8/6/23	Maxen Power Supply Limited	Spam calls using overseas call centres.	£120,000
Data security, data controls.	30/5/23	Thames Valley Police	Release of witness details to suspected criminals. Various breach issues including security and controls.	Reprimand
Data security	23/5/23	Parkside Community Primary School	School in breach for lack of data security and other controls, including when special type data of students was disclosed. Infringements of Arts 5(1)(f), 24(1) and 32 of UK GDPR.	Reprimand
Calls	16/5/23	Ice Telecommunications Ltd	Over 70,000 spam calls	80,000
Spam calls	16/5/23	UK Direct Business Solutions Limited	Over 400,000 spam calls.	£100,000
Child data	4/4/23	TikTok	Lack of consent to collect child data.	£12.7 million
Data security	9/3/23	NHS Highland	Health data emails CCd not blind copied.	Reprimand
Security Accurate Up to date Systems	7/3/23	University Hospitals Bristol and Weston NHS	Data transfer from legacy system, data not tested, discovery of unsuccessful transfer after older system finished.	TBD
Security Process Testing Policy Procedure	3/3/23	NHS Blood and Transplant	Release of untested development code into live system for matching transplant list patients with donated organs.	Reprimand
Accuracy, testing, verification	2/3/23	Metropolitan Police Service	No appropriate checks to ensure crime records data uploaded was accurate.	Reprimand

Issue	Date	Party	Breach	Penalty
Hack	21/2/23	Chartered Institute for Securities & Investment	Known vulnerability allowed breach hack attack, exposing financial personal data.	TBD
Unauthorised access	17/2/23	Swan	Ex-employee illegal access to data.	Prosecution
Spam calls	15/2/23	It's OK Limited	1.7m calls to people on TPS.	£200,000
Unauthorised access	1/2/23	Khan	Ex-employee unauthorised access.	Prosecution
Spam emails and text	14/12/22	Monetise Media Limited	3.5m spam emails and texts.	£125,000
Text spam	14/12/22	Ryan Hill Partners	463,360 text spam, with 409,468 delivered.	£70,000
Spam calls	7/12/22	Allapplianceservices UK Ltd	100,000 spam calls.	£85,000
Spam calls	7/12/22	Boiler Cover Breakdown Limited	Two related companies made 9,000 and 350,000 spam calls to TPS registrants.	£120,000 and £140,000
Spam calls	7/12/22	Repair Plans UK Limited	21,000 targeted spam calls to elderly.	£70,000
Spam calls	7/12/22	Utility Guard Limited	2,000 calls to TPS registrants.	£20,000
Data security breach	6/12/22	Power Leisure Bookmakers	Whether appropriate data security measures.	Reprimand
Spam calls	11/11/22	Zuwyco Limited	100,000 spam calls.	£160,000
Data storage, data security	10/11/22	Royal Free London NHS	Hysteroscopy scans were saved to three USB sticks over years.	TBD
Data security	2/11/22	Department for Education	Allowing third parties to access systems remotely, further offsite processing. Lack of security.	Reprimand
Data security	31/10/22	Department for Work and Pensions	Inappropriate disclosure of individuals personal data. No testing or data protection impact assessment (DPIA) was completed before implementing.	Reprimand
Data security	24/11/22	Interserve Limited	Lack of adequate security. Data hack breach. Data of 113,000 employees affected.	£4.4 million
Spam calls	19/10/22	Apex	122 calls to TPS registrants.	£230,000
Data security	7/10/22	Secretary of State for the Home Department	Envelope containing four documents classified 'Official Sensitive' found at a venue in London, by venue staff.	Reprimand

Issue	Date	Party	Breach	Penalty
Lawfulness (DPA). Spam (PECR).	5/10/22	Easylife	Contravened Art 5(1)(a) GDPR, serious deficiencies in how it collected, processed, and used personal and special category data of 145,400 individuals. 1,345,732 unsolicited direct marketing calls.	£1.5 million
Spam calls	3/10/22	Green Logic	12,000 spam calls.	£40,000
Spam calls	3/10/22	Eco Spray	180,000 spam calls.	£100,000
Spam calls	3/10/22	Euroseal Windows	170,000 spam calls.	£80,000
Spam calls	3/10/22	Posh Windows	460,000 spam calls.	£150,000
Time limits SARs	23/9/22	Kent Police	40% of access reports not replied on time.	TBD
Time limits SARs	23/9/22	London Borough of Lambeth	26% of access reports not replied on time.	TBD
Data security	22/9/22	Wakefield Council	Papers prepared as a court bundle, in relation to child protection proceedings, to the parents. Documents contained a child protection medical report which included home address of mother and her children.	Reprimand
Time limits SARs	21/9/22	London Borough of Hackney	40% of access reports not replied on time.	TBD
Time limits SARs	21/9/22	Home Office	21,000 access notices not responded to within time.	TBD
Time limits SARs	20/9/22	Virgin Media	14% of access reports not replied on time.	Reprimand
Spam email	6/9/22	Halfords	498,179 spam emails.	£30,000
Accuracy Up to date	6/9/22	National Crime Agency	Due to oversight reports not actioned and led to incorrect arrest.	Reprimand
Data security. Review. Accuracy.	26/8/22	Ministry of Justice	A bulk access to amend/ input for a limited period continued; incorrect data entered was automatically carried over to another system reflecting incorrect convictions.	Reprimand
Disclosures of data	26/8/22	South Wales Police	Two incidents of data disclosure.	Reprimand
Disclosure breach	19/8/22	Quinn	Two child reports disclosed to wrong party.	Reprimand
Data access, collection, use issues	16/8/22	Home Office	Employee conducted sensitive interviews and uploaded content online.	Reprimand
Data loss	12/8/22	Crown Prosecution Service	Employee and 3 data loss events.	Reprimand

Issue	Date	Party	Breach	Penalty
Illegal data access. Security. Controls.	3/8/22	O'Brien	Former health advisor unlawfully accesses hospital records of 14 people he knew.	Prosecution Fine, conviction, and compensation to each data subject
SARs	27/7/22	Ministry of Defence	SAR backlogs.	Reprimand
Prior information. Policies	26/7/22	GrindR	Lack of adequate prior information to users.	Reprimand
Hack data breach	19/8/22	Direct Clothing	Site hacked and customers defrauded by hackers. Number of vulnerabilities. Confusion on whether third party providing security services.	Only reprimand
Disclosures Controls Data security	11/7/22	DHSC	Private communication channels but lack of controls.	TBD
Data security	3/6/22	Tavistock & Portman NHS	Bulk emails in breach of GDPR Arts 5(1)(f) (security), and 32(1), (2) (security).	£78,400
Consent Procedures	29/6/22	Allied Health	Data accessible without consent.	Reprimand
Disclosure	7/6/22	Bolton at Home	Voice mail for person A left on phone of person B.	Reprimand
Data deletion order	26/5/22	Clearview AI	Facial recognition company and databases collected.	Enforcement Notice to delete all UK data
Facial and other images illegally collected	26/5/22	Clearview AI	Facial recognition company and databases collected illegally.	£7.5 million
Data security	17/5/22	Warrington and Halton Hospitals NHS	Uploading patient data to wrong system.	TBD
PECR	22/4/22	Reed Online	PECR breach.	£40,000
PECR	13/4/22	Finance Giant	500,000 spam texts and emails.	£60,000
PECR	8/4/22	Bizfella	225,000 spam texts.	£30,000
Disclosure	7/4/22	North Yorkshire County Council	Correspondence sent to wrong recipient.	Reprimand
Disclosure	7/4/22	Epsom and St Helier University Hospitals	Incorrect test data disclosed.	Reprimand
Spam	31/3/22	H&L Business Consulting	450,000 spam texts.	£80,000
Spam	16/3/22	UK Platinum Home Care Services	400,000 spam calls.	£110,000

Issue	Date	Party	Breach	Penalty
Spam	16/3/22	Domestic Support Ltd	70,000 spam calls.	£80,000
Spam	16/3/22	Seaview Brokers	5,000 spam calls.	£15,000
Spam	16/3/22	Home Sure Solutions	230,000 spam calls.	£100,000
Spam	16/3/22	UK Appliance Cover	40,000 spam calls.	£100,000
Data security Ransomware breach	10/3/22	Tuckers Solicitors	Breach GDPR Art 5(1)(f), data security and ransomware attack.	£98,000
PECR Breach notice	8/3/22	Royal Mail	RM notified that it may have breached PECR on a campaign. Over 200,000 people contacted who already opted out.	£20,000
Holding	7/3/22	Smith, Law & Shepherds IFA	Breach GDPR Art 15 (confirmation of holding data).	Enforcement Notice
Misused data Not accurate	2/3/22	North Yorkshire Police	Data duplicated resulting in incorrect double conviction; not accurate data as required.	Reprimand
Spam	17/2/22	Money Hive Limited	750,000 spam texts.	£50,000
Spam	9/2/22	Tempcover Ltd	30,000 spam texts.	£85,000
Spam	2/2/22	Home2sense Limited	500,000 spam calls.	£200,000
Spam	20/1/22	Energy Suite Limited	1,000 spam calls.	£2,000
SARs	18/1/22	Ministry of Justice	Failure to delay with SARS, enforcement notice issues.	Enforcement notice
Spam	17/12/21	Northern Gas & Power	Spam calls.	£75,000
Spam	8/12/21	Virgin Media	450,000 spam emails.	£50,000
Breach	2/12/21	Cabinet Office	Addresses disclosed online.	£500,000
Spam	1/12/21	EB Associates	100,000 spam calls.	£140,000
Spam	25/10/21	Unite the Union	60,000 spam calls.	45,000
Breach Security	22/10/21	HIV Scotland	Email sent to group disclosing data, including inference of health data, of some of the individuals.	£10,000
Spam	22/9/21	Your Home Improvements Ltd	2,000 spam calls.	£20,000
Spam	15/9/21	We Buy Any Car Ltd	191.4 million spam emails and 3.6 million spam SMS.	£200,000
Spam	15/9/21	Saga Services	130,000 spam emails.	£150,000
Spam	15/9/21	Sports Direct	2.5 m spam emails.	£70,000
Spam	5/9/21	DialADeal Scotland	Spam calls.	£150,000
Spam	19/8/21	Parkin Beacher Ltd	Spam calls.	£50,000

Issue	Date	Party	Breach	Penalty
Spam	2/8/21	Yes Consumer Solutions	Spam calls to clocking company.	£170,000
Data security	8/7/21	Mermaids	Failure to keep data secure.	£25,000
Calls	1/7/21	Brazier Consulting Services	11 million unlawful calls.	£200,000
Spam	23/6/21	ColourCoat Limited	Large number of spam calls.	£130,000
Spam	15/6/21	Global One 2015	Over 500,000 spam messages. Charity.	£10,000
Spam	15/6/21	Papa John's (GB) Ltd	168,022 spam messages.	£10,000
Spam	8/6/21	Solarwave Limited	73,000 spam calls.	£100,000
Spam	8/6/21	LTH Holdings Limited	1.4 m spam calls.	£145,000
Spam	8/6/21	Colour Car Sales Ltd	Spam texts. Difficulty in contacting company.	£170,000
Spam	3/6/21	Conservative Party	51 spam emails.	£10,000
Spam	20/5/21	American Express Services Europe Ltd	4 million spam messages.	£90,000
Spam	18/5/21	Tested.me Ltd	84,000 spam emails.	£8,000
Nuisance calls	27/3/20	Black Lion Marketing Ltd	Unsolicited direct marketing calls.	£171,000
Access	13/3/20	Young	Town clerk prosecuted for blocking access and deleting records to frustrate access.	Prosecution
Data security	4/3/20	Cathay Pacific Airways Ltd	Failure to protect and secure customer data, leading to hack exposure. Lack of appropriate data security over four years.	£500,000
Automated nuisance calls	2/3/20	CRDNN Ltd	193 million automated nuisance spam marketing calls.	£500,000
Automated nuisance calls	2/3/20	CRDNN Ltd	193 million automated nuisance spam marketing calls.	Enforcement Notice
Disclosure breach	15/3/20	Kirk	Former social worker disclosed data on service users to third party service firm.	Prosecution
Data breach hack	9/1/20	DSG Retail Ltd	14 million customers exposed after point of sale hack attack.	£500,000
Data security	20/12/19	Doorstep Dispensaree Ltd	500,000 medical record data documents left in unsecure manner.	£275,000
Access breach	5/12/19	Shaw	Former reablement officer accessed care record data without any business need.	Prosecution

Issue	Date	Party	Breach	Penalty
Access breach	2/12/19	Shipsey	Former Social Services support officer accessed care record data without any business need.	Prosecution
Nuisance calls	17/9/19	Superior Style Home Improvements Ltd	Unsolicited direct marketing calls. Call to telephone preference service (TPS) opted-out numbers.	£150,000
Nuisance calls	17/9/19	Superior Style Home Improvements Ltd	Unsolicited direct marketing calls. Call to TPS opted-out numbers.	Enforcement Notice
Access right	12/8/19	Hudson Bay Finance Ltd	Enforcement Notice for failing to fulfil data access right.	Enforcement Notice
Nuisance calls	2/8/19	Making it Easy Ltd	Unsolicited direct marketing calls. Calls to TPS opted-out numbers.	£160,000
Nuisance calls	2/8/19	Making it Easy Ltd	Unsolicited direct marketing calls. Calls to TPS opted-out numbers.	Enforcement Notice
Disclosure breach	19/7/19	Life at Parliament View Ltd	Failure to secure customer data; left exposed for two years.	£80,000
Access	25/6/19	Metropolitan Police Service (MPS)	Data access right; repeat fulfilment breaches.	Enforcement Notice
Nuisance texts	24/6/19	EE Ltd	2.5 million direct marketing text communications.	£100,000
Collection breaches. Sale breaches.	24/6/19	Cullen	Former managing director involved in illegal data collections and data sale for insurance claims.	Prosecution
Nuisance calls	13/6/19	Smart Home Protection Ltd	Unsolicited direct marketing calls. Calls to TPS opted-out numbers.	£90,000
Access breach	7/6/19	Masterson	Former customer service advisor accessed anti-social behaviour record data without any business need.	Prosecution
Access breach	6/6/19	Baines	Restorative Justice Case Worker victim and offender record data to personal email without any business need.	Prosecution
Collection breach. Consent breach.	10/5/19	Her Majesty's Revenue and Customs (HMRC)	Failure to obtain adequate consent to collect caller personal data.	Enforcement Notice
Nuisance texts	7/5/19	Hall and Hanley Ltd	Sending over 3.5 million direct marketing text communications.	£120,000

Issue	Date	Party	Breach	Penalty
Nuisance calls	16/4/19	Avalon Direct Ltd	Over 50,000 unsolicited direct marketing calls. Calls to TPS opted-out numbers.	£80,000
Nuisance calls	16/4/19	Avalon Direct Ltd	Over 50,000 unsolicited direct marketing calls. Calls to TPS opted-out numbers.	Enforcement Notice
Disclosure breach	11/4/19	Bounty (UK) Ltd	Illegal sharing and disclosure of personal data.	£400,000
Collection Consent Transparency breaches	10/4/19	True Visions Productions	Illegal filming in maternity ward. Transparency. Consent. Prior information.	£120,000
Disclosure breach. Data security.	4/4/19	London Borough of Newham	Illegal disclosure of data of persons on police database.	£145,000
Nuisance emails	26/3/19	Grove Pension Solutions Ltd	Two million unsolicited direct marketing emails. Relying on 'misleading' professional advices.	£40,000
Nuisance texts	19/3/19	Vote Leave Ltd	Political. Unsolicited direct marketing text communications.	£40,000
Compliance	7/2/19	Magnacrest Ltd	Prosecution for failure to comply with Enforcement Notice re data access right.	Prosecution
Nuisance marketing	1/2/19	Leave.EU Group Ltd (2)	Political. 300,000 unsolicited communications.	£15,000
Nuisance marketing	1/2/19	Leave.EU Group Ltd (1)	Political. Unsolicited communications without consent.	£45,000
Nuisance emails	1/2/19	Eldon Insurance Services Ltd (TA GoSkippy Insurance)	Unsolicited direct marketing emails without consent.	£60,000
Nuisance emails	1/2/19	Eldon Insurance Services Ltd (TA GoSkippy Insurance)	Unsolicited direct marketing emails without consent.	Enforcement Notice
Nuisance calls	31/1/19	A Green Legal Services Ltd	Unsolicited direct marketing emails without consent.	£80,000
Nuisance calls	31/1/19	A Green Legal Services Ltd	Unsolicited direct marketing emails without consent.	Enforcement Notice
Nuisance calls	22/1/19	NWR Ltd	Over 800,000 unsolicited direct marketing calls. Calls to TPS opted-out numbers.	Enforcement Notice
Nuisance texts	13/12/18	Tax Returned Ltd	14.8 million unsolicited direct marketing text communications.	£200,000
Nuisance texts	13/12/18	Tax Returned Ltd	14.8 million unsolicited direct marketing text communications.	Enforcement Notice

Issue	Date	Party	Breach	Penalty
Data security. Hack.	26/11/18	Uber	Failure to secure customer data against hack attack.	£385,000
Nuisance calls	26/11/18	Solartech North East Ltd	Almost 75,000 unsolicited direct marketing calls. Calls to TPS opted-out numbers.	Enforcement Notice
Nuisance calls	23/11/18	DM Design Bedrooms Ltd	1.6 million unsolicited direct marketing calls. Calls to TPS opted-out numbers.	£160,000
Nuisance calls	23/11/18	Solartech North East Ltd	Almost 75,000 unsolicited direct marketing calls. Calls to TPS opted-out numbers.	£90,000
Nuisance calls	23/11/18	DM Design Bedrooms Ltd	1.6 million unsolicited direct marketing calls. Calls to TPS opted-out numbers.	Enforcement Notice
Various	16/11/18	Metropolitan Police Service (MPS)	Crime data, profiling, gangs database matrix. Processing data for longer than necessary. Excessive processing of personal data. Processing not fair or lawful.	Enforcement Notice
Nuisance calls	31/10/18	Secure Home Systems Ltd	Almost 85,000 unsolicited direct marketing calls. Calls to TPS opted-out numbers.	£80,000
Nuisance calls	30/10/18	ACT Response Ltd	Over 495,000 unsolicited direct marketing calls. Calls to TPS opted-out numbers.	£140,000
Social media data breach and profiling	24/10/18	Facebook	Re Cambridge Analytica political data harvesting and data breaches.	£500,000
Social media data breach and profiling	24/10/18	Aggregate IQ Data Service Ltd	Data analytics for political profiling and other activities.	Enforcement Notice
Nuisance calls	9/10/18	Boost Finance Ltd	Millions of unsolicited direct marketing calls.	£90,000
Data security	8/10/18	Heathrow Airport Ltd (HAL)	USB lost by employee with personal data, lack of encryption.	£120,000
Nuisance calls	1/10/18	Oakland Assist UK Ltd	Unsolicited direct marketing calls.	£150,000
Data security	28/9/18	BUPA Insurance Services Ltd	Data security breaches failing to secure persona data.	£175,000
Data breach. Hack.	20/9/18	Equifax Ltd	Failure to secure personal data of 15 million citizens in hack attack.	£500,000
Access	6/9/18	London Borough of Lewisham	Enforcement Notice order regarding data access rights.	Enforcement Notice
Nuisance emails	5/9/18	Everything DM Ltd	1.43 million unsolicited marketing emails.	£60,000

Issue	Date	Party	Breach	Penalty
Nuisance emails	5/9/18	Everything DM Ltd	1.43 million unsolicited marketing emails.	Enforcement Notice
Collection breach. Sale breach.	9/8/18	Lifecycle Marketing (Mother and Baby) Ltd	Illegal collection, use and sale of persona data, including mothers and children.	£140,000
Nuisance calls	1/8/18	AMS Marketing Ltd	Over 75,000 unsolicited direct marketing calls. Calls to TPS opted-out numbers.	£100,000
Compliance	3/7/18	Noble Design and Build Ltd	Failure to comply with Information Notice	Prosecution
Sensitive data breach	18/7/17	Independent Inquiry into Child Sexual Abuse (IICSA)	Breach of identity of child sex abuse victims.	£200,000
Spam	28/6/18	Our Vault Ltd	Spam calls.	£70,000
Spam	20/6/18	BT	Email marketing spam.	£77,000
Sensitive data breach	11/6/18	Gloucestershire Police	Revealed abuse victim details in bulk email.	£80,000
Hacking	7/6/18	British & Foreign Bible Society	Responsible for exposure of computer system to hacking attack.	£100,000
Records, security	23/5/18	Bayswater Medical	Special personal data and medical records left in unattended building.	£35,000
Data breach	21/5/18	Yahoo! UK	Mass data breach. ISP.	£250,000
Security breach	21/5/18	University of Greenwich	Serious security breach, data of 20K people, included sensitive personal data.	£120,000
Data breach, security, offence, unlawful obtaining	17/5/18	Daniel Short	Recruitment agent took candidate details for new job.	Prosecution
Security, encryption	16/5/18	Crown Prosecution Service (CPS)	Loss of police interviews on DVD, not encrypted.	£325,000
Unlawful access	23/4/18	Michelle Harrison	Hospital health employee accessing patient records without need.	Prosecution
Unlawful identification	16/4/16	Royal Borough of Kensington & Chelsea	Unlawfully identified people.	£120,000
Security	5/4/18	Humberside Police	Rape victim interview recording on disk lost.	£130,000
Unlawful access	7/2/18	Philip Bagnall	Unlawfully obtaining customer data of former employer.	Prosecution
Consent	31/1/18	Holmes Financial Services	Automated marketing calls. without consent	£300,000
Nuisance calls	15/9/17	Your Money Rights Ltd	146 million illegal nuisance and heavy-handed nuisance Spam calls.	£350,000

Issue	Date	Party	Breach	Penalty
Special heath data breach. Unlawful access and disclosure	11/8/17	Brioney Woolfe	Former Colchester hospital employee prosecuted for (a) unlawfully obtaining sensitive heath data of friends and (b) unlawfully disclosing sensitive health data.	Prosecuted at Colchester Magistrates Court. Convicted
Data breach	11/8/17	TalkTalk	Customer data breach.	£100,000
Nuisance calls	3/8/17	Laura Anderson TA Virgo Home Improvements	Nuisance calls and breach of do not call register telephone preference service.	£80,000
Nuisance calls	3/8/17	HPAS TA Safestyle	Nuisance calls and breach of do not call register telephone preference service.	£70,000
Unlawful disclosure	21/7/17	Stuart Franklin	Unlawful disclosure of CVs of applicants to then employer, the Controller, to third party.	Birmingham Magistrates Court. Conviction.
Span email	20/7/17	Moneysupermarket.com	Price comparison website fined for.	£80,000
Spam texts	17/7/17	Provident Personal Credit Union	Spam marketing texts.	£80,000
Data breach	3/7/17	Royal Free	Sensitive health data. Various unlawful data breaches by hospital to third party research company DeepMind.	Curiously no fine. Curiously no deletion.
Website data breach	27/7/17	Boomerang Video	Website cyber attack. Did not take preventative steps.	£60,000
Nuisance calls	22/6/17	MyHome Installations	Nuisance calls and breach of do not call register telephone preference service.	£50,000
Marketing emails	16/6/17	Morrisons supermarkets	Incorrect use of data and customer marketing.	£10,500
Data breach	12/6/17	Gloucester City Council	Cyber attack and access to special employee data.	£100,000
Blagging calls	8/6/17	Joseph Walker	Blagging calls to obtain data from insurance companies re claims and to resell data.	Prosecution
Data breach	31/5/17	Basildon Borough Council	Unlawfully publishing special data about a family in online planning documents.	£150,000
Spam texts	17/5/17	Concept Car Credit	Spam texts.	£40,000
Spam calls	17/5/17	Brighter Home Solutions	Nuisance calls and breach of do not call register telephone preference service.	£50,000
Unlawful access	16/5/17	Sally Anne Day	Employee unlawful access of sensitive patient health data.	Prosecution. Conviction.
Spam texts	16/5/17	Onecom	Spam texts.	£100,000

Issue	Date	Party	Breach	Penalty
Spam calls	10/5/17	Keourboom Communications	99.5m Spam calls.	'Record' £400,000
Data breach	4/5/17	Greater Manchester Police	3 DVDs lost with videos of special sex crime victim interviews lost.	£150,000
Data breach	2/5/17	Construction Materials Online	Failed to protect customer data.	£55,000
Spam texts	19/4/17	Moneva	Spam texts.	£40,000
Various breaches	5/4/17	Great Ormond Street Hospital Childrens Charity	Sharing records with other charities. Profiling. Matching data from other data sources not provided directly.	£11,000
Collection breach	5/4/17	Battersea Dogs and Cats Home	Finding personal data not provided.	£9,000
Various breaches	5/4/17	Cancer Research UK	Profiling. Matching data from other data sources not provided directly.	£16,000
Unlawful disclosure	5/4/17	Cancer Support UK	Sharing data with others regardless of cause.	£16,000
Various breaches	5/4/17	Macmillan Cancer Support	Profiling. Matching data from other data sources not provided directly.	£14,000
Various breaches	5/4/17	NSPCC	Profiling. Matching data from other data sources not provided directly.	£12,000
Matching	5/4/17	Oxfam	Matching data from other data sources not provided directly.	£6,000
Various breaches	5/4/17	Guide Dogs for Blind	Profiling. Matching data from other data sources not provided directly.	£15,000
Various breaches	5/4/17	International Fund for Animal Welfare	Sharing data with others regardless of cause. Profiling. Matching data from other data sources not provided directly.	£18,000
Various breaches	5/4/17	Royal British Legion	Profiling. Matching data from other data sources not provided directly.	£12,000
Various breaches	5/4/17	WWF UK	Profiling. Matching data from other data sources not provided directly.	£9,000

Issue	Date	Party	Breach	Penalty
Unlawful accesss	5/4/17	Eileen McMillan	Hospital employee unlawfully access sensitive health files on estranged family members.	Prosecution
Spam texts	30/3/17	PRS Media	Spam texts without consent of 4.4m people.	£140,000
Spam calls	30/3/17	Xternal Property	Nuisance calls and breach of do not call register telephone preference service.	£80,000
Spam emails	27/3/17	Flybe	3.3m spam emails despite objection opt outs.	£70,000
Emails	27/3/17	Honda	PECR breach.	£13,000
Data breach	20/3/17	Norfolk County Council	Old files including special data left in cabinet given to second-hand shop.	£60,000
Breach	16/3/17	Barrister	Senior barrister failed to keep client file secure.	£1,000
Unlawful obtaining	16/3/17	Gregory Oram	Leaving employee unlawfully obtaining personal data from employer and emailing to personal email to start rival recruitment firm.	Prosecution
Spam texts	14/3/17	Munee Hut	Outsourcing spam texts.	Prosecution. Also fined £20,000
Spam calls	9/3/17	Media Tactics	22m spam calls.	£270,000
Unlawful access	3/3/17	Elaine Lewis	Former nurse unlawfully accessed sensitive medical records.	Prosecution
Security	28/2/17	HCA International	Health company failed to keep IVF fertility records secure.	£200,000
Spam texts	15/2/17	Digitonomy	Spam texts.	£120,000
Sale and spam	2/2/17	Data Supply Company	Sale of records, resulting in purchaser spam texts.	£20,000
CCTV	1/2/17	Karthikesu	Newsagent uses CCTV. Section 17 offence.	Prosecution
Texts	24/1/17	LAD Media	Spam texts.	£50,000
Unlawful obtaining	18/1/17	Rebecca Gray	Employee leaving recruitment company emails client personal data when moving to new recruitment firm.	Prosecution
Spam calls	16/1/17	IT Project Ltd	Nuisance calls and breach of do not call register telephone preference service.	£40,000
Data loss	10/1/17	Royal & Sun Alliance	Data loss of 60,000 customers.	£150,000

Issue	Date	Party	Breach	Penalty
Unlawful access	10/1/17	Minty, Leong & Craddock	Unlawful access (blagging) of insurance data to make claims.	Prosecution
Access	20/12/16	Wainwrights Estate	Failure to comply with information notice after failure to comply with access request.	Prosecution
Unlawful processing	9/12/16	British Heart Foundation	Secretly screened and profiled to target for money.	£18,000
Unlawful processing	9/12/16	RSPCA	Matching, profiling, screening for wealth targeting.	£25,000
Unlawful access	2/12/16	Monnapula	Former health employee unlawfully accessed special heath files of people she knew.	Prosecution
Spam texts	30/12/16	Oracle Insurance Brokers	Spam texts.	£30,000
Spam texts	29/11/16	Silver City	Spam texts.	£100,000
Unlawful access Blagging	11/11/16	Severs and Billington	Unlawful access. Blagging.	Prosecution
Spam calls	10/11/16	Assist Law	Nuisance calls and breach of do not call register telephone preference service.	£30,000
Spam texts	7/11/16	Nouveau Finance	2.2m spam texts.	£70,000
Unlawful use	2/11/16	Tandon	Email data to personal email and sold to third party.	Prosecution
Unlawful access	28/10/16	Evans	Former NHS employee unlawful accessed special data of girlfriend of partner.	Prosecution
Unlawful access	25/10/16	Wooltorton	Former hospital employee unlawfully accessing special data of people she knew.	Prosecution
Spam texts	13/10/16	Rainbow (UK) Ltd	Spam texts.	£20,000
Data breach	5/10/16	Talk Talk	Data breach. Cyber attack accessing customer data. 160,000 customers.	£400,000
Spam texts	28/9/16	Ocean Finance	Spam texts.	£130,000
Spam texts	15/9/16	CarFinance 247	Spam texts.	£30,000
Texts	8/9/16	Vincent Bond	Unsolicited texts.	£40,000
Spam calls	8/9/16	Omega	1.6m spam calls.	£60,000
Security	25/8/16	Whitehead Nursing	Not protecting special data.	£15,000
Data breach	16/8/16	Hampshire County Council	Personal data files found in disused building.	£100,000
Unlawful disclosure	11/8/16	Regal Chambers Surgery	Unlawful disclosure of data of woman and family to estranged husband.	£40,000

Issue	Date	Party	Breach	Penalty
Information notice	21/7/16	Clarity Leeds	Failure to comply with information notice after failure to comply with access request.	Prosecution
Spam calls	9/6/16	Advanced VOIP	Spam calls.	£180,000
Spam texts	9/6/16	Quigley & Carter	Spam texts.	£80,000
Data breach	8/6/16	Chief Constable of Dyfed-Powys	Email identifying sex offenders sent to member of public in error.	£150,000
Spam calls	16/5/16	Check Point Claims	17.5m spam calls.	£250,000
Spam texts	11/5/16	Better for the Country	500,000 spam Brexit texts	£50,000
Unlawful disclosure	9/5/16	Chelsea & Westminster Hospital	Revealed emails of HIV patients.	£180,000
Data breach. Unlawful disclosure	4/5/16	Blackpool Teaching Hospitals NHS Foundation Trust	Inadvertently published online workers' confidential data including their National Insurance number, date of birth, religious belief and sexual orientation.	£185,000
Nuisance calls	27/4/16	Nevis Home Improvements Ltd	2.5 million recorded phone calls.	£50,000
Data breach/ Unlawful disclosure	21/4/16	Chief Constable of Kent Police	Fined after sensitive personal details of woman who accused her partner of domestic abuse passed to the suspect.	£80,000
Trying to buy data without consent	7/4/16	David Barlow Lewis	Former LV employee David Barlow Lewis prosecuted at Bournemouth Magistrates' Court for attempting to commit a s 55 offence, by attempting to obtain personal data without the controller's consent. Pleaded guilty to trying to get an existing LV employee to sell him customer data.	Prosecution and fine.
Failure to comply with notice	5/4/16	Keurboom Communications Limited and director Gregory Rudd	Both prosecuted at Luton Magistrates' Court for failing to comply with a third party information notice issued by the Commissioner in relation to an investigation for PECR breaches. The communication company pleaded guilty to the s 47 offence.	Prosecution of company and directors. Company fined £1,500, plus costs and director fined £1,000
Nuisance calls with fake number	1/4/16	Advice Direct Ltd	Fined by ICO.	£20,000

Issue	Date	Party	Breach	Penalty
Failure to comply with breach notification rules	24/3/16	TalkTalk Telecom Group Plc	Data breach and failure to comply with breach notification rules. Privacy and Electronic Communications (EC Directive) Regulations 2003.	£1,000 per reg 5C(2) of PECR
Nuisance calls	17/3/16	FEP Heatcare	Spam calls. 2.6m calls.	£180,000
Access request	29/3/16	MI Wealth Management Ltd	Failure to comply with access request	Ordered to comply
Security of data	10/3/16	Chief Constable Wiltshire Constabulary	Investigation file lost. Data breach.	Undertaking to comply with Seventh Principle
Nuisance calls	29/2/16	Prodial Ltd	Spam calls. 46m calls.	£350,000
Spam texts	22/11/15	UKMS Money Solutions Ltd (UKMS)	Spamming. 1.3m spam texts.	£80,000
Spam calls	10/11/15	Oxygen Ltd	Unsolicited automated marketing calls.	£120,000
Stolen laptops	4/11/15	Crown Prosecution Service (CPS)	Stolen laptops with police interview videos of victims and witnesses, mostly for ongoing violent or sexual type cases.	£200,000
Spam texts	27/10/15	Help Direct UK Ltd	Unsolicited marketing text messages.	£200,000
	20/10/15	Pharmacy 2U Ltd	Online pharmacy sold details of more than 20,000 customers to marketing companies. No consent. No notification to customers.	£130,000
Information notice	8/10/15	Nuisance Call Blocker Ltd	Failing to respond to information notice.	Prosecuted
Automated marketing calls	30/9/15	Home Energy & Lifestyle Management Ltd (HELM)	6m automated marketing calls. Breach of marketing call regulations.	£200,000
Unsolicited marketing calls	16/9/15	Cold Call Elimination Ltd	Unsolicited marketing calls.	£75,000
Enforcement notice Right to be Forgotten	20/8/15	Google Inc	Ordered to remove nine search results after ICO ruled the information linked was no longer relevant.	Enforcement notice
Nuisance calls	10/8/15	Point One Marketing Ltd (previously Conservo Digital Ltd)	Nuisance calls.	£50,000
Lost data	6/8/15	The Money Shop	Loss of computer equipment with significant amount of customer details.	£180,000

Issue	Date	Party	Breach	Penalty
Non-notification	4/8/15	Consumer Claims Solutions Ltd	Personal injury claims telemarketing company.	Prosecution. Guilty plea to the s17 non-notification offence
Loss of unencrypted DVDs	18/5/15	South Wales Police	Fine for losing a video recording which formed part of the evidence in a sexual abuse case. Despite containing a graphic and disturbing account, DVDs were unencrypted and left in a desk drawer.	£160,000
Non-notification	16/4/15	Lismore Recruitment Ltd	Failing to notify with the ICO.	Prosecution. Guilty plea
Spam calls	1/4/15	Direct Assist Ltd	Direct marketing calls to people without their consent.	£80,000
Unauthorised disclosure	30/3/15	Serious Fraud Office	Witness in a serious fraud, bribery and corruption investigation mistakenly sent evidence relating to 64 other people in case.	£180,000
Spam texts	24/3/15	Sweet Media Ltd	Enforcement notice to stop sending nuisance Spam texts. ICO raid. SIM cards and computers seized. Sent over 4.5m texts.	Enforcement notice
Spam texts	17/3/15	Help Direct UK	Order to stop spam texts.	Enforcement notice
Unlawful access	12/3/15	Yasir Manzoor	Former customer service assistant at Lloyds Banking Group prosecuted for unlawfully accessing a former partner's bank account.	Prosecution
Unlawful access	26/2/15	Bernard Fernandes	Former support clerk at Transport for London prosecuted for unlawfully accessing the oyster card records of family and neighbours.	Prosecution
Hack Security Breach	24/2/15	Staysure.co.uk Ltd	IT security failings let hackers access customer records. More than 5,000 customers had their credit cards used by fraudsters after the attack on the online holiday insurance company. Hackers potentially accessed over 100,000 live credit card details, and customers' medical details. Credit card CVV numbers were also accessible despite industry rules that they should not be stored at all.	£175,000

Issue	Date	Party	Breach	Penalty
Privacy Policy	30/1/15	Google Inc	Google Inc signs undertaking committing to making further changes to its amalgamated Privacy Policy in order to ensure compliance with the first principle of DPA 1998.	Privacy Policy
Failure to respond to information notice	6/1/15	Tivium Ltd	Failure to respond to information notice.	Prosecution. Fined £5000, plus compensation plus costs.
Spam texts	6/1/15	Optical Express (Westfield) Ltd	Enforcement notice to stop Spam texts.	Enforcement notice
Spam calls	27/12/14	Kwik Fix Plumbers Ltd	Nuisance spam calls targeting vulnerable victims. In several cases, the calls resulted in elderly people being tricked into paying for boiler insurance they did not need.	£90,000
Failure to report breach	19/12/14	Vodafone	Failure to comply with the personal data breach reporting requirements under the Privacy and Electronic Communications (EC Directive) Regulations 2003.	£1,000
Spam texts	5/12/14	Parklife Manchester Ltd	Unsolicited marketing texts. Texts sent to 70,000 people bought tickets to last year's event, and appeared on recipients' mobile phone as sent by 'Mum'.	70,000
Enforcement notice Data breach	19/11/14	Grampian Health Board (NHS Grampian)	ICO ordered NHS Grampian to ensure patients' information better protected. Six data breaches in 13 months where papers containing sensitive personal data were left abandoned in public areas of a hospital. In one case the data was found at a local supermarket.	Enforcement notice
Unlawful access	13/11/14	Harkanwarjit Dhanju	Former West Sussex Primary Care Trust pharmacist prosecuted for unlawfully accessing medical records of family members, work colleagues and local health professionals.	Prosecution
Spam calls	12/11/14	Hot House Roof Company	Enforcement notice to stop Spam calls.	Enforcement notice

Issue	Date	Party	Breach	Penalty
Company director	11/11/14	Matthew Devlin	Company director Matthew Devlin fined after illegally accessing Everything Everywhere's (EE) customer database, to target them with services of his own telecoms companies.	Prosecution
Hack Security Breach	5/11/14	Worldview Ltd	Serious data breach when vulnerability on company's site allowed hackers to access full payment card details of 3,814 customers.	£7,500
Spam email	21/10/14	Abdul Tayub	Enforcement notice. Sending unsolicited marketing mail by electronic means without providing information as to his identity and without prior consent.	Enforcement notice
Spam calls	1/10/14	EMC Advisory Services Ltd	Spam calls. Also failure to ensure persons registered with TPS, or who previously asked not to be contacted, were not called.	£70,000
Spam email	12/9/14	All Claims Marketing Ltd	Enforcement notice. Spam email and without providing information as to its identity.	Enforcement notice
Spam calls	3/9/14	Winchester and Deakin Limited (also trading as Rapid Legal and Scarlet Reclaim)	Enforcement notice. Spam calls. Included calls to people who had registered with the TPS, or who had asked not to be contacted.	Enforcement notice
Breach	24/8/14	Ministry of Justice	Serious failings in the way prisons handed people's information.	£180,000
Unlawful access	22/8/14	Dalvinder Singh	Santander banker fined for reading 11 colleagues' bank accounts, to see their salary and bonuses.	Prosecution
Failure to notify with ICO	6/8/14	A Plus Recruitment Limited	Failure to notify with ICO.	Prosecution
Failure to notify with ICO	5/8/14	1st Choice Properties (SRAL)	Failure to notify with ICO.	Prosecution
Spam calls	28/7/14	Reactiv Media Ltd	Spam calls. Calls to people who registered with TPS.	£50,000
Hack Security Breach	23/7/14	Think W3 Limited	Online travel services company. Serious breach of DPA 1998. Thousands of people's data accessed by hacker.	£150,000

Issue	Date	Party	Breach	Penalty
Company owner Failure to notify ICO of changes to his notification	15/7/14	Jayesh Shah	Owner of a marketing company (Vintels) prosecuted for failing to notify ICO of changes to his notification.	Prosecution. Fined £4000, plus costs and victim surcharge
Failure to notify with ICO	14/7/14	Hayden Nash Consultants	Recruitment company. Failure to notify with ICO.	Prosecution
Unlawful access Unlawful sale	10/7/14	Stephen Siddell	Former branch manager for Enterprise Rent-A-Car prosecuted for unlawfully stealing the records of almost two thousand customers and selling them to a claims management company.	Prosecution
Failure to notify with ICO	9/7/14	Global Immigration Consultants Ltd	Failure to notify with ICO.	Prosecution.
Spam calls	16/6/14	DC Marketing Ltd	Enforcement notice. Spam calls.	Enforcement notice
Director Failure to notify with ICO	6/6/14	Darren Anthony Bott	Director of pensions review company prosecuted for failure to notify with ICO.	Prosecution. Guilty plea
Failure to comply with information notice	5/6/14	API Telecom	Failure to comply with information notice.	Prosecution
Unlawful disclosure	29/5/14	Wolverhampton City Council	Investigation into a data breach at the council that occurred in January 2012, when a social worker who had not received data protection training, sent a report to a former service user detailing their time in care. The social worker failed to remove highly sensitive information about the recipient's sister that should not have been included.	Enforcement notice
Failure to notify with ICO	13/5/14	QR Lettings	Failure to notify with ICO.	Prosecution
Failure to notify with ICO	25/4/14	Allied Union Ltd	Failure to notify with ICO.	Prosecution
Spam calls	3/4/14		Unsolicited spam calls to people who registered with TPS.	£50,000

Issue	Date	Party	Breach	Penalty
Failure to notify with ICO	25/3/14	Help Direct UK Ltd	Failure to notify with ICO.	Prosecution
Security Unlawful access	19/3/14	Kent Police	Highly sensitive and confidential information, including copies of police interview tapes, were left in a basement at the former site of a police station.	£100,000
Directors and company Failure to notify with ICO	12/3/14	Boilershield Limited	Failure to notify with ICO.	Prosecution. Both fined £1,200, plus costs and surcharge
Failure to notify with ICO	11/3/14	Becoming Green (UK) Ltd	Failure to notify with ICO.	Prosecution
Spam calls	10/3/14	Isisbyte Limited	Enforcement notice, Spam calls.	Enforcement notice
Spam calls	10/3/14	SLM Connect Limited	Enforcement notice. Spam calls.	Enforcement notice
Hack Security Breach	7/3/14	British Pregnancy Advice Service (BPAS)	Hacker threatened to publish thousands of names of people who sought advice on abortion, pregnancy and contraception.	£200,000
Blagging	24/1/14	ICU Investigations Ltd	Blagging. Six men who were part of a company that tricked organisations into revealing personal details about customers has today been sentenced for conspiring to breach the DPA.	Prosecution
Security Unlawful disclosure	11/1/14	Department of Justice Northern Ireland	A monetary penalty notice has been served on Department of Justice Northern Ireland after a filing cabinet containing details of a terrorist incident was sold at auction.	£185,000
Spam texts	16/12/13	First Financial (UK) Ltd	Millions of spam texts.	£175,000
Security. Unlawful disclosure No encryption	29/10/13	North East Lincolnshire Council	Loss of an unencrypted memory device containing personal data and special personal data relating to 286 children.	£80,000
Security Unlawful disclosure	22/10/13	Ministry of Justice	Failure to keep personal data securely, after spreadsheets showing prisoners' details were emailed to members of the public in error.	£140,000

Issue	Date	Party	Breach	Penalty
Data breach	2/1/13	Sony	Hack breach	£250,000
Unlawful access Customer financial data Bank employee	6/11/12	Lara Davies	Bank employee obtained unlawfully access to bank statements of her partner's ex-wife. Court prosecution. Pleaded guilty to 11 DPA offences.	Court conviction. Fined. Lost job.
Spam	28/11/12	Christopher Niebel and Gary McNeish, joint owners of Tetrus Telecoms	An ICO monetary penalty was issued. The company had sent millions of unlawful Spam texts to the public over the past three years. This case involved the prosecution of Directors.	£300,000 £140,000
Data Loss/ Data Breach Unlawful disclosure Sensitive data	22/11/12	Plymouth City Council	An ICO monetary penalty issued for a serious breach of the seventh data protection principle. A social worker sent part of a report relating to family A, to family B due to printing issues. The photocopied report contained confidential and highly special personal data relating to the two parents and their four children, including of allegations of child neglect in on-going care proceedings.	£60,000
Incorrect storage and processing Potential loss and damage Financial institution	6/11/12	Prudential	An ICO monetary penalty issued after a mix-up over the administration of two customers' accounts led to tens of thousands of pounds, meant for an individual's retirement fund, ending up in the wrong account. This was the first case in relation to a fine for incorrect storage and processing.	£50,000
Data Loss/ Data Breach Unlawful disclosure Sensitive data	25/10/12	Stoke-on-Trent City Council	An ICO monetary penalty issued following a serious breach of the Data Protection Act that led to sensitive information about a child protection legal case being emailed to the wrong person.	£120,000

Issue	Date	Party	Breach	Penalty
Data Loss/ Data Breach Police	16/10/12	Greater Manchester Police	An ICO monetary penalty issued after the theft of a memory stick containing special personal data from an officer's home. The device, which had no password protection, contained details of more than a thousand people with links to serious crime investigations.	£150,000
Data Loss/ Data Breach Charity	10/10/12	Norwood Ravenswood Ltd	An ICO monetary penalty issued after highly special information about the care of four young children was lost after being left outside a London home. This was a charity which was fined.	£70,000
Data Loss/ Data Breach	11/9/12	Scottish Borders Council	An ICO monetary penalty issued after former employees' pension records were found in an over-filled paper recycle bank in a supermarket car park.	£250,000
Unlawful disclosure Special data	6/8/12	Torbay Care Trust	An ICO monetary penalty issued after special personal information relating to 1,373 employees was published on the Trust's website.	£175,000
Unlawful disclosure Special data	12/7/12	St George's Healthcare NHS Trust	An ICO monetary penalty issued after a vulnerable individual's special medical details were sent to the wrong address.	£60,000
Data Loss/ Data Breach	5/7/12	Welcome Financial Services Ltd	An ICO monetary penalty issued following a serious breach of the Data Protection Act. The breach led to the personal data of more than half a million customers being lost.	£150,000
Data Loss/ Data Breach Special data	19/6/12	Belfast Health and Social Care Trust	An ICO monetary penalty issued following a serious breach of the Data Protection Act. The breach led to the special personal data of thousands of patients and staff being compromised. The Trust also failed to report the incident to the ICO.	£225,000

Issue	Date	Party	Breach	Penalty
Unlawful disclosure Special data	6/6/12	Telford & Wrekin Council	An ICO monetary penalty issued for two serious breaches of the seventh data protection principle. A social worker sent a core assessment report to the child's sibling instead of the mother. The assessment contained confidential and highly special personal data. Whilst investigating the first incident, a second incident was reported to the ICO involving the inappropriate disclosure of foster carer names and addresses to the children's mother. Both children had to be re-homed.	£90,000
Unlawful disclosure Special data Security	1/6/12	Brighton and Sussex University Hospitals NHS Trust	An ICO monetary penalty issued following the discovery of highly special personal data belonging to tens of thousands of patients and staff – including some relating to HIV and Genito Urinary Medicine patients – on hard drives sold on an Internet auction site in October and November 2010.	£325,000
Unlawful disclosure Special data	21/5/12	Central London Community Healthcare NHS Trust	An ICO monetary penalty issued for a serious contravention of the DPA, which occurred when special personal data was faxed to an incorrect and unidentified number. The contravention was repeated on 45 occasions over a number of weeks and compromised 59 Data Subjects' personal data.	£90,000
Data Loss/ Data Breach Special data	15/5/12	London Borough of Barnet	An ICO monetary penalty issued following the loss of special information relating to 15 vulnerable children or young people, during a burglary at an employee's home.	£70,000
Unlawful disclosure Special data	30/4/12	Aneurin Bevan Health Board	An ICO monetary penalty issued following an incident where a sensitive report – containing explicit details relating to a patient's health – was sent to the wrong person.	£70,000

Issue	Date	Party	Breach	Penalty
Unlawful disclosure Special data	14/3/12	Lancashire Constabulary	An ICO monetary penalty issued following the discovery of a missing person's report containing special personal information about a missing 15 year old girl.	£70,000
Unlawful disclosure Special data	15/1/12	Cheshire East Council	An ICO monetary penalty issued after an email containing special personal information about an individual of concern to the police was distributed to 180 unintended recipients.	£80,000
Data Loss/ Data Breach Special data	13/2/12	Croydon Council	An ICO monetary penalty issued after a bag containing papers relating to the care of a child sex abuse victim was stolen from a London pub.	£100,000
Unlawful disclosure Special data	13/2/12	Norfolk County Council	An ICO monetary penalty issued for disclosing information about allegations against a parent and the welfare of their child to the wrong recipient.	£80,000
Unlawful disclosure Special data	30/1/12	Midlothian Council	An ICO monetary penalty issued for disclosing sensitive personal data relating to children and their carers to the wrong recipients on five separate occasions. The penalty is the first that the ICO has served against an organisation in Scotland.	£140,000
Unlawful disclosure Special data	6/12/11	Powys County Council	An ICO monetary penalty issued for a serious breach of the Data Protection Act after the details of a child protection case were sent to the wrong recipient.	£130,000
Unlawful disclosure Special data	28/11/11	North Somerset Council	An ICO monetary penalty issued for a serious breach of the Data Protection Act where a council employee sent five emails, two of which contained highly special and confidential information about a child's serious case review, to the wrong NHS employee.	£60,000

Issue	Date	Party	Breach	Penalty
Unlawful disclosure Special data	28/11/11	Worcestershire County Council	An ICO monetary penalty issued for an incident where a member of staff emailed highly special personal information about a large number of vulnerable people to 23 unintended recipients.	£80,000
Unlawful disclosure Special data	9/6/11	Surrey County Council	An ICO monetary penalty issued for a serious breach of the Data Protection Act after special personal information was emailed to the wrong recipients on three separate occasions.	£120,000
Unlawful disclosure Special Data Security	10/5/11	Andrew Jonathan Crossley, formerly trading as solicitors firm ACS Law	An ICO monetary penalty issued for failing to keep special personal information relating to around 6,000 people secure.	£1,000
Data Loss/ Data Breach Laptop Encryption	8/2/11	Ealing Council	An ICO monetary penalty issued following the loss of an unencrypted laptop which contained personal information. Ealing Council breached the Data Protection Act by issuing an unencrypted laptop to a member of staff in breach of its own policies.	£80,000
Data Loss/ Data Breach Laptop Encryption	8/2/11	Hounslow Council	An ICO monetary penalty issued following the loss of an unencrypted laptop which contained personal information. Hounslow Council breached the Act by failing to have a written contract in place with Ealing Council. Hounslow Council also did not monitor Ealing Council's procedures for operating the service securely.	£70,000

Conclusion

11.30   One comment on the above is that it is worrying how many problem issues arise with regard to health data, and which amounts to special personal data.

It should also be noted that company directors (and other officers) can be personally prosecuted and fined.

If a request for information or other notice is received from the ICO it may be appropriate to seek immediate legal advice. The ICO can also issue enforcement notices. In addition, the ICO may also issue monetary penalty notices or fines. It is important to note the emphasis now under the GDPR regime on teams dealing with the nuanced respective data protection (and security) issues; DPOs; assessing data protection risks and dealing with them appropriately; and the related rules. Organisations should ensure proper policies; awareness and ongoing training are in operation across all personnel who have an impact and responsibility regarding data protection operations. It appears that fines, prosecutions and Data Subject damage and access litigation will increase.

Chapter 12

Security of Personal Data

Introduction

12.01   Personal data and 'personally identifiable information (PII) data has become the prime target of hackers and cyber-criminals. It can be exploited in many ways, from identity theft, spamming and phishing right through to cyber-espionage.'[1] The data protection regime sets information and data security obligations on all Controllers, as well as Processors. These IT and personal data security requirements must be complied with. Data security risks have increased with the internet, electronic communications, and increasing numbers of electronic devices.[2] However, data security risk issues are not just limited to the organisation's internet or email communications.

The growing number of data security breaches, including through inadequate data security, as well as internet usage and social media, cloud computing and online abuse, will all increase the attention on data security and data protection. Yahoo! has suffered a large number of data breaches, with the data of 500 million users exposed in one incident, and over a billion users in another. Cathay Pacific was fined £500,000 for failing to protect customer data during a computer data breach where passport and other data was exposed. Uber was fined £385,000 in the UK (and €600,000 in the Netherlands) for failing to protect user data in a data breach incident. Sony was fined £250,000 in relation to a hacking data breach incident. Facebook was fined £500,000 regarding abuses of social media harvested data (Cambridge Analytica). Telco Talk-Talk was hacked in a data breach incident. The MD of TalkTalk has said that 'cyber criminals are becoming increasingly sophisticated and attacks against companies which do business online are becoming more frequent'. Retailers have been hacked, as evidenced by the ICO data fine of £500,000 on DSG Retail. Even children's toy manufacturer Vtech was hacked, which carries the added risk to child data as well as parent data. Some organisations may not have realised that they can be held responsible for errant third party hack attacks where they have contributed to or enabled the attack by failure to implement and update adequate data security precautions.

Appropriate Security Measures

12.02   Organisations should be aware that data security and appropriate security measures extends beyond IT or technical data security. Doorstep Dispensaree and its

---

1   Y Rozenberg, 'Challenges in PII Data Protection,' *Computer Fraud & Security* (2012) 5–9, at 5.
2   'Security of the Internet and the Known Unknowns,' *Communications of the ACM* (2012) (55) 35–37.

fine of £275,000 by the data regulator arose out of the storing of physical file records in an insecure manner.[3]

There are specific requirements with regard to the security measures that need to be implemented under the Data Protection Act 2018 (DPA 2018), UK GDPR, GDPR – and to be updated by the Data Protection and Digital Information (No 2) Bill (DPDI Bill) (eg clauses 22 and 23).

Organisations and Controllers must take appropriate security measures against unauthorised access to, or unauthorised alteration, disclosure or destruction of, the data, in particular where the processing involves the transmission of data over a network, and against all other unlawful forms of processing. As these risks grow,[4] so too must the efforts of the organisation. It is not the case that one solution, on one occasion, will be sufficient.

The requirements regarding security of processing previously contained in the seventh Data Protection Principle (DPA 1998, Sch 1, Pt I, para 7) are now expanded under the EU General Data Protection Regulation (GDPR) (Principle 6 and Article 32) and UK GDPR. The Controller must take appropriate technical and organisational measures against unauthorised or unlawful processing of personal data and against accidental loss or destruction of, or damage to personal data.

The Controller must ensure the following:

'Taking into account the state of the art, the costs of implementation and the nature, scope, context and purposes of processing as well as the risk of varying likelihood and severity for the rights and freedoms of natural persons, the Controller and the Processor shall implement *appropriate technical and organisational measures* to ensure a level of security appropriate to the risk.'

The GDPR and UK GDPR places significant emphasis on risk and risk assessment. Organisations need to be compliant with these obligations. Note that the DPDI Bill proposes amendments in relation to certain data, namely, processing for research etc purposes (clauses 22 and 23; also see Schedule 12). There is also a new provision in relation to confidentiality and data protection (clause 73).

Ensuring Appropriate Security Measures

12.03 What are security and 'appropriate technical and organisational measures'? What must the organisation do? In determining appropriate technical and organisational measures, a Controller may have regard to:

- the state of technological development and the cost of implementing any measures;
- the harm that might result from such unauthorised or unlawful processing or accidental loss, destruction or damage; and
- the nature of the data to be protected.

Article 32 sets out various additional factors.

Employees and Security

12.04 The Controller must take reasonable steps to ensure the reliability of any employees of the organisation who have access to the personal data.

---

3   *ICO v Doorstep Dispensaree Limited* [2019] 20 December 2019.
4   See, for example, 'The Cybersecurity Risk,' *Communications of the ACM* (2012) (55) 29–32.

Organisations should be aware that they could be held liable, whether with the ICO or in a civil court, in relation to data breaches and data security breaches occasioned by their employees. Organisations may also begin to face claims in relation to online abuse caused, initiated or participated in by their employees while using the organisation's network and devices. Indeed, this applies in relation to their other servants and agents also.

There can be no full data security policy across the organisation unless employees embrace the measures taken, and are appropriately trained in data security issues.

Engaging Data Processors

12.05 Processors[5] also have obligations in relation to processing personal data and security.

Where processing of personal data is carried out by a Processor on behalf of a Controller, then the Controller must have a contract in writing with the Processor, containing certain clauses and obligations.

The contracts with Processors must address the following,

- processing must be carried out in pursuance of a contract in writing;
- contract must provide that the Processor carries out the processing only on and subject to the instructions of the Controller;
- Processor must comply with the above *security* requirements.

There are also certain other requirements. The Controller:

- must ensure Processors provide sufficient guarantees in respect of the technical security measures and organisational measures governing the processing;
- must take reasonable steps to ensure compliance with these measures.

There are specific requirements where Processors are engaged and relied upon. Where Controllers engage Processors then the Controller must:

- have a contract in writing or other equivalent form which provides that the Processor will act only on instructions of the Controller and that it will comply with the data security measures to which the Controller is subject;
- ensure that the Processor provides sufficient guarantees in respect of the technical security measures and organisational measures it implements;
- takes reasonable steps to ensure compliance with such matters.

What actions should an organisation take if third parties process their organisation's data? Organisations should consider:

- ideally, that an organisation should have advance procedures and policies in place to cater for such an eventuality, for example ensuring that an appropriate senior manager/board member has an assigned role and takes responsibility for date protection compliance, including dealing with breaches, and also having a documented IT security incident handling procedure policy in place. Needless to say, it must be properly policed, implemented, reviewed and updated appropriately;
- once a breach does occur, a proper procedure can assist in containing the breach and recovering from same; assessing the ongoing risk; notify the breach as appropriate; evaluating and reacting to the breach and the risk;

---

5   Note generally, for example, R Morgan, 'Data Controllers, Data Processors and Data Sharers,' SCL *Computers and Law*, 4 March 2011.

- all of the appropriate personnel within the organisation should be aware of the procedures and consulted as appropriate, including for example managing director, legal, IT, media/press officer;
- a part of the procedure will have a designated list of external contact points, some or all of whom may need to be notified and contacted, as appropriate;
- obviously the nature of organisations, and of breaches themselves, differ and the IT security incident handling procedure policy will need to be tailored. After all, the cause of a data security breach can be any of a number of potential reasons;
- also, such a policy while covering breaches of data protection and privacy, may well encompass wider issues, such as outsourcing, backups, disaster recovery, business continuity, etc;
- if an organisation does business in other jurisdictions it may need to take additional measures. For example, if it owns or has access to personal information of Californian residents then it may have a legal duty to notify those individuals if that information (such as names and credit card details) has been accessed illegally.

Over time the length of these contracts has become longer as the nature of the issues that need to be incorporated become longer and more complex.

Security and the EDPB

12.06 The influential European Data Protection Board (EDPB) (previously WP29) has previously published a document relating to personal data and information security.[6] It refers to the surveillance of employee's electronic communications. In terms of compliance it raises a number of policy concerns for organisations to consider when dealing with their policies and activities regarding such personal data. It suggests that organisations asking if the proposed processing of the employee's personal data is:

- transparent?
- necessary?
- fair?
- proportionate?
- for what purpose?

It also suggests that organisations should consider if each proposed processing activity can be achieved through some other less obtrusive means.

It also refers to informing those outside of the organisation as appropriate in relation to the proposed processing.

It also refers to issues of proportionality in suggesting that an organisation in processing personal data should adopt the minimum processing necessary, and pursuing a strategy of prevention versus detection. Detection leans more towards blanket monitoring of employees, whereas prevention is viewed as more appropriate and employee privacy friendly. Of course, where some issue comes to the organisation's attention, they could then investigate that issue, as opposed to actively monitoring all employees 24/7. An example would be using IT filtering systems, which alert the IT manager that there may be an issue to look at further, rather than the IT manager actively looking at and monitoring all employee communications.

---

6   This was published on 29 May 2002.

Security and the GDPR and UK GDPR

12.07   Security is particularly emphasised as being important under the new data protection regime. The EU General Data Protection Regulation (GDPR) Recitals refer to security as follows: network and information security, Computer Emergency Response Teams (CERTs) and Computer Security Incident Response Teams (CSIRTs); guidance for appropriate measures; appropriate technical and organisational measures; security and risk evaluation; high risk and impact assessments; and impact assessments; and large scale processing operations; consultations; data breach and data breach notification; Commission delegated acts. Chapter IV, Section 2 of the GDPR relates to data security.

Security of Processing

12.08   Taking into account the state of the art, the costs of implementation and the nature, scope, context and purposes as well as the risk of varying likelihood and severity for the rights and freedoms of natural persons, the Controller and the Processor shall implement appropriate technical and organisational measures to ensure a level of security appropriate to the risk, including *inter alia*, as appropriate:

- the pseudonymisation and encryption of personal data;
- the ability to ensure the ongoing confidentiality, integrity, availability and resilience of processing systems and services;
- the ability to restore the availability and access to personal data in a timely manner in the event of a physical or technical incident;
- a process for regularly testing, assessing and evaluating the effectiveness of technical and organisational measures for ensuring the security of the processing (GDPR, Article 32(1)).

In assessing the appropriate level of security account shall be taken in particular of the risks that are presented by data processing, in particular from accidental or unlawful destruction, loss, alteration, unauthorised disclosure of, or access to personal data transmitted, stored or otherwise processed (Article 32(2)).

Adherence to an approved code of conduct pursuant to Article 40 or an approved certification mechanism pursuant to Article 42 may be used as an element by which to demonstrate compliance with the requirements set out in Article 32(1) (Article 32(3)).

The Controller and Processor shall take steps to ensure that any person acting under the authority of the Controller or the Processor who has access to personal data shall not process them except on instructions from the Controller, unless they are required to do so by EU or state law (Article 32(4)).

Notification of a Data Breach to Supervisory Authority

12.09   In the case of a personal data breach, the Controller shall without undue delay and, where feasible, not later than 72 hours after having become aware of it, notify the personal data breach to the supervisory authority, unless the personal data breach is unlikely to result in a risk for the rights and freedoms of natural persons. Where the notification to the supervisory authority is not made within 72 hours, it shall be accompanied by reasons for the delay (Article 33(1)).

The Processor shall notify the Controller without undue delay after becoming aware of a personal data breach (Article 33(2)).

Contents of Notification

12.10   The notification must at least:

- describe the nature of the personal data breach including where possible, the categories and approximate number of Data Subjects concerned and the categories and approximate number of data records concerned;
- communicate the name and contact details of the data protection officer (DPO) or other contact point where more information can be obtained;
- describe the likely consequences of the personal data breach;
- describe the measures taken or proposed to be taken by the Controller to address the personal data breach, including, where appropriate, measures to mitigate its possible adverse effects (Article 33(2)).

Where, and in so far as, it is not possible to provide the information at the same time, the information may be provided in phases without undue further delay (Article 33(4)).

The Controller shall document any personal data breaches, comprising the facts relating to the personal data breach, its effects and the remedial action taken. This documentation must enable the supervisory authority to verify compliance with this Article (Article 33(5)).

Communication of a Data Breach to Data Subject

12.11   When the personal data breach is likely to result in a high risk to the rights and freedoms of individuals the Controller shall communicate the personal data breach to the Data Subject without undue delay (Article 34(1)).[7]

The communication to the Data Subject shall describe in clear and plain language the nature of the personal data breach and contain at least the information and the recommendations provided for in Article 31(3)(b), (d) and (e) (Article 32(2)).

The communication to the Data Subject referred to in Article 32(1) must not be required if:

- the Controller has implemented appropriate technical and organisational protection measures, and that those measures were applied to the personal data affected by the personal data breach, in particular those that render the data unintelligible to any person who is not authorised to access it, such as encryption; or
- the Controller has taken subsequent measures which ensure that the high risks to the rights and freedoms of Data Subjects referred to in para 1 is no longer likely to materialise; or
- it would involve disproportionate effort. In such a case, there shall instead be a public communication or similar measure whereby the Data Subjects are informed in an equally effective manner (Article 34(3)).

If the Controller has not already communicated the personal data breach to the Data Subject, the supervisory authority, having considered the likelihood of the breach to result in a high risk, may require it to do so or may decide that any of the conditions referred to in Article 34(3) are met (Article 34(4)).

---

7   Note, for example, P Wainman, 'Data Protection Breaches: Today and Tomorrow,' SCL *Computers and Law*, 30 June 2012. Also see M Dekker, Dr, C Christoffer Karsberg and B Daskala, *Cyber Incident Reporting in the EU* (2012).

Data Protection Impact Assessment and Prior Consultation

12.12   Chapter IV, Section 3 of the GDPR refers to Impact Assessments and Prior Consultations.

Data Protection Impact Assessment

12.13   Where a type of processing, in particular using new technologies, and taking into account the nature, scope, context and purposes of the processing, is likely to result in a high risk for the rights and freedoms of natural persons, the Controller shall, prior to the processing, carry out an assessment of the impact of the envisaged processing operations on the protection of personal data. A single assessment may address a set of similar processing operations that present similar high risks (Article 35(1)).

The Controller shall seek the advice of the DPO, where designated, when carrying out a data protection impact assessment (Article 35(2)).

A data protection impact assessment shall particularly be required where there is:

- a systematic and extensive evaluation of personal aspects relating to natural persons which is based on automated processing, including profiling, and on which decisions are based that produce legal effects concerning the natural person or similarly significantly affect the individual;
- processing on a large scale of special categories of data referred to in Article 9(1), or of personal data relating to criminal convictions and offences referred to in Article 10; or
- a systematic monitoring of a publicly accessible area on a large scale (Article 35(2)).

The supervisory authority shall establish and make public a list of the kind of processing operations which are subject to the requirement for a data protection impact assessment pursuant to Article 35(1). The supervisory authority shall communicate those lists to the EDPB (Article 35(4)).

The supervisory authority may also establish and make public a list of the kind of processing operations which are subject to requirement for a data protection impact assessment. The supervisory authority shall communicate those lists to the EDPB (Article 35(4)).

The supervisory authority may also establish and make public a list of the kind of processing operations for which no data protection impact assessment is required. The supervisory authority shall communicate those lists to the Board.

Prior to the adoption of the lists referred to above, the competent supervisory authority shall apply the consistency mechanism referred to in Article 63 where such lists involve processing activities which are related to the offering of goods or services to Data Subjects or to the monitoring of their behaviour in several states, or may substantially affect the free movement of personal data within the EU (Article 35(6)).

The EDPB has also issued the following document:

- Recommendation 01/2019 on the draft list of the European Data Protection Supervisor regarding the processing operations subject to the requirement of a data protection impact assessment (Article 39.4 of regulation (EU) 2018/1725.

In terms of the UK, the DPDI Bill proposes amendments in relation risk assessments and reporting/consultation with the ICO. These are referred to in clauses 17 and 18.

Contents of Data Protection Impact Assessment

12.14 The assessment shall contain at least:

- a systematic description of the envisaged processing operations and the purposes of the processing, including where applicable the legitimate interest pursued by the Controller;
- an assessment of the necessity and proportionality of the processing operations in relation to the purposes;
- an assessment of the risks to the rights and freedoms of Data Subjects;
- the measures envisaged to address the risks, including safeguards, security measures and mechanisms to ensure the protection of personal data and to demonstrate compliance with the GDPR taking into account the rights and legitimate interests of Data Subjects and other persons concerned (Article 35(7)).

Compliance with approved codes of conduct referred to in Article 38 by the relevant Controllers or Processors shall be taken into due account in assessing the impact of the processing operations performed by such Controllers or Processors, in particular for the purposes of a data protection impact assessment (Article 35(8)).

Where appropriate, the Controller shall seek the views of Data Subjects or their representatives on the intended processing, without prejudice to the protection of commercial or public interests or the security of the processing operations (Article 35(9)).

Where the processing pursuant to Article 6(1)(c) or (e) has a legal basis in EU law, or the law of the state to which the Controller is subject, and such law regulates the specific processing operation or set of operations in question, and a data protection impact assessment has already been carried out as part of a general impact assessment in the context of the adoption of that legal basis, Article 35(1) to (7) shall not apply, unless states deem it necessary to carry out such assessment prior to the processing activities (Article 35(10)).

Where necessary, the Controller shall carry out a review to assess if the processing of personal data is performed in compliance with the data protection impact assessment at least when there is a change of the risk represented by the processing operations (Article 35(11)).

The DPDI Bill proposes amendments in relation risk assessments and reporting/consultation with the ICO. These are referred to in clauses 17 and 18.

Prior Consultation

12.15 The Controller shall consult the supervisory authority prior to the processing of personal data where a data protection impact assessment indicates that the processing would result in a high risk in the absence of measures taken by the Controller to mitigate the risk (Article 36(1)).

Where the supervisory authority is of the opinion that the intended processing referred to in Article 36(2) would infringe the GDPR, in particular where the Controller has insufficiently identified or mitigated the risk, the supervisory authority shall, within a period of up to eight weeks of receipt of the request for consultation give written advice to the Controller, and where applicable the Processor in writing, and may use any of its powers referred to in Article 58. This period may be extended for a further six weeks, taking into account the complexity of the intended processing (Article 36(2)).

When consulting the supervisory authority pursuant to Article 36(1), the Controller shall provide the supervisory authority with:

- where applicable, the respective responsibilities of the Controller, joint Controllers and Processors involved in the processing, in particular for processing within a group of undertakings;
- the purposes and means of the intended processing;
- the measures and safeguards provided to protect the rights and freedoms of Data Subjects pursuant to the GDPR;
- where applicable, the contact details of the DPO;
- the data protection impact assessment provided for; and
- any other information requested by the supervisory authority (Article 36(3)).

States shall consult the supervisory authority during the preparation of a proposal for a legislative measure to be adopted by a national parliament, or of a regulatory measure based on such a legislative measure, which relates to processing (Article 36(4)).

Notwithstanding Article 36(1), states' law may require Controllers to consult with, and obtain prior authorisation from, the supervisory authority in relation to the processing by a Controller for the performance of a task carried out by the Controller in the public interest, including the processing of such data in relation to social protection and public health (Article 36(5)).

The DPDI Bill proposes amendments in relation risk assessments (clause 17) and consultation with the ICO (clause 18).

Organisational Security Awareness

12.16   There is a need to ensure security awareness within the organisation. Controllers and Processors must take all reasonable steps to ensure that persons employed by them and other persons at the place of work, are aware of and comply with the relevant security measures (note DPA 1998, Sch 1, Pt II, para 10).

Identifying and Controlling Organisational IT Security

12.17   Who needs to be in charge of IT and data security in an organisation? What organisational security measures should be in place?

The DPA does not require that a named individual be appointed with responsibility for security compliance. A titled officer is highly recommended and under the GDPR a formal DPO is now a requirement. There are specific organisational responsibilities, regarding security, which are set out in the DPA and these include a specific requirement that all staff are aware of and comply with the security standards set out in the data protection regime.

These security requirements apply where an organisation collects and processes any personal data. Typically personal data would include information which identifies living individuals such as employees or customers. Accordingly, for most organisations, data protection compliance is likely to be an issue that crosses various aspects of the business such as human resources, IT and customer support. It is not necessarily just an IT function. An organisational decision as to who should be responsible for IT and data security should be made with this in mind.

The security standards set out in the Data Protection Act can be summarised as obliging the organisation to take 'appropriate' security measures to guard against unauthorised access, alteration, disclosure or destruction of any personal data.

In determining what is 'appropriate', the organisation can have regard to the state of technological development and the cost of implementing the security measures. However, the organisation is obliged to ensure that the measures it decides to adopt provide a level of security appropriate to the harm that might result from a security compromise given the nature of the data concerned. For example, a hospital processing sensitive health data would be expected to adopt a particularly high security standard while a corner shop processing personal data for a paper round might be subject to a less onerous standard.

In light of some high profile cases of data theft or loss, readers should note also that the ICO's office has taken the view that an appropriate level of security for laptop computers used in the financial services and sensitive health industries requires the use of encryption in respect of the data stored on the hard drive (over and above the use of user name and password log-in requirements).

In adopting security measures within an organisation, they should note that the legal standard governing personal data is over and above any other legal obligations of confidentiality which could be owed to third parties at common law or under a contract which contains confidentiality provisions.

Appraising Employees

12.18 What guidance should be given to an organisation's employees regarding IT and data security? An organisation might consider these issues.

The overriding principle here is that, for it to be effective, an employee must have clear notice of all aspects of the IT and data security policy. The following might be included.

General Policy: Seek to reserve the right to appropriately monitor use of the computer and telephone system, including email. Disclosure of special or confidential information about the company or personal data about any individual without authorisation should be forbidden.

Email: Employees should be made aware that email is an essential business tool but not without its risks. Business communications should be suitable and not too casual or contain inappropriate material. Personal use of email must be reasonable.

Internet Access: Downloading of any software without approval should be forbidden. No improper or illegal activities (hacking, etc) should be tolerated. Access to certain types of websites (abuse, adult, criminal, hate, violent, etc) should be expressly restricted. Origination or dissemination of inappropriate material should be forbidden.

Mobile Telephones and Devices: Downloading of any software without approval should be forbidden. No improper or illegal activities (hacking, etc) should be tolerated. Access to certain types of websites (adult, criminal, hate, violent, etc) should be expressly restricted. Origination or dissemination of inappropriate material should be forbidden.

Vehicles: Increasingly tracking and other data from vehicles can be related to identified employees. It is important for organisations to consider these personal data issues first.

Internet Social Media: Downloading of any software without approval should be forbidden. No improper or illegal activities (hacking, etc) should be tolerated. Access to certain types of websites (adult, criminal, hate, violent, etc) should be expressly restricted. Origination or dissemination of inappropriate material should be forbidden, eg abuse.

Software Installation and Management: Purchase and/or installation of software not approved in advance should be forbidden. All software must be required to be tested before installation on the system to ensure that it is free from viruses, malware, etc.

Password Security: Clear guidelines as to the use of passwords should be given including the strength of password required, the importance of keeping one's password confidential, the changing of passwords at regular intervals and (in the light of recent events) the application of password security to laptops, mobile phones and PDAs. At least, in some businesses, stronger encryption may be appropriate and employees should be required to comply with procedures in this regard. Carrying company data on vulnerable media such as memory sticks should be discouraged.

Connecting Hardware: Employees should be required not to connect any hardware (memory sticks, hard drives, etc) without following specified procedures and obtaining appropriate authorisation.

Remote Access: For many businesses, remote access, including web-based remote access, is a vital tool. However, policies should deal with such matter as accessing remotely from insecure locations as internet cafes, etc and emphasise the importance of logging off effectively.

Organisational Security Measures

12.19   What measures should an organisation take? Some suggestions may include:

- ensure that the organisation has the appropriate security equipment and software to protect the systems if granting third party access. If providing access to a third party involves the business opening its systems up to a public network such as the Internet, it is essential that suitable security measures are taken;
- obtain a complete listing of the IT provider personnel who have access to the systems and detail their level, status (full time/contractor) and ensure that their employment contracts incorporate terms similar to above.

Third parties should be granted access to the systems only when the:

- relevant individuals in the organisation (eg a business manager, in conjunction with IT staff) have agreed that there is a business need for such access to be granted. Access should only be for a temporary period and renewed at regular intervals;
- third party computer accounts should be monitored (subject to legal agreements between the organisation and the third party and in accordance with legal requirements) and disabled as soon as access is no longer required;
- ensure that sensitive files segregated in secure areas/computer systems and available only to qualified persons;
- ensure that the organisation has inventoried the various types of data being stored and classified it according to how important it is and how costly it would be for the company if it were lost or stolen;
- scan computers (especially servers) for unauthorised programs that transmit information to third parties such as hackers;
- programs that have a hidden purpose are known as Trojans. Individuals may have inadvertently or deliberately downloaded free programs from the Internet that send back information such as passwords to hackers or Internet usage information to marketers to build up trends of people's tastes;
- ensure that third parties only have access to information and computer settings on a 'need-to-know' basis;
- the System Administrator for the computer systems should set up computer accounts for third parties so that these third parties do not have access to all information on the systems or have the permission to install non-standard software and change computer settings;
- when engaging an external business to destroy records or electronic media, ensure references are checked. Draft a contract setting out the terms of the relationship.

Ensure that destruction is done on-site and require that a certificate of destruction be issued upon completion.

Breach Laws to Consider

12.20 What laws might affect an organisation if an organisation has an IT or data security breach? Suggested legal issues and laws to consider include,

- DPA 2018;
- UK GDPR;
- GDPR;
- DPDI Bill with new provisions plus amendments to DPA 2018 and UK GDPR;
- ePrivacy regulation;
- Electronic Commerce (EC) Regulations 2002;
- Criminal Damage Act 1971;
- evidence;
- Fraud Act 2006;
- Theft Act 1968;
- civil liability law;
- Protection of Children Act 1978;
- Criminal Justice and Public Order Act 1994;
- European Convention on Human Rights;
- PECR, PECR Amendment, and DPDI Bill amendments PEC (Part 4).

Other issues to consider include:

- official guidance and current stated positions of regulators and guidance bodies;
- international standards organisations eg technical security standards, etc;
- the new proposals in relation to digital verification services (see DPDI Bill, Part 2); and proposals in relation to trust services (see DPDI Bill, Part 4).

Third Party Security Providers

12.21 What actions should an organisation take if a third party is responsible for IT security or has access to its IT system? Some issues to consider include:

- this is becoming increasingly popular in practice through outsourcing arrangements and vendor agreements;
- it is prudent to understand the security framework and document stakeholder exposure throughout it;
- measures to take with the organisation's IT provider;
- ensure that one engages lawyers to draft appropriate contracts that secure what the IT provider is securing;
- ensure that data protection and confidentiality clauses are included to protect all of your intellectual property assets;
- have the IT provider supply a complete security document outlining the hardware, topology, software and methodologies deployed;
- ensure that the IT provider has staff participate in regular training programs to keep abreast of technical and legal issues;
- ensure that the IT provider develops a security breach response plan in the event that your company experiences a data breach; also develop security guidelines for laptops and other portable computing devices when transported off-site;

- have the IT provider ensure that all employees follow strict password and virus protection procedures and develop a mechanism where employees are required to change passwords often, using safe methods especially for terminating employees;
- ensure that the IT provider has a records retention/disposal schedule for personally identifiable information, whether stored in paper, micrographic or magnetic/electronic (computer) media.

Raising Awareness

12.22 An EU Council Resolution[8] indicates the recognition and official concern in relation to the loss of personal data, and the fact that technology has changed significantly since the EU Data Protection Directive 1995 (DPD 1995).

It refers to the dangers of information loss, attacks on organisations, and issues of network and information security for organisations and individuals.

It indicated that EU states should engage in information campaigns addressing the issues of security and personal data.

It recognises the need to promote best practice, such as the internationally recognised standards for IT and security set by international and standards setting organisation eg ISO 27001, ISO 15408, PCI DSS, ISO 31000, BS10012:2009, ISO/IEC 18043, ISO 22301, National Information Security Technology (NIST) standards, Center for Internet Security (CIS) standards, etc.

It also recognises the increase in eGovernment and the need to promote secure eGovernment.

It also notes that in the increase of attacks on the security of personal data though technology, some of the solutions may also come from new technologies. Some of these are referred to as privacy enhancing technologies, or PETs.[9] (See PbD and DPbD, Part 4.)

In addition it also refers to the increase of mobile and wireless communications technologies and the need for introducing and enhancing wireless security.

Note also the network and information systems rules applicable to certain digital service providers.[10] Separate rules also relate to electronic identification and trust services.[11]

Keeping on top of the increasing threats to information security is an ongoing task. The threats are ever changing, and so equally should be the effort to prevent breaches, and to deal with them if and when they occur. Some of the most current information security threats are highlighted annually by various IT security vendors as well as police and investigative officials. Many security risk reports are published annually.

---

8   EU Council Resolution 2002/C43/02 of 28 January 2002.
9   See, for example, B Beric and G Carlisle, 'Investigating the Legal Protection of Data, Information and Knowledge Under the EU Data Protection Regime,' *International Review of Law, Computers & Technology* (2009) (23) 189–201.
10 See Network and Information Systems Regulations 2018 (UK), as amended by the Network and Information Systems (Amendment) Regulations 2018 (UK), and also the European Commission Regulation 2018/151.
11 See Regulation (EU) 910/2014 on electronic identification and trust services for electronic transactions in the internal market.

ICO Guidance

12.23 The ICO has also issued a guide entitled *A Practical Guide to IT Security, Ideal for Small Businesses*[12] which is useful. The ICO has also commented in relation to encryption issues.[13] Of course, as threats advance, so must data security measures and precautions.

The ICO also provides the following tips and suggestions[14] for maintaining and implementing IT security for personal data, namely:

For Computer Security

- install a firewall and virus-checking on the computers;
- make sure that the operating system is set up to receive automatic updates;
- protect the computer by downloading the latest patches or security updates, which should cover vulnerabilities;
- only allow staff access to the information they need to do their job and do not let them share passwords;
- encrypt any personal information held electronically that would cause damage or distress if it were lost or stolen;
- take regular back-ups of the information on your computer system and keep them in a separate place so that if one loses computers, one does not lose the information;
- securely remove all personal information before disposing of old computers (by using technology or destroying the hard disk);
- consider installing an anti-spyware tool. Spyware can secretly monitor ones computer activities, etc. Spyware can be unwittingly installed within other file and program downloads, and their use is often malicious. They can capture passwords, banking credentials and credit card details, and then relay them back to fraudsters. Anti-spyware helps to monitor and protect the computer from spyware threats, and it is often free to use and update.

For Using Emails Securely

- consider whether the content of the email should be encrypted or password protected. The IT or security team should be able to assist with encryption;
- when starting to type in the name of the recipient, some email software will suggest similar addresses one has used before. If one has previously emailed several people whose name or address starts the same way – eg 'Dave' – the auto-complete function may bring up several 'Dave's.' Make sure to choose the right address before clicking send;
- if one wants to send an email to a recipient without revealing their address to other recipients, make sure to use blind carbon copy (bcc), not carbon copy (cc). When one uses cc every recipient of the message will be able to see the address it was sent to;
- be careful when using a group email address. Check who is in the group and make sure you really want to send your message to everyone;
- if sending a sensitive email from a secure server to an insecure recipient, security will be threatened. One may need to check that the recipient's arrangements are secure enough before sending the message.

---

12 At https://ico.org.uk.
13 ICO, Our Approach to Encryption, at https://ico.org.uk.
14 ICO, Security Measures, at https://ico.org.uk.

For Using Faxes Securely

- consider whether sending the information by a means other than fax is more appropriate, such as using a courier service or secure email. Make sure to only send the information that is required;
- make sure to double check the fax number you are using. It is best to dial from a directory of previously verified numbers;
- check that you are sending a fax to a recipient with adequate security measures in place. For example, the fax should not be left uncollected in an open plan office;
- if the fax is sensitive, ask the recipient to confirm that they are at the fax machine, they are ready to receive the document, and there is sufficient paper in the machine;
- ring up or email to make sure the whole document has been received safely;
- use a cover sheet. This will let anyone know who the information is for and whether it is confidential or sensitive, without them having to look at the contents.

For Other Security

- shred all your confidential paper waste;
- check the physical security of your premises;
- training staff,
  - so they know what is expected of them;
  - to be wary of people who may try to trick them into giving out personal details;
  - so that they can be prosecuted if they deliberately give out personal details without permission;
  - to use a strong password – these are long (at least seven characters) and have a combination of upper and lower case letters, numbers and the special keyboard characters like the asterisk or currency symbols;
  - not to send offensive emails about other people, their private lives or anything else that could bring your organisation into disrepute;
  - not to believe emails that appear to come from your bank that ask for your account, credit card details or your password (a bank would never ask for this information in this way);
  - not to open Spam – not even to unsubscribe or ask for no more mailings. Tell them to delete the email and either get Spam filters on your computers or use an email provider that offers this service.[15]

ICO and Security Breaches

12.24 The ICO advises that under the Regulations (PECR updated), public electronic communications service providers are required to notify the ICO if a personal data breach occurs. (Note the ePrivacy Regulation refers to further rules and updates). A personal data breach is defined to mean:

'a breach of security leading the accidental or unlawful destruction, loss, alteration, unauthorised disclosure of, or access to, personal data transmitted, stored or otherwise processed in connection with the provisions of a public electronic communications service.'

---

15   ICO, Security Measures, at https://ico.org.uk.

The ICO advises[16] that the following must be complied with:

Keep a log of personal data breaches

You must keep a record of all personal data breaches in an inventory or log. It must contain:

- the facts surrounding the breach;
- the effects of that breach; and
- remedial action taken.

We have produced a template log to help you record the information you need.

Notify breaches to the ICO

You must notify the ICO of any personal data breaches. This notification must include at least a description of,

- the nature of the breach;
- the consequences of the breach; and
- the measures taken or proposed to be taken by the provider to address the breach.

To make this process easier, we suggest that you send your log to us on a monthly basis. This means one will not have to record the information twice and will meet the organisation's requirement to notify any security breaches without unnecessary delay.

However, if the breach is of a particularly serious nature you need to notify us about the breach as soon as possible, by filling in the security breach notification form (PECR).

When thinking about whether a breach is of a serious nature, we recommend that one considers,

- the type and sensitivity of the data involved;
- the impact it could have on the individual, such as distress or embarrassment; and
- the potential harm, such as financial loss, fraud, theft of identity.

Please email all security breach notifications to us at data security breach@ico.gsi.gov.uk.

Failure to comply with the requirement to submit breach notifications can incur a ... fine.

For more practical information on how to notify us about PECR security breaches please see our guidance for service providers.

Notify breaches to your subscribers

You may also need to tell your subscribers. If the breach is likely to adversely affect their personal data or privacy you need to, without unnecessary delay, notify them of the breach. You need to tell them,

- the nature of the breach;
- contact details for your organisation where they can get more information; and
- how they can mitigate any possible adverse impact of the breach.

You do not need to tell your subscribers about a breach if you can demonstrate that you have measures in place which would render the data unintelligible and that those measures were applied to the data concerned in the breach.

If you don't tell subscribers, the ICO can require you do so, if it considers the breach is likely to have an adverse effect on them.[17]

---

16 ICO, Security Breaches, at https://ico.org.uk.
17 ICO, Security Measures, at https://ico.org.uk.

Disposal of Computer Hardware

12.25 Particular care is needed when considering the disposal of IT hardware, equipment and software. They may still contain personal data files. It may also include commercial or other confidential information relating to the organisation. This can continue to be the case even when it appears that files have been wiped or deleted. It is always advised to take professional legal, IT and or forensic advice.

Disposal can occur from the organisation. However, organisations need to be aware that there can be a security breach as well a breach of the data protection regime if devices and hardware are donated to charity or otherwise given away but there remains corporate and personal data on the devices. Even when it appears data may be deleted, it can sometimes be recovered with the right skills. There have also been instances where equipment is meant to be decommissioned and disposed of but employees or contractors do not fulfil the job, and the devices get into third party hands with data still on them.

This can raise other issues. If an employee leaves, they will be leaving their company laptop, etc behind. This can be reassigned to another employee. However, is the new employee appropriately designated to access to the level and importance of the data on the laptop? Hierarchies of access control need to be considered.

Particular sensitivity also arises if it is intended to recycle or give to charity particular devices. Real consideration should be given to the personal data (and other data) thereon in deciding if and how to so dispose of such devices.

Conclusion

12.26 Security is a legal data protection compliance requirement, as well as best business practice. This is one of the more prominent areas of compliance where time never stands still. The security risks and needs must constantly be appraised and updated. It is also essential to ensure that outsourced data processing activities are also undertaken in an appropriately secure manner. Increasingly the area of appraisals and procedures surrounding security breaches and data loss instances is regulated. If such an event arises, the ICO as well as individual Data Subjects may have to be informed. Liability issues should also be a constant concern for organisations as regards security and risk. Maintaining data security is an ongoing task. What may be secure and data protection compliant last month, may not be so next month. Constant vigilance is required.

Chapter 13

Outsourcing and Data Processors

Introduction

13.01 While many organisations may feel they do not engage third parties to deal with their personal data, processes and databases, closer inspection often indicates that this is not correct. Many organisations, and across all sectors of activity, engage third parties or outsource certain of their internal processing activities.[1]

One example is where an organisation may find it more convenient to outsource its payroll functions to an organisation specialising in such activities. It is necessary, therefore, that the employee personal data, or certain of it, is transferred to the third party organisation for processing. This third party is a data Processor acting for the organisation. A contract must be in place and appropriate security standards implemented.

Sometimes organisations outsource other activities, such as marketing, recruitment, employment of consultants or agents or part time employees. Organisations increasingly outsource market research and customer satisfaction surveys to third parties. These are all Processors where personal data is involved.

If an organisation must transfer or export personal data outside of the UK and lawfully permit transfers outside of the transfer restriction, it must satisfy, as appropriate, one of the following:

- an export to one of the safe permitted countries; or
- UK permitted third countries; or
- an export pursuant to the new UK accepted standard contractual clauses (Controller to Processor); or
- an export pursuant to the new UK accepted standard contractual clauses (Controller to Controller); or
- an export pursuant to UK accepted binding corporate rules (BCRs).

The government presented new UK data transfer contract rules on 2 February 2022. They are entitled:

(1) International Data Transfer Agreement (IDTA); and
(2) International Data Transfer Addendum (UK Addendum).

---

1   See generally V Alsenoy, 'Allocating Responsibility Among Controllers, Processors, and "Everything In Between": The Definition of Actors and Roles in Directive 95/46/EC,' *Computer Law & Security Review* (2012) (28) 25–43; R Morgan, 'Data Controllers, Data Processors and Data Sharers,' SCL *Computers and Law*, 04 March 2011.

These contract models became UK law from 21 March 2022. These were issued under section 119A of the Data Protection Act 2018.

The Data Protection and Digital Information (No 2) Bill (DPDI Bill) also contains new provisions in relation to data transfers, such as transfers of personal data to third countries (clause 21); transfers of personal data to third countries, etc: general processing (Schedule 5); and transfers of personal data to third countries, etc: consequential and transitional provisions (Schedule 7).

(Note that UK data transfers to the US,[2] and EU data transfers to the UK require more attention as a result of the Brexit process, and ongoing amendments in this particular area. The UK successfully applied for an obtained EU adequacy decision in order to facilitate the ongoing transfer of data from the EU to the UK after Brexit.) (See Lambert, *Data Protection and Data Transfers Law.*)

Processors and Data Security

13.02   Processors also have obligations in relation to processing personal data and security.

Where processing of personal data is carried out by a Processor on behalf of a Controller, then the Controller must have a contract in writing in place with the Processor, containing certain clauses and obligations.

The contracts with Processors must address the following:

● processing must be carried out in pursuance of a contract in writing or another equivalent form;
● the contract must provide that the Processor carries out the processing only on and subject to the instructions of the Controller;
● the Processor must comply with the 'security' requirements (see above).

There are also certain other requirements. The Controller:

● must ensure the Processor provides sufficient guarantees in respect of the technical security measures and organisational measures governing the processing;
● must take reasonable steps to ensure compliance with these measures.

Cloud and data security issues must also be considered as they arise.

Engaging Processors

13.03   Where processing of personal data is carried out by a Processor on behalf of a Controller, the Controller should:

● choose a Processor providing sufficient guarantees in respect of the technical and organisational security measures governing the processing to be carried out; and
● take reasonable steps to ensure compliance with those measures.

---

2   Note that the original Safe Harbour agreement, and the replacement Privacy Shield, were each struck down by the Court of Justice.

Relying on Third Party Processors

13.04   There are specific requirements where Processors are engaged. Where Controllers engage Processors then the Controller must:

- have a contract in writing or other equipment form which provides that the Processor will act only on instructions of the Controller and that it will comply with the data security measures to which the Controller is subject;
- ensure the Processor provides sufficient guarantees in respect of the technical security measures and organisational measures it implements;
- takes reasonable steps to ensure compliance with such matters.

What actions should an organisation take if third parties process their organisation's data? Organisations should consider:

- implementing advanced procedures and policies to ensure and cater for such an eventuality;
- ensuring that an appropriate senior manager/board member has an assigned role and takes responsibility for data protection compliance, including dealing with breaches, and also having a documented IT security incident handling procedure policy in place. Needless to say, it must be properly policed, implemented, reviewed and updated appropriately;
- that once a breach does occur, a proper procedure can assist in containing the breach and recovering from same; assessing the ongoing risk; notifying the breach as appropriate; evaluating and reacting to the breach and the risk;
- ensuring that all of the appropriate personnel within the organisation are aware of the procedures and consulted as appropriate, including for example, the managing director, legal, IT, media/press officer;
- that a part of the procedure will have a designated list of external contact points, some or all of whom may need to be notified and contacted, as appropriate;
- that obviously the nature of organisations, and of the breaches themselves, differ and the IT security incident handling procedure policy will need to be tailored accordingly. After all, the cause of a data security breach can be due to any of a number of potential reasons; also
- that such a policy while covering breaches of data protection and privacy, may well encompass wider issues, such as outsourcing, backups, disaster recovery, business continuity, etc;
- that if doing business in other jurisdictions one may need to take additional measures. For example, if the business owns or has access to personal information of Californian residents then there may be a legal duty to notify those individuals if that information (such as names and credit card details) has been accessed illegally.

Conclusion

13.05   It is also important that the organisation undertake ongoing assessments and checks regarding the operation of the data processing undertaken by the Processor. This should also include the security and compliance measures. Issues of risk, security breach and data protection compliance must be assessed on an ongoing basis. The issue of the relationship and the appropriate contract documentation required when outsourcing is becoming increasingly complex. It can even be more complicated when data services occur across jurisdictional borders invoking the data transfer regime in addition to the data Processor regime.

Part 2

Inward Facing Organisational DP Obligations

Chapter 14

Processing Employee Personal Data

Introduction

14.01 Organisations sometimes focus on their customer related data compliance issues. It is important for new and existing organisations to look inwards, as there are important inward facing data protection obligations. Personal data includes the personal data of employees also. The employees of the organisation also have Data Subject rights which must be respected.

The variety of inward-facing data protection issues which organisations need to deal with on a daily basis are ever increasing. Some of these include whether to allow employees to access devices, communications, bring their own devices (BYOD) into the organisation, and place organisational data onto such devices. If something is permitted, or even not permitted, this should be expressly specified in a transparent manner in an appropriate policy – or even in layered documentation.

The ability for organisations to track their employees off-site is also a new consideration. This can include technologies onboard vehicles as well as satellite and location technologies. It also includes the organisation's (and employee's own) smart phone (and other) devices. The issues of monitoring and unjustified monitoring are also big considerations. Organisations should not assume that monitoring, much less all types of monitoring, of employees is permitted, and or permitted at all times during the day.

Clearly, there are many more means by which new and/or expanded sets of personal data may be collected and used by an organisation. However, it is equally necessary to consider the data protection compliance issues at the earliest opportunity, and what collections are permissible and which are not.

Organisations should also note that the fields or categories of potential employee data are ever increasing. These are no longer limited to a hard copy personnel or HR file, nor limited to the physical location of the personnel department.

New Inward Facing Changes

14.02 Some of the new EU General Data Protection Regulation (GDPR) and UK GDPR changes which apply to inward facing organisational issues include:

- repeal of EU Data Protection Directive 1995 (DPD 1995) (Article 94);
- WP29 and European Data Protection Board (Recitals 72, 77, 105, 119, 124, 136, 139, 140, 143, 168; Articles 35, 40–43, 47, 51, 52, 58–62, 64 and 65, 94);
- background and rationale (Recitals 1–8, 11–13);
- context objectives, scope of GDPR (Articles 1, 2 and 3);

- obligations (Recitals 32, 39, 40, 42, 43–47);
- security (Recitals 2, 16, 19, 39, 49, 50, 52, 53, 71, 73, 75, 78, 81, 83, 91, 94, 104, 112; Articles 2, 4, 5, 9, 10, 30, 32, 35, 40, 45, 47);
- processing;
- rights (Recitals 1, 2, 3, 4, 9, 10, 11, 13, 16, 19, 38, 39, 41, 47, 50–54, 57, 59, 63, 65, 66, 68–71, 73–81, 84–86, 89, 91, 94, 98, 102, 104, 108, 109, 111, 113, 114, 116, 122, 129, 137, 139, 141–143, 153–156, 162, 164, 166, 173; Articles 1, 4–7, 9–22);
- proceedings (Recitals 52, 80, 129, 143–147; Articles 23, 40, 78, 79, 81, 82);
- establishment (Recitals 22, 36, 52, 65, 100, 117, 122, 124, 126, 127, 145; Articles 3, 4, 9, 17, 18, 21, 37, 42, 49, 54, 56, 57, 60, 62, 65, 70, 79);
- transfers (Recitals 6, 48, 101–103, 107, 108, 110–114, 153; Articles 4, 13, 14, 15, 23, 28, 30, 40, 42, 44–49, 70, 83, 85, 88, 96);
- new bodies (Recital 142; Articles 9, 80);
- notification/registration replaced (Recital 89);
- exceptions/exemptions (Recitals 14, 15, 17);
- lawful processing and consent (Recital 10, 32, 33, 38–40, 42–46, 49–51, 54, 63, 65, 68, 69, 71, 83, 111, 112, 116, 138, 155, 161, 171; Articles 4–9, 13, 14, 17, 18, 20, 22, 23, 32, 40, 49, 82, 83);
- online identifiers (Recitals 30, 64; Articles 4, 87);
- sensitive and special personal data (Recitals 10, 51, 53, 54, 59, 65, 71, 80, 91, 97; Articles 6, 9, 22, 27, 30, 35, 37, 47);
- health data (Recital 35, 45, 52–54, 63, 65, 71, 73, 75, 91, 112, 155, 159; Articles 4, 9, 17, 23, 36, 88);
- GDPR definitions (Article 4);
- new processing rules: obligations (Articles 5–11);
- new (data protection) Principles (Article 5);
- lawfulness of processing: lawful processing conditions (Article 6);
- processing special categories of personal data (Article 9);
- processing re criminal convictions and offences data (Article 10);
- processing not requiring identification (Article 11);
- Controllers and Processors (Chapter IV);
- responsibility of the Controller (Article 24);
- joint Controllers (Article 26);
- Processor (Article 28);
- processing under authority of Controller and Processor (Article 29);
- records of processing activities (Article 30);
- representatives of Controllers not established in EU (Article 27);
- security of processing (Article 32);
- notifying data breach to supervisory authority (Article 33);
- communicating data breach to Data Subject (Article 34);
- data protection impact assessment and prior consultation (Chapter IV, Section 3);
- data protection impact assessment (Article 35);
- prior consultation (Article 36);
- new Data Protection Officer (DPO) (Chapter IV; Section 4; Article 37);
- position (Article 38) and tasks (Article 39) of new DPO;
- general principle for transfers (Recitals 6, 48, 101–103, 107, 108, 110–114, 153; Articles 4, 13, 14, 15, 23, 28, 30, 40, 42, 44–49, 70, 83, 85, 88, 96; Article 44);
- transfers via adequacy decision (Article 45);
- transfers via appropriate safeguards (Article 46);
- transfers via binding corporate rules (Article 47);
- transfers or disclosures not authorised by EU law (Article 48);

- derogations for specific situations (Article 49);
- new processing rules: Data Subject rights (Recitals 1–4, 9–11, 13, 16, 19, 38, 39, 41, 47, 50–54, 57, 59, 63, 65, 66, 68–71, 73–81, 84–86, 89, 91, 94, 98, 102, 104, 108, 109, 111, 113, 114, 116, 122, 129, 137, 139, 141–143, 153–156, 162, 164, 166, 173; Articles 1, 4–7, 9–22; Chapter III);
- right to transparency (Recitals 13, 39, 58, 60, 71, 78, 100, 121; Chapter III, Section 1; Articles 5, 12–14, 26, 40–43, 53, 88);
- data access rights (Chapter III, Section 2);
- right to prior information: directly obtained data (Article 13);
- right to prior information: indirectly obtained data (Article 14);
- right of confirmation and right of access (Article 15);
- rectification and erasure (Chapter III, Section 3);
- right to rectification (Article 16);
- right to erasure (Right to be Forgotten) (RtbF) (Article 17);
- right to restriction of processing (Article 18);
- notifications re rectification, erasure or restriction (Article 19);
- right to data portability (Article 20);
- right to object (Article 21);
- rights against automated individual decision making, including profiling (Article 22);
- Data Protection by Design and by Default (DPbD) (Article 25);
- security rights;
- data protection impact assessment and prior consultation;
- communicating data breach to Data Subject (Article 34);
- DPO (contact);
- remedies, liability and sanctions (Chapter VIII);
- right to effective judicial remedy against Controller or Processor (Article 79);
- representation of Data Subjects (Article 80);
- right to compensation and liability (Article 82);
- general conditions for imposing administrative fines (Article 83);
- penalties (Article 84);
- specific data processing situations (Chapter IX);
- processing in employment context (Article 88).

The Data Protection Act 2018 (DPA 2018) at Sch 1, Pt 1 refers to conditions relating to employment (and other issues). It refers to conditions relating to employment and special categories of data. It states that '[t]his condition is met if':

- 'the processing is necessary for the purposes of performing or exercising obligations or rights which are imposed or conferred by law on the controller or the data subject in connection with employment …';
- 'when the processing is carried out, the controller has an appropriate policy document in place …'

Data Protection Officer (DPO)

14.03　There may have been a traditional view within organisations that the role of the person tasked with dealing with data protection issues was limited to dealing with *outward facing* data protection queries such as access requests, data protection website queries and the like. There may have been an understanding that personnel managers were responsible for dealing with all employee related queries, including references to and copies of employee documentation and personal data.

This is no longer the case. Now there must be a designated DPO appointed in organisations. Furthermore, the role and tasks of the DPO are not limited to outward facing issues. The DPO will also be concerned with inward facing issues. Employees and similar internal facing individuals have data protection rights and will be able to address queries to the DPO quite separate from the human resource functions.

Therefore, organisations must consider DPO issues and the GDPR in terms of internal facing functions. Chapter IV, Section 4 of the new GDPR refers to DPOs and the obligation for organisations to appoint DPOs. The Controller and the Processor shall designate a DPO in any case where:

- the processing is carried out by a public authority or body, except for courts acting in their judicial capacity; or
- the core activities of the Controller or the Processor consist of processing operations which, by virtue of their nature, their scope and/or their purposes, require regular and systematic monitoring of Data Subjects on a large scale; or
- the core activities of the Controller or the Processor consist of processing on a large scale of special categories of data pursuant to Article 9 and data relating to criminal convictions and offences referred to in Article 10 (Article 37(1)).

A group of undertakings may appoint a single DPO provided that the DPO is easily accessible from each establishment (Article 37(2)).

Where the Controller or the Processor is a public authority or body, a single DPO may be designated for several such authorities or bodies, taking account of their organisational structure and size (Article 37(3)).

In cases other than those referred to in Article 37(1), the Controller or Processor or associations and other bodies representing categories of Controllers or Processors may or, where required by EU or state law shall, designate a DPO. The DPO may act for such associations and other bodies representing Controllers or Processors (Article 37(4)).

The DPO shall be designated on the basis of professional qualities and, in particular, expert knowledge of data protection law and practices and the ability to fulfil the tasks referred to in Article 39 (Article 37(5)).

The DPO may be a staff member of the Controller or Processor, or fulfil the tasks on the basis of a service contract (Article 37(6)).

The Controller or the Processor shall publish the contact details of the DPO and communicate these to the supervisory authority (Article 37(7)).

The Controller or the Processor shall ensure that the DPO is involved, properly and in a timely manner, in all issues which relate to the protection of personal data (Article 38(1)).

The Controller or Processor shall support the DPO in performing the tasks referred to in Article 39 by providing resources necessary to carry out these tasks as well as access to personal data and processing operations, and to maintain their expert knowledge (Article 38(2)).

The Controller or Processor shall ensure that the DPO does not receive any instructions regarding the exercise of those tasks. He or she shall not be dismissed or penalised by the Controller or the Processor for performing their tasks. The DPO shall directly report to the highest management level of the Controller or the Processor (Article 38(3)).

Data Subjects may contact the DPO with regard to all issues related to the processing of their personal data and the exercise of their rights under the GDPR (Article 38(4)).

The DPO shall be bound by secrecy or confidentiality concerning the performance of their tasks, in accordance with EU or state law (Article 38(5)). (The Data Protection and Digital Information (No 2) Bill (DPDI Bill) refers to confidentiality and data protection at cl 73.)

The DPO may fulfil other tasks and duties – which must not result in a conflict of interests (Article 38(6)).

The Controller or Processor shall ensure that any such tasks and duties do not result in a conflict of interests (Article 38(6)).

The DPO shall have at least the following tasks:

- to inform and advise the Controller or the Processor and the employees who carry out processing of their obligations pursuant to the GDPR and to other EU or state data protection provisions;
- to monitor compliance with the GDPR, with other EU or state data protection provisions and with the policies of the Controller or Processor in relation to the protection of personal data, including the assignment of responsibilities, awareness-raising and training of staff involved in processing operations, and the related audits;
- to provide advice where requested as regards the data protection impact assessment and monitor its performance pursuant to Article 35;
- to cooperate with the supervisory authority;
- to act as the contact point for the supervisory authority on issues related to the processing of personal data, including the prior consultation referred to in Article 36, and to consult, where appropriate, with regard to any other matter (Article 37(1)).

The DPO shall in the performance of their tasks have due regard to the risk associated with the processing operations, taking into account the nature, scope, context and purposes of the processing (Article 39(2)).

Inward Facing Issues

14.04 Organisations must comply with the data protection regime as regards their inward facing personal data. This primarily relates to the employees of the organisation. This raises a number of issues both in terms of whom are the employees, what personal data is being collected and processed, for what purpose or purposes, where is it located, does anyone else obtain the data, etc, and how the organisation ensures that it is data protection compliant in relation to same.

In relation to employee personal data, organisations must ensure compliance with the:

- Principles of data protection;
- Legitimate Processing Conditions;
- Special Personal Data Legitimate Processing Conditions;
- data security requirements;
- risk assessments and privacy impact assessments;
- employee (etc) Data Subject rights;
- new DPO.

Those Covered

14.05 Who is covered by the inward facing organisational data protection obligations? While full time employees are the most obvious example, they are not the only ones. Organisations must consider the inward facing personal data of:

- full time employees;
- part time employees;
- other workers such as temps and casual staff;

- agency staff;
- contractors;
- ex-employees;
- retired employees;
- spouses;
- job applicants, including unsuccessful applicants;
- volunteers;
- apprentices and trainees;
- work experience staff;
- indirectly engaged persons, such as actors (after the Sony film 'The Interview' massive data breach incident – after which the online publication of internal disparaging emails regarding certain actors caused significant reputational damage and potential lawsuits. It also cost key personnel their jobs).

Where an organisation engages with the data of any of the above, it will have to ensure that the data protection regime is complied with.

Compliance with the Principles of Data Protection

14.06   In dealing with employee personal data, as well as potential employees and any of the categories outlined above, it is necessary for the organisation to comply with the Principles of data protection.

The data protection Principles apply in the work environment as well as elsewhere. Employee personal data must be:

(1) processed lawfully, fairly and transparently;
(2) collected for specified, explicit and legitimate purposes;
(3) adequate, relevant and limited to purpose;
(4) accurate and kept up to date;
(5) kept no longer than is necessary;
(6) processed in line with security, integrity and confidentiality;
(7) processed in an accountable manner.

All of the Principles must be complied with. Compliance with the Principles of data protection applies to all employee and inward-facing personal data collected and or processed by an organisation. It also applies regardless of registration requirements (if any).

These can be summarised in the new GDPR and UK GDPR as:

- lawful, fair and transparent processing;
- purpose limited processing;
- data minimisation;
- ongoing accuracy of data;
- time storage limitations;
- appropriate security, integrity and confidentiality.

The Controller must demonstrate compliance and accountability.

Ordinary Personal Data Lawful Processing Conditions

14.07   When dealing with the above inward-facing categories of employees, agents, contractors, etc, the Lawful Processing Conditions are required to be complied with, *in addition* to the Principles of data protection.

The GDPR and UK GDPR contains the general Lawful Processing Conditions, eg, employee non sensitive personal data. In order to comply with the general personal data Lawful Processing Conditions, the organisation must fall within *one* of the following conditions, namely:

- the individual whom the personal data is about has consented to the processing;
- the processing is necessary for the performance of a contract to which the Data Subject is a party or in order to take steps at the request of the data subject is party or in order to take steps at the request of the Data Subject prior to entering into a contract;
- the processing is necessary for compliance with a legal obligation to which the Controller is subject;
- the processing is necessary to protect the 'vital interests' of the Data Subject or another natural person;
- the processing is necessary for the performance of a task carried out in the public interest or in the exercise of official authority vested in the Controller;
- the processing is necessary for the 'legitimate interests' of the Controller or a third party, except where overridden by the interests or fundamental rights of the Data Subject, in particular where the Data Subject is a child.

Article 7 also sets out conditions which apply in relation to consent. The Controller, if relying on consent (and if appropriate in the first instance), must be able to demonstrate that the Data Subject has consented. These conditions need to be considered carefully in advance.

(There are also additional conditions which apply for particular children's consent, eg if information is held in relation to the children of an employee.)

Lawful Processing and Organisation's Employees

14.08   Unlike certain other areas, the legitimate processing of employee personal data does not require employee consent. However, many organisations would have originally expected and proceeded on the basis that consent was so required. They would have incorporated (deemed) consent clauses into employment contracts, etc.

As indicated above, organisations can rely upon the legitimate processing condition that processing is necessary for the purposes of *legitimate interests* pursued by the Controller or by the third party or parties to whom the data are disclosed, except where the processing is unwarranted in any particular case by reason of prejudice to the rights and freedoms or legitimate interests of the Data Subject.

An alternative could be to say that the processing is necessary as part of a contract to which the employee is a party, in particular the employment contract.

Special Personal Data Lawful Processing Conditions

14.09   Organisations may also feel the need on occasion to store and use special personal data in relation to employees, such as medical and health data. In the case of special personal data, an organisation must, in addition to satisfying all of the data protection Principles, be able to comply or fall within one of the Special Personal Data Lawful Processing Conditions.

The GDPR sets out conditions relevant for the purposes of the processing of Special Personal Data. The organisation should be familiar with what constitutes Special Personal Data, namely, personal data revealing racial or ethnic origin, political opinions, religious or philosophical beliefs, or trade union membership, and the processing of genetic data, biometric data for the purpose of uniquely identifying a natural person, data concerning health data or data concerning a natural person's sex life or orientation. Such data *by default* may not be used (such '[p]rocessing ... shall be prohibited'). The organisation must fall within one of the specified exemptions to be able to process Special Personal Data. In the context of employees and inward-facing personal data, the conditions or exceptions provided are:

(1) the employee Data Subject has given explicit consent to the processing of the personal data for a specified purpose;

(2) the processing is necessary for the purposes of carrying out obligations or rights under employment law;

(3) the processing is necessary to protect the vital interests of the Data Subject or another natural person where the Data Subject is incapable of consent;

(4) the processing is carried out in the course of its legitimate activities with appropriate safeguards by a foundation, association or not for profit body and relates to its members;

(5) the processing relates to personal data which are manifestly made public by the Data Subject;

(6) the processing is necessary for the establishment, exercise or defence of legal claims;

(7) the processing is necessary for reasons of substantial public interest, on the basis of Union or state law which shall be proportionate to the aim pursued, respect the essence of the right to data protection and provide for suitable and specific measures to safeguard the fundamental rights and the interests of the Data Subject;

(8) the processing is necessary for preventative or occupational medicine, for the assessment of the working capacity of the employee, medical diagnosis, the provision of health or social care or treatment;

(9) the processing is necessary for public health;

(10) the processing is necessary for archiving purposes in the public interest, scientific or historical research purposes or statistical purposes.

The DPA 2018 at ss 10 and 11 also sets out further provisions in relation to Special Personal Data; as well as Sch 1 of the Act.

Furthermore, regulations can also set out further obligations in relation to the processing of special personal data.

The DPDI Bill makes further provisions and amendments, albeit not expressly referring to employee data by name.

Special Data Lawful Processing and Organisation's Employees

14.10 However, where sensitive personal data is involved, the organisation may have to obtain consent, unless otherwise specifically permitted in relation to one of the other particular purpose conditions set out above.

Consent

14.11 If it is the case that none of the condition criteria apply or permit a specific data processing use, then the organisation must obtain appropriate consent.

In considering the legitimising criteria the organisation should pay particular attention to the conditional word 'necessary.' If not strictly necessary, and demonstrably so, in the event that it is ever necessary to justify it when subsequently queried, it means that it may be necessary to fall back to the consent criteria.

Explicit consent, for example, with special personal data usage, can mean having to obtain written consent. There is also a reference to freely given, specific, informed and unambiguous consent (see definition of 'consent'). Where employee consent is utilised or required, an issue can sometimes arise as to whether it is voluntarily and freely given. If the employee feels forced into giving consent they, or the ICO, might subsequently say that the consent is invalid, thus compromising the legitimacy of the processing.

Compliance and Policies

14.12 It is essential for all organisations to implement appropriate written policies. These will vary, as there are different types of policy. In addition, each policy will be specifically tailored to meet the needs and circumstances of the particular organisation.

Once finalised, the policy or policies should be properly and effectively communicated to all employees. It may also have to be made available to others who work in or for the organisation eg contractors.

Those in the organisation with responsibility for dealing with personal data also need to be particularly familiarised with the policies, security measures, data protection processes, as well as effectively trained in relation to all aspects of data protection compliance.

As with all legal, business and organisational policies relating to regulatory compliance, data protection policies need to be regularly monitored and updated as requirement dictates. This can be because of legal changes, ICO guideline changes, business and activity changes, changing security and risk requirements, changing technology, etc.

ICO Codes

14.13 It is recommended that the organisation consult the most relevant ICO guidance and codes in terms of implementing, or tailoring, IT data processing and data protection compliance practices.[1]

Responsible Person for Data Protection Compliance

14.14 Organisations will have to appoint a particular identified person in the organisation to deal with and be responsible for all data protection processes and related compliance issues. This includes ensuring that the organisation is data protection compliant in accordance with the DPA and the ICO Employment Practices Code.[2]

In addition to a data protection supervisor or DPO it is also recommended that an individual at Board level be appointed to be responsible for overseeing and dealing with data protection compliance within the organisation. The contemporary importance and significance of data protection ensures that it is now clearly a boardroom issue.

Responsibilities include ongoing compliance, policies, strategies, processes, training, monitoring, reviewing and updating, coordinating, engaging appropriate expertise

1   ICO Employment Practices Code, at https://ico.org.uk.
2   See above.

and advices, audits, DPbD, education, courses, notification and registration, incident response, etc, as regards data protection.

Personnel Contracts

14.15 The organisation's contracts of employment need to incorporate appropriate notifications, consent clauses (only if appropriate), and references to the organisational policies relevant to data protection, such as corporate communications usage policies, internet policies, devices, security, breaches, etc. There may also be reference to where these policies are located and where the latest and most up to date version will always be available. This might be a staff handbook, intranet, etc.

These documents will all be different depending on the organisation, the sector and the data protection practices ie the types of personal data, what it is used for and why. Issues such as compliance, security and confidentiality should be emphasised.

Training

14.16 Staff induction sessions as well as ongoing staff training should all incorporate guidance in relation to dealing with and handling personal data.

Employee Handbooks

14.17 Most organisations provide an employee handbook to their employees. These handbooks should contain guidance and polices of data protection, corporate communications, usage policies, etc.

Notices, Communications, Internet, Intranet

14.18 All of these provide an opportunity for the organisation to set out and reinforce the organisational requirements regarding the data protection regime. These can be user friendly and instantaneous, and hence provide an easy means of notifying new and urgent changes, notices, etc.

Personnel Department

14.19 While the personnel department or personnel Director will be required to be familiar with data protection, the role and responsibility of operating data protection compliance is not a personnel role. It needs to be someone outside of the employment and personnel function. However, the person responsible for data protection will need to liaise regularly with the personnel department, including training and keeping personnel staff up to date in relation to new developments in data protection compliance.

Employees and Data Security

14.20 The security of employee personal data is an essential obligation under the data protection regime.

The Controller must take reasonable steps to ensure the reliability of any employees of the organisation who have access to the personal data. There are a number of cases where issues arise, including prosecutions, where an employee has engaged in unauthorised access to personal data which they had no work function or purpose to do so (eg, snooping); and also where an employee leaving the organisation takes personal data seeking to use it in their next employment (eg, customer databases).

Lynda McDonald[3] refers to security indicating that the following would be required to be checked, namely:

- access to buildings, computer rooms and offices where personal data is held;
- access to computer and other equipment where unauthorised access could have a detrimental effect on security;
- that manual records are put away at night in locked filing cabinets before the cleaners arrive;
- that passwords are not written down so that others can access them;
- that strict rules are in force within the business about what personal information can be accessed by which organisations, for example, the information that line managers can access about their staff may be different to (and less than) that which a personnel manager can access;
- that there is an efficient and effective security system in place to prevent employees from seeing other employee data;
- that mechanisms are in place to detect any breach of security, and procedures in place to investigate such breaches;
- that all staff have undergone training on the organisation's data protection policy and how it works in practice, either as part of their induction or at specialist sessions which are appropriate to their job role, position and function.[4]

Even where an employee is working off-site or at home, or indeed travelling, it is still the organisation's responsibility to ensure appropriate security measures and processes are in place.

These scenarios are increasingly prominent but the organisation should ensure that they occur on a planned and permission basis. Unregulated activities enhance the level of risk as well as increasing the level on unknown, uncontrollable activities.

Stuart Room in *Cyber and Data Security Law and Practice* also provides many detailed suggestions in relation to security issues.

Data Access Right of Employees

14.21 Employees are individuals and are hence able to rely upon their data protection rights, such as requesting a copy of the personal data relating to them. In the instance of an employee access request being made, the organisation should assess the request to see if the appropriate (minimum) fee has been paid and whether any exemptions apply which would prevent a disclosure being made. In addition, while the employee's personal data may have to be disclosed, certain third party personal data should be taken out or redacted. It may also be the case that clarification may have to be obtained to further clarify what particular personal data is being sought. It should not be a mere mechanism to avoid so complying.

Now the access request must be complied with without delay and at latest within one month (reduced from 40 calendar days).

MacDonald[5] refers to some examples of the types of employee related personal data that may often be subject to access requests, such as:

- performance reviews or appraisals;
- sickness records;

---

3   L AC MacDonald, *Data Protection: Legal Compliance and Good Practice for Employers* (Tottel, 2008) 11–12.
4   See above.
5   See above at 51.

- warnings or minutes of disciplinary interviews; training records; statements about pay; emails or electronic documents of which they are the subject; and
- expressions of opinion regarding eg prospects for promotion.

Information relating to automated individual decisions regarding employees are also relevant and may be requested.

Conclusion

14.22 Organisations need to actively have considered data protection compliance issues and the recording of compliance even before an employee is engaged. Data protection and personal data arises at recruitment, selection and interview stages. The organisation must also note relevant policies. Unless data protection issues and policy issues are properly incorporated into the employment relationship, the organisation may be non-compliant. In addition, it may not be able to enforce and rely upon particular contract terms, policies, employee obligations, disciplinary rules and such like.

Chapter 15

Employee Data Protection Rights

Introduction

15.01   Just as other parties whose personal data are being collected and processed have data protection rights, employees also have Data Subject rights.

The Data Protection Rights of Employees

15.02   The rights of employees can be summarised as including:

- right of access;
- right to establish if personal data exists;
- right to be informed of the logic in automatic decision taking;
- right to prevent processing likely to cause damage or distress;
- right to prevent processing for direct marketing;
- right to prevent automated decision taking;
- right to compensation (see Data Protection Act 2018 (DPA 2018), ss 168 and 169);
- right to rectify inaccurate data;
- right to rectification, blocking, erasure and forgetting, and destruction;
- right to complain to ICO;
- right to go to court.

Chapter III of the EU General Data Protection Regulation (GDPR) refers to the rights of Data Subjects. These include:

- right to transparency (Article 5; Article 12);
- right to prior information: directly obtained data (Article 14);
- right to prior information: indirectly obtained data (Article 14);
- right of confirmation and right of access (Article 15);
- right to be informed of third country safeguards (Article 15(2));
- right to rectification (Article 16);
- right to erasure (Right to be Forgotten) (RtbF) (Article 17);
- right to restriction of processing (Article 18);
- notifications re rectification, erasure or restriction (Article 19);
- right to data portability (Article 18);
- right to object (Article 19);
- rights re automated individual decision making, including profiling (Article 20);
- DPbD (Article 23);
- security rights;

- data protection impact assessment and prior consultation;
- communicating data breach to Data Subject;
- Data Protection Officer (DPO);
- remedies, liability and sanctions (Chapter VIII).

However, there are additional rights related issues to consider. Employers should recall that there can be obligations to notify Data Subjects of the existence of certain rights that they can enforce. There is little consideration of how this may apply in terms of relevance to the employment context.

In addition, employers will recall that there are various record keeping obligations. Consideration should also be given to how and to what extent this is applied in the employment context, separate to the outward-facing data protection rules.

In addition to employee specific references that can occur in data laws, companies, employees and employee representatives need to monitor for when changes occur to general data rights under data protection legislation. An example is the Data Protection and Digital Information (No 2) Bill (DPDI Bill) which proposes potential data rights changes. The final version will need to be monitored once in force.

Rights under the GDPR/UK GDPR

Access Right

15.03   There are various rights for individual Data Subjects. How these can apply in the work environment for employees is set out below.

Article 15 of the GDPR relates to the right of access for the employee. Employees and the other categories of person referred to above are covered by the data access right.

The employee shall have the right to obtain from the Controller confirmation as to whether or not personal data concerning them are being processed, and access to the data and the following information:

- the purposes of the processing;
- the categories of personal data concerned;
- the recipients or categories of recipient to whom the personal data have been or will be disclosed, in particular to recipients in third countries or international organisations;
- where possible, the envisaged period for which the personal data will be stored, or if not possible, the criteria used to determine that period;
- the existence of the right to request from the Controller rectification or erasure of personal data or restriction of processing of personal data concerning the employee or to object to the processing;
- the right to lodge a complaint to a SA;
- where the personal data are not collected from the employee, any available information as to their source;
- the existence of automated decision making including profiling referred to in Article 22(1) and (4) and at least in those cases, meaningful information about the logic involved, as well as the significance and the envisaged consequences of such processing for the employee (Article 15(1)).

Where personal data are transferred to a third country or to an international organisation, the employee shall have the right to be informed of the appropriate safeguards pursuant to Article 46 relating to the transfer (Article 15(2)).

The Controller shall provide a copy of the personal data undergoing processing. For any further copies requested by the employee, the Controller may charge a reasonable fee based on administrative costs. Where the Data Subject makes the request in electronic form, and unless otherwise requested by the employee, the information shall be provided in a commonly used electronic form (Article 15(3)).

The right to obtain a copy referred to in para (3) shall not adversely affect the rights and freedoms of others (Article 15(4)).

The DPDI Bill refers to time limits for companies responding to requests by Data Subjects (clause 8), information to be provided to Data Subjects (clauses 9 and 10), and complaints (Schedule 8).

Rectification Right

15.04 Chapter III, Section 3 of the GDPR refers to rectification and erasure. The employee shall have the right to obtain from the Controller without undue delay the rectification of inaccurate personal data concerning them. Taking into account the purposes of the processing, the employee shall have the right to have incomplete personal data completed, including by means of providing a supplementary statement (Article 16).

Right to Erasure (Right to be Forgotten)

15.05 The GDPR states that Data Subject shall have the right to obtain from the Controller the erasure of personal data concerning them without undue delay and the Controller shall have the obligation to erase personal data without undue delay where one of the following grounds applies:

- the personal data are no longer necessary in relation to the purposes for which they were collected or otherwise processed;
- the employee withdraws consent on which the processing is based according to Article 6(1)(a), or Article 9(2)(a), and where there is no other legal ground for the processing;
- the Data Subject objects to the processing pursuant to Article 21(1) and there are no overriding legitimate grounds for the processing, or the employee objects to the processing to Article 21(2);
- the personal data have been unlawfully processed;
- the personal data have to be erased for compliance with a legal obligation in EU or state law to which the Controller is subject;
- the data have been collected in relation to the offering of information society services referred to in Article 8(1) (Article 17(1)).

Where the Controller has made the personal data public and is obliged pursuant to Article 17(1) to erase the personal data, the Controller, taking account of available technology and the cost of implementation, shall take reasonable steps, including technical measures, to inform Controllers which are processing the personal data that the employee has requested the erasure by such Controllers of any links to, or copy or replication of, those personal data (Article 17(2)).

Article 17(1) and (2) shall not apply to the extent that processing is necessary:

- for exercising the right of freedom of expression and information;
- for compliance with a legal obligation which requires processing by EU or state law to which the Controller is subject or for the performance of a task carried out in the public interest or in the exercise of official authority vested in the Controller;

- for reasons of public interest in the area of public health in accordance with Article 9(2)(h) and (i) as well as Article 9(3);
- for archiving purposes in the public interest, or scientific and historical research purposes or statistical purposes in accordance with Article 89(1) in so far as the right referred to in Article 17(1) is likely to render impossible or seriously impair the achievement of the objectives of that processing; or
- for the establishment, exercise or defence of legal claims (Article 17(3)).

Notification Obligation re Rectification, Erasure or Restriction

15.06 The GDPR states that the Controller shall communicate any rectification, erasure or restriction of processing carried out in accordance with Articles 16, 17(1) and 18 to each recipient to whom the data have been disclosed, unless this proves impossible or involves disproportionate effort. The Controller shall inform the employee about those recipients if the employee requests it (Article 19).

Right to Restriction of Processing

15.07 Article 18 of the GDPR refers to the right to restriction of processing. The employee shall have the right to obtain from the Controller the restriction of the processing where one of the following applies:

- the accuracy of the data is contested by the employee, for a period enabling the Controller to verify the accuracy of the data;
- the processing is unlawful and the employee opposes the erasure of the personal data and requests the restriction of their use instead;
- the Controller no longer needs the personal data for the purposes of the processing, but they are required by the employee for the establishment, exercise or defence of legal claims;
- the Data Subject has objected to processing pursuant to Article 21(1) pending the verification whether the legitimate grounds of the Controller override those of the employee (Article 18(1)).

Where processing has been restricted under Article 18(1), such personal data shall, with the exception of storage, only be processed with the employee's consent or for the establishment, exercise or defence of legal claims or for the protection of the rights of another natural or legal person or for reasons of important public interest of the EU or of a state (Article 18(2)).

An employee who has obtained the restriction of processing pursuant to Article 18(1) shall be informed by the Controller before the restriction of processing is lifted (Article 18(3)).

Right to Data Portability

15.08 The GDPR states that the employee shall have the right to receive the personal data concerning them, which they have provided to a Controller, in a structured, commonly used and machine-readable format and have the right to transmit those data to another Controller without hindrance from the Controller to which the personal data have been provided, where:

- the processing is based on consent pursuant to Article 6(1)(a) or Article 9(2)(a) or on a contract pursuant to Article 6(1)(b); and
- the processing is carried out by automated means (Article 20(1)).

In exercising their right to data portability pursuant to Article 20(1), the employee has the right to have the data transmitted directly from Controller to Controller, where technically feasible (Article 20(2)).

The exercise of the right shall be without prejudice to Article 17. The right shall not apply to processing necessary for the performance of a task carried out in the public interest or in the exercise of official authority vested in the Controller (Article 20(3)).

The right shall not adversely affect the rights and freedoms of others (Article 20(4)).

Automated Individual Decision Making Right

15.09   Chapter III, Section 4 of the GDPR refers to the right to object and automated individual decision making.

The DPDI Bill refers to potential changes regarding automated processing and automated processing decisions at Schedule 3. The final version will need to be considered.

Right to Object

15.10   The GDPR states that the employee shall have the right to object, on grounds relating to their particular situation, at any time to the processing of personal data concerning them which is based on Article 6(1)(e) or (f), including profiling based on these provisions. The Controller shall no longer process the personal data unless the Controller demonstrates compelling legitimate grounds for the processing which override the interests, rights and freedoms of employee or for the establishment, exercise or defence of legal claims (Article 21(1)).

Where personal data are processed for direct marketing purposes, the Data Subject shall have the right to object at any time to processing of personal data concerning them for such marketing, which includes profiling to the extent that it is related to such direct marketing (Article 21(2)).

Where the employee objects to processing for direct marketing purposes, the personal data shall no longer be processed for such purposes (Article 21(3)).

At the latest at the time of the first communication with the employee, the right referred to in Article 21(1) and (2) shall be explicitly brought to the attention of the employee and shall be presented clearly and separately from any other information (Article 19(4)).

In the context of the use of information society services, and notwithstanding Directive 2002/58/EC,[1] the employee may exercise their right to object by automated means using technical specifications (Article 21(5)).

Where personal data are processed for scientific and historical research purposes or statistical purposes pursuant to Article 89(1), the employee, on grounds relating to their particular situation, shall have the right to object to processing of personal data concerning them, unless the processing is necessary for the performance of a task carried out for reasons of public interest (Article 21(6)).

Automated Individual Decision Making, Including Profiling

15.11   The GDPR states that the employee shall have the right not to be subject to a decision based solely on automated processing, including profiling, which produces legal effects concerning them or similarly significantly affects them (Article 22(1)).

---

1   Directive 2002/58/EC of the European Parliament and of the Council of 12 July 2002 concerning the processing of personal data and the protection of privacy in the electronic communications sector (Directive on privacy and electronic communications). Also note ePrivacy Regulation and updated ePrivacy rules.

Article 22(1) shall not apply if the decision:

- is necessary for entering into, or performance of, a contract between the employee and a Controller [a]; or
- is authorised by EU or state law to which the Controller is subject and which also lays down suitable measures to safeguard the employee's rights and freedoms and legitimate interests; or
- is based on the Data Subject's explicit consent (Article 22(2)) [c].

In cases referred to in Article 22(2)(a) and (c) the Controller shall implement suitable measures to safeguard the employee's rights and freedoms and legitimate interests, at least the right to obtain human intervention on the part of the Controller, to express their point of view and to contest the decision (Article 22(3)).

Decisions referred to in Article 22(2) shall not be based on special categories of personal data referred to in Article 9(1), unless Article 9(2)(a) or (g) applies and suitable measures to safeguard the employee's rights and freedoms and legitimate interests are in place (Article 22(4)).

As noted, the DPDI Bill refers to potential changes regarding automated processing and automated processing decisions which are set out at Schedule 3. The final version of the changes will need to be considered.

Express Employee Provision

15.12   There are a limited number of situations which are expressly referred to in the GDPR in addition to the general provisions. One specific provision refers to the employment sector. This is referred to in GDPR Article 88. It provides that:

'Member States may, by law or by collective agreements, provide for more specific rules to ensure the protection of the rights and freedoms in respect of the processing of employees' personal data in the employment context, in particular for the purposes of the recruitment, the performance of the contract of employment, including discharge of obligations laid down by law or by collective agreements, management, planning and organisation of work, equality and diversity in the workplace, health and safety at work, protection of employer's or customer's property and for the purposes of the exercise and enjoyment, on an individual or collective basis, of rights and benefits related to employment, and for the purpose of the termination of the employment relationship.'

It continues that:

'Those rules shall include suitable and specific measures to safeguard the data subject's human dignity, legitimate interests and fundamental rights, with particular regard to the transparency of processing, the transfer of personal data within a group of undertakings, or a group of enterprises engaged in a joint economic activity and monitoring systems at the work place.'

Conclusion

15.13   Organisations need to respect the data protection rights of their employees, and even potential employees. In addition, particular care and attention needs to be paid to access requests from employees. Compliance is an ongoing issue as, for example, new changes and business practices will always present new challenges internally.

Chapter 16

Employee Considerations

Introduction

16.01   A large number of issues arise in terms of dealing with employee personal data, both in terms of audits, access, planning and compliance.

Contract

16.02   The starting point for informing and appraising employees of the importance of data protection, confidentiality and security in the organisation, and in relation to the employee's personal data should be to begin with the employment contract. There should be clauses referring to data protection and also to security.

Policies

16.03   There should also be policies relating to data protection furnished to all actual (and prospective) employees. These need to be updated regularly as the issues covered change constantly.

These policies may be separate or may be incorporated into an employee handbook.

Organisations need to be aware that if there is an important change made, unless this is notified and recorded to employees, the organisation may not be able to rely upon the changed clause. For example, if there is a new activity banned or regulated in an updated policy but the new policy is not notified to employees, it may be impossible to use the new policy to disciple an errant employee. They and their lawyers will strongly argue that the new policy was not notified, is not part of the employment relationship, and would be unlawful to apply. There are many examples of this problem occurring in practice.

Data Protection Policy

16.04   In considering what policies to implement, the organisation will have to consider many issues and separate policies, with data protection being just one. Others include health and safety, environmental, etc. The data protection policy will perhaps be the most dynamic given the wide range of data, individuals, processes, activities and technologies involved, and which are ever changing. Someone within the organisation needs to be responsible for examining and implementing ongoing changes as the requirement arises.

Internet Usage Policy

16.05   In addition to a general data protection policy, further specific data protection related policies may be required. The foremost of these relates to the employees' use of the internet on the organisation's systems.

Mobile and Device Usage Policies

16.06   Increasingly, employees use not just desktop computers but also laptops, mobile phones, smart phones, handheld devices, Blackberrys, iPads, etc. Unless explicitly incorporated into one of the above policies, then additional, or extended, policies need to be implemented. One particular issue for an organisation to consider is the employees' own devices, employee devices the bills for which are paid by the organisation, and devices supplied and paid for by the organisation. Somewhat different considerations may need to be applied.

Vehicle Use Policy

16.07   Vehicles must also be considered by organisations in terms of policy and employee usage. Increasingly tracking and other data from vehicles can be related to identified employees. Sometimes this may be as a result of the organisation furnishing a vehicle to the employee for work related business. However, this need not be the case. Even where an employee is using their own vehicle, it is possible for the organisation to be collecting or accessing personal data. In addition, organisations must also be aware that vehicle technology, both in-built and added, can result in greater collections of data, including personal data, being potentially accessible. Tracking, incident and accident reports, etc, are just some examples. It is important for organisations to consider these personal data issues.

Biometrics

16.08   A number of data regulators have said that added justification and diligence is needed if an employer wishes to consider the introduction of collections of biometric employee data – outside of normal health and welfare considerations. The data protection regime has also been interpreted as preventing or circumscribing the mandated collection of employee personal data which is biometric in nature and which is for non-health purposes. Some employers have felt that because biometrics can be used for access control, and even less serious uses, that they want to introduce such data collections. Questions of purpose, necessity, proportionality, fairness, alternatives, etc, must be considered. A company should not automatically assume that because biometric technologies exist, that they should be applied to employees without a full legal assessment.

The Data Protection and Digital Information (No 2) Bill (DPDI Bill) also refers to changes in relation to biometric data protection issues. Part 5 refers to oversight of retention and use of biometric material (clause 104); removal of provision for regulation of CCTV, etc (clause 105); and oversight of biometrics databases (clause 106).

On Site

16.09 Each of the activities that an employee is engaged in when working need to be considered. The types of data that may be created in relation to an employee also need to be considered, including if each type is permitted to be collected and used under the data protection regime.

Off Site

16.10 An altogether different assessment may be needed in relation to the proposed collection and use of employee data which is created or comes to exist in off site locations away from the physical location of the employer's business. In addition, added diligence is needed to consider these off site issues in the context of the employee's home – especially outside of work hours.

Obviously these issues may have been complicated by home working as a result of the Covid-19 pandemic.

There is, however, also a trend whereby employees also have a right to be able to switch off or turn off. This particularly relates to work-based communications such as emails and text messages. Some countries have begun to expressly refer to these rights to turn off issues in legal rules.

Transfers of Undertaking

16.11 Transfers of undertakings or TUPE,[1] as it is known, refers to organisations being transferred to a new owner, whether in whole or in part. Situations like this are an everyday part of the commercial business environment.

The Transfer of Undertakings (Protection of Employment) Regulations 2006[2] provide certain protections for employees where the business is being transferred to a new owner. While primarily directed at the protection of employees' employment related rights, it is also noteworthy in that employee personal data will also be transferred to the new employer or organisation. There are various types of personal data to consider. The same rights, interests, terms, contracts, etc, as applied with the old employer are to apply with the new employer, which included data protection user rights, and possibly corporate communications usage, etc.

Evidence

16.12 Disputes naturally arise between employers and employees from time to time. In such disputes the organisation may need to rely upon documents, information and materials which will contain personal data. While this may fit under the legitimate interests and legal interest provisions, employers should be careful about using less obvious personal data. This might include private emails communications over which

---

1   See generally, L AC MacDonald, *Data Protection: Legal Compliance and Good Practice for Employers* (Tottel, 2008) 44–48.
2   SI 2006/246. Please consider any changes, updates and/or replacements as may occur.

an employee may argue privacy and confidentiality. Particular concerns arise in cases where covert monitoring has been used. Before commencing covert activities of this type the organisation should seek advices. Otherwise, any evidence gathered may possibly be ruled inadmissible subsequently.

Organisations also need to be careful in that computer, electronic and mobile data can change, expire and or be amended quickly. It can be important to act quickly. Advance policies, procedures and protocols assist in this regard.

Enforceability

16.13   An important issue for all organisations to consider is that if they ever wish to be able to discipline an errant employee, including up to dismissal, consequent upon their activities regarding personal data, internet usage, security breach, etc, the organisation needs to be able to point to a breach of an explicit contract or policy clause. If the breach is not explicit, or there is not written into the policy and contract, the employee can argue that there is no breach, perhaps regardless of the seriousness of the instant issue arising.

While online abuse is an issue to be dealt with, organisations need to be conscious of reputational damage from such incidents. However, they also need to consider what would happen if any of their employees are involved, whether by way of participation or orchestration, in an incident of abuse. One would have to consider what the contracts and policies say, as well as develop reaction strategies.

Data Breach

16.14   Employee involvement is critical in dealing with – and preparing for – data breach incidents. Various teams of employees will be involved.

Notification of Employee Data Breaches

16.15   However, as employee personal data can also be the subject of a data breach incident, employees may also need to be specifically considered in this context. For example, they may need to be separately informed that there is a breach relating to their personal data and what actions and safeguards are being followed by the organisation to deal with the issue. If the employees need to take specific actions, they may also need to be appraised of this possibility. Potentially liability issues may also arise. For example, employees in the massive Sony data breach incidents may have considered suing Sony for breaches in relation to their data.

Employee Data Organisations

16.16   It is increasingly possible for an organisation to represent Data Subjects, in terms of dealing with particular data protection issues but also in terms of representation and litigation.

While employee unions may represent their members in dealing with data protection issues, it is possible that employers may also have to deal with new organisations in relation to employees' personal data. This may involve breach incidents in particular.

Location

16.17 Increasingly technology permits organisations to track devices and hence employees. However, a very careful prior analysis needs to be conducted in advance to consider whether this is strictly needed, desirable, proportionate, transparent and complies with the data protection regime. As with many of these new issues, a question of balance is needed and just because something is technically possible does not equate with it being prudent or lawful.

Conclusion

16.18 These are all issues that need to be addressed well in advance of an incident arising. It may be too late to start implementing policies, etc, after the event.

Employee data protection compliance is a complicated and ongoing obligation for organisations. It also needs to involve the DPOs, appropriate board member, human resources, IT personnel and legal. On occasion, others may also have to become involved also.

Organisations should also ensure that employees are fully appraised of the need for respect for personal data, data security, and understanding of the respective policies to protect personal data. Where an employee accesses, uses or – worse – discloses personal data, whether of customers or employees, the employer will be held responsible (notwithstanding any employee responsibility issues). The data regulator will seek to know what the employer did or did not do that may have prevented to employee breach arising. Data security is also very important and ranges from access controls, segregation, hierarchies of access on a need-to-access basis, passwords, encryption, device policies, and on-site and off-site usage rules. These issues, and where risks and gaps may arise, are ongoing compliance requirements and cannot be left static over time.

Chapter 17

Employee Monitoring Issues

Introduction

17.01 One of the more contentious areas of employee data protection practice relates to the issue of the monitoring of employee email, internet, etc usage. More recently, concerns have arisen as to the use of technology to monitor employee activities generally, and to monitor their location and movement.

Employers are concerned about certain risks that can arise as result of the activities of employees in the workplace, but sometimes proceed without considering data protection compliance, the need for proportionality, and that while certain monitoring activities may be permissible, others will not be. Employers need to engage in a careful diligence exercise prior to rolling out any monitoring-type activities. It is also unwise be assume that just because one monitoring use or activity may be possible, that additional unrelated forms of monitoring technology will also be legally permitted. Various data regulators receive complaints from employees that refer to employer monitoring issues, from CCTV, to email, to location, to biometrics, etc.

Sample Legal Issues Arising

17.02 Some examples of the legal issues and concerns that can arise for employers and organisations as a result of the actions of their employees include:

- vicarious liability;[1]
- defamation;
- copyright infringement;
- confidentiality breaches and leaks;
- data protection;
- contract;
- inadvertent contract formation;
- harassment;
- abuse;
- discrimination;
- computer crime;
- interception offences;
- criminal damage;

---

1   Note the recent Morrisons case, where the employer was not held vicariously liable for an errant employee's internet upload of employee personal data. See *Morrison v Various* [2020] UKSC 12 (1 April 2020). Employers should not assume generally, however, that they may never become vicariously liable.

- data loss;
- data damage;
- computer crime;
- criminal damage;
- eCommerce law;
- arms and dual use good export restrictions;
- non-fatal offences against the person;
- child pornography;
- policies;
- on-site/off-site;
- work day/home time;
- bring your own device (BYOD), etc;
- online abuse, snooping, etc.

These are examples of an expanding list of concerns for organisations. Obviously, some of these will be recalibrated in importance depending on the type of organisation, the business sector and what its activities are. Confidentiality, for example, may be critically important for certain organisations, but less important for other organisations.

Employee Misuse of Email, Internet, etc

17.03   Even before the increase in data breach and data loss examples, there is a significant number of examples where problems have arisen for organisations as a result of the activities of certain employees. Increasingly, organisations face the problem that the activity of an errant employee on the internet, television, or social networks can go viral instantly on a global scale, with adverse reputational damage for the organisation.

There are many instances where organisations have felt the need to dismiss or otherwise discontinue relationships with employees. Some examples include Equifax, Uber, Yahoo!, Swedish Transport Authority, Norwich EU Healthcare; Lois Franxhi; Royal & Sun Alliance Liverpool; C&W Birmingham; Rolls Royce Bristol; Claire Swire/Bradley Chait; Ford; Weil Gotshal; Sellafield, Target, Sony, etc. As these instances are ever expanding it would be impossible to provide a definitive list.

The frequency and scale of recent breaches of security eg, Yahoo! (500 million users), Cambridge Analytica, TalkTalk, Cathay Pacific, DSG Retail, Sony Playstation (70 million individual's personal data[2] and 25 million in another[3]) make the topicality and importance of data security compliance ever more important. Even after that, Sony was hacked again in the example of the film 'The Interview,' which was arguably even more costly and damaging. The largest UK data losses appear to be Yahoo! and Revenue and Customs (loss of discs with the names, dates of birth, bank and address details for 25 million individuals).[4] Marks and Spencer was also involved in a data breach as were a number of hotels, and the mobile company TalkTalk.

There are many UK cases involving substantial fines for data protection breaches. These include where there was data relating to large numbers of Data Subjects, to

2   See, for example, G Martin, 'Sony Data Loss Biggest Ever,' *Boston Herald*, 27 April 2011.
3   See, for example, C Arthur, 'Sony Suffers Second Data Breach With Theft of 25m More User Details,' *Guardian*, 3 May 2011.
4   See, for example, 'Brown Apologises for Record Loss, Prime Minister Gordon Brown has said he "Profoundly Regrets" the Loss of 25 Million Child Benefit Records,' *BBC*, 21 November 2007, at http://news.bbc.co.uk/2/hi/7104945.stm.

small numbers or even single Data Subjects but which were particularly special or sensitive. These range across commercial, non-profit and state organisations. The Crown Prosecution Service (CPS) was fined £325,000. Humberside Police was fined £130,000 relating to a data loss incident regarding one Data Subject (but involving particularly special and sensitive data – a rape victim interview on disc). Brighton and Sussex University Hospitals NHS Trust was fined £325,000 by the ICO in relation to a data loss incident.[5] Zurich Insurance was fined £2.3m for losing data of 46,000 customers.[6] Sony was fined £250,000. Even the British & Foreign Bible Society was fined £100,000. Note, these are all even prior to the new EU General Data Protection Regulation (GDPR) level fines and penalties.

The retail group DSG Retail was fined £500,000 for a breach affecting 14 million individuals.[7] Airline Cathay Pacific was fined £500,000 for breaches lasting four years.[8] Doorstep Dispenseree was fined for £275,000 for data storage and data security issues.[9]

HP suspended 150 employees in one instance, which is one of the potential actions available.

Prudential was also fined in relation to the mishandling of personal data, while a Barclays employee was fined in court for personal use and access to customer account personal data.

Senior executives at Sony and Target lost their jobs as a result of data breach incidents. Some of the examples where employees have lost their jobs as a result of data breach incidents include senior management as well as IT and tech executives. It is probable that many more junior employees have lost jobs and positions out of the headlines.

In a more creative solution Ford issued a deletion amnesty to 20,000 employees to delete objected to material before a new or amended policy would kick in.

Some of the legal concerns referred to above will now be looked at in greater detail.

Contract

17.04 It is possible for employees to agree and enter into contract via electronic communications. This is increasingly a concern since the legal recognition of electronic contract in the eCommerce legislation.

This can include the inadvertent creation of legally binding contracts for the organisation.

In addition, it is possible that an employee may create or agree particular contract terms, delivery dates, etc, electronically which they would not otherwise do.

These can be contracts, or terms, which the organisation would not like to be bound by.

It is also possible that breach of contract issues could arise.

---

5 See, for example, 'Largest Ever Fine for Data Loss Highlights Need for Audited Data Wiping,' *ReturnOnIt*.
6 See, for example, J Oates, 'UK Insurer Hit With Biggest Ever Data Loss Fine,' *The Register*, 24 August 2010, at https://www.theregister.com/2010/08/24/data_loss_fine/. This was imposed by the Financial Services Authority (FSA).
7 *ICO v DSG Retail* [2020] 9/1/20.
8 *ICO v Cathay Pacific Airways Limited* [2020] 4/3/2020.
9 *ICO v Doorstep Dispensaree Limited* [2019] 20/12/19.

Employment Equality

17.05   It can be illegal to discriminate, or permit discrimination, on grounds of, for example:

- gender;
- race;
- age;
- sexual orientation;
- family status;
- religious beliefs;
- disability;
- member of minority groups.

Instances of such discrimination can occur on the organisation's computer systems. Even though the organisation may not be initially aware of the instance, it can still have legal consequences.

Harassment

17.06   Harassment via the organisation's computer systems is also something which could cause consequences for an organisation. Examples could include the circulation of written words, pictures or other material which a person may reasonably regard as offensive. The organisation could be held liable for employees' discriminatory actions unless it took reasonable steps to prevent them, or to deal with them appropriately once they arise. See Protection from Harassment Act (as amended). Note that there have been a number of official hearings on internet related harassment and abuse, with proposals for new legislation emanating in the Online Safety Bill. Various changes have been made, so it is not yet clear what the final form and rules therein may be. It requires to be reviewed, however, once finalised.

Online Abuse

17.07   This is a growing problem. However, it is also an issue for organisations when their employees are the victims or perpetrators of online abuse. It is only a matter of time before organisations are sued for the actions of their employees using the organisation's systems. Organisations can also assist in tackling these issues, and some indeed have more of an ability to do so than others. Note the Online Safety Bill referred to above.

Offline Abuse

17.08   Offline abuse or offline disparagement, defamation, etc can also arise. In the Sony data breach incident regarding the film 'The Interview' there are examples of employee details being published online after the breach. In addition various emails were published where senior employees were at least disparaging of others directly or indirectly engaged by the organisations. In instances such as this, as well as being other than best practice for both the employees and the organisation, liability issues can also arise. Note the Online Safety Bill referred to above, for example, where online activity is followed into the offline world.

Child Pornography

17.09 There is a serious risk and concern for organisations where this could occur on the organisation's computer systems or devices. See, for example, the Protection of Children Act 1978 (as amended), Criminal Justice Act 1988 (as amended), and the Criminal Justice and Public Order Act 1994 (as amended).

Dealing with the Employee Risks

17.10 It is important for all organisations to engage in a process of risk assessment of exposures which can be created as a result of their employee's use of its computer systems and devices.

Organisations should:

- identify the areas of risk;
- assess and evaluate those risks;
- engage in a process to eliminate/reduce the risks identified as appropriate;
- formalise an overall body of employee corporate communications usage policies;
- implement appropriate and lawful technical solutions appropriate to dealing with the identified risks;
- implement an ongoing strategy to schedule reviews of the new and emerging risks, and to update and or implement appropriate procedures and policies, including the existing employee corporate communications usage policies;
- data security for employee related data;
- risk assessment and indeed impact assessments, particularly where changes happen in relation to employee related data;
- advising all employees of the official policy if and when a breach incident may arise – and for the avoidance of doubt, well in advance of breach problem issues arising;
- advising and ensuring that the specific employees who might have to deal with breach issues directly are fully aware of and trained on their functions. This will be an ongoing task and will also involve different teams of employees (and others who may be external experts and professional advisors, eg IT, IT forensics, lawyers, counsel, public relations, crisis management, etc).

Employee Corporate Communications Usage Policies

17.11 Given the general risks, and the risks specific to an organisation identified in a review process, it is critical that the organisation implement appropriate policies in an overall body of employee corporate communications usage policies.

It is important to note that there is no one fixed solution, or one single policy on its own which is sufficient to deal with these issues. Equally, a single policy on its own would not be sufficient to give comfort to the organisation in terms of (a) dealing with the risks and issues, and (b) ensuring that the organisation has implemented sufficient policies that allows it to act appropriately to meet specific risks, including disposal, as they arise.

For example, if an organisation discovers a particular unauthorised activity on its computer systems undertaken by one of its employees, eg illegal file sharing or an employee hosting an illegal gambling website on its servers, it may decide that it wishes to dismiss the errant employee. But can it legally dismiss the employee? In the first instance, the organisation should ideally be in the position of being able to point to a specific clause in the employees written contract of employment and a specific breach, or breaches, of one or more of the organisation's employee corporate communications usage policies.

If it can, then the likelihood is that the organisation's legal advisors would be comfortable recommending that the dismissal is warranted, justified and lawful. However, if the answer is no, in that there is no written clause which is clearly breached as a result of the specific activities, even though carried out during the hours of employment, at the organisation's office, on the organisations computer system and utilising the organisation's computer servers, the organisation would not have any legal comfort in dismissing the employee.

The organisation may not be able to obtain pro-dismissal legal advice. If the company decided to proceed with the dismissal in any event it could run the legal risk that the employee may decide to legally challenge the dismissal under employment law. The employee would be assisted in that there is no express written clause which is breached. Unfortunately, the organisation may have to defend such an action on the basis of common law or implied obligations and duties owed by the employee. There may be no guarantee of success.

Focus of Organisational Communications Usage Policies

17.12   Organisations have a need for a comprehensive suite of organisational communications usage policies. This includes use of the organisation's devices, telephone, voicemail, email and Internet. The policies need to address:

- security;
- telephone;
- email;
- text;
- internet;
- mobile and portable devices;
- electronic storage devices;
- home and off-site usage;
- vehicle usage and location usage;
- employee Internet of Things (IoT) usage as it may affect the organisation.

This will involve an ongoing task, not just a one-off exercise. It also needs coordinated team responsibility.

Key Issues to Organisational Communications Usage Policies

17.13   The key aspects to consider in relation to the employee corporate communications usage policies, include:

- ownership;
- usage;
- authorisation;
- confidentiality;
- authentication;
- retention and storage;
- viruses;
- disciplinary matters;
- dismissal matters;

- security;
- awareness;
- transparency;
- breach notification;
- DPOs;
- planning and data protection by design and by default;
- safety/abuse.

These will vary depending on each organisation.

From a data protection regime perspective, one of the key issues for an organisation is the ability to monitor employees if and when needed, as distinct from general monitoring which may be difficult or not permissible.

Data Protection and Employee Monitoring

17.14 Organisations may wish to monitor for various reasons. Some of these include:

- continuity of operations during staff illness;
- maintenance;
- preventing/investigating allegations of misuse;
- assessing/verifying compliance with software licensing obligations;
- complying with legal and regulatory requests for information, etc.

Organisations may also wish to monitor in order to prevent risks and to identify problems as they arise. When issues arise they will wish to deal appropriately with the employee.

Employers and agencies recruiting for them need to carefully consider the legality of internet and social media monitoring of employees and applicants. It is a growing practice by all accounts, and appears more permissible in the US than the EU. However, organisations should not assume that they are permitted to monitor, record, keep files, and make decisions based upon personal information and personal data gathered online/electronically unknown to the individual employee or applicant.[10]

The issue of the right to privacy and data protection of the employee and the rights and interests of the organisation arise. The issue of the right to privacy is a complex subject beyond the scope of this discussion. However, it is an expanding area, particularly after the introduction of the Human Rights Act 1998 (as amended).[11] (Note that there has been some discussion as to whether some or all of the Human Rights Act may be repealed after Brexit. This issue will require careful review in order to identify any such changes, and their implications.) Monitoring raises interlinking issues of privacy, human rights and data protection.

---

10 See, for example, C Brandenburg, 'The Newest Way to Screen Job Applicants: A Social Networker's Nightmare,' *Federal Communications Law Journal* (2007–2008) (60) 597; D Gersen, 'Your Image, Employers Investigate Job Candidates Online More than Ever. What Can You Do to Protect Yourself?' *Student Law* (2007–2008) (36) 24; AR Levinson, 'Industrial Justice: Privacy Protection for the Employed,' *Cornell Journal of Law and Public Policy* (2009) (18) 609–688; I Byrnside, 'Six Degrees of Separation: The Legal Ramifications of Employers Using Social Networking Sites to Research Applicants,' *Vanderbilt Journal of Entertainment and Technology Law* (2008) (2) 445–477; and M Maher, 'You've Got Messages, Modern Technology Recruiting Through Text Messaging and the Intrusiveness of Facebook,' *Texas Review of Entertainment and Sports Law* (2007) (8) 125–151.
11 Human Rights Act 1998, at https://www.legislation.gov.uk/ukpga/1998/42/contents.

Monitoring activities which seek to involve biometric data need added diligence. Note also that the Data Protection and Digital Information (No 2) Bill (DPDI Bill) seeks to make certain amendments in relation to biometric issues.

Human Rights

17.15 The following is subject to continuing Brexit considerations. The Human Rights Act 1998 (as amended)[12] means that the European Convention for the Protection of Human Rights and Fundamental Freedoms[13] is incorporated into and applicable in the UK.

Article 8 of the Convention provides that everyone has right to private and family life, and their home and correspondence. It states that:

'(1) Everyone has the right to respect for ... private and family life, ... home and ... correspondence;

(2) There shall be no interference by a public authority with the exercise of this right except such as is in accordance with the law and is necessary in a democratic society in the interests of national security, public safety or the economic wellbeing of the country, for the prevention of disorder or crime, for the protection of health or morals, or for the protection of the rights and freedoms of others.'[14]

The *Halford* case[15] is an example of the interface of human rights and data protection. The Leveson inquiry on press hacking, and recommendations, are also relevant in considering these issues.

As noted above, the nature and extent of any changes to human rights legislation and/or divergencies from EU norms hold large potential significance.

Application of Data Protection Regime

17.16 In terms of employee monitoring, employers are entitled to exercise reasonable control and supervision over their employees and their use of organisational resources.

Employers are also entitled to promulgate policies to protect their property and good name and to ensure that they do not become inadvertently liable for the misbehaviour of employees.

Equally, however, employees do retain privacy rights and data protection rights that must be respected by the organisation.

Organisations must consider:

- the culture of organisation;
- whether there is understanding and expectation that employees can use the organisation's computers for personal use;
- whether the organisation accessing the employee's communications without permission would be unfair and unlawful obtaining;
- history and practice of adherence to existing policies – or, worse, accepted conduct of non-compliance with existing policies.

12 Human Rights Act 1998, at https://www.legislation.gov.uk/ukpga/1998/42/contents.
13 At https://www.echr.coe.int/documents/d/echr/Convention_ENG. See also Balla, R, 'Constitutionalism – Reform on Data Protection Law and Human Rights,' *Cerentul Juridic* (2011) (47) 61–74.
14 At https://www.echr.coe.int/documents/d/echr/Convention_ENG.
15 *Halford v UK* (1997) IRLR 471, (1997) 24 EHRR 523.

Monitoring involves careful consideration of policy, practice as well as interrelated legal issues of privacy/human rights/data protection.

Monitoring or accessing employee emails or tracking of employee web browsing without permission would likely be unfair obtaining. Location issues are increasingly important – for a number of reasons. In terms of employees, particular issues arise as to if and when an organisation can, or should, monitor or record the location of employees eg via their electronic and hardware devices, etc. It is important, therefore, that organisations have appropriate mechanisms and policies to reduce the risks, and then also to deal with issues as they arise. Reactively responding and trying to set up policies once a problem has arisen should be avoided. As pointed out above, if it is not explicitly in place before the incident, then a bad policy (or indeed an outdated policy) cannot be relied upon in invoking particular terms against the employee.

ILO Code

17.17   Organisations should also consider the ILO Code of Practice on Protection of Workers Personal Data,[16] which recommends that:

- employees must be informed in advance of reasons, time schedule, methods and techniques used and the personal data collected;
- the monitoring must minimise the intrusion on privacy of employees;
- secret monitoring must be in conformity with legislation or on foot of suspicion of criminal activity or serious wrongdoing;
- continuous monitoring should only occur if required for health and safety or protection of property.

EDPB/WP29

Processing in the Employment Context

17.18   The WP29, now replaced by the European Data Protection Board (EDPB), has long been concerned about employee monitoring and surveillance issues in terms of privacy and personal data. It issued an Opinion on the Processing of Personal Data in the Employment Context.[17] It states that 'no business interest may ever prevail on the principles of transparency, lawful processing, legitimisation, proportionality, necessity and others contained in data protection laws.'

It states that when processing workers' personal data, employers should always bear in mind fundamental data protection principles such as the following:

- FINALITY: Data must be collected for a specified, explicit and legitimate purpose and not further processed in a way incompatible with those purposes;
- TRANSPARENCY: As a very minimum, workers need to know which data the employer is collecting about them (directly or from other sources), which are the purposes of processing operations envisaged or carried out with these data presently or in the future. Transparency is also assured by granting the Data Subject the right to access to his/her personal data and with the Controllers' obligation of notifying supervisory authorities as provided in national law;

---

16   At   https://www.ilo.org/wcmsp5/groups/public/---ed_protect/---protrav/---safework/documents/normativeinstrument/wcms_107797.pdf.

17   Opinion 8/2001 on the processing of personal data in the employment context, WP48.

- LEGITIMACY: The processing of workers' personal data must be legitimate. Article 7 of the Directive lists the criteria making the processing legitimate;
- PROPORTIONALITY: The personal data must be adequate, relevant and not excessive in relation to the purposes for which they are collected and/or further processed. Assuming that workers have been informed about the processing operation and assuming that such processing activity is legitimate and proportionate, such a processing still needs to be fair with the worker;
- ACCURACY AND RETENTION OF THE DATA: Employment records must be accurate and, where necessary, kept up to date. The employer must take every reasonable step to ensure that data inaccurate or incomplete, having regard to the purposes for which they were collected or further processed, are erased or rectified;
- SECURITY: The employer must implement appropriate technical and organisational measures at the workplace to guarantee that the personal data of his workers is kept secured. Particular protection should be granted as regards unauthorised disclosure or access;
- AWARENESS OF THE STAFF: Staff in charge or with responsibilities in the processing of personal data of other workers' need to know about data protection and receive proper training. Without an adequate training of the staff handling personal data, there could never be appropriate respect for the privacy of workers in the workplace.[18]

In relation to consent, the WP29 adds that where as a necessary and unavoidable consequence of the employment relationship an employer has to process personal data it is misleading if it seeks to legitimise this processing through consent.[19] Reliance on consent as a legitimising mechanism should be confined to cases where the worker has a genuine free choice and is subsequently able to withdraw the consent without detriment.[20] Consent is thus nuanced, considered, specific, and confined.

More recently the EDPB has issued the following:

- Guidelines 1/2020 on processing in the context of connected vehicles and mobility related applications;
- Guidelines 3/2019 on processing of personal data through video devices.

Electronic Communications

17.19   WP29 also issued an opinion on the review of ePrivacy rules.[21]

Under the heading Data Protection by Design (DPbD) it advocates the application of the principle of *data minimisation* and the deployment of Privacy Enhancing Technologies (PETs) by Controllers. It also calls upon legislators to re-enforce this principle.[22] More recently the EDPB issued Guidelines 4/2019 on Article 25 Data Protection by Design and by Default.

WP29 also issued a working document on the surveillance of electronic communications in the workplace.[23]

---

18   At Opinion 8/2001 on the processing of personal data in the employment context, WP48.
19   See above.
20   See above.
21   Opinion 2/2008 on the review of the Directive 2002/58/EC on privacy and electronic communications (ePrivacy Directive), WP150.
22   Opinion 2/2008 on the review of the Directive 2002/58/EC on privacy and electronic communications (ePrivacy Directive), WP150.
23   Working document on the surveillance of electronic communications in the workplace, WP55.

It also issued an Opinion on the concept of personal data which is also relevant in considering the definition of personal data.[24]

In relation to employee health records, also note the Working Document on the processing of personal data relating to health in electronic health records (EHR).[25]

When outsourcing and dealing with Processors it is worth considering the Opinion on the concepts of data 'Controller' and data 'Processor.'[26]

In relation to video surveillance, WP29 issued an Opinion on the processing of personal data by means of video surveillance.[27]

Employment Contracts, Terms, Policies

17.20   As indicated above, organisations need to consider:

- whether the contract provision has been properly incorporated;
- issues of limitation of liability;
- issues of exclusion of warranties;
- disclaimers;
- graduated disclaimers;
- ongoing risk assessment;
- continual review and updating;
- risk, risk identification, risk assessment, and risk minimisation;
- enforceability;
- etc.

Processing Compliance Rules

17.21   If an organisation is collecting and processing personal data, it must comply with the data protection regime in respect of:

- Principles of data protection;
- non-sensitive personal data Lawful Processing Conditions;
- special personal data Lawful Processing Conditions;
- direct marketing (DM) requirements;
- data security requirements;
- Processor contract requirements;
- transfer requirements;
  - risk;
  - risk assessment.

Guideline Considerations

17.22   Some suggested guidelines to consider generally are set out below. However, it is always suggested that appropriate professional legal and technical advice be sought in particular circumstances:

---

24 Opinion 4/2007 on the concept of personal data. At https://ec.europa.eu/justice/article-29/documentation/opinion-recommendation/files/2007/wp136_en.pdf.

25 At http://ec.europa.eu/justice/article-29/documentation/opinion-recommendation/files/2007/wp131_en.pdf.

26 WP29, Opinion 1/2010. At http://ec.europa.eu/justice/article-29/documentation/opinion-recommendation/files/2010/wp169_en.pdf.

27 WP29, Opinion 4/2004. At http://ec.europa.eu/justice/article-29/documentation/opinion-recommendation/files/2004/wp89_en.pdf.

- comply with the processing compliance rules set out above;
- ensure fair obtaining, collecting and processing of personal data;
- compliance must be ensured at the time of data capture NOT subsequently;
- get it right first time;
- the lessons of *British Gas* and other examples are that in a worst case you may have to delete the database and start again from the beginning, or re-do your collection and notification process;
- consider opt-in and opt-out consent changes;
- consider the purpose or purposes for the data collection and which must be specified;
- provide information to the Data Subject when collecting;
- consider whether the Data Subject is the source (direct) or whether a third-party is the source (indirect);
- specified and lawful;
- use or purpose to which the data collected will be put must be clear and defined. Otherwise it could be deemed too vague and unfair and ultimately an unfair collection which would undermine the initial consent given;
- if disclosure occurs, it must be specified, clear and defined;
- data security measures must be assessed and implemented;
- data security includes physical security;
- data security also includes technical security;
- measures must be put in place to prevent loss, alteration or destruction;
- other legislation may also apply such as in relation to hacking, criminal damage, etc;
- the personal data must be kept accurate and kept up to date;
- personal data must be kept for no longer than is necessary;
- consider that there are many different types of personal data;
- the organisational or business need requirement must be identified;
- how personal data is collected must be considered, planned and recorded;
- check Principles of data protection;
- check Lawful Processing Conditions;
- explicit consent may be required for collecting and processing special personal data;
- identify and deal with new processes and procedures in advance to ensure data protection compliance. One cannot assume that the organisation can obtain a fair and lawful consent after a go-live. This is increasingly the case after the GDPR;
- identify new contacts, contracts, collections and consents in advance to ensure data protection compliance;
- policy for protecting and securing employee's personal data;
- policy for notifying employees of data breaches involving their personal data;
- insurance issues, particularly regarding data breaches;
- risk assessment and planning issues.

The Rights of Employee Data Subjects

17.23   The rights of Data Subjects can be summarised as including:

- right of access;
- right to establish if personal data exists;
- right to be informed of the logic in automatic decision taking;
- right to prevent processing likely to cause damage or distress;
- right to prevent processing for direct marketing;

- right to prevent automated decision taking;
- right to compensation;
- right to rectify inaccurate data;
- right to rectification, blocking, erasure and destruction;
- right to complain to ICO;
- right to go to court.

Chapter III of the new GDPR/UK GDPR refers to rights of Data Subjects. These include:

- right to transparency (Article 5; Article 12);
- right to prior information: directly obtained data (Article 13);
- right to prior information: indirectly obtained data (Article 14);
- right of confirmation and right of access (Article 15);
- right to rectification (Article 16);
- right to erasure (Right to be Forgotten) (RtbF) (Article 17);
- right to restriction of processing (Article 18);
- notifications re rectification, erasure or restriction (Article 19);
- right to data portability (Article 20);
- right to object (Article 21);
- rights re automated individual decision making, including profiling (Article 22);
- DPbD (Article 25);
- security rights;
- data protection impact assessment and prior consultation;
- communicating data breach to Data Subject (Article 34);
- Data Protection Officer (DPO);
- remedies, liability and sanctions (Chapter VIII).

Monitoring Case

17.24   There has been considerable publicity in relation to the ECHR case of *Bărbulescu v Romania*.[28] This was frequently reported as holding that employers can monitor employee communications. The ECHR press release heading states: 'Monitoring of an employee's use of the internet and his resulting dismissal was justified'. Popular commentary suggested and implied that all employers can monitor all employee communications including email and internet. A strong and significant word of caution should be noted by organisations. The previous edition noted:

- the case does not find on a general basis that employers can monitor all employee email;
- the case does not find on a general basis that employers can monitor all employee internet usage;
- the case does not find on a general basis that employers can monitor all employee communications;
- the case technically related to a claim that national laws are insufficient, it is not a case per se between the employee and the employer;
- there is a significant dissent encompassed within the judgment – which some will feel is a more correct assessment of the law – and provides better guidance to employers;

28   *Bărbulescu v Romania*, ECHR, Case No 61496/08, 12 January 2016.

- the majority decision acknowledges difficult legal and factual issues and certain matters missing from the claim file from the respective sides;
- the employer had accessed two online communications' accounts of the employee, one ostensibly for business and one personal;
- notwithstanding that the personal account was clearly personal and private, and there being various apparent issues, the majority seemed to ignore this clear breach by the employer;
- details of one or both accounts were then disclosed to other employees in the organisation and discussed by them openly – this further breach by the employer was also ignored by the majority;
- in terms of the account established ostensibly for business purposes and which was accessed by the employer, this contained personal data and sensitive personal data;
- the employer was not able to establish any reason or suspicion of wrongdoing to trigger a wish to access or monitor this account;
- as such, a considered analysis would suggest that there was no basis for general monitoring in this instance, and seems to lead to the conclusion that there is also a breach by the employer here;
- this important point is ignored in the majority decision;
- it is well established and recognised that employees do not give up their privacy and data protection rights at the door of the employer. The majority decision appears to ignore and not take into account that employers must have some genuine reason or suspicion in the specific case to go beyond the employee's rights to monitor and access online communications. The issue related to Yahoo Messenger accounts, not the official company email;
- it does not appear that specific warnings to employees beyond a general communications policy (which did not refer to monitoring issues) was issued, or issued to the employee in question, or at least this was not established. For some the majority decision ignores this important point. Again, this leans strongly towards there being an employer breach.

It was also queried whether a different result would have been achieved before the EU Court of Justice in this instance.

On balance, it was suggested in the previous edition that employers should remain cautious against global employee monitoring in the UK and EU. Employees, supervisory authorities, EDPB and others might suggest the decision is regressive not progressive, or is simply wrong or must be interpreted cautiously and confined to unusual facts and an unusual decision. The logic of the majority decision could be criticised as being in contrast with the established body of law and legal understanding in relation to these issues. The majority suggests a logic which means that the result justifies the means and issues of law, rights and process are irrelevant. The majority do not point to any lawful basis for employer monitoring and access prior to any problem issue being raised with the employee. It has to be cautioned that organisations may better be guided by the dissent analysis than the frequently misunderstood blanket monitoring headline of the case.

Since the last edition it can now be noted that the previous level of understanding has been restored. The case *Bărbulescu v Romania* was the subject of a more superior decision in the Grand Chamber of ECHR in 2017.[29] This resulted in a different decision

29 *Bărbulescu v Romania*, ECHR, Case No 61496/08, Grand Chamber, 5 September 2017.

in favour of the employee. The court said that the employee's rights were not properly considered.

The court concludes that the applicant's communications in the workplace were covered by the concept of 'private life' and 'correspondence'. In the circumstances of the case, Article 8 of the Convention was applicable.

The original courts did not sufficiently examine whether the aim pursued by the employer could have been achieved by less intrusive methods than accessing the actual contents of the employee's communications. The original court also failed to consider the seriousness of the consequences of the monitoring and the subsequent disciplinary proceedings. The Grand Chamber noted that the employee had received the most severe disciplinary sanction, namely dismissal. It held that:

> 'the domestic courts failed to determine, in particular, whether the applicant had received prior notice from his employer of the possibility that his communications on Yahoo Messenger might be monitored; nor did they have regard either to the fact that he had not been informed of the nature or the extent of the monitoring, or to the degree of intrusion into his private life and correspondence. In addition, they failed to determine, firstly, the specific reasons justifying the introduction of the monitoring measures; secondly, whether the employer could have used measures entailing less intrusion into the applicant's private life and correspondence; and thirdly, whether the communications might have been accessed without his knowledge'.

> '[T]he Court considers that the domestic authorities did not afford adequate protection of the applicant's right to respect for his private life and correspondence and that they consequently failed to strike a fair balance between the interests at stake. There has therefore been a violation of Article 8 of the Convention'.

Conclusion

17.25   Organisations at different times may feel a tension to engage in monitoring of employees. No matter how tempting, this needs to be checked in order to see if it is possible and to remain data protection compliant. While there are naturally risks and issues to deal with, the starting point will always be one of proportionate responses which ensure data protection compliance. The need, or more limited circumstance, of notification with the ICO will need to be fully considered by organisations. Employee data security breaches will also require the employer to consider the rules on notifying the ICO of the event and circumstances of the data breach. There are also a number of trend issues which mean that the somewhat settled area of employee data protection is more susceptible to change issues, such as Covid, home working, monitoring, biometrics, right to turn off, and new forms of data collection in relation to employees and the work that they are undertaking.

Part 3

Outward Facing Organisational
DP Obligations

Chapter 18

Outward Facing Issues

Introduction

18.01 Beyond the inward facing employee related sphere, organisations also need to consider the outward facing sphere. For many organisations the outward facing data protection issues frequently dominate more. They can also be the most contentious. These issues raise significant data protection concerns and compliance issues to be dealt with.

Because these issues are related to consumers, they are more obvious to the media and gain more public attention when things go wrong – whereas employee data issues are less obvious or less transparent.

Some of the queries that can arise include:

- consumer data rights;
- data over-collection;
- data misuse by corporations;
- hidden collections;
- hidden uses;
- consent issues;
- data breach issues and how breaches arose;
- whether individuals are notified frequently enough and early enough of breach events;
- whether companies take sufficient remedial measures after a breach arises and whether they should pay breach monitoring and insurance for the individuals affected (eg Equifax data breach and the monitoring for third party use of breach victim details by errant third parties);
- designated Data Protection Officers (DPOs);
- new senior responsible individuals (as referred to in the Data Protection and Digital Information (No 2) Bill (DPDI Bill) (clause 14);
- new decision makers (as referred to in the DPDI Bill (clause 66);
- forms of outward facing personal data to consider;
- compliance with the data protection regime when dealing with existing customers;
- how organisations contact potential customers yet remain data protection compliant;
- whether an organisation can engage in direct marketing (DM);
- whether profiling is possible generally, or even in more limited circumstances;
- whether users who are not customers can raise additional issues;
- whether security considerations still arise;
- the possible existence of even more security issues to consider;
- higher security obligations for customers and users;

- how the erasure and Right to be Forgotten regime works;
- the new risk assessment and impact assessment provisions.

The general increase in internet usage, profiling, advertising, marketing and social media are also important issues to consider. Abuse whether online or via social media or related websites is increasingly recognised as a problem to be dealt with. Civil sanctions and actions are likely to increase in the instances where it needs to be invoked. In some instances and in some jurisdictions organisations may also need to consider criminal law sanctions.

New Outward Facing Changes

18.02 Some of the new Data Protection Act 2018 (DPA 2018) changes which apply to outward facing organisational issues include:

- reducing the child age in relation to information society services from the EU General Data Protection Regulation (GDPR) from 16 to 13 years of age (DPA 2018, s 9);
- numerous clarification and changes from the GDPR in terms of Special Personal Data;
- variations in relation rights issues from the GDPR;
- safeguards and related issues (eg DPA 2018, s 19);
- codes of practice (DPA 2018, ss 121–128);
- enforcement (DPA 2018, Part 6);
- offences (DPA 2018, ss 196–200);
- restrictions on requirement to produce certain records (DPA 2018, s 184);
- avoidance of certain contractual terms relating to health records (DPA 2018, s 185);
- rights issues (DPA 2018, s 186);
- new representation bodies acting for Data Subject whom will have to be dealt with (see DPA 2018, ss 187–190);
- provisions relating to Special Personal Data (eg. DPA 2018, Sch 1).

Some of the GDPR and UK changes which apply to outward facing organisational issues include:

- repeal of the EU Data Protection Directive (DPD 1995) (Article 94);
- WP29 and EDPB (Recitals 72, 77, 105, 119, 124, 136, 140, 143, 168; Articles 35, 40–43, 47, 51, 52, 58–62, 64, and 65);
- background and rationale (Recitals 1, 8, 11, 13);
- context, objectives, scope of GDPR (Articles 1, 2 and 3);
- obligations (Recitals 32, 39, 40, 42, 43–47);
- security (Recitals 2, 16, 19, 39, 49, 50, 52, 53, 71, 73, 75, 78, 81, 83, 91, 94, 104, 112; Articles 2, 4, 5, 9, 10, 30, 32, 35, 40, 47);
- processing;
- rights (Recitals 1, 2, 4, 9, 10, 11, 13, 16, 19, 38, 39, 41, 47, 50–54, 57, 63, 65, 66, 68–71, 73–81, 84–86, 89, 91, 94, 98, 102, 104, 108, 109, 111, 113, 114, 116, 122, 129, 137, 139, 141–143, 153–156, 162, 164, 166, 173; Articles 1, 4–7, 9–22);
- proceedings (Recitals 52, 80, 129, 143, 147; Articles 23, 40, 78, 79, 81, 82);
- establishment (Recitals 22, 36, 52, 65, 100, 117, 122, 124, 126, 127; Articles 3, 4, 9, 17, 18, 21, 37, 42, 49, 54, 56, 57, 60, 62, 65, 70, 79);
- transfers (Recitals 6, 48, 101–103, 107, 108, 110–114, 153; Articles 4, 13–15, 23, 28, 30, 40, 42, 44–49, 70, 83, 85, 88, 96);
- ICO, etc;

- new bodies (Recital 142; Articles 9, 80);
- notification/registration replaced (Recital 89);
- exceptions/exemptions (Recitals 14, 15, 17);
- lawful processing and consent (Recitals 10, 32, 33, 38–40, 42–46, 49–51, 54, 63, 65, 68, 69, 71, 83, 111, 112, 116, 138, 155, 161, 171; Articles 4–9, 13, 14, 17, 18, 20, 22, 23, 32, 40, 49, 82, 83);
- online identifiers (Recitals 30, 64; Articles 4, 87);
- sensitive and special personal data (Recitals 10, 51, 53, 54, 59, 65, 71, 80, 91, 97; Articles 6, 9, 22, 27, 30, 35, 37, 47);
- children (Recital 38);
- health data (Recitals 35, 45, 52–54, 63, 65, 71, 73, 75, 91, 112, 155, 159: Article 4, 9, 17, 23, 36, 88);
- GDPR definitions (Article 4);
- new processing rules: obligations (Articles 5–11);
- new (data protection) Principles (Article 5);
- lawfulness of processing: lawful processing conditions (Article 6);
- child's consent;
- processing special categories of personal data (Article 9);
- processing re criminal convictions and offences data (Article 10);
- processing not requiring identification (Article 11);
- Controllers and Processors (Chapter IV);
- responsibility of the Controller (Article 24);
- joint Controllers (Article 26);
- Processor (Article 28);
- processing under authority of Controller and Processor (Article 29);
- records of processing activities (Article 30);
- representatives of Controllers not established in EU (Article 27);
- co-operation with supervisory authority;
- security of processing (Article 32);
- notifying data breach to supervisory authority (Article 33);
- communicating data breach to Data Subject (Article 34);
- data protection impact assessment and prior consultation (Chapter IV, Section 3);
- data protection impact assessment (Article 35);
- prior consultation (Article 36);
- new DPO (Chapter IV; Section 4; Article 37);
- position (Article 38) and tasks of new Data Protection Officer (DPO) (Article 39);
- general principle for transfers (Recitals 6, 48, 101–103, 107, 108, 110–114, 153; Articles 4, 13–15, 23, 28, 30, 40, 42, 44–49, 70, 83, 85, 88, 96; Articles 44);
- transfers via adequacy decision (Article 45);
- transfers via appropriate safeguards (Article 46);
- transfers via binding corporate rules (Article 47);
- transfers or disclosures not authorised by EU law (Article 48);
- derogations for specific situations (Article 49);
- new processing rules: Data Subject rights (Recitals 1–4, 9–11, 13, 16, 19, 38, 39, 41, 47, 50–54, 57, 59, 63, 65, 66, 68–71, 73–81, 84–86, 89, 91, 94, 98, 102, 104, 108, 109, 111, 113, 114, 116, 122, 129, 137, 141–143, 153–156, 162, 164, 166, 173; Articles 1, 4–7, 9–22; Chapter III);
- right to transparency (Recitals 13, 39, 58, 60, 71, 78, 100, 121; Articles 5; Chapter III, Section 1; Articles 12–14, 26, 40–43, 53, 88);
- data access rights (Chapter III, Section 2);
- right to prior information: directly obtained data (Article 13);
- right to prior information: indirectly obtained data (Article 14);

- right of confirmation and right of access (Article 15);
- rectification and erasure (Section 3);
- right to rectification (Article 16);
- right to erasure (Right to be Forgotten) (RtbF) (Article 17);
- right to restriction of processing (Article 18);
- notifications re rectification, erasure or restriction (Article 19);
- right to data portability (Article 20);
- right to object (Article 21);
- rights against automated individual decision making, including profiling (Article 22);
- Data Protection by Design and by Default (DPbD) (Article 25);
- security rights;
- data protection impact assessment and prior consultation;
- communicating data breach to Data Subject (Article 34);
- DPO (contact details);
- remedies, liability and sanctions (Chapter VIII);
- right to judicial remedy against supervisory authority;
- right to effective judicial remedy against Controller or Processor (Article 79);
- representation of Data Subjects (Article 80);
- suspension of proceedings (Article 81);
- right to compensation and liability (Article 82);
- codes of conduct and certification;
- general conditions for imposing administrative fines (Article 83);
- penalties (Article 84);
- specific data processing situations (Chapter IX);
- safeguards and derogations: public interest/scientific/historical research/statistical archiving processing;
- obligations of secrecy (Article 90).

In addition, the DPDI Bill seeks to makes changes to the DPA 2018 and UK GDPR, as well as other new provisions. Some of these include:

- changes to definitions (clauses 1–4);
- changes to Principles and lawful processing (clauses 5–6; Schedules 1, 2);
- changes to data rights (clauses 7–10);
- changes to automated decision making (clause 11; Schedule 3);
- changes re obligations of Controllers and Processors (clauses 12–20; Schedule 4);
- changes re data transfers (clause 21; Schedules 5, 6, 7);
- changes re safeguards for processing for research, etc, purposes (clauses 22–23);
- changes re Information Commissioner/Commission (clauses 27–33; 100–103; 86; Schedule 13);
- changes re enforcement (clauses 34–42);
- changes re protection of prohibitions, restrictions and rights (clause 43);
- UK GDPR regulations (clause 44);
- new digital verification services (clauses 46–60);
- changes re customer data and business data (clauses 61–77);
- changes re PEC and PECR (clauses 78–86; Schedule 10);
- trust services (clauses 87–91);
- sharing information (clauses 92–93);
- changes to ICO data regulator regime (clauses 100–103; Schedules 8 and 13);
- changes re biometric data (clauses 104–106).

The final version of such changes will need to be carefully considered.

Data Protection Officer

18.03   Chapter IV, Section 4 of the new GDPR refers to Data Protection Officers (DPOs) and the obligation for organisations to appoint DPOs.

The Controller and the Processor shall designate a DPO in any case where:

- the processing is carried out by a public authority or body, except for courts acting in their judicial capacity;
- the core activities of the Controller or the Processor consist of processing operations which, by virtue of their nature, their scope and/or their purposes, require regular and systematic monitoring of Data Subjects on a large scale; or
- the core activities of the Controller or the Processor consist of processing on a large scale of special categories of data pursuant to Article 9 and data relating to criminal convictions and offences referred to in Article 10 (Article 37(1)).

A group of undertakings may appoint a single DPO provided that a DPO is easily accessible from each establishment (Article 37(2)).

Where the Controller or the Processor is a public authority or body, a single DPO may be designated for several such authorities or bodies, taking account of their organisational structure and size (Article 37(3)).

In cases other than those referred to in Article 37(1), the Controller or Processor or associations and other bodies representing categories of Controllers or Processors may or, where required by EU or state law shall, designate a DPO. The DPO may act for such associations and other bodies representing Controllers or Processors (Article 37(4)).

The DPO shall be designated on the basis of professional qualities and, in particular, expert knowledge of data protection law and practices and the ability to fulfil the tasks referred to in Article 39 (Article 37(5)).

The DPO may be a staff member of the Controller or Processor, or fulfil the tasks on the basis of a service contract (Article 37(6)).

The Controller or the Processor shall publish the contact details of the DPO and communicate them to the supervisory authority (Article 37(7)).

The Controller or the Processor shall ensure that the DPO is involved, properly and in a timely manner, in all issues which relate to the protection of personal data (Article 38(1)).

The Controller or Processor shall support the DPO in performing the tasks referred to in Article 39 by providing resources necessary to carry out those tasks and access to personal data and processing operations, and to maintain their expert knowledge (Article 38(2)).

The Controller or Processor shall ensure that the DPO does not receive any instructions regarding the exercise of those tasks. He or she shall not be dismissed or penalised by the Controller or the Processor for performing their tasks. The DPO shall directly report to the highest management level of the Controller or the Processor (Article 38(3)).

Data Subjects may contact the DPO on all issues related to the processing of the Data Subject's data and the exercise of their rights under the GDPR (Article 38(4)).

The DPO shall be bound by secrecy or confidentiality concerning the performance of their tasks, in accordance with EU or state law (Article 38(5)).

The DPO may fulfil other tasks and duties. The Controller or Processor shall ensure that any such tasks and duties do not result in a conflict of interests (Article 38(6)).

The DPO shall have at least the following tasks:

- to inform and advise the Controller or the Processor and the employees who are processing personal data of their obligations pursuant to the GDPR and to other EU or state data protection provisions;
- to monitor compliance with the GDPR, with other EU or state data protection provisions and with the policies of the Controller or Processor in relation to the protection of personal data, including the assignment of responsibilities, awareness-raising and training of staff involved in the processing operations, and the related audits;
- to provide advice where requested as regards the data protection impact assessment and monitor its performance pursuant to Article 33;
- to cooperate with the supervisory authority;
- to act as the contact point for the supervisory authority on issues related to the processing, including the prior consultation referred to in Article 36, and consult, where appropriate, with regard to any other matter (Article 39(1)).

The DPO shall in the performance of their tasks have due regard to the risk associated with the processing operations, taking into account the nature, scope, context and purposes of processing (Article 39(2)).

The implications of the new concepts of 'senior responsible individual' (clause 14) and 'decision-makers' (clause 66) contained in the DPDI Bill will need to be considered.

Data Protection by Design and by Default

18.04 There are new obligations for organisations. This applies particularly as regards the introduction of outward facing uses and changes which involve personal data (see details below).

Types of Outward Facing Personal Data

Customers, Prospects and Users

18.05 What forms of outward facing personal data must organisations be concerned with? The types of personal data which are considered relate to:

- current customers;
- past customers;
- prospective customers;
- users whom may not be registered customers;
- distinguishing adults and children.

Organisations will be often concerned with collecting personal preferences, account details, etc, from customers and leads. Direct marketing (DM) and additional avenues for commercialisation are also a frequent business imperative. Increasingly commercial organisations may be tempted by profiling technologies. Retailers may also be tempted by increasing sophistication in camera and visual recognition technology for commercial uses.[1]

---

1   This issue arose for consideration in the first data protection audit of Facebook by the Irish supervisory authority. See also, for example, S Monteleone, 'Privacy and Data Protection at the time of Facial Recognition: Towards a New Right to Digital Identity?' *European Journal of Law and Technology* (2012) (3:3).

In addition, there may be individuals who access the organisations website but who are not actual customers. Indeed, they may never become customers. Yet certain personal data may still be collected by the organisation. In this instance, it is also necessary for the organisation to comply with the data protection Principles and related obligations.

How to be Outward Facing Compliant

Customers, Prospects and Users

18.06   How can an organisation focus on the elements that will ensure data protection compliance when dealing with the personal data of customers, prospects and/or users. In terms of personal data collected and processed relating to the above categories, the following must be complied with, namely:

- prior information requirements;
- data protection Principles;
- Lawful Processing Conditions;
- Special Personal Data Lawful Processing Conditions;
- security requirements;
- notification requirements (note new changes in this regard);
- risk and risk assessments, particularly as regards new processes and activities;
- response plans to remediate data breach;
- response plans to notify the data regulator (or data regulators) and notify individuals;
- response plans to assist individuals to monitor and protect against their data being misued by errant third party attackers.

Particular considerations can also arise in relation to users whom may not be customers in the normal and contractual sense.

Note that the DPDI Bill makes suggested amendments regarding lawful processing and purpose limitation (see clauses 5 and 6).

Prior Information Requirements

18.07   The organisation is obliged to inform customers, etc, in a fair and transparent manner that it is intending to collect and process their personal data. It must identify exactly whom the Controller is, ie the legal entity collecting and processing the personal data. The categories of personal data being collected must be outlined, as well as the purposed linked to the categories of personal data. If any third parties will be involved in processing the personal data, these must be referred to and identified, at least by category, when the personal data is being collected. Particular information must also be produced where it is envisaged that the personal data may be transferred outside of the jurisdiction.

The DPDI Bill makes suggested amendments regarding the information to be provided (see clause 9).

Compliance with the Outward Facing Principles

18.08   In dealing with customer personal data, as well as potential customers, etc, it is necessary for the organisation to comply with the Principles of data protection.

Chapter II of the new GDPR refers to the Principles of data protection in Article 5 as follows.

Personal data must be:

(a) processed lawfully, fairly and in a transparent manner in relation to the Data Subject ('lawfulness, fairness and transparency');

(b) collected for specified, explicit and legitimate purposes and not further processed in a manner incompatible with those purposes; further processing for archiving purposes in the public interest, scientific or historical research purposes or statistical purposes shall, in accordance with Article 89(1), not be considered incompatible with the initial purposes ('purpose limitation');

(c) adequate, relevant and limited to what is necessary in relation to the purposes for which they are processed ('data minimisation');

(d) accurate and, where necessary, kept up to date; every reasonable step must be taken to ensure that personal data that are inaccurate, having regard to the purposes for which they are processed, are erased or rectified without delay ('accuracy');

(e) kept in a form which permits identification of Data Subjects for no longer than is necessary for the purposes for which the personal data are processed; personal data may be stored for longer periods insofar as the data will be processed solely for archiving purposes in the public interest, scientific or historical research purposes or statistical purposes in accordance with Article 89(1) subject to implementation of the appropriate technical and organisational measures required by the Regulation in order to safeguard the rights and freedoms of the Data Subject ('storage limitation');

(f) processed in a manner that ensures appropriate security of the personal data, including protection against unauthorised or unlawful processing and against accidental loss, destruction or damage, using appropriate technical or organisational measures ('integrity and confidentiality') (Article 5(1)).

The Controller shall be responsible for and be able to demonstrate compliance with Article 5(1) ('accountability' principle) (Article 5(2)).

These can be summarised as:

- lawful, fair and transparent processing;
- use purpose limitation;
- data minimisation;
- accuracy principle;
- storage limitation principle;
- security, integrity and confidentiality.

The Controller must demonstrate compliance accountability.

Compliance with the Principles of data protection applies to all customers, etc, personal data collected and or processed by an organisation. It also applies regardless of registration notification requirements.

This requires that each of the Principles of data protection must be considered separately and individually assessed by the organisation to ensure that it can, and will continue to be in compliance if and when it collects and processes personal data of customers, etc.

This will involve particular consideration of the contacting model with customers, how contracts are formed, the instant that they are formed and how records are maintained in the event that these need to be examined and evidenced subsequently. Integral to this contract model process is how the data protection elements, data protection policies, data protection clauses, data protection prior information requirements and customers consent, as appropriate, are complied with. Is the organisation proposing to ask questions which are not strictly required for the provision of the service or goods? Are questions being asked which are wholly unrelated to the actual service or product? If so, the third Principle of data protection may be breached. If the product or service is time limited, and no further product or service is envisaged, it would be difficult for the organisation to permanently keep the personal data. This could conflict with the second, third and or fifth Principle of data protection.

Depending on the type of service, products and or relationship with customers etc, whether physical and online, can mean that even more particular attention needs to be paid to fulfilling compliance with certain Principles of data protection.

Customers, etc, and Ordinary Personal Data Lawful Processing Conditions

18.09   What are the Lawful Processing Conditions when an organisation is processing personal data regarding customers, etc? The Lawful Processing Conditions are required to be complied with, in addition to the Principles of data protection. In order to collect and process personal data, in addition to complying with the above Principles of data protection, organisations must comply or fall within one of the following general personal data Lawful Processing Conditions in dealing with customer, etc, personal data:

- the customer, etc, whom the personal data is about has consented to the processing for a specified purpose;
- the processing is necessary for the performance of a contract to which the customer is party or in order to take steps at the request of the customer prior to entering into a contract;
- the processing is necessary for compliance with a legal obligation to which the Controller is subject;
- the processing is necessary in order to protect the vital interests of the customer or of another natural person;
- the processing is necessary for the performance of a task carried out in the public interest or in the exercise of official authority vested in the controller;
- the processing is necessary for the purposes of the legitimate interests pursued by the Controller or by a third party, except where such interests are overridden by the interests or fundamental rights and freedoms of the customer which require protection of personal data, in particular where the customer is a child.

Organisations prior to collecting and processing customer, etc, personal data should identify what personal data it is seeking, why, and which of the Lawful Processing Conditions it will be complying with. This will differ according to the organisation, sector and particular activity envisaged.

Frequently, organisations may wish to rely upon the consent option. In that instance, there should be documented policies and/or contact whereby the customer is informed and appraised of the proposed data processing and freely consents to same. The manner of consent should be recorded. If it is not recorded, it could present difficulties subsequently where it is needed to be proven that consent was obtained for a particular customer or for a whole database of customers.

A further issue arises. Many organisations over a long period of time will make changes to their business activities. There may also be changes to the contract and transaction models which can mean changes to the processing activities and contacts, policies, etc, relating to data protection and consent. The date of the changeover, the nature of the changes, and means of recording and maintaining a record of the consent also needed to be maintained by the organisation in an easily accessible manner. The *obligation of records* is a critical practical and compliance issue for organisations.

These issues can be more pronounced for organisations which change their business models and processes more frequently. Many internet companies will, therefore, have frequent additional challenges.

As noted above, frequently, an organisation would seek to fall within the contract consent or legitimate interests condition above in relation to customers, etc.

However, an organisation may seek to maintain compliance based on the legitimate interests condition. This could mean, on occasion, that an organisation seeks to legitimise processing activities by saying the customer has entered a contact and that the processing is a legitimate and necessary consequence of that. However, organisations seeking to adopt this model should seek professional advice beforehand. It is quite easy for an organisation to feel that it is compliant, but then for additional activities, commercialisation and or direct marketing to occur which may not be transparent, fair or warranted.

In any event, the Principles of data protection must be complied with regardless of the particular Lawful Processing Condition.

It is important to note that the DPDI Bill makes suggested amendments in this area. Part 3 of the Bill distinguishes customer data and business data, some of which may be made by further regulations. This will need to be monitored carefully as it progresses.

The DPDI Bill also makes changes in relation to marketing, PEC, and PECR (see Part 4 of the Bill).

Customers, etc, Special Personal Data Lawful Processing Conditions

18.10 Organisations generally, or more frequently organisations involved in particular sectors, may wish to know certain information which falls within the special personal data categories eg, health data; sexual data. In the case of customers, etc, special personal data, an organisation must, in addition to the data protection Principles, be able to comply or fall within one of the Special Personal Data Lawful Processing Conditions.

The Special Personal Data Lawful Processing Conditions require one of the following:

1   the Data Subject has given explicit consent to the processing of those personal data for one or more specified purposes, except where Union or state law provide that the prohibition may not be lifted by the Data Subject;

2   processing is necessary for the purposes of carrying out the obligations and exercising specific rights of the Controller or of the Data Subject in the field of employment and social security and social protection law in so far as it is authorised by Union or state law or a collective agreement pursuant to state law providing for appropriate safeguards for the fundamental rights and the interests of the Data Subject;

3   processing is necessary to protect the vital interests of the Data Subject or of another natural person where the Data Subject is physically or legally incapable of giving consent;

4   processing is carried out in the course of its legitimate activities with appropriate safeguards by a foundation, association or any other not-for-profit body with a political, philosophical, religious or trade union aim and on condition that the processing relates solely to the members or to former members of the body or to

persons who have regular contact with it in connection with its purposes and that the personal data are not disclosed outside that body without the consent of the Data Subjects;

5   processing relates to Personal Data which are manifestly made public by the Data Subject;

6   processing is necessary for the establishment, exercise or defence of legal claims or whenever courts are acting in their judicial capacity;

7   processing is necessary for reasons of substantial public interest, on the basis of Union or state law which shall be proportionate to the aim pursued, respect the essence of the right to data protection and provide for suitable and specific measures to safeguard the fundamental rights and the interests of the Data Subject;

8   processing is necessary for the purposes of preventive or occupational medicine, for the assessment of the working capacity of the employee, medical diagnosis, the provision of health or social care or treatment or the management of health or social care systems and services on the basis of law or pursuant to contract with a health professional and subject to the conditions and safeguards referred to in paragraph 3;

9   processing is necessary for reasons of public interest in the area of public health, such as protecting against serious cross-border threats to health or ensuring high standards of quality and safety of health care and of medicinal products or medical devices, on the basis of law which provides for suitable and specific measures to safeguard the rights and freedoms of the data subject, in particular professional secrecy;

10 processing is necessary for archiving purposes in the public interest, scientific or historical research purposes or statistical purposes in accordance with Article 89(1) based on Union or state law which shall be proportionate to the aim pursued, respect the essence of the right to data protection and provide for suitable and specific measures to safeguard the fundamental rights and the interests of the Data Subject.

Furthermore, regulations enacted also set out further obligations in relation to the processing of special personal data.

It should be noted that the ability of an organisation to actually come within one of the Special Personal Data Lawful Processing Conditions is more restricted that the general personal data conditions. This is because the data protection regime considers that organisations have less legitimate interest in the processing of special personal data. It also recognises the greater importance that legislators and individuals attach to the sensitive categories of personal data.

Customers, etc, and Data Security Requirements

18.11   What (data) security issues arise for customer, etc, related personal data? Customers, etc, will be concerned to ensure that their personal data is not inadvertently accessed, disclosed or used in a manner which they have not consented to and are unaware of. This is a legal requirement under the data protection regime. Appropriate security measures must also be established. These obligations are becoming ever more present with examples of unauthorised access, disclosure, hacks, etc, such as Yahoo!, Cathay Pacific, Uber, DSG Retail, TalkTalk, Sony, Ashley Madison, Vtech (the children's toy manufacturer), Hyatt hotels, etc.

In the case of outward facing personal data, such categories will generally present significant differences to employee related personal data. Generally there will be more customer, etc, related personal data. It will also be more widely accessible within the organisation. Fewer people within an organisation need to have access to employee files and personal data. Customers, etc, personal data tends to be spread across more than one single location or database. Frequently, the personal data are obtained through a variety of sources, and which are more diverse than inward facing personal data. This all means that there are greater data security issues and access issues to be considered by the organisation.

Increasingly, attacks and breaches that come to public attention tend to relate to outward facing personal data. This means that there is greater reason to maintain and or enhance these security measures to avoid the consequences of publicity, official enquiries, enforcement proceedings, or complaints and or proceedings from Data Subjects.

Data security is also an issue to carefully consider in relation to the new and developing areas of cloud computing, outsourcing, and new models and categories of data processing.

Organisations should be aware of the importance of maintaining separate databases and maintaining these in a non accessible or open manner. Encryption, access restrictions, separate locations, etc, are just some of the security precautions to be considered.

Direct Marketing

18.12   Most commercial organisations will wish to engage in direct marketing (DM). For some organisations this will be an important core activity.

The data protection regime has extensive provisions dealing with direct marketing. There are requirements to inform the Data Subject that they may object by a written request and free of charge to their personal data being used for direct marketing (DM) purposes.

If the Controller anticipates that personal data kept by it will be processed for purposes of direct marketing it must inform the persons to whom the data relates that they may object by means of a request in writing to the Controller and free of charge.

However, a customer is entitled at any time by notice in writing to a Controller to require the Controller at the end of such period (as is reasonable in the circumstances) to cease, or not to begin, processing for the purposes of direct marketing (DM) personal data in respect of which they are the Data Subject.

Two individuals (ie, separate to the organisation) were fined £440,000 by the ICO for sending unsolicited marketing Spam messages.[2] More recently, Black Lion Marketing was fined £171,000 for unsolicited texts;[3] CRDNN Limited was fined £500,000 for 193 million unsolicited calls;[4] and True Visions Productions was fined £120,000 for consent and transparency failings.[5]

Note the updated rules under the ePrivacy Regulation (and PECR) once finalised.

In addition, the DPDI Bill makes suggested changes in this area too (see Part 4). These include: the PEC Regulations (clause 78); storing information on terminal equipment (clause 79); unreceived communications (clause 80); meaning of 'direct marketing' (clause 81); email for direct marketing (clause 82); political marketing

---

2   *ICO v Niebel* and *ICO v McNeish* at https//:ico.org.uk. Note, case was appealed.
3   *ICO v Black Lion Marketing Limited* [2020] 27/3/2020.
4   *ICO v CRDNN Limited* [2020] 2/3/2020.
5   *ICO v True Visions Productions Limited* [2019] 10/4/19.

(clauses 83–84); duty to notify ICO of unlawful direct marketing (clause 85); ICO enforcement powers (clause 86).

Consequences of Non-Compliance

18.13   If the organisation fails to assess and organise compliance procedures in advance of undertaking the collection and processing of personal data of customers, etc, it will inevitable be operating in breach of the data protection regime. Any personal data collected will be illicit.

Equally, if originally compliant but during operation one of the data protection Principles, Lawful Processing Conditions, and/or security requirements are breached, the personal data processed will be questionable, particularly if new personal data is involved or has new activities and uses.

What are the consequences? The collection and/or processing are illegal. The organisation, as the Controller, can be the subject of complaints, investigations and enforcement proceedings from the ICO. Depending on the severity of the non-compliance, prosecutions can also involve the directors and employees of the organisation, in addition to the organisation itself.

If convicted, the organisation could face significant fines. These will be in addition to the bad publicity and media attention which a prosecution can bring.

There can be other consequences too. If the organisation relies heavily on direct marketing (DM), or is a particular type of internet company, the customer database of personal data can be one of the most significant assets of the organisation. If the database is collected in breach of the data protection regime, the organisation will not be able to establish compliant data collections and consents. It could, therefore, be ordered to delete the database.

Alternatively, an organisation may wish to sell its business or to seek investors for the business. This is frequently the case in the technology sector. However, as part of a potential purchaser or investor assessing whether to proceed, it will undertake a due diligence examination of the processes, procedures and documentation of the organisation. It will request to see documented evidence of data protection compliance and that the valuable database, etc, are fully data protection compliant. If this cannot be established, serious question marks will arise and the transaction may not proceed.

The DPDI Bill, once finalised, will need to be monitored.

Users versus Customers

18.14   Do separate issues arise for users and their personal data? Where someone is a customer, there is more direct contact and therefore more direct means for the organisation to engage with the customer in a measured contract formation process. Consequently, it is possible to ensure compliance though a considered and documented data protection compliance process and to engage consent appropriately at an early stage from the individual customer or potential customer.

Users, however, may not be customers. Therefore, customer contact models which incorporate consent or other data protection legitimising procedures for customers may leave a gap where non-customer users are not presented with the same documentation, notices and sign up document sets. Organisations therefore need to consider users as separate from normal customers. They must assess where the organisation interacts with such users, physically or online, and what personal data may be collected. Where personal data is collected from users, the organisation needs to ensure compliance. This may mean that the organisation needs to have a separate additional set of notices, policies and consent documentation in relation to users.

Conclusion

18.15   When organisations begin to look outwards, a separate range of data collection possibilities will arise. The avenues for data collection are more diverse. In addition, the intended uses to which the organisation will put this type of personal data will be potentially greater. The data protection Principles and Lawful Processing Conditions require particular consideration and configuration to the intended data processing activities of customer, etc personal data. Different security and enforcement risks can arise and need to be protected against. It cannot be assumed that everyone that the organisation may wish to collect personal data from will be an actual customer. Therefore, organisations need to consider how to ensure separate consent and notifications to this category of person. An example of this may be cookies which may obtain personal data. Even on the narrow issue of cookies, we see that consent and transparency are no longer linear, and now to be compliant must be multi-faceted and multi layered. Consent and compliance from a wider perspective are also increasingly complex. The many competing interests that must be met by outward facing data protection compliance mean it is more difficult, but it also becomes easier to miss a gap and become non-compliant.

Chapter 19

Data Protection and Privacy by Design

Introduction

19.01 It has been suggested that 'law should play a more active role in establishing best practices for emerging online trends.'[1] Data Protection by Design (DPbD) and data protection by default are prime examples. One of the most important and developing practical areas of data protection is the concept of DPbD as referred to in the EU General Data Protection Regulation (GDPR). Originally developed as a follow on from the data protection legal regime, it is now being recognised more widely, and is also being explicitly referred to and recognised in primary legislation itself.

DPbD/PbD and data protection by default are important for organisations both in terms of being a legal obligation but also commercially in terms of being a competitive advantage.[2]

Background

19.02 The concept of PbD is complementary to data protection law and regulation. The idea is acknowledged to have started with Dr Ann Cavoukian, previously the Information and Privacy Commissioner for Ontario, Canada. She states that:

> 'the increasing complexity and interconnectedness of information technologies [requires] building privacy right into system design ... the concept of Privacy by Design (PbD), ... describe[s] the philosophy of embedding privacy proactively into technology itself – making it the default.'[3]

Principles of PbD

19.03 The Information and Privacy Commissioner for Ontario refers to seven principles of PbD.[4] These are set out below.

---

1 W McGeveran, 'Disclosure, Endorsement, and Identity in Social Marketing,' *Illinois Law Review* (2009)(4) 1105–1166, at 1105.
2 See, for example, A Mantelero, 'Competitive Value of Data Protection: The Impact of Data Protection Regulation on Online Behaviour,' *International Data Privacy Law* (2013) (3:4) 229.
3 At http://privacybydesign.ca/about/. Also see: https://www.ipc.on.ca/wp-content/uploads/Resources/7foundationalprinciples.pdf.
4 At http://www.privacybydesign.ca/content/uploads/2009/08/7foundational principles.pdf. Also see: https://www.ipc.on.ca/wp-content/uploads/Resources/7foundationalprinciples.pdf, and related pages.

1   Proactive not Reactive; Preventative not Remedial

The Privacy by Design (PbD) approach is characterised by proactive rather than reactive measures. It anticipates and prevents privacy invasive events before they happen. PbD does not wait for privacy risks to materialise, nor does it offer remedies for resolving privacy infractions once they have occurred – it aims to prevent them from occurring. In short, PbD comes before-the-fact, not after.

2   Privacy as the Default Setting

One point is certain – the default rules PbD seek to deliver the maximum degree of privacy by ensuring that personal data are automatically protected in any given IT system or business practice. If an individual does nothing, their privacy still remains intact. No action is required on the part of the individual to protect their privacy – it is built into the system, by default.

3   Privacy Embedded into Design

PbD is embedded into the design and architecture of IT systems and business practices. It is not bolted on as an add-on, after the fact. The result is that privacy becomes an essential component of the core functionality being delivered. Privacy is integral to the system, without diminishing functionality.

4   Full Functionality – Positive-Sum, not Zero-Sum

PbD seeks to accommodate all legitimate interests and objectives in a positive-sum 'win-win' manner, not through a dated, zero-sum approach, where unnecessary trade-offs are made. PbD avoids the pretence of false dichotomies, such as privacy vs security, demonstrating that it is possible to have both.

5   End-to-End Security – Full Lifecycle Protection

PbD, having been embedded into the system prior to the first element of information being collected, extends securely throughout the entire lifecycle of the data involved – strong security measures are essential to privacy, from start to finish. This ensures that all data are securely retained, and then securely destroyed at the end of the process, in a timely fashion. Thus, PbD ensures cradle to grave, secure lifecycle management of information, end-to-end.

6   Visibility and Transparency – Keep it Open

PbD seeks to assure all stakeholders that whatever the business practice or technology involved, it is in fact, operating according to the stated promises and objectives, subject to independent verification. Its component parts and operations remain visible and transparent, to users and providers alike. Remember, trust but verify.

7   Respect for User Privacy – Keep it User-Centric

Above all, PbD requires architects and operators to keep the interests of the individual uppermost by offering such measures as strong privacy defaults, appropriate notice, and empowering user-friendly options. Keep it user-centric.[5]

---

5   At http://www.privacybydesign.ca/content/uploads/2009/08/7foundational principles.pdf. Also see: https://www.ipc.on.ca/wp-content/uploads/Resources/7foundationalprinciples.pdf.

GDPR/UK GDPR

Data Protection by Design (DPbD)

19.04 The Commission proposed an enhanced data protection regime including DPbD.[6] Article 25 of the GDPR refers to data protection by design and by default. This is an increasingly important area in data protection.

Data Subject's rights and freedoms and legitimate interests and compliance increasingly require planning and pre-problem solving.

Data Protection by Design and by Default (DPbD)

19.05 Article 25 of the new GDPR refers to DPbD and by default. (Note also the related concept of Privacy by Design (PbD). In some ways PbD is the impetus for the current DPbD rules).

Taking into account the state of the art, the cost of implementation and the nature, scope, context and purposes of the processing as well as the risks of varying likelihood and severity for rights and freedoms of natural persons posed by the processing, the Controller shall, both at the time of the determination of the means for processing and at the time of the processing itself, implement appropriate technical and organisational measures, such as pseudonymisation, which are designed to implement data protection principles, such as data minimisation, in an effective manner and to integrate the necessary safeguards into the processing in order to meet the requirements of the GDPR and protect the rights of Data Subjects (Article 25(1)).

The Controller shall implement appropriate technical and organisational measures for ensuring that, by default, only personal data which are necessary for each specific purpose of the processing are processed. This applies to the amount of data collected, the extent of their processing, the period of their storage and their accessibility. In particular, such measures shall ensure that by default personal data are not made accessible without the individual's intervention to an indefinite number of natural persons (Article 25(2)).

An approved certification mechanism pursuant to Article 42 may be used as an element to demonstrate compliance with the requirements set out in this Article.

Prior to the new GDPR, the ICO has issued recommendations in relation to privacy notices, namely:

- Privacy Impact Assessment Code of Practice (see below).

This now needs to be read in light of the GDPR changes.

ICO

19.06 DPbD is embraced by the ICO in the UK. The ICO refers to DPbD by saying that 'Privacy by Design is an approach whereby privacy and data protection compliance is designed into systems holding information right from the start, rather than being bolted on afterwards or ignored, as has too often been the case.'[7]

6   See GDPR, S Spiekermann, 'The Challenges of Privacy by Design,' *Communications of the ACM* (2012) (55) 38–40; S Spiekermann and LF Cranor, 'Engineering Privacy,' *IEEE Transactions on Software Engineering* (2009) (35) 67–82; L Tielemans and M Hildebrandt, 'Data Protection by Design and Technology Neutral Law,' *Computer Law and Security Review* (2013) (29:5) 509.
7   ICO, *Privacy by Design* at https://ico.org.uk.

It provides[8] the following documents and guidance:

- Privacy by Design report;[9]
- Privacy by Design implementation plan;[10]
- Privacy Impact Assessment (PIA) handbook;[11]
- ICO technical guidance note on Privacy Enhancing Technologies (PETs);[12]
- Enterprise Privacy Group paper on PETs;
- HIDE (Homeland security, biometric Identification and personal Detection Ethics);
- Glossary of privacy and data protection terms;
- Privacy Impact Assessments – international study (Loughborough University).

Privacy by Design Report

19.07   The ICO report on Privacy by Design Foreword notes that:

'The capacity of organisations to acquire and use our personal details has increased dramatically since our data protection laws were first passed. There is an ever increasing amount of personal information collected and held about us as we go about our daily lives … we have seen a dramatic change in the capability of organisations to exploit modern technology that uses our information to deliver services, this has not been accompanied by a similar drive to develop new effective technical and procedural privacy safeguards. We have seen how vulnerable our most personal of details can be and these should not be put at risk.'[13]

In the report, Toby Stevens, Director, of the Enterprise Privacy Group, adds that:

'This report is the first stage in bridging the current gap in the development and adoption of privacy-friendly solutions as part of modern information systems. It aims to address the current problems related to the handling of personal information and put into place a model for privacy by design that will ensure privacy achieves the same structured and professional recognition as information security has today.'[14]

The report describes PbD as follows:

'The purpose of privacy by design is to give due consideration to privacy needs prior to the development of new initiatives – in other words, to consider the impact of a system or process on individuals' privacy and to do this throughout the systems lifecycle, thus ensuring that appropriate controls are implemented and maintained.'[15]

The report refers to the various lifecycles that arise in an organisation.[16] These can be products, services, systems and processes:

'For a privacy by design approach to be effective, it must take into account the full lifecycle of any system or process, from the earliest stages of the system business case, through requirements gathering and design, to delivery, testing, operations, and out to the final decommissioning of the system.

---

8   See above.
9   See above.
10 ICO, *PbD ICO Implementation Plan*, at https://ico.org.uk.
11 ICO, *Privacy Impact Assessment*, at https://ico.org.uk.
12 ICO, *Privacy by Design, An Overview of Privacy Enhancing Technologies*, 26 November 2008. At https://ico.org.uk.
13 ICO, *Privacy by Design* (2008). At https://ico.org.uk.
14 See above at 2.
15 See above at 7.
16 ICO, *Privacy by Design* (2008).

This lifetime approach ensures that privacy controls are stronger, simpler and therefore cheaper to implement, harder to by-pass, and fully embedded in the system as part of its core functionality.

However, neither current design practices in the private and public sectors, nor existing tools tend to readily support such an approach. Current privacy practices and technologies are geared towards 'spot' implementations and 'spot' verifications to confirm that privacy designs and practices are correct at a given moment within a given scope of inspection.'[17]

ICO Recommendations

19.08 The ICO report makes a number of recommendations in relation to PbD practice in the UK.[18] These are:

'Working with industry bodies to build an **executive mandate for privacy by design**, supported by sample business cases for the costs, benefits and risks associated with the processing of personal information, and promotion of executive awareness of key privacy and identity concepts so that privacy is reflected in the business cases for new systems.

Encouraging widespread use of **privacy impact assessments throughout the systems lifecycle**, and ensuring that these assessments are both maintained and published where appropriate to demonstrate transparency of privacy controls.

Supporting the development of **cross-sector standards for data sharing** both within and between organisations, so that privacy needs are harmonised with the pressures on public authorities and private organisations to share personal information.

Nurturing the development of **practical privacy standards** that will help organisations to turn the legal outcomes mandated under data protection laws into consistent, provable privacy implementations.

Promoting current and future research into PETs that deliver commercial products to manage consent and revocation, privacy-friendly identification and authentication, and prove the effectiveness of privacy controls.

Establishing more rigorous compliance and enforcement mechanisms by assigning responsibility for privacy management within organisations to nominated individuals, urging organisations to demonstrate greater clarity in their personal information processing, and empowering and providing the ICO with the ability to investigate and enforce compliance where required.

The government, key industry representatives and academics, and the ICO are urged to consider, prioritise and set in motion plans to deliver these recommendations and hence make privacy by design a reality.'[19]

The report highlights the need and context for PbD in relation to the many instances of data loss in the UK (and internationally). It states that:

'Consumer trust in the ability of public authorities and private organisations to manage personal information is at an all-time low ebb. A stream of high-profile privacy incidents in the UK over the past year has shaken confidence in the data sharing agenda for government with associated impacts on high-profile data management programmes, and businesses are having to work that much harder to persuade customers to release personal information to them.'[20]

---

17 ICO, *Privacy by Design* (2008). At https://ico.org.uk, at 7–8.
18 See above, summarised at 3, and in detail at 22–31.
19 ICO, *Privacy by Design* (2008), note emphasis in original.
20 ICO, *Privacy by Design* (2008). At https://ico.org.uk, at 6.

PbD is part of the solution whereby 'the evolution of a new approach to the management of personal information that ingrains privacy principles into every part of every system in every organisation.'[21]

Organisations need to address many key data protection issues, such as:

'assessing information risks from the individual's perspective; adopting transparency and data minimisation principles; exploiting opportunities for differentiation through enhanced privacy practices; and ensuring that privacy needs influence their identity management agenda (since identity technologies are invariably needed to deliver effective privacy approaches).'[22]

The ICO has also issued more recent guidance on risk and assessment issues in light of the GDPR.[23]

EDPB

19.09 In addition to the above, the EDPB has more recently set out further guidance documentation, namely;

- Guidelines 4/2019 on Article 25 Data Protection by Design and by Default;
- Recommendation 01/2019 on the draft list of the European Data Protection Supervisor regarding the processing operations subject to the requirement of a data protection impact assessment (Article 39.4 of Regulation (EU) 2018/1727).

Commercial Adoption

19.10 Many multinationals and other organisations are embracing PbD and DPbD. Microsoft, for example, has endorsed PbD for many years.

The EU data protection authorities, under WP29 and the French data protection authority (CNIL) while investigating particular policy amalgamation and changes, in *WP29 and Data Protection Authorities/Google*,[24] found certain changes to be in breach of data protection law. Various remedial changes were required. One of these included that Google incorporate the policy of DPbD into its products and services. In addition to mandated DPbD per the new GDPR, it may be that specific DPbD requirements or recommendations come to be included in individual decisions of SAs when dealing with audits, complaints and investigations.

Conclusion

19.11 An organisation must be proactive and not reactive. Data protection considerations need to be considered and built in from the earliest stage in processes which

---

21 See above.
22 See above.
23 See ICO,' Data Protection Impact Assessments' at https://ico.org.uk/for-organisations/guide-to-data-protection/guide-to-the-general-data-protection-regulation-gdpr/accountability-and-governance/data-protection-impact-assessments/.
24 See WP29 Letter to Google: https://www.cnil.fr/fileadmin/documents/en/20121016-letter_google-article_29-FINAL.pdf; Appendix: https://www.cnil.fr/fileadmin/documents/en/GOOGLE_PRIVACY_POLICY-_RECOMMENDATIONS-FINAL-EN.pdf; French DP regulator (CNIL) statement: https://www.cnil.fr/english/news-and-events/news/article/googles-new-privacy-policy-incomplete-information-and-uncontrolled-combination-of-data-across-ser/.

potentially impact data protection. They must be transparent and visible. Problem issues are addressed and solutions incorporated into the process design and process cycle so that pre-problem solving is achieved for personal data. DPbD needs to be built in, not merely added or considered once a problem arises at the end or after go-live. However, PbD and DPbD means incorporating these considerations into the whole life cycle and not just at the beginning and or the end. It is also incorporated into engineering processes and not just system consideration and data categories. PbD and DPbD is now a key concept and requirement under the new GDPR. There is increasing emphasis on privacy engineering as a part of the mechanisms needed to achieve DPbD. DPbD is one of the more important innovations in data protection generally. This is reflected in the GDPR. All organisations will need to appraise themselves of the concept and the regulatory compliance issues. The above Google requirement to implement DPbD is also timely and reflects the importance that enterprise, both large and small, needs to engage the benefits, as well as the requirements, of DPbD.

Privacy impact assessments[25] are also referred to in the GDPR and may also be relevant in the context of DPbD. DPbD, privacy impact assessments are also relevant in the context of developing cloud services.[26] Cloud services also raise important data protection and security considerations and these should be carefully considered by customers as well as providers.[27] WP29 (now the EDPB) has also commented in relation to Cloud issues,[28] big data issues,[29] Internet of Things (IoT),[30] drones,[31] apps on smart devices,[32] cookies,[33] device fingerprinting,[34] anonymisation and pseudonomisation techniques,[35] purpose limitation,[36] smart devices,[37] learning analytics, etc.

In terms of impact assessments and risk assessments, note that there are potential changes to come with the Data Protection and Digital Information (No 2) Bill, such as assessment of high risk processing (clause 17); and consulting with the ICO prior to processing (clause 18).

25 Wright, D, 'The State of the Art in Privacy Impact Assessments,' *Computer Law & Security Review* (2012) (28) 54–61.
26 Cloud and data protection reliability and compliance issues are referred to in R Clarke 'How Reliable is Cloudsourcing? A Review of Articles in the Technical Media 2005–11,' *Computer Law & Security Review* (2012) (28) 90–95. King and Raja also research the area of the protections of sensitive personal data and cloud computing, see NJ King and VT Raja 'Protecting the Privacy and Security of Sensitive Customer Data in the Cloud,' *Computer Law & Security Review* (2012) (28) 308–319; J Peng, 'A New Model of Data Protection on Cloud Storage,' *Journal of Networks* (03/2014) (9:3) 666.
27 See, for example ICO, *Guidance on the Use of Cloud Computing*, at https://ico.org.uk. WP29, *Opinion 05/2012 on Cloud Computing*, WP 196, 1 July 2012; P Lanois, 'Caught in the Clouds: The Web 2.0, Cloud Computing, and Privacy?,' *Northwestern Journal of Technology and Intellectual Property* (2010) (9) 29–49; FM Pinguelo and BW Muller 'Avoid the Rainy Day: Survey of US Cloud Computing Caselaw,' *Boston College Intellectual Property & Technology Forum* (2011) 1–7; IR Kattan, 'Cloudy Privacy Protections: Why the Stored Communications Act Fails to Protect the Privacy of Communications Stored in the Cloud,' *Vandenburg Journal of Entertainment and Technology Law* (2010–2011) (13) 617–656.
28 WP29, Opinion 02/2015 on C-SIG Code of Conduct on Cloud Computing; and Opinion 05/2012 on Cloud Computing.
29 WP29, Statement on Statement of the WP29 on the impact of the development of big data on the protection of individuals with regard to the processing of their personal data in the EU, 2014. The ICO also issued guidance on big data and data protection issues prior to the new GDPR in 2014.
30 WP29, Opinion 8/2014 on the Recent Developments on the Internet of Things.
31 WP29, Opinion 01/2015 on Privacy and Data Protection Issues relating to the Utilisation of Drones.
32 WP29, Opinion 02/2013 on apps on smart devices.
33 WP29, Cookie sweep combined analysis 2015; Opinion 04/2012 on Cookie Consent Exemption.
34 WP29, Opinion 9/2014 on the application of Directive 2002/58/EC to device fingerprinting.
35 WP29, Opinion 05/2014 on Anonymisation Techniques. The ICO has previously issued guidance on anonymisation techniques prior to the GDPD in an anonymisation code of practice (2012).
36 WP29, Opinion 03/2013 on purpose limitation.
37 WP29, Opinion 02/2013 on apps on smart devices.

Chapter 20

Enforcement Powers

Introduction

20.01 What happens if an organisation does not comply with the data protection regime when dealing with customers, etc, personal data?

When things go wrong, there can be legal and publicity consequences for the organisation. The impact of a data protection breach can mean an immediate cross team effort to deal with the data protection breach.

In dealing with an incident, and in planning for compliance with customer, etc personal data, organisations should be aware of the various ICO enforcement powers. These emphasise the importance of consequences for non-compliance. Enforcement proceedings can be issued by the ICO. Significant fines and penalties can result. Potentially also, individual customers may decide to sue for damage, loss and breach of their personal data rights.

Data protection compliance is also an important due diligence issue when organisations are reviewed at time of sale and purchase, and indeed at other times also. It can affect a sale or purchase as well as the value involved. In some instances where there is non-compliance, a customer database, which in some instances is the most valuable asset of a commercial organisation, may have to be deleted. That is a real cost of non compliance and not getting things right from day one.

This is an area subject to further change, in particular due to the Data Protection and Digital Information (No 2) Bill, once finalised.

Enforcement Notices

20.02 The ICO may issue enforcement notices to organisations. If the ICO is satisfied that a Controller has contravened or is contravening any of the data protection Principles, in relation to the use of customer, etc personal data, the ICO may serve a notice ('an enforcement notice'). The enforcement notice will require compliance by the organisation with the data protection Principles, or principle in question and as specified in the notice.

Where the ICO is satisfied that a person has failed, or is failing, it may give the person a written notice which requires the person:

- to take steps specified in the notice; or
- to refrain from taking steps specified in the notice;
- or both.

Breaches which might give rise to an enforcement notice can be varied but include:

- a breach of the Principles;
- a breach of rights;
- a breach of obligations of Controllers and Processors;
- a breach of a requirement to communicate a data breach to the ICO or to Data Subjects;
- a breach of the transfer restrictions.

There are also other types of breaches referred to which can also give rise to an enforcement notice.

The enforcement notice is, therefore, very wide in terms of what the ICO can require. It can encompass all types of non-compliance or breach in relation to customer, etc, personal data. The ICO considers whether the contravention has caused or is likely to cause personal damage or distress, in deciding whether to serve an enforcement notice (Data Protection Act 2018 (DPA 2018), s 150(2)). This would encompass non-compliance in terms of collecting and processing customer, etc personal data. However, the ICO may reserve such notices for more serious instances of non-compliance or breach. It may be argued that an actual data breach or data loss instance is naturally a serious incident and therefore may lean towards investigation and enforcement. This might be particularly the case if the breach has not been remedied by the time of notification of the breach to the ICO.

20.03   Section 151 of the DPA 2018 also refers to enforcement notices in the context of rectification and erasure of personal data. The provisions are detailed and would require attention when procedures are designed to comply with the Principles, rights and other requirement of the data protection legislation. Where a Data Subject feels that there is non compliance with their rights and/or a request in the context of rectification or erasure, there is potential for these issues to arise if the request is being refused, whether in whole or in part.

Assessment Notices

20.04   Organisations also need to be aware of assessment notices that may be issued by the ICO. Section 146 of the DPA 2018 relates to assessment notices. The ICO may serve a Controller with a notice (referred to as an 'assessment notice') for the purpose of enabling the ICO to carry out an assessment of whether the Controller or Processor has complied or is complying with the data protection legislation.

An assessment notice may require the Controller or Processor to do any of a range of particular actions, including permitting the ICO to enter the premises. (Note that the ICO previously had to apply to court for an order to enter the Cambridge Analytica premises).

Limitations and Restrictions

20.05   DPA 2018, s 147 refers to assessment notices and limitations and restrictions. These should be consulted in the event of such a notice arising.

Destroying/Falsifying Information and Document

20.06   DPA 2018, s 148 refers to particular provisions and consequences which may arise in the event of destroying or falsifying information as regards information notices and assessment notices. Various offences can arise.

Powers of Entry and Inspection

20.07   Section 154 and Sch 15 of the DPA 2018 refer to powers of entry and inspection.

Request for Audit

20.08   DPA 2018, s 129 refers to a request for a consensual audit, which organisations can request from the ICO.

Information Notices

20.09   DPA 2018, s 142 refers to information notices. The ICO may issue an information notice:

* requiring a Controller or Processor to provide information for the purposes of carrying out the ICO's functions; or
* require any person to provide information required for investigating suspected breaches or offences, or for determining whether the processing of personal data is carried out by an individual in the course of a purely personal or household activity.

It is an offence in response to an information notice to make a statement which is false or reckless.

Information Orders

20.10   DPA 2018, s 145 refers to special information orders. The ICO can apply to court from an information order where a person fails to comply with an information notice. The order would essentially direct that certain action or information be provided.

Failure to Comply

20.11   A failure to comply with a notice regardless of type can have serious consequences. Further investigations and actions, including court actions directing assistance to the ICO can occur. In addition, depending on what the ICO finds, penalties, fines and prosecutions can also ensue.

Unlawful Obtaining etc of Personal Data

20.12   Section 170 of the DPA 2018 refers to unlawful obtaining etc, of personal data. It is an offence for a person knowingly or recklessly:

* to obtain or disclose personal data without the consent of the Controller;
* to procure the disclosure of personal data to another person without the consent of the Controller or Processor; or
* after obtaining personal data, to retain it without the consent of the person who was the Controller in relation to the personal data when it was obtained.

This is likely to be utilised increasingly frequently, particularly where employees or agents seek to use, access, copy or transfer personal data in a manner other than as envisaged by the Controller.

Re-identifying De-identified Personal Data

20.13 The DPA 2018 also introduces provisions in relation to re-identifying personal data which was originally de-identified. Section 171 provides that it is an offence for a person knowingly or recklessly to re-identify information that is de-identified personal data without the consent of the controller responsible for de-identifying the personal data. This will be one of the more interesting sections to look at to see how it might be interpreted and applied by organisations, researchers, the ICO and by the courts. The extent of the defences specified will need to be considered.

Re-identification and Testing

20.14 There is also a related provision in s 172 of the DPA 2018 relating to effectiveness testing conditions and re-identification. This follows on from some of the defence related provisions in s 171. An individual or organisation will have to be particularly careful and considered (even in advance) in order to avoid the offences and or avail of the defences. Issues of public interest and knowledge and intent may also be involved, which are always difficult to definitively confirm or assess in advance as to how it may be interpreted by a court.

Power of ICO to Impose Monetary Penalty

20.15 Section 155 of the DPA 2018 refers to the ICO imposing monetary penalties and penalty notices. If the ICO is satisfied that a person:

- has failed or is failing as specified; or
- has failed to comply with an information notice, an assessment notice, or an enforcement),

it can require the person to pay the amount specified.

The ICO must have regard to particular issues when deciding to issue such a notice. A detailed list of such matters are contained in s 155(2) and (3).

Some examples include:

- the nature, gravity and duration of the failure;
- the intentional or negligent character of the failure;
- any action taken by the Controller or Processor to mitigate the damage or distress suffered by Data Subjects;
- past failures, etc.

Section 157 refers to the maximum amount of penalties. It states that in relation to an infringement of the EU General Data Protection Regulation (GDPR), the maximum amount of the penalty that may be imposed by a penalty notice is the amount specified in GDPR, Article 83, or if an amount is not specified there, the standard maximum amount.

There are also provisions in relation to penalty amounts as regards the DPA 2018. The Secretary of State is also permitted to make addition rules as regards penalty issues.

Prohibition of Requirement to Produce Certain Records

20.16 Section 184 refers to a prohibition on requirements to produce certain records. It is an offence to require a person to provide or provide access to relevant records in connection with:

- the recruitment of an employee;
- the continued employment of a person; or
- a contract for the provision of services to them.

It is also an offence to require a person to give or give access to a relevant record if:

- involved in the provision of goods, facilities or services to the public or a section of the public; and
- the requirement is a condition of providing or offering to provide goods, facilities or services to the other person or a third party.

Section 185 also provides for the avoidance of certain contractual terms relating to health records. If prohibited terms are included they are deemed to be void.

Tasks

20.17 Without prejudice to other tasks set out under the GDPR, each supervisory authority shall:

- monitor and enforce the application of the GDPR;
- promote public awareness and understanding of the risks, rules, safeguards and rights in relation to processing. Activities addressed specifically to children shall receive specific attention;
- advise, in accordance with national law, the national parliament, the government, and other institutions and bodies on legislative and administrative measures relating to the protection of natural person's rights and freedoms with regard to processing;
- promote the awareness of Controllers and Processors of their obligations under the GDPR;
- upon request, provide information to any Data Subject concerning the exercise of their rights under the GDPR and, if appropriate, co-operate with the supervisory authorities in other states to this end;
- handle complaints lodged by a Data Subject, or by a body, organisation or association in accordance with Article 80, and investigate, to the extent appropriate, the subject matter of the complaint and inform the complainant of the progress and the outcome of the investigation within a reasonable period, in particular if further investigation or coordination with another supervisory authority is necessary;
- co-operate with, including sharing information and provide mutual assistance to other supervisory authorities with a view to ensuring the consistency of application and enforcement of the GDPR;

- conduct investigations on the application of the GDPR, including on the basis of information received from another supervisory authority or other public authority;
- monitor relevant developments, insofar as they have an impact on the protection of personal data, in particular the development of information and communication technologies and commercial practices;
- adopt standard contractual clauses referred to in Articles 28(8) and 46(2)(d);
- establish and maintain a list in relation to the requirement for data protection impact assessment pursuant to Article 35(4);
- give advice on the processing operations referred to in Article 36(2);
- encourage the drawing up of codes of conduct pursuant to Article 40(1) and give an opinion and approve such codes of conduct which provide sufficient safeguards, pursuant to Article 40(5);
- encourage the establishment of data protection certification mechanisms and of data protection seals and marks pursuant to Article 42(1), and approve the criteria of certification pursuant to Article 42(5);
- where applicable, carry out a periodic review of certifications issued in accordance with Article 42(7);
- draft and publish the criteria for accreditation of a body for monitoring codes of conduct pursuant to Article 41 and of a certification body pursuant to Article 43;
- conduct the accreditation of a body for monitoring codes of conduct pursuant to Article 41 and of a certification body pursuant to Article 43;
- authorise contractual clauses and provisions referred to in Article 46(3);
- approve binding corporate rules pursuant to Article 47;
- contribute to the activities of the EDPB;
- keep internal records of breaches of the GDPR and of measures taken in accordance with Article 58(2);
- fulfil any other tasks related to the protection of personal data (Article 57(1)).

Each supervisory authority shall facilitate the submission of complaints referred to in Article 57(1)(f), by measures such as a complaint submission form which can also be completed electronically, without excluding other means of communication (Article 57(2)).

The performance of the tasks of each supervisory authority shall be free of charge for the Data Subject and, where applicable, for the DPO (Article 57(3)).

Where requests are manifestly unfounded or excessive, in particular because of their repetitive character, the supervisory authority may charge a reasonable fee based on administrative costs, or refuse to act on the request. The supervisory authority shall bear the burden of demonstrating the manifestly unfounded or excessive character of the request (Article 57(4)).

The DPA 2018, ss 115–117, and Schs 12 and 13, also refers to the general functions of the ICO. Other sections also specify that certain report and reviews must be undertaken by the ICO (eg ss 139–141; Sch 17).

Powers

20.18 Pursuant to the new GDPR, each supervisory authority shall have the following investigative powers:

- to order the Controller and the Processor, and, where applicable, the Controller's or the Processor's representative to provide any information it requires for the performance of its tasks;
- to carry out investigations in the form of data protection audits;

- to carry out a review on certifications issued pursuant to Article 42(7);
- to notify the Controller or the Processor of an alleged infringement of the GDPR;
- to obtain, from the Controller and the Processor, access to all personal data and to all information necessary for the performance of its tasks;
- to obtain access to any premises of the Controller and the Processor, including to any data processing equipment and means, in accordance with EU law or state procedural law (Article 58(1)).

Each supervisory authority shall have the following corrective powers:

- to issue warnings to a Controller or Processor that intended processing operations are likely to infringe provisions of the GDPR;
- to issue reprimands to a Controller or a Processor where processing operations have infringed provisions of the GDPR;
- to order the Controller or the Processor to comply with the Data Subject's requests to exercise their rights pursuant to the GDPR;
- to order the Controller or Processor to bring processing operations into compliance with the provisions of the GDPR, where appropriate, in a specified manner and within a specified period;
- to order the Controller to communicate a personal data breach to the Data Subject;
- to impose a temporary or definitive limitation including a *ban on processing*;
- to order the rectification or erasure of data pursuant to Articles 16, 17 and 18 and the notification of such actions to recipients to whom the personal data have been disclosed pursuant to Articles 17(2) and 19;
- to withdraw a certification or to order the certification body to withdraw a certification issued pursuant to Articles 42 and 43, or to order the certification body not to issue certification if the requirements for the certification are not or no longer met;
- to impose an administrative fine pursuant to Articles 83, in addition to, or instead of measures referred to in this paragraph, depending on the circumstances of each individual case;
- to order the suspension of data flows to a recipient in a third country or to an international organisation (Article 58(2)).

Each supervisory authority shall have the following authorisation and advisory powers:

- to advise the Controller in accordance with the prior consultation procedure referred to in Article 36;
- to issue, on its own initiative or on request, opinions to the national parliament, the state government or, in accordance with national law, to other institutions and bodies as well as to the public on any issue related to the protection of personal data;
- to authorise processing referred to in Article 36(5), if the law of the state requires such prior authorisation;
- to issue an opinion and approve draft codes of conduct pursuant to Article 40(5);
- to accredit certification bodies pursuant to Article 43;
- to issue certifications and approve criteria of certification in accordance with Article 42(5);
- to adopt standard data protection clauses referred to in Article 28(8) and in Article 43(2)(d);
- to authorise contractual clauses referred to in Article 46(3)(a);
- to authorise administrative agreements referred to in Article 46(3)(b);
- to approve binding corporate rules pursuant to Article 47 (Article 58(3)).

The exercise of the powers conferred on the supervisory authority pursuant to this Article shall be subject to appropriate safeguards, including effective judicial remedy and due process, set out in EU and state law in accordance with the Charter of Fundamental Rights of the EU (Article 58(4)).

Each state shall provide by law that its supervisory authority shall have the power to bring infringements of the GDPR to the attention of the judicial authorities and where appropriate, to commence or engage otherwise in legal proceedings, in order to enforce the provisions of the GDPR (Article 58(5)).

Each state may provide by law that its supervisory authority shall have additional powers to those referred to in Article 58(1), (2) and (3). The exercise of these powers shall not impair the effective operation of Chapter VII (Article 58(6)).

General Conditions for Imposing Administrative Fines

20.19   The new GDPR provides that each supervisory authority shall ensure that the imposition of administrative fines pursuant to the GDPR referred to in Article 83(4), (5) and (6) shall in each individual case be effective, proportionate and dissuasive (Article 83(1)).

Administrative fines shall, depending on the circumstances of each individual case, be imposed in addition to, or instead of, measures referred to in Article 83(a) to (h) and (j). When deciding whether to impose an administrative fine and deciding on the amount of the administrative fine in each individual case due regard shall be given to the following:

● the nature, gravity and duration of the infringement taking into account the nature, scope or purpose of the processing concerned as well as the number of Data Subjects affected and the level of damage suffered by them;
● the intentional or negligent character of the infringement;
● action taken by the Controller or Processor to mitigate the damage suffered by Data Subjects;
● the degree of responsibility of the Controller or Processor taking into account technical and organisational measures implemented by them pursuant to Articles 25 and 32;
● any relevant previous infringements by the Controller or Processor;
● the degree of co-operation with the supervisory authority, in order to remedy the infringement and mitigate the possible adverse effects of the infringement;
● the categories of personal data affected by the infringement;
● the manner in which the infringement became known to the supervisory authority, in particular whether, and if so to what extent, the Controller or Processor notified the infringement;
● where measures referred to Article 58(2), have previously been ordered against the Controller or Processor concerned in regard to the same subject-matter, compliance with these measures;
● adherence to approved codes of conduct pursuant to Article 40 or approved certification mechanisms pursuant to Article 42; and
● any other aggravating or mitigating factor applicable to the circumstances of the case, such as financial benefits gained, or losses avoided, directly or indirectly, from the infringement (Article 83(2)).

If a Controller or Processor intentionally or negligently, for the same or linked processing operations, infringes several provisions of the GDPR, the total amount of the administrative fine shall not exceed the amount specified for the gravest infringement (Article 83(3)).

Infringements of the following provisions shall, in accordance with Article 83(2), be subject to administrative fines up to 10,000,000 EUR, or in case of an undertaking, up to two percent of the total worldwide annual turnover of the preceding financial year, whichever is higher:

- the obligations of the Controller and the Processor pursuant to Articles 8, 11, 25–39 and 42 and 43;
- the obligations of the certification body pursuant to Articles 42 and 43;
- the obligations of the monitoring body pursuant to Article 41(4) (Article 83(4)).

Infringements of the following provisions shall, in accordance with Article 83(2), be subject to administrative fines up to 20,000,000 EUR, or in case of an undertaking, up to four percent of the total worldwide annual turnover of the preceding financial year, whichever is higher:

- the basic principles for processing, including conditions for consent, pursuant to Articles 5, 6, 7 and 9;
- the Data Subjects' rights pursuant to Articles 12–22;
- the transfers of personal data to a recipient in a third country or an international organisation pursuant to Articles 44–49;
- any obligations pursuant to state laws adopted under Chapter IX;
- non-compliance with an order or a temporary or definite limitation on processing or the suspension of data flows by the supervisory authority pursuant to Article 58(2) or does not provide access in violation of Article 53(1) (Article 83(5)).

Non-compliance with an order by the supervisory authority as referred to in Article 58(2) shall, in accordance with Article 83(2), be subject to administrative fines up to 20,000,000 EUR, or in case of an undertaking, up to four percent of the total worldwide annual turnover of the preceding financial year, whichever is higher (Article 83(6)).

Without prejudice to the corrective powers of supervisory authorities pursuant to Article 58(2), each state may lay down the rules on whether and to what extent administrative fines may be imposed on public authorities and bodies established in that state (Article 83(7)).

The exercise by the supervisory authority of its powers under this Article shall be subject to appropriate procedural safeguards in conformity with EU law and state law, including effective judicial remedy and due process (Article 83(8)).

Where the legal system of the state does not provide for administrative fines, Article 83 may be applied in such a manner that the fine is initiated by the competent supervisory authority and imposed by competent national courts, while ensuring that these legal remedies are effective and have an equivalent effect to the administrative fines imposed by supervisory authorities. In any event, the fines imposed shall be effective, proportionate and dissuasive. Those states shall notify to the Commission the provisions of their laws which they adopt pursuant to this paragraph by 25 May 2018 and, without delay, any subsequent amendment law or amendment affecting them (Article 83(9)).

Penalties

20.20 The new GDPR provides that states shall lay down the rules on penalties applicable to infringements of the GDPR in particular for infringements which are not subject to administrative fines pursuant to Article 83, and shall take all measures necessary to ensure that they are implemented. Such penalties shall be effective, proportionate and dissuasive (Article 84(1)).

Each state must notify to the Commission those provisions of its law which it adopts pursuant to Article 84(1), by 25 May 2018 and, without delay, any subsequent amendment affecting them (Article 84(2)).

DPDI Bill

20.21 The above issues also need to be considered in light of proposed changes contained in the Data Protection and Digital Information (No 2) Bill (DPDI Bill) – once finalised and enacted. For present purposes, readers should note that the proposals include new change provisions regarding:

- ICO power to require documents (clause 34);
- ICO power to require a report (clause 35);
- interview notices (clause 36);
- penalty notices (clause 37);
- ICO electronic marketing and PECR enforcement powers (clause 86; Schedule 10).

Conclusion

20.22 Data protection is important. Personal data is considered important and sensitive to customers. This should be respected by organisations. Organisations are not permitted to collect nor process customer, etc, personal data without being data protection compliant. It is in this context that there can be severe consequences for organisations for non-compliance, whether in collecting personal data initially, or in the subsequent processing of the personal data. The ICO can impose penalties financially, or can prosecute for non-compliance. Alternatively, enforcement notices can be imposed which specify certain actions that must be implemented by the organisation. Certain types of organisation can be the recipient of separate types of notices, namely assessment notices. In any of these events, customers, etc, will be particularly concerned that their personal data has been collected, is being processed in a certain manner and or may have been subject to a breach event. This can have its own consequences. Overall, it should also be noted that the consequences of breach or non-compliance are becoming increasingly important as enforcement actions and penalties are increasing, in frequency, number and financial scale. The new regime also further enhances the enforcement rules. Subject to the above, further Brexit consequent regulations are also expected.

Chapter 21

Transfers of Personal Data

Introduction

21.01 Organisations are under ever increasing pressure to reduce costs. This can sometimes involve consideration of outsourcing to countries outside of the jurisdiction. Any transfers of personal data, unless specifically exempted, are restricted. In addition, the global nature of commercial activities means that organisations as part of normal business processes may seek to transfer particular sets of personal data to group entities whom may be located outside of the jurisdiction. There can be similar situations where an organisation wishes to make cross border data flows to agents, partners or outsourced Processors. Companies are also ever keen to target customers inside and outside of a given jurisdiction. It is the nature of internet commerce. This trend of transfers has increased, however, as more and more activity is carried out online, such as eCommerce and social media. Personal data is frequently transferred or mirrored on computer servers in more than one country as a matter of apparent technical routine.

The data protection regime controls and regulates the transfers of personal data[1] from the UK to jurisdictions outside of the jurisdiction. The transfer of personal data outside of the jurisdiction is variously known as: data transfer; trans border data flow (TBDF); and cross border transfer.[2] Frequently, organisations would have transferred personal data to other sections within their international organisation, such as banks. This could be personal data in relation to customers as well as employees (eg where the personnel or payroll section may be in a different country). Such transfers are included in the default ban on transfers, unless specifically exempted.

Organisations need to be aware that any transfer of personal data of UK (and EU) citizens needs to be in compliance with the data protection regime. One of the obligations is that transfers of personal data may not occur.[3] This *default position* or starting point can be derogated from if one of a limited number of specific permission

---

1   See A Nugter, *Transborder Flow of Personal Data within the EC* (Kluwer Law and Taxation Publishers, 1990).
2   CT Beling, 'Transborder Data Flows: International Privacy Protection and the Free Flow of Information,' *Boston College International and Comparative Law Review* (1983)(6) 591–624; 'Declaration on Transborder Data Flows,' *International Legal Materials* (1985)(24) 912–913; Council Recommendation Concerning Guidelines Governing the Protection of Privacy and Transborder Flows of Personal Data,' *International Legal Materials* (1981)(20) 422–450; 'Draft Recommendation of the Council Concerning Guidelines the Protection of Privacy and Transborder Flows of Personal Data,' *International Legal Materials* (1980)(19) 318–324.
3   For one article noting the difficulties that the data protection regime creates in terms of trans border data flows, see L Kong, 'Data Protection and Trans Border Data Flow in the European and Global Context,' *European Journal of International Law* (2010)(21) 441–456.

channels are satisfied. If none of the permission channels apply (and the respective criteria for that channel are satisfied), the default position of the data protection regime is that the data transfer cannot take place.

For more specific details readers can also look to *Data Protection and Data Transfers Law* (2023, Bloomsbury).

Transfer Ban

21.02   Transfers outside of the UK (and outside the EU) are prohibited *per se*. The policy focus is directed upon the possibility of reduced standards of data protection elsewhere and the dangers of uncontrolled transfers of personal data.

The Data Protection Act 1998 (DPA 1998) stated previously that:

> 'Personal data shall not be transferred to a country or territory outside the European Economic Area [EEA] unless that country or territory ensures an adequate level of protection for the rights and freedoms of Data Subjects in relation to the processing of personal data.'

Data protection compliance practice for organisations means that they will have to include an international compliance assessment as well as an assessment of the risks associated with transfers of personal data outside of the jurisdiction. This applies to transfers from parent to subsidiary or to a branch office in the same way as a transfer to an unrelated company or entity. However, different exemptions can apply in different scenarios which makes the data transfer regime quite involved. Below is a headline description of some of the permission channels. These originate in the EU but also apply, and have applied, in the UK.

Country Adequate Protection Channel

21.03   If the recipient country has already been deemed by the UK or EU to already have an adequate level of protection for personal data, then the transfer can be permitted. This is a general permission channel deemed on country specific adequacy. A transfer can occur where there has been a positive Community finding in relation to the type of transfer proposed. A Community finding means a finding that a country or territory outside the EEA/EU does, or does not, ensure an adequate level of protection.

Therefore, if there has been a positive community finding in relation to a named country outside of the jurisdiction, this means that that country is deemed to have a level of protection in its laws comparable to the UK and EU data protection regime. This then makes it possible for organisations to make transfers to that specific country.

The EU Commission provides a list of Commission decisions on the adequacy of the protection of personal data in named third countries. Most importantly for present purposes, there has been an adequacy decision for the UK.[4] The EU Commission has thus far recognised: Andorra; Argentina; Canada (commercial organisations); Faroe Islands; Guernsey; Israel; Isle of Man; Japan; Jersey; New Zealand; Republic of Korea; Switzerland; UK; and Uruguay. This list will expand over time.

---

4   'EU Adopts "Adequacy" Decisions Allowing Data to Continue Flowing Freely to the UK,' Press Statement, Department for Digital, Culture, Media and Sport, 28 June 2021.

(There is separate recognitions for the EU-US Privacy Framework rules (if signed up and adhered to), and the transfer of air passenger name record to the United States Bureau of Customs and Border Protection (as specified) as providing adequate protection for personal data.)

In determining whether a third country ensures an adequate level of protection, the factors to be taken into account include:

- where the transfer is necessary for obtaining legal advice or in connection with legal proceedings or prospective proceedings;
- (subject to certain conditions) where it is necessary in order to prevent injury or damage to the health or property of the Data Subject, or in order to protect his or her vital interests;
- where the transfer is required or authorised by law;
- whether the ICO has authorised the transfer where the Controller has given or adduced adequate safeguards; or
- whether the contract relating to the transfer of the data embodies appropriate contract clauses as specified in a 'finding'.

Individual Specific Channels

21.04　If the recipient country's protection for personal data is not determined by a formal finding as adequate, or is not ascertainable, but it is intended that transfers are still commercially desired, the organisation should ascertain if the transfer comes within one of the other more individual or specific permission channels. Transfers of personal data from the UK to outside of the UK (or EU) jurisdiction cannot occur unless it falls within one of the transfer channels.

The individual specific channels from the transfer restriction ban (on the basis of the EU rules and if there is a UK equivalent of the EU rule) regime) would be:

- the Data Subject has given consent;
- the transfer is necessary for performance of contract between Data Subject and Controller;
- the transfer is necessary for taking steps at the request of the Data Subject with a view to entering into a contract with the Controller;
- the transfer is necessary for conclusion of a contract between Controller and a person other than Data Subject that is entered into at request of Data Subject and is in the interests of the Data Subject;
- the transfer is necessary for the performance of such a contract;
- the transfer is required or authorised under any enactment or instrument imposing international obligation on UK;
- the transfer is necessary for reasons of substantial public interest;
- the transfer is necessary for purposes of or in connection with legal proceedings or prospective legal proceedings;
- the transfer is necessary in order to prevent injury or damage to the health of the Data Subject or serious loss of or damage to the property of the Data Subject or otherwise to protect vital interests;
- subject to certain conditions the transfer is only part of personal data on a register established by or under an enactment;
- the transfer has been authorised by a supervisory authority where the Controller adduces adequate safeguards;
- the transfer is made to a US entity that has signed up to the EU/US 'Privacy Framework' arrangements (or UK equivalent);

- the UK/EU Model Contracts (the UK and EU has set out model contracts which if incorporated into the data exporter – data importer/recipient relationship can act as a permission channel thus permitting the transfer to occur).

Other potential permission categories may be where:

- the transfers are substantially in the public interest;
- the transfers are made in connection with any (legal) claim;
- the transfers are in the vital interests of the Data Subject;
- there are public protections;
- the transfer is necessary for the performance of a contract. (This will depend on the nature of the goods or services provided under the contract. The transfer must be necessary for the benefit of the transferee and not just convenient for the organisation.)

Creating Adequacy

Through Consent

21.05   One of the possible transfer solutions is 'creating adequacy' through consent. Obtaining consent of pre-existing customers may pose a problem so in some cases may not be possible or practical. For example, it may not be possible to retrospectively change existing contracts and terms.

Through Contract

21.06   One of the other exemptions relates to transfers permitted as a result of adopting the UK/EU model contracts into the legal relationship between the data exporter and the data importer/recipient. The EU have recently updated its version of the model contracts; and the UK has also issued its similar version of the model contracts to apply to data transfers from the UK. Transfers of data to a third country may be made even though there is not adequate protection in place in the third country, *if* the Controller secures the necessary level of protection through contractual obligations. These contractual protections are the model contract clauses emanating from the UK and EU. The UK/EU has issued what it considers to be adequate clauses which, when incorporated into the legal contract relationship of the data exporter and data importer, then provide an adequate level of protection. (The UK clauses follow broadly the EU clauses.)

Binding Corporate Rules

21.07   The GDPR, Commission, and WP29[5] (now the EDPB) also developed a policy of recognising adequate protection of certain policies of multinational organisations transferring personal data to satisfy the determined binding corporate rules (BCR) transfer channel.[6] This relates to transfers internally between companies

---

5   WP29, Recommendation 1/2007 on the Standard Application for Approval of Binding Corporate Rules for the Transfer of Personal Data; Working Document setting up a table with the elements and principles to be found in Binding Corporate Rules, WP 153 (2008); Working Document Setting up a framework for the structure of Binding Corporate Rules, WP154 (2008); Working Document on Frequently Asked Questions (FAQs) related to Binding Corporate Rules, WP155 (2008).
6   See L Moerel, *Binding Corporate Rules, Corporate Self-Regulation of Global Data Transfers* (OUP, 2012).

within a related group of large multinational companies. It therefore differs from the model contract clauses above, which generally relate to non-related companies, rather than group companies.

Organisations which have contracts, policies and procedures which satisfy the BCR, and are so accepted as doing so once approved after a (lengthy) formal official review process, can transfer personal data outside of the jurisdiction within the group organisation.

Some of the official guidance documents in relation to the BCR channel include:

- Recommendations 1/2022 on the Application for Approval and on the elements and principles to be found in Controller Binding Corporate Rules (Article 47 GDPR) (EDPB) issued on 17 November 2022;
- Working Document on Transfers of personal data to third countries: Applying Article 26 (2) of the EU Data Protection Directive to Binding Corporate Rules for International Data Transfers (WP74);
- Model Checklist, Application for approval of Binding Corporate Rules (WP102);
- Working Document Setting Forth a Co-Operation Procedure for Issuing Common Opinions on Adequate Safeguards Resulting From Binding Corporate Rules (WP107);
- Working Document Establishing a Model Checklist Application for Approval of Binding Corporate Rules (WP108);
- Recommendation on the Standard Application for Approval of Binding Corporate Rules for the Transfer of Personal Data;
- Working Document setting up a table with the elements and principles to be found in Binding Corporate Rules (WP153);
- Working Document Setting up a framework for the structure of Binding Corporate Rules (WP154);
- Working Document on Frequently Asked Questions (FAQs) related to Binding Corporate Rules.

The BCR[7] appear to be increasingly popular to large multinational organisation in relation to their data processing and data transfer compliance obligations. The ICO also refers to the BCR rules.

It is envisaged that the popularity of the BCR transfer channel will increase. However, the formal review process with a data authority (such as the ICO) can take some considerable time given the complexity involved.

GDPR/UK GDPR: The New Transfers Regime

Transfers Restricted

21.08 Cross border data transfers are referred to in Recitals 6, 48, 101–103, 107, 108, 110–115, 153. Chapter V of the new EU General Data Protection Regulation (GDPR) refers to data transfers and transfer of personal data to third countries or international organisations. Any transfer of personal data which are undergoing processing or are intended for processing after transfer to a third country or to an international organisation shall only take place if, subject to the other provisions of the GDPR, the conditions laid down in this Chapter are complied with by the Controller and Processor, including for onward transfers of personal data from the third country

---

7   See also L Moerel, *Binding Corporate Rules, Corporate Self-Regulation and Global Data Transfers* (OUP, 2012).

or an international organisation to another third country or to another international organisation. All provisions in this Chapter shall be applied in order to ensure that the level of protection of natural persons guaranteed by the GDPR/UK GDPR are not undermined (Article 44).

Transfers Restricted on Adequacy Decision

21.09   A transfer of personal data to a third country or an international organisation may take place where the Commission/UK authority has decided that the third country, a territory or one or more specified sectors within that third country, or the international organisation in question ensures an adequate level of protection. Such transfer shall not require any specific authorisation (Article 45(1)).

When assessing the adequacy of the level of protection, the regulator should (at least in terms of the original GDPR), in particular, take account of the following elements:

- the rule of law, respect for human rights and fundamental freedoms, relevant legislation, both general and sectoral, including concerning public security, defence, national security and criminal law and the access of public authorities to personal data, as well as the implementation of such legislation, data protection rules, professional rules and security measures, including rules for onward transfer of personal data to another third country or international organisation, which are complied with in that country or international organisation, case law, as well as effective and enforceable Data Subject rights and effective administrative and judicial redress for the Data Subjects whose personal data are being transferred;
- the existence and effective functioning of one or more independent supervisory authorities in the third country or to which an international organisation is subject, with responsibility for ensuring and enforcing compliance with the data protection rules, including adequate enforcement powers, for assisting and advising the Data Subjects in exercising their rights and for co-operation with the supervisory authorities of the states; and
- the international commitments the third country or international organisation concerned has entered into, or other obligations arising from legally binding conventions or instruments as well as from its participation in multilateral or regional systems, in particular in relation to the protection of personal data (Article 45(2)).

The regulator, after assessing the adequacy of the level of protection, may decide, by means of implementing act, that a third country, a territory or one or more specified sectors within a third country, or an international organisation ensures an adequate level of protection within the meaning of Article 45(3). The implementing act shall provide for a mechanism for a periodic review, at least every four years, which shall take into account all relevant developments in the third country or international organisation. The implementing act shall specify its territorial and sectorial application and, where applicable, identify the supervisory authority or authorities referred to in Article 45(2)(b). The implementing act shall be adopted in accordance with the examination procedure referred to in Article 93(2) (Article 45(3)).

The regulator shall, on an on-going basis, monitor developments in third countries and international organisations that could affect the functioning of decisions adopted pursuant to para 3 and decisions adopted on the basis of Article 25(6) of the EU Data Protection Directive 1995 (DPD) (Article 45(4)).

The regulator shall, where available information reveals, in particular following the review referred to in Article 45(3), that a third country, a territory or one or more specified sectors within a third country, or an international organisation no longer ensures an adequate level of protection within the meaning of Article 45(2), to the extent necessary, repeal, amend or suspend the decision referred to in Article 45(3) without retro-active effect. Those implementing acts shall be adopted in accordance with the examination procedure referred to in Article 87(2), or, in cases of extreme urgency, in accordance with the procedure referred to in Article 93(2) (Article 45(5)). On duly justified imperative grounds of urgency, the regulator shall adopt immediately applicable implementing acts in accordance with the procedure referred to in Article 93(3) (Article 45(5)).

The regulator shall enter into consultations with the third country or international organisation with a view to remedying the situation giving rise to the decision made pursuant to Article 45(5) (Article 45(6)).

A decision pursuant to paragraph 5 is without prejudice to transfers of personal data to the third country, territory or one or more specified sectors within that third country, or the international organisation in question pursuant to Articles 46 to 49 (Article 45(7)).

The regulator shall publish in the Official Journal of the EU and on its website a list of those third countries, territories and specified sectors within a third country and international organisations for which it has decided that an adequate level of protection is or is no longer ensured (Article 45(8)).

Decisions adopted by the regulator on the basis of Article 25(6) of the DPD 1995 shall remain in force until amended, replaced or repealed by a Commission Decision adopted in accordance with Article 45(3) or (5) (Article 45(9)).

(Caution is needed in the event of Brexit or post-Brexit changes from the prior EU rules.)

Transfers Subject to Appropriate Safeguards

21.10   In the absence of a decision pursuant to Article 45(3), a Controller or Processor may transfer personal data to a third country or an international organisation only if the Controller or Processor has provided appropriate safeguards, and on condition that enforceable Data Subject rights and effective legal remedies for Data Subjects are available (Article 46(1)).

The appropriate safeguards referred to in Article 46(1) may be provided for, without requiring any specific authorisation from a supervisory authority, by:

- a legally binding and enforceable instrument between public authorities or bodies;
- binding corporate rules in accordance with Article 47;
- standard data protection clauses adopted by the Commission in accordance with the examination procedure referred to in Article 93(2); or
- standard data protection clauses adopted by a supervisory authority and approved by the Commission pursuant to the examination procedure referred to in Article 93(2); or
- an approved code of conduct pursuant to Article 40 together with binding and enforceable commitments of the Controller or Processor in the third country to apply the appropriate safeguards, including as regards Data Subjects' rights; or
- an approved certification mechanism pursuant to Article 42 together with binding and enforceable commitments of the Controller or Processor in the third country to apply the appropriate safeguards, including as regards Data Subjects' rights (Article 46(2)).

Subject to the authorisation from the competent supervisory authority, the appropriate safeguards referred to in Article 46(1) may also be provided for, in particular, by:

- contractual clauses between the Controller or Processor and the Controller, Processor or the recipient of the personal data in the third country or international organisation; or

- provisions to be inserted into administrative arrangements between public authorities or bodies which include enforceable and effective Data Subject rights (Article 46(3)).

The supervisory authority shall apply the consistency mechanism referred to in Article 63 in the cases referred to in Article 46(3) (Article 46(4)), at least in the case of EU based regulators.

(Authorisations by a state or supervisory authority on the basis of Article 26(2) of the prior DPD95 before the GDPR shall remain valid until amended, replaced or repealed, if necessary, by that supervisory authority. Decisions adopted by the Commission on the basis of Article 26(4) of DPD 1995 shall remain in force until amended, replaced or repealed, if necessary, by a Commission Decision adopted in accordance with Article 46(2) (Article 42(5)).)

Binding Corporate Rules

21.11 The competent supervisory authority shall approve binding corporate rules (BCR) in accordance with the consistency mechanism set out in Article 63, provided that they:

- are legally binding and apply to and are enforced by every member concerned of the group of undertakings or groups of enterprises engaged in a joint economic activity, including their employees;
- expressly confer enforceable rights on Data Subjects with regard to the processing of their personal data;
- fulfil the requirements laid down in Article 47(2) (Article 47(1)).

The binding corporate rules shall specify at least:

- the structure and contact details of the concerned group of undertakings or group of enterprises engaged in a joint economic activity and of each of its members;
- the data transfers or set of transfers, including the categories of personal data, the type of processing and its purposes, the type of Data Subjects affected and the identification of the third country or countries in question;
- their legally binding nature, both internally and externally;
- the application of the general data protection Principles, in particular purpose limitation, data minimisation, limited storage periods, data quality, data protection by design and by default (DPbD), legal basis for the processing, processing of special categories of personal data, measures to ensure data security, and the requirements in respect of onward transfers to bodies not bound by the binding corporate rules [d];
- the rights of Data Subjects in regard to processing and the means to exercise these rights, including the right not to be subject to decisions based solely on automated processing, including profiling in accordance with Article 22, the right to lodge a complaint before the competent supervisory authority and before the competent courts of the states in accordance with Article 79, and to obtain redress and, where appropriate, compensation for a breach of the binding corporate rules [e];
- the acceptance by the Controller or Processor established on the territory of a state of liability for any breaches of the binding corporate rules by any member concerned not established in the EU; the Controller or the Processor shall be exempted from this liability, in whole or in part, only if it proves that that member is not responsible for the event giving rise to the damage [f];
- how the information on the binding corporate rules, in particular on the provisions referred to in this Article 47(2)(d), (e) and (f) is provided to the Data Subjects in addition to Articles 13 and 14;

- the tasks of any DPO designated in accordance with Article 37 or any other person or entity in charge of the monitoring compliance with the binding corporate rules within the group of undertakings, or group of enterprises engaged in a joint economic activity, as well as monitoring the training and complaint handling;
- the complaint procedures;
- the mechanisms within the group of undertakings, or group of enterprises engaged in a joint economic activity, for ensuring the verification of compliance with the binding corporate rules. Such mechanisms shall include data protection audits and methods for ensuring corrective actions to protect the rights of the Data Subject. Results of such verification should be communicated to the person or entity referred under point (h) and to the board of the controlling undertaking or of the group of enterprises engaged in a joint economic activity, and should be available upon request to the competent supervisory authority [i];
- the mechanisms for reporting and recording changes to the rules and reporting these changes to the supervisory authority;
- the co-operation mechanism with the supervisory authority to ensure compliance by any member of the group of undertakings, or group of enterprises engaged in a joint economic activity, in particular by making available to the supervisory authority the results of verifications of the measures referred to in this Article 47(2)(j);
- the mechanisms for reporting to the competent supervisory authority any legal requirements to which a member of the group of undertakings, or group of enterprises engaged in a joint economic activity is subject in a third country which are likely to have a substantial adverse effect on the guarantees provided by the binding corporate rules; and
- the appropriate data protection training to personnel having permanent or regular access to personal data (Article 47(2)).

There may be future changes and requirements too. The Commission may specify the format and procedures for the exchange of information between Controllers, Processors and supervisory authorities for binding corporate rules. Those implementing acts shall be adopted in accordance with the examination procedure set out in Article 93(2) (Article 48(3)).

Transfers Not Authorised by (EU) Law

21.12 Any judgment of a court or tribunal and any decision of an administrative authority of a third country requiring a Controller or Processor to transfer or disclose personal data may only be recognised or enforceable in any manner if based on an international agreement, such as a mutual legal assistance treaty, in force between the requesting third country and the EU or a state, without prejudice to other grounds for transfer pursuant to this Chapter of the GDPR (Article 48).

Derogations

21.13 In the absence of an adequacy decision pursuant to Article 45(3), or of appropriate safeguards pursuant to Article 46, including binding corporate rules, a transfer or a set of transfers of personal data to a third country or an international organisation shall take place only on one of the following conditions:

- the Data Subject has explicitly consented to the proposed transfer, after having been informed of the possible risks of such transfers for the Data Subject due to the absence of an adequacy decision and appropriate safeguards; [a]
- the transfer is necessary for the performance of a contract between the Data Subject and the Controller or the implementation of pre-contractual measures taken at the Data Subject's request; [b]

- the transfer is necessary for the conclusion or performance of a contract concluded in the interest of the Data Subject between the Controller and another natural or legal person; [c]
- the transfer is necessary for important reasons of public interest;
- the transfer is necessary for the establishment, exercise or defence of legal claims;
- the transfer is necessary in order to protect the vital interests of the Data Subject or of other persons, where the Data Subject is physically or legally incapable of giving consent;
- the transfer is made from a register which according to EU or state law is intended to provide information to the public and which is open to consultation either by the public in general or by any person who can demonstrate a legitimate interest, but only to the extent that the conditions laid down in EU or state law for consultation are fulfilled in the particular case. [g]

Where a transfer could not be based on a provision in Articles 45 or 46, including the provision of binding corporate rules, and none of the derogations for a specific situation pursuant to para (1) is applicable, a transfer to a third country or an international organisation may take place only if the transfer is not repetitive, concerns only a limited number of Data Subjects, is necessary for the purposes of compelling legitimate interests pursued by the Controller which are not overridden by the interests or rights and freedoms of the Data Subject, and the Controller has assessed all the circumstances surrounding the data transfer and has on the basis of that assessment provided suitable safeguards with respect to the protection of personal data. The Controller shall inform the supervisory authority of the transfer. The Controller shall in addition to the information referred to in Article 13 and Article 14, inform the Data Subject about the transfer and on the compelling legitimate interests pursued by the Controller (Article 49(1)). [h]

A transfer pursuant to paragraph Article 49(1)(g) shall not involve the entirety of the personal data or entire categories of the personal data contained in the register. Where the register is intended for consultation by persons having a legitimate interest, the transfer shall be made only at the request of those persons or if they are to be the recipients (Article 49(2)).

Article 49(1)(a), (b) and(c) and para (2) shall not apply to activities carried out by public authorities in the exercise of their public powers (Article 49(3)).

The public interest referred to in Article 49(1)(g) shall be recognised in EU law or in the law of the state to which the Controller is subject (Article 49(5)).

In the absence of an adequacy decision, EU law or state law may, for important reasons of public interest, expressly set limits to the transfer of specific categories of personal data to a third country or an international organisation. States shall notify such provisions to the Commission (Article 49(5)).

The Controller or Processor shall document the assessment as well as the suitable safeguards referred to in Article 49(1) (second subparagraph) in the records referred to in Article 30 (Article 44(6)).

International Cooperation

21.14 In relation to third countries (which now includes the UK as it relates to the EU) and international organisations, the Commission and supervisory authorities shall take appropriate steps to:

- develop international co-operation mechanisms to facilitate the effective enforcement of legislation for the protection of personal data;

- provide international mutual assistance in the enforcement of legislation for the protection of personal data, including through notification, complaint referral, investigative assistance and information exchange, subject to appropriate safeguards for the protection of personal data and other fundamental rights and freedoms;
- engage relevant stakeholders in discussion and activities aimed at furthering international co-operation in the enforcement of legislation for the protection of personal data;
- promote the exchange and documentation of personal data protection legislation and practice, including on jurisdictional conflicts with third countries (Article 50).

Derogations

21.15   Chapter III, Section 5 of the new GDPR refers to restrictions. EU or state law to which the Controller or Processor is subject may restrict by way of a legislative measure the scope of the obligations and rights provided for in Articles 12 to 22 and Article 34, as well as Article 5 in so far as its provisions correspond to the rights and obligations provided for in Articles 12 to 20, when such a restriction respects the essence of the fundamental rights and freedoms and is a necessary and proportionate measure in a democratic society to safeguard:

- national security [a];
- defence [b];
- public security [c];
- the prevention, investigation, detection or prosecution of criminal offences or the execution of criminal penalties, including the safeguarding against and the prevention of threats to public security [d];
- other important objectives of general public interests of EU or of a state, in particular an important economic or financial interest of EU or of a state, including monetary, budgetary and taxation matters, public health and social security [e];
- the protection of judicial independence and judicial proceedings;
- the prevention, investigation, detection and prosecution of breaches of ethics for regulated professions [g];
- a monitoring, inspection or regulatory function connected, even occasionally, to the exercise of official authority in cases referred to in (a) to (e) and (g);
- the protection of the Data Subject or the rights and freedoms of others;
- the enforcement of civil law claims (Article 23(1)).

In particular, any legislative measure referred to in Article 23(1) shall contain specific provisions at least, where relevant, as to:

- the purposes of the processing or categories of processing;
- the categories of personal data;
- the scope of the restrictions introduced;
- the safeguards to prevent abuse or unlawful access or transfer;
- the specification of the Controller or categories of Controllers;
- the storage periods and the applicable safeguards taking into account the nature, scope and purposes of the processing or categories of processing;
- the risks for the rights and freedoms of Data Subjects; and
- the right of Data Subjects to be informed about the restriction, unless this may be prejudicial to the purpose of the restriction (Article 23(2)).

Issues

21.16   Certain issues may arise in relation to:

- What is a 'transfer'? Is there a difference between transfer versus transit?
- 'Data' and anonymised data, is there a restriction on transfers of anonymised data? For example, can certain anonymised data fall outside the definition of personal data?
- 'Third country' currently includes the EU countries and EEA countries of Iceland, Norway, Liechtenstein. The EU countries are expanding over time. In addition, the list of permitted additional third countries is also expanding over time, for example, safe harbour.
- How EU/US transfers will be resolved after the ECJ/CJEU struck down the original EU–US Safe Harbour data transfer agreement, and challenges face the new EU-US Privacy Shield replacement.[8] Many organisations used this as the legitimising basis for the lawful transfer of personal data from the EU to the US;
- Brexit and post-Brexit changes, and especially if any of these differ significantly from the EU rules.

Transfer and Restriction Assessment

21.17   Assessing if the export ban applies and if a transfer channel is available includes asking the following questions:

- does the organisation wish to transfer personal data?
- is there a transfer to a 'third country'?
- does that third country have an adequate level of protection?
- does it involve transfers to the EU-US Privacy Shield or other transfer mechanism?
- does it involve white list countries?
- what constitutes adequacy?
- what is the nature of the data?
- how is it to be used?
- what laws and practices are in place in the third country?
- is it a transfer by Controller to Processor?
- are they transfers within an international or multinational company or group of companies where an internal privacy code or agreement is in place?
- are they transfers within a consortium established to process international transactions, for example, banking?
- are they transfers between professionals such as lawyers or accountants where a clients business has on international dimension?
- the Commission has identified core principles which must be present in the foreign laws or codes of practice or regulations in order to achieve the requisite standard of 'adequacy' in third party countries – are these principles present?
- has the personal data been processed for a specific purpose?
- is the personal data accurate and up to date?
- has the Data Subject been provided with adequate information in relation to the transfer?
- have technical and organisational security measures been taken by the Controller?
- is there a right of access to the data by the Data Subject?

---

8   *Digital Rights Ireland and Seitlinger and Others*, Joined Cases C-293/12 and C-594/12, Court of Justice, 8 April 2014.

- is there a prohibition on onward transfer of data?
- is there an effective procedure or mode of enforcement?

Contracts, consent and binding corporate rules take on a new significance as the concepts of permissibility and adequacy receive renewed scrutiny. Given the controversy and striking out of the EU-US Safe Harbours and Privacy Shield arrangements, all Controllers engaged in processing, and those considering transfers, should very carefully consider all of the implications, current changes and the new Privacy Shield arrangement – and also how the UK may seek to replicate something similar to the Privacy Framework for the UK and US.

Transfer Compliance

21.18 Organisations may consider the following queries:

- does the organisation transfer customer, etc, personal data outside of the jurisdiction?
- is there a transfer to the US? If so, is the recipient of the data a Privacy Shield recipient? If yes, then the organisation can transfer the data. If not, the organisation needs to: (i) assess the adequacy of the protection measures in place; (ii) see if that transfer is exempted; (iii) create adequacy through consent or appropriate contract.
- is the recipient country a Commission permitted white list country? If so, transfer is permitted.
- are there data protection rules in place or codes of practice and if so did they incorporate the adequate and equivalent protections?
- if there is inadequate protection is it practical to obtain the consent of the Data Subject?
- if not, then is it practical to enter into an appropriate contract with the recipient?
- are the Commission model data contract clauses is available?

The ICO also asks:

1. does the organisation need to transfer personal data abroad?
2. is the organisation transferring the personal data to a country outside of the jurisdiction or will it just be in transit through a non-EEA country?
3. has the organisation complied with all the other data protection Principles?
4. is the transfer to a country on the EU Commission's white list of countries or territories (per a Community finding) accepted as providing adequate levels of protection for the rights and freedoms of Data Subjects in connection with the processing of their personal data?
5. if the transfer is to the US, has the US recipient of the personal data signed up to the EU-US Department of Commerce Privacy Shield scheme [or any alternative mechanism]?
6. is the personal data passenger name record information (PNR)? If so, particular rules may apply.

   [Note: No 7 missing in the original]

8. can the organisation assess that the level of protection for Data Subjects' rights as 'adequate in all the circumstances of the case'?.
9. if not, can the organisation put in place adequate safeguards to protect the rights of the Data Subjects whose data is to be transferred?
10. can the organisation rely on another exception from the restriction on international transfers of personal data?

Brexit

21.19   Also see Chapter 24 with regard to Brexit and the impact on EU data transfers to the UK after Brexit is completed. The important issue of a UK adequacy decision and the complicating issues involved are necessary considerations. While an adequacy decision has issued for the UK, it needs to be reviewed on a regular basis and is not guaranteed as being permanent, or beyond the scope of third party challenge. Given that change is still an ongoing issue in the UK data protection legal landscape, caution and constant monitoring should be maintained.

Issues to monitor and note are:

- the EU adequacy decision for the UK;[9]
- new and updated EU standard or model contracts issues;[10]
- new UK standard or model contract issued (the International Data Transfer Agreement (IDTA) and International Data Transfer Addendum (UK Addendum), 2 February 2022 but effective from 21 March 2022 (issued under s 119A DPA 2018);
- UK data protection consultation process of possible further changes, including to UK GDPR;
- proposed changes to DPA 2018;
- proposed changes to UK GDPR;
- proposed changes in Data Protection and Digital information (No 2) Bill (DPDI Bill) re data transfers (eg clauses 13, 21; and Schedules 5, 6, and 7);
- proposed changes to a wide range of EU legacy laws in the UK.

The DPDI proposed changes regarding data transfers refer to:

- clause 13 (removal of requirement for representatives for controllers, etc, outside the UK);
- clause 21 (transfers of personal data to third countries and international organisations);
- Schedule 5 (transfers of personal data to third countries, etc: general processing);
- Schedule 6 (transfers of personal data to third countries, etc: law enforcement processing); and
- Schedule 7 (transfers of personal data to third countries, etc: consequential and transitional provisions).

Conclusion

21.20   Data protection compliance practice for organisations means that they will have to include a compliance assessment, as well as an assessment of associated risks, in relation to potential transfers of personal data outside of the jurisdiction. This applies to transfers from parent to subsidiary or to a branch office as well as transfers to any unrelated company or entity.

The ICO also provides useful guidance in relation to:

---

9   'EU Adopts "Adequacy" Decisions Allowing Data to Continue to Flow Freely to UK,' Press Release. Department for Digital, Culture, Media and Sport, 28 June 2021; Decision on the Adequate Protection of Personal Data by the United Kingdom – General Data Protection Regulation, EU Commission, 28 June 2021.

10   'Standard Contractual Clauses for International Transfers, Modernised Standard Contractual Clauses for the Transfer of Personal Data to Third Countries' EU Commission, Justice and Consumers, 4 June 2021.

- Assessing Adequacy;
- Model Contract Clauses;
- Binding Corporate Rules;
- Outsourcing;
- Brexit/post-Brexit issues.

There is also the following ICO guidance which can be a useful reference for organisations, namely, the:

Data Protection Act;

International Data Transfers;

The Information Commissioner's Recommended Approach to Assessing Adequacy Including Consideration of the Issue of Contractual Solutions, Binding Corporate Rules.

Organisations should be aware that if they wish to transfer personal data outside of the UK/EU, that additional considerations arise and that unless there is a specific exemption, then the transfer may not be permitted. Once a transfer possibility arises, the organisation should undertake a compliance exercise to assess if the transfer can be permitted, and if so, how. Additional compliance documentation and contracts may be required. The increasing locations and methods by which personal data may be collected by organisations, in particular internet, communications and social media, will increasingly be scrutinised in terms of transparency, consent and compliance. Equally, cloud computing is receiving particular data protection attention. Apps are also being considered as is the developing area of the Internet of Things (IoT) and related data protection compliance issues.

Chapter 22

ePrivacy and Marketing (EU)

Introduction

22.01   There is increasing use of electronically transmitted personal data. It arises in mobile devices, desktops, and more recently an even wider range of electronic or connected devices. The personal communications data is protected and regulated, in certain respects, separate from the general data protection regime under the General Data Protection Regulation (GDPR) and UK GDPR. In addition, there are also protections against electronic marketing directed towards individuals, and regulation of such activities when they may be permitted. The two most well-known forms of such electronic marketing are emails and texts. These are sometimes referred to as unsolicited emails/texts or spam emails/texts.

The rules governing such activities, which are separate to the main GDPR/UK GDPR rules, are sometimes referred to as the ePrivacy rules. All companies should be aware of these rules, but especially those wishing to engage in heavy electronic marketing activities. This chapter refers mainly to the EU rules which provide the background to the rules as they exist in the UK. The following chapter shall refer to these rules as they apply specifically in the UK (known as the Privacy and Electronic Communications Regulations, or PEC and PECR[1]) .

Background

22.02   Originally the regulation of telecommunications related personal data centred on telecoms companies. It is now recognised as encompassing telecoms companies and certain companies engaged in activities involving the collection or transmission of particular personal data over electronic communications networks, including the internet. It can also be extended even more widely as modern communications technologies such as internet, email, SMS and MMS text messaging can be utilised by almost any company.

Organisations concerned with compliance relating to marketing, email marketing, text marketing, telephone marketing, fax marketing, the use of location-based data, cookies (and cookie replacement technologies), identification regarding telephone calls, and other telephone issues need to consider the additional data protection rules ie the ePrivacy rules which exist separate to the GDPR.

The GDPR indicates that it shall not impose additional obligations on natural or legal persons in relation to the processing of personal data in connection with the

---

1   Privacy and Electronic Communications (EC Directive) Regulations 2003, SI 2003/2426.

provision of publicly available electronic communications services in public communication networks in the EU in relation to matters for which they are subject to specific obligations with the same objective set out in Directive 2002/58/EC[2] (Article 89).

However, other ePrivacy specific rules need to be complied with by companies engaging in electronic based marketing activities – currently in the form of the EU ePrivacy Directive (and to be replaced by the ePrivacy Regulations (once finalised)). Very careful review is needed when seeking engagement in these types of marketing activities.

There has been a long separation in EU law between the general data protection issues (covered originally in EU Data Protection Directive 1995 (DPD 1995)), and the regulation of personal data in the sphere of (tele)communications networks. The later were legislated for in the Data Protection Directive of 1997.[3] This was replaced with the ePrivacy Directive (ePD). The ePD was amended by Directive 2006/24/EC and Directive 2009/136/EC. The ePrivacy Directive still governs these issues in the EU. However, there is a proposal for a new ePrivacy Regulation to encompass more modern communications issues. It was originally hoped that the ePrivacy Regulation would become law at the same time, or closely after, the GDPR. This has not occurred. Currently the proposed ePrivacy Regulation is still going through the legislative and amendment process. It is currently described as 'Proposal for a regulation on privacy and electronic communications, In A Europe Fit for the Digital Age'.[4] It is hoped and expressed that the ePrivacy Regulation will be enacted during 2023, with a 24-month transition period.

This will have major significance as UK companies targeting marketing to the EU market will have to comply with the new EU ePrivacy rules. In addition, the UK rules (PECR) may also be updated and amended to closely follow some, or all of the rules as will be set out in the final version of the EU ePrivacy Regulation.

Organisations need to be aware of the updated provisions coming with the ePrivacy Regulation, and also monitor when it will be finalised and enacted. The GDPR had a significant big bang effect and was arguably the most widely publicised law, certainly in relation to data protection issues, to date. The enactment and go live of the ePrivacy Regulation may not receive the exact same level of attention, but it will be significant nonetheless.

Scope of the ePD

22.03 The current ePD[5] concerns the processing and protection of personal data and privacy in the electronic communications sector. It is also known as the Directive on privacy and electronic communications, hence ePD. One of the concerns has been how electronic communications and electronic information are increasingly used for profiling for marketing purposes, including by electronic means.[6] (Indeed, this is also reflected in the cookie rules.)

---

2 Directive 2002/58/EC of the European Parliament and of the Council of 12 July 2002 concerning the processing of personal data and the protection of privacy in the electronic communications sector (Directive on privacy and electronic communications).
3 Directive 97/66/EC.
4 Initially published on 10 January 2017.
5 Directive 2002/58/EC of 12 July 2002.
6 See, for example, W McGeveran, 'Disclosure, Endorsement, and Identity in Social Marketing,' *University of Illinois Law Review* (2009) (4) 1105–1166.

The ePD broadly relates to and encompasses the following, namely:

- definitions;
- security;
- confidentiality;
- traffic data;
- non itemised bills;
- call and connected line identification;
- location data;
- exceptions;
- directories;
- unsolicited communications;
- technical features.

It also provides rules in relation to:

- email marketing;
- text marketing;
- telephone marketing;
- fax marketing;
- cookies, etc.

Marketing

22.04   How should organisations go about ensuring data protection compliance for direct marketing (DM)? When is DM permitted? All organisations should carefully assess compliance issues when considering any direct marketing activities. Getting it wrong can be costly and can have ICO enforcement and investigation consequences as well as penalties.

Article 13 of the ePD refers to unsolicited communications. Article 13(1) in particular provides that the use of the following, namely:

- automated calling systems without human intervention (automatic calling machines);
- facsimile machines (fax); or
- electronic mail,

for the purposes of direct marketing may *only* be allowed in respect of subscribers who have given their *prior consent*.

This means that there is a default rule prohibiting DM without prior consent. Many marketing orientated organisations may be surprised, if not dismayed by this.

Existing Customers' Email

22.05   However, in the context of existing customers, there is a possibility to direct market using emails. Article 13(2) of the ePD provides that notwithstanding Article 13(1), where an organisation obtains from its customers their electronic contact details for email, in the context of the sale of a product or a service, in accordance with the DPD, the organisation may use these electronic contact details for DM of its own similar products or services provided that customers clearly and distinctly are given the opportunity to object, free of charge and in an easy manner, to such use of electronic contact details when they are collected and on the occasion of each message in case the customer has not initially refused such use.

Therefore, once the email details are obtained at the time of a product or service transaction, it will be possible to use that email for direct marketing purposes. Conditions or limitations apply however. Firstly, the organisation is only permitted to market and promote similar products or services. This, therefore, rules out unrelated, non-identical and non-similar products and services. Secondly, at the time of each subsequent act of DM, the customer must be given the opportunity in an easy manner to opt-out or cancel the DM. Effectively, they must be taken off the DM list.

National Opt-out Registers

22.06 Article 13(3) of ePD provides that appropriate measures must ensure that, free of charge, unsolicited communications for purposes of direct marketing, in cases other than those referred to in paras 1 and 2, are not allowed either without the consent of the subscribers concerned or in respect of subscribers who do not wish to receive these communications, the choice between these options to be determined by national legislation. This means that each state must determine and provide a means for individuals to opt-out of receiving DM in advance.[7]

Marketing Emails Must Not Conceal Their Identity

22.07 Article 13(4) of ePD provides that the practice of sending electronic mail for purposes of DM disguising or concealing the identity of the sender on whose behalf the communication is made shall be prohibited. This means that organisations cannot conceal their identity if permitted to engage in direct marketing. If these are not complied with, what might otherwise be permissible DM can be deemed to be impermissible. Complaints, investigations or enforcement proceedings can thus arise.

Marketing Emails Must Have an Opt-Out

22.08 In addition, Article 13(4) of ePD provides that the practice of sending electronic mail for purposes of DM without a valid address to which the recipient may send a request that such communications cease, shall be prohibited. This means that organisations must also include an easy contact address or other details at which the recipient can contact if they wish to object to receiving any further DM. If these are not complied with, what might otherwise be permissible DM can be deemed to be impermissible. Complaints, investigations or enforcement proceedings can thus also arise.

Marketing Protection for Organisations

22.09 Article 13(5) of ePD provides that Article 13(1) and (3) shall apply to subscribers who are natural persons. States shall also ensure, in the framework of EU law and applicable national legislation, that the legitimate interests of subscribers other than natural persons with regard to unsolicited communications are sufficiently protected. This means that protection from unsolicited DM can also be extended to organisations.

Scope

22.10 ePD Article 1 refers to the scope and aim of the Directive. Article 1(1) provides that the Directive harmonises the provisions of the states to ensure an equivalent level of protection of fundamental rights and freedoms, and in particular the right to privacy, with respect to the processing of personal data in the electronic

---

7   See ICO, *Marketing*, at https://ico.org.uk.

communication sector and to ensure the free movement of such data and of electronic communication equipment and services in the EU.

Article 1(2) provides that the provisions of the Directive particularise and complement DPD 1995 for the purposes mentioned in Article 1(1). Moreover, they provide for protection of the legitimate interests of subscribers who are legal persons.

Article 1(3) provides that the ePD shall not apply to activities which fall outside the scope of the Treaty establishing the European Community, such as those covered by Titles V and VI of the Treaty on EU, and in any case to activities concerning public security, defence, State security (including the economic well-being of the State when the activities relate to State security matters) and the activities of the State in areas of criminal law.

Definitions

22.11 Article 2 of the ePD refers to definitions. The definitions in GDPR and in the ePD shall apply. The following additional definitions shall also apply: user, traffic data, location data, communication, call, consent, value added consent, electronic mail.

Services

22.12 Article 3 relates to the services concerned. Article 3(1) provides that the ePD shall apply to the processing of personal data in connection with the provision of publicly available electronic communications services in public communications networks in the EU.

Article 3(2) provides that Articles 8, 10 and 11 shall apply to subscriber lines connected to digital exchanges and, where technically possible and if it does not require a disproportionate economic effort, to subscriber lines connected to analogue exchanges.

Article 3(3) provides that cases where it would be technically impossible or require a disproportionate economic effort to fulfil the requirements of Articles 8, 10 and 11 shall be notified to the Commission by the states.

Unsolicited Communications

22.13 Article 13 refers to unsolicited communications. Article 13(1) provides that the use of automated calling systems without human intervention (automatic calling machines), facsimile machines (fax) or electronic mail for the purposes of direct marketing may only be allowed in respect of subscribers who have given their prior consent.

Article 13(2) provides that notwithstanding Article 13(1), where a natural or legal person obtains from its customers their electronic contact details for electronic mail, in the context of the sale of a product or a service, in accordance with DPD 1995, the same natural or legal person may use these electronic contact details for direct marketing of its own similar products or services provided that customers clearly and distinctly are given the opportunity to object, free of charge and in an easy manner, to such use of electronic contact details when they are collected and on the occasion of each message in case the customer has not initially refused such use.

Article 13(3) provides that states shall take appropriate measures to ensure that, free of charge, unsolicited communications for purposes of direct marketing, in cases other than those referred to in Article 13(1) and (2), are not allowed either without the consent of the subscribers concerned or in respect of subscribers who do not wish to receive these communications, the choice between these options to be determined by national legislation.

Article 13(4) provides that in any event, the practice of sending electronic mail for purposes of direct marketing disguising or concealing the identity of the sender on whose behalf the communication is made, or without a valid address to which the recipient may send a request that such communications cease, shall be prohibited.

Article 13(5) provides that Article 13(1) and (3) shall apply to subscribers who are natural persons. States shall also ensure, in the framework of EU law and applicable national legislation, that the legitimate interests of subscribers other than natural persons with regard to unsolicited communications are sufficiently protected.

Security

22.14 Article 4 relates to security. Article 4(1) provides that the provider of a publicly available electronic communications service must take appropriate technical and organisational measures to safeguard security of its services, if necessary in conjunction with the provider of the public communications network with respect to network security. Having regard to the state of the art and the cost of their implementation, these measures shall ensure a level of security appropriate to the risk presented. Obviously, these can change over time as risks and as technology change.

Article 4(2) provides that in case of a particular risk of a breach of the security of the network, the provider of a publicly available electronic communications service must inform the subscribers concerning such risk and, where the risk lies outside the scope of the measures to be taken by the service provider, of any possible remedies, including an indication of the likely costs involved.

Confidentiality

22.15 Article 5 refers to confidentiality of the communications. Article 5(1) provides that states shall ensure the confidentiality of communications and the related traffic data by means of a public communications network and publicly available electronic communications services, through national legislation. In particular, they shall prohibit listening, tapping, storage or other kinds of interception or surveillance of communications and the related traffic data by persons other than users, without the consent of the users concerned, except when legally authorised to do so in accordance with Article 15(1). This paragraph shall not prevent technical storage which is necessary for the conveyance of a communication without prejudice to the principle of confidentiality.

Article 5(2) provides that para 1 shall not affect any legally authorised recording of communications and the related traffic data when carried out in the course of lawful business practice for the purpose of providing evidence of a commercial transaction or of any other business communication.

Article 5(3) provides that states shall ensure that the use of electronic communications networks to store information or to gain access to information stored in the terminal equipment of a subscriber or user is only allowed on condition that the subscriber or user concerned is provided with clear and comprehensive information, inter alia about the purposes of the processing, and is offered the right to refuse such processing by the Controller. This shall not prevent any technical storage or access for the sole purpose of carrying out or facilitating the transmission of a communication over an electronic communications network, or as strictly necessary in order to provide an information society service explicitly requested by the subscriber or user.

Traffic Data

22.16 Article 6 refers to traffic data. Article 6(1) provides that traffic data relating to subscribers and users processed and stored by the provider of a public communications network or publicly available electronic communications service must be erased or made anonymous when it is no longer needed for the purpose of the transmission of a communication without prejudice to Article 6(2), (3) and (5) and Article 15(1).

Article 6(2) provides that traffic data necessary for the purposes of subscriber billing and interconnection payments may be processed. Such processing is permissible only up to the end of the period during which the bill may lawfully be challenged or payment pursued.

Article 6(3) provides that for the purpose of marketing electronic communications services or for the provision of value added services, the provider of a publicly available electronic communications service may process the data referred to in Article 6(1) to the extent and for the duration necessary for such services or marketing, if the subscriber or user to whom the data relate has given his/her consent. Users or subscribers shall be given the possibility to withdraw their consent for the processing of traffic data at any time.

Article 6(3) provides that the service provider must inform the subscriber or user of the types of traffic data which are processed and of the duration of such processing for the purposes mentioned in Article 6(2) and, prior to obtaining consent, for the purposes mentioned in Article 6(3).

Article 6(3) provides that processing of traffic data, in accordance with Article 6(1), (2), (3) and (4), must be restricted to persons acting under the authority of providers of the public communications networks and publicly available electronic communications services handling billing or traffic management, customer enquiries, fraud detection, marketing electronic communications services or providing a value added service, and must be restricted to what is necessary for the purposes of such activities.

Article 6(6) provides that Articles 6(1), (2), (3) and (5) shall apply without prejudice to the possibility for competent bodies to be informed of traffic data in conformity with applicable legislation with a view to settling disputes, in particular interconnection or billing disputes.

Non-Itemised Billing

22.17 Article 7 relates to itemised billing. Article 7(1) provides that subscribers shall have the right to receive non-itemised bills. Article 7(2) provides that states shall apply national provisions in order to reconcile the rights of subscribers receiving itemised bills with the right to privacy of calling users and called subscribers, for example by ensuring that sufficient alternative privacy enhancing methods of communications or payments are available to such users and subscribers.

Calling and Connected Line Identification

22.18 Article 8 relates to presentation and restriction of calling and connected line identification. Article 8(1) provides that where presentation of calling line identification is offered, the service provider must offer the calling user the possibility, using a simple means and free of charge, of preventing the presentation of the calling line identification on a per-call basis. The calling subscriber must have this possibility on a per-line basis.

Article 8(2) provides that where presentation of calling line identification is offered, the service provider must offer the called subscriber the possibility, using a simple means and free of charge for reasonable use of this function, of preventing the presentation of the calling line identification of incoming calls.

Article 8(3) provides that where presentation of calling line identification is offered and where the calling line identification is presented prior to the call being established, the service provider must offer the called subscriber the possibility, using a simple means, of rejecting incoming calls where the presentation of the calling line identification has been prevented by the calling user or subscriber.

Article 8(4) provides that where presentation of connected line identification is offered, the service provider must offer the called subscriber the possibility, using a simple means and free of charge, of preventing the presentation of the connected line identification to the calling user.

Article 8(5) provides that Article 8(1) shall also apply with regard to calls to third countries originating in the EU. Paragraphs (2), (3) and (4) shall also apply to incoming calls originating in third countries.

Article 8(6) provides that states shall ensure that where presentation of calling and/or connected line identification is offered, the providers of publicly available electronic communications services inform the public thereof and of the possibilities set out in paras (1), (2), (3) and (4).

Location Data other than Traffic Data

22.19   Article 9 of the ePD relates to location data other than traffic data. Article 9(1) provides that where location data other than traffic data, relating to users or subscribers of public communications networks or publicly available electronic communications services, can be processed, such data may only be processed when they are made anonymous, or with the *consent* of the users or subscribers to the extent and for the duration necessary for the provision of a value added service. The service provider must inform the users or subscribers, prior to obtaining their consent, of the type of location data other than traffic data which will be processed, of the purposes and duration of the processing and whether the data will be transmitted to a third party for the purpose of providing the value added service. Users or subscribers shall be given the possibility to withdraw their consent for the processing of location data other than traffic data at any time.

This is increasingly important as more and more smart phones and electronic devices permit the capture of location based data relating to individuals and/or their personal equipment.

Article 9(1) provides that where consent of the users or subscribers has been obtained for the processing of location data other than traffic data, the user or subscriber must continue to have the possibility, using a simple means and free of charge, of temporarily refusing the processing of such data for each connection to the network or for each transmission of a communication.

Article 9(1) provides that processing of location data other than traffic data in accordance with Articles 9(1) and (2) must be restricted to persons acting under the authority of the provider of the public communications network or publicly available communications service or of the third party providing the value added service, and must be restricted to what is necessary for the purposes of providing the value added service.

Exceptions

22.20   Article 10 relates to exceptions.

Directories

22.21   Article 12 refers to directories of subscribers. Article 12(1) provides that states shall ensure that subscribers are informed, free of charge and before they are included in the directory, about the purpose(s) of a printed or electronic directory of subscribers available to the public or obtainable through directory enquiry services, in which their personal data can be included and of any further usage possibilities based on search functions embedded in electronic versions of the directory.

Article 12(2) provides that states shall ensure that subscribers are given the opportunity to determine whether their personal data are included in a public directory, and if so, which, to the extent that such data are relevant for the purpose of the directory as determined by the provider of the directory, and to verify, correct or withdraw such data. Not being included in a public subscriber directory, verifying, correcting or withdrawing personal data from it shall be free of charge.

Article 12(3) provides that states may require that for any purpose of a public directory other than the search of contact details of persons on the basis of their name and, where necessary, a minimum of other identifiers, additional consent be asked of the subscribers.

Article 12(4) provides that Articles 12(1) and (2) shall apply to subscribers who are natural persons. states shall also ensure, in the framework of EU law and applicable national legislation, that the legitimate interests of subscribers other than natural persons with regard to their entry in public directories are sufficiently protected.

ePrivacy Regulation

22.22   There have been over a dozen draft updated versions of the ePrivacy Regulation. Some of the main provisions are:

- consent;
- confidentiality of electronic communications data;
- permitted processing of electronic communications data;
- permitted processing of electronic communications content;
- permitted processing of electronic communications metadata;
- compatible processing of electronic communications metadata;
- storage and erasure of electronic communications data;
- protection of end-users' terminal equipment information;
- restrictions;
- presentation and restriction of calling and connected line identification;
- exceptions to presentation and restriction of calling and connected line identification in relation to emergency communications;
- blocking unwanted, malicious or nuisance calls;
- publicly available directories;
- unsolicited and direct marketing communications;
- supervisory authorities;
- European Data Protection Board;
- cross-border cooperation;
- remedies;
- right to compensation and liability;
- general conditions for imposing administrative fines;
- penalties;
- exercise of the delegation;
- repeal.

These issues and new legal requirements will need to be incorporated into the compliance processes of companies engaging in the covered activities. Attention will be needed to ensure that the enactment and go live date issues are adhered to.

Conclusion

22.23   Originally envisaged as relating to telecoms type data only, this secondary aspect of the data protection regime has expanded in substance, scope and detail. While much of it is still specific to telecoms companies and entities involved in the transfer of electronic communications, certain issues are more generally applicable. The ePD as amended applies to all organisations who wish to engage in direct marketing through a variety of means. Compliance is necessary and needs to be planned in advance. If not specifically exempted from the default rule it is difficult to envisage permissible direct marketing (DM).

The ePD and the above comments all need to be read in light of the final version of the provisions formulated in the new ePrivacy Regulation, as well as national regulations which may be repealed, amended or updated as a result. However, it is critically important for companies and organisations to ensure that they become aware of the implications of the ePrivacy Regulation once it is (finally) enacted.

Chapter 23

ePrivacy and Marketing (UK)

Introduction

23.01 Direct marketing (DM) tends to be one of the most contentious areas of data protection practice. It also receives probably most attention by data regulators on foot of public complaints, with the possible exceptions of data breach/data loss issues (eg Cathay Pacific Airways ICO data breach fine of £500,000 for failing to protect customers' personal data) and internet/social media data protection issues (eg recent TikTok investigation and ICO fine of £12.7 million).

Most organisations need to engage in (DM) at some stage, some more heavily than others. Many organisations may even go so far as to say that DM is an essential ingredient of their continued commercial success.

However, DM is sometimes viewed as Spam and unsolicited commercial communications which are unwanted and also unlawful. The data protection regime (and eCommerce legal regime) refers to permissible DM and sets out various obligatory requirements while at the same time setting a default position of prohibiting non-exempted or non-permitted electronic direct marketing.

The EU General Data Protection Regulation (GDPR) does not impose additional obligations on natural or legal persons in relation to the processing of personal data in connection with the provision of publicly available electronic communications services in public communication networks in the EU in relation to matters for which they are subject to specific obligations with the same objective set out in Directive data 2002/58/EC[1] (Article 95 of the GDPR). The issues of e-marketing and ePrivacy are instead more directly encompassed within the ePrivacy Directive (ePD). The UK ePrivacy data protection regime mirrors what is contained in the ePrivacy Directive. This is contained in the Privacy and Electronic Communications Regulations (PECR).[2] These were enacted in the UK while the UK was an EU member state.

The ePrivacy Regulation, once finalised, will repeal the ePrivacy Directive and change the EU ePrivacy legal regime. This necessitates careful review for UK companies looking towards the EU in their business focus. It will also require attention insofar as the PECR may be amended by further changes to mirror the ePrivacy Regulation.

In addition, readers will need to carefully consider the final enacted version of the Data Protection and Digital Information (No 2) Bill, as this will also make changes to the ePrivacy regime in the UK.

---

1   Directive 2002/58/EC of the European Parliament and of the Council of 12 July 2002 concerning the processing of personal data and the protection of privacy in the electronic communications sector (Directive on privacy and electronic communications).
2   Privacy and Electronic Communications (EC Directive) Regulations 2003, SI 2003/2426.

However, in the meantime, companies need to remain aware of and compliant with the current version of the PECR.

Direct Marketing (DM)

23.02 If the organisation anticipates that personal data kept by it will be processed for the purposes of DM, it must inform the persons to whom the data relates that they may object by means of a request in writing to the Controller and free of charge.[3]

Unsolicited Communications

23.03 Article 13 of the ePD, which provides the backdrop to the UK PECR, refers to unsolicited communications. Article 13(1) provides that the use of automated calling systems without human intervention (automatic calling machines), facsimile machines (fax) or electronic mail for the purposes of direct marketing may only be allowed in respect of subscribers who have given their prior consent.

Article 13(2) provides that notwithstanding Article 13(1), where a natural or legal person obtains from its customers their electronic contact details for email, in the context of the sale of a product or a service, in accordance with the DPD, the same natural or legal person may use these electronic contact details for direct marketing of its own similar products or services provided that customers clearly and distinctly are given the opportunity to object, free of charge and in an easy manner, to such use of electronic contact details when they are collected and on the occasion of each message in case the customer has not initially refused such use.

Article 13(3) provides that states shall take appropriate measures to ensure that, free of charge, unsolicited communications for purposes of DM, in cases other than those referred to in Article 13(1) and (2), are not allowed either without the consent of the subscribers concerned or in respect of subscribers who do not wish to receive these communications, the choice between these options to be determined by national legislation.

Article 13(4) provides that in any event, the practice of sending electronic mail for purposes of DM disguising or concealing the identity of the sender on whose behalf the communication is made, or without a valid address to which the recipient may send a request that such communications cease, shall be prohibited.

Article 13(5) provides that Article 13(1) and (3) shall apply to subscribers who are natural persons. states shall also ensure that the legitimate interests of subscribers other than natural persons with regard to unsolicited communications are sufficiently protected.

Marketing Default Position

23.04 How should organisations go about data protection compliance DM? When is DM permitted? All organisations should carefully assess compliance issues when considering any DM activities. Getting it wrong can be costly and can have ICO enforcement and investigation consequences, not to mention penalties. Indeed, a penalty of £440,000, for example, was imposed in relation to spam DM (see ICO cases chart).

---

3   See, for example, L Edwards, 'Consumer Privacy Law 1: Online Direct Marketing,' and L Edwards and J Hatcher, 'Consumer Privacy Law: Data Collection, Profiling and Targeting,' each in L Edwards and C Waelde, eds, *Law and the Internet* (Hart, 2009) 489 *et seq*, and 511 *et seq* respectively.

Article 13 of the ePD provides a number of rules in relation to unsolicited communications. Article 13(1) provides that:

- automated calling systems without human intervention (automatic calling machines);
- facsimile machines (fax); or
- electronic mail,

for the purposes of DM may *only* be allowed in respect of subscribers who have given their *prior consent*.

Therefore, there is a default rule prohibiting the forms of DM referred to above *without* prior consent. Many marketing orientated organisations may consider this a hindrance to what may have been considered legitimate marketing and business activities.

Limited Direct Marketing Permitted

23.05 Limited direct marketing is permitted, namely, of subscribers or customers whom have given their prior consent. This implies consent in advance of receiving the DM or simultaneous to the DM.

However, in terms of DM by email, this is further restricted.

Direct Marketing to Existing Customers' Email

23.06 In the context of existing customers, there is a possibility to DM using emails. Article 13(2) of the ePD provides that where an organisation obtains from its customers their electronic contact details for email, in the context of the sale of a product or a service, in accordance with the DPD, the organisation may use these electronic contact details for DM of its own similar products or services provided that customers clearly and distinctly are given the opportunity to object, free of charge and in an easy manner, to such use of electronic contact details when they are collected and on the occasion of each message in case the customer has not initially refused such use.

Therefore, once the email details are obtained at the time of a product or service transaction, it will be possible to use that email for direct marketing purposes. Conditions or limitations apply however. Firstly, the organisation is only permitted to market and promote similar products or services. This, therefore, rules out unrelated, non-identical and non-similar products and services. Secondly, at the time of each subsequent act of DM, the customer must be given the opportunity in an easy and accessible manner to opt out or cancel the DM. Effectively, they must be taken off of the organisation's DM list.

National Marketing Opt-out Registers

23.07 Article 13(3) of ePD provides that states shall take appropriate measures to ensure that, free of charge, unsolicited communications for purposes of direct marketing, in cases other than those referred to in Article 13(1) and (2), are not allowed either without the consent of the subscribers concerned or in respect of subscribers who do not wish to receive these communications, the choice between these options to be determined by national legislation. This means that each state must determine and provide a means for individuals to opt-out of receiving DM in advance.[4]

---

4   See ICO, *Marketing*, at https://ico.org.uk.

Various of the cases where marketing breach data fines are imposed by the ICO involve unsolicited marketing calls being made to telephone numbers registered on the telephone preference service (TPS), whereby individuals can register their preference not to be the recipients of marketing calls. Examples of illegal TPS marketing call breaches include:

- It's OK Limited – fined £200,000;[5]
- Boiler Cover Breakdown Limited – fined £120,000;[6]
- Boiler Breakdown Limited – fined £140,000;[7]
- Superior Style Home Improvements – fined £150,000;[8]
- Making it Easy – fined £160,000;[9]
- Smart Home Protection – fined £90,000;[10]
- Avalon Direct – fined £80,000;[11]
- Solartech North East – fined £90,000;[12]
- DM Design Bedrooms – fined £160,000;[13]
- Secure Home Systems – fined £80,000;[14]
- ACT Response – fined £140,000;[15]
- AMS Marketing – fined £100,000.[16]

Deceptive Emails: Marketing Emails Must Not Conceal Identity

23.08 Article 13(4) of ePD provides that the practice of sending email for purposes of DM disguising or concealing the identity of the sender on whose behalf the communication is made shall be prohibited. This means that organisations cannot conceal their identity if permitted to engage in direct marketing. If these are not complied with, what might otherwise be permissible DM can be deemed to be impermissible. Complaints, investigations or enforcement proceedings can thus arise.

Marketing Emails Must Provide Opt-Out

23.09 In addition, Article 13(4) of ePD provides that the practice of sending email for purposes of DM without a valid address to which the recipient may send a request that such communications cease, shall be prohibited. This means that organisations must also include an easy contact address or other details at which the recipient can contact if they wish to object to receiving any further DM. If these are not complied with, what might otherwise be permissible DM can be deemed to be impermissible. Complaints, investigations or enforcement proceedings can thus also arise.

Marketing Protection for Organisations

23.10 Article 13(5) of the ePD provides that Article 13(1) and (3) shall apply to subscribers who are natural persons. States shall also ensure, in the framework of

---

5   *ICO v It's OK Limited* [2023] 15/2/2023.
6   *ICO v Boiler Cover Breakdown Limited* [2022] 7/12/2022.
7   *ICO v Boiler Breakdown Limited* [2022] 7/12/2022.
8   *ICO v Superior Style Home Improvements Limited* [2019] 17/9/2019.
9   *ICO v Making it Easy Limited* [2019] 2/8/2019.
10 *ICO v Smart Home Protection Limited* [2019] 13/6/2019.
11 *ICO v Avalon Direct* [2019] 16/4/2019.
12 *ICO v Solartech North East Limited* [2018] 23/11/2018.
13 *ICO v DM Design Bedrooms* [2018] 23/11/2018.
14 *ICO v Secure Home Systems* [2018] 31/10/2018.
15 *ICO v ACT Response* [2018] 30/10/2018.
16 *ICO v AMS Marketing* [2018] 1/8/2018.

EU law and applicable national legislation, that the legitimate interests of subscribers other than natural persons with regard to unsolicited communications are sufficiently protected. This means that protection from unsolicited DM can also be extended to organisations.

PECR

23.11   Detailed provisions governing direct marketing by electronic communications are set out in the UK PECR (Privacy and Electronic Communications (EC Directive) Regulations 2003[17]) (originally implementing the ePD in the UK prior to Brexit). Note that PECR will likely be updated, amended and/or replaced once the full extent of the enacted ePrivacy Regulation is known.

It provides rules in relation to automated calling machine; fax; email; unsolicited call by automated calling machine or fax; unsolicited telephone call; disguising or concealing identity; contact address; opt in/opt out; and 'soft opt in.'

The PECR are also interesting in that they apply to both legal and natural persons. Generally, rights are not recognised for organisations in the data protection regime.

The PECR refer to the implementation of the rules regarding electronic communications and direct marketing DM).

Regulation 21A refers to calls for direct marketing of claims management services.[18] Regulation 21B refers to calls for direct marketing in relation to pension schemes.[19]

Regulations 22 and 23 refer to email marketing.[20] Regulation 22 of the PECR provides as follows:

'(1)   This regulation applies to the transmission of unsolicited communications by means of electronic mail to individual subscribers.

(2)   Except in the circumstances referred to in paragraph (3), a person shall neither transmit, nor instigate the transmission of, unsolicited communications for the purposes of direct marketing by means of electronic mail unless the recipient of the electronic mail has previously notified the sender that he consents for the time being to such communications being sent by, or at the instigation of, the sender.

(3)   A person may send or instigate the sending of electronic mail for the purposes of direct marketing where:

  (a)   that person has obtained the contact details of the recipient of that electronic mail in the course of the sale or negotiations for the sale of a product or service to that recipient;

  (b)   the direct marketing is in respect of that person's similar products and services only; and

  (c)   the recipient has been given a simple means of refusing (free of charge except for the costs of the transmission of the refusal) the use of his contact details for the purposes of such direct marketing, at the time that the details were initially collected, and, where he did not initially refuse the use of the details, at the time of each subsequent communication.

(4)   A subscriber shall not permit his line to be used in contravention of paragraph (2).'

---

17   SI 2003/2426.
18   See the Privacy and Electronic Communications (EC Directive) Regulations 2003, SI 2003/2426.
19   Ibid.
20   Privacy and Electronic Communications (EC Directive) Regulations 2003, at https://www.legislation.gov.uk/uksi/2003/2426/contents/made.

Regulation 23 of the PECR[21] provides as follows:

'A person shall neither transmit, nor instigate the transmission of, a communication for the purposes of direct marketing by means of electronic mail:

(a) where the identity of the person on whose behalf the communication has been sent has been disguised or concealed; ...

(b) where a valid address to which the recipient of the communication may send a request that such communications cease has not been provided;

[(c) where that electronic mail would contravene regulation 7 of the Electronic Commerce (EC Directive) Regulations 2002; or

(d) where that electronic mail encourages recipients to visit websites which contravene that regulation.]'

Regulation 24 of the PECR is also relevant in that it provides the information which must be furnished with the direct marketing so that the recipient may contact the organisation to opt-out, namely:

● the name of the organisation; and

● either the address of the person or a telephone number on which he can be reached free of charge.

Regulation 19 of the PECR prohibits the use of automated calling machines for the purposes of direct marketing.

The use of fax machines for the purposes of direct marketing is restricted in reg 20 of the PECR.

See https://ico.org.uk/for-organisations/direct-marketing-and-electronic-communications/ guide-to-pecr/guidance-on-direct-marketing-using-electronic-mail/. It is expected that once the EU ePrivacy rules are finalised, the PECR in the UK will be amended or replaced.

ICO PECR Guidance

23.12 The ICO's previous guidance stated as follows:

'The Regulations define electronic mail as "any text, voice, sound, or image message sent over a public electronic communications network which can be stored in the network or in the recipient's terminal equipment until it is collected by the recipient and includes messages sent using a short message service" (Regulation 2 "Interpretation" applies).

In other words, email, text, picture and video marketing messages are all considered to be "electronic mail". Marketing transmitted in WAP messages is considered to be "electronic mail". WAP Push allows a sender to send a specially formatted SMS message to a handset which, when received, allows a recipient through a single click to access and view content stored online, through the browser on the handset.

We consider this rule also applies to voicemail and answerphone messages left by marketers making marketing calls that would otherwise be "live". So there are stricter obligations placed on you if you make live calls but then wish to leave messages on a person's voicemail or answerphone.

Faxes are not considered to be "electronic mail". Fax marketing is covered elsewhere in the Regulations. These regulations also do not cover so-called silent calls or calls where a fax

---

21 As amended by the Privacy and Electronic Communications (EC Directive) (Amendment) Regulations 2011 (SI 2011/1208).

or other electronic signal is transmitted; this is because no marketing material is transmitted during these calls.'[22]

It adds that:

'This is what the law requires:

- You cannot transmit, or instigate the transmission of, unsolicited marketing material by electronic mail to an individual subscriber unless they have previously notified you, the sender, that they consent, for the time being, to receiving such communications. There is an exception to this rule which has been widely referred to as the soft opt in (Regulation 22 (2) refers).
- You cannot transmit, or instigate the transmission of, any marketing by electronic mail (whether solicited or unsolicited) to any subscriber (whether corporate or individual) where:
  - Your identity has been disguised or concealed; or
  - You have not provided a valid address to which the recipient can send an opt-out request.
  - That electronic mail would contravene regulations 7 or 8 of the Electronic Commerce (EC Directive) Regulations 2002 (SI 2002/2013); or
  - That electronic mail encourages recipients to visit websites which contravene those regulations (Regulation 23 refers).
- A subscriber must not allow their line to be used to breach Regulation 22 (2) (Regulation 22 (4) refers).'[23]

This is an area that is apt for change in both rules and official guidance so it is an area where ongoing review of the ICO guidance is recommended. Certain current ICO guidance is titled 'Guidance on direct marketing using electronic mail'.[24]

Offences by Direct Marketers under PECR

23.13   Offences arise in relation to activities referred to under PECR. These include:

- sending unsolicited marketing messages to individuals by fax, SMS, email or automated dialling machine;
- sending unsolicited marketing by fax, SMS, email or automated dialling machine to a business if it has objected to the receipt of such messages;
- marketing by telephone where the subscriber has objected to the receipt of such calls;
- failing to identify the caller or sender or failing to provide a physical address or a return email address;
- failing to give customers the possibility of objecting to future email and SMS marketing messages with each message sent;
- concealing the identity of the sender on whose behalf the marketing communication was made.

Fines can be significant. Organisations can be fined up to £500,000 by the ICO for unwanted marketing phone calls and emails in accordance with the updated amended PECR. It is also envisaged that fines will increase significantly under the GDPR and ePrivacy Regulation.

---

22 ICO, *Electronic Mail*, at https://ico.org.uk.
23 See above.
24 See https://ico.org.uk/for-organisations/direct-marketing-and-privacy-and-electronic-communications/ guide-to-pecr/guidance-on-direct-marketing-using-electronic-mail/.

ICO Monetary Penalties

23.14 The ICO was also empowered under the Criminal Justice and Immigration Act 2008 (CJIA 2008) to impose penalties of a monetary variety. Section 77 of the CJIA 2008 provides power to alter penalty for unlawfully obtaining etc personal data. Fines and penalties for electronic marketing related offences are being increased under the GDPR and ePrivacy Regulation.

Civil Sanctions

23.15 Individual Data Subjects can also sue for compensation under the data protection rules. Where a person suffers damage as a result of a failure by a Controller or Processor to meet their data protection obligations, then the Controller or Processor may be subject to civil sanctions by the person affected. Damage suffered by a Data Subject will include damage to reputation, financial loss and mental distress.

This will vary from organisation to organisation, sector to sector, the type of personal data involved, the risks of damage, loss, etc, the nature of the security risks, the security measures and procedures adopted, the history of risk, loss and damage in the organisation and sector.

Certain types of data will convey inherent additional risks over others, such as loss of financial personal data. This can be argued to require higher obligations for the organisation.

One interesting area to consider going forward is online damage, such as viral abuse, publication, defamation, bulletin boards, discussion forums and websites (or sections of websites), and social media websites. Where damage occurs as a result of misuse or loss of personal data or results in defamation, abuse and threats, liability could arise for the individual tortfeasors as well as the website.

While there are eCommerce defences in the eCommerce Directive, one should recall that the data protection regime (and its duty of care and liability provisions) are separate and stand alone from the eCommerce Directive legal regime. Indeed, even in terms of the eCommerce defences one should also recall that (a) an organisation must first fall within an eCommerce defence, and not lost that defence, in order to avail of it; and (b) there is no automatic entitlement to an internet service provider (ISP) or website to a global eCommerce defence, as in fact there in not one eCommerce defence but three specific defences relating to specific and technical activities. Not all or every ISP activity will fall into one of these defences. Neither will one activity fall into all three defences.

It is also possible to conceive of a website which has no take down procedures, inadequate take down defences, or non-expeditious take down procedures or remedies, and which will face potential liability under privacy and data protection as well as eCommerce liability. For example, an imposter social media profile which contains abuse, personal data and defamatory material could attract liability for the website operator under data protection, and under normal liability if none of the eCommerce defences were unavailable or were lost. The later could occur if, for example, the false impersonating profile was notified to the website (or it was otherwise aware) but it did not do anything.[25]

---

25 This is a complex and developing area of law, common law, civil law, GDPR, forthcoming ePrivacy Regulation and case law, both in the UK and internationally. A full detailed analysis is beyond this current work.

PECR implemented ePD (also known as the ePrivacy Directive) regarding the protection of privacy in the electronic communications sector. In 2009 ePD was amended by Directive 2009/136/EC. This included changes to Article 5(3) of ePD requiring consent for the storage or access to information stored on a subscriber or users terminal equipment ie a requirement for organisations to obtain consent for cookies and similar technologies.[26] The ePrivacy Regulation will add/import updates and replacements to this area which organisations will need to incorporate and comply with.

Call and Fax Opt Out Registers

23.16 The Telephone Preference Service (TPS) and Fax Preference Service (FPS), operated by the Direct Marketing Association, are registers that allow people to register their numbers and their preference to opt out of receiving unsolicited calls or faxes. Therefore, an organisation proposing to use call or fax for DM, must first consult these registers to ensure that no contact details are used which are already registered on these registers.

The Spam Problem

23.17 Spam is just one of a number of names taken to describe the problem of unsolicited electronic commercial marketing materials. The Spam name comes originally from a Monty Python comic sketch. However, electronic Spam is far from comic and costs industry hundreds of millions of pounds each year in employee lost time and resources, in lost bandwidth, in reduced capacity and network speed, as well as other problems.

Spam Internationally

23.18 The growing recognition of the problems caused by Spam, such as scams, viruses, lost productivity and bandwidth, has meant an increasing number of local and national laws specifically dedicated to preventing Spam.

In the US for example there a large number of local state laws[27] and national federal laws dedicated to tackling Spam. These include both new specific laws and Spam specific amendments to pre-existing laws. A US federal Spam act known as the CANSPAM Act was introduced.[28]

Related Issues

23.19 Certain related issues also arise, which are beyond detailed analysis presently but which may be used for specific organisations to consider further.

One example is the increasingly controversial area of profiling, advertising and direct marketing in relation to children.[29]

---

26 The same comments apply, see above.
27 See www.spamlaws.com.
28 See VJ Reid, 'Recent Developments in Private Enforcement of the Can-Spam Act,' *Akron Intellectual Property Journal* (2010) (4) 281–307.
29 U Munukutla-Parker, 'Unsolicited Commercial E-mail, Privacy Concerns Related to Social Network Services, Online Protection of Children, and Cyberbullying,' *I/S: A Journal of Law and Policy* (2006) (2) 628–650.

Online behavioural advertising (OBA) and the behavioural targeting of internet advertising is increasingly debated.[30]

Commentators, and media, often focus on the issue of threats to privacy, data protection and reputation rights caused by web 2.0 activities such as social media, search engine services, etc. The query arises as to whether revenue versus privacy is better respected by certain online services providers?[31]

Cases

23.20   There are many official cases, prosecutions and fines in relation to Spam. Some of the largest fines from the ICO have been in relation to Spam and unsolicited marketing (in addition to the growing area of data breaches).

DPDI and PECR

23.21   The Data Protection and Digital Information (No 2) Bill (DPDI Bill), separate and in addition to any changes which may occur after the ePrivacy Regulation, seeks to make changes in relation to the ePrivacy and PECR in the UK.

Part 4 of the DPDI Bill refers to privacy and electronic communications. It contains provisions and amendments in relation to:

- the REC Regulation (ie PECR) (clause 78);
- storing information in the terminal equipment of a subscriber or user (clause 79);
- unreceived communications (clause 80);
- meaning of 'direct marketing' (clause 81);
- use of electronic mail for direct marketing purposes (clause 82);
- direct marketing for the purposes of democratic engagement (clause 83);
- meaning of expressions in clause 83 (clause 84);
- duty to notify the Commissioner of unlawful direct marketing (clause 85);
- Commissioner's enforcement powers (clause 86).

Conclusion

23.22   Few organisations will not be interested in DM and advertising. The key is to get it right. The consequences of sending unlawful electronic communications can amount to offences, prosecutions official enforcement and investigations as well as being sued or prosecuted. This is one of the areas which is consistently an area of focus from ICO investigation. These issues become more important as: (a) increased competition puts pressure on organisations to engage, or increase, marketing and profiling efforts; and (b) the software, devices and technologies available to facilitate such efforts are increasing in significance. Over time, cost efforts also decrease in terms of adopting these new tools. As always, however, organisations are cautioned to ensure data protection compliance. They might also, on occasion, pause to question general ethical consideration in certain instances. Depending on the sector, there may also be an obligation to consider and comply with certain third party organisational

---

30   Deane-Johns, 'Behavioural Targeting of Internet Advertising,' *Computers and Law* (2009) (20) 22.
31   L Edwards and C Waelde, eds, *Law and the Internet* (Oxford: Hart, 2009) 539.

rules, particularly as regards direct marketing issues. Indeed, the new regime also provides the impetus for representative organisations to increasingly consider industry-wide data protection Codes of Conduct. These are encouraged by the ICO and the new data protection regime. It is also important to look out for the changes that may occur as a result of the ePrivacy Regulation once available.

Part 4
UK Regime

Chapter 24

Background to the UK Regime

Introduction

24.01 The UK data protection regime is fundamentally changed. It should not be viewed as a big bang development, however. Rather, as the ICO has pointed out, it is an 'evolution' not a 'revolution.'[1] The previous data protection regime was over 20 years' old and required substantial redevelopment and updating.

Pre-Brexit Uncertainty

A New Act

24.02 'The [new Act] will bring the European Union's [GDPR] into UK law, helping Britain prepare for a successful Brexit.'[2] This is only partly correct, as the Data Protection Act 2018 (DPA 2018) only partly implements the GDPR.

Data protection was one of the more significant complicating factors leading up to Brexit transition – both during official negotiations and from the perspective of all of the sought after certainty that industry wished for. Indeed, it is still one of the more significant post-Brexit issues given the commercial significance of maintaining the ability, or restoring the ability, of commercial data transfers from the EU into the UK. In order to trade with the EU and for EU personal data to be transferred to the UK (as is required in many trade, banking, service, travel and education examples), it must deal with the default transfer ban. EU personal data may only be transferred to countries and/or entities deemed to have proper and equivalent data security and data protection standards as the EU data protection regime. With that in mind it is obvious that the UK wishes to continue to maintain an equivalent EU standard for the protection, collection, use and storage of personal data. Indeed, the government has indicated that it wishes to even go further than the GDPR standards.[3] Julian David, the CEO of techUK, states:

---

1   Steve Wood, Deputy Commissioner (Policy), 'GDPR is an Evolution in Data Protection, Not a Burdensome Revolution,' ICO, 25 August 2017.
2   'A New Law Will Ensure That the United Kingdom Retains Its World-Class Regime Protecting Personal Data.' *The Queen's Speech and Associated Background Briefing, on the Occasion of the Opening of Parliament on Wednesday 21 June 2017* (Prime Minister's Office, 10 Downing Street, London, SW1A 2AA) (21 June 2017).
3   'UK's proposed Data Protection Bill looks to go further than GDPR,' Information-Age.com, 8 August 2017. This is also interesting from the perspective of some standards exceeding the GDPR, but other standards which might be argued to be less than the GDPR level. Even if there are one or two aspects which are below the GDPR level, that is very problematic to an adequacy decision application.

'techUK supports the aim of a Data Protection [Act] that implements GDPR in full, puts the UK in a strong position to secure unhindered data flows once it has left the EU, and gives businesses the clarity they need about their new obligations.'[4]

Queen's Speech

24.03 The 2017 Queens Speech[5] forecast the Data Protection Act 2018 (DPA 2018) changes as follows:

'A new law [to] ensure that the United Kingdom retains its world-class regime protecting personal data, and ... a new digital charter ... to ensure that the United Kingdom is the safest place to be online.'

Background Briefing Document

24.04 A government official document[6] also states that the main purpose is 'Make our data protection framework suitable for our new digital age, allowing citizens to better control their data.' The main benefits are:

- 'to meet the manifesto commitments to give people new rights to "require major social media platforms to delete information held about them at the age of 18" ... and to "bring forward a new data protection law".
- To ensure that our data protection framework is suitable for our new digital age, and cement the UK's position at the forefront of technological innovation, international data sharing and protection of personal data.
- To allow police and judicial authorities to continue to exchange information quickly and easily with our international partners in the fight against terrorism and other serious crimes.
- To implement the [GDPR] and the new Directive which applies to law enforcement data processing, meeting our obligations while we remain an EU member state and helping to put the UK in the best position to maintain our ability to share data with other EU member states and internationally after we leave the EU.'

The main elements of the DPA 2018 are described as:

- 'To establish a new data protection regime for non-law enforcement data processing ... The new rules strengthen rights and empower individuals to have more control over their personal data, including a right to be forgotten when individuals no longer want their data to be processed, provided that there are no legitimate grounds for retaining it.
- To modernise and update the regime for data processing by law enforcement agencies. The regime will cover both domestic processing and cross-border transfers of personal data.
- To update the powers and sanctions available to the [ICO].'

---

4   'A New Law Will Ensure That the United Kingdom Retains Its World-Class Regime Protecting Personal Data.' *The Queen's Speech and Associated Background Briefing, on the Occasion of the Opening of Parliament on Wednesday 21 June 2017* (Prime Minister's Office, 10 Downing Street, London, SW1A 2AA) (21 June 2017).
5   Queen's Speech 2017, 21 June 2017.
6   'A New Law Will Ensure That the United Kingdom Retains Its World-Class Regime Protecting Personal Data.' *The Queen's Speech and Associated Background Briefing, on the Occasion of the Opening of Parliament on Wednesday 21 June 2017* (Prime Minister's Office, 10 Downing Street, London, SW1A 2AA) (21 June 2017).

Digital Charter and Internet Safety

24.05   The official background briefing document also refers to a Digital Charter and issues of online safety. It states 'proposals for a new digital charter will be brought forward to ensure that the United Kingdom is the safest place to be online.' More specifically it states:

- 'We will develop a Digital Charter that will create a new framework which balances users' and businesses' freedom and security online.
- The Charter will have two core objectives: making the UK the best place to start and run a digital business *and the safest place in the world to be online.*[7]
- We will work with technology companies, charities, communities and international partners to develop the Charter; and we will make sure it is underpinned by an effective regulatory framework.
- We are optimistic about the opportunities on offer in the digital age, but we understand these opportunities come with new challenges and threats – to our security, privacy, emotional wellbeing, mental health and the safety of our children. We will respond to these challenges, assuring security and fairness in the new digital age and strengthening the UK's position as one of the world's leading digital economies.
- We strongly support a free and open internet. But, as in the offline world, freedoms online must be balanced with protections to ensure citizens are protected from the potential harms of the digital world. We will not shy away from tackling harmful behaviours and harmful content online – be that extremist, abusive or harmful to children. And we will make sure that technology companies do more to protect their users and improve safety online.
- Many of these challenges are of an international nature, so we will open discussions with other like-minded democracies and work with them to develop a shared approach. The Prime Minister has already started this process, securing an agreement with G7 countries to strengthen their work with tech companies on this vital agenda.
- Britain's future prosperity will be built on our technical capability and creative flair. Through our Modern Industrial Strategy and digital strategy, we will help digital companies at every stage of their growth, including by supporting access to the finance, talent and infrastructure needed for success and by making it easier for companies and consumers to do business online.'

Ministerial Statement

24.06   A Ministerial Statement[8] described how individuals are intended to 'have more control over their personal data and be better protected in the digital age under [the] new measures.' The DPA 2018 is indicated to:

- ensure the public 'have greater control over personal data – including right to be forgotten';
- ensure a '[n]ew right to require social media platforms to delete information on children and adults when asked.'

---

7   Emphasis added.
8   'Government to Strengthen UK Data Protection Law,' Department for Digital, Culture, Media & Sport and The Rt Hon Matt Hancock MP, 7 August 2017.

In terms of consent issues it states:

'The reliance on default opt-out or pre-selected "tick boxes", which are largely ignored, to give consent for organisations to collect personal data will also become a thing of the past.'

It adds that:

'Businesses will be supported to ensure they are able to manage and secure data properly. The data protection regulator, the [ICO], will also be given more power to defend consumer interests and issue higher fines, of up to £17 million or 4 per cent of global turnover, in cases of the most serious data breaches.'

The Minister of State for Digital states the DPA 2018 is:

'designed to support businesses in their use of data, and give consumers the confidence that their data is protected and those who misuse it will be held to account.

The new Data Protection [Act] ... give[s] us one of the most robust, yet dynamic, set of data laws in the world. The [DPA 2018] ... give[s] people more control over their data, require[s] more consent for its use, and prepare[s] Britain for Brexit. We have some of the best data science in the world and this new law will help it to thrive.'

In addition, it states that the updated data protection regime:

- makes it simpler for individuals to *withdraw consent* for the use of their personal data;
- allows individuals to ask for their personal data held by companies to be *erased*;
- enables *parents and guardians* to give consent for their *child's data* to be used;
- requires *'explicit' consent* to be necessary for processing *sensitive personal data*;
- expands the *definition of 'personal data'* to include IP addresses, internet cookies and DNA;
- updates and strengthens data protection law to reflect the changing nature and scope of the *digital economy*;
- makes it easier and free for individuals to require an organisation to disclose the personal data it holds on them (*assess* issues);
- makes it easier for customers to move data between service providers (*data portability*).

New criminal offences 'are created to deter organisations from either intentionally or recklessly creating situations where someone could be identified from anonymised data.' Re-identification issues are increasingly complex and problematic. This is particularly important as the concept of anonymisation has been seen as one of the tools available to data protection, data life cycles, security and safety.

The data protection rules 'are made clearer for those who handle data but they will be made more accountable for the data they process with the priority on personal privacy rights.' Also,

'Those organisations carrying out high-risk data processing will be obliged to carry out impact assessments to understand the risks involved.'

Negotiations and Transition

24.07 While the referendum on the UK's membership of the EU occurred on 23 June 2016, that was only the beginning of a very long and complicated set of processes, including the UK Government have negotiated the form of what 'Brexit' might look like, important interim exit deal strategies, ultimately the passing of the EU (Withdrawal Agreement) Act 2020 in January 2020. Indeed, many complicated process aspects of Brexit are still continuing.

Notwithstanding the interim negotiations and the EU (Withdrawal Agreement) Act 2020 passing, there was for some time a possibility of a so-called 'no deal Brexit' whereby Brexit Day may have arrived without a formal exit arrangement having been agreed, and which would have caused even more problems than the final agreed version of Brexit that ultimately transpired.

The possibility of a no deal was so concerning that the Bank of England, for example, advised lenders in June to ramp up preparations for the nightmare of a no-deal Brexit.[9]

However, regardless of the exit strategy, there still undoubtedly many areas of EU law that will continue to have an effect on UK business, for example, because they remain part of UK law itself or because compliance and or equivalence is necessary in order to effectively do business with EU Member States, and the inherently cross-jurisdictional nature of the internet. Certain politicians would much prefer to excise these incorporated EU laws for political policy reasons regardless of any counter effects arising.

The 2017 Queen's Speech proposed, amongst other legislation, a European Union (Withdrawal) Bill, a Trade Bill, a Customs Bill and a Data Protection Bill – all of which may have implications in the ecommerce/Brexit field.

A draft Brexit Agreement was issued on 14 November 2018, was approved by the Cabinet, and by EU Member States on 25 November 2018. Parliament approval was ultimately obtained after a general election and the formation of a new government. (The initial attempt to obtain parliamentary approval was shelved in late 2018.) Brexit Day (also referred to as Exit Day in the European Union (Withdrawal) Act 2018) (having been triggered per the Article 50 procedure) was originally 29 March 2019 and was then delayed.

On or before the Withdrawal Treaty there were expected to be various new national laws catering for the new arrangements (and catering for equivalency as between the UK and EU legal norms).

As regards data protection, and in particular catering for ongoing data transfers, an Adequacy Decision from the EU as regards permitting data transfers on the basis of UK law being equivalent in terms of personal data is ideally required. Recall that the Data Protection Act 2018 did not implement the General Data Protection Regulation 2016/679 into the UK. While the official position is progressing in terms of a final deal or treaty.

Prior to the transition period, there was also increased focus on seeking to provide official guidance in terms of the possibility of a no deal Brexit, as that was a real possibility at that stage.

While we are in the immediate post Brexit period, the previous advice, opinions and documentation regarding a no deal Brexit and preparing for Brexit remain relevant for a number of reasons. First, most important of these is perhaps the lesson that should not be forgotten – ie how complicated Brexit overall, and data protection Brexit issues, actually are. Second, we have arguably not yet arrived in a calm, certain, and assuring position for data protection in the UK. All of the past guidance, etc is relevant to consider until we do arrive on terra firma. Third, the past guidance, etc is also useful to reassess as and when future UK data protection and Brexit controversies arise, as they will for at least a period.

In addition to UK based guidance that occurred, a number of external data protection supervisory authorities also sought to address the demand and concern for guidance.

---

9   See W Schomberg, 'Brexit: Bank of England Tells Lenders to Ramp Up Preparations For No Deal' *Independent*, 3 June 2020.

The issue of Brexit generally, and in particular what may happen in terms of data protection and data transfers, was an obvious concern for commercial entities and their advisors. Some of these concerns of course remain – even after the EU/UK adequacy decision.

Guidance

24.08   The lead up to Brexit was sometimes contentious but for concerned observers wishing for clarity in order to understand their data protection obligations, the various guidance and political discussions were not always helpful. A lot of uncertainly existed (and to an extent continues as changes continue to be made). The guidance can also be classified as pre and post-Brexit. Some of the pre-Brexit guidance can also be classified as forecasting a negotiated exit, and some anticipating a non-negotiated deal exit. While many of these are now superseded by events, they still serve as illustrative examples of the difficulties and uncertainty sometimes created as a consequence of Brexit and the Brexit process.

The ICO issued the following no deal guidance in late 2018: Announcements, descriptions and statements on No Deal Brexit; Six Steps to Take guide on No Deal Brexit; 'Broader' guidance document on leaving EU if no withdrawal agreement; and Overview FAQs guidance on No Deal Brexit.

There is also ICO guidance and commentary on data protection, transfers and: the European Union (Withdrawal) Act 2018; Department update. There is also ICO guidance, partly in relation to the possibility of a no deal Brexit arising, including a press release and related statements and electronic announcements. The release acknowledged that: '[w]hile the basis on which the UK will leave the EU has still to be decided, the ICO has today published new guidance and practical tools to help organisations understand the implications in the event of a no deal.'

The ICO documentation included: announcements and descriptions (press statement, blog post, etc); 'Six Steps to Take' guide; 'broader' guidance document on leaving EU if no withdrawal agreement; and 'Overview FAQs' guidance.

An ICO blog notes that the 'Government has made clear that the [GDPR] will be absorbed into UK law at the point of exit, so there will be no substantive change.' The GDPR was (apparently) directly effective during the transition. The blog suggests that the 'two-way free flow of personal information will no longer be the case if the UK leaves the EU without a withdrawal agreement that specifically provides [and hopefully expressly so provide] for the continued flow of personal data.' The ICO blog advises organisations to take 'precautionary preparations' to 'ensure these data flows continue' in the event of no deal. However, there was uncertainty even in the event of a deal. The official advice is to 'carefully consider alternative transfer mechanisms to maintain data flows.' One of these is the standard contractual clauses route.

'Six Steps to Take' ICO Guide

24.09   The ICO has also issued a six-step assistance guide. It states that '[i]f you operate in the EEA, you may need to comply with both the UK data protection regime and the EU regime after the UK exits the EU. You may also need to appoint a representative in the EEA.' The six steps for 'Leaving the EU' refers to: continue to comply; transfers to the UK; transfers from the UK; European operations; documentation; organisational awareness.

The first step (continue to comply) states, inter alia, that:

'The [DPA 2018] will remain in place. The government intends to bring the GDPR directly into UK law on exit, to sit alongside it. There will be some technical adjustments to the UK version of the GDPR so that it works in a UK-only context – for example, amending provisions referring to EU law and enforcement cooperation.'

The second step (transfers to the UK) states, inter alia, that organisations need to:

'Review your data flows and identify where you receive data from the EEA, including from suppliers and processors. Think about what GDPR safeguards you can put in place to ensure that data can continue to flow once we are outside the EU.'

It continues that this 'means the sender needs to make sure there are adequate safeguards in place, or one of the exceptions listed in the GDPR.'

It also refers to the importance of the adequacy decision issue.

The ICO guidance advises that '[y]ou may want to consider putting standard contractual clauses (SCCs) in place if you are receiving data from the EEA.'

The third step (transfers from the UK) refers to transfers from the UK to the EU; and also to transfers from the UK to countries outside the European Economic Area (EEA). In terms of the latter, the guidance states, inter alia, [w]e expect the UK government to confirm that the UK will reflect existing EU adequacy decisions, approved EU SCCs and BCRs.' It then cross-refers to the more detailed guidance. Readers will note that this is descriptive of some future governmental and legal decisions and rules. It is unclear specifically what this as yet refers to, nor when.

The fourth step (European operations) states inter alia that '[i]f you operate across Europe, you should review your structure, processing operations and data flows to assess how the UK's exit from the EU will affect the data protection regimes that apply to you.'

It also refers to data protection regimes and reiterates that organisations may need to comply with the EU and the UK data protection regimes, highlighting the need for dual compliance exercises. Issues of branches and establishments within the post-Brexit EU need to be considered. A further consideration is having to deal with the UK and one or more respective data protection authorities.

The need to appoint a representative located in the EU is also highlighted. Note that the Data Protection and Digital Information (No 2) Bill refers to such representatives and seeks to remove this obligation (cl 13).

The fifth step (documentation) highlights the need to review the organisation's locations, documentation, flows, processes and relationships. This applies inward facing and outward facing. Once changes occur there will be additional changes, such as identifying and differentiating EU and UK law references in documentation, policies, notices, etc.

The sixth step (organisational awareness) reiterates the need for training and internal awareness raising processes. Reference is also made to the need for organisations to have, and to update, their risk register.

'Broader' ICO Guidance

24.10 The ICO also issued a broader Brexit transfer guidance. It highlights that the (various) guidance is particularly relevant to organisations which: operate in the EEA, which includes the EU; or send personal data outside the UK; or receive personal data from the EEA.

It is also indicated to be relevant where the following apply to the organisation: the Privacy and Electronic Communications (EC Directive) Regulations 2003 (SI 2003/2426) (PECR); the Network and Information Systems Regulations 2018 (SI 2018/506) (NIS); or EU Regulation 910/2014 on electronic identification and trust services for electronic transactions in the internal market (eIDAS).

The guidance refers to the DPA 2018. It points out that it came into force at the same time as the GDPR, and covers four data protection regimes, namely: Part 2, Chapter 2: General processing – the GDPR – 'this chapter supplements the GDPR so that it operates in a UK context'; Part 2, Chapter 3: Other general processing – 'this chapter applies a UK version of the GDPR (the "applied GDPR") to those areas outside the scope of EU law, such as defence'; Part 3: Law enforcement processing – 'this chapter brings into UK law the EU Data Protection Directive 2016/680 (the Law Enforcement Directive)'; Part 4: Intelligence services processing.

ICO Overview FAQs Guidance

24.11   The ICO frequently asked questions (FAQs) guidance refers to the following guidance questions and answers:

- Will the GDPR still apply if we leave EU without a deal?
- What will the UK data protection law be if we leave without a deal?
- Is the old ICO guidance still relevant?
- Can we still transfer data to and from Europe if we leave without a deal?
- Do PECR rules still apply?
- Do network and information system (NIS) rules still apply?
- Do the electronic identification and trust services for electronic transactions in the internal market (eIDAS) rules still apply?
- Do FOIA still apply?
- Do the environmental information regulations (EIR) still apply?
- Will ICO be producing more guidance?

The first question advises that:

'The GDPR is an EU Regulation and, in principle, it will no longer apply to the UK if we leave the EU on 29 March 2019 without a deal. However, if you operate inside the UK, you will need to comply with UK data protection law. The government *intends* to incorporate the GDPR into UK data protection law when we exit the EU – so in practice there will be little change to the core data protection principles, rights and obligations found in the GDPR.' [emphasis added and 29 March 2019 has now been superseded by extensions]

In terms of organisations wishing to continue dealing with EU, its adds that the 'GDPR may also still apply directly to you if you operate in Europe, offer goods or services to individuals in Europe, or monitor the behaviour of individuals in Europe.' The GDPR will also 'still apply to any organisations in Europe who send you data, so you may need to help them decide how to transfer personal data to the UK in line with the GDPR.' The guidance cross refers to the six points above.

Question two above indicates that the DPA 2018, 'which currently supplements and tailors the GDPR within the UK, will continue to apply.' Again, referring to the future intent, it states that the 'government also intends to incorporate the provisions of the GDPR directly into UK law if we leave the EU without a deal, to sit alongside the DPA 2018.' In addition, the ICO 'expect the government to use new legislation to make technical amendments to the GDPR so that it works in a UK-only context.'

Question four above asks if an organisation can still transfer data to and from Europe if the UK leaves without a deal. The ICO guidance states as follows:

'The government has said that transfers of data from the UK to the European Economic Area (EEA) will not be restricted. However, if we leave the EU without a deal, GDPR transfer rules will apply to any data coming from the EEA into the UK. You need to consider what GDPR safeguards you can put in place to ensure that data can continue to flow into the UK.'

In terms of question five, referring to the Privacy and Electronic Communications Regulations (PECR),[10] the ICO states:

'Yes. The current PECR rules cover marketing, cookies and electronic communications. They derive from EU law but are set out in UK law. They will continue to apply after we exit the EU.'

Other EU changes are also noted. 'The EU is replacing the current e-privacy law with a new e-privacy Regulation (ePR). The new ePR is not yet agreed. It is unlikely to be finalised before the UK exists the EU. This means the ePR will not form part of UK law if we leave without a deal.'

Question six refers to NIS rules. The guidance advises, inter alia, that organisations may need to appoint local representatives in the EU, and review and comply with local NIS rules.

This guidance concludes by saying that '[i]n the meantime, given that we expect UK data protection law to remain aligned with the GDPR, our Guide to GDPR remains a good source of advice and guidance on how to comply with UK and EU data protection rules both now and after we leave the EU.' The guidance also notes the guidance will be variously updates as changes and new developments occur.

Further ICO Guidance

24.12   Given concerns regarding the potential for a 'final' no deal Brexit (including in relation to data protection, data transfers, etc), the ICO issues further guidance.

The ICO commented that '[w]hen the UK exits the EU, the EU GDPR will no longer be law in the UK. The UK government intends to write the GDPR into UK law, with necessary changes to tailor its provisions for the UK (the "UK GDPR"). The government has published a "Kneeling Schedule" for the GDPR, which shows planned amendments.'

In planning for a no deal Brexit scenario, the ICO gave guidance such as: 'Data Protection If There's No Brexit Deal'; 'International data transfers'; 'EU representatives'; 'One Stop Shop regulatory oversight by a lead data protection authority'.

It is the Government's intention that:

'the UK GDPR also applies to controllers and processors based outside the UK if their processing activities relate to:

- offering goods or services to individuals in the UK; or
- monitoring the behaviour of individuals taking place in the UK.'[11]

The ICO gives examples where transfers by a UK business to its consumers outside the UK are permitted; while transfers to third party organisations or service providers (including cloud services) can trigger the GDPR or UK GDPR.

Those who currently make data transfers to outside of the EEA should 'already' have compliance strategies in place.

On Exit Day, organisations needed to consider if they were intending to make restricted transfers outside of the UK (permissible *if* covered by an adequacy decision; or an appropriate safeguard; or an exception); and if they were receiving personal data from outside of the UK.

The ICO also referred to the European Data Protection Board (EDPB) advice in relation to transfers even in the event of a no deal Brexit; the ICO data transfers guide; as well as future guidance.

---

10   Privacy and Electronic Communications (EC Directive) Regulations 2003, SI 2003/2426.
11   See ico.org.uk/for-organisations/data-protection-and-the-eu/data-protection-and-the-eu-in-detail/the-uk-gdpr/.

Various detailed references and examples are made to adequacy decisions and appropriate safeguards (eg standard contractual clauses; binding corporate rules) for restricted transfers. These should be considered in detail as appropriate. Some of this is contingent on future UK legislation, however.

As regards those in the UK who propose to continue to receive personal data from the EU, it was reiterated that the GDPR applies to such transfers and to the transferor. Immediately upon Exit Day the UK became a so-called third country (outside of the EU), in which case additional restrictions apply on transfers. The ICO has further transfer guidance, as does the EDPB. Organisations should 'take a broad interpretation of [what is] a restricted transfer' (ICO). The EU transferor would 'only' be able to make the transfer to the UK transferee organisation if one of the following applied:

- There was an EU adequacy decision (eg adequacy decision; appropriate safeguards; standard contractual clauses. (Additional provisions may apply to public bodies)). (Unfortunately, from the UK perspective, '[a]t exit date there may not be an adequacy decision by the European Commission regarding the UK' (ICO) [that would seem to be an understatement at present].
- An exception outside of the above applied – but which is interpreted very narrowly and restrictively (such as medical emergencies; explicit consent; occasional contract transfers; occasional public interest transfers; occasional legal defence transfers; transfers from public registers; exceptional compelling legitimate interest transfers). The transferor would decide if applicable, not the UK recipient.

There is particular guidance in relation to transfers from jurisdictions covered by an EU adequacy decision (as opposed to the EU itself). Organisations, therefore, need to consider where potential post-Brexit transfers to the UK may come from.

Compliance

24.13 The ICO advised that preparation was necessary and that organisations should: assess their data flows and transfers in order to identify problem restricted transfers in advance; consider if and how transfers may continue, especially in the absence of a possible future EU adequacy decision, which may not have issued yet; consider standard contractual clauses with the counterparty (note the ICO tool available, and draft template contracts); update binding corporate rules, if previously utilised; update documentation and privacy notices; undertake compliance vetting by the transferor entity.

Particular considerations also arose for UK entities which did not have an office, branch or establishment in the EU or EEA after Exit Day. Other entities may have had to appoint a representative in the EU for GDPR purposes. The ICO provided commentary on these situations. Indeed, many organisations already had established branches outside the UK or even moved outside of the UK as a result of preparing for Brexit. GDPR compliance needs to be considered. Details and commentary on these scenarios are referred to in the ICO guidance.

Organisations may need to review their:

- agreements, contracts and appointments;
- terms, contracts, policies and websites;
- rights of data subjects;
- transfer documentation;
- data protection impact assessments (DPIAs);
- Data Protection Officer or Officers;
- further ICO and other official guidance.

EU Guidance

24.14 The European Data Protection Supervisor (EDPS) also issued guidance in relation to the possibility of a No Deal Brexit scenario ('Information Note on International Data Transfers After Brexit,' 16 July 2019).

The EDPS noted that the UK would be a third country as referred to under the data protection rules, and transfer restrictions would automatically kick in.

The EDPS noted that a No-Deal Brexit 'would have [immediate] repercussions for the protection pf personal data ... because ... EU ... law, including data protection law, will cease to apply in the UK.' The GDPR requirements and restrictions on data transfers to less safe or non-equivalent third countries will apply (see Chapter V, GDPR). There is a default transfer ban, unless one of the limited number of transfer mechanisms can be established for particular data transfers or transactions involving personal data.

The level of protection for the data being transferred must not be undermined (GDPR Article 46).

Businesses and their advisers at one stage therefore had to consider what would happen if there was a No-Deal Brexit scenario. If so, the organisation needs to assess how best to establish safeguards and the application of one of the limited number of transfer mechanism in this scenario 'to enable the transfer to a third country' – namely, the UK in this instance.

The EDPS referred to:

- adequacy decisions (see GDPR Article 47 regarding adequate levels of protection);
- appropriate safeguards (GDPR Article 48), eg:
    - standard contractual clauses expressly adopted by the Commission for such purposes (transfers to controllers 2001/497, 2004/915) (transfers to processors 2010/87);
    - binding corporate rules (BCRs) (applicable to a group of companies – and importantly approved by one of the respective data protection supervisory authorities. Note, prior BCRs can continue to apply but may need certain amendments post the GDPR. Currently, BCRs may be applied for in the UK, but take time, and it remains unclear how the ICO could approve BCRs in a no deal Brexit) (see GDPR Articles 46–48);
    - codes of conduct and certification mechanisms. (However, the exact nature of how this would work is not fully established and more guidance is awaited);
    - ad hoc contractual clauses. However, prior authorisation from a data protection supervisory authority would be necessary (GDPR Article 48(3)(a));
    - derogations (GDPR Article 50(1)).

The EDPS noted that a common feature in the above is that Data Subject rights must be enforceable and effective.

In terms of derogations, the EDPS noted that these are exhaustively mentioned in the GDPR Article 50:

- explicit consent of the individual to the transfer – 'after having been provided with all necessary information about the risks associated with the transfer';
- where the transfer is necessary for contract performance to which the Data Subject is a part;
- where the transfer is necessary to conclude or perform a contract concluded in the interest of the Data Subject;
- where the transfer is necessary for important public interest reasons;
- where the transfer is necessary for legal claims;

- where the transfer is necessary to protect the vital interests of the data subject (or someone else) and the data subject is physically or legally incapable of giving consent;
- where the transfer is made from a public register.

The EDPS also noted that the Commission in a Position Paper[12] said that personal data transferred (to the UK) before the Withdrawal Date would continue to be processed during the transition.

However, a note of caution is advised in that data processing activities must be judged both at the time of collection, processing and storage. That initial collection may be lawful and permissible, does not absent an organisation from the assessment of ascertaining a current lawful basis for current processing – especially the further-in-time current processing for the time being moves away from the initial date of collection, and more so in the event of secondary uses or purposes of processing. Later storage also requires a separate assessment of the basis for ongoing storage.

The EDPS referring to the Commission Position Paper reads as follows:

> 'The European Commission in the Position Paper on the Use of Data and Protection of Information Obtained or Processed Before the Withdrawal Date concludes that UK based controllers and processors may continue to process personal data transferred before the withdrawal date only if these data enjoy the protection of EU data protection law. Such protection will be guaranteed, in the case that a Withdrawal Agreement is put in place.'

The above caution should be noted, however, as anything to do with Brexit and data transfers is far from simple or assured in the current climate, and data processing activities can be varied and more nuanced than a headline description may suggest.

The EDPS acknowledged and cautioned that '[t]he developments on this sensitive issue should be closely followed and the EDPS [and others] may provide further guidance' as necessary. After all, this is a very fluid situation.

The EDPS set out five steps in preparation for Brexit, which businesses and organisations should consider, namely:

- map data processing activities;
- check the most suitable available data transfer mechanisms;
- implement the correct data transfer mechanism before 1 November 2019;
- update internal documentation;
- update data protection notices.

(These steps are also included in guidance from the European Data Protection Board (EDPB) in guidance of 12 February 2019.)

In addition to the above Position Paper referred to by the EDPS, the Commission also issued a 'Notice to Stakeholders Withdrawal of the United Kingdom From the Union and EU Rules in the Field of Data Protection' on 9 January 2018.

This noted that given the Article 50 notice submitted by the UK (on 29 March 2017) that EU law ceased to apply in the UK – unless there was a validated Withdrawal Agreement providing for data protection, transfers and other arrangements.

The Commission's 'Notice to Stakeholders' noted the 'considerable uncertainties' and that 'all stakeholders processing personal data are reminded of legal repercussions, which need to be considered when the [UK] becomes a third country.' The Commission highlighted the possibility and need to consider:

---

12 Commission, 'Position paper on the Use of Data and Protection of Information Obtained or Processed Before the Withdrawal Date,' 20 September 2017.

- standard data protection clauses (as approved by the Commission);
- binding corporate rules (but which generally only apply to certain large group entities, and in any event require prior approval from a data protection supervisory authority);
- approved codes of conduct; and
- approved certification mechanisms.

The Commission noted that the rules relating to some of these mechanisms have been simplified in the GDPR as compared with the prior DPD95/46.

The European Data Protection Board (EDPB) issued guidance entitled 'Information Note on Data Transfers Under the GDPR in the Event of a No Deal Brexit' (12 February 2019). It reiterated the need to consider: standard or ad hoc data protection clauses; binding corporate rules; codes of conduct and certification mechanisms; and derogations. It also includes reference to the five steps referred to above.

It noted that at that time, '[a]ccording to the UK Government, the current practice, which permits personal data to flow freely from the UK to the EEA, will continue in the event of a no-deal Brexit.' However, matters have shifted politically since then and the immediate next steps remain somewhat less certain, which is unfortunate for business entities which require the ability to plan ahead. The 'UK Government's and the ICO's website should be regularly consulted.' While there is uncertainty, organisations wishing to continue dealing and receiving personal data from their unconnected business partners located inside the EU must implement most likely standard contractual clauses, given that binding corporate rules will only apply to the largest of organisations and in a pre-approved manner. In addition, there will be increased pressure on parties in the EU wishing to continue to deal with UK entities, to implement appropriate mechanisms and safeguards from their end, in which case they will be raising queries directly with their UK counter parties.

Of course, may of the above guides have been somewhat overtaken by events. They are illustrative of the great concern for companies and individuals to be assured as mush as possible as to what the data protection regime would be in the UK, and how it would be affected by Brexit, both immediately and on an ongoing basis.

Brexit and Post-Brexit

Data and the European Union (Withdrawal) Act 2018

24.15 Official guidance by way of correspondence with the author from the Department for Digital, Culture, Media and Sport indicates that:

> 'The EU (Withdrawal) Act 2018 (EUWA) retains the GDPR in UK law. The fundamental principles, obligations and rights that organisations and data subjects have become familiar with will stay the same. To ensure the UK data protection framework continues to operate effectively when the UK is no longer as EU Member State, the government will make appropriate changes to the GDPR and Data Protection Act 2018 using regulation-making powers under the EUWA.'

One of the main aims is to maintain (most) pre-existing EU law already applicable in the UK after Brexit. There is also power, in the future, for various ministerial changes.

The European Union (Withdrawal) Act 2018 (EUWA 2018) received Royal Assent on 26 June 2018. The definitions are referred to throughout. The following are relevant to consider.

Section 20 refers to interpretation, including:

- a definition of the Charter of Fundamental Rights;
- 'exit day' ('means 29 March 2019 at 11.00pm ...' (this was extended by the European Union (Withdrawal) Act 2018 (Exit Day) (Amendment) Regulations 2019 (SI 2019/718) in the UK and at EU level by European Council Decision 2019/476/EU), and further extended to 31 October 2019 (this highlights again how complex Brexit was and is; and how even future issues which may need to be negotiated may not occur within the original time frame envisaged, for example, future extensions or applications regarding data transfers);
- 'EU regulation' ('means a regulation within the meaning of Article 288 of the Treaty on the Functioning of the European Union');
- 'EU directive';
- 'retained direct EU legislation' ('means any direct EU legislation which forms part of domestic law by virtue of section (as modified by or under this Act or by other domestic law from time to time, and including any instruments made under it on or after exit day)';
- 'withdrawal agreement'.

Section 20(4) provides that:

'A Minister of the Crown may by regulations –

(a) Amend the definition of "exit day" in subsection (1) to ensure that the day and time specified in the definition are the day and time that the Treaties are to cease to apply to the United Kingdom, and

(b) Amend subsection (2) in consequence of such amendment.'

Section 9(1) provides that 'A Minister ... may by regulation make such provision as the Minister considers appropriate for the purposes of implementing the withdrawal agreement if the Minister considers that such provision should be in force on or before exit day, subject to the prior enactment of a statute by Parliament approving the final terms of withdrawal of the United Kingdom from the EU.' Note that 'regulations under this section may not ... amend, repeal or revoke the Human Rights Act 1998 or any subordinate legislation made under it' (s 9(3)(e)). Also '[n]o regulations may be made under this section after exit day' (s 9(4)).

Section 2 refers to 'Saving for EU-derived domestic legislation.' It includes the following:

'EU-derived domestic legislation, as it has effect in domestic law immediately before exit day, continues to have effect in domestic law and after exit day.'

This potentially includes the DPA 2018.

Section 3, states that:

'Direct EU legislation, so far as operative immediately before exit day, forms part of domestic law on and after exit day' (s 3(1)).

This should seem to include an EU regulation – which may then include the GDPR. However, there remains some uncertainty, not least as the organisation may have to refer to the DPA 2018, the EUWA, any ministerial legislation, and any other legislation that may also ensue plus the withdrawal agreement itself.

There is also a definition of 'direct EU legislation' (s 3(2)(a)). This includes reference to 'any EU regulation ...'

Section 4 refers to a saver for rights, powers, liabilities, obligations, restrictions, remedies and procedures which were in effect immediately before exit day.

There are also provisions in relation to exceptions for saving and incorporations (s 5). This refers to the principle of supremacy of EU ceasing for laws after exit day (s 5(1)). However, it may apply to 'relevant' issues of interpretation (see s 5(2)).

The Charter 'is not part of domestic law on or after exit day (s 5(4)). (This may have potential to interact with issues of a future transfer adequacy decision assessment process.) However, note IN s 5(5) that:

'Subsection (4) does not affect the retention in domestic law on or after exit day in accordance with this Act of any fundamental rights or principles which exist irrespective of the charter (and references to the Charter in any case law are, so far as necessary for this purpose, to be read as if they were references to any corresponding retaining fundamental rights or principles)'.

This may require closer examination.

Section 6 refers to interpretation of 'retained EU law.' This section confirms that courts are not bound by 'any principles laid down, or any decision made, on or after exit day by the European Court' (s 6(1)). UK courts cannot continue to refer matters to the European Court (s 6(1)(b)). Having said that, UK courts 'may have regard to anything done on or after exit day by the European court, another EU entity or the EU so far as it is relevant to any other matter before the court' (s 6(2)).

Also, the Supreme Court and High Court are 'not bound' by any retailed EU case law (see s 6(4)). 'In deciding whether to depart from any retained EU case law, the Supreme Court or the High Court ... must apply the same test as it would apply in deciding whether to depart from its own case law' (s 695)).

There are also definitions for 'retained case law', 'retained EU law', 'retained general principles of EU law' amongst others set out in s 6(7).

Section 7 refers to status of retained EU law. It provides that:

'Anything which –

(a)   Was, immediately before exit day, primary legislation of a particular kind, subordinate legislation of a particular kind or another enactment of a particular kind, and
(b)   Continues to be domestic law as an enactment of the same kind' (s 7(1)).

'Retained direct principal EU legislation cannot be modified other than as specified (s 7(2)).

There is also a reference to the Human Rights Act 1998 in s 7(5)(f).

It also has a definition of 'retained direct principal EU legislation' (s 7(6)).

There are also detailed explanatory notes available with the EUWA. The Overview indicates that the EUWA 'repeals the European Communities Act 1972 (ECA) on the day the United Kingdom leaves the European Union'; and ends the supremacy of EU law. The query arises as to whether this means the entire EUWA only become active 'on' exit day.

The 'principal purpose of the Act is to provide a functioning statute book on the day the UK leaves the EU' (explanatory note (EN) 10). 'As a general rule, the same rules and laws will apply on the day after exit as on the day before. It will then be for Parliament and, where appropriate, the devolved legislatures to make any future changes' (EN10). It adds that:

'The approach in the act to preserving EU law is to ensure that all EU laws which are directly applicable in the UK and all laws which have been made in the UK in order to implement our obligations as a member of the EU are converted into domestic law on the day the UK leaves the EU, subject to some limited exceptions' (EN 48).

Section 1 repeals the European Communities Act 1972 (EN74). EU legislation is 'given legal effect in the UK via section 2(1) of the ECA, which described how such legislation is to have effect "in accordance with the EU treaties". It is this which ensures that, for example, EU regulations are directly applicable and fully binding in all member states' (EN81).

The guidance adds that 'Section 3 … convert[s] "direct EU legislation" into domestic legislation at the point of exit' (EN82). 'Subsection (1) therefore provides for the conversion into domestic law of this direct EU legislation' (EN83).

> 'Subsection (2)(a) converts EU regulations, certain EU decisions and EU tertiary legislation (now known as delegated and implementing acts), as they have effect immediately before exit day. These terms are defined at section 20. Section 20 and Schedule 6 provide that certain instruments are exempt EU instruments. These exemptions reflect that certain EU instruments did not apply to the UK because the UK did not adopt the Euro, or because the UK did not participate in certain aspects of the EU *acquis*, in the area of freedom, security and justice. EU decisions which are addressed only to a member state other than the UK are also not converted into domestic law. Additionally, so far as EU-derived domestic legislation under section 2 reproduces the effect of an EU regulation, decision or tertiary legislation, these instruments are not converted under this section. This is to avoid duplication on the statute book after exit' (EN84).

Brexit and EU (Withdrawal Agreement) Act 2020

24.16 The EU (Withdrawal Agreement) Act 2020 became law on 23 January 2020. The so-called Exit Date was confirmed as 31 January 2020. This triggered the transition period during which negotiations proceeded and agreement was made over the fine text with regard to all outstanding issues and the important future relationship between the UK and the EU.

The EU (Withdrawal Agreement) Act 2020 refers to the transition period as the 'Implementation Period.'

The EU (Withdrawal Agreement) Act 2020 operates by repealing the European Communities Act 1972, which brought the UK into the (then) EU. However, the carve-out in order to keep EU law during the transition period operates by reinstating temporarily the European Communities Act. In light of that, in the event of late extension (between July and December 2020) it may be that any necessary extension Amendment Act may be required to provide for the extension, and the continuation, of EU law during the extension period. It may well be that there is an element of politics involved in seeking to put pressure on the EU negotiators by having ruled out an extension at and prior to June.

There is also reference to the Court or Justice of the European Union and to EU law issues as they apply in the UK. However, the EU (Withdrawal Agreement) Act 2020 allows all courts – as opposed to just the Supreme Court (as previously referred to) – to depart from CJEU jurisprudence (section 26).

A final point to note is that as a result of the EU (Withdrawal Agreement) Act 2020 UK officials are no longer represented at EU institutions, bodies and agencies. This means that the ICO is no longer a member of the EDPB.

UK GDPR

24.17 There are, however, some changes, where a limited number of changes are required for language and localisation reasons. Where countries adopt their own local data protection legislation in addition to the GDPR, the local name of the data protection supervisory authority is often different and needs to be expressly referred to.

In the case of the UK, the GDPR is no longer directly effective – unlike other EU member states. It was deemed necessary to establish a UK version of the GDPR because upon Brexit occurring, the previously directly effective main GDPR would cease to be directly and legally effective in the UK.

It appears that there may have been some additional changes in addition to pure localisation issues.

It also appears that there is a certain political willingness to make even more changes.

However, as more changes occur a reckoning needs to be considered whereby some might argue that at a certain tipping point so many changes will have occurred that the UK version of the GDPR is no longer reconcilable with or fully equivalent to the original EU version of the GDPR. This raises political, policy, and legal issues.

From the point of view of users, industry, and advisors the real issue is that these post Brexit data protection changes create uncertainty. Industry does not like uncertainty. It makes it more difficult to be satisfied that legal contracts and data protection processes will not be impacted or that legal challenges may not arise. Legal and process costs also arise in the event that further changes have to be accommodated.

It is worth noting that in addition to direct changes to the UK version of the GDPR, some politicians have also expressed a desire to make changes to hundreds of other EU related laws in the UK, some of which potentially also impact data protection issues. This would have further potential to create uncertainty. This serves to highlight the point that while we have in one sense moved beyond the pre Brexit uncertainties, some of which are referred to above, current and ongoing changes to UK data protection rules (both direct and indirect), create new uncertainties and revive past uncertainties.

Data Protection and Digital Information (No 2) Bill

24.18   The Data Protection and Digital Information (No 2) Bill (DPDI Bill) makes further changes to the UK data protection regime, both with new provisions and changes to the UK GDPR. These will require careful examination once enacted, and no doubt further official guidance will also be issued.

Readers should note that in addition to changes proposed directly within the DPDI Bill, the earlier consultation process suggests that there are a number of additional changes also being actively considered. If some or all of these additional changes were to come to fruition in future, there will be changes required to the enacted version of the DPDI Bill.

Conclusion

24.19   The above provides an introduction to some of the change considerations and the intentions behind the new UK data protection regime. The documentation referred to above, in particular the Ministerial Statement document, provides very detailed policy background in relation to the need and benefit of updating the UK data protection regime and aligning, or continuing to align, with the EU regime. This announced policy arguably jars somewhat with some of the changes that have occurred to UK data protection immediately after Brexit – but potentially jars more so with some of the suggested further changes that politicians have referred to. This is discomforting to industry generally (and their advisors) because we have not arrived at a position where we are assured in saying that the UK legal position on data protection has settled.

One point is that there has already been significant change brought to the UK data protection regime as a result of Brexit. – some might even suggest tumultuous change and associated uncertainty awaiting the change and wondering what the nuanced changes would be. A further suite of changes result from the DPDI Bill. Even after this, further changes are also indicated as being contemplated as a result of the consultation regarding UK data protection law and effects. It cannot be lost on industry figures and their advisors that a variety of risks still exist before arriving at safe waters with relative certainty. While EU/UK data transfers might represent this uncertainty best, wider international perceptions of whether and to what extent UK data protection law is actually fully equivalent to EU data protection law is also significant. If recent opinion polls are to believed we may be at (or near) the high mark of Brexit data protection divergence. These polls suggest that most people now perceive Brexit differently. While it is still speculative, it is possible that the UK may re-enter the EU at some stage in the future – at which stage one might assume that the standards of the EU GDPR would apply and industry and users can be much more assured on data protection than is arguably the position currently. A word caution is needed in two respects. First, if this was to occur it will take time. Second, even though the end result may be significantly more certainty as regards data protection issues, a not dissimilar level of official discussion and process as occurred to create Brexit as to end Brexit may have to be navigated. These comments are, however, contingent on political and policy developments. In the meantime the ongoing turbulence of question marks over whether some or all UK data protection is truly close enough to EU data protection to be satisfied that it is equivalent – and whether it can withstand a legal challenge – remains a constant concern.

Chapter 25

Data Protection Act 2018

Introduction

25.01   The UK Data Protection Act 2018 is the most important development in UK data protection law in over 20 years.

Repeal

25.02   The Data Protection Act 1998 (DPA 1998) is repealed – as specified in Sch 19, para 44 of the Data Protection Act 2018 (DPA 2018).

Breakdown

25.03   The DPA 2018 is long and complex, comprising:

- 215 sections over 130 pages; and
- 20 Schedules (comprising 1–9 Parts depending on the Schedule) over 208 pages.

The Act is also complicated by the fact that it addresses more than just the EU General Data Protection Regulation (GDPR) itself, and consequent repeal of the prior legislation.

In addition to the GDPR related issues, the DPA 2018 also encompasses the following:

- Part 3: Law Enforcement Processing;
- Part 4: Intelligence Services Processing;
- Part 2, Chapter 3: applying the GDPR rules via the Act to other information and data not covered by the GDPR.

Part 3 refers to Law Enforcement Processing and makes provision about the processing of personal data by competent authorities for law enforcement purposes and implements the EU Law Enforcement Directive in the UK.

Part 4 refers to Intelligence Services Processing and makes provision about the processing of personal data by the intelligence services.

Specific Changes from GDPR

25.04   There are many changes from the GDPR. Some of these are referred to below.

DPA 2018 Changes from GDPR

GDPR	Description	Change	DPA 2018
Art 8	Age for information society services: 16	Change to: 13	s 9
GDPR	GDPR	Extends GDPR to additional information areas	Part 2
Art 4(7)	Meaning of 'Controller'	Change to definition	s 6(2) s 209 s 210
	Meaning of 'public authority' and 'public body'	Specifying UK public authorities	s 7
Art 6(1)(e)	Lawfulness of processing: public interest, etc	Specifies examples for UK	s 8
Art 9(1)	Special categories of personal data & criminal convictions	Makes provisions in UK: re (b) Employment, social security & social protection; re (g) Substantial public interest; re (h) Health & social care; re (i) Public health; re (j) Archiving, research & statistics	s 10
Art 9(2)(h)	Processing for health or social care purposes	Special categories of personal data: supplementary/ health or social care	s 11
Art 15(1)–(3)	Controller obligations	Obligations of credit reference agencies	s 13
Art 22(1), (2)(b)	Automated decisions	Makes exception Art 22(1). Automated decision making authorised by law: safeguards	s 14
GDPR	GDPR	Schedules 2, 3, 4 make exemptions from, and restrictions and adaptation on GDPR	s 15
Arts 13–21, and 34	Prior information requirements; Right of access; Right of rectification; Right of erasure and forgetting; Right to restriction of processing; Notification obligation; Right to data portability; Right to object; Communicating breach to Data Subject	Adaptation or restriction on Arts 13–21, and 34	Sch 2, Part 1

GDPR	Description	Change	DPA 2018
Arts 13–21, and 34	Prior information requirements; Right of access; Right of rectification; Right of erasure and forgetting; Right to restriction of processing; Notification obligation; Right to data portability; Right to object; Communicating breach to Data Subject	Restriction on Arts 13–21, and 34	Sch 2, Part 2
Art 15	Right of access	Restriction from Art 15	Sch 2, Part 3
Arts 13–15	Prior information requirements; Right of access	Restriction on Arts 13 – 15	Sch 2, Part 4
Chs II, III, IV, and VII	Principles; Rights of Data Subjects; Controllers & Processors; Cooperation & consistency	Exemptions and derogation on GDPR Chapters II, III, IV, & VII	Sch 2, Part 5
Arts 15, 16, 18, 19, 20 and 21	Right of access; Right of rectification; Right to restriction of processing; Notification obligation; Right to data portability; Right to object	Derogations from rights in Arts 15, 16, 18, 19, 20 and 21	Sch 2, Part 6
Arts 13–21	Prior information requirements; Right of access; Right of rectification; Right of erasure and forgetting; Right to restriction of processing; Notification obligation; Right to data portability; Right to object	Restricting rules in Arts 13–21 to health, social work, education and child abuse data	Sch 3
Arts 13–21	Prior information requirements; Right of access; Right of rectification; Right of erasure and forgetting; Right to restriction of processing; Notification obligation; Right to data portability; Right to object	Restricting rules in Arts 13–21	Sch 4

GDPR	Description	Change	DPA 2018
Art 89(1)	Safeguards and derogations re processing for archiving in public interest, scientific or historic research purposes or statistical purposes	Makes provision re archiving, research and statistical purposes: safeguards	s 19
Art 80	Representation of Data Subjects	Further specifics on bodies representing Data Subjects	s 187
GDPR	GDPR various	Various	Schedules

Comment

25.05   The DPA 2018 is quite a complex piece of legislation and will require organisations and their representatives undertaking careful re-reading even in order to get an overview understanding.

Large elements of the DPA 2018 will not be relevant in the ordinary course of dealing for most organisations, in particular Part 3 and Part 4. The GDPR extended section (Part 2, Chapter 3) (eg freedom of information) will also not be directly relevant to most organisations, especially those in the commercial sphere. Note that these elements of the Act while so encompassed, are outside of core data protection and are beyond the preset scope of this book.

In terms of the remainder data protection sections of the DPA 2018, it should be noted that these differ from the DPA 1998. The DPA 1998 was intended to implement the EU Data Protection Directive 1995 (DPD 1995) into the UK. EU Directives by their nature need local law implementation.

EU Regulations are different. The GDPR is directly effective in all states – including the UK. The DPA 2018 is not technically required to implement the GDPR in the UK as it is already applicable directly.

However, like many other states, the UK recognises that it needs a new law to repeal the old law (ie the DPA 1998); and in order to deal with specific local law issues. In addition, the GDPR specifies that certain provisions from the GDPR can be tailored in each individual state depending on the local issues and environment. For example, while the GDPR provides that information society services must have an age of consent of 16, it provides that states may derogate from this. The UK utilises this derogation to apply an age of consent of 13 instead of 16. Numerous other derogations and changes are made in the DPA 2018.

Regard is also needed to the EU Adequacy Decision for data transfers; and proposed changes to the UK GDPR meant to be brought about by the Data Protection and Digital Information (No 2) Bill.

Future

25.06   While the UK was in the EU, the GDPR was directly effective. This was regardless of the DPA 2018. After Brexit and with the EU (Withdrawal Agreement) Act 2020 of 23 January 2020 and with Brexit Exit Day occurring, the GDPR direct effect position ceased to be. The EU GDPR ceased to be directly effective in the UK. Ultimately, the UK introduced its own UK GDPR (in large part reflecting the same provisions, with certain amendments).

However, certain politicians have voiced intentions to repeal hundreds if not thousands of EU legacy related laws in the UK. An impact assessment will be needed to see if and how this may affect the UK data protection regime directly, and also how it might indirectly affect the EU Adequacy Decision for the UK and in particular if it may undermine this decision for data transfers.

In addition, the final version of the changes referred to in the Data Protection and Digital Information (No 2) Bill will need to be scrutinised.

Part 5

EU Regime

Chapter 26

EU Data Protection Regime

Introduction

26.01   The EU data protection regime is fundamentally updated and expanded.[1] Many things have changed since the introduction of the EU Data Protection Directive 1995 (DPD 1995). Data processing activities have changed, as well as increases in scale and complexity. New data processing activities and issues are constantly evolving. The EU undertook a formal review of the data protection regime. Partly on foot of the review, it was decided to update DPD 1995, ultimately via the new EU Regulation, namely the EU General Data Protection Regulation (GDPR).

Formal Nature of Regulations and Directives

26.02   As noted above, DPD 1995 is replaced by a Regulation, the GDPR. The final version of the GDPR was agreed in April 2016. However, it is important to note that an EU Regulation differs from a Directive under formal EU law.[2] A Regulation is immediately directly effective in all EU states – without the need for national implementing laws. A Directive requires national implementing measures, whereas a Regulation does not. The GDPR Regulation applied in the UK for a period (prior to the Brexit exit date[3]) as in other EU countries. It changed the UK data protection regime as well as commercial practice. The reforms introduced are described as being 'comprehensive.'[4] Notwithstanding Brexit, the UK is indicated to maintain a UK version of the GDPR (not titled the UK GDPR, in addition to the DPA 2018). This will arguably necessitate further data protection regulation changes if and when further EU changes occur, in order to maintain equivalence. There is a tension, however, insofar as certain political statements have suggested and intention to move quite significantly away from the GDPR and EU model.

---

1   European Commission – Press release, 'Agreement on Commission's EU Data Protection Reform Will Boost Digital Single Market,' Brussels (15 December 2015); R Graham, 'Prepare for European Data Protection Reform,' *SCL Computer and Law*, 30 November 2011.
2   Generally see, for example, A Biondi and P Eeckhout, eds, *EU Law after Lisbon* (2012); N Foster, *Foster on EU Law* (2011); O'Neill, A, *EU Law for UK Lawyers* (2011); Steiner, J, *EU Law* (2011). Also, HCFJA de Waele, 'Implications of Replacing the Data Protection Directive by a Regulation. A Legal Perspective,' *Privacy & Data Protection* (2012) (12) 3.
3   See EU (Withdrawal Agreement) Act 2020, enacted on 23 January 2020.
4   In Brief, *Communications Law* (2012) (17) 3.

Review Policy

26.03 The Commission and others recognised that technology and commercial changes have meant that the data protection regime required updating.[5] Indeed, the Council of Europe Convention on data protection[6] which pre-dates DPD 1995 and which was incorporated into the national law of many EU (and other states) prior to DPD 1995, is also in the process of being updated.[7] The WP29 (prior to the new European Data Protection Board) also refers to the need for future data protection measures in its Opinion regarding *The Future of Privacy*.[8] Indeed, there have also been calls for greater political activism in relation to particular data protection issues.[9] Others[10] have also highlighted new problematic developments in relation to such things as location data and location based services, which need to be dealt with.[11] Online abuse and offline abuse issues are other issues which need to be addressed. Rebecca Wong refers to some of the areas of concern which the GDPR proposes to address.[12] These include:

- the data protection regime in the online age;
- social media;
- cloud computing;
- minimum/maximum standards;
- the data protection Principles.[13]

The Commission states[14] that the policy in reviewing the data protection regime is to:

- modernise the EU legal system for the protection of personal data, in particular to meet the challenges resulting from globalisation and the use of new technologies;
- strengthen individuals' rights, and at the same time reduce administrative formalities to ensure a free flow of personal data within the EU and beyond;
- improve the clarity and coherence of the EU rules for personal data protection and achieve a consistent and effective implementation and application of the fundamental right[15] to the protection of personal data in all areas of the EU's activities.[16]

---

5 For example, see also from a US perspective, N Roethlisberger, 'Someone is Watching: The Need for Enhanced Data Protection', *Hastings Law Journal* (2011) (62:6) 1793.
6 Convention for the Protection of Individuals with regard to Automatic Processing of Personal Data, Council of Europe (1982).
7 See S Kierkegaard et al, '30 Years On – The Review of the Council of Europe Data Protection Convention 108,' *Computer Law & Security Review* (2011) (27) 223–231.
8 The Future of Privacy, WP29, referred to in R Wong, 'Data Protection: The Future of Privacy,' *Computer Law & Security Review* (2011) (27) 53–57.
9 A Ripoll Servent and A MacKenzie, 'Is the EP Still a Data Protection Champion? The Case of SWIFT,' *Perspectives on European Politics & Society* (2011) (12) 390–406.
10 C Cuijpers and M Pekarek, 'The Regulation of Location-Based Services: Challenges to the European Union Data Protection Regime,' *Journal of Location Based Services* (2011) (5) 223–241.
11 See, for example, M Hildebrandt, 'Location Data, Purpose Binding and Contextual Integrity: What's the Meggase,' in L Florida, ed, *Protection of Information and the Right to Privacy – A New Equilibrium* (Springer 2014) 31.
12 R Wong, 'The Data Protection Directive 95/46/EC: Idealisms and Realisms,' *International Review of Law, Computers & Technology* (2012) (26) 229–244.
13 See above.
14 Reform of Data Protection Legal Framework, Commission, Justice Directorate, at http://ec.europa.eu/justice/data-protection/index_en.htm.
15 In relation to data protection as a fundamental right, see, for example S Rodata, 'Data Protection as a Fundamental Right,' in S Gutwirth, Y Poullet, P de Hert, C de Terwangne and S Nouwt, *Reinventing Data Protection?* (Springer, 2009) 77. A Mantelero notes that 'If legislators consider data protection as a fundamental right, it is necessary to reinforce its protection in order to make it effective and not conditioned by the asymmetries which characterize the relationship between Data Subject and data controllers,' A Mantelero, 'Competitive Value of Data Protection: The Impact of Data Protection Regulation on Online Behaviour,' *International Data Privacy Law* (11/2013) (3:4) 98.
16 Reform of Data Protection legal Framework, Commission, Justice Directorate, at http://ec.europa.eu/justice/data-protection/index_en.

It is also to enhance consumer confidence in eCommerce.[17] In addition, it should also bring comprehensive savings to organisations as the compliance obligations of complying with somewhat differing national data protection regimes will be reduced if not eliminated.[18]

The review[19] summarised the need for new data protection rules, as follows:

'The current EU data protection rules date from 1995. Back then, the internet was virtually unknown to most people. Today, 250 million people use the internet daily in Europe.

Think how that has changed our personal data landscape through the explosion of ecommerce, social networks, online games and cloud computing.

The European Commission has therefore adopted proposals for updating data protection rules to meet the challenges of the digital age. In particular, the proposals will strengthen protection of your personal data online.'

These proposals were debated in some detail.[20] Commentators described the GDPR as 'a long (and ambitious) text'.[21] In addition, the process which has arrived at this stage is described as being herculean.[22] The details of the changes were agreed in December 2015, and finalised and enacted in April 2016, with a go live date of May 2018.

Importance

26.04   Costa and Poullet indicate that as the GDPR 'comes into force, the document will be the new general legal framework of data protection, repealing [the DPD] more than twenty-seven years after its adoption.'[23] The GDPR, as well as Article 8(1) of the EU Charter of fundamental rights of 2000 and Article 16(1) of the Lisbon Treaty, reassert the importance of privacy and data protection 'as a fundamental right'.[24] '[E]ffective and more coherent protection' is required[25] (see below).

In terms of policy as between modernising via a Directive or via a Regulation 'in order to ensure a full consistent and high level of protection equivalent in EU states, a Regulation was judged as the adequate solution to ensure full harmonisation'[26] throughout the EU. The Commission may also oversee and monitor the national supervisory authorities.[27]

Individuals are rarely aware about how their data are collected and processed while they are surfing on the internet at home, using their cell phones, walking down a

---

17 In Brief, *Communications Law* (2012) (17) 3.
18 See above.
19 See details of some of the steps and consultations, at http://ec.europa.eu/justice/data-protection/index_en.htm.
20 See Commission, *Why Do We Need New Data Protection Rules Now?*, at http://ec.europa.eu/justice/data-protection/document/review2012/factsheets/1_en.pdf.
21 P De Hert and V Papakonstantinou, 'The Proposed Data Protection Regulation Replacing Directive 95/46/EC: A Sound System for the Protection of Individuals,' *Computer Law & security Review* (2012) (28) 130–142. Note also, IN Walden and RN Savage, 'Data Protection and Privacy Laws: Should Organisations be Protected?,' *International and Comparative Law Quarterly* (1988) (37) 337–347.
22 See above.
23 L Costa and Y Poullet, 'Privacy and the Regulation of 2012,' *Computer Law & Security Review* (2012) (28) 254–262, at 254.
24 See above, 254.
25 See above.
26 See above, 255.
27 See above.

video-surveyed street or with an RFID tag embedded in their clothes, and so on.[28] There is a need for greater transparency. As regards data processing, 'transparency translates the widening of the knowledge about information systems … coupled with fairness.'[29]

Fundamental Right

26.05 Personal data protection is now recognised as a fundamental right for individuals, both in the GDPR and the EU Charter of Fundamental Rights of 2000, Lisbon Treaty (Treaty on the Functioning of the European Union) and the Council of Europe Convention.

'**EU Charter (Article 8(1))**

Protection of Personal Data

Everyone has the right to the protection of personal data concerning him or her.'

'**EU Lisbon Treaty (Article 16(1))**

Everyone has the right to the protection of personal data concerning them.'

While the UK is indicated to have adopted a UK GDPR post-Brexit, it is unclear if an equivalence to the Charter or Treaty will also be sought to be maintained. The point is that the EU data protection regime is wider than just the EU GDPR. There have also been some suggestions that the UK Human Rights Act 1998 is to be repealed after Brexit, or at least watered down by way of amendment. There have also been comments that a wide range of other EU laws in the UK are intended to be repealed, extending to hundreds of such laws. If there is no relationship or equivalence to EU norms such as in the Charter, Treaties or human rights law, this holds the potential for difficulties in the EU recognising the UK protections for personal data in a formal adequacy decision. This is notwithstanding the actual UK GDPR. The UK GDPR and application for an adequacy decision could thus be undermined by other UK law changes.

Innovations

26.06 Commentators have indicated that parts of the GDPR contain particular 'legislative innovation.'[30] Some examples of this innovation are indicated to be the:

- Principles of data protection;
- Data Subjects' rights;
- Controllers' and Processors' obligations;
- Regulation issues regarding technologies.[31]

It has been noted that while DPD 1995 emphasises protection for the fundamental right and freedoms of individuals 'and in particular their right to privacy,' the GDPR

---

28 See above, 256.
29 L Costa and Y Poullet, 'Privacy and the Regulation of 2012,' *Computer Law & Security Review* (2012) (28) 254–292.
30 See above.
31 See above.

in Articles 1 and 2 stresses the need to protect the fundamental right and freedoms of individuals 'and in particular their right to the protection of personal data.'[32] Further references also emphasise data protection as a stand-alone concept from privacy, such as data protection risk assessments and pre-problem solving via data protection by design (DPbD) and by default.

There is a consistency mechanism whereby the national data protection authorities are obliged to cooperate with each other and with the Commission.[33] Two examples given include: data protection assessments; and the obligation of notifying Data Subjects in relation to data breaches.[34]

The obligations in terms of sufficient security and data breaches are more detailed in the GDPR than previously.[35] The obligations are now more detailed than those in relation to telcos and ISPs in the ePD.[36] Data breaches are referred to in the GDPR. In the event of a data breach the Controller must notify the ICO. In addition the Controller must also communicate to the Data Subjects if there is a risk of harm to their privacy or personal data.

Data portability is a newly expressed right. It 'implies the right of Data Subjects to obtain from the Controller a copy of their personal data in a structured and commonly used format ... data portability is a kind of right to backup and use personal information under the management of the data Controller. Second, data portability grants the right to transmit personal data and other information provided by the Data Subject from one automated processing system to another one ... therefore the right to take personal data and leave.'[37]

DPD 1995 stated that Controller must not process personal data excessively. However, this is now more limited. The GDPR states that data collection and processing must be transparent, fair and limited to the minimum.

Broader parameters are contained in the GDPR in relation to consent. The definition and conditions are broader than previously. The inclusion of the words freely given, specific, informed and unambigious appears more specific than the previous 'unambiguously' consented.

DPD 1995, Article 15 protection in relation to automated individual decisions 'is considerably enlarged'[38] regarding profiling in GDPR. The use of, *inter alia*, the word 'measure' in the GDPR as opposed to 'decision' in DPD 1995 now makes the category of activity encompassed within the obligation much wider.[39] There is greater Data Subject protection. While there were previously two exemptions, in terms of contract and also a specific law, the GDPR adds a third in terms of consent from the Data Subject. However, Controllers will need to ensure a stand alone consent for profiling separate from any consent for data collection and processing per se.[40]

---

32 See above, 255.
33 Chapter VII, section 10, see L Costa and Y Poullet, 'Privacy and the Regulation of 2012,' *Computer Law & Security Review* (2012) (28) 254–262, at 255.
34 See above.
35 L Costa and Y Poullet, 'Privacy and the Regulation of 2012,' *Computer Law & Security Review* (2012) (28) 254–262, at 256.
36 See above.
37 See above, at 256.
38 See above, at 258. Also see Council of Europe Recommendation regarding profiling (25 November 2010).
39 L Costa and Y Poullet, 'Privacy and the Regulation of 2012,' *Computer Law & Security Review* (2012) (28) 254–262, at 258–259.
40 See above, at 258. Also see Council of Europe Recommendation regarding profiling (25 November 2010) 259.

The GDPR also moves significantly further than DPD 1995 in terms of creating obligations, responsibility and liability on Controllers.[41] Appropriate policies must be implemented by Controllers, as well as complaint data processing, secure data processing, the undertaking of data protection impact assessments, shared liability as between joint Controllers, appointing representatives within the EU where the Controllers are located elsewhere and provisions regarding Processors.[42]

While DPD 1995 imposed compensation obligations on Controllers in the case of harm to Data Subjects, the GDPR extends liability to Processors.[43] In addition, where harm is suffered by Data Subjects any joint Controller and or Processors shall be 'jointly and severally liable for the entire amount of the damage.'[44]

The concepts of data protection by design (DPbD), data protection by default and impact assessments all emphasise the ability of the data protection regime to become involved in standards setting and the regulation of particular technologies and technical solutions.[45] The previous Ontario Data Protection Commissioner, Anne Cavoukian, refers to PbD (the precursor to DPbD).[46] The GDPR describes it as follows, by indicating that:

> '[h]aving regard to the state of the art and the cost of implementation and taking account of the nature, scope, context and purposes of the processing as well as the risks of varying likelihood and severity for rights and freedoms of individuals posed by the processing, the Controller shall, both at the time of the determination of the means for processing and at the time of the processing itself, implement appropriate technical and organisational measures, such as pseudonymisation, which are designed to implement data protection principles, such as data minimisation, in an effective way and to integrate the necessary safeguards into the processing in order to meet the requirements of [the GDPR] and protect the rights of Data Subjects.' (Article 23(1)).

Data protection by default is referred to and defined as follows:

> 'The Controller shall implement mechanisms for ensuring that, by default, only those personal data are processed which are necessary for each specific purpose of the processing and are especially not collected or retained beyond the minimum necessary for those purposes, both in terms of the amount of the data and the time of their storage. In particular, those mechanisms shall ensure that by default personal data are not made accessible to an indefinite number of individuals' (Article 23(2)).

These accord with the general principle of data minimisation, whereby non-personal data should be processed first and where the collection and processing of personal data is required, it must be the minimum data as opposed to the minimum data which is so processed. This is referred to in Article 5(1)(c).

Data Subjects have more control over their personal data. In the context of social networks, 'individual profiles should be kept private from others by default.'[47]

---

41 See above.
42 See above.
43 See above.
44 See above.
45 See above.
46 For example, Anne Cavoukian, DPA Ontario, Privacy Guidelines for RFID Information Systems, at www.ipc.on.ca, says the privacy and security must be built into the solution from the outset, at the design stage. Referred to *ibid*.
47 L Costa and Y Poullet, 'Privacy and the Regulation of 2012,' *Computer Law & Security Review* (2012) (28) 254–262, at 260, and referring to European data Protection Supervisor on the Communications from Commission to the European Parliament, the Council, the Economic and Social Committee and the Committee of the Regions, 'A Comprehensive Approach on Personal Data Protection in the European Union,' at 23.

The concept of DPbD and data protection by default as provided in the GDPR are predicted to soon impact upon organisational contracts and contracting practices relating to data processing activities.[48]

As mentioned above, one of the new areas is the obligation to engage in data protection impact assessments. Article 35(1) provides that that:

> '[w]here a type of processing in particular using new technologies, and taking into account the nature, scope, context and purposes of the processing, is likely to result in a high risk for the rights and freedoms of natural persons, the Controller shall, prior to the processing, carry out an assessment of the impact of the envisaged processing operations on the protection of personal data. A single assessment may address a set of similar processing operations that present similar high risks.'

This is particularly so where the envisaged processing could give rise to specific risks.

A further addition is the possibility of mass group claims or claims through representative organisations. This is referred to as 'collective redress' and allows data protection and privacy NGOs to complain to both the ICO and to the courts (see Recital 143 and Article 80).[49] 'Civil procedure rules'[50] may also need to be introduced.

The regime as regards cross border data transfers are 'significantly altered.'[51] These are included in Articles 44–50.

Enhanced Provisions and Changes

26.07 One of the more important extensions and enhancements relates to the expanded Right to be Forgotten. The 'right to be forgotten and to erasure, which consists of securing from the Controller the erasure of personal data as well prevention of any further dissemination of his data.'[52] (It is also said to interface with the new right to data portability[53]).

The erasure and forgetting right is even more enhanced in instances where the personal data was originally disclosed when the Data Subject was a child. Some commentators refer to the option of an entire 'clean slate.'[54]

> 'The use of data from social networks in employment contexts is a representative example. Personal data such as photos taken in private contexts have been used to refuse job positions and fire people. But forgetfulness is larger. It is one dimension of how people deal with their own history, being related not only to leaving the past behind but also to living in the present without the threat of a kind of "Miranda" warning, where whatever you say can be used against you in the future. In this sense the right to be forgotten is closely related to entitlements of dignity and self-development. Once again, privacy appears as the pre-requisite of our liberties, assuring the possibility to freely express ourselves and move freely on the street ...'[55]

---

48 See above, 260.
49 See also Commission on a common framework for collective redress, at http://ec.europa.eu/consumers/redress_cons/collective_redress_en.htm.
50 L Costa and Y Poullet, 'Privacy and the Regulation of 2012,' *Computer Law & Security Review* (2012) (28) 254–262, at 261.
51 See above.
52 See above, at 256.
53 See above.
54 See above, at 257.
55 See above.

The erasure and forgetting right is most clearly associated and related to the following in particular:

- where the personal data are no longer necessary in relation to the purposes for which they were originally collected and processed (and the associated finality principle);
- where the Data Subject has withdrawn their consent for processing;
- where Data Subjects object to the processing of the personal data concerning them;
- where the processing of the personal data does not comply with the GDPR.[56]

The GDPR and the erasure and forgetting right 'amplifies the effectiveness of data protection Principles and rules.'[57]

Data Subjects can have their data erased under the right to be forgotten when there is no compliance, in addition to instances where they simply withdraw their consent.[58] User control and Data Subject control are, therefore, enhanced.

The right creates compliance obligations, such as:

- erasing personal data and not processing it further;
- informing third parties that the Data Subject has requested the deletion of the personal data;
- taking responsibility for publication by third parties under the Controller's authority[59] (Articles 17, 2 and 8).

The GDPR also enhances and expands the various powers of the national supervisory authorities, such as the ICO.[60]

Some of the key changes are referred to below. In some respects, these could also be seen as advantages of the GDPR data protection regime:

- administrative costs are to be reduced with a single EU wide set of rules and obligations;
- there may be less need to interact with the ICO, as more responsibility and accountability is passed to the organisational level;
- the consent requirement is clarified as to mean explicit consent (whereas previously there were references to different categories of consent);
- rights are improved with easier access to personal data, as well as its transferability;
- the enhanced Right to be Forgotten will improve the position of Data Subjects and the ability to delete and erase data;
- the EU data protection regime applies to non-EU entities operating with regard to EU personal data and EU citizens;
- the national authorities will be able to impose fines based on a percent of global turnover[61] (see below).

The ICO welcomes the GDPR, stating:

'it strengthens the position of individuals, recognises important concepts such as privacy by design and privacy impact assessments and requires organisations to be able to

---

56 L Costa and Y Poullet, 'Privacy and the Regulation of 2012,' *Computer Law & Security Review* (2012) (28) 254–262.
57 See above.
58 See above, at 257.
59 See above.
60 See above, at 260.
61 In Brief, *Communications Law* (2012) (17) 3.

demonstrate that they have measures in place to ensure personal information is properly protected.'[62]

The EU Commission's press statement dated 15 December 2015 issued once the GDPR text was agreed notes that the GDPR 'will enable people to better control their personal data. At the same time modernised and unified rules will allow businesses to make the most of the opportunities of the Digital Single Market by cutting red tape and benefiting from reinforced consumer trust.'[63]

The Commission also refers to the benefits of the changes. It states:

'The reform will allow people to regain control of their personal data. Two-thirds of Europeans (67%), according to a recent Eurobarometer survey, stated they are concerned about not having complete control over the information they provide online. Seven Europeans out of ten worry about the potential use that companies may make of the information disclosed. The data protection reform will strengthen the right to data protection, which is a fundamental right in the EU, and allow them to have trust when they give their personal data.

The new rules address these concerns by strengthening the existing rights and empowering individuals with more control over their personal data. Most notably, these include,

- **easier access to your own data**: individuals will have more information on how their data is processed and this information should be available in a clear and understandable way;
- **a right to data portability**: it will be easier to transfer your personal data between service providers;
- **a clarified "Right to be Forgotten"**: when you no longer want your data to be processed, and provided that there are no legitimate grounds for retaining it, the data will be deleted;
- **the right to know when your data has been hacked:** For example, companies and organisations must notify the national supervisory authority of serious data breaches as soon as possible so that users can take appropriate measures.

Clear modern rules for businesses

In today's digital economy, personal data has acquired enormous economic significance, in particular in the area of big data. By unifying Europe's rules on data protection, lawmakers are creating a business opportunity and encouraging innovation.

One continent, one law: The regulation will establish one single set of rules which will make it simpler and cheaper for companies to do business in the EU.

One-stop-shop: businesses will only have to deal with one single supervisory authority. This is estimated to save €2.3 billion per year.

European rules on European soil: companies based outside of Europe will have to apply the same rules when offering services in the EU.

Risk-based approach: the rules will avoid a burdensome one-size-fits-all obligation and rather tailor them to the respective risks.

Rules fit for innovation: the regulation will guarantee that data protection safeguards are built into products and services from the earliest stage of development (Data protection by Design (DPbD)). Privacy-friendly techniques such as pseudonomysation will be encouraged, to reap the benefits of big data innovation while protecting privacy.

---

62 Referred to in In Brief, *Communications Law* (2012) (17) 3.
63 European Commission – Press release, 'Agreement on Commission's EU Data Protection Reform Will Boost Digital Single Market,' Brussels (15 December 2015).

Benefits for big and small alike

The data protection reform will stimulate economic growth by cutting costs and red tape for European business, especially for small and medium enterprises (SMEs). The EU's data protection reform will help SMEs break into new markets. Under the new rules, SMEs will benefit from four reductions in red tape:

- **No more notifications**: Notifications to supervisory authorities are a formality that represents a cost for business of €130 million every year. The reform will scrap these entirely.
- **Every penny counts**: Where requests to access data are manifestly unfounded or excessive, SMEs will be able to charge a fee for providing access.
- **Data Protection Officers**: SMEs are exempt from the obligation to appoint a data protection officer insofar as data processing is not their core business activity.
- **Impact Assessments**: SMEs will have no obligation to carry out an impact assessment unless there is a high risk.

...

Better protection of citizens' data

Individuals' personal data will be better protected, when processed for any law enforcement purpose including prevention of crime. It will protect everyone – regardless of whether they are a victim, criminal or witness. All law enforcement processing in the Union must comply with the principles of necessity, proportionality and legality, with appropriate safeguards for the individuals. Supervision is ensured by independent national data protection authorities, and effective judicial remedies must be provided.

The Data Protection Directive for Police and Criminal Justice Authorities provides clear rules for the transfer of personal data by law enforcement authorities outside the EU, to ensure that the level of protection of individuals guaranteed in the EU is not undermined.'[64]

In one survey, 72 percent of internet users were concerned that they gave away too much personal data.[65] However, red tape reduction and economic growth are also commercial issues considered under the regime. New technological changes are also recognised and encompassed. European harmonisation issues are also a central consideration.

The Data Protection Regime

Introducing the GDPR Changes

26.08   Some of the headline changes include:

- new and updated fundamental principles, such as fairness and legality, processing conditions, prior information, consent, transparency, accuracy, lawfulness of processing, definitions;
- DPOs;
- special rules concerning children in relation to information society services;
- expanded rights including subject access rights;
- new enforcement and sanctions provisions;
- Right to be Forgotten;

---

64   European Commission – Press release, 'Agreement on Commission's EU Data Protection Reform Will Boost Digital Single Market,' Brussels (15 December 2015).
65   Eurobarometer, 'Attitudes on Data Protection and Electronic Identity in the EU' (June 2011).

- right to data portability;
- new security and breach provisions;
- provisions regarding single supervisory authority or one-stop-shop;
- risk based approach, risk minimisation, consultations and reporting.

Some of the new detailed changes include:

- repeal of DPD 1995 (Article 94);
- WP29 and European Data Protection Board (EDPB) (Articles 35, 40–43, 51, 52, 58–63, 64, 65 and 94);
- background and rationale (Recitals 1, 8, 11, 13);
- context objectives, scope of GDPR (Articles 1, 2 and 3);
- obligations (Recitals 32, 39, 40, 42, 43–47);
- security (Articles 2, 4, 5, 9, 10, 30, 32, 35, 40, 45 and 47);
- processing;
- rights (Articles 1, 4–7, 9–22);
- proceedings (Articles 23, 40, 78, 79, 81 and 82);
- establishment (Articles 3, 4, 9, 17, 18, 21, 37, 42, 49, 54, 56, 57, 60, 62, 65, 70 and 79);
- transfers (Articles 44–50);
- ICO, etc;
- new bodies (Recital 142; Articles, 9 and 80);
- notification/registration replaced (Recital 89);
- exceptions/exemptions (Article 23);
- lawful processing and consent (Articles 4–9, 13, 14, 17, 18, 20, 22, 23, 32, 40, 49, 82, 83);
- online identifiers (Recital 30; Articles 4, 87);
- sensitive and special personal data (Articles 6, 9, 22, 27, 30, 35, 37, 47);
- children (Articles 6, 8, 12, 40, 57);
- health data (Articles 4, 9, 17, 23, 36, 88);
- DPR definitions (Article 4);
- new processing rules: obligations (Articles 5–11);
- new (data protection) Principles (Article 5);
- lawfulness of processing: legitimate processing conditions (Article 6);
- child's consent: conditions for information society services (Article 8);
- processing special categories of personal data (Article 9);
- processing re criminal convictions and offences data (Article 10);
- processing not requiring identification (Article 11);
- Controllers and Processors (Chapter IV);
- responsibility of the Controller (Article 24);
- joint Controllers (Article 26);
- Processor (Article 28);
- processing under authority of Controller and Processor (Article 29);
- records of processing activities (Article 30);
- representatives of Controllers not established in EU (Article 27);
- co-operation with supervisory authority;
- security of processing (Article 32);
- notifying data breach to supervisory authority (Article 33);
- communicating data breach to Data Subject (Article 34);
- data protection impact assessment and prior consultation (Chapter IV, Section 3);
- data protection impact assessment (Article 35);
- prior consultation (Article 36);
- new Data Protection Officer (DPO) (Chapter IV, Section 4; Article 37);

- position (Article 38) and tasks of new DPO (Article 39);
- general principle for transfers (Article 44);
- transfers via adequacy decision (Article 45);
- transfers via appropriate safeguards (Article 46);
- transfers via binding corporate rules (Article 47);
- transfers or disclosures not authorised by EU law (Article 48);
- derogations for specific situations (Article 49);
- new processing rules: Data Subject rights (Chapter III);
- right to transparency (Article 5; Chapter III, Section 1; Articles 12–14, 26, 40–43, 88);
- data access rights (Chapter III, Section 2);
- right to prior information: directly obtained data (Article 13);
- right to prior information: indirectly obtained data (Article 14);
- right of confirmation and right of access (Article 15);
- rectification and erasure (Chapter III, Section 3).
- right to rectification (Article 16);
- right to erasure (Right to be Forgotten) (RtbF) (Article 17);
- right to restriction of processing (Article 18);
- notifications re rectification, erasure or restriction (Article 19);
- right to data portability (Article 20);
- right to object (Article 21);
- rights against automated individual decision making, including profiling (Article 22);
- Data protection by design (DPbD) and by default (Article 25).
- security rights;
- data protection impact assessment and prior consultation;
- communicating data breach to Data Subject (Article 34);
- Data Protection Officer (DPO) (contact);
- remedies, liability and sanctions (Chapter VIII);
- right to lodge complaint with supervisory authority (Article 77);
- right to judicial remedy against supervisory authority (Article 78);
- right to effective judicial remedy against Controller or Processor (Article 79);
- representation of Data Subjects (Article 80);
- suspension of proceedings (Article 81);
- right to compensation and liability (Article 82);
- codes of conduct and certification (Chapter IV, Section 5; Articles 40–43);
- international co-operation on personal data (Articles 50, 60);
- Supervisory Authorities (Chapter VI, Section 1; Article 81);
- general conditions for imposing administrative fines (Article 83);
- penalties (Article 84);
- specific data processing situations (Chapter IX);
- processing and freedom of expression and information (Article 85);
- processing and public access to official documents (Article 86);
- processing national identification numbers (Article 87);
- processing in employment context (Article 88);
- safeguards and derogations: public interest/scientific/historical research/statistical processing (Article 89);
- obligations of secrecy (Article 90);
- churches and religious associations (Article 91);
- delegated acts and implementing acts (Chapter X);
- exercise of the delegation (Article 92);

- relationship to Directive 2002/58/EC (Article 95);
- relationship to previously concluded agreements (Article 96);
- review of other EU data protection instruments (Article 98);
- restrictions.

Definitions

26.09   Article 4 of the GDPR sets out the definitions for the new data protection regime.

Prior to the GDPR, the ICO has issued recommendations in relation to personal data, definitions, etc, namely:

- Determining What is Personal Data;
- What is 'Data' for the Purposes of the DPA?;
- What is Personal Data? – A Quick Reference Guide.

These now need to be read in light of the GDPR changes.

GDPR Recitals

26.10   The Recitals to the GDPR are also instructive in relation to the purposes and themes covered. They include reference to, for example: DPD 1995 being repealed; WP29/EDPB; background and rationale; obligations; security; processing; rights; proceedings; establishment; transfers; supervisory authorities; new bodies; lawful processing and consent; online identifiers; special personal data; children; and health data. The importance of data protection and health data is also referred to by the OECD.[66]

Main Provisions and Changes of GDPR

26.11   The main GDPR provisions and changes are referred to below.

Repeal of DPD95

26.12   DPD 1995 is repealed. It is repealed with effect from 25 May 2018 (Article 94(1)). References to the repealed DPD 1995 shall be construed as references to the GDPR (Article 94(2)).

WP29 and European Data Protection Board

26.13   A European Data Protection Board (EDPB) is established. This effectively replaces the WP29. References to the previous WP29 shall be construed as references to the EDPB established by the GDPR (Article 94(2)). Chapter IV, Section 3 of the GDPR provides for the EDPB. The EDPB is established as body of the EU and shall have legal personality (Article 68(1)). The EDPB shall be composed of the head of one supervisory authority of each state and of the European Data Protection Supervisor, or their respective representatives (Article 68(3)). The EDPB shall act independently when performing its tasks or exercising its powers pursuant to Articles 70 and 71 (Article 69(1)).

---

66 *Strengthening Health Information Infrastructure for Health Care Quality Governance: Good Practices, New Opportunities, and Data Privacy Protection Challenges*, OECD (2013).

Context of GDPR

26.14 The initial provisions refer to the context of the GDPR, namely, the subject matter and objectives (Article 1); material scope (Article 2); and territorial scope (Article 3).

GDPR Definitions

26.15 Article 4 of the GDPR sets out the important definitions for the new data protection regime.

Processing Rules: Obligations

26.16 The processing rules as set out in the GDPR regime are set out below.

The Recitals refer to the following: data processing must be lawful and fair (Recital 39); processing necessary for a contract (Recital 40); processing for a legal obligation (Recital 40); processing necessary to protect life (Recital 46); the legitimate interests of the Controller (Recital 47).

Principles

26.17 Article 5 of the GDPR sets out the Principles relating to data protection. Personal data must be:

- processed lawfully, fairly and in a transparent manner in relation to the Data Subject ('lawfulness, fairness and transparency');
- collected for specified, explicit and legitimate purposes and not further processed in a manner that is incompatible with those purposes; further processing for archiving purposes in the public interest, scientific or historical research purposes or statistical purposes shall, in accordance with Article 89(1), not be considered to be incompatible with the initial purposes ('purpose limitation');
- adequate, relevant and limited to what is necessary in relation to the purposes for which they are processed ('data minimisation');
- accurate and, where necessary, kept up to date; every reasonable step must be taken to ensure that personal data that are inaccurate, having regard to the purposes for which they are processed, are erased or rectified without delay ('accuracy');
- kept in a form which permits identification of Data Subjects for no longer than is necessary for the purposes for which the personal data are processed; personal data may be stored for longer periods insofar as the personal data will be processed solely for archiving purposes in the public interest, scientific or historical research purposes or statistical purposes in accordance with Article 89(1) subject to implementation of the appropriate technical and organisational measures required by the GDPR in order to safeguard the rights and freedoms of the Data Subject ('storage limitation');
- processed in a way that ensures appropriate security of the personal data, including protection against unauthorised or unlawful processing and against accidental loss, destruction or damage, using appropriate technical or organisational measures ('integrity and confidentiality').

The Controller must be responsible for and be able to demonstrate compliance with the above ('accountability').

These can be summarised as:

- processed lawfully, fairly and transparently ('lawfulness, fairness and transparency');

- for specified, explicit and legitimate purposes and not further processed incompatibly with the purpose; (with a carveout) ('purpose limitation');
- adequate, relevant and limited to what is necessary for the purposes ('data minimisation');
- accurate and, where necessary, kept up to date; every reasonable step must be taken to ensure that personal data that are inaccurate, having regard to the purposes for which they are processed, are erased or rectified without delay ('accuracy');
- kept in a form which permits identification for no longer than is necessary; (with a carveout) ('storage limitation');
- appropriate security, including protection against unauthorised or unlawful processing and against accidental loss, destruction or damage, using appropriate technical or organisational measures ('integrity and confidentiality').

The Controller must demonstrate compliance ('accountability').

Lawfulness of Processing: Lawful Processing Conditions

26.18   Article 6 of the GDPR sets out the provisions in relation to the lawfulness of processing. Processing of personal data shall be lawful only if and to the extent that at least one of the following applies:

- the Data Subject has given *consent* to the processing of their personal data for one or more specific purposes (see section below at para **26.19** and also Article 7);
- processing is necessary for the performance of a contract to which the Data Subject is party or in order to take steps at the request of the Data Subject prior to entering into a contract;
- processing is necessary for compliance with a legal obligation to which the Controller is subject;
- processing is necessary in order to protect the vital interests of the Data Subject or of another natural person;
- processing is necessary for the performance of a task carried out in the public interest or in the exercise of official authority vested in the Controller;
- processing is necessary for the purposes of the legitimate interests pursued by the Controller or by a third party, except where such interests are overridden by the interests or fundamental rights and freedoms of the Data Subject which require protection of personal data, in particular where the Data Subject is a child. This shall not apply to processing carried out by public authorities in the performance of their tasks (Article 6(1)).

States may maintain or introduce more specific provisions to adapt the application of the rules of the GDPR with regard to the processing of personal data for compliance with Article 6(1)(c) and (e) by determining more precisely specific requirements for the processing and other measures to ensure lawful and fair processing including for other specific processing situations as provided for in Chapter IX (Article 6(2)). The basis for the processing referred to in Article 6(1)(c) and (e) must be laid down by EU law, or state law to which the Controller is subject.

The purpose of the processing shall be determined in this legal basis or as regards the processing referred to in Article 6(1)(e), shall be necessary for the performance of a task carried out in the public interest or in the exercise of official authority vested in the Controller. This legal basis may contain specific provisions to adapt the application of rules of the GDPR, *inter alia* the general conditions governing the lawfulness of processing by the Controller, the type of data which are subject to the processing, the Data Subjects concerned; the entities to, and the purposes for which the data may be disclosed; the purpose limitation; storage periods and processing operations and processing procedures, including measures to ensure lawful and fair processing, such as those for other specific processing situations as provided for in Chapter IX. EU law or the state law must meet an objective of public interest and be proportionate to the legitimate aim pursued (Article 6(3)).

Where the processing for another purpose than the one for which the data have been collected is not based on the Data Subject's consent or on EU or state law which constitutes a necessary and proportionate measure in a democratic society to safeguard the objectives referred to in Article 23(1), the Controller shall, in order to ascertain whether processing for another purpose is compatible with the purpose for which the personal data are initially collected, take into account, *inter alia*:

- any link between the purposes for which the data have been collected and the purposes of the intended further processing;
- the context in which the personal data have been collected, in particular regarding the relationship between Data Subjects and the Controller;
- the nature of the personal data, in particular whether special categories of personal data are processed, pursuant to Article 9 or whether personal data related to criminal convictions and offences are processed, pursuant to Article 10;
- the possible consequences of the intended further processing for Data Subjects;
- the existence of appropriate safeguards, which may include encryption or pseudonymisation (Article 7(4)).

Prior to the GDPR, the ICO issued recommendations in relation to marketing personal data issues, namely:

- Direct Marketing;
- Direct Marketing Checklist – Ideal for Small Businesses;
- Companies Receiving Unwanted Marketing;
- Guidance on Political Campaigning.

These now need to be read in light of the GDPR changes.

Consent for Processing: Conditions for Consent

26.19   Consent is an important issue under the new GDPR.[67] Lawful processing and consent are referred to in Recital 40. The WP29 also refers to consent issues.[68]

Article 7 of the GDPR refers to conditions for consent as follows. Where processing is based on consent, the Controller shall be able to demonstrate that the Data Subject has consented to the processing of their personal data (Article 7(1)).

If the Data Subject's consent is given in the context of a written declaration which also concerns other matters, the request for consent must be presented in a manner which is *clearly distinguishable* from other matters, in an *intelligible and easily accessible form*, using *clear and plain language*. Any part of such a declaration which constitutes an infringement of the GDPR shall not be binding (Article 7(2)).

The Data Subject shall have the *right to withdraw his or her consent at any time*. The withdrawal of consent shall not affect the lawfulness of processing based on consent before its withdrawal. Prior to giving consent, the Data Subject must be informed thereof. It shall be as easy to withdraw consent as to give consent (Article 7(3)).

---

67   JP Vandenbroucke and J Olsen, 'Informed Consent and the New EU Regulation on Data Protection,' *International Journal of Epidemiology* (2013) (42: 6) 1891.

68   WP29 Opinion 15/2011 Consent; Working Document 02/2013 providing guidance on obtaining consent for cookies, 201; Opinion 04/2012 on Cookie Consent Exemption.

When assessing whether consent is freely given, utmost account shall be taken of the fact whether, *inter alia*, the performance of a service, is conditional on consent to the processing of personal data that is not necessary for the performance of this contract (Article 7(4)).

Children

26.20 The issue of children in the data protection regime have been steadily rising. The increased use of social media and Web 2.0 services enhance the exposures and risks for children and the uninitiated.[69]

This concern has included children's groups, regulators and also the EDPB (previously the WP29). WP29 issued Opinion 2/2009 on the Protection of Children's Personal Data (General Guidelines and the Special Case of Schools) in 2009 and also Working Document 1/2008 on the Protection of Children's Personal Data (General Guidelines and the Special Case of Schools). Schools are being encouraged to be proactive and to have appropriate codes and policies for children's social media and internet usage.[70]

There is now an explicit acknowledgement of children's interest in the EU data protection regime, unlike with DPD95 which contained no explicit reference. The GDPR refers to a 'child' including as below the age of 16 years. This is significant amongst other things in relation consent, contracting, etc. It is also significant for websites which have significant numbers of children. Up until now it was common for certain social networks to purport to accept users only over the age of 13. A child was defined in the first and final version of the GDPR as up to 18 years of age. Therefore, the potential implications will require careful assessment. This includes, for example, social contracts, consent, notices, terms of use, contract terms, payment and purchase issues, related process models, sign-ups, social media, internet, etc. Note, however, that the UK has adopted a change whereby it specifies the age as being 13 for the UK (Data Protection Act 2018 (DPA 2018), s 9).

Article 8 of the original proposal for the GDPR contained provisions in relation to the processing of personal data of a child. The final version of Article 8(1) provided that where Article 6(1)(a) applies, in relation to the offer of information society services directly to a child, the processing of the personal data of a child shall be lawful where the child is at least 16 years old. Where the child is below the age of 16 years, such processing shall be lawful only if and to the extent that consent is given or authorised by the holder of parental responsibility over the child. The original Article 8(1) proposal provided that Article 8(1) shall not affect the general contract law of states, such as the rules on the validity, formation or effect of a contract in relation to a child. Under the original Article 8(3) the Commission is empowered to adopt delegated acts in accordance with Article 86 for the purpose of further specifying the criteria and requirements for the methods to obtain verifiable consent referred to in Article 8(1). In doing so, the Commission shall consider specific measures for micro, small and medium-sized enterprises (original draft Article 8(3)). In addition,

---

69 See, for example, D Gourlay and G Gallagher, 'Collecting and Using Children's Information Online: the UK/US Dichotomy,' SCL *Computers and Law*, 12 December 2011.

70 Note generally, for example, JS Groppe, 'A Child's Playground or a Predator's Hunting Ground? – How to Protect Children on Internet Social Networking Sites,' *CommLaw Conspectus* (2007)(16) 215–245; EP Steadman, 'MySpace, But Who's Responsibility? Liability of Social Networking Websites When Offline Sexual Assault of Minors Follows Online Interaction,' *Villanova Sports and Entertainment Law Journal* (2007)(14) 363–397; DC Beckstrom, 'Who's Looking at Your Facebook Profile? The Use of Student Conduct Codes to Censor College Students' Online Speech,' *Willamette Law Review* (2008) 261–312.

the Commission may lay down standard forms for specific methods to obtain verifiable consent referred to in Article 8(1). Those implementing acts shall be adopted in accordance with the examination procedure referred to in Article 87(2) (original draft Article 8(4)).

The explicit reference to children is new, and some would argue overdue. Increasingly, the activities of children on the internet and on social media, poses risks and concerns.[71] This has been further emphasised of late with tragic events involving online abuse, in particular cyber bullying. Risks arise obviously from their activities online (eg inappropriate content, cyber bullying, but also from the collection and use of their personal data online and collected online, sometimes without their knowledge or consent). Their personal data and privacy is more vulnerable than that of older people.

It is important for organisation to note the 'child' provisions in the GDPR. This will have implications in how organisations:

- consider the interaction with children and what personal data may be collected and processed;
- ensure that there is appropriate compliance for such collection and processing for children as distinct from adults.

Regard might be had in due course to the UK Online Safety Bill once finalised.

Child's Consent: Conditions for Information Society Services

26.21 Processing of children's personal data are referred to in Recital 38. Article 8 of the GDPR makes new provisions in relation to conditions for children's consent for Information Society services. Where Article 6(1)(a) applies, in relation to the offer of information society services directly to a child, the processing of personal data of *a child shall be lawful where the child is at least 16* years old. Where the child is *below the age of 16 years*, such processing shall only be lawful if and to the extent that consent is given or authorised by the holder of *parental responsibility* over the child (Article 8(1)).

The Controller shall make reasonable efforts to verify in such cases that consent is given or authorised by the holder of parental responsibility over the child, taking into consideration available technology (Article 8(2)). This shall not affect the general contract law of states such as the rules on the validity, formation or effect of a contract in relation to a child (Article 8(3)).

Processing Special Categories of Personal Data

26.22 Sensitive personal data are referred to in Recitals 10 and 51 and special categories of personal data are referred to in Recitals 10, 51, 52, 53, 54, 71, 80, 91 and 97.

Article 9 refers to the processing of special categories of personal data. The processing of personal data, revealing racial or ethnic origin, political opinions, religious or philosophical beliefs, or trade-union membership, and the processing of genetic data, biometric data for the purpose of uniquely identifying a natural person, data concerning health or data concerning a natural person's sex life and sexual orientation shall be *prohibited* (Article 9(1)).[72]

---

71 See, for example, L McDermott, 'Legal Issues Associated with Minors and Their Use of Social Networking Sites,' *Communications Law* (2012) (17) 19–24.

72 In relation to genetic data generally, see for example D Hallinan, PJA de Hert and M Friedewald, 'Genetic Data and the Data Protection Regulation: Anonymity, Multiple Subjects, Sensitivity and a Prohibitionary Logic Regarding Genetic Data?,' *Computer Law and Security Review* (2013) (29: 4) 317.

The above shall not apply if one of the following applies:

- the Data Subject has given *explicit consent* to the processing of those personal data for one or more specified purposes, except where EU law or state law provide that the above prohibition may not be lifted by the Data Subject;
- processing is necessary for the purposes of carrying out the obligations and exercising specific rights of the Controller or of the Data Subject in the field of employment and social security and social protection law in so far as it is authorised by EU law or state law or a collective agreement pursuant to state law providing for adequate safeguards for the fundamental rights and the interests of the Data Subject;
- processing is necessary to protect the vital interests of the Data Subject or of another natural person where the Data Subject is physically or legally incapable of giving consent;
- processing is carried out in the course of its legitimate activities with appropriate safeguards by a foundation, association or any other not-for-profit-seeking body with a political, philosophical, religious or trade union aim and on condition that the processing relates solely to the members or to former members of the body or to persons who have regular contact with it in connection with its purposes and that the personal data are not disclosed outside that body without the consent of the Data Subjects;
- processing relates to personal data which are manifestly made public by the Data Subject;
- processing is necessary for the establishment, exercise or defence of legal claims or whenever courts are acting in their judicial capacity;
- processing is necessary for reasons of substantial public interest, on the basis of EU or state law which shall be proportionate to the aim pursued, respect the essence of the right to data protection and provide for suitable and specific measures to safeguard the fundamental rights and the interests of the Data Subject;
- processing is necessary for the purposes of preventive or occupational medicine, for the assessment of the working capacity of the employee, medical diagnosis, the provision of health or social care or treatment or the management of health or social care systems and services on the basis of EU law or state law or pursuant to contract with a health professional and subject to the conditions and safeguards referred to in Article 9(3); [h] or
- processing is necessary for reasons of public interest in the area of public health, such as protecting against serious cross-border threats to health or ensuring high standards of quality and safety of health care and of medicinal products or medical devices, on the basis of EU law or state law which provides for suitable and specific measures to safeguard the rights and freedoms of the Data Subject, in particular professional secrecy;
- processing is necessary for archiving purposes in the public interest, scientific or historical research purposes or statistical purposes in accordance with Article 89(1) based on EU or state law which shall be proportionate to the aim pursued, respect the essence of the right to data protection and provide for suitable and specific measures to safeguard the fundamental rights and the interests of the Data Subject (Article 9(2)).

Personal data referred to in Article 9(1) may be processed for the purposes referred to in Article 9(2)(h) when those data are processed by or under the responsibility of a professional subject to the obligation of professional secrecy under EU or state law or rules established by national competent bodies or by another person also subject to an obligation of secrecy under EU or state law or rules established by national competent bodies (Article 9(3)).

States may maintain or introduce further conditions, including limitations, with regard to the processing of genetic data, biometric data or health data (Article 9(5)).

Health Research

26.23 The issue of health research was just one of the matters which proved to be of some controversy during the discussions for the GDPR. The final provisions include the following. The special data processing prohibition in Article 9(1) shall not apply in the following health research instances, namely where:

- processing is necessary for the purposes of preventive or occupational medicine, for the assessment of the working capacity of the employee, medical diagnosis, the provision of health or social care or treatment or the management of health or social care systems and services on the basis of EU or state law or pursuant to contract with a health professional and subject to the conditions and safeguards referred to in paragraph 3 (Article 9(2)(h));
- processing is necessary for reasons of public interest in the area of public health, such as protecting against serious cross-border threats to health or ensuring high standards of quality and safety of health care and of medicinal products or medical devices, on the basis of EU or state law which provides for suitable and specific measures to safeguard the rights and freedoms of the data subject, in particular professional secrecy (Article 9(2)(i)).

Personal data referred to in Article 9(1) may be processed for the purposes referred to in Article 9(2)(h) when those data are processed by or under the responsibility of a professional subject to the obligation of professional secrecy under Union or state law or rules established by national competent bodies or by another person also subject to an obligation of secrecy under EU or state law or rules established by national competent bodies (Article 9(3)).

The EDPB recently issued data protection and health guidance specific to the Covid pandemic, namely,

- Guidelines 03/2020 on the processing of data concerning health for the purpose of scientific research in the context of the Covid-19 outbreak.

Note that the Data Protection and Digital Information (No 2) Bill (DPDI Bill) refers to certain health data issues.

Processing re Criminal Convictions and Offences Data

26.24 Article 10 refers to processing of data relating to criminal convictions and offences. Processing of personal data relating to criminal convictions and offences or related security measures based on Article 6(1) shall be carried out only under the control of official authority or when the processing is authorised by EU law or state law providing for adequate safeguards for the rights and freedoms of Data Subjects. Any comprehensive register of criminal convictions may be kept only under the control of official authority.

Processing Not Requiring Identification

26.25 Article 11 refers to processing not requiring identification. If the purposes for which a Controller processes personal data *do not or do no longer require* the identification of a Data Subject by the Controller, the Controller shall not be obliged to maintain, acquire or process additional information in order to identify the Data Subject for the sole purpose of complying with the GDPR (Article 11(1)).

Where, in such cases the Controller is able to demonstrate that it is not in a position to identify the Data Subject, the Controller shall inform the Data Subject accordingly, if possible. In such cases, Articles 15 to 20 shall not apply except where the Data Subject, for the purpose of exercising their rights under these articles, provides additional information enabling their identification (Article 11(2)).

Controllers and Processors

26.26   Chapter IV of the GDPR refers to Controllers and Processors. Chapter IV, Section 1 refers to general obligations. The WP29 also refers to Controller and Processor issues.[73]

Responsibility of the Controller

26.27   Taking into account the nature, scope, context and purposes of the processing as well as the risks of varying likelihood and severity for the rights and freedoms of individuals, the Controller shall implement appropriate technical and organisational measures to ensure and be able to demonstrate that the processing of personal data is performed in compliance with the GDPR. Those measures shall be reviewed and updated where necessary (Article 24(1)).

Where proportionate in relation to the processing activities, the measures referred to in Article 24(1) shall include the implementation of appropriate data protection policies by the Controller (Article 24(2)).

Adherence to approved codes of conduct pursuant to Article 40 or an approved certification mechanism pursuant to Article 42 may be used as an element to demonstrate compliance with the obligations of the Controller (Article 24(3)).

Joint Controllers

26.28   Where two or more Controllers jointly determine the purposes and means of the processing of personal data, they are joint Controllers. They shall, in a transparent manner, determine their respective responsibilities for compliance with the obligations under the GDPR, in particular as regards the exercising of the rights of the Data Subject and their respective duties to provide the information referred to in Articles 13 and 14, by means of an arrangement between them unless, and in so far as, the respective responsibilities of the Controllers are determined by EU or state law to which the Controllers are subject. The arrangement may designate a point of contact for Data Subjects (Article 26(1)).

The arrangement shall duly reflect the joint Controllers' respective effective roles and relationships vis-à-vis Data Subjects. The essence of the arrangement shall be made available for the Data Subject (Article 26(2)).[74]

Irrespective of the terms of the arrangement referred to in Article 24(1), the Data Subject may exercise their rights under the GDPR in respect of and against each of the Controllers (Article 24(3)).

The CJEU has also dealt with the issue of who might be joint controllers, and related issues, in a number of cases, namely the so called Facebook fan page case

---

73   WP29 Opinion 1/2010 on the concepts of 'controller' and 'processor.'
74   Generally see J Mäkinen, 'Data Quality, Sensitive Data and Joint Controllership as Examples of Grey Areas in the Existing Data Protection Framework for the Internet of Things,' *Information & Communications Technology Law* (2015) (24:3) 262.

where Facebook and the operator of a fan page were found to be joint controllers;[75] and the Fashion ID case.[76]

Processor

26.29   Where a processing is to be carried out on behalf of a Controller, the Controller shall use only Processors providing sufficient guarantees to implement appropriate technical and organisational measures in such a manner that the processing will meet the requirements of the GDPR and ensure the protection of the rights of the Data Subject (Article 28(1)).

The Processor shall not engage another Processor without the prior specific or general written authorisation of the Controller. In the case of general written authorisation, the Processor shall inform the Controller on any intended changes concerning the addition or replacement of other Processors, thereby giving the Controller the opportunity to object to such changes (Article 28(2)).

The carrying out of processing by a Processor shall be governed by a contract or other legal act under EU or state law, that is binding the Processor with regard to the Controller and that sets out the subject-matter and duration of the processing, the nature and purpose of the processing, the type of personal data and categories of Data Subjects and the obligations and rights of the Controller. The contract or other legal act shall stipulate, in particular, that the Processor:

- process the personal data only on documented instructions from the Controller, including with regard to transfers of personal data to a third country or an international organisation, unless required to do so by EU or state law to which the Processor is subject; in such a case, the Processor shall inform the Controller of that legal requirement before processing the data, unless that law prohibits such information on important grounds of public interest;
- ensure that persons authorised to process the personal data have committed themselves to confidentiality or are under an appropriate statutory obligation of confidentiality;
- take all measures required pursuant to Article 32;
- respect the conditions referred to in Article 28(2) and (4) for engaging another Processor;
- taking into account the nature of the processing, assist the Controller by appropriate technical and organisational measures, insofar as this is possible, for the fulfilment of the Controller's obligation to respond to requests for exercising the Data Subject's rights laid down in Chapter III;
- assist the Controller in ensuring compliance with the obligations pursuant to Articles 32 to 36 taking into account the nature of processing and the information available to the Processor;
- at the choice of the Controller, deletes or returns all the personal data to the Controller after the end of the provision of services relating to processing, and deletes existing copies unless EU or state law requires storage of the personal data;
- make available to the Controller all information necessary to demonstrate compliance with the obligations laid down in this Article and allow for and contribute to audits, including inspections, conducted by the Controller or another auditor

---

75 *Unabhängiges Landeszentrum für Datenschutz Schleswig-Holstein v Wirtschaftsakademie Schleswig-Holstein GmbH*, CJEU [2018] Case C-210/16 (5 June 2018).
76 *Fashion ID GmbH & Co.KG v Verbraucherzentrale NRW eV*, CJEU [2019] Case C-40/17 (29 July 2019).

mandated by the Controller. (With regard to this point, the Processor shall immediately inform the Controller if, in its opinion, an instruction breaches the GDPR or EU or state data protection provisions) (Article 28(3).)

Where a Processor engages another Processor for carrying out specific processing activities on behalf of the Controller, the same data protection obligations as set out in the contract or other legal act between the Controller and the Processor as referred to in Article 28(3) shall be imposed on that other Processor by way of a contract or other legal act under EU or state law, in particular providing sufficient guarantees to implement appropriate technical and organisational measures in such a manner that the processing will meet the requirements of the GDPR. Where that other Processor fails to fulfil its data protection obligations, the initial Processor shall remain fully liable to the Controller for the performance of that other Processor's obligations (Article 28(4)).

Adherence of the Processor to an approved code of conduct pursuant to Article 40 or an approved certification mechanism pursuant to Article 42 may be used as an element to demonstrate sufficient guarantees referred to in Article 28(1) and (4) (Article 28(5)).

Without prejudice to an individual contract between the Controller and the Processor, the contract or the other legal act referred to in Article 26(3) and (4) may be based, in whole or in part, on standard contractual clauses referred to in Article 28(7) and (8), including when they are part of a certification granted to the Controller or Processor pursuant to Articles 42 and 43 (Article 28(6)).

The Commission may lay down standard contractual clauses for the matters referred to in Article 28(3) and (4) and in accordance with the examination procedure referred to in Article 93(2) (Article 28(7)).

A supervisory authority may adopt standard contractual clauses for the matters referred to in Article 28(3) and (4) and in accordance with the consistency mechanism referred to in Article 63 (Article 28(8)).

The contract or the other legal act referred to in Article 28(3) and (4) shall be in writing, including in an electronic form (Article 28(9)).

Without prejudice to Articles 82, 83 and 84, if a Processor infringes the GDPR by determining the purposes and means of data processing, the Processor shall be considered to be a Controller in respect of that processing (Article 28(10)).

Organisations acting as Processors should recall that while they may indeed be Processors, they can also at the same time be Controllers in relation to different sets of personal data.

Processing Under Authority of Controller and Processor

26.30 The Processor and any person acting under the authority of the Controller or of the Processor who has access to personal data shall not process them except on instructions from the Controller, unless required to do so by EU or state law (Article 29).

Records of Processing Activities

26.31 Each Controller and where applicable the Controller's representative, shall maintain a record of processing activities under its responsibility. This record shall contain all of the following information:

- the name and contact details of the Controller and where applicable the joint Controller, the Controller's representative and the DPO;
- the purposes of the processing;

- a description of categories of Data Subjects and of the categories of personal data;
- the categories of recipients to whom the personal data have been or will be disclosed including recipients in third countries or international organisations;
- where applicable, transfers of data to a third country or an international organisation, including the identification of that third country or international organisation and, in case of transfers referred to in Article 49(1), the documentation of suitable safeguards;
- where possible, the envisaged time limits for erasure of the different categories of data;
- where possible, a general description of the technical and organisational security measures referred to in Article 32(1) (Article 30(1)).

Each Processor and, where applicable, the Processor's representative shall maintain a record of all categories of processing activities carried out on behalf of a Controller, containing:

- the name and contact details of the Processor or Processors and of each Controller on behalf of which the Processor is acting, and where applicable of the Controller's or the Processor's representative, and the DPO;
- the categories of processing carried out on behalf of each Controller;
- where applicable, transfers of data to a third country or an international organisation, including the identification of that third country or international organisation and, in case of transfers referred to in Article 49(1), the documentation of suitable safeguards;
- where possible, a general description of the technical and organisational security measures referred to in Article 32(1) (Article 30(2)).

The records referred to in Article 30(1) and (2) shall be in writing, including in an electronic form (Article 30(3)).

The Controller and the Processor and, where applicable, the Controller's or the Processor's representative, shall make the record available to the supervisory authority on request (Article 30(4)).

The obligations referred to in Article 30(1) and (2) shall not apply to an enterprise or an organisation employing fewer than 250 persons unless the processing it carries out is likely to result in a risk to the rights and freedoms of Data Subject, the processing is not occasional, or the processing includes special categories of data as referred to in Article 9(1) or personal data relating to criminal convictions and offences referred to in Article 10 (Article 30(5)).

The records-rules may be one of the more underappreciated areas of the new data protection regime, but holds the potential for substantial bite. Already data regulators are looking at how businesses and organisations document and record how they are compliant. It is perhaps only a matter of time before party opponents seek to direct attention to this area also.

Representatives of Controllers Not Established in EU

26.32 Where Article 3(2) applies, the Controller or the Processor shall designate in writing a representative in the EU (Article 27(1)).

This obligation shall not apply to:

- processing which is occasional, does not include, on a large scale, processing of special categories of data as referred to in Article 9(1) or processing of personal data relating to criminal convictions and offences referred to in Article 10, and is

unlikely to result in a risk for the rights and freedoms of natural persons, taking into account the nature, context, scope and purposes of the processing; or
● a public authority or body (Article 27(2)).

The representative shall be established in one of the states where the Data Subjects whose personal data are processed in relation to the offering of goods or services to them, or whose behaviour is monitored, are (Article 27(3)).

The representative shall be mandated by the Controller or the Processor to be addressed in addition to or instead of the Controller or the Processor by, in particular, supervisory authorities and Data Subjects, on all issues related to the processing, for the purposes of ensuring compliance with the GDPR (Article 27(4)).

The designation of a representative by the Controller or the Processor shall be without prejudice to legal actions which could be initiated against the Controller or the Processor themselves (Article 28(5)).

Cooperation with Supervisory Authority

26.33   The Controller and the Processor and, where applicable, their representatives, shall co-operate, on request, with the supervisory authority in the performance of its tasks (Article 31).

Data Protection by Design (DPbD) and by Default

26.34   Article 25 refers to data protection by design and by default. Note also the related concept, or precursor concept, of Privacy by Design (PbD). In some ways PbD is the impetus for the current DPbD rules.

Taking into account the state of the art and the cost of implementation and the nature, scope, context and purposes of the processing as well as the risks of varying likelihood and severity for rights and freedoms of natural persons posed by the processing, the Controller shall, both at the time of the determination of the means for processing and at the time of the processing itself, implement appropriate technical and organisational measures, such as pseudonymisation, which are designed to implement data protection Principles, such as data minimisation, in an effective manner and to integrate the necessary safeguards into the processing in order to meet the requirements of the GDPR and protect the rights of Data Subjects (Article 25(1)).

The Controller shall implement appropriate technical and organisational measures for ensuring that, by default, only personal data which are necessary for each specific purpose of the processing are processed. That obligation applies to the amount of data collected, the extent of their processing, the period of their storage and their accessibility. In particular, such measures shall ensure that by default personal data are not made accessible without the individual's intervention to an indefinite number of natural persons (Article 27(2)).

An approved certification mechanism pursuant to Article 42 may be used as an element to demonstrate compliance with the requirements set out in Article 25(1) and (2) (Article 25(3)).

Rectification and Erasure

26.35   See details of obligations below.

Data Security

26.36   The Recitals refer to: network and information security, Computer Emergency Response Teams (CERTs) and Computer Security Incident Response Teams (CSIRTs); appropriate technical and organisational measures; security and risk evaluation; high risk and impact assessments; and impact assessments; and large scale processing operations; consultations; data breach and data breach notification; Commission delegated acts.

Chapter IV, Section 2 of the GDPR refers to security in detail.

Note that the EDPB also registers details in relation to certification, seals, and related tools, each of which also impact data security issues.

Security of Processing

26.37   Having regard to the state of the art and the costs of implementation and taking into account the nature, scope, context and purposes of the processing as well as the risk of varying likelihood and severity for the rights and freedoms of natural persons, the Controller and the Processor shall implement appropriate technical and organisational measures, to ensure a level of security appropriate to the risk, including, *inter alia*, as appropriate:

- the pseudonymisation and encryption of personal data;
- the ability to ensure the ongoing confidentiality, integrity, availability and resilience of processing systems and services;
- the ability to restore the availability and access to data in a timely manner in the event of a physical or technical incident;
- a process for regularly testing, assessing and evaluating the effectiveness of technical and organisational measures for ensuring the security of the processing (Article 32(1)).

In assessing the appropriate level of security account shall be taken in particular of the risks that are presented by processing, in particular from accidental or unlawful destruction, loss, alteration, unauthorised disclosure of, or access to personal data transmitted, stored or otherwise processed (Article 32(2)).

Adherence to an approved code of conduct pursuant to Article 40 or an approved certification mechanism pursuant to Article 42 may be used as an element to demonstrate compliance with the requirements set out in Article 32(1) (Article 32(3)).

The Controller and Processor shall take steps to ensure that any natural person acting under the authority of the Controller or the Processor who has access to personal data shall not process them except on instructions from the Controller, unless he or she is required to do so by EU or state law (Article 32(4)).

Prior to the GDPR, the ICO has issued recommendations in relation security issues, namely:

- A Practical Guide to IT Security: Ideal for the Small Business;
- Guidance on Data Security Breach Management;
- Notification of Data Security Breaches to the Information Commissioner's Office;
- Notification of Privacy and Electronic Communications Security Breaches;
- eIDAS;
- The Guide to NIS;
- Data Protection Impact Assessments.

These now need to be read in light of the GDPR changes.

Notifying Data Breach to Supervisory Authority

26.38   In the case of a personal data breach, the Controller shall without undue delay and, where feasible, not later than 72 hours after having become aware of it, notify the personal data breach to the supervisory authority competent in accordance with Article 55, unless the personal data breach is unlikely to result in *a* risk for the rights and freedoms of natural persons. Where the notification to the supervisory authority is not made within 72 hours, it shall be accompanied by a reason for the delay (Article 33(1)).

The Processor shall notify the Controller without undue delay after becoming aware of a personal data breach (Article 33(2)).

The notification referred to in Article 33(1) must at least:

- describe the nature of the personal data breach including where possible, the categories and approximate number of Data Subjects concerned and the categories and approximate number of data records concerned;
- communicate the name and contact details of the DPO or other contact point where more information can be obtained;
- describe the likely consequences of the personal data breach;
- describe the measures taken or proposed to be taken by the Controller to address the personal data breach, including, where appropriate, measures to mitigate its possible adverse effects (Article 33(2)).

Where, and in so far as, it is not possible to provide the information at the same time, the information may be provided in phases without undue further delay (Article 33(4)).

The Controller shall document any personal data breaches, comprising the facts relating to the personal data breach, its effects and the remedial action taken. This documentation must enable the supervisory authority to verify compliance with this Article (Article 33(5)).

Organisations should obviously review their security procedures. However, in accordance with the GDPR obligations and in accordance with planned preparedness, organisations should have procedures for how and when they notify the ICO. (Depending on the organisation and sector, other regulators may also need to be notified).

Each organisation should have a prepared notification procedure and letter for the ICO in the event that it is needed. This may be incorporated into an overall data breach procedure for the organisation.

WP29 also refers to breach and breach notification issues in one of its official documents.[77]

Communicating Data Breach to Data Subject

26.39   When the personal data breach is likely to result in a high risk to the rights and freedoms of natural persons, the Controller shall communicate the personal data breach to the Data Subject without undue delay (Article 34(1)).

The communication to the Data Subject referred to in Article 34(1) shall describe in clear and plain language the nature of the personal data breach and contain at least the information and measures referred to in Article 33(3)(b), (c) and (d) (Article 34(2)).

The communication to the Data Subject shall not be required if:

- the Controller has implemented appropriate technical and organisational protection measures, and that those measures were applied to the data affected by the

---

77 WP29, Opinion 03/2014 on Personal Data Breach Notification. Also see WP29; Working Document 01/2011 on the current EU personal data breach framework and recommendations for future policy developments; Opinion 06/2012 on the draft Commission Decision on the measures applicable to the notification of personal data breaches under Directive 2002/58/EC on privacy and electronic communications.

personal data breach, in particular those that render the data unintelligible to any person who is not authorised to access it, such as encryption;

- the Controller has taken subsequent measures which ensure that the high risk for the rights and freedoms of Data Subjects referred to in Article 34(3) is no longer likely to materialise;
- it would involve disproportionate effort. In such a case, there shall instead be a public communication or similar measure, whereby the Data Subjects are informed in an equally effective manner (Article 34(3)).

If the Controller has not already communicated the personal data breach to the Data Subject, the supervisory authority, having considered the likelihood of the personal data breach resulting in a high risk, may require it to do so or may decide that any of the conditions referred to in Article 34(3) are met (Article 34(4)).

Each organisation should have a prepared Data Subject notification procedure and letter/email for the Data Subject in the event that it is needed. This may be incorporated into an overall data breach procedure for the organisation.

Data Protection Impact Assessment and Prior Consultation

26.40   Chapter IV, Section 3 of the GDPR refers to impact assessments and prior consultations. The WP29 also refers to impact assessments.[78] The ICO also has a guide entitled 'Data Protection Impact Assessments'.[79]

Data Protection Impact Assessment

26.41   Where a type of processing in particular using new technologies, and taking into account the nature, scope, context and purposes of the processing, is likely to result in a high risk for the rights and freedoms of natural persons, the Controller shall, prior to the processing, carry out an assessment of the impact of the envisaged processing operations on the protection of personal data. A single assessment may address a set of similar processing operations that present similar high risks (Article 35(1)).

The Controller shall seek the advice of the DPO, where designated, when carrying out a data protection impact assessment (Article 35(2)).

A data protection impact assessment referred to in Article 35(1) shall in particular be required in the case of:

- a systematic and extensive evaluation of personal aspects relating to natural persons which is based on automated processing, including profiling, and on which decisions are based that produce legal effects concerning the individual person or similarly significantly affect the natural person;

---

78 WP29 Opinion 03/2014 on Personal Data Breach Notification; Opinion 07/2013 on the Data Protection Impact Assessment Template for Smart Grid and Smart Metering Systems ('DPIA Template') prepared by Expert Group 2 of the Commission's Smart Grid Task Force; Opinion 04/2013 on the Data Protection Impact Assessment Template for Smart Grid and Smart Metering Systems ('DPIA Template') prepared by Expert Group 2 of the Commission's Smart Grid Task Force; Opinion 9/2011 on the revised Industry Proposal for a Privacy and Data Protection Impact Assessment Framework for RFID Applications (and Annex: Privacy and Data Protection Impact Assessment Framework for RFID Applications); Opinion 5/2010 on the Industry Proposal for a Privacy and Data Protection Impact Assessment Framework for RFID Applications; Statement on the role of a risk-based approach in data protection legal framework, 2014.
79 ICO 'Data Protection Impact Assessments,' at https://ico.org.uk/for-organisations/guide-to-data-protection/guide-to-the-general-data-protection-regulation-gdpr/accountability-and-governance/data-protection-impact-assessments/.

- processing on a large scale of special categories of data referred to in Article 9(1), or of personal data relating to criminal convictions and offences referred to in Article 10;
- a systematic monitoring of a publicly accessible area on a large scale (Article 35(3)).

The supervisory authority shall establish and make public a list of the kind of processing operations which are subject to the requirement for a data protection impact assessment pursuant to Article 35(1). The supervisory authority shall communicate those lists to the EDPB (Article 35(4)).

The supervisory authority may also establish and make public a list of the kind of processing operations for which no data protection impact assessment is required. The supervisory authority shall communicate those lists to the EDPB (Article 35(5)).

Prior to the adoption of the lists referred to in Article 35(4) and (5) the competent supervisory authority shall apply the consistency mechanism referred to in Article 63 where such lists involve processing activities which are related to the offering of goods or services to Data Subjects or to the monitoring of their behaviour in several states, or may substantially affect the free movement of personal data within the EU (Article 35(6)).

The assessment shall contain at least:

- a systematic description of the envisaged processing operations and the purposes of the processing, including where applicable the legitimate interest pursued by the Controller;
- an assessment of the necessity and proportionality of the processing operations in relation to the purposes;
- an assessment of the risks to the rights and freedoms of Data Subjects referred to in Article 35(1); and
- the measures envisaged to address the risks, including safeguards, security measures and mechanisms to ensure the protection of personal data and to demonstrate compliance with the GDPR taking into account the rights and legitimate interests of Data Subjects and other persons concerned (Article 35(7)).

Compliance with approved codes of conduct referred to in Article 40 by the relevant Controllers or Processors shall be taken into due account in assessing the impact of the processing operations performed by such Controllers or Processors, in particular for the purposes of a data protection impact assessment (Article 35(8)).

Where appropriate, the Controller shall seek the views of Data Subjects or their representatives on the intended processing, without prejudice to the protection of commercial or public interests or the security of the processing operations (Article 35(9)).

Where the processing pursuant to Article 6(1)(c) or (e) has a legal basis in EU law, or the law of the state to which the Controller is subject, that law regulates the specific processing operation or set of operations in question, and a data protection impact assessment has already been carried out as part of a general impact assessment in the context of the adoption of that legal basis, Article 35(1)–(7) shall not apply, unless states deem it to be necessary to carry out such an assessment prior to the processing activities (Article 35(10)).

Where necessary, the Controller shall carry out a review to assess if the processing is performed with the data protection impact assessment at least when there is a change of the risk represented by the processing operations (Article 35(11)).

Organisations must assess their obligations in terms of implementing procedures for, and undertaking of, DPIAs.[80]

The DPDI Bill seeks to make provision in relation to impact and risk assessments.

Prior Consultation

26.42 The Controller shall consult the supervisory authority prior to the processing where a data protection impact assessment as provided for in Article 35 indicates that the processing would result in a high risk in the absence of measures taken by the Controller to mitigate the risk (Article 36(1)).

Where the supervisory authority is of the opinion that the intended processing referred to in Article 36(2) would infringe the GDPR, in particular where the Controller has insufficiently identified or mitigated the risk, it shall within a maximum period of eight weeks following the request for consultation provide written advice to the Controller and, where applicable to the Processor, and may use any of its powers referred to in Article 58. This period may be extended by six weeks, taking into account the complexity of the intended processing. The supervisory authority shall inform the Controller and, where applicable, the Processor, of any such extension within one month of receipt of the request for consultation together with the reasons for the delay. Those periods may be suspended until the supervisory authority has obtained information it has requested for the purposes of the consultation. (Article 36(2)).

When consulting the supervisory authority pursuant to Article 36(3), the Controller shall provide the supervisory authority with:

- where applicable, the respective responsibilities of Controller, joint Controllers and Processors involved in the processing, in particular for processing within a group of undertakings;
- the purposes and means of the intended processing;
- the measures and safeguards provided to protect the rights and freedoms of Data Subjects pursuant to the GDPR;
- where applicable, the contact details of the DPO;
- the data protection impact assessment provided for in Article 35; and
- any other information requested by the supervisory authority (Article 36(3)).

States shall consult the supervisory authority during the preparation of a proposal for a legislative measure to be adopted by a national parliament or of a regulatory measure based on such a legislative measure, which relates to the processing (Article 36(4)).

Notwithstanding Article 36(1), states' law may require Controllers to consult with, and obtain prior authorisation from, the supervisory authority in relation to the processing by a Controller for the performance of a task carried out by the Controller in the public interest, including processing in relation to social protection and public health (Article 36(5)).

The DPDI Bill seeks to make provision in relation to prior consultations with the ICO.

Data Protection Officer

26.43 See obligations below (at para **26.72**).

---

80 Generally note D Wright and P de Hert, eds, *Privacy Impact Assessment* (Springer 2012).

Data Transfers

26.44 For a more detailed discussion of UK data transfer rules and issues see Lambert, *Data Protection and Data Transfers Law* (Bloomsbury).

Recitals 101–115 refer to cross border data transfers. The WP29 also refers to transfers.[81]

Chapter V of the GDPR refers to data transfers and transfer of personal data to third countries or international organisations.

Prior to the new GDPR, the ICO has issued recommendations in relation to personal data transfer issues, namely:

- Assessing Adequacy;
- International Transfers – Legal Guidance;
- Model Contract Clauses;
- Outsourcing – A Guide for Small and Medium-Sized Businesses.

These now need to be read in light of the new changes.

There have also been significant data transfer changes in the UK with the EU Adequacy Decision, new EU contracts, new UK contacts, and changes now proposed in the DPDI Bill.

General Principle for Transfers

26.45 Any transfer of personal data which are undergoing processing or are intended for processing after transfer to a third country or to an international organisation shall take place only if, subject to the other provisions of the GDPR, the conditions laid down in this Chapter are complied with by the Controller and Processor, including for onward transfers of personal data from the third country or an international organisation to another third country or to another international organisation. All provisions in this Chapter shall be applied in order to ensure that the level of protection of natural persons guaranteed by the GDPR are not undermined (Article 44).

Transfers via Adequacy Decision

26.46 A transfer of personal data to a third country or an international organisation may take place where the Commission has decided that the third country, a territory or one or more specified sectors within that third country, or the international organisation in question ensures an adequate level of protection. Such transfer shall not require any specific authorisation (Article 45(1)).

When assessing the adequacy of the level of protection, the Commission shall, in particular, take account of the following elements:

- the rule of law, respect for human rights and fundamental freedoms, relevant legislation, both general and sectoral, including concerning public security, defence,

---

81 WP29 Statement on the implementation of the judgement of the Court of Justice of the European Union of 6 October 2015 in the *Maximilian Schrems v Data Protection Commissioner case* (C-362/14); Recommendation 1/2012 on the Standard Application form for Approval of Binding Corporate Rules for the Transfer of Personal Data for Processing Activities; Opinion 3/2009 on the Draft Commission Decision on standard contractual clauses for the transfer of personal data to processors established in third countries, under Directive 95/46/EC (data controller to data processor); FAQs in order to address some issues raised by the entry into force of the EU Commission Decision 2010/87/EU of 5 February 2010 on standard contractual clauses for the transfer of personal data to processors established in third countries under Directive 95/46/EC 2010; Recommendation 1/2007 on the Standard Application for Approval of Binding Corporate Rules for the Transfer of Personal Data.

national security and criminal law and the access of public authorities to personal data, as well as the implementation of this legislation, data protection rules, professional rules and security measures, including rules for onward transfer of personal data to another third country or international organisation, which are complied with in that country or international organisation, case law, as well as effective and enforceable Data Subject rights and effective administrative and judicial redress for the Data Subjects whose personal data are being transferred;

- the existence and effective functioning of one or more independent supervisory authorities in the third country or to which an international organisation is subject, with responsibility for ensuring and enforcing compliance with the data protection rules, including adequate enforcement powers for assisting and advising the Data Subjects in exercising their rights and for assisting and advising the Data Subjects in exercising their rights and for co-operation with the supervisory authorities of the states; and

- the international commitments the third country or international organisation concerned has entered into, or other obligations arising from legally binding conventions or instruments as well as from its participation in multilateral or regional systems, in particular in relation to the protection of personal data (Article 45(2)).

The Commission, after assessing the adequacy of the level of protection, may decide by means of implementing act, that a third country, or a territory or one or more specified sectors within that third country, or an international organisation ensures an adequate level of protection within the meaning of Article 45(3).

The Commission shall, on an on-going basis, monitor developments in third countries and international organisations that could affect the functioning of decisions adopted pursuant to Article 45(3) and decisions adopted on the basis of Article 25(6) of DPD 1995 (Article 45(4)).

The Commission shall publish in the Official Journal of the EU and on its website a list of those third countries, territories and specified sectors within a third country and international organisations where it has decided that an adequate level of protection is or is no longer ensured (Article 45(8)).

Decisions adopted by the Commission on the basis of Article 25(6) of DPD 1995 shall remain in force until amended, replaced or repealed by a Commission Decision adopted in accordance with Article 45(3) or (5) (Article 45(9)).

Note that the EU-US Safe Harbour data transfer regime was struck down by the Court of Justice in the *Schrems* case.[82] The Safe Harbour regime was held to be invalid. Notwithstanding the GDPR, the previous Safe Harbour regime needed to be replaced. Negotiations between the EU Commission and the US authorities ensued. Agreement may be reached and a new agreement implemented in early 2016. The replacement is entitled EU-US Privacy Shield.

It should be noted also that there have been some concerns that the same or similar reasons for the striking down of the Safe Harbour regime may cause concerns for some of the other transfer legitimising mechanisms. It remains to be seen if further challenges or concerns will undermine the Privacy Shield, standard clauses, etc.

---

82 *Schrems v Commissioner*, Court of Justice, Case C-362/14, 6 October 2015. The case technically related to Prism and Facebook Europe and transfers to the US. However, the wider import turned out to be the entire EU-US Safe Harbour Agreement and data transfers to the US. Note WP29 statement on the case, Statement on the implementation of the judgement of the Court of Justice of the European Union of 6 October 2015 in the *Maximilian Schrems v Data Protection Commissioner case* (C-362/14).

The issues of data transfers and adequacy decision has added significance in the UK now that Brexit has been passed by Parliament (in the form of the EU (Withdrawal Agreement) Act 2020), and the transition period is well advanced, and the UK is seeking a formal adequacy decision from the EU in order ease and facilitate the continued use of EU data transfers into the UK. (See also Chapter 24.)

Transfers via Appropriate Safeguards

26.47   In the absence of a decision pursuant to Article 45(3), a Controller or Processor may transfer personal data to a third country or an international organisation only if the Controller or Processor has provided appropriate safeguards, and on condition that enforceable Data Subject rights and effective legal remedies for Data Subjects are available (Article 46(1)).

The appropriate safeguards referred to in Article 46(1) may be provided for, without requiring any specific authorisation from a supervisory authority, by:

- a legally binding and enforceable instrument between public authorities or bodies;
- binding corporate rules in accordance with Article 47;
- standard data protection clauses adopted by the Commission in accordance with the examination procedure referred to in Article 93(2);
- standard data protection clauses adopted by a supervisory authority and approved by the Commission pursuant to the examination procedure referred to in Article 93(2);
- an approved code of conduct pursuant to Article 40 together with binding and enforceable commitments of the Controller or Processor in the third country to apply the appropriate safeguards, including as regards Data Subjects' rights; or
- an approved certification mechanism pursuant to Article 42 together with binding and enforceable commitments of the Controller or Processor in the third country to apply the appropriate safeguards, including as regards Data Subjects' rights (Article 46(2)).

Subject to the authorisation from the competent supervisory authority, the appropriate safeguards referred to in Article 46(1) may also be provided for, in particular, by:

- contractual clauses between the Controller or Processor and the Controller, Processor or the recipient of the personal data in the third country or international organisation; or
- provisions to be inserted into administrative arrangements between public authorities or bodies which include enforceable and effective Data Subject rights (Article 46(3)).

The supervisory authority shall apply the consistency mechanism referred to in Article 63 in the cases referred to in Article 46(3) (Article 46(4)).

Authorisations by a state or supervisory authority on the basis of Article 26(2) of DPD95 shall remain valid until amended, replaced or repealed, if necessary, by that supervisory authority. Decisions adopted by the Commission on the basis of Article 26(4) of DPD95 shall remain in force until amended, replaced or repealed, if necessary, by a Commission Decision adopted in accordance with Article 46(2) (Article 46(5)).

Transfers via Binding Corporate Rules

26.48   The competent supervisory authority shall approve binding corporate rules in accordance with the consistency mechanism set out in Article 63, provided that they:

- are legally binding and apply to and are enforced by every member concerned of the group of undertakings or groups of enterprises engaged in a joint economic activity, including their employees;
- expressly confer enforceable rights on Data Subjects with regard to the processing of their personal data; and
- fulfil the requirements laid down in Article 47(2) (Article 47(1)).

The binding corporate rules shall specify at least:

- the structure and contact details of the group of enterprises engaged in a joint economic activity and of each of its members;
- the data transfers or set of transfers, including the categories of personal data, the type of processing and its purposes, the type of Data Subjects affected and the identification of the third country or countries in question;
- their legally binding nature, both internally and externally;
- the application of the general data protection Principles, in particular purpose limitation, data minimisation, limited storage periods, data quality, data protection by design (DPbD) and by default, legal basis for the processing, processing of special categories of personal data, measures to ensure data security, and the requirements in respect of onward transfers to bodies not bound by the binding corporate rules [d];
- the rights of Data Subjects in regard to processing and the means to exercise these rights, including the right not to be subject to decisions based solely on automated processing, including profiling in accordance with Article 22, the right to lodge a complaint with the competent supervisory authority and before the competent courts of the states in accordance with Article 79, and to obtain redress and, where appropriate, compensation for a breach of the binding corporate rules [e];
- the acceptance by the Controller or Processor established on the territory of a state of liability for any breaches of the binding corporate rules by any member concerned not established in the EU; the Controller or the Processor shall be exempted from this liability, in whole or in part, only if it proves that that member is not responsible for the event giving rise to the damage [f];
- how the information on the binding corporate rules, in particular on the provisions referred to in this Article 47(2)(d), (e) and (f) is provided to the Data Subjects in addition to Articles 13 and 14;
- the tasks of any DPO designated in accordance with Article 37 or any other person or entity in charge of monitoring compliance with the binding corporate rules within the group of undertakings, or group of enterprises engaging in a joint economic activity, as well as monitoring training and complaint handling;
- the complaint procedures;
- the mechanisms within the group of undertakings, or group of enterprises engaging in a joint economic activity for ensuring the verification of compliance with the binding corporate rules. Such mechanisms shall include data protection audits and methods for ensuring corrective actions to protect the rights of the Data Subject. Results of such verification should be communicated to the person or entity referred under point (h) and to the board of the controlling undertaking or of the group of enterprises engaged in a joint economic activity, and should be available upon request to the competent supervisory authority;
- the mechanisms for reporting and recording changes to the rules and reporting those changes to the supervisory authority;
- the co-operation mechanism with the supervisory authority to ensure compliance by any member of the group of undertakings, or group of enterprises engaging

in a joint economic activity, in particular by making available to the supervisory authority the results of verifications of the measures referred to in this Article 47(2)(j);

- the mechanisms for reporting to the competent supervisory authority any legal requirements to which a member of the group of undertakings, or group of enterprises engaging in a joint economic activity is subject in a third country which are likely to have a substantial adverse effect on the guarantees provided by the binding corporate rules; and
- the appropriate data protection training to personnel having permanent or regular access to personal data (Article 47(2)).

The Commission may specify the format and procedures for the exchange of information between Controllers, Processors and supervisory authorities for binding corporate rules. Those implementing acts shall be adopted in accordance with the examination procedure set out in Article 93(2) (Article 47(4)).

Given that the EU-US Safe Harbour data transfer regime was struck down by the Court of Justice in the *Schrems* case,[83] there have been some concerns that a similar strike down problem could arise for other transfer legitimising mechanisms, including BCRs. The WP29 also refers to BCR issues, including the *Schrems* case.[84]

Transfers or Disclosures Not Authorised by EU Law

26.49   Any judgment of a court or tribunal and any decision of an administrative authority of a third country requiring a Controller or Processor to transfer or disclose personal data may only be recognised or enforceable in any manner if based on an international agreement, such as a mutual legal assistance treaty, in force between the requesting third country and the EU or a state, without prejudice to other grounds for transfer pursuant to this Chapter (Article 48).

Derogations for Specific Situations

26.50   In the absence of an adequacy decision pursuant to Article 45(3), or of appropriate safeguards pursuant to Article 46, including binding corporate rules, a transfer or a set of transfers of personal data to a third country or an international organisation shall take place only on one of the following conditions:

- the Data Subject has explicitly consented to the proposed transfer, after having been informed of the possible risks of such transfers for the Data Subject due to the absence of an adequacy decision and appropriate safeguards; [a]

---

83 *Schrems v Commissioner*, Court of Justice, Case C-362/14, 6 October 2015.
84 WP29 Statement on the implementation of the judgement of the Court of Justice of the European Union of 6 October 2015 in the *Maximilian Schrems v Data Protection Commissioner case* (C-362/14); Explanatory Document on the Processor Binding Corporate Rules, Revised version May 2015 – WP 204; Opinion 02/2014 on a Referential for requirements for Binding Corporate Rules submitted to national Data Protection Authorities in the EU and Cross Border Privacy Rules submitted to APEC CBPR Accountability Agents; Opinion 07/2013 on the Data Protection Impact Assessment Template for Smart Grid and Smart Metering Systems ('DPIA Template') prepared by Expert Group 2 of the Commission's Smart Grid Task Force; Opinion 04/2013 on the Data Protection Impact Assessment Template for Smart Grid and Smart Metering Systems ('DPIA Template') prepared by Expert Group 2 of the Commission's Smart Grid Task Force; Working Document 02/2012 setting up a table with the elements and principles to be found in Processor Binding Corporate Rules; Recommendation 1/2012 on the Standard Application form for Approval of Binding Corporate Rules for the Transfer of Personal Data for Processing Activities; Opinion 5/2010 on the Industry Proposal for a Privacy and Data Protection Impact Assessment Framework for RFID Applications.

- the transfer is necessary for the performance of a contract between the Data Subject and the Controller or the implementation of pre-contractual measures taken at the Data Subject's request; [b]
- the transfer is necessary for the conclusion or performance of a contract concluded in the interest of the Data Subject between the Controller and another natural or legal person; [c]
- the transfer is necessary for important reasons of public interest;
- the transfer is necessary for the establishment, exercise or defence of legal claims;
- the transfer is necessary in order to protect the vital interests of the Data Subject or of other persons, where the Data Subject is physically or legally incapable of giving consent;
- the transfer is made from a register which according to EU or state law is intended to provide information to the public and which is open to consultation either by the public in general or by any person who can demonstrate a legitimate interest, but only to the extent that the conditions laid down in EU or state law for consultation are fulfilled in the particular case. [g]

Where a transfer could not be based on a provision in Article 45 or 46, including the provisions on binding corporate rules, and none of the derogations for a specific situation referred to in the first subparagraph of this paragraph is applicable, a transfer to a third country or an international organisation may take place only if the transfer is not repetitive, concerns only a limited number of data subjects, is necessary for the purposes of compelling legitimate interests pursued by the Controller which are not overridden by the interests or rights and freedoms of the Data Subject, and the Controller has assessed all the circumstances surrounding the data transfer and has on the basis of that assessment provided suitable safeguards with regard to the protection of personal data. The Controller shall inform the supervisory authority of the transfer. The Controller shall, in addition to providing the information referred to in Articles 13 and 14, inform the Data Subject of the transfer and on the compelling legitimate interests pursued (Article 49(1)).

A transfer pursuant to Article 49(1)(g) shall not involve the entirety of the personal data or entire categories of the personal data contained in the register. Where the register is intended for consultation by persons having a legitimate interest, the transfer shall be made only at the request of those persons or if they are to be the recipients (Article 49(2)).

Article 47(1)(a), (b), (c) and the second subparagraph shall not apply to activities carried out by public authorities in the exercise of their public powers (Article 49(3)).

The public interest referred to in Article 47(1)(d) must be recognised in EU law or in the law of the state to which the Controller is subject (Article 49(4)).

In the absence of an adequacy decision, EU law or state law may, for important reasons of public interest, expressly set limits to the transfer of specific categories of personal data to a third country or an international organisation. States shall notify such provisions to the Commission (Article 49(5)).

The Controller or Processor shall document the assessment as well as the suitable safeguards referred to in Article 49(1) in the records referred to in Article 30 (Article 49(6)).

Data Subject Rights

26.51 The Recitals refer to: Data Subject rights; principles of fair and transparent processing; prior information requirements; right of access; right of rectification and right to be forgotten (RtbF); right to complain to single supervisory authority; automated processing.

Chapter III of the GDPR refers to the rights of Data Subjects. These include:

- right to transparency (Article 5; Article 12);
- right to prior information: directly obtained data (Article 13);
- right to prior information: indirectly obtained data (Article 14);
- right of confirmation and right of access (Article 15);
- right to rectification (Article 16);
- right to erasure (Right to be Forgotten) (RtbF) (Article 17);
- right to restriction of processing (Article 18);
- notifications re rectification, erasure or restriction (Article 19);
- right to data portability (Article 20);
- right to object (Article 21);
- rights re automated individual decision making, including profiling (Article 22);
- DPbD (Article 25);
- security rights;
- data protection impact assessment and prior consultation;
- communicating data breach to data subject;
- Data Protection Officer (DPO);
- remedies, liability and sanctions (Chapter VIII).

Transparency

26.52   Article 5 of the GDPR provides that personal data shall be 'processed … in a transparent manner in relation to the Data Subject.' Transparency:

> 'require[s] greater awareness among citizens about the processing going on: its existence, its content and the flows generated in and out by using terminals.
>
> Transparency also relates to security of data and risk management.'[85]

Some commentators have suggested the GDPR could go further. It has been suggested that 'the greater the flow of information systems the more opaque it becomes in modern information systems and with new ICT applications. In that case the right to transparency must increase alongside these new processes.'[86]

Article 5 of the new GDPR in the data protection Principles first principle now reads that personal data shall be:

> 'processed lawfully, fairly and in a transparent manner in relation to the Data Subject ("lawfulness, fairness and transparency").'

Article 12 refers to transparent information, communication and modalities for exercising the rights of the Data Subject.

The Controller shall take appropriate measures to provide any information referred to in Articles 13 and 14 and any communication under Articles 15–22, and 34 relating to processing to the Data Subject in a concise, transparent, intelligible and easily accessible form, using clear and plain language, in particular for any information addressed specifically to a child. The information shall be provided in writing, or by other means, where appropriate, by electronic form. When requested by the Data Subject, the information may be provided orally, provided that the identity of the Data Subject is proven by other means (Article 12(1)).

---

85   L Costa and Y Poullet, 'Privacy and the Regulation of 2012,' *Computer Law & Security Review* (2012) (28) 254–262, at 256.
86   See above, at 256.

The Controller shall facilitate the exercise of Data Subject rights under Articles 15–22. In cases referred to in Article 11(2) the Controller shall not refuse to act on the request of the Data Subject for exercising their rights under Articles 15–22, unless the Controller demonstrates that it is not in a position to identify the Data Subject (Article 12(2)).

The Controller shall provide information on action taken on a request under Articles 15–22 to the Data Subject without undue delay and in any event within one month of receipt of the request. That period may be extended by two further months when necessary, taking into account the complexity and the number of the requests. The Controller shall inform the Data Subject of any such extension within one month of receipt of the request, together with the reasons for the delay. Where the Data Subject makes the request by electronic means, the information shall be provided by electronic means where possible, unless otherwise requested by the Data Subject (Article 12(3)).

If the Controller does not take action on the request of the Data Subject, the Controller shall inform the Data Subject without delay and at the latest within one month of receipt of the request of the reasons for not taking action and on the possibility of lodging a complaint to a supervisory authority and seeking a judicial remedy (Article 12(4)).

Information provided under Articles 13 and 14 and any communication and any actions taken under Articles 15–22 and 34 shall be provided free of charge. Where requests from a Data Subject are manifestly unfounded or excessive, in particular because of their repetitive character, the Controller may either charge a reasonable fee taking into account the administrative costs for providing the information or the communication or taking the action requested; or refuse to act on the request. The Controller shall bear the burden of demonstrating the manifestly unfounded or excessive character of the request (Article 12(4)).

Without prejudice to Article 11, where the Controller has reasonable doubts concerning the identity of the natural person making the request referred to in Articles 15–21, the Controller may request the provision of additional information necessary to confirm the identity of the Data Subject (Article 12(6)).

The information to be provided to Data Subjects pursuant to Articles 13 and 14 may be provided in combination with standardised icons in order to give in an easily visible, intelligible and clearly legible manner, a meaningful overview of the intended processing. Where the icons are presented electronically they shall be machine-readable (Article 12(7)).

The Commission shall be empowered to adopt delegated acts in accordance with Article 92 for the purpose of determining the information to be presented by the icons and the procedures for providing standardised icons (Article 12(8)).

Prior to the new GDPR, the ICO has issued recommendations in relation to privacy notices, namely:

- Getting It Right: Collecting Information about Your Customers;
- Privacy Notices Code of Practice.

These now need to be read in light of the GDPR changes.

Data Access Rights

26.53   Chapter III, Section 2 of the GDPR refers to data access. It should be noted that the prior information requirements might have previously been viewed as Controller compliance obligations. However, they are now reformulated as part of the Data Subject rights. This therefore is a change in emphasis.

Right to Prior Information: Directly Obtained Data

26.54   Article 13 refers to information to be provided where the data are collected from the Data Subject. Where personal data relating to a Data Subject are collected from the Data Subject, the Controller shall, at the time when personal data are obtained, provide the Data Subject with the following information:

- the identity and the contact details of the Controller and, where applicable, of the Controller's representative;
- the contact details of the DPO, where applicable;
- the purposes of the processing for which the personal data are intended as well as the legal basis for the processing;
- where the processing is based on Article 6(1)(f), the legitimate interests pursued by the Controller or by a third party;
- the recipients or categories of recipients of the personal data, if any;
- where applicable, the fact that the Controller intends to transfer personal data to a third country or international organisation and the existence or absence of an adequacy decision by the Commission, or in the case of transfers referred to in Articles 46 or 47, or the second subparagraph of Article 49(1), reference to the appropriate or suitable safeguards and the means by which to obtain a copy of them or where they have been made available (Article 13(1)).

In addition to the information referred to in Article 13(1), the Controller shall, at the time when personal data are obtained, provide the Data Subject with the following further information necessary to ensure fair and transparent processing:

- the period for which the personal data will be stored, or if that is not possible, the criteria used to determine that period;
- the existence of the right to request from the Controller access to and rectification or erasure of personal data or restriction of processing concerning the Data Subject or to object to the processing as well as the right to data portability;
- where the processing is based on Article 6(1)(a) or Article 9(2)(a), the existence of the right to withdraw consent at any time, without affecting the lawfulness of processing based on consent before its withdrawal;
- the right to lodge a complaint to a supervisory authority;
- whether the provision of personal data is a statutory or contractual requirement, or a requirement necessary to enter into a contract, as well as whether the Data Subject is obliged to provide the data and of the possible consequences of failure to provide such data;
- the existence of automated decision making including profiling referred to in Article 22(1) and (4) and at least in those cases, meaningful information about the logic involved, as well as the significance and the envisaged consequences of such processing for the Data Subject (Article 13(2)).

Where the Controller intends to further process the data for a purpose other than that for which the personal data were collected, the Controller shall provide the Data Subject prior to that further processing with information on that other purpose and with any relevant further information as referred to in Article 13(2) (Article 13(2)).

Article 13(1), (2) and (3) shall not apply where and insofar as the Data Subject already has the information (Article 13(4)).

Right to Prior Information: Indirectly Obtained Data

26.55   Article 14 refers to information to be provided where the data have not been obtained from the Data Subject. Where personal data have not been obtained from the Data Subject, the Controller shall provide the Data Subject with the following information:

- the identity and the contact details of the Controller and, where applicable, of the Controller's representative;
- the contact details of the DPO, where applicable;
- the purposes of the processing for which the personal data are intended as well as the legal basis of the processing;
- the categories of personal data concerned;
- the recipients or categories of recipients of the personal data, if any;
- where applicable, that the Controller intends to transfer personal data to a recipient in a third country or international organisation and the existence or absence of an adequacy decision by the Commission, or in case of transfers referred to in Article 46 or 47, or the second subparagraph of Article 49(1), reference to the appropriate or suitable safeguards and the means to obtain a copy of them or where they have been made available (Article 14(1)).

In addition to the information referred to in Article 14(1), the Controller shall provide the Data Subject with the following information necessary to ensure fair and transparent processing in respect of the Data Subject:

- the period for which the personal data will be stored, or if this is not possible, the criteria used to determine that period;
- where the processing is based on Article 6(1)(f), the legitimate interests pursued by the Controller or by a third party;
- the existence of the right to request from the Controller access to and rectification or erasure of personal data or restriction of processing concerning the Data Subject and to object to processing as well as the right to data portability;
- where processing is based on Article 6(1)(a) or Article 9(2)(a), the existence of the right to withdraw consent at any time, without affecting the lawfulness of processing based on consent before its withdrawal;
- the right to lodge a complaint to a supervisory authority;
- from which source the personal data originate, and if applicable, whether it came from publicly accessible sources;
- the existence of automated decision making including profiling referred to in Article 22(1) and (4) and at least in those cases, meaningful information about the logic involved, as well as the significance and the envisaged consequences of such processing for the Data Subject (Article 14(2)).

The Controller shall provide the information referred to in Article 14(1) and (2),

- within a reasonable period after obtaining the data, but at the latest within one month, having regard to the specific circumstances in which the data are processed; or
- if the data are to be used for communication with the Data Subject, at the latest at the time of the first communication to that Data Subject; or
- if a disclosure to another recipient is envisaged, at the latest when the data are first disclosed (Article 14(3)).

Where the Controller intends to further process the data for a purpose other than the one for which the data were obtained, the Controller shall provide the Data Subject prior to that further processing with information on that other purpose and with any relevant further information as referred to in Article 14(2) (Article 14(4)).

Article 14(1) to (4) shall not apply where and insofar as:

- the Data Subject already has the information;
- the provision of such information proves impossible or would involve a dispro-portionate effort, in particular for processing for archiving purposes in the public interest, scientific or historical research purposes or statistical purposes subject to the conditions and safeguards referred to in Article 89(1) or in so far as the obligation referred to in Article 14(1) is likely to render impossible or seriously impair the achievement of the objectives of that processing. In such cases the Controller shall take appropriate measures to protect the Data Subject's rights and freedoms and legitimate interests, including making the information publicly available;
- obtaining or disclosure is expressly laid down by EU or state law to which the Controller is subject and which provides appropriate measures to protect the Data Subject's legitimate interests; or
- where the data must remain confidential subject to an obligation of professional secrecy regulated by EU or state law, including a statutory obligation of secrecy (Article 14(5)).

Right of Confirmation and Right of Access

26.56   The Data Subject shall have the right to obtain from the Controller confir-mation as to whether or not personal data concerning them are being processed, and where that is the case, access to the personal data and the following information:

- the purposes of the processing;
- the categories of personal data concerned;
- the recipients or categories of recipients to whom the personal data have been or will be disclosed, in particular recipients in third countries or international organisations;
- where possible, the envisaged period for which the personal data will be stored, or if possible, this the criteria used to determine that period;
- the existence of the right to request from the Controller rectification or erasure of personal data or restriction of the processing of personal data concerning the Data Subject or to object to the processing;
- the right to lodge a complaint to a supervisory authority;
- where the personal data are not collected from the Data Subject, any available information as to their source;
- the existence of automated decision making including profiling referred to in Article 22(1) and (4) and at least in those cases, meaningful information about the logic involved, as well as the significance and the envisaged consequences of such processing for the Data Subject (Article 15(1)).

Where personal data are transferred to a third country or to an international organisa-tion, the Data Subject shall have the right to be informed of the appropriate safeguards pursuant to Article 46 relating to the transfer (Article 15(2)).

The Controller shall provide a copy of the personal data undergoing processing. For any further copies requested by the Data Subject, the Controller may charge a rea-sonable fee based on administrative costs. Where the Data Subject makes the request by electronic means, and unless otherwise requested by the Data Subject, the informa-tion shall be provided in a commonly used electronic form (Article 15(3)).

The right to obtain a copy referred to in Article 15(3) shall not adversely affect the rights and freedoms of others (Article 15(4)).

Prior to the new GDPR, the ICO has issued recommendations in relation data access issues, namely:

- Access to Information Held in Complaint Files;
- Enforced Subject Access (section 56);
- How to Disclose Information Safely – Removing Personal Data from Information Requests and Datasets;
- Regulatory Activity Exemption;
- Subject Access: Code of Practice;
- Subject Access: Responding to a Request Checklist.

These now need to be read in light of the GDPR changes.

Right to be Informed of Third Country Safeguards

26.57 Where personal data are transferred to a third country or to an international organisation, the Data Subject shall have the right to be informed of the appropriate safeguards pursuant to Article 46 relating to the transfer (Article 15(2)). This has added relevance as part of the potential ripples from the *Schrems* Court of Justice decision.

Rectification and Erasure

26.58 Chapter III, Section 3 of the GDPR refers to rectification and erasure. This was already an important and topical issue and is now even more important on foot of the *Google Spain* case (see below) and also issues such as online abuse.

Right to Rectification

26.59 The Data Subject shall have the right to obtain from the Controller without undue delay the rectification of inaccurate personal data concerning them. Taking into account the purposes of the processing, the Data Subject shall have the right to have incomplete personal data completed, including by means of providing a supplementary statement (Article 16).[87]

Right to Erasure (Right to be Forgotten) (RtbF)

26.60 The Data Subject shall have the right to obtain from the Controller the erasure of personal data concerning them without undue delay where one of the following grounds applies:

- the personal data are no longer necessary in relation to the purposes for which they were collected or otherwise processed;
- the Data Subject withdraws consent on which the processing is based according to Article 6(1)(a), or Article 9(2)(a), and where there is no other legal ground for the processing;
- the Data Subject objects to the processing of personal data pursuant to Article 21(1) and there are no overriding legitimate grounds for the processing, or the Data Subject objects to the processing of personal data pursuant to Article 21(2);
- the personal data have been unlawfully processed;

---

87   See P Lambert, *The Right to be Forgotten* (Bloomsbury, 2019).

- the personal data have to be erased for compliance with a legal obligation in EU or state law to which the Controller is subject;
- the data have been collected in relation to the offer of information society services referred to in Article 8(1) (Article 17(1)).

Where the Controller has made the personal data public and is obliged pursuant to Article 17(1) to erase the personal data, the Controller, taking account of available technology and the cost of implementation, shall take reasonable steps, including technical measures, to inform Controllers which are processing the personal data that the Data Subject has requested the erasure by such Controllers of any links to, or copy or replication of those personal data (Article 17(2)).

Article 17(1) and (2) shall not apply to the extent that processing is necessary:

- for exercising the right of freedom of expression and information;
- for compliance with a legal obligation which requires processing of personal data by EU or Member state law to which the Controller is subject or for the performance of a task carried out in the public interest or in the exercise of official authority vested in the Controller;
- for reasons of public interest in the area of public health in accordance with Article 9(2)(h) and (i) as well as Article 9(3);
- for archiving purposes in the public interest, or scientific and historical research purposes or statistical purposes in accordance with Article 89(1) in so far as the right referred to in Article 17(1) is likely to render impossible or seriously impair the achievement of the objectives of that processing; or
- for the establishment, exercise or defence of legal claims (Article 17(3)).[88]

In the *Google Spain* case, the Court of Justice held that:

'Article 2(b) and (d) of [the DPD] ... are to be interpreted as meaning that, first, the activity of a search engine consisting in finding information published or placed on the internet by third parties, indexing it automatically, storing it temporarily and, finally, making it available to internet users according to a particular order of preference must be classified as "processing of personal data" within the meaning of Article 2(b) when that information contains personal data and, second, the operator of the search engine must be regarded as the "controller" in respect of that processing, within the meaning of Article 2(d).

Article 4(1)(a) of [DPD 1995] is to be interpreted as meaning that processing of personal data is carried out in the context of the activities of an establishment of the controller on the territory of a Member State, within the meaning of that provision, when the operator of a search engine sets up in a Member State a branch or subsidiary which is intended to promote and sell advertising space offered by that engine and which orientates its activity towards the inhabitants of that Member State.'[89]

The WP29 also refers to RtbF issues as well as the *Google Spain* case.[90] This includes WP29 'Guidelines on the implementation of the Court of Justice of the European

---

88 In relation to the original draft, etc, see for example, G Sartor, 'The Right to be Forgotten in the Draft Data Protection Regulation,' *International Data Privacy Law* (2015) (5;1) 64. Also A Mantelero, 'The EU Proposal for a general data protection regulation and the roots of the "right to be forgotten,"' *Computer Law and Security Report* (2013) (29:3) 229.

89 *Google Spain SL and Google Inc v Agencia Española de Protección de Datos (AEPD) and Mario Costeja González*, Case C-131/12, 13 May 2014. Also see, for example, P Lambert, *The Right to be Forgotten* (Bloomsbury, 2019); P Lambert, *International Handbook of Social Media Laws* (Bloomsbury 2014); P Lambert, *Social Networking: Law, Rights and Policy* (Clarus Press 2014); V Mayer-Schönberger, *Delete: the Virtue of Forgetting in the Digital Age* (Princeton, 2009).

90 WP29 Guidelines on the implementation of the Court of Justice of the European Union judgment on 'Google Spain and Inc v Agencia Española de Protección de Datos (AEPD) and Mario Costeja

Union judgment on *"Google Spain and Inc v Agencia Española de Protección de Datos (AEPD) and Mario Costeja González."'*

There have also been recent cases, including a case against the French data regulator (regarding special categories of data)[91]; a case taken by the French data regulator against Google (regarding jurisdictional takedowns);[92] and the first UK High Court RtbF cases, *NT1* and *NT2*.[93]

Note also the EDPB guidance:

- Guidelines 5/2019 on the criteria of the Right to be Forgotten in the search engines cases under the GDPR (part 1).

Right to Restriction of Processing

26.61 Article 18 refers to the right to restriction of processing. The Data Subject shall have the right to obtain from the Controller the restriction of the processing where one of the following applies:

- the accuracy of the personal data is contested by the Data Subject, for a period enabling the Controller to verify the accuracy of the personal data;
- the processing is unlawful and the Data Subject opposes the erasure of the personal data and requests the restriction of their use instead;
- the Controller no longer needs the personal data for the purposes of the processing, but they are required by the Data Subject for the establishment, exercise or defence of legal claims;
- the data subject has objected to processing pursuant to Article 21(1) pending the verification whether the legitimate grounds of the Controller override those of the Data Subject (Article 18(1)).

Where processing of personal data has been restricted under Article 18(1), such personal data shall, with the exception of storage, only be processed with the Data Subject's consent or for the establishment, exercise or defence of legal claims or for the protection of the rights of another natural or legal person or for reasons of important public interest of the EU or of a state (Article 18(2)).

A Data Subject who obtained the restriction of processing pursuant to Article 18(1) shall be informed by the Controller before the restriction of processing is lifted (Article 18(3)).

Notifications re Rectification, Erasure or Restriction

26.62 The Controller shall communicate any rectification or erasure of personal data or restriction of processing carried out in accordance with Articles 16, 17(1) and 18 to each recipient to whom the personal data have been disclosed, unless this proves impossible or involves disproportionate effort. The Controller shall inform the Data Subject about those recipients if the Data Subject requests this (Article 19).

González' C-131/121; Opinion 8/2010 on applicable law (WP29 adds as follows: 'In its judgment in Google Spain the Court of Justice of the European Union decided upon certain matters relating to the territorial scope of Directive 95/46/EC. The WP29 commenced an internal analysis of the potential implications of this judgment on applicable law and may provide further guidance on this issue during the course of 2015, including, possibly, additional examples.').

91 *GC and Others v Commission Nationale de l'Informatique et des Libertés (CNIL) (Déréférencement de données sensibles)*, CJEU [2019] Case C-136/17.

92 *Google LLC, successor in law to Google Inc v Commission Nationale de l'Informatique et des Libertes (CNIL)*, CJEU [2019] Case C-507/17.

93 *NT1 and NT2 v Google LLC* [2018] EWHC 799 (QB; [2018] EMLR 18; [2018] HRLR 13.

Right to Data Portability

26.63   The Data Subject shall have the right to receive the personal data concerning him or her, which he or she has provided to a Controller, in a structured, commonly used, machine-readable format and have the right to transmit those data to another Controller without hindrance from the Controller to which the personal data have been provided, where:

- the processing is based on consent pursuant to Article 6(1)(a) or Article 9(2)(a) or on a contract pursuant to Article 6(1)(b); and
- the processing is carried out by automated means (Article 20(1)).

In exercising his or her right to data portability pursuant to Article 20(1), the Data Subject has the right to obtain that the data is transmitted directly from Controller to Controller where technically feasible (Article 20(2)).

The exercise of this right shall be without prejudice to Article 17. The right shall not apply to processing necessary for the performance of a task carried out in the public interest or in the exercise of official authority vested in the Controller (Article 20(3)).

The right shall not adversely affect the rights and freedoms of others (Article 20(4)).

Right Against Automated Individual Decision Making

26.64   Chapter III, Section 4 of the GDPR refers to the right to object and automated individual decision making.

Right to Object

26.65   The Data Subject shall have the right to object, on grounds relating to his or her particular situation, at any time to the processing of personal data concerning him or her which is based on Article 6(1)(e) or (f), including profiling based on these provisions. The Controller shall no longer process the personal data unless the Controller demonstrates compelling legitimate grounds for the processing which override the interests, rights and freedoms of the Data Subject or for the establishment, exercise or defence of legal claims (Article 21(1)).

Where personal data are processed for direct marketing purposes, the Data Subject shall have the right to object at any time to the processing of personal data concerning him or her for such marketing, which includes profiling to the extent that it is related to such direct marketing (Article 20(2)).

Where the Data Subject objects to the processing for direct marketing purposes, the personal data shall no longer be processed for such purposes (Article 21(3)).

At the latest at the time of the first communication with the Data Subject, the right referred to in Article 21(1) and (2) shall be explicitly brought to the attention of the Data Subject and shall be presented clearly and separately from any other information (Article 21(4)).

In the context of the use of information society services, and notwithstanding Directive 2002/58/EC,[94] the Data Subject may exercise his or her right to object by automated means using technical specifications (Article 21(5)).

Where personal data are processed for scientific or historical research purposes or statistical purposes pursuant to Article 89(1), the Data Subject, on grounds relating to

---

94   Directive 2002/58/EC of the European Parliament and of the Council of 12 July 2002 concerning the processing of personal data and the protection of privacy in the electronic communications sector (Directive on privacy and electronic communications).

his or her particular situation, shall have the right to object to processing of personal data concerning him or her, unless the processing is necessary for the performance of a task carried out for reasons of public interest (Article 21(6)).

Rights re Automated Individual Decision Making, Including Profiling

26.66 There is often a wide concern as to the data protection impact of increased profiling techniques.[95]

The new GDPR provides that the Data Subject shall have the right not to be subject to a decision based solely on automated processing, including profiling,[96] which produces legal effects concerning him or her or similarly significantly affects him or her (Article 22(1)).

Article 22(1) shall not apply if the decision:

- is necessary for entering into, or performance of, a contract between the Data Subject and a Controller [a];
- is authorised by EU or state law to which the Controller is subject and which also lays down suitable measures to safeguard the Data Subject's rights and freedoms and legitimate interests; or
- is based on the Data Subject's explicit consent (Article 22(1)) [c].

In cases referred to in Article 22(2)(a) and (c) the Controller shall implement suitable measures to safeguard the Data Subject's rights and freedoms and legitimate interests, at least the right to obtain human intervention on the part of the Controller, to express his or her point of view and to contest the decision (Article 22(3)).

Decisions referred to in Article 22(2) shall not be based on special categories of personal data referred to in Article 9(1), unless Article 9(2)(a) or (g) applies and suitable measures to safeguard the Data Subject's rights and freedoms and legitimate interests are in place (Article 22(4)).

Data Protection by Design and by Default

26.67 Article 25 refers to data protection by design and by default. Note also the related concept of Privacy by Design (PbD). In some ways PbD is the impetus or precursor for the current DPbD rules.

Taking into account the state of the art and the nature, scope, context and purposes of the processing as well as the risks of varying likelihood and severity for rights and freedoms of natural persons posed by the processing, the Controller shall, both at the time of the determination of the means for processing and at the time of the processing itself, implement appropriate technical and organisational measures, such as pseudonymisation, which are designed to implement data protection Principles, such as data minimisation, in an effective way and to integrate the necessary safeguards into the processing in order to meet the requirements of the GDPR and protect the rights of Data Subjects (Article 25(1)).

The Controller shall implement appropriate technical and organisational measures for ensuring that, by default, only personal data which are necessary for each specific purpose of the processing are processed. That obligation applies to the amount of data collected, the extent of their processing, the period of their storage and their

---

95 This is in the EU as well as the US (and elsewhere). From a US perspective, see N Roethlisberger, 'Someone is Watching: The Need for Enhanced Data Protection,' *Hastings Law Journal* (2011) (62:6) 1793.

96 See, for example, M Hildebrandt, 'Who is Profiling Who? Invisible Visibility,' in S Gutwirth, Y Poullet, P de Hert, C de Terwange and S Nouwt, *Reinventing Data Protection?* (Springer, 2009) 239.

accessibility. In particular, such measures shall ensure that by default personal data are not made accessible without the individual's intervention to an indefinite number of natural persons (Article 23(2)).

An approved certification mechanism pursuant to Article 42 may be used as an element to demonstrate compliance with the requirements set out in Article 25(1) and (2) (Article 25(3)).

Note also the EDPB guidance:

● Guidelines 4/2019 on Article 25 Data Protection by Design and by Default.

Security Rights

26.68   See above (paras **26.36** and **26.37**).

Data Protection Impact Assessment and Prior Consultation

Data Protection Impact Assessment

26.69   Chapter IV, Section 3 of the GDPR refers to Impact Assessments and Prior Consultations.

Where a type of processing in particular using new technologies, and taking into account the nature, scope, context and purposes of the processing, is likely to result in a high risk for the rights and freedoms of natural persons, the Controller shall, prior to the processing, carry out an assessment of the impact of the envisaged processing operations on the protection of personal data. A single assessment may address a set of similar processing operations that present similar high risks (Article 35(1)).

The Controller shall seek the advice of the DPO, where designated, when carrying out a data protection impact assessment (Article 35(2)).

A data protection impact assessment referred to in Article 35(1) shall in particular be required in the case of:

● a systematic and extensive evaluation of personal aspects relating to natural persons which is based on automated processing, including profiling, and on which decisions are based that produce legal effects concerning the natural person or similarly significantly affect the natural person;
● processing on a large scale of special categories of data referred to in Article 9(1), or of personal data relating to criminal convictions and offences referred to in Article 10; or
● a systematic monitoring of a publicly accessible area on a large scale (Article 35(3)).

The supervisory authority shall establish and make public a list of the kind of processing operations which are subject to the requirement for a data protection impact assessment pursuant to Article 35(1). The supervisory authority shall communicate those lists to the EDPB (Article 35(4)).

The supervisory authority may also establish and make public a list of the kind of processing operations for which no data protection impact assessment is required. The supervisory authority shall communicate those lists to the EDPB (Article 35(5)).

Prior to the adoption of the lists referred to in Article 35(4) and (5) the competent supervisory authority shall apply the consistency mechanism referred to in Article 63 where such lists involve processing activities which are related to the offering of goods or services to Data Subjects or to the monitoring of their behaviour in several states, or may substantially affect the free movement of personal data within the EU (Article 35(6)).

The assessment shall contain at least:

- a systematic description of the envisaged processing operations and the purposes of the processing, including where applicable the legitimate interest pursued by the Controller;
- an assessment of the necessity and proportionality of the processing operations in relation to the purposes;
- an assessment of the risks to the rights and freedoms of Data Subjects referred to in Article 35(1);
- the measures envisaged to address the risks, including safeguards, security measures and mechanisms to ensure the protection of personal data and to demonstrate compliance with the GDPR taking into account the rights and legitimate interests of Data Subjects and other persons concerned (Article 35(7)).

Compliance with approved codes of conduct referred to in Article 40 by the relevant Controllers or Processors shall be taken into due account in assessing the impact of the processing operations performed by such Controllers or Processors, in particular for the purposes of a data protection impact assessment (Article 35(8)).

Where appropriate, the Controller shall seek the views of Data Subjects or their representatives on the intended processing, without prejudice to the protection of commercial or public interests or the security of the processing operations (Article 35(9)).

Where the processing pursuant to Article 6(1)(c) or (e) has a legal basis in EU law or the law of the state to which the Controller is subject, that law regulates the specific processing operation or set of operations in question, and a data protection impact assessment has already been carried out as part of a general impact assessment in the context of the adoption of this legal basis, Article 35(1)–(7) shall not apply, unless states deem it necessary to carry out such assessment prior to the processing activities (Article 35(10)).

Where necessary, the Controller shall carry out a review to assess if the processing is performed in compliance with the data protection impact assessment at least when there is a change of the risk represented by the processing operations (Article 35(11)).

Prior Consultation

26.70 The Controller shall consult the supervisory authority prior to the processing where a data protection impact assessment as provided for in Article 33 indicates that the processing would result in a high risk in the absence of measures taken by the Controller to mitigate the risk (Article 36(1)).

Where the supervisory authority is of the opinion that the intended processing referred to in Article 36(1) would infringe the GDPR, in particular where the Controller has insufficiently identified or mitigated the risk, it shall within a period of up to eight weeks of receipt of the request for consultation, provide written advice to the Controller and, where applicable the Processor, and may use any of its powers referred to in Article 58. That period may be extended for six weeks, taking into account the complexity of the processing. The supervisory authority shall inform the Controller, and where applicable the Processor of any such extension within one month of receipt of the request for consultation together with the reasons for the delay. Those periods may be suspended until the supervisory authority has obtained any information it has requested for the purposes of the consultation (Article 36(2)).

When consulting the supervisory authority pursuant to Article 36(1), the Controller shall provide the supervisory authority with:

- where applicable, the respective responsibilities of Controller, joint Controllers and Processors involved in the processing, in particular for processing within a group of undertakings;
- the purposes and means of the intended processing;
- the measures and safeguards provided to protect the rights and freedoms of Data Subjects pursuant to the GDPR;
- where applicable, the contact details of the DPO;
- the data protection impact assessment provided for in Article 35; and
- any other information requested by the supervisory authority (Article 36(3)).

States shall consult the supervisory authority during the preparation of a proposal for a legislative measure to be adopted by a national parliament or of a regulatory measure based on such a legislative measure, which relates to the processing (Article 36(4)).

Notwithstanding Article 36(1), states' law may require Controllers to consult with, and obtain prior authorisation from, the supervisory authority in relation to the processing by a Controller for the performance of a task carried out by the Controller in the public interest, including processing in relation to social protection and public health (Article 36(5)).

Communicating Data Breach to Data Subject

26.71 Individual data subjects are to be notified in the event of a data breach. Further details are set out above in para **26.39**.

Data Protection Officer

26.72 Section 4 of the new GDPR refers to Data Protection Officers (DPOs) and the obligation for organisations to appoint DPOs. See Chapter 31 for particular details.

Remedies, Liability and Sanctions

26.73 Chapter VIII refers to remedies, liability issues and sanctions regarding data protection.

The Recitals refer to proceedings against Controllers, Processors and jurisdiction; damages and compensation; the prevention, investigation, detection or prosecution of criminal offences or the execution of criminal penalties, including public security.

Right to Lodge Complaint with Supervisory Authority

26.74 Without prejudice to any other administrative or judicial remedy, every Data Subject shall have the right to lodge a complaint with a supervisory authority, in particular in the state of his or her habitual residence, place of work or place of the alleged infringement if the Data Subject considers that the processing of personal data relating to him or her infringes the GDPR (Article 77(1)).

The supervisory authority with which the complaint has been lodged shall inform the complainant on the progress and the outcome of the complaint including the possibility of a judicial remedy pursuant to Article 78 (Article 77(2)).

Right to Judicial Remedy Against Supervisory Authority

26.75 Without prejudice to any other administrative or non-judicial remedy, each natural or legal person shall have the right to an effective judicial remedy against a legally binding decisions of a supervisory authority concerning them (Article 78(1)).

Without prejudice to any other administrative or non-judicial remedy, each Data Subject shall have the right to an effective judicial remedy where the supervisory authority which is competent in accordance with Article 55 and Article 56 does not handle a complaint or does not inform the Data Subject within three months on the progress or outcome of the complaint lodged under Article 77 (Article 78(2)).

Proceedings against a supervisory authority shall be brought before the courts of the state where the supervisory authority is established (Article 78(3)).

Where proceedings are brought against a decision of a supervisory authority which was preceded by an opinion or a decision of the EDPB in the consistency mechanism, the supervisory authority shall forward that opinion or decision to the court (Article 78(4)).

Right to Effective Judicial Remedy Against Controller or Processor

26.76 Without prejudice to any available administrative or non-judicial remedy, including the right to lodge a complaint with a supervisory authority pursuant Article 77, each Data Subject shall have the right to an effective judicial remedy where they consider that their rights under the GDPR have been infringed as a result of the processing of their personal data in non-compliance with the GDPR (Article 79(1)).

Proceedings against a Controller or a Processor shall be brought before the courts of the state where the Controller or Processor has an establishment. Alternatively, such proceedings may be brought before the courts of the state where the Data Subject has his or her habitual residence, unless the Controller or Processor is a public authority of a state acting in the exercise of its public powers (Article 79(2)).

Representation of Data Subjects

26.77 The Data Subject shall have the right to mandate a not-for-profit body, organisation or association, which has been properly constituted according to the law of a state, has statutory objectives which are in the public interest and is active in the field of the protection of Data Subject's rights and freedoms with regard to the protection of their personal data to lodge the complaint on his or her behalf, to exercise the rights referred to in Articles 77, 78 and 79 on his or her behalf and to exercise the right to receive compensation referred to in Article 82 on his or her behalf where provided for by state law (Article 80(1)).

States may provide that any body, organisation or association referred to in Article 80(1), independently of a Data Subject's mandate, has the right to lodge, in that state, a complaint with the supervisory authority competent in accordance with Article 77 and to exercise the rights referred to in Articles 78 and 79 if it considers that the rights of a Data Subject under the GDPR have been infringed as a result of the processing (Article 80(2)).

Right to Compensation and Liability

26.78 Any person who has suffered material or non-material damage as a result of an infringement of the GDPR shall have the right to receive compensation from the Controller or Processor for the damage suffered (Article 82(1)).

Any Controller involved in the processing shall be liable for the damage caused by the processing which infringes the GDPR. A Processor shall be liable for the damage caused by the processing only where it has not complied with obligations of the GDPR specifically directed to Processors or where it has acted outside or contrary to lawful instructions of the Controller (Article 82(2)).

A Controller or Processor shall be exempt from liability under Article 82(2) if it proves that it is not in any way responsible for the event giving rise to the damage (Article 82(3)).

Where more than one Controller or Processor or both a Controller and a Processor are involved in the same processing and, where they are, in accordance with Article 82(2) and (3), responsible for any damage caused by the processing, each Controller or Processor shall be held liable for the entire damage, in order to ensure effective compensation of the Data Subject (Article 82(4)).

Where a Controller or Processor has, in accordance with Article 82(4), paid full compensation for the damage suffered, that Controller or Processor shall be entitled to claim back from the other Controllers or Processors involved in the same processing that part of the compensation corresponding to their part of responsibility for the damage in accordance with the conditions set out in Article 82(2) (Article 82(5)).

Court proceedings for exercising the right to receive compensation shall be brought before the courts competent under the law of the state referred to in Article 79(2) (Article 82(6)).

Codes of Conduct and Certification

26.79   Chapter IV, Section 5 of the GDPR refers to Codes of Conduct and Certification.

Codes of Conduct

26.80   The states, the supervisory authorities, the EDPB and the Commission shall encourage the drawing up of codes of conduct intended to contribute to the proper application of the GDPR, taking account of the specific features of the various data processing sectors and the specific needs of micro, small and medium-sized enterprises (Article 40(1)).

Associations and other bodies representing categories of Controllers or Processors may prepare codes of conduct, or amend or extend such codes, for the purpose of specifying the application of the GDPR, such as:

- fair and transparent data processing;
- the legitimate interests pursued by Controllers in specific contexts;
- the collection of data;
- the pseudonymisation of personal data;
- the information of the public and of Data Subjects;
- the exercise of the rights of Data Subjects;
- the information provided to, and the protection of children and the manner in which the consent of the holders of parental responsibility over children to be obtained;
- the measures and procedures referred to in Article 24 and measures to ensure security of processing referred to in Article 32;
- the notification of personal data breaches to supervisory authorities and the communication of such personal data breaches to Data Subjects;
- transfer of personal data to third countries or international organisations; or
- out-of-court proceedings and other dispute resolution procedures for resolving disputes between Controllers and Data Subjects with regard to the processing, without prejudice to the rights of the Data Subjects pursuant to Articles 75 and 79 (Article 40(2)).

In addition to adherence by Controller or Processor subject to the Regulation, codes of conduct approved pursuant to Article 40(5) and having general validity pursuant to

Article 40(9) may also be adhered to by Controllers or Processors that are not subject to this Regulation pursuant to Article 3 in order to provide appropriate safeguards within the framework of personal data transfers to third countries or international organisations under the terms referred to in Article 46(2)(e). Such Controllers or Processors shall make binding and enforceable commitments, via contractual or other legally binding instruments, to apply those appropriate safeguards including with regard to the rights of Data Subjects (Article 40(3)).

Such a code of conduct shall contain mechanisms which enable the body referred to in Article 41(1) to carry out the mandatory monitoring of compliance with its provisions by the Controllers or Processors which undertake to apply it, without prejudice to the tasks and powers of the supervisory authority competent pursuant to Article 55 or 56 (Article 40(4)).

Associations and other bodies referred to in Article 40(2) which intend to prepare a code of conduct or to amend or extend an existing code, shall submit the draft code, amendment or extension to the supervisory authority which is competent pursuant to Article 55. The supervisory authority shall provide an opinion on whether the draft code, or, amendment or extension complies with the GDPR and shall approve such draft code, amendment or extension if it finds that it provides sufficient appropriate safeguards (Article 40(5)).

Where the draft code, or amendment or extension is approved, and where the code of conduct concerned does not relate to processing activities in several states, the supervisory authority shall register and publish the code (Article 40(6)).

Where a draft code of conduct relates to processing activities in several states, the supervisory authority which is competent shall, before approving the draft code, amendment or extension, submit it to the EDPB which shall provide an opinion on whether the draft code, amendment or extension complies with the GDPR or, in the situation referred to in Article 40(3), provides appropriate safeguards (Article 40(7)).

Where the opinion referred to in Article 40(7) confirms that the draft code, amendment or extension complies with the GDPR, or, in the situation referred to in Article 40(3), provides appropriate safeguards, the EDPB shall submit its opinion to the Commission (Article 40(8)).

The Commission may by way of implementing acts decide that the approved codes of conduct, amendments or extensions submitted to it pursuant to Article 40(3) have general validity within the EU. Those implementing acts shall be adopted in accordance with the examination procedure set out in Article 93(2) (Article 40(9)).

The Commission shall ensure appropriate publicity for the approved codes which have been decided as having general validity in accordance with Article 40(9) (Article 40(10)).

The EDPB shall collate all approved codes of conduct, amendments and extensions in a register and shall make them publicly available by way of appropriate means (Article 40(11)).

Certification

26.81 The states, the supervisory authorities, the EDPB and the Commission shall encourage, in particular at EU level, the establishment of data protection certification mechanisms and of data protection seals and marks, for the purpose of demonstrating compliance with the GDPR of processing operations by Controllers and Processors. The specific needs of micro, small and medium-sized enterprises shall be taken into account (Article 42(1)).

In addition to adherence by Controllers or Processors subject to the GDPR, data protection certification mechanisms, seals or marks approved pursuant to Article 42(5) may be established for the purpose of demonstrating the existence of appropriate safeguards provided by Controllers or Processors that are not subject to the GDPR according to Article 3 within the framework of personal data transfers to third countries or international organisations under the terms referred to in Article 46(2)(f). Such Controllers or Processors shall make binding and enforceable commitments, via contractual or other legally binding instruments, to apply those appropriate safeguards, including with regard to the rights of Data Subjects (Article 42(2)).

The certification shall be voluntary and available via a process that is transparent (Article 42(3)).

A certification pursuant to this Article does not reduce the responsibility of the Controller or the Processor for compliance with the GDPR and is without prejudice to the tasks and powers of the supervisory authorities which are competent pursuant to Article 55 or 56 (Article 42(4)).

A certification pursuant to this Article shall be issued by the certification bodies referred to in Article 43, or by the competent supervisory authority on the basis of the criteria approved by that competent supervisory authority pursuant to Article 58(3), or by the EDPB. Where the criteria approved by the EDPB this may result in a common certification, the European Data Protection Seal (Article 42(5)).

The Controller or Processor which submits its processing to the certification mechanism shall provide the certification body, the competent supervisory authority, with all information and access to its processing activities which are necessary to conduct the certification procedure (Article 42(6)).

The certification shall be issued to a Controller or Processor for a maximum period of three years and may be renewed under the same conditions, provided that the relevant requirements continue to be met. Certification shall be withdrawn, as applicable, by the certification bodies referred to in Article 43, or by the competent supervisory authority where the requirements for the certification are not or no longer met (Article 42(7)).

The EDPB shall collate all certification mechanisms and data protection seals and marks in a register and shall make them publicly available by any appropriate means (Article 42(8)).

Specific Data Processing Situations

26.82 Chapter IX of the GDPR refers to provisions regarding specific data processing situations.

Processing and Freedom of Expression and Information

26.83 States shall by law reconcile the right to the protection of personal data pursuant to the GDPR with the right to freedom of expression and information, including the processing of personal data for journalistic purposes and the purposes of academic, artistic or literary expression (Article 85(1)).

For processing carried out for journalistic purposes or the purpose of academic artistic or literary expression, states shall provide for exemptions or derogations from the provisions in Chapter II (Principles), Chapter III (Rights of the Data Subject), Chapter IV (Controller and Processor), Chapter V (transfer of personal data to third countries or international organisations), Chapter VI (independent supervisory authorities), Chapter VII (cooperation and consistency) and Chapter IX (specific data processing situations) if they are necessary to reconcile the right to the protection of personal data with the freedom of expression and information (Article 85(2)).

Each state shall notify to the Commission those provisions of its law which it has adopted pursuant to Article 85(2) and, without delay, any subsequent amendment law or amendment affecting them (Article 85(3)).

Processing in Employment Context

26.84 Issues related to employee personal data are continuing to grow in importance.[97]

The new GDPR provides that states may, by law or by collective agreements, provide for more specific rules to ensure the protection of the rights and freedoms in respect of the processing of employees' personal data in the employment context, *in particular* for the purposes of the recruitment, the performance of the contract of employment, including discharge of obligations laid down by law or by collective agreements, management, planning and organisation of work, equality and diversity in the workplace, health and safety at work, protection of employer's or customer's property and for the purposes of the exercise and enjoyment, on an individual or collective basis, of rights and benefits related to employment, and for the purpose of the termination of the employment relationship (Article 88(1)).

These rules shall include suitable and specific measures to safeguard the Data Subject's human dignity, legitimate interests and fundamental rights, with particular regard to the transparency of processing, the transfer of data within a group of undertakings or group of enterprises engaged in a joint economic activity and monitoring systems at the work place (Article 88(2)).

Each state shall notify to the Commission those provisions of its law which it adopts pursuant to Article 88(1), by 25 May 2018 and, without delay, any subsequent amendment affecting them (Article 88(3)).

Prior to the new GDPR, the ICO has issued recommendations in relation to personal data employment issues, namely:

- Employment Practices Code;
- Employment Practices Code – A Quick Guide;
- Employment Practices Code – Supplementary Guidance;
- Disclosure of Employee Information under TUPE;
- Getting it Right: A brief Guide to Data Protection for Small Businesses;
- Monitoring under Section 75 of the Northern Ireland Act 1998.

These now need to be read in light of the GDPR changes.

Safeguards and Derogations: Public Interest/Scientific/Historical Research/Statistical Archiving Processing

26.85 There are also provisions in relation to safeguards and derogations for processing personal data for archiving purposes in the public interest, scientific or historical research purposes or statistical purposes.

Processing for archiving purposes in the public interest, scientific or historical research purposes or statistical purposes, shall be subject to appropriate safeguards for the rights and freedoms of the Data Subject. These safeguards shall ensure that technical and organisational measures are in place in particular in order to ensure the respect of the principle of data minimisation. These measures may include pseudonymisation, provided that those purposes can be fulfilled in that manner. Where those purposes can be fulfilled by further processing which does not permit or no longer permits the identification of Data Subjects these purposes shall be fulfilled in that manner (Article 89(1)).

Where personal data are processed for scientific and historical research purposes or statistical purposes, EU or state law may provide for derogations from the rights

---

97 See, for example, Chapters 16–19 and Article 82 of the GDPR.

referred to in Articles 15, 16, 18 and 21 subject to the conditions and safeguards referred to in Article 89(1) in so far as such rights are likely to render impossible or seriously impair the achievement of the specific purposes, and such derogations are necessary for the fulfilment of those purposes (Article 89(2)).

Where personal data are processed for archiving purposes in the public interest, EU or state law may provide for derogations from the rights referred to in Articles 15, 16, 18, 19, 20 and 21 subject to the conditions and safeguards referred to in Article 89(1) in so far as such rights are likely to render impossible or seriously impair the achievement of the specific purposes, and such derogations are necessary for the fulfilment of these purposes (Article 89(3)).

Where processing referred to in Article 89(2) and (3) serves at the same time another purpose, the derogations shall apply only to processing for the purposes referred to in those paragraphs (Article 89(4)).

Obligations of Secrecy

26.86   States may adopt specific rules to set out the powers by the supervisory authorities laid down in Article 58(1)(e) and (f) in relation to Controllers or Processors that are subject, under EU or state law or rules established by national competent bodies to an obligation of professional secrecy or other equivalent obligations of secrecy where this is necessary and proportionate to reconcile the right of the protection of personal data with the obligation of secrecy. Those rules shall only apply with regard to personal data which the Controller or Processor has received as a result of, or has obtained in, an activity covered by that obligation of secrecy (Article 90(1)).

Each state shall notify to the Commission the rules adopted pursuant to Article 90(1), by 25 May 2018 and without delay, any subsequent amendment affecting them (Article 90(2)).

New Data Protection Officer Obligation

Introduction

26.87   Now organisations need to have a designated Data Protection Officer (DPO) to deal with the data protection compliance obligations, dealing with Data Subject access requests, etc. That is not to say that board and management responsibility for data protection compliance is in any way removed.

DPO

26.88   Chapter IV, Section 4 of the new GDPR refers to DPOs and the obligation for organisations to appoint DPOs.

The Controller and the Processor shall designate a DPO in all cases specified by the GDPR, in particular in Article 35. (For further details see Chapter 31).

Position of DPO

26.89   The Controller or the Processor shall ensure that the DPO is involved, properly and in a timely manner in all issues which relate to the protection of personal data (Article 38(1)).

The Controller or Processor shall support the DPO in performing the tasks referred to in Article 39 by providing resources necessary to carry out those tasks as well as access to personal data and processing operations, and to maintain his or her expert knowledge (Article 38(2)).

The Controller or Processor shall ensure that the DPO does not receive any instructions regarding the exercise of the tasks. He or she shall not be dismissed or penalised by the Controller or the Processor for performing the tasks. The DPO shall directly report to the highest management level of the Controller or the Processor (Article 38(3)).

Data Subjects may contact the DPO with regard to all issues relating to the processing of their personal data and to the exercise of their rights under the GDPR (Article 38(4)).

The DPO shall be bound by secrecy or confidentiality concerning the performance of their tasks, in accordance with EU or state law (Article 38(5)).

The DPO may fulfil other tasks and duties. The Controller or Processor shall ensure that any such tasks and duties do not result in a conflict of interests (Article 38(6)).

Tasks of DPO

26.90 The DPO shall have at least the following tasks:

- to inform and advise the Controller or the Processor and the employees who carry out processing of their obligations pursuant to the GDPR and to other EU or state data protection provisions;
- to monitor compliance with the GDPR, with other EU or state data protection provisions and with the policies of the Controller or Processor in relation to the protection of personal data, including the assignment of responsibilities, awareness-raising and training of staff involved in processing operations, and the related audits;
- to provide advice where requested as regards the data protection impact assessment and monitor its performance pursuant to Article 39;
- to cooperate with the supervisory authority;
- to act as the contact point for the supervisory authority on issues related to the processing, including the prior consultation referred to in Article 36, and consult, where appropriate, on any other matter (Article 39(1)).

The DPO shall in the performance of his or her tasks have due regard to the risk associated with the processing operations, taking into account the nature, scope, context and purposes of processing (Article 39(2)).

Importance

26.91 The new profession and new mandated requirement for a DPO will prove to be one of the game changes in data protection practice and protection for personal data. While the DPO will be promoting data protection compliance, adherence to the new data protection regime, pre-problem solving (such as data protection by design and by default) and the understanding of data protection throughout the organisation, the protection of the DPO's independence will ensure that the temptation by some in an organisation to ignore or downgrade data protection in favour of (new) collections and processing, and maximum use compared to proportionate and limited data use, can be more robustly resisted. The independence of the DPO is also protected by ensuring that they report directly to the highest level which will generally be a board member. This counters junior managers or others seeking to adversely influence, ignore or overrule the DPO in the proper performance of their functions and role. See *The Data Protection Officer, Profession, Rules and Role*.

Conclusion

26.92 All organisations need to become very familiar with the GDPR. While in some instances the current compliance mechanisms are continued, there are many new requirements to compliance. Organisations need to start now in terms of ensuring preparation and compliance. Indeed, the most prudent organisations will continually be adopting best practice, and data protection compliance is an area where best practice has positive benefits above and beyond mere compliance.

While the GDPR is now established, what is less certain is how the envisaged UK GDPR will look like in final draft and how it will be applied. Critical to assessing it – especially from an EU perspective – will be any associated laws or changes, such as the cessation or diminution of the Human Rights Act 1998.

Part 6
Particular Issues

Chapter 27

Data Breach

Introduction

27.01   Data breach issues are one of the most important and consequential areas of data protection (and security) for organisations to pay attention to. Given the unfortunate increase in the number of data breaches, it is inevitable that there will be increasing regulator attention. The EU General Data Protection Regulation (GDPR) also increases data protection security obligations; and the consequence of significant fines and penalties where breaches occur.

The GDPR defines 'personal data breach' as a 'breach of security leading to the accidental or unlawful destruction, loss, alteration, unauthorised disclosure of, or access to, personal data transmitted, stored or otherwise processed'. The importance attached to dealing with data breaches and data breach incidents is highlighted in the GDPR. Now data breaches must be notified to the supervisory authority and the Data Subjects. (Bear in mind that employees can also be Data Subjects.) Data Subjects can suffer loss and damage if there has been a data breach, and particularly so if they are unaware of it and are not notified when the organisation becomes aware in order that, for example, remedial measures can be undertaken by the Data Subject. For example, they may wish to change passwords or cancel credit cards, depending on the nature of the breach. Indeed, in some instances organisations may need to recommend remedial or safety measures to Data Subjects after a data breach.

Data Breach Incidents in Context

27.02   The issue and frequency of data breaches and data breach incidents are highlighted in Part 1. In addition, it is clear that national supervisory authorities take data breaches very seriously. Significant fines are now regularly levelled at organisations, including large organisations and public organisations, in relation to data breaches. Additionally, even smaller organisations have been fined.

The ICO, and other supervisory authorities, can carry out audits and inspections of organisations, which can include security and data breach preparedness, as well as the implications which result from a recent data breach incident. In fact, many data breaches result in media publicity for the organisation, in which case the ICO is likely to contact the organisation.

Notification of a Data Breach to Supervisory Authority

27.03   In the case of a personal data breach, the GDPR requires that the Controller shall without undue delay and, where feasible, not later than 72 hours after having become aware of it, notify the personal data breach to the supervisory authority competent in accordance with Article 33, unless the personal data breach is unlikely to result in a risk for the rights and freedoms of natural persons. Where the notification to the supervisory authority is not made within 72 hours, it shall be accompanied by reasons for delay (Article 33(1)).

The Processor shall notify the Controller without undue delay after becoming aware of a personal data breach (Article 33(2)).

The notification referred to in Article 33(1) must at least:

- describe the nature of the personal data breach including where possible, the categories and approximate number of Data Subjects concerned and the categories and approximate number of data records concerned;
- communicate the name and contact details of the data protection officer (DPO) or other contact point where more information can be obtained;
- describe the likely consequences of the personal data breach;
- describe the measures taken or proposed to be taken by the Controller to address the personal data breach, including, where appropriate, to mitigate its possible adverse effects (Article 33(3)).

Where, and in so far as, it is not possible to provide the information at the same time, the information may be provided in phases without undue further delay (Article 33(4)).

The Controller shall document any personal data breaches, comprising the facts relating to the personal data breach, its effects and the remedial action taken. This documentation shall enable the supervisory authority to verify compliance with this Article (Article 33(5)).

Note that there can be data security breach issues which can lead to data regulator sanction, but separately and in addition, the failure to notify when required can itself be an instance of breach of the data protection regime.

Communication of a Data Breach to Data Subject

27.04 When the personal data breach is likely to result in a high risk to the rights and freedoms of natural persons the Controller shall communicate the personal data breach to the Data Subject without undue delay (GDPR Article 34(1)).[1]

The communication to the Data Subject referred to in Article 34(2) shall describe in clear and plain language the nature of the personal data breach and contain at least the information and measures referred to in Article 33(3)(b), (c) and (d) (Article 34(2)).

The communication to the Data Subject referred to in Article 34(1) may not be required if:

- the Controller has implemented appropriate technical and organisational protection measures, and that those measures were applied to the personal data affected by the personal data breach, in particular those that render the personal data unintelligible to any person who is not authorised to access it, such as encryption;
- the Controller has taken subsequent measures which ensure that the high risk for the rights and freedoms of Data Subjects referred to in para 1 is no longer likely to materialise;

---

1   Note, for example, P Wainman, 'Data Protection Breaches: Today and Tomorrow,' SCL *Computers and Law*, 30 June 2012. Also see M Dekker, Dr, C Christoffer Karsberg and B Daskala, *Cyber Incident Reporting in the EU* (2012).

- it would involve disproportionate effort. In such cases, there shall instead be a public communication or similar measure whereby the Data Subjects are informed in an equally effective manner (Article 34(3)).

If the Controller has not already communicated the personal data breach to the Data Subject, the supervisory authority, having considered the likelihood of the personal data breach resulting in a high risk, may require it to do so or may decide that any of the conditions referred to in Article 34(4) are met (Article 34(4)).

Employee Data Breaches

27.05   Employee involvement is critical in dealing with – and preparing for – data breach incidents. Various teams of employees will be involved.

However, as employee personal data can also be the subject of a data breach incident, employees may need to be specifically considered in this context also. For example, they may need to be separately informed that there is a breach relating to their personal data and what actions and safeguards are being followed by the organisation to deal with the issue. If the employees need to take specific actions, they may also need to be appraised of this possibility. Potentially liability issues may also arise. For example, employees in the massive Sony data breach incidents may have considered suing Sony for breaches in relation to their data. Employees did sue their employer in the Morrison case, albeit unsuccessful in the specific matter apparently sued for.[2] A note of caution should be applied as to if any how this immunises all employers. This text would suggest that there may indeed still be circumstances upon which an employer may indeed be vicariously liable to employees and third parties.

Notification Timelines

27.06   Organisations will need to assess the categories of personal data they have that may be involved in a data breach. They also need to assess what type of organisation or sector they are involved in. These factors may dictate how the data protection regime may impose time limits for respective notification of breaches. (See Chapter 10).

Notification Processes

27.07   DPOs and organisations need to develop, and update as appropriate, breach notification procedures. There needs to be an appropriate response plan for the different types of breach incidents, ICO, other regulators if appropriate or required, Data Subjects and other organisations, whether partners, Processors, outsource security, etc.

Contracts and agreements should also be reviewed to ensure appropriate breach, notification and security provisions.

---

2   See *Morrison v Various* [2020] UKSC 12 (1 April 2020).

Data Security Standards

27.08 The requirement to comply with the GDPR regime, to maintain security and to prevent and to deal with data breaches increasingly directs attention to detailed standards and implementation measures. One example is compliance with ISO 27001 international standard for confidentiality and security. In particular it refers to:

- security policies;
- organisational information security;
- HR security issues (including employees, families, contractors previously and currently);
- asset identification and control;
- encryption;
- physical and environmental security factors;
- operational security;
- communications security;
- acquisition, development and maintenance of systems;
- supplier relations;
- security incident management;
- security issues and business continuity;
- compliance with internal policies and external issues such as a data protection regime and other laws.

Also consider ISO 31000 on international risk management standards, and BS10012:2009 a standard for personal information management systems. There are also a variety of other data security technical rules which can be considered.

Organisations, including Processors, must implement appropriate security measures, considering:

- PIAs;
- anonymising data;
- deleting after use purpose;
- confidentiality;
- integrity;
- availability;
- access controls and restrictions;
- Approved Codes of Conduct and Certification;
- separating, segregating and securing different data sets;
- encryption.

There are also various other technical data security standards and guides, such as ISO 15408; ISO/IEC 27001 and 27002; ANSI/ISA 62443 (Formerly ISA-99); IEC 62443; NERC; NIST: and also the GDPR provisions in relation to data protection impact assessments, certification, and codes of conduct.

Incident Response

27.09 Some of the incident response and action points include, and not in order of priority:

- incident detection and reporting;
- incident notification to organisation (eg notification or demand from hacker, posting online, etc);

- internal notification(s);
- team notifications;
- risk assessment;
- PIAs;
- disciplinary action;
- hacker relation action;
- supervisory authority external breach notification;
- Data Subject breach notification;
- customer breach notification.

Conclusion

27.10   Security and data breach issues are significant considerations for organisations. The data protection regime re-emphasises this. Data breach issues should be considered in conjunction with the various risk reduction mechanisms referred to under the GDPR regime, such as impact assessments, Data Protection by Design and by default, mandatory breach reporting, mandatory prior consultations with the supervisory authority in the case of identified high risks, codes of conduct and certification mechanisms. The enhanced penalties will also be applied in the worst breach cases. There is an increasing trend for data penalties and third party litigation claims when corporate data protection breaches occur.

Chapter 28

Data Protection Impact Assessment

Data Protection Impact Assessment and Prior Consultation

28.01 Chapter IV, Section 3 of the EU General Data Protection Regulation (GDPR) refers to data protection impact assessments (DPIAs) (sometimes also referred to as privacy impact assessments (PIAs)) and prior consultations. As a result of the new GDPR regime there is now a mandatory data protection impact assessment regime. These assessments must be undertaken when data processing activities involve specific data protection and privacy risks. In particular when new products and services, or other changes to existing products and services arise, the organisation should ensure that these activities are the subject of a data protection impact assessment (DPIA).

These impact assessments will help organisations to identify and understand current and new risks in proposed processing activities, or indeed to existing processing activities. Considerations include:

- identifying when a project involves the collection of new information about individuals;
- identifying whether information about individuals will be disclosed to organisations or people who have not previously had routine access to the information;
- identifying whether the project involves the use of new technology which may raise privacy and data protection issues, such as overreach or privacy intrusion;
- identifying whether the personal data raises issues or concerns or is in some way objectionable.

Data Protection Impact Assessment

The New Requirement

28.02 Where a type of processing in particular using new technologies, and taking into account the nature, scope, context and purposes of the processing, is likely to result in a high risk for the rights and freedoms of natural persons, the Controller shall, prior to the processing, carry out an assessment of the impact of the envisaged processing operations on the protection of personal data. A single assessment may address a set of similar processing operations that present similar high risks (Article 35(1)).

The Controller shall seek the advice of the data protection officer (DPO), where designated, when carrying out a DPIA (Article 35(2)).

A DPIA referred to in Article 35(1) shall in particular be required in the following cases:

- a systematic and extensive evaluation of personal aspects relating to natural persons which is based on automated processing, including profiling, and on which decisions are based that produce legal effects concerning the natural person or similarly significantly affect the natural person;
- processing on a large scale of special categories of data referred to in Article 9(1), or of personal data relating to criminal convictions and offences referred to in Article 10;
- a systematic monitoring of a publicly accessible area on a large scale (Article 35(3)).

The supervisory authority shall establish and make public a list of the kind of processing operations which are subject to the requirement for a DPIA pursuant to Article 35(1). The supervisory authority shall communicate those lists to the European Data Protection Board (EDPB) (Article 35(4)).

The supervisory authority may also establish and make public a list of the kind of processing operations for which no DPIA is required. The SA shall communicate those lists to the EDPB (Article 35(5)).

Prior to the adoption of the lists referred to in Article 35(4) and (5) the competent supervisory authority shall apply the consistency mechanism referred to in Article 57 where such lists involve processing activities which are related to the offering of goods or services to Data Subjects or to the monitoring of their behaviour in several states, or may substantially affect the free movement of personal data within the EU (Article 35(6)).

The assessment shall contain at least:

- a systematic description of the envisaged processing operations and the purposes of the processing, including where applicable the legitimate interest pursued by the Controller;
- an assessment of the necessity and proportionality of the processing operations in relation to the purposes;
- an assessment of the risks to the rights and freedoms of Data Subjects referred to in Article 35(1);
- the measures envisaged to address the risks, including safeguards, security measures and mechanisms to ensure the protection of personal data and to demonstrate compliance with the GDPR taking into account the rights and legitimate interests of Data Subjects and other persons concerned (Article 35(7)).

Compliance with approved codes of conduct referred to in Article 40 by the relevant Controllers or Processors shall be taken into due account in assessing the impact of the processing operations performed by such Controllers or Processors, in particular for the purposes of a DPIA (Article 35(8)).

Where appropriate, the Controller shall seek the views of Data Subjects or their representatives on the intended processing, without prejudice to the protection of commercial or public interests or the security of the processing operations (Article 35(9)).

Where the processing pursuant to Article 6(1)(c) or (e) has a legal basis in EU law, or the law of the state to which the Controller is subject, that law regulates the specific processing operations in question, and a DPIA has already carried out as part of a general impact assessment in the context of the adoption of this legal basis, Article 35(1)–(7) shall not apply, unless states deem it necessary to carry out such assessment prior to the processing activities (Article 35(10)).

Where necessary, the Controller shall carry out a review to assess if processing is performed in accordance with the DPIA at least when there is a change of the risk represented by processing operations (Article 35(11)).

ICO Guidance

28.03   The ICO also refers to these issues, post the GDPR, in guidance.[1] It stresses that '[a] DPIA should begin early in the life of a project, before you start your processing, and run alongside the planning and development process.'

It refers to the following steps, namely:

- identify need for a DPIA;
- describe the processing;
- consider consultation;
- assess necessity and proportionality;
- identify and assess risks;
- identify measures to mitigate risk;
- sign off and record outcomes;
- integrate outcomes into plan;
- keep under review.

Reasons for Assessment

28.04   Vodafone refer to the following reasons for assessments:

- *accountability*: to demonstrate that the assessment process was performed appropriately and in accordance with the programme of assessments agreed with the board sponsor for data protection;
- *provides basis for post implementation review*: to ensure any data protection risks identified are allocated a business owner and a timetable for delivery mitigation actions, therefore providing the DPO with a mechanism for ensuring that the agreed actions are delivered within agreed timescales;
- *provides a basis for audit*: Vodafone distinguishes between a review which is undertaken by the DPO who is responsible for ensuring it is implemented and the controls required are delivered, and the audit which is an objective and neutral assessment undertaken by the group or local audit function or any other suitably qualified audit function that is not part of delivering the overall Data Protection Risk Management System;
- *provides corporate memory*: ensuring the information gained is available to those completing new assessments if original staff have left or use a part of a subsequent assessment of the same business or commercial unit or activity;
- enables the experience gained during the project to be shared with the future assessment teams and others outside the organisation.[2]

Nokia also give reasons for undertaking assessments:

- 'to measure the implementation of privacy requirements, to get an understanding of the current status (risk, controls, root causes, etc)';[3]

---

1   ICO, 'Data Protection Impact Assessments,' at https://ico.org.uk/for-organisations/guide-to-data-protection/guide-to-the-general-data-protection-regulation-gdpr/accountability-and-governance/data-protection-impact-assessments/.
2   S Deadman and A Chandler, 'Vodafone's Approach to Privacy Impact Assessments,' in D Wright and P de Hert, eds, *Privacy Impact Assessment* (Springer, 2012) 298.
3   T Brautigam, 'PIA: Cornerstone of Privacy Compliance in Nokia,' in D Wright and P de Hert, eds, *Privacy Impact Assessment* (Springer, 2012) 260–261.

- the assessment is part of technical and organisational measures. It assists to find out if new projects follow the data protection requirements; project management; communicate fulfilment of requirements; help to generate status reports for management teams; an effective tool for assigning responsibility and fixing problems;
- the DPIA assessment serves as 'a repository for information requests from authorities and consumers. Consumers might ask Nokia where and for how long their data is stored. A data protection authority might, for example, ask how consumers are informed about privacy practices or who the controller of the data is. Privacy assessment might also be used to prepare notifications for data protection authorities';[4]
- 'a means to improve general awareness. The assessment process ... builds up competencies and privacy awareness, as it offers an extensive set of questions that might be relevant for privacy compliance.'[5]

Key Elements of Assessment Report

28.05 Some key elements of an assessment report are as follows:

- the scope of the assessment undertaken;
- summary of the consultative process undertaken;
- the project background paper(s) provided to those consulted (appendices);
- analysis of the data protection issues and risks arising from the assessment;
- the business case justifying data protection intrusion and implications, treatment or mitigating action, together with timelines for implementation;
- references to relevant laws, codes and guidelines, including internal local group policies.[6]

Assessment Characteristics

28.06 Common characteristics of impact assessments:

- *Statement of problem*: Is government intervention both necessary and desirable?
- *Definition of alternative remedies*: these include different approaches, such as the use of economic incentives or voluntary approaches;
- *Determination of physical effects of each alternative, including potential unintended consequences*: the net should be cast wide. Generally speaking, regulations or investments in many areas of public policy can have social, environmental and other implications that must be kept in mind;
- *Estimation of benefits and costs of each alternative*: benefits should be quantified and where possible monetised. Costs should be true opportunity and not simply expenditures;
- *Assessment of other economic impacts*: including effects on competition, effects on small firms, international trade implications;
- *Identification of winners and losers*: those in the community who stand to gain and lose from each alternative and, if possible, the extent of their gains and losses;
- *Communication with the interested public, including the following activities*: notification of intent to regulate, request for compliance costs and other data, public disclosure of regulatory proposals and supporting analysis, and consideration of and response to public comments;
- *A clear choice of the preferred alternative*, plus a statement defending that choice;

---

4 See above.
5 See above.
6 S Deadman and A Chandler, above, 299.

- *Provision of a plan for ex post analysis of regulatory outcomes*: it is important to establish a benchmark against which to measure performance. Planning is needed to ensure that procedures are in place for the collection of date to permit such benchmarking.[7]

Some assessment characteristics distinguishing it from other privacy related processes include:

- an assessment focuses on a particular initiative or project;
- an assessment is performed at depth, through the project life cycle, and involves engagement with stakeholders;
- an assessment assesses a project against the needs, expectations and concerns of all stakeholders, including but not limited to legal requirements;
- an assessment assesses all aspects of privacy and data protection;
- an assessment adopts a multi-perspective approach, taking into account the costs and benefits as perceived by all stakeholders;
- an assessment adopts a multi perspective approach, taking into account the risks as perceived by all stakeholders;
- an assessment is a process used to establish what undertakings an organisation needs to give;
- an assessment is the process that identifies the problems and identifies solutions to them;
- an assessment is conducted before and in parallel with a project, and ensures that harmful and expensive problems that an audit would later expose are involved, and that unavoidable negative impacts on privacy are minimised and harms mitigated.[8]

Key Steps and Methodologies

28.07 The key steps and methodologies in an assessment include:

- identifying all of the personal data related to a programme or service and looking at how it will be used;
- mapping where personal data is sent after collection;
- identifying privacy and data protection risks and the level of the risks;
- finding methods to eliminate or reduce the risks.[9]

Some Assessment Issues

28.08 Organisations might consider issues such as the following:

- preparation;
- undertaking of the assessment;
- the timing of the assessment;
- cost and resourcing the assessment;
- whom the report is for;

---

7   OECD, 'Regulatory Performance: Ex Post Evaluation of Regulatory Tools and Institutions,' Working Party on Regulatory Management and Reform, Draft Report by the Secretariat, OECD, Paris (2004), 7; referred to in D Parker, '(Regulatory) Impact Assessment and Better Regulation,' in D Wright and P de Hert, eds, *Privacy Impact Assessment* (Springer, 2012) 80.
8   R Clarke, 'PIAs in Australia: A Work-In-Progress Report,' in D Wright and P de Hert, eds, *Privacy Impact Assessment* (Springer, 2012) 121.
9   Office of the Privacy Commissioner of Canada, Fact Sheet on Privacy Impact Assessment. Also note OIPC of Alberta, 'Commissioner Accepts Privacy Impact assessment for the Alberta Security Screening Directive,' press release, 16 January 2003.

- issues and problems raised;
- independence of those undertaking the assessment;
- any constraints;
- legal professional privilege and confidentiality;
- after undertaking the assessment, draft report/comments/final report;
- whether the assessment is a one off or an ongoing assessment in a (rolling) series?

DPDI Bill

28.09   The Data Protection and Digital Information (No 2) Bill (DPDI Bill) seeks to make amendments in relation to risk assessments (clause 17). The UK GDPR is sought to be amended as follows:

'17 Assessment of high risk processing

(1)   The UK GDPR is amended in accordance with subsections (2) to (4).
(2)   In the heading of Section 3 of Chapter 4, for "Data protection impact assessment" substitute "Assessment of high risk processing".
(3)   In Article 35 (data protection impact assessment)—
    (a)   for the heading substitute "Assessment of high risk processing",
    (b)   in paragraph 1, for "natural persons" substitute "individuals",
    (c)   omit paragraphs 2 to 5,
    (d)   for paragraph 7 substitute—

      "7 The controller must produce a document recording compliance with this Article which includes at least—

      (a)   a summary of the purposes of the processing,
      (b)   an assessment of whether the processing is necessary for those purposes,
      (c)   an assessment of the risks to individuals referred to in paragraph 1, and
      (d)   a description of how the controller proposes to mitigate those risks.",

    (e)   in paragraph 8, for ", in particular for the purposes of a data protection impact assessment" substitute "for the purposes of an assessment required by paragraph 1",
    (f)   omit paragraph 9,
    (g)   in paragraph 10—
      (i)   for "a data protection impact assessment" substitute "an assessment of the envisaged processing operations on the protection of personal data", and
      (ii)   omit "for the processing", and
    (h)   in paragraph 11—
      (i)   omit "Where necessary,", and
      (ii)   for "to assess if processing is performed in accordance with the data protection impact assessment" substitute "of an assessment pursuant to paragraph 1 where necessary and".
(4)   In Article 57(1) (Information Commissioner's tasks), for paragraph (k) substitute—

    "(k)   produce and publish a document containing examples of types of processing which the Commissioner considers are likely to result in a high risk to the rights and freedoms of individuals (for the purposes of Articles 27A, 30A and 35);".

(5)   The 2018 Act is amended in accordance with subsections (6) and (7).
(6)   Before section 64 insert—

    "Risk assessment and prior consultation".

(7)   In section 64 (data protection impact assessment)—
    (a)   for the heading substitute "Assessment of high risk processing",
    (b)   in subsection (1), for "a data protection impact assessment" substitute 15 "an assessment of the impact of the envisaged processing operations on the protection of personal data",

(c)   omit subsection (2), and

(d)   for subsection (3) substitute—

"(3) The controller must produce a document recording compliance 20 with this section which includes at least—

(a)   a summary of the purposes of the processing,

(b)   an assessment of whether the processing is necessary for those purposes,

(c)   an assessment of the risks to the rights and freedoms 25 of individuals referred to in subsection (1), and

(d)   a description of how the controller proposes to mitigate those risks.'"

Prior Consultation

28.10   The Controller shall consult the supervisory authority *prior to* processing where a DPIA as provided for in Article 35 indicates that the processing would result in a high risk in the absence of measures taken by the Controller to mitigate the risk (Article 36(1)).

Where the supervisory authority is of the opinion that the intended processing referred to in Article 36(1) would infringe the GDPR, in particular where the Controller has insufficiently identified or mitigated the risk, it shall within a period of up to eight weeks of receipt of the request for consultation, provide written advice to the Controller and, where applicable the Processor, and may use any of its powers referred to in Article 53. That period may be extended for a further six weeks, taking into account the complexity of the intended processing. The supervisory authority shall inform the Controller and, where applicable, the Processor, of any such extension within one month of receipt of the request for consultation together with the reasons for the delay. Those periods may be suspended until the supervisory authority has obtained information it may have requested for the purposes of the consultation (Article 36(2)).

When consulting the supervisory authority pursuant to Article 36(1), the Controller shall provide the supervisory authority with:

- where applicable, the respective responsibilities of the Controller, joint Controllers and Processors involved in the processing, in particular for processing within a group of undertakings;
- the purposes and means of the intended processing;
- the measures and safeguards provided to protect the rights and freedoms of Data Subjects pursuant to the GDPR;
- where applicable, the contact details of the DPO;
- the DPIA provided for in Article 35; and
- any other information requested by the supervisory authority (Article 36(3)).

States shall consult the supervisory authority during the preparation of a proposal for a legislative measure to be adopted by a national parliament, or of a regulatory measure based on such a legislative measure, which relates to processing (Article 37(4)).

Notwithstanding Article 36(1), states' law may require Controllers to consult with, and obtain prior authorisation from, the supervisory authority in relation to the processing of personal data by a Controller for the performance of a task carried out by the Controller in the public interest, including processing in relation to social protection and public health (Article 36(5)).

28.11   The DPDI Bill seeks to make amendments in relation to consulting the ICO prior to processing (clause 18). The UK GDPR is sought to be amended as follows:

'18 Consulting the Commissioner prior to processing

(1)   Article 36 of the UK GDPR (prior consultation) is amended in accordance with subsections (2) and (3).
(2)   In paragraph 1—
    (a)   for "shall" substitute "may",
    (b)   for "a data protection impact assessment" substitute "an assessment",
and
    (c)   after "high risk" insert "to the rights and freedoms of individuals".
(3)   In paragraph 3—
    (a)   in point (d), for "data protection officer" substitute "senior responsible individual", and
    (b)   in point (e) omit "data protection impact".
(4)   Section 65 of the 2018 Act (prior consultation) is amended in accordance with subsections (5) and (6).
(5)   In subsection (2)—
    (a)   for "must" substitute "may",
    (b)   for "if a data protection impact assessment prepared" substitute "where an assessment", and
    (c)   for "(in the absence of measures to mitigate the risk)" substitute "in the absence of measures taken by the controller to mitigate the risk".
(6)   In subsection (3)—
    (a)   for "is required to consult" substitute "consults",
    (b)   omit paragraph (a) (and the "and" after it), and
    (c)   in paragraph (b), omit "other".'

Conclusion

28.12   Carrying out impact assessments and the like helps to not only identify privacy and data protection problems, which can then be addressed, but also helps to raise these at the earliest stage possible. Therefore, the least expensive and least problematic time to make remedial changes is engaged. Carrying out such assessments is a requirement under the GDPR regime. This is especially so for high risk activities and when sensitive personal data may be involved. These assessments ensure organisations understand the data they hold, and the problem issues likely to arise. The organisation, its processes, and the ultimate customer relationship, will all be improved. Impact assessments are ultimately one of the mechanisms under the GDPR for assessing, and thus minimising, risk in the personal data environment.

Organisations must now be proactive and assess when processing activities are likely to raise risks in relation to personal data and processing. The DPO and other relevant parties/teams must be involved. Assessments must be more systematic. Risk identification and evaluation are now key considerations. Measures to mitigate and address risks must be considered and documented, including risk assessments. In situations where there are substantial risk issues, it may be necessary to consult with the ICO.

Chapter 29

Social Media

Introduction

29.01   New technologies 'permit easy dissemination and using of information. Current ICT allows individuals to share [sometimes unknowingly] their personal preferences and behaviour information on an unprecedented scale. This could lead to people losing control of personal information.'[1] The internet is an increasing part of our daily lives. One of its more popular examples is social media. What are the legal implications of social media?[2] One of the most controversial issues in relation to social media websites is their data processing and respect for privacy and personal data.[3] This is only part of the story. There are many discrete issues, such as:

- employers using social networks to vet and screen job applicants;[4]
- employers monitoring their employees' social media;[5]
- recruiting through social media;[6]
- universities monitoring student usage of social media;
- universities using social media websites to vet applicants;
- new forms of digital evidence, both criminal and civil.

One example of note is the (then) Facebook investigation of particular data protection issues by one of the EU national supervisory authorities. LinkedIn has also been audited in the EU. Recently, the ICO investigated the significant implications surrounding Cambridge Analytica; and also separately, particular Brexit campaign issues.

---

1   T Stanimir, 'Personal Data Protection and the New Technologies,' *Proceedings of the International Conference on Information Technologies* (2011) 333–344.
2   S Nelson, J Simek and J Foltin, 'The Legal Implications of Social Networking,' *Regent University Law Review*, (2009–2010) (22) 1–34. Also, P Viscounty, J Archie, F Alemi and J Allen, 'Social Networking and the Law,' *Business Law Today* (2008–009) (58) 18.
3   See, for example, P Roth, 'Data Protection Meets Web 2.0: Two Ships Passing in the Night,' *UNSW Law Journal* (2010) (33) 532–561. NJ Slabbert, 'Orwell's Ghost: How Teletechnology is Reshaping Civil Society,' *CommLaw Conspectus* (2007–2008) (16) 349–359.
4   C Brandenburg, 'The Newest Way to Screen Job Applicants: A Social Networker's Nightmare,' *Federal Communications Law Journal* (2007–2008) (60) 597. D Gersen, 'Your Image, Employers Investigate Job Candidates Online More than Ever. What can You Do to Protect Yourself?' *Student Law* (2007–2008) (36) 24; I Byrnside, 'Six Degrees of Separation: The Legal Ramifications of Employers Using Social Networking Sites to Research Applicants,' *Vanderbilt Journal of Entertainment and Technology Law* (2008) (2) 445–477.
5   AR Levinson, 'Industrial Justice: Privacy Protection for the Employed,' *Cornell Journal of Law and Public Policy* (2009) (18) 609–688.
6   M Maher, 'You've Got Messages, Modern Technology Recruiting Through Text Messaging and the Intrusiveness of Facebook,' *Texas Review of Entertainment and Sports Law* (2007) (8) 125–151.

Prior to the EU General Data Protection Regulation (GDPR), the ICO has issued recommendations in relation to online and computing personal data issues, namely:

- Bring Your Own Device (BYOD) guidance;
- Cloud Computing;
- IT Asset Disposal;
- Personal Information Online Code of Practice;
- Personal Information Online: Small Business Checklist;
- Privacy in Mobile Apps: Guidance for App Developers;
- Social Media and Online Forums – When Does the DPA apply?

These now need to be read in light of the GDPR changes. This also applies to the ongoing changes and shifts as occur when there are successful challenges in relation to certain transfers of personal data to the United States. Even post-Brexit, the EU challenges, ongoing challenges, and the new Privacy Framework should also be considered in the UK. The final versions of the Data Protection and Digital Information (No 2) Bill, and the Online Safety Bill, will each need careful examination for implications for internet companies, e-commerce, and social media activities. It appears that there will be a lot of change both inside the UK and in the EU in relation to these services. The EU is also seeking to impose more robust legislation in this sector, in addition to the GDPR. There is also potential for change in the United States in relation to certain online activities. The coming changes over the next number of years will have many impacts for this sector.

The Digital, Culture, Media and Sport (DCMS) Committee investigated social media, disinformation and fake news, and recommended more scrutiny, responsibility, and detailed regulation for social media firms, particularly in terms of what it referred to as 'online harms'. The final report is entitled 'Disinformation and "Fake News"': Final Report'.[7] Damian Collins MP, Chair of the DCMS Committee stated inter alia that:

'The big tech companies are failing in the duty of care they owe to their users to act against harmful content, and to respect their data privacy rights.

Companies like Facebook exercise massive market power which enables them to make money by bullying the smaller technology companies and developers who rely on this platform to reach their customers.

These are issues that the major tech companies are well aware of, yet continually fail to address. The guiding principle of the 'move fast and break things' culture often seems to be that it is better to apologise than ask permission.

We need a radical shift in the balance of power between the platforms and the people. The age of inadequate self regulation must come to an end. The rights of the citizen need to be established in statute, by requiring the tech companies to adhere to a code of conduct written into law by Parliament, and overseen by an independent regulator.

We also have to accept that our electoral regulations are hopelessly out of date for the internet age. We need reform so that the same principles of transparency of political communications apply online, just as they do in the real world. More needs to be done to require major donors to clearly establish the source of their funds.

---

7   Digital, Culture, Media and Sport (DCMS) Committee, 'Disinformation and "Fake News": Final Report' (18 February 2019). Available at www.parliament.uk/business/committees/committees-a-z/commons-select/digital-culture-media-and-sport-committee/news/fake-news-report-published-17-19/.

Much of the evidence we have scrutinised during our inquiry has focused on the business practices of Facebook; before, during and after the Cambridge Analytica data breach scandal.

We believe that in its evidence to the Committee Facebook has often deliberately sought to frustrate our work, by giving incomplete, disingenuous and at times misleading answers to our questions.'[8]

Controllers and Joint Controllers

29.02   Some may have assumed that the social media company was automatically the Controller in terms of the data held on the site. However, a CJEU case made clear that such a situation can be more nuanced. In the Facebook fan page case[9] it was held that the operator of a fan page on Facebook was a Joint Controller, in conjunction with Facebook, of the respective data held. The court stated that 'the concept of "[C]ontroller" within the meaning of that provision encompasses the administrator of a fan page hosted on a social network.'

The issue of Joint Controllers is also considered in the Fashion ID case.[10] This relates to a website which incorporated a social medial plugin whereby certain data was collected and transmitted to a third party in addition to the website operator.

One wonders if there may be a potential situation where there are three Joint Controllers. Consider two companies creating a form of joint venture, which as part of its activities also takes direction from each respective entity. Another scenario might be a lecturer who posts on Facebook or a blogging website. Perhaps the lecturer, university and the site are each a Joint Controller.

Investigations

29.03   Social media organisations can be officially investigated and audited much like any other organisations can. One audit,[11] for example, reviewed certain specific aspects of social media data protection compliance. This arose after a number of complaints regarding specific aspects of an organisation. The following issues were looked at, namely:

- privacy policies;
- advertising;
- access requests;
- retention;
- cookies/social plug-ins;
- third part apps;
- disclosures to third parties;
- facial recognition/tag suggest;
- data security;
- deletion of accounts;
- friend finder;

8   Ibid.
9   *Unabhängiges Landeszentrum für Datenschutz Schleswig-Holstein v Wirtschaftsakademie Schleswig-Holstein GmbH*, CJEU [2018] Case C-210/16 (5 June 2018).
10 *Fashion ID GmbH & Co.KG v Verbraucherzentrale NRW eV*, CJEU [2019] Case C-40/17 (29 July 2019).
11 Facebook Ireland Limited, *Report of Re-Audit, Data Protection Commissioner*, 21 September 2012.

- tagging;
- posting on other profiles;
- credits;
- pseudonymous profiles;
- abuse reporting;
- compliance management/governance.

That is not to suggest that every potential data protection issue was considered. It was not. Other issues and complaints can arise in future, as well as further investigations.[12]

The audit investigation forced the social media organisation to make particular changes to certain aspects of its data protection practices. These are referred to in the reports. The entity in the EU, the entity which was investigated, was responsible for its data protection compliance for everywhere outside of the US and Canada. Therefore, these changes should see an impact even beyond the EU. In addition it is noted that the controversial use of facial recognition technology by the organisation also had to be turned off for users in the EU. This is a direct result of the complaints and the official audit investigation.

Originally, it did not permit users to delete their accounts. However, it has now been made clear to the organisation that it must permit users the right and functional ability to delete their accounts. It will be recalled that one of the data protection Principles refers to personal data being held no longer than is necessary. User consent to processing can also be withdrawn.

The organisation settled litigation in the US relating to an advertising feature which it had launched and later cancelled. The case was meant to have been settled for approximately $20m. Note, also that there was a strong dissenting judgement criticising the settlement as, inter alia, too low.[13]

Social Media and Leveson

29.04   Amongst the many witnesses at the *Leveson Inquiry* were Facebook, Google and Twitter. One of the headline issues relates to what activities and services they engage in, respectively, and what they can and cannot do in terms of specific content. These are controversial and evolving issues in terms of both data protection compliance as well as take downs and liability for material on (and via) their websites. This is an area which will continue to expand. It is a critical area of contention in litigation (and policy discussion). Sony has been fined £250,000 by the ICO and Google was sued by UK Apple users.[14] Potential individual or group actions also arise in the

---

12 The *Europe Against Facebook* group also point out that there are particular issues and complaints outstanding. See http://www.europe-v-facebook.org/EN/en.html. There was also a group created in the US by MoveOn.org called *Petition: Facebook, Stop Invading My Privacy*, similarly objecting to certain practices of the social media website. A Morganstern, 'In the Spotlight: Social Network Advertising and the Right of Publicity,' *Intellectual Property Law Bulletin* (2007–2008) (1) 181–198; R Podolny, 'When "Friends" Become Adversaries: Litigation in the Age of Facebook,' *Manitoba Law Journal* (2009) (33) 391–408; Y Hashemi, 'Facebook's Privacy Policy and Its Third-Party Partnerships: Lucrativity and Liability,' *BU Journal of Science & Technology Law* (2009) (15) 140–161. Also P Nyoni and M Velempini, 'Data Protection Laws and Privacy on Facebook,' *SA Journal of Information Management* (2015) (17:1) 1.

13 The Beacon advertising feature. See appeal and lower court in the case of *McCall v Facebook*. The appeal case is *McCall v Facebook*, US Court of Appeals for the Ninth Circuit. See also, for example, W McGeveran, 'Disclosure, Endorsement, and Identity in Social Marketing,' *Illinois Law Review* (2009) (4) 1105–1166.

14 See *Google Inc v Vidal-Hall* [2015] EWCA Civ 311 (27 March 2015).

context of some of the Cambridge Analytica activities, but which may be complicated by the act that the company has sought to close down. Facebook was fined £500,000 by the ICO regarding Cambridge Analytica issues.

Social Media Data Transfers: Processors

29.05 Any social media organisation may quite legitimately need to engage third parties or outsource particular tasks. However, it is not always clear that the website will have ensured that an appropriate written contract is in place and that appropriate security measures are in place with the outsourced Processor as regards the personal data received and processed by it. Users should also be informed of such outsourcing and be assured of the security measures. Consent, transparency and prior information are equally important compliance issues.

Apps: Social Media Data Transfers

29.06 Increasingly, social networks provide and facilitate third party apps or applications on their websites.[15] Frequently, as part of this practice, personal data is disclosed to the third party companies operating or developing the apps. Unfortunately, there appears to be an overly loose compliance relationship as regards the transfer and protection of users' personal data. Sometimes, data would be accessible or transferred without regard to users' personal data rights, user knowledge, contracts and security. In addition, there could sometimes be no restriction on the apps developers using the personal data for more than one purpose and for activities unrelated to the initial intended purpose.

The GDPR also recognises that apps raise data protection issues.

Awareness

29.07 Increasingly potential employers, schools and universities use social media profile information in making assessments on applications regarding specific individuals. Unfortunately, one of the issues relates to the consequence of this for individuals, sometimes adverse consequences.[16] In addition, many users, and particularly those of a younger age, will not (fully) appreciate that such activities and consequences can arise from their social media.

There is arguably more to be done by social networks in terms of informing and appraising users of the issues which can arise. This is particularly emphasised when children and teenagers are concerned.

WP29 in its Opinion regarding social media, recognises the dangers arising from apps.[17] Compliance with the GDPR must be ensured. There is also a UK Home Office Good Practice Guidance for the Providers of Social Networks.[18] Arguably, these could be updated. This is an area where significant ongoing research is needed.

15 See, for example, Y Hashemi, 'Facebook's Privacy Policy and its Third-Party Partnerships: Lucrativity and Liability,' *BUJ Science & Technology Law* (2009) (15) 140–161.
16 See discussion at L Edwards and C Waelde, eds, above, 481.
17 WP29, Opinion 5/2009 on online social networking.
18 At https://www.gov.uk/government/uploads/system/uploads/attachment_data/file/251456/industry_guidance_social_networking.pdf.

In addition, it should be noted that social media companies have also recognised that their own awareness and preparedness needs to increased following the revelations surrounding the attack on the US election of 2016; and the ongoing Cambridge Analytica developments. The ICO is also investigating the latter and will no doubt issue findings and a report in due course. It cannot be ruled out at this remove as to whether the ICO may find sufficient evidence to mount prosecutions in relation to offences committed.

Tagging and Identification

29.08   It is possible that people are visible online in photographs uploaded to social networks which they would not want, may be unaware of, and also have not consented to.

In addition, social media websites can permit people to be tagged and labelled in uploaded photographs, without their consent.

These concerns are even more enhanced. Facebook developed enhanced capacity to index and reveal information and photographs from its website (Facebook Graph Search tool as well as new facial recognition applications). There has been some controversy as to what jurisdictions these types of tools may be applied to, and which not. It is also noted that users are being requested to submit nude photographs in order to be scanned in such a manner as to aid in dealing with revenge porn attacks. By submitting such photographs and presumably furnishing associated specific terms and acknowledgements, there may be an intention to obtain not just consent, but explicit consent.

Transparency and User Friendly Tools

29.09   Social media frequently appear to value membership numbers over fully transparent, obvious and user friendly privacy protection and complaint tools. The on-site tools (when present) are 'frequently unobvious or difficult to use. The cynical might imagine that this is because ... the revenue stream from the SNS comes from third parties – advertisers – having access to as much data, on as many profiles, as possible.'[19]

One part solution is to have privacy and friend restricted access as the default model for social media websites. This is suggested particularly in relation to children by the Home Office code of conduct for social networks.[20]

WP29 in the context of online behavioural advertising indicates that an icon in itself can be insufficient. In that context it was particularly concerned with consent issues. However, significant research remains to be undertaken in order to properly assess the adequacy of icons, notices, tools, information, information notices, report buttons, reports processes, report teams, response times, resolutions times, etc, in relation to online abuse and social media websites. There is as yet a distinct shortage of research and literature on this topic. This is despite the media reports of online abuse and many examples of tragic consequences.

19 L Edwards and C Waelde, eds, *Law and the Internet* (Hart, 2009) 483.
20 In 2008. At https://www.gov.uk/government/uploads/system/uploads/attachment_data/file/251456/ industry_guidance_social_networking.pdf.

Abuse, Attacks, Threats, Trolling, Victims

29.10 It is clear that these problem issues are significant and appear to be increasing. Pierre Trudel, for example, notes that the risks to individuals increase from many online activities, including in relation to data protection, safety, etc.[21]

Popular social media websites, such as Twitter, Reddit and now Facebook, are recognising that more needs to be done to address issues of online abuse and will progress changes to assist in dealing with the problem.

The Olympics in London brought to the fore the disadvantages of social media, where social networks such as Twitter, Facebook, etc, can be used for abuse.[22] There is a growing and troubling number of instances of suicides arising as a result of abuse and threats occurring on social media websites. Social networks, and other websites, also contain controversial material in relation to self-harm.

YouTube and Google also embrace 'real name' posting policies (in part). Such policies may assist somewhat in reducing trolling and attacks online, as well as the unfortunate consequences thereof.[23]

The problem of cyber bullying is incontrovertible, with increasing high-profile suicides recently. If anyone is still unclear about the devastation caused to victims and families, the video posted by Canadian teenager Amanda Todd is required viewing. Indeed it should be required viewing for parents, educators and policymakers.

The cyberbullying of teenagers is just one facet of online abuse, which can range from threats to defamation, harassment to stalking, grooming and breaches of privacy and data protection. There are also overlaps. The cyberbullying of children can involve harassment, threats, verbal abuse and defamation, or in the case of Amanda Todd, privacy and data-protection breaches later expanding to threats. The solutions are multifaceted. Much of the recent commentary points to education, educators and parents. While this is correct, it is only one aspect.

One point missing from the current discussion is that it is legally possible to find anonymous abusers. Victims and the police can apply to court for the disclosure of user details from relevant websites and service providers. These are frequently known as *Norwich Pharmacal* orders. Online abusers can face civil as well as criminal consequences, even if they are children or teenagers. It goes without saying the police must properly follow up reports. It is clear from recent media commentary that the UK police are proactive and considered in this area.

Much of this abuse occurs on social media websites, but it does also occur via mobile telephones and smartphones. An article in the *Guardian* states that the 'Mobile internet is now just the internet.'[24] Some social media sites provide 'tools' or 'reporting processes.' However, many of them, and indeed other Web 2.0 websites, do not do all they could to deal with these issues. Even some of the largest social networks have been slower to implement reporting procedures for certain forms of abuse than

21 P Trudel, 'Privacy Protection on the Internet: Risk Management and Networked Normativity,' in S Gutwirth, Y Poullet, P de Hert, C de Terwange and S Nouwt, *Reinventing Data Protection?* (Springer, 2009) 317.

22 J Rosenberg, 'Tom Daley, Twitter Abuse and the Law,' *Guardian*, 31 July 2012; S James, 'Man Cautioned After Mark Halsey Twitter Abuse,' *Guardian*, 27 September 2012; LL Baughmanm, 'Friend Request or Foe? Confirming the Misuse of Internet and Social Networking Sites by Domestic Violence Perpetrators,' *Widener Law Journal* (2010) (19) 933–966. Generally, also see JJ Ator, 'Got Facebook?' *GPSolo* (March, 2009) 4–5.

23 Generally note, for example, B Kane, 'Balancing Anonymity, Popularity, & Micro-Celebrity: The Crossroads of Social Networking & Privacy,' *Albany Law Journal of Science and Technology* (2010) (20) 327–363.

24 J Naughton, 'Mobile internet is Now Just the Internet,' *Guardian*, 27 December 2015.

should be the case. Some websites also have particular tools available which they use for certain activities, but are reluctant to extend to abuse victims.

But no matter how many 'report buttons' there are on a given website, they are entirely useless without protocols, policies and procedures behind the scenes to follow through on reports that are made. A complaints procedure is meaningless unless there are enough people investigating abuse reports.

It would be interesting to examine and compare the number of people employed in abuse investigation teams across various social media websites. Should there be a minimum number of employees assigned per number of users of a social media website? Or should there be a minimum number of employees per amount of abuse reports made? The turnover of such websites could easily absorb hiring more staff.

A further point arises regarding social media and related websites. Some are happy to publish statistics about the level of reports and complaints received relating to copyright infringement. This appears commercially driven. There is significantly less 'transparency' as regards the level of abuse reports and complaints made to social media websites, and around how, and how quickly, these abuse reports are resolved.

As much as we are presently shocked by the dark side of internet abuse, cyberbullying and the terrible consequences, it may be that we would be further shocked at the scale of abuse being reported, when the facility is available to do so. That may be a useful line of pursuit for anyone who is officially concerned about this issue. It is also worth considering that whatever a website may say at first blush may not always be the whole picture.

We are now beginning to realise that, on occasion, social media and other websites can have a dark side.

Unfortunately, there are large gaps in our knowledge, research and understanding of these developing issues. More research is needed to appraise ourselves of all potential solutions and policy decisions as well as assisting websites to fully engage their own (corporate, moral and legal) responsibilities and functional capabilities.

There are also business case advantages. The EU Commission and websites have recently developed a code of conduct initiative for online hate takedowns.

Employment and Social Media

29.11 Employers are increasingly considering access to employees' social media materials.[25] A general policy of such monitoring is not permitted under EU data protection law. Nor can employees be forced to disclose or permit access to their social media accounts by way of enforced access. However, it is the case that social media evidential material is increasingly frequent in employment disputes and employment litigation. Organisations should seek legal advice in advance of seeking to utilise or rely upon such materials, otherwise potential litigation, dismissals or disciplinary actions can be deemed to be illegal.[26]

---

25 A Blank, 'On the Precipe of e-Discovery: Can Litigants Obtain Employee Social Networking Web Site Information Through Employers?' *CommLaw Conspectus* (2009–2010) (18) 487–516. Also, I Byrnside, 'Six Clicks of Separation: The Legal Ramifications of Employers using Social Networking Sites to Research Applicants,' *Vanderbilt Journal of Entertainment and Technology Law* (2008) (10) 445–477.

26 See also M Maher, 'You've Got Messages: Modern technology Recruiting Through Text-Messaging and the Intrusiveness of Facebook,' *Texas Review of Entertainment & Sports Law*, (2007) (8) 125–151; C Brandenburg, 'The Newest Way to Screen Job Applicants: A Social Networker's Nightmare,' *Federal Communications Law Journal* (2007–2008) (60) 597–626.

Electronic Evidence

29.12 There are growing digital evidence opportunities for litigation, which can include personal data.[27] These can include service of documents[28] and civil discovery.[29] Social media have been described as electronic footprints.[30] This can also include employees' social media activity.[31]

The Rights of Data Subjects

29.13 It is noted that '[o]ne aspect of privacy and data protection is a remedy against intrusiveness and loss of control of the circulation of a person's informational image.'[32] In addition, '[s]uch intrusiveness and its loss do not only exist when someone is or can be identified; for instance, the acts of being observed and being traced are privacy threats, even without knowing the name of the observed or traced person.'[33]

Even with social media, the rights of Data Subjects remain. The rights of Data Subjects, including for social media, can be summarised as including:

- right of access;
- right to establish if personal data exists;
- right to be informed of the logic in automatic decision taking;
- right to prevent processing likely to cause damage or distress;
- right to prevent processing for direct marketing;
- right to prevent automated decision taking;
- right to compensation;
- right to rectify inaccurate data;
- right to rectification, blocking, erasure and destruction;
- right to complain to ICO;
- right to go to court.

27 K Minotti, 'The Advent of Digital Diaries: Implications of Social Networking Web Sites for the Legal Profession,' *South Carolina Law Review* (2009) (60) 1057–1074; JS Wilson, 'MySpace, Your Space or Our Space? New Frontiers in Electronic Evidence,' *Oregon Law Review* (2007) (86) 1201–1240; AC Payne, 'Twitigation: Old Rules in a New World,' *Washburn Law Journal* (2010) (49) 842–870.

28 AL Shultz, AL, 'Superpoked and Served: Service of Process via Social Networking Sites,' 43 *University Richmond Law Review* (2008–2009) (43) 1497–1528. RJ Hedges, Rashbaum and AC Losey, 'Electronic Service of Process at Home and Abroad: Allowing Domestic Electronic Service of Process in Federal Courts,' *Federal Courts Law Review* (2010) (4) 54–76.

29 SC Bennett, 'Civil Discovery of Social Networking Information,' *Southwestern Law Review* (2009–2010) (39) 413–431. Also, DS Witte, 'Your Opponent Does Not Need a Friend Request to See Your Page: Social Networking Sites and Electronic Discovery,' *McGeorge Law Review* (2009–2010) (41) 891–903; RA Ward, 'Discovering Facebook: Social Network Subpoenas and the Stored Communications Act,' *Harvard Journal of Law & Technology* (2011) (24) 563–588.

30 EM Marsico, Jr, 'Social Networking Websites: Are Myspace and Facebook the Fingerprints of the Twenty-first Century?' *Widener Law Journal* (2010) (19) 967–976. Also, EE North, 'Facebook Isn't Your Space Anymore: Discovery of Social Networking Website,' *University of Kansa Law Review* (2009–2010) (58) 1279–1309; TM Williams, 'Facebook: Ethics, Traps, and Reminders,' *Litigation News* (2009–2010) (35) 4.

31 For example, see, L Thomas, 'Social Networking in the Workplace: Are Private Employers Prepared to Comply With Discovery Requests for Posts and Tweets?' *SMU Law Review* (2010) (63) 1373–1402.

32 L Costa and Y Poullet, 'Privacy and the Regulation of 2012,' *Computer Law & Security Review* (2012) (28) 254–262, at 256.

33 See above.

These expand under the GDPR. Chapter III of the GDPR refers to the rights of Data Subjects. These include:

- right to transparency (Article 5; Article 12);
- right to prior information: directly obtained data (Article 13);
- right to prior information: indirectly obtained data (Article 14);
- right of confirmation and right of access (Article 15);
- right to rectification (Article 16);
- right to erasure (Right to be Forgotten) (RtbF) (Article 17);
- right to restriction of processing (Article 18);
- notifications re rectification, erasure or restriction (Article 19);
- right to data portability (Article 20);
- right to object (Article 21);
- rights re automated individual decision making, including profiling (Article 22);
- DPbD (Article 25);
- security rights;
- data protection impact assessment and prior consultation;
- communicating data breach to Data Subject;
- Data Protection Officer;
- remedies, liability and sanctions (Chapter VIII).

Consent and Social Media

29.14   It is noted that social media websites:

> 'are of course data Controllers, and so under [data protection] law they must, in pursuit of "fair processing," gain the consent of their users to process their personal data – and indeed, "explicit consent" in the case of sensitive personal data (which abounds on SNA [social networking service] – on almost every Facebook profile a user reveals his or her race, politics, sexuality or religious beliefs, since these predetermined fields in the user profile, which most users fill in without much thought).'[34]

Frequently, social media websites seek to comply with the consent requirement by providing that it is 'required as part of registration before "admission" to the site is granted. Consent is usually obtained by displaying a privacy policy [or privacy statement] on the site and asking the user to accede to them by ticking a box. As there is no chance to negotiate, and little or no evidence that users either read or understand these conditions, it is hard to see how this consent is "free and informed" … yet business practice for the entire sector seems to regard this consent is satisfactory.'[35]

There are other difficulties.

> 'A further problem arises where SNS users display facts or images about other users – eg commonly, photographs featuring multiple persons. Such users rarely seek prior consent and such software tools as are made available usually only facilitate post factum removal, for example, of "tags" on Facebook.'[36]

> 'Also, the question arises as to whether ordinary users should be subject to the full panopoly of [data protection] obligations vis-a-vis their peers, and if they are not, how invasions of privacy by users rather than the site itself should be controlled. One suggestion has been that

34   L Edwards and C Waelde, eds, *Law and the Internet* (Hart, 2009) 479.
35   See above.
36   See above.

sites should be subject to liability for invasion of privacy if they do not take down expediently on complaint.'[37]

Consent is an important issue under the GDPR.[38] Lawful processing and consent are referred to in Recitals 32 and 40. The WP29 also refers to consent issues.[39]

Article 7 of the GDPR refers to conditions for consent as follows. Where processing is based on consent, the Controller shall be able to demonstrate that the Data Subject has consented to processing of their personal data (Article 7(1)).

If the Data Subject's consent is given in the context of a written declaration which also concerns other matters, the request for consent must be presented in a manner which is *clearly distinguishable* from the other matters, in an *intelligible and easily accessible form*, using *clear and plain language*. Any part of the declaration which constitutes an infringement of the GDPR shall not be binding (Article 7(2)).

The Data Subject shall have the *right to withdraw his or her consent at any time*. The withdrawal of consent shall not affect the lawfulness of processing based on consent before its withdrawal. Prior to giving consent, the Data Subject must be informed thereof. It shall be as easy to withdraw consent as to give it (Article 7(3)).

When assessing whether consent is freely given, utmost account shall be taken of whether, inter alia, the performance of a contract, including the provision of a service, is conditional on the consent to the processing of data that is not necessary for the performance of that contract (Article 7(4)).

The issue of children in the data protection regime has been steadily rising. The increased use of social media and Web 2.0 services enhance the exposures and risks for children and the uninitiated.[40]

This has included children's groups, regulators and also the EDPB (previously the WP29). WP29 issued Opinion 2/2009 on the Protection of Children's Personal Data (General Guidelines and the Special Case of Schools) in 2009 and also Working Document 1/2008 on the Protection of Children's Personal Data (General Guidelines and the Special Case of Schools) in 2008. Schools are being encouraged to be proactive and to have appropriate codes and policies for children's social media and internet usage.[41]

There is now an express acknowledgement of children's interests in the EU data protection regime, unlike with the DPD 1995 which contained no explicit reference. The GDPR expressly refers to a 'child' for the first time. This is significant amongst other things in relation to consent, contracting, etc. It is also significant for social networks which have significant numbers of children. Up until now it was common for certain social networks to purport to accept users only over the age of 13. Now that the age of a child in the context of information society services is considered by

---

37 See above.
38 JP Vandenbroucke and J Olsen, 'Informed Consent and the New EU Regulation on Data Protection,' *International Journal of Epidemiology* (2013) (42: 6) 1891.
39 WP29 Opinion 15/2011 Consent; Working Document 02/2013 providing guidance on obtaining consent for cookies, 201; Opinion 04/2012 on Cookie Consent Exemption.
40 See, for example, D Gourlay and G Gallagher, 'Collecting and Using Children's Information Online: the UK/US Dichotomy,' SCL *Computers and Law*, 12 December 2011.
41 Note generally, for example, JS Groppe, 'A Child's Playground or a Predator's Hunting Ground? – How to Protect Children on Internet Social Networking Sites,' *CommLaw Conspectus* (2007) (16) 215–245; EP Steadman, 'MySpace, But Who's Responsibility? Liability of Social Networking Websites When Offline Sexual Assault of Minors Follows Online Interaction,' *Villanova Sports and Entertainment Law Journal* (2007) (14) 363–397; DC Beckstrom, 'Who's Looking at Your Facebook Profile? The Use of Student Conduct Codes to Censor College Students' Online Speech,' *Willamette Law Review* (2008) 261–312.

the GDPR to be at least 16 years old, it may require careful assessment in relation to social media contracts, terms, processes, sign ups, etc. (Note, states may additionally make provisions in relation to the age of children in this regard in addition to the above, for example, not below the age of 13 years old (see Article 8), which the UK has availed of (see Data Protection Act 2018 (DPA 2018), s 9).

The explicit reference to children is new, and some would argue overdue. Increasingly, the activities of children on the internet and on social media poses risks and concerns.[42] This has been further emphasised of late with tragic events involving online abuse, in particular cyber bullying. Risks arise obviously from their activities online (eg inappropriate content, cyber bullying, but also from the collection and use of their personal data online and collected online, sometimes without their knowledge or consent). Their personal data and privacy is more vulnerable than that of older people.

It is important for organisations to note the definition of 'child' in the GDPR. This will have implications in how organisations;

● consider the interaction with children and what personal data may be collected and processed;
● ensure that there is appropriate compliance for such collection and processing for children as distinct from adults.

Processing of children's personal data are referred to in Recitals 58, 65, 71 and 75.

The German Federal court has affirmed lower courts holding unlawful Facebook's 'friend finder' function which accesses users' email lists and promoted/advertised to these contacts even if not members of the website.[43]

The GDPR can be taken to be part of the increasing willingness to critically assess both the arguments raised by internet companies, or at least social media internet companies, and the responsibility of such companies. The express inclusion of the right of data protection bodies to act on behalf of groups of Data Subjects in the GDPR will undoubtedly increase the potential for more actions targeted at social media internet companies (and indeed other companies).

Website Discretion, Liability and Obligations

29.15   On occasion certain websites will argue that they are not responsible for certain activities occurring on their websites. A particular example is user generated content. One frequent argument relates to the issue of the limited ISP defences of *caching, hosting* and *mere conduit* in the ECD.[44] There is also an argument raised by certain websites that they can target and deal with European consumers and users, yet are not responsible in relation to the collection and processing of users' personal data. This later point is based on the argument that if the website company is based outside of the EU, even though the users are in the EU, they do not have to comply with the data protection regime. There is an irony here. These website companies seek to avail of EU law as regards EU law defences of mere conduit, caching and hosting, yet then

---

42   See, for example, L McDermott, 'Legal Issues Associated with Minors and Their Use of Social Networking Sites,' *Communications Law* (2012) (17) 19–24.

43   *Federation of German Consumer Organisations (VZBV) v Facebook*, German Federal Court of Justice, 14 January 2016.

44   Directive 2000/31/EC of the European Parliament and of the Council of 8 June 2000 on certain legal aspects of information society services, in particular electronic commerce, in the Internal Market ('Directive on electronic commerce').

argue their preferred policy of ignoring EU data protection law. Are such websites immune to the EU data protection regime? Can websites pick and choose one set of EU laws to benefit them, but ignore entirely other laws which create rights for their users? Caselaw and the GDPR confirm compliance liability.

These issues in relation to websites, social media and jurisdiction are commented upon later.

Third Party Controllers and EU Data Subjects

29.16 DPD 1995 Recital 20 stated that the fact that the processing of data is carried out by a person established in a third country must not stand in the way of the protection of individuals provided for in this Directive. In these cases, the processing should be governed by the law of the state in which the means used are located, and there should be guarantees to ensure that the rights and obligations provided for in this Directive are respected in practice.

Specific Processing Risks

29.17 DPD 1995 Recital 53 stated that certain processing operations are likely to pose specific risks to the rights and freedoms of Data Subjects by virtue of their nature, their scope or their purposes, such as that of excluding individuals from a right, benefit or a contract, or by virtue of the *specific use of new technologies*; it is for states, if they so wish, to specify such risks in their legislation.

DPD 1995 Recital 54 stated that with regard to all the processing undertaken in society, the amount posing such specific risks should be very limited. States must provide that the supervisory authority, or the data protection official in cooperation with the authority, check such processing prior to it being carried out. Following this prior check, the supervisory authority may, according to its national law, give an opinion or an authorisation regarding the processing. Such checking may equally take place in the course of the preparation either of a measure of the national parliament or of a measure based on such a legislative measure, which defines the nature of the processing and lays down appropriate safeguards.

The GDPR also continues this trajectory with the obligations to proactively examine risk and gap issues, and to carry out audits and assessments. While most organisations will have engaged in GDPR compliance exercises leading up to May 2018, it must be stressed that data protection compliance is an ongoing exercise, not a one moment in time action. In addition, there is a new emphasis in being able to record and demonstrate compliance, as opposed to merely making statements without appropriate backup.

Rights

Right to Prevent Data Processing Likely to Cause Damage or Distress

29.18 Data Subjects have a right to prevent processing likely to cause damage or distress. This can also be considered relevant to social media.

Right to Prevent Data Processing for DM

29.19 Data Subjects have the right to prevent processing for purposes of direct marketing. This can also be considered relevant to social media.

Compensation for Data Subjects

29.20   Data Subjects are entitled to damages and compensation for failure to comply with certain requirements, particularly where there is material or non material damage. This can be relevant to social media.

Rectification, Blocking, Erasure and Destruction Rights

29.21   Data Subjects have rights in relation to rectification, blocking, erasure and forgetting, and destruction. This can also be relevant to social media.

Automated Decision Taking/Making Processes

29.22   Automated decision taking/making processes can also be considered in the social media context. Controllers may not take decisions which produce legal effects concerning a Data Subject or which otherwise significantly affect a Data Subject and which are based solely on processing by automatic means of personal data and which are intended to evaluate certain personal matters relating to the Data Subject such as, performance at work, credit worthiness, reliability of conduct.

GDPR

Definitions and Social Media

29.23   The GDPR is relevant to social media. The GDPR definitions include:

'personal data breach'	means a breach of security leading to the accidental or unlawful destruction, loss, alteration, unauthorised disclosure of, or access to, personal data transmitted, stored or otherwise processed;
'main establishment'	means:

- as regards a Controller with establishments in more than one Member State, the place of its central administration in the EU, unless the decisions on the purposes and means of the processing of personal data are taken in another establishment of the Controller in the EU and the latter establishment has the power to have such decisions implemented, in which case the establishment having taken such decisions is to be considered to be the main establishment;

- as regards a Processor with establishments in more than one Member State, the place of its central administration in the EU, or, if the Processor has no central administration in the EU, the establishment of the Processor in the EU where the main processing activities in the context of the activities of an establishment of the Processor take place to the extent that the Processor is subject to specific obligations under the GDPR.

'representative'	means any natural or legal person established in the EU who, designated by the Controller or Processor in writing pursuant to Article 27, represents the Controller or Processor, with regard to their respective obligations under the GDPR;
'enterprise'	means any natural or legal person engaged in an economic activity, irrespective of its legal form, including partnerships or associations regularly engaged in an economic activity;
'group of undertakings'	means a controlling undertaking and its controlled undertakings.

The originally proposed definition of a child appears deleted in the final version of the GDPR.

However, see reference to children below.

Right to Object, Profiling and Social Media

29.24 Electronic identity or eID's are also an area being considered.[45]

Transparency

29.25 Article 12 refers to transparent information, communication and modalities for exercising the rights of the Data Subject. The Controller shall take appropriate measures to provide any information referred to in Articles 15–22 and 34 relating to the processing to the Data Subject in a concise, transparent, intelligible and easily accessible form, using clear and plain language, in particular for any information addressed specifically to a child. When requested by the Data Subject, the information may be provided orally, as long as the identity of the Data Subject is proven by other means (Article 12(1)).

The Controller shall facilitate the exercise of Data Subject rights under Articles 15–22. In cases referred to in Article 11(2), the Controller shall not refuse to act on the request of the Data Subject for exercising their rights under Articles 15–22, unless the Controller demonstrates that it is not in a position to identify the Data Subject (Article 12(2)).

The Controller shall provide information on action taken on a request under Articles 15–22 to the Data Subject without undue delay and in any event within one month of receipt of the request. This period may be extended by two further months where necessary, taking into account the complexity of the request and the number of the requests. The Controller shall inform the Data Subject of any extensions within one month of receipt of the request, together with the reasons for the delay. Where the Data Subject makes the request in electronic form means, the information shall be provided in electronic form where possible, unless otherwise requested by the Data Subject (Article 12(3)).

If the Controller does not take action on the request of the Data Subject, the Controller shall inform the Data Subject without delay and at the latest within one month of receipt of the request of the reasons for not taking action and on the possibility of lodging a complaint to a supervisory authority and seeking a judicial remedy (Article 12(4)).

Information provided under Articles 13 and 14 and any communication and any actions taken under Articles 15–22 and 34 shall be provided free of charge. Where requests from a Data Subject are manifestly unfounded or excessive, in particular because of their repetitive character, the Controller may either charge a reasonable fee taking into account the administrative costs of providing the information or communication or taking the action requested; or, refuse to act on the request. In these cases, the Controller shall bear the burden of demonstrating the manifestly unfounded or excessive character of the request (Article 12(5)).

Without prejudice to Article 11, where the Controller has reasonable doubts concerning the identity of the individual making the request referred to in Articles 15–21,

---

45 See, for example, Norberto Nuno Gomes de Ardrade, 'Regulating Electronic Identity in the European Union: An Analysis of the Lisbon Treaty's Competences and Legal Basis for eID,' *Computer Law and Security Review* (2012) (28) 153–162, at 153. European Commission, *Communication from the Commission – a Digital Agenda for Europe* (Brussels: European Commission 2010) 11.

the Controller may request the provision of additional information necessary to confirm the identity of the Data Subject (Article 12(6)).

The information to be provided to Data Subjects pursuant to Articles 13 and 14 may be provided in combination with standardised icons in order to give in an easily visible, intelligible and clearly legible manner a meaningful overview of the intended processing. Where the icons are presented electronically they shall be machine-readable (Article 12(7)).

The Commission shall be empowered to adopt delegated acts in accordance with Article 92 for the purpose of determining the information to be presented by the icons and the procedures for providing standardised icons (Article 12(8)).

Child's Consent: Conditions for Information Society Services

29.26 Processing of children's personal data are referred to in Recital 38. Article 8 of the GDPR makes provisions in relation to conditions for children's consent for information society services. Where Article 6(1)(a) applies, in relation to the offer of information society services directly to a child, the processing of personal data of a child shall be lawful where the child is at least 16 years old. Where the child is below the age of 16 years, such processing shall be lawful only if and to the extent that such consent is given or authorised by the holder of parental responsibility over the child (Article 8(1)). (States may provide by law for a lower age for those purposes provided that such lower age is not below 13 years (Article 8(1)) – as the UK has done (DPA 2018, s 9). The Controller shall make reasonable efforts to verify in such cases that consent is given or authorised by the holder of parental responsibility over the child, taking into consideration available technology (Article 8(2)). This shall not affect the general contract law of states such as the rules on the validity, formation or effect of a contract in relation to a child (Article 8(3)).

Data Access Rights

29.27 Chapter III, Section 2 of the GDPR refers to data access. It should be noted that the prior information requirements might have previously been viewed as Controller compliance obligations. However, they are now reformulated as part of the Data Subject information and access rights. This would therefore be a change in emphasis.

Right to Prior Information: Directly Obtained Data

29.28 Article 13 refers to information to be provided where the data are collected from the Data Subject. Where personal data relating to a Data Subject are collected from the Data Subject, the Controller shall, at the time when personal data are obtained, provide the Data Subject with *all* of the following information:

- the identity and the contact details of the Controller and, where applicable, of the Controller's representative;
- the contact details of the DPO, where applicable;
- the purposes of the processing for which the personal data are intended as well as the legal basis of the processing;
- where the processing is based on Article 6(1)(f), the legitimate interests pursued by the Controller or by a third party;
- the recipients or categories of recipients of the personal data, if any;
- where applicable, the fact that the Controller intends to transfer personal data to a third country or international organisation and the existence or absence of an adequacy decision by the Commission, or in case of transfers referred to in

Article 46 or 47, or Article 49(1) (second subparagraph), reference to the appropriate or suitable safeguards and the means by which to obtain a copy of them or where they have been made available (Article 13(1)).

In addition to the information referred to in Article 13(1), the Controller shall, at the time when personal data are obtained, provide the Data Subject with the following further information necessary to ensure fair and transparent processing:

- the period for which the personal data will be stored, or if this is not possible, the criteria used to determine this period;
- the existence of the right to request from the Controller access to and rectification or erasure of personal data or restriction of processing concerning the Data Subject or to object to the processing as well as the right to data portability;
- where the processing is based on Article 6(1)(a) or Article 9(2)(a), the existence of the right to withdraw consent at any time, without affecting the lawfulness of processing based on consent before its withdrawal;
- the right to lodge a complaint with a supervisory authority;
- whether the provision of personal data is a statutory or contractual requirement, or a requirement necessary to enter into a contract, as well as whether the Data Subject is obliged to provide the data and of the possible consequences of failure to provide such data;
- the existence of automated decision making, including profiling, referred to in Article 22(1) and (4) and at least in those cases, meaningful information about the logic involved, as well as the significance and the envisaged consequences of such processing for the Data Subject (Article 13(2)).

Where the Controller intends to further process the personal data for a purpose other than the one for which the data were collected, the Controller shall provide the Data Subject prior to that further processing with information on that other purpose and with any relevant further information as referred to in Article 13(2) (Article 13(3)).

Article 13(1), (2) and (3) shall not apply where and insofar as the Data Subject already has the information (Article 13(4)).

Right to Prior Information: Indirectly Obtained Data

29.29 Article 14 refers to information to be provided where the personal data have not been obtained from the Data Subject. Where personal data have not been obtained from the Data Subject, the Controller shall provide the Data Subject with the following information:

- the identity and the contact details of the Controller and, where applicable, of the Controller's representative;
- the contact details of the DPO, where applicable;
- the purposes of the processing for which the personal data are intended as well as the legal basis of the processing;
- the categories of personal data concerned;
- the recipients or categories of recipients of the personal data, if any;
- where applicable, that the Controller intends to transfer personal data to a recipient in a third country or international organisation and the existence or absence of an adequacy decision by the Commission, or in case of transfers referred to in Article 46 or 47, or the second subparagraph of Article 49(1), reference to the appropriate or suitable safeguards and the means to obtain a copy of them or where they have been made available (Article 14(1)).

In addition to the information referred to in Article 14(1), the Controller shall provide the Data Subject with the following information necessary to ensure fair and transparent processing in respect of the Data Subject:

- the period for which the personal data will be stored, or if this is not possible, the criteria used to determine that period;
- where the processing is based on Article 6(1)(f), the legitimate interests pursued by the Controller or by a third party;
- the existence of the right to request from the Controller access to and rectification or erasure of the personal data or restriction of processing of data concerning the Data Subject and to object to the processing as well as the right to data portability;
- where processing is based on Article 6(1)(a) or Article 9(2)(a), the existence of the right to withdraw consent at any time, without affecting the lawfulness of processing based on consent before its withdrawal;
- the right to lodge a complaint to a supervisory authority;
- from which source the personal data originate, and if applicable, whether it came from publicly accessible sources;
- the existence of automated decision making including profiling referred to in Article 22(1) and (4) and at least in those cases, meaningful information about the logic involved, as well as the significance and the envisaged consequences of such processing for the Data Subject (Article 14(2)).

The Controller shall provide the information referred to in Article 14(1) and (2):

- within a reasonable period after obtaining the personal data, but at the latest within one month, having regard to the specific circumstances in which the personal data are processed;
- if the personal data are to be used for communication with the Data Subject, at the latest at the time of the first communication to that Data Subject; or
- if a disclosure to another recipient is envisaged, at the latest when the personal data are first disclosed (Article 14(3)).

Where the Controller intends to further process the personal data for a purpose other than that for which the data were obtained, the Controller shall provide the Data Subject prior to that further processing with information on that other purpose and with any relevant further information as referred to in Article 14(2) (Article 14(4)).

Article 14(1)–(4) shall not apply where and insofar as:

- the Data Subject already has the information;
- the provision of such information proves impossible or would involve a disproportionate effort, in particular for processing for archiving purposes in the public interest, scientific or historical research purposes or statistical purposes, subject to the conditions and safeguards referred to in Article 89(1) or in so far as the obligation referred to in Article 14(1) is likely to render impossible or seriously impair the achievement of the objectives of that processing. In such cases the Controller shall take appropriate measures to protect the Data Subject's rights and freedoms and legitimate interests, including making the information publicly available;
- obtaining or disclosure is expressly laid down by EU or state law to which the Controller is subject and which provides appropriate measures to protect the Data Subject's legitimate interests; or
- where the personal data must remain confidential subject to an obligation of professional secrecy regulated by EU or state law, including a statutory obligation of secrecy (Article 14(5)).

Right of Confirmation and Right of Access

29.30   The Data Subject shall have the right to obtain from the Controller confirmation as to whether or not personal data concerning them are being processed, and where that is the case, access to the personal data and the following information:

- the purposes of the processing;
- the categories of personal data concerned;
- the recipients or categories of recipients to whom the personal data have been or will be disclosed, in particular recipients in third countries or international organisations;
- where possible, the envisaged period for which the personal data will be stored, or if not possible, the criteria used to determine that period;
- the existence of the right to request from the Controller rectification or erasure of personal data or restriction of processing of personal data concerning the Data Subject or to object to such processing;
- the right to lodge a complaint to a supervisory authority;
- where the personal data are not collected from the Data Subject, any available information as to their source;
- the existence of automated decision making including profiling referred to in Article 22(1) and (4) and at least in those cases, meaningful information about the logic involved, as well as the significance and the envisaged consequences of such processing for the Data Subject (Article 15(1)).

Where personal data are transferred to a third country or to an international organisation, the Data Subject shall have the right to be informed of the appropriate safeguards pursuant to Article 46 relating to the transfer (Article 15(2)).

The Controller shall provide a copy of the personal data undergoing processing. For any further copies requested by the Data Subject, the Controller may charge a reasonable fee based on administrative costs. Where the Data Subject makes the request by electronic means, and unless otherwise requested by the Data Subject, the information shall be provided in a commonly used electronic form (Article 15(3)).

The right to obtain a copy referred to in Article 15(3) shall not adversely affect the rights and freedoms of others (Article 15(4)).

Prior to the GDPR, the ICO issued recommendations in relation to data access, namely:

- Access to Information Held in Complaint Files;
- Enforced Subject Access (section 56);
- How to Disclose Information Safely – Removing Personal Data from Information Requests and Datasets;
- Regulatory Activity Exemption;
- Subject Access: Code of Practice;
- Subject Access: Responding to a Request Checklist.

These now need to be read in light of the GDPR changes.

Rectification and Erasure

29.31   Chapter III, Section 3 of the GDPR refers to rectification and erasure.

Prior to the GDPR, the ICO issued recommendations in relation to personal data deletion issues, namely:

- Deleting Personal Data.

This now needs to be read in light of the GDPR changes.

Right to Rectification

29.32 The Data Subject shall have the right to obtain from the Controller without undue delay the rectification of personal data concerning them. Taking into account the purposes of the processed, the Data Subject shall have the right to obtain completion of incomplete personal data completed, including by means of providing a supplementary statement (Article 16).

Right to Erasure (Right to be Forgotten) (RtbF)

29.33 The Data Subject shall have the right to obtain from the Controller the erasure and forgetting of personal data concerning them without undue delay and the Controller shall have the obligation to erase personal data without undue delay where one of the following grounds applies:

- the data are no longer necessary in relation to the purposes for which they were collected or otherwise processed;
- the Data Subject withdraws consent on which the processing is based according to Article 6(1)(a), or Article 9(2)(a), and where there is no other legal ground for the processing;
- the Data Subject objects to the processing pursuant to Article 21(1) and there are no overriding legitimate grounds for the processing, or the Data Subject objects to the processing pursuant to Article 21(2);
- the personal data have been unlawfully processed;
- the data have to be erased for compliance with a legal obligation in EU or state law to which the Controller is subject;
- the personal data have been collected in relation to the offer of information society services referred to in Article 8(1) (Article 17(1)).

Where the Controller has made the personal data public and is obliged pursuant to Article 17(1) to erase the personal data, the Controller, taking account of available technology and the cost of implementation, shall take reasonable steps, including technical measures, to inform Controllers which are processing the personal data that the Data Subject has requested the erasure by such Controllers of any links to, or copy or replication of, that personal data (Article 17(2)).

Article 17(1) and (2) shall not apply to the extent that processing is necessary:

- for exercising the right of freedom of expression and information;
- for compliance with a legal obligation which requires processing of personal data by EU or state law to which the Controller is subject or for the performance of a task carried out in the public interest or in the exercise of official authority vested in the Controller;
- for reasons of public interest in the area of public health in accordance with Article 9(2)(h) and (i) as well as Article 9(3);
- for archiving purposes in the public interest, scientific or historical research purposes or statistical purposes in accordance with Article 89(1) in so far as the right referred to in Article 17(1) is likely to render impossible or seriously impair the achievement of the objectives of that processing; or
- for the establishment, exercise or defence of legal claims (Article 17(3)).

Right to Restriction of Processing

29.34 Article 18 refers to the right to restriction of processing. The Data Subject shall have the right to obtain from the Controller the restriction of the processing where one of the following applies:

- the accuracy of the data is contested by the Data Subject, for a period enabling the Controller to verify the accuracy of the data;
- the processing is unlawful and the Data Subject opposes the erasure of the personal data and requests the restriction of their use instead;
- the Controller no longer needs the personal data for the purposes of the processing, but they are required by the Data Subject for the establishment, exercise or defence of legal claims;
- the Data Subject has objected to processing pursuant to Article 21(1) pending the verification whether the legitimate grounds of the Controller override those of the Data Subject (Article 18(1)).

Where processing has been restricted under Article 18(1), such personal data shall, with the exception of storage, only be processed with the Data Subject's consent or for the establishment, exercise or defence of legal claims or for the protection of the rights of another natural or legal person or for reasons of important public interest of the EU or of a state (Article 18(2)).

A Data Subject who obtained the restriction of processing pursuant to Article 18(1) shall be informed by the Controller before the restriction of processing is lifted (Article 18(3)).

Notification re Rectification, Erasure or Restriction

29.35 The Controller shall communicate any rectification or erasure of personal data or restriction of processing carried out in accordance with Articles 16, 17(1) and 18 to each recipient to whom the personal data have been disclosed, unless this proves impossible or involves disproportionate effort. The Controller shall inform the Data Subject about those recipients if the Data Subject requests it (Article 19).

Right to Data Portability

29.36 The Data Subject shall have the right to receive the personal data concerning them, which they have provided to a Controller, in a structured and commonly used and machine-readable format and have the right to transmit those data to another Controller without hindrance from the Controller to which the data have been provided, where:

- the processing is based on consent pursuant to Article 6(1)(a) or Article 9(2)(a) or on a contract pursuant to Article 6(1)(b); and
- the processing is carried out by automated means (Article 20(2)).

In exercising their right to data portability pursuant to Article 20(1), the Data Subject has the right to have the data transmitted directly from Controller to Controller where technically feasible (Article 20(2)).

The exercise of this right shall be without prejudice to Article 17. That right shall not apply to processing necessary for the performance of a task carried out in the public interest or in the exercise of official authority vested in the Controller (Article 20(3)).

The right referred to in Article 20(4) shall not adversely affect the rights and freedoms of others (Article 20(4)).

Right Against Automated Individual Decision Making

29.37 Chapter III, Section 4 of the GDPR refers to the right to object and automated individual decision making.

Right to Object

29.38 The Data Subject shall have the right to object, on grounds relating to their particular situation, at any time to processing of personal data concerning them which is based on Article 6(1)(e) or (f), including profiling based on these provisions. The Controller shall no longer process the personal data unless the Controller demonstrates compelling legitimate grounds for the processing which override the interests, rights and freedoms of the Data Subject or for the establishment, exercise or defence of legal claims (Article 21(1)).

Where personal data are processed for direct marketing purposes, the Data Subject shall have the right to object at any time to the processing of personal data concerning them for such marketing, which includes profiling to the extent that it is related to such direct marketing (Article 21(2)).

Where the Data Subject objects to the processing for direct marketing purposes, the personal data shall no longer be processed for such purposes (Article 21(3)).

At the latest at the time of the first communication with the Data Subject, the right referred to in Article 21(1) and (2) shall be explicitly brought to the attention of the Data Subject and shall be presented clearly and separately from any other information (Article 21(4)).

In the context of the use of information society services, and notwithstanding Directive 2002/58/EC,[46] the Data Subject may exercise their right to object by automated means using technical specifications (Article 21(5)).

Where personal data are processed for scientific or historical research purposes or statistical purposes pursuant to Article 89(1), the Data Subject, on grounds relating to their particular situation, shall have the right to object to processing of personal data concerning them, unless the processing is necessary for the performance of a task carried out for reasons of public interest (Article 21(6)).

Rights re Automated Individual Decision Making, Including Profiling

29.39 The Data Subject shall have the right not to be subject to a decision based solely on automated processing, including profiling, which produces legal effects concerning them or similarly significantly affects them (Article 22(1)).

Article 22(1) shall not apply if the decision:

- is necessary for entering into, or performance of, a contract between the Data Subject and a Controller [a];
- is authorised by EU or state law to which the Controller is subject and which also lays down suitable measures to safeguard the Data Subject's rights and freedoms and legitimate interests; or
- is based on the Data Subject's explicit consent (Article 22(1)) [c].

In cases referred to in Article 22(2) (a) and (c) the Controller shall implement suitable measures to safeguard the Data Subject's rights and freedoms and legitimate interests, at least the right to obtain human intervention on the part of the Controller, to express his or her point of view and to contest the decision (Article 22(3)).

Decisions referred to in Article 22(4) shall not be based on special categories of personal data referred to in Article 9(1), unless Article 9(2)(a) or (g) applies and suitable measures to safeguard the Data Subject's rights and freedoms and legitimate interests are in place (Article 22(4)).

---

46 Directive 2002/58/EC of the European Parliament and of the Council of 12 July 2002 concerning the processing of personal data and the protection of privacy in the electronic communications sector (Directive on privacy and electronic communications).

Communicating Data Breach to Data Subject

29.40   When a personal data breach is likely to result in a high risk to the rights and freedoms of natural persons, the Controller shall communicate the personal data breach to the Data Subject without undue delay (Article 34(1)).

The communication to the Data Subject shall describe in clear and plain language the nature of the personal data breach and contain at least the information referred to in Article 33(3)(b), (c) and (d) (Article 34(2)).

The communication to the Data Subject shall not be required if:

- the Controller has implemented appropriate technical and organisational protection measures, and those measures were applied to the personal data affected by the personal data breach, in particular those that render the personal data unintelligible to any person who is not authorised to access it, such as encryption;
- the Controller has taken subsequent measures which ensure that the high risk for the rights and freedoms of Data Subjects referred to in Article 34(1) is no longer likely to materialise;
- it would involve disproportionate effort. In such cases, there shall instead be a public communication or similar measure whereby the Data Subjects are informed in an equally effective manner (Article 34(3)).

If the Controller has not already communicated the personal data breach to the Data Subject, the supervisory authority, having considered the likelihood of the breach to result in a high risk, may require it to do so or may decide that any of the conditions referred to in Article 34(3) are met (Article 34(4)).

Security of Processing

29.41   Taking into account the state of the art, the costs of implementation and the nature, scope, context and purposes of the processing as well as the risk of varying likelihood and severity for the rights and freedoms of natural persons, the Controller and the Processor shall implement appropriate technical and organisational measures, to ensure a level of security appropriate to the risk, including inter alia, as appropriate:

- the pseudonymisation and encryption of personal data;
- the ability to ensure the ongoing confidentiality, integrity, availability and resilience of processing systems and services;
- the ability to restore the availability and access to personal data in a timely manner in the event of a physical or technical incident;
- a process for regularly testing, assessing and evaluating the effectiveness of technical and organisational measures for ensuring the security of the processing (Article 32(1)).

In assessing the appropriate level of security account shall be taken in particular of the risks that are presented by data processing, in particular from accidental or unlawful destruction, loss, alteration, unauthorised disclosure of, or access to personal data transmitted, stored or otherwise processed (Article 32(2)).

Adherence to an approved code of conduct pursuant to Article 40 or an approved certification mechanism pursuant to Article 39 may be used as an element to demonstrate compliance with the requirements set out in Article 32(1) (Article 32(3)).

The Controller and Processor shall take steps to ensure that any natural person acting under the authority of the Controller or the Processor who has access to personal data shall not process them except on instructions from the Controller, unless he or she is required to do so by EU or state law (Article 32(4)).

Representatives of Controllers Not Established in EU

29.42 Where Article 3(2) applies, the Controller or the Processor shall designate in writing a representative in the EU (Article 27(1)).

This obligation shall not apply to:

- processing which is occasional, does not include, on a large scale, processing of special categories of data as referred to in Article 9(1) or processing of personal data relating to criminal convictions and offences referred to in Article 10, and is unlikely to result in a risk for the rights and freedoms of natural persons, taking into account the nature, context, scope and purposes of the processing; or
- a public authority or body (Article 27(2)).

The representative shall be established in one of the states where the Data Subjects whose personal data are processed in relation to the offering of goods or services to them, or whose behaviour is monitored (Article 27(3)).

The representative shall be mandated by the Controller or the Processor to be addressed in addition to or instead of the Controller or the Processor by, in particular, supervisory authorities and Data Subjects, on all issues related to the processing, for the purposes of ensuring compliance with the GDPR (Article 27(4)).

The designation of a representative by the Controller or the Processor shall be without prejudice to legal actions which could be initiated against the Controller or the Processor themselves (Article 27(5)).

Chapter IV, Section 3 of the GDPR refers to Impact Assessments and Prior Consultations.

Data Protection Impact Assessment

29.43 Where a type of processing in particular using new technologies, and taking into account the nature, scope, context and purposes of the processing, is likely to result in a high risk for the rights and freedoms of natural persons, the Controller shall, prior to the processing, carry out an assessment of the impact of the envisaged processing operations on the protection of personal data. A single assessment may address a set of similar processing operations that present similar high risks (Article 35(1)).

The Controller shall seek the advice of the DPO, where designated, when carrying out a data protection impact assessment (Article 35(2)).

A data protection impact assessment referred to in Article 35(1) shall in particular be required in the case of:

- a systematic and extensive evaluation of personal aspects relating to natural persons which is based on automated processing, including profiling, and on which decisions are based that produce legal effects concerning the individual or similarly significantly affect the individual;
- processing on a large scale of special categories of data referred to in Article 9(1), or of data relating to criminal convictions and offences referred to in Article 10;
- a systematic monitoring of a publicly accessible area on a large scale (Article 35(3)).

The supervisory authority shall establish and make public a list of the kind of processing operations which are subject to the requirement for a data protection impact assessment pursuant to Article 35(1). The supervisory authority shall communicate those lists to the EDPB (Article 68(4)).

The supervisory authority may also establish and make public a list of the kind of processing operations for which no data protection impact assessment is required. The supervisory authority shall communicate those lists to the EDPB (Article 35(5)).

Prior to the adoption of the lists referred to above the competent supervisory authority shall apply the consistency mechanism referred to in Article 63 where such lists involve processing activities which are related to the offering of goods or services to Data Subjects or to the monitoring of their behaviour in several states, or may substantially affect the free movement of personal data within the EU (Article 35(6)).

The assessment shall contain at least:

- a systematic description of the envisaged processing operations and the purposes of the processing, including where applicable the legitimate interest pursued by the Controller;
- an assessment of the necessity and proportionality of the processing operations in relation to the purposes;
- an assessment of the risks to the rights and freedoms of Data Subjects referred to in Article 35(1); and
- the measures envisaged to address the risks, including safeguards, security measures and mechanisms to ensure the protection of personal data and to demonstrate compliance with the GDPR taking into account the rights and legitimate interests of Data Subjects and other persons concerned (Article 35(7)).

Compliance with approved codes of conduct referred to in Article 40 by the relevant Controllers or Processors shall be taken into due account in assessing the impact of the processing operations performed by such Controllers or Processors, in particular for the purposes of a data protection impact assessment (Article 35(8)).

Where appropriate, the Controller shall seek the views of Data Subjects or their representatives on the intended processing, without prejudice to the protection of commercial or public interests or the security of the processing operations (Article 35(9)).

Where the processing pursuant to Article 6(1)(c) or (e) has a legal basis in EU law, or the law of the state to which the Controller is subject, that law regulates the specific processing operation or set of operations in question, and a data protection impact assessment has already been carried out as part of a general impact assessment in the context of the adoption of this legal basis, Article 35(1) to (7) shall not apply unless states deem it to be necessary to carry out such an assessment prior to the processing activities (Article 35(10)).

Where necessary, the Controller shall carry out a review to assess if the processing is performed in accordance with the data protection impact assessment at least when there is a change of the risk represented by the processing operations (Article 35(11)).

Prior Consultation

29.44 The Controller shall consult the supervisory authority prior to the processing where a data protection impact assessment as provided for in Article 35 indicates that the processing would result in a high risk in the absence of measures taken by the Controller to mitigate the risk (Article 36(1)).

Where the supervisory authority is of the opinion that the intended processing referred to in Article 36(1) would infringe the GDPR, in particular where the Controller has insufficiently identified or mitigated the risk, it shall within a maximum period of eight weeks following the request for consultation give written advice to the Controller and, where applicable the Processor, and may use any of its powers referred to in Article 58. This period may be extended by six weeks, taking into account the complexity of the intended processing. The supervisory authority shall inform the Controller and, where applicable, the Processor, of any such extension within one month of receipt of the request for consultation together with the reasons for the delay. These periods may be suspended until the supervisory authority has obtained any information it has requested for the purposes of the consultation (Article 36(2)).

When consulting the supervisory authority pursuant to Article 36(1), the Controller shall provide the supervisory authority with:

- where applicable, the respective responsibilities of Controller, joint Controllers and Processors involved in the processing, in particular for processing within a group of undertakings;
- the purposes and means of the intended processing;
- the measures and safeguards provided to protect the rights and freedoms of Data Subjects pursuant to the GDPR;
- where applicable, the contact details of the DPO;
- the data protection impact assessment provided for in Article 35; and
- any other information requested by the supervisory authority (Article 36(3)).

States shall consult the supervisory authority during the preparation of a proposal for a legislative measure to be adopted by a national parliament, or of a regulatory measure based on such a legislative measure, which relates to the processing (Article 36(4)).

Notwithstanding Article 36(1), states' law may require Controllers to consult with, and obtain prior authorisation from, the supervisory authority in relation to the processing by a Controller for the performance of a task carried out by the Controller in the public interest, including processing in relation to social protection and public health (Article 36(5)).

As mentioned earlier, this area is likely to undergo a large variety of data law and related law changes in the coming years, and from a variety of sources apart from the UK. All of these will need to be carefully considered.

Chapter 30

Press and Data Protection

Introduction

30.01 While it may seem somewhat discrete to those more familiar with corporate and consumer data protection compliance issues, data protection practice in the press and media sphere is both interesting as well as important. Arguably, it gets less attention than it deserves. In fact, it is deserving of a volume dedicated specifically to the topic.

It raised issues of how journalism interests interface with the personal data rights of individuals. From one perspective there could be argued to be a clash of interests. There are also issues of parents and children at play in many media stories.

The Right to be Forgotten is also evident in the media sphere, and again there can sometimes be perceived to be a clash of interests.

This area is also clouded by media transgressions such as the phone hacking scandals as occurred by or on behalf of certain media entities. Some of the resulting cases are still ongoing into 2023. One of the fallouts is the Leveson Inquiry. The UK Leveson Report deals with (certain) data protection issues in detail, namely the recommendations relating to data protection and journalism. The evidence and issues are more fully described in Part H, 5 of the Report.

Exemption

30.02 The Data Protection Act 1998 (DPA 1998) s 32 (now repealed) referring to journalism activities, provided:

'(1) Personal data which are processed only for the special purposes are exempt from any provision to which this subsection relates if—
  (a) the processing is undertaken with a view to the publication by any person of any journalistic, literary or artistic material,
  (b) the data Controller reasonably believes that, having regard in particular to the special importance of the public interest in freedom of expression, publication would be in the public interest, and
  (c) the data controller reasonably believes that, in all the circumstances, compliance with that provision is incompatible with the special purposes.
(2) Subsection (1) relates to the provisions of—
  (a) the data protection principles except the seventh data protection principle,
  (b) section 7,
  (c) section 10,
  (d) section 12, and
  (e) section 14(1) to (3).

(3) In considering for the purposes of subsection (1)(b) whether the belief of a data Controller that publication would be in the public interest was or is a reasonable one, regard may be had to his compliance with any code of practice which—
    (a) is relevant to the publication in question, and
    (b) is designated by the [Secretary of State] by order for the purposes of this subsection.
(4) Where at any time ('the relevant time') in any proceedings against a data Controller under section 7(9), 10(4), 12(8) or 14 or by virtue of section 13 the data Controller claims, or it appears to the court, that any personal data to which the proceedings relate are being processed—
    (a) only for the special purposes, and
    (b) with a view to the publication by any person of any journalistic, literary or artistic material which, at the time twenty-four hours immediately before the relevant time, had not previously been published by the data Controller,
the court shall stay the proceedings until either of the conditions in subsection (5) is met.
(5) Those conditions are—
    (a) that a determination of the Commissioner under section 45 with respect to the data in question takes effect, or
    (b) in a case where the proceedings were stayed on the making of a claim, that the claim is withdrawn.
(6) For the purposes of this Act 'publish', in relation to journalistic, literary or artistic material, means make available to the public or any section of the public.'

Lord Lester of Herne Hill is referred to in the Report (p 1067) as having 'warned at length that, as drafted and because of cl 31, the DPA failed to implement the Directive and authorised interference by the press with the right to privacy in breach of Art 8 of the ECHR.'
At page 1068 of the Report, it refers to:

'Mr Coppel's arguments ... would be that on the current state of the UK authorities, s 32 fails to implement the Directive from which it derives, and is inconsistent with the relevant parts of the ECHR to which it is intended to give effect, because the relationship between privacy and expression rights has got out of balance. A proper balance is a fundamental obligation. The UK is therefore positively *required* to change the law to restore the balance. That is indeed Mr Coppel's own contention: that UK data protection law currently fails to implement our obligations, and that Lord Lester's concerns had proved to be prescient.'

The Report itself then states:

'2.11 Without going so far as that, even if the current balance were within the spectrum permitted by our international obligations, the argument could be expressed in terms that it is at an extreme end of that spectrum, and the UK can as a matter of law, and should as a matter of policy, restore a more even-handed approach, not least given the asymmetry of risks and harms as between the individual and the press.

2.12 Put at its very lowest, the point could be made that the effect of the development of the case law has been to push personal privacy law in media cases out of the data protection regime and into the more open seas of the Human Rights Act. This has happened for no better reason than the slowness of the legal profession to assimilate data protection law and, in the case of the judiciary, its greater familiarity with (and, he suggests, perhaps a preference for) the latitude afforded by the human rights regime over the specificity of data protection. But this, the argument goes, is undesirable because the data protection regime is much more predictable, detailed and sophisticated in the way it protects and balances rights, and significantly reduces the risks, uncertainties and expense of litigation concomitant on more open-textured law dependent on a court's discretion. Where the law has provided specific answers, the fine-nibbed pen should be grasped and not the broad brush. The balancing of competing rights in a free democracy is a highly sophisticated exercise; appropriate tools have been provided for the job and should be used.'

Leveson Recommendations

To the Ministry of Justice

30.03   The Leveson Report makes the following recommendations, namely:

'48. The exemption in section 32 of the Data Protection Act 1998 should be amended so as to make it available only where:49 (a) the processing of data is necessary for publication, rather than simply being in fact undertaken with a view to publication; (b) the data Controller reasonably believes that the relevant publication would be or is in the public interest, with no special weighting of the balance between the public interest in freedom of expression and in privacy; and (c) objectively, that the likely interference with privacy resulting from the processing of the data is outweighed by the public interest in publication.

49. The exemption in section 32 of the Data Protection Act 1998 should be narrowed in scope, so that it no longer allows, by itself, for exemption from:50 (a) the requirement of the first data protection principle to process personal data fairly (except in relation to the provision of information to the Data Subject under paragraph 2(1)(a) of Part II Schedule 1 to the 1998 Act) and in accordance with statute law; (b) the second data protection principle (personal data to be obtained only for specific purposes and not processed incompatibly with those purposes); (c) the fourth data protection principle (personal data to be accurate and kept up to date); (d) the sixth data protection principle (personal data to be processed in accordance with the rights of individuals under the Act); (e) the eighth data protection principle (restrictions on exporting personal data); and (f) the right of subject access. The recommendation on the removal of the right of subject access from the scope of section 32 is subject to any necessary clarification that the law relating to the protection of journalists' sources is not affected by the Act.

50. It should be made clear that the right to compensation for distress conferred by section 13 of the Data Protection Act 1998 is not restricted to cases of pecuniary loss, but should include compensation for pure distress.

51. The procedural provisions of the Data Protection Act 1998 with special application to journalism in: (a) section 32(4) and (5) (b) sections 44 to 46 inclusive should be repealed.

52. In conjunction with the repeal of those procedural provisions, consideration should be given to the desirability of including in the Data Protection Act 1998 a provision to the effect that, in considering the exercise of any powers in relation to the media or other publishers, the Information Commissioner's Office should have special regard to the obligation in law to balance the public interest in freedom of expression alongside the public interest in upholding the data protection regime.

53. Specific provision should be made to the effect that, in considering the exercise of any of its powers in relation to the media or other publishers, the Information Commissioner's Office must have regard to the application to a data Controller of any relevant system of regulation or standards enforcement which is contained in or recognised by statute.

54. The necessary steps should be taken to bring into force the amendments made to section 55 of the Data Protection Act 1998 by section 77 of the Criminal Justice and Immigration Act 2008 (increase of sentence maxima) to the extent of the maximum specified period; and by section 78 of the 2008 Act (enhanced defence for public interest journalism).

55. The prosecution powers of the Information Commissioner should be extended to include any offence which also constitutes a breach of the data protection principles.

56. A new duty should be introduced (whether formal or informal) for the Information Commissioner's Office to consult with the Crown Prosecution Service in relation to the exercise of its powers to undertake criminal proceedings.

57. The opportunity should be taken to consider amending the Data Protection Act 1998 formally to reconstitute the Information Commissioner's Office as an Information Commission, led by a Board of Commissioners with suitable expertise drawn from the worlds of regulation, public administration, law and business, and active consideration should be given in that context to the desirability of including on the Board a Commissioner from the media sector.'

To the ICO

30.04   The Leveson Report also makes recommendation to the ICO. These are:

'58. The Information Commissioner's Office should take immediate steps to prepare, adopt and publish a policy on the exercise of its formal regulatory functions in order to ensure that the press complies with the legal requirements of the data protection regime.

59. In discharge of its functions and duties to promote good practice in areas of public concern, the Information Commissioner's Office should take immediate steps, in consultation with the industry, to prepare and issue comprehensive good practice guidelines and advice on appropriate principles and standards to be observed by the press in the processing of personal data. This should be prepared and implemented within six months from the date of this Report.

60. The Information Commissioner's Office should take steps to prepare and issue guidance to the public on their individual rights in relation to the obtaining and use by the press of their personal data, and how to exercise those rights.

61. In particular, the Information Commissioner's Office should take immediate steps to publish advice aimed at individuals (Data Subjects) concerned that their data have or may have been processed by the press unlawfully or otherwise than in accordance with good practice.

62. The Information Commissioner's Office, in the Annual Report to Parliament which it is required to make by virtue of section 52(1) of the Act, should include regular updates on the effectiveness of the foregoing measures, and on the culture, practices and ethics of the press in relation to the processing of personal data.

63. The Information Commissioner's Office should immediately adopt the Guidelines for Prosecutors on assessing the public interest in cases affecting the media, issued by the Director of Public Prosecutions in September 2012.

64. The Information Commissioner's Office should take immediate steps to engage with the Metropolitan Police on the preparation of a long-term strategy in relation to alleged media crime with a view to ensuring that the Office is well placed to fulfil any necessary role in this respect in the future, and in particular in the aftermath of Operations Weeting, Tuleta and Elveden.

65. The Information Commissioner's Office should take the opportunity to review the availability to it of specialist legal and practical knowledge of the application of the data protection regime to the press, and to any extent necessary address it.

66. The Information Commissioner's Office should take the opportunity to review its organisation and decision-making processes to ensure that large-scale issues, with both strategic and operational dimensions (including the relationship between the culture, practices and

ethics of the press in relation to personal information on the one hand, and the application of the data protection regime to the press on the other) can be satisfactorily considered and addressed in the round.'

Increased Sentencing for Data Breach

30.05 The Leveson Report also makes other law recommendations. These are:

'67. On the basis that the provisions of s 77–78 of the Criminal Justice and Immigration Act 2008 are brought into effect, so that increased sentencing powers are available for breaches of s 55 of the Data Protection Act 1998.

68. The Secretary of State for Justice should use the power vested in him by s 124(1)(a)(i) of the Coroners and Justice Act 2009 to invite the Sentencing Council of England and Wales to prepare guidelines in relation to data protection offences (including computer misuse).'

Comparison

30.06 A comparison of the DPA 1998 and the Leveson comments is set out below.

DPA 1998 (s 32)	Leveson

(1) Personal data which are processed only for the special purposes are exempt from any provision to which this subsection relates if—
  (a) the processing is undertaken with a view to the publication by any person of any journalistic, literary or artistic material,
  (b) the data Controller reasonably believes that, having regard in particular to the special importance of the public interest in freedom of expression, publication would be in the public interest, and
  (c) the data Controller reasonably believes that, in all the circumstances, compliance with that provision is incompatible with the special purposes.
(2) Sub-s (1) relates to the provisions of—
  (a) the data protection principles except the seventh data protection principle,
  (b) s 7,
  (c) s 10,
  (d) s 12, and
  (e) s 14(1) to (3).
(3) In considering for the purposes of sub-s (1)(b) whether the belief of a data Controller that publication would be in the public interest was or is a reasonable one, regard may be had to his compliance with any code of practice which—
	48 The exemption in s 32 of the Data Protection Act 1998 should be amended so as to make it available only where:(a) the processing of data is necessary for publication, rather than simply being in fact undertaken with a view to publication; (b) the data Controller reasonably believes that the relevant publication would be or is in the public interest, with no special weighting of the balance between the public interest in freedom of expression and in privacy; and (c) objectively, that the likely interference with privacy resulting from the processing of the data is outweighed by the public interest in publication.
	49 The exemption in s 32 of the Data Protection Act 1998 should be narrowed in scope, so that it no longer allows, by itself, for exemption from: (a) the requirement of the first data protection principle to process personal data fairly (except in relation to the provision of information to the Data Subject under paragraph 2(1)(a) of Part II Schedule 1 to the 1998 Act) and in accordance with statute law; (b) the second data protection principle (personal data to be obtained only for specific purposes and not processed incompatibly with those purposes); (c) the fourth data protection principle (personal data to be accurate and

(a) is relevant to the publication in question, and

(b) is designated by the [Secretary of State]by order for the purposes of this sub-section.

(4) Where at any time ('the relevant time') in any proceedings against a data Controller under s 7(9), 10(4), 12(8) or 14 or by virtue of s 13 the data Controller claims, or it appears to the court, that any personal data to which the proceedings relate are being processed—

(a) only for the special purposes, and

(b) with a view to the publication by any person of any journalistic, literary or artistic material which, at the time twenty-four hours immediately before the relevant time, had not previously been published by the data Controller, the court shall stay the proceedings until either of the conditions in sub-s (5) is met.

(5) Those conditions are—

(a) that a determination of the Commissioner under s 45 with respect to the data in question takes effect, or

(b) in a case where the proceedings were stayed on the making of a claim, that the claim is withdrawn.

(6) For the purposes of this Act 'publish', in relation to journalistic, literary or artistic material, means make available to the public or any section of the public.

kept up to date); (d) the sixth data protection principle (personal data to be processed in accordance with the rights of individuals under the Act); (e) the eighth data protection principle (restrictions on exporting personal data); and (f) the right of subject access. The recommendation on the removal of the right of subject access from the scope of s 32 is subject to any necessary clarification that the law relating to the protection of journalists' sources is not affected by the Act.

50 It should be made clear that the right to compensation for distress conferred by s 13 of the Data Protection Act 1998 is not restricted to cases of pecuniary loss, but should include compensation for pure distress.

51 The procedural provisions of the Data Protection Act 1998 with special application to journalism in: (a) s 32(4) and (5); (b) ss 44 – 46 inclusive should be repealed.

52 In conjunction with the repeal of those procedural provisions, consideration should be given to the desirability of including in the Data Protection Act 1998 a provision to the effect that, in considering the exercise of any powers in relation to the media or other publishers, the Information Commissioner's Office should have special regard to the obligation in law to balance the public interest in freedom of expression alongside the public interest in upholding the data protection regime.

53 Specific provision should be made to the effect that, in considering the exercise of any of its powers in relation to the media or other publishers, the Information Commissioner's Office must have regard to the application to a data controller of any relevant system of regulation or standards enforcement which is contained in or recognised by statute.

Conclusion

30.07 The Data Protection Act 2018 (DPA 2018), s 177 makes provision for the ICO to produce guidance in relation to the steps needed in seeking redress in relation to media organisations. In addition, DPA 2018, s 179 states that the Secretary of State issue reports on the effectiveness of media related dispute resolution procedures. Schedule 17 also refers to reviews of processing of personal data for journalism purposes. As indicated above, there are important interests and rights involved in this space, and sometimes conflicts and litigation can arise. A larger volume is justified on these issues alone.

Chapter 31

Data Protection Officer

Introduction

31.01 Organisations are now required to have a Data Protection Officer (DPO). In addition, the role and task requirements are now more explicit. The DPO must also have an appropriate independence in their activities and cannot be compromised or dictated to in a manner which undermines their role and duties in relation to personal data. It is now clear that the profession of the independent and expert DPO has arrived.

Role of DPO

31.02 Chapter IV, Section 4 of the EU General Data Protection Regulation (GDPR) refers to the role and requirement of DPOs and the obligation for organisations to appoint DPOs.

The Controller and the Processor shall designate a DPO in any case where:

- the processing is carried out by a public authority or body, except for courts acting in their judicial capacity;
- the core activities of the Controller or the Processor consist of processing operations which, by virtue of their nature, their scope and/or their purposes, require regular and systematic monitoring of Data Subjects on a large scale;
- the core activities of the Controller or the Processor consist of processing on a large scale of special categories of data pursuant to Article 9 and personal data relating to criminal convictions and offences referred to in Article 10 (Article 37(1)).

Tasks and Role

31.03 The Controller or the Processor shall ensure that the DPO is involved, properly and in a timely manner in all issues which relate to the protection of personal data (GDPR Article 38(1)).

The DPO shall have at least the following tasks:

- to inform and advise the Controller or the Processor and the employees who carry out processing of their obligations pursuant to the GDPR and to other EU or state data protection provisions;
- to monitor compliance with the GDPR, with other EU or state data protection provisions and with the policies of the Controller or Processor in relation

to the protection of personal data, including the assignment of responsibilities, awareness-raising and training of staff involved in the processing operations, and the related audits;
- to provide advice where requested as regards the data protection impact assessment and monitor its performance pursuant to Article 35;
- to cooperate with the supervisory authority;
- to act as the contact point for the supervisory authority on issues related to the processing, including the prior consultation referred to in Article 34, and consult, as appropriate, on any other matter (Article 39(1)).

The DPO shall in the performance of their tasks have due regard to the risk associated with the processing operations, taking into account the nature, scope, context and purposes of the processing (Article 39(2)).

The DPO may fulfil other tasks and duties. The Controller or Processor shall ensure that any such tasks and duties do not result in a conflict of interests (Article 38(6)).

The DPO will also supervise, advise and/or assist in relation to PIAs and monitor performance and make recommendations. They will also monitor and deal with any requests from the supervisory authority and also be the designated contact for the supervisory authority.

It is important that the DPO has regard to the risks that may arise specific to the organisation in relation to personal data and processing issues (including security issues). Depending on the sector, there may also be a Code of Conduct and/or certification issues for the DPO to be also concerned with. Data protection seals and certification are meant to help organisations demonstrate compliance.

Group DPO

31.04   A group of undertakings may appoint a single DPO provided that a DPO is easily accessible from each establishment (Article 37(2)).

Where the Controller or the Processor is a public authority or body, a single DPO may be designated for several such authorities or bodies, taking account of their organisational structure and size (Article 37(3)).

In cases other than those referred to in Article 37(1), the Controller or Processor or associations and other bodies representing categories of Controllers or Processors may or, where required by EU or state law shall, designate a DPO. The DPO may act for such associations and other bodies representing Controllers or Processors (Article 37(4)).

Qualifications and Expertise of DPO

31.05   The DPO shall be designated on the basis of professional qualities and, in particular, expert knowledge of data protection law and practices and the ability to fulfil the tasks referred to in Article 39 (Article 37(5)).

The DPO may be a staff member of the Controller or Processor, or fulfil the tasks on the basis of a service contract (Article 37(6)).

Contact Details

31.06   The Controller or the Processor shall publish the contact details of the DPO and communicate these to the supervisory authority (Article 37(7)).

Data Subjects may contact the DPO on all issues related to the processing of the Data Subject's personal data and the exercise of their rights under the GDPR (Article 38(4)).

Reporting

31.07   The DPO shall directly report to the highest management level of the Controller or the Processor (Article 38(3)).

Independent in Role and Tasks

31.08   The Controller or Processor shall ensure that the DPO does not receive any instructions regarding the exercise of their tasks. He or she shall not be dismissed or penalised by the Controller or the Processor for performing their tasks (Article 38(3)).

Resources

31.09   The Controller or Processor shall support the DPO in performing the tasks referred to in Article 39 by providing resources necessary to carry out those tasks and access to personal data and processing operations, and to maintain his or her expert knowledge (Article 38(2)).

Review of DPOs

31.10   The EU data regulators and European Data Protection Board (which replaced the WP29) announced that they have launched a coordinated enforcement investigation into the role of DPOs. This was announced in an official statement in March 2023 as follows:[1]

> 'As intermediaries between DPAs, individuals and the business units of an organisation, data protection officers have an essential role in contributing to compliance with data protection law and promoting effective protection of data subject rights.'

It continues:

> 'To gauge whether DPOs have the position in their organisations required by Art 37–39 GDPR and the resources needed to carry out their tasks, participating DPAs will implement the CEF at national level in a number of ways:
>
> – DPOs will be sent questionnaires to aid fact-finding exercise or questionnaires to identify if a formal investigation is warranted;
> – commencement of a formal investigation;
> – follow-up of ongoing formal investigations.
>
> The results of the joint initiative will be analysed in a coordinated manner and the DPAs will decide on possible further national supervision and enforcement actions. In addition, results will be aggregated, generating deeper insight into the topic and allowing targeted follow-up at EU level. The EDPB will publish a report on the outcome of this analysis once the actions are concluded.'

The review process is intended to last for one year.

Data Protection and Digital Information (No 2) Bill

31.11   The Data Protection and Digital Information (No 2) Bill (DPDI Bill) in the UK refers to new concepts of 'senior responsible individual' and 'decision-makers'

---

1   See https://edpb.europa.eu.

(clauses 14 and 66). These should be consulted in relation to these changes and or overlap with the role or activities of the DPO.

Summary

31.12   In summary, organisations must designate a DPO to:

- monitor internal compliance with the GDPR regime and rules;
- ensure governance of the organisation's data management;
- draft and update compliant data protection policies;
- implement systems, changes and functions in terms of being compliant.

The DPO should be qualified and have particular expertise in data protection law and practice. They need to be able to fulfil their tasks in compliance and conformity with the GDPR. It appears they may be an employee or a contractor.

The DPO details must be made available publicly and the supervisory authority (such as the ICO) should be notified.

The organisation must involve the DPO in a timely manner in relation to all issues in relation to the protection of personal data and Data Subject issues. Proper and adequate resources must be supplied to the DPO by the organisation in order that they can undertake their tasks. There is an obligation that the DPO has independence in their role and functions, and that they cannot be controlled or micromanaged or instructed in relation to their tasks.

The DPO will report to the Board or highest management level as appropriate. This also emphasises the increasing importance attached to data protection understanding and compliance.

The DPO advises the organisation and employees in relation to their data protection obligations under national law and the GDPR. They will also monitor compliance with the data protection legal regime as well as internal policies. They will also be involved in assigning responsibilities, raising awareness and staff education and training.

DPOs should be highlighting the changes and the new GDPR to the organisation. Key issues need to be identified to appropriate management. New and ongoing change and compliance issues need appropriate resourcing. The DPO should assess what personal data the organisation collects and processes, for what purpose, and where it is located and secured. Particular attention is needed with regard to outsourcing issues and contracts with Processors. Contracts, including service level agreements in relation to IT systems, cloud, etc may be assessed. The various IT hardware, software and systems that employees use need to be considered.

The structure of the organisation needs to be considered, as well as jurisdiction and location issues. The life cycles, storage and disposal of personal data is also an important consideration for the new DPO.

The processes, policies and documentation must be maintained by the organisation, which places particular obligations on the DPO to consider the different documentation sets.

For further details see *The Data Protection Officer, Profession, Rules and Role*.[2] The ICO also provides commentary on the importance of the DPO.[3]

---

2   Paul Lambert, *The Data Protection Officer, Profession, Rules and Role* (Routledge, Taylor & Francis, 2017).

3   ICO, 'Data Protection Officers,' at https://ico.org.uk/for-organisations/guide-to-data-protection/guide-to-the-general-data-protection-regulation-gdpr/accountability-and-governance/data-protection-officers/.

Chapter 32

Additional Parties

Introduction

32.01 For a considerable time under the data protection regime the only parties that one had to consider were Controllers (and sometimes Processors acting for Controllers), the individual Data Subjects themselves, and sometimes the data regulator (eg ICO). In a number of areas, this is changing, and with significant consequences.

New Additional Parties

32.02 Increasingly there needs to be an awareness of new additional parties. These are:

- entities which may advocate on aspects of data protection policy and proposed data law changes, including to formal legislative processes and consultations;
- entities which may make complaints to data regulators and even take cases on behalf of individuals or groups of Data Subjects;
- entities which actually intervene in data litigation cases with a view to promoting societal, public or general Data Subject perspectives on the data issues being litigated.

In terms of the latter, there have always been occasional, even rare, instances of amicus briefs being permitted in certain legal cases. These interventions are becoming much more frequent in the case of data litigation. Having said that, there have also been recent interventions on both sides of the data litigation in question. For example, industry or representative bodies on the one side, and privacy advocacy groups on the other.

This demonstrates that while the instances of data litigation are increasing, so too are the number of parties involved. The same goes for interventions to try to influence the course of new data laws.

Impact

32.03 Some of these new parties and interventions are not merely academic – they can have a real impact. In some instances, the very course of data protection law and practice can be changed; and even international relations can be impacted.

There are examples of this which would have been hard to have contemplated just a few short years ago.

One example is the *Schrems v Data Protection Commissioner* case[1] (Schrems I) which related to data transfers to the US under the Safe Harbour arrangement, the Safe Harbour arrangement previously agreed between the EU and US was declared invalid. This all resulted from privacy advocates making complaints to the Irish data regulator, and ultimately being referred to the ECJ/CJEU.

Another case is the *Digital Rights Ireland* case[2] which successfully challenged the then Data Retention Directive as being overly broad and disproportionate.

The Schrems PRISM case[3] (*Schrems II*) successfully challenged the Privacy Shield arrangement agreed between the EU and US as a replacement for the earlier invalidated Safe Harbour.

The decision has important implications for companies and citizens in the UK, and (other) EU member states – not to mention the Commission and US authorities. Significant data transfers occur between the EU and US, and a large number (over 5,300) of US companies have registered in the US as being compliant with the EU–US Privacy Shield, and no doubt made representations to that effect to their EU business partners. (There was knock-on implications for the separate Swiss–US Privacy Shield, which was to a large extent modelled on the EU–US Privacy Shield.)

The issues at stake in *Schrems II* were the interpretation and legality of the:

● standard contractual clause data transfers (ie the EU SCC Decision providing for such contracts for data transfers); and
● Privacy Shield data transfers (ie the EU Privacy Shield Decision providing for such data transfers).

As indicated earlier, data transfers of personal data from inside the EU to outside it are subject to a default transfer ban (see GDPR Art 44). Only if a particular transfer can fit within one of the limited exemption or legitimising mechanisms may a data transfer become permissible.

The EU recognises a mechanism for data transfers from the EU to third countries based on standard contractual clauses (SCC) per the SCC Decision. These standard contracts are expressly provided for in the official decision,[4] and provide a legal mechanism for parties to provide a lawful mechanism for individualised data transfers by way of contracts incorporating particular clauses and safeguards specified by the Commission (the so-called SCC Decision).[5]

The *Schrems II* decision upholds the validity of the SCC Decision – and hence the existing data transfer contracts and clauses which are compliant with the SCC Decision. Data transfers can continue insofar as they are compliant with this transfer mechanism – but importantly new such contracts may have to be read in light on this new decision (see below). New data contracts will become more involved and

---

1   *Schrems v Data Protection Commissioner*, joined party: Digital Rights Ireland Ltd, Case C-362/14, ECJ, 6 October 2015.
2   *Digital Rights Ireland Ltd v Minister for Communications, Marine and Natural Resources and Kärntner Landesregierung*, Joined Cases C-293/12 and C-594/12, ECJ, 8 April 2014.
3   *Data Protection Commissioner v Facebook Ireland and Maximillian Schrems (Schrems II)*, Case C-311/18, ECLI:EU:C:2020:559, 16 July 2020.
4   In fact, and technically speaking, there are two such standard contract mechanisms. One refers to data transfers from a Controller to a Controller, and the other refers to data transfers from a Controller to a Processor. While only one of the SCC mechanisms is the focus in this case, there is growing commentary that the same principles elucidated in the case should apply to both mechanisms.
5   See the interpretation and validity of Commission Decision 2010/87/EU of 5 February 2010 on standard contractual clauses for the transfer of personal data to processors established in third countries under Directive 95/46 (OJ 2010 L 39, p 5), as amended by Commission Implementing Decision (EU) 2016/2297 of 16 December 2016 (OJ 2016 L 344, p 100). This is the Commission Decision 2010/87.

complicated as a result of the decision. Indeed, it would also be wise, if not recommended, for those with existing SCC contracts in place, particularly older ones, to review them. It may be that some or all existing SCC contracts may benefit from being updated or have further provisions added by way of supplementary agreement.

It will be recalled that the Privacy Shield was effectively a negotiated agreement between EU and US authorities providing a lawful data transfer mechanism for all data transfers by organisations signing up to the Privacy Shield registration process and thereby agreeing to regulate their data transfers in accordance with the Privacy Shield rules.

The need for the Privacy Shield arose as the result of an earlier data transfer mechanism known as the Safe Harbour arrangement being declared invalid.[6] The replacement Privacy Shield Decision[7] was effectively being challenged in *Shrems II*.

The case ultimately invalidated the Privacy Shield and the EU and US have had to come up with a third attempt to legitimise data transfers, now known as the Privacy Framework.

Decisions

32.04 The court invalidated the Privacy Shield in what is the most directly and immediately impactful part of the decision. The official summary states that:

> '[T]he Court examines the validity of Decision 2016/1250 in the light of the requirements arising from the GDPR, read in the light of the provisions of the Charter guaranteeing respect for private and family life, personal data protection and the right to effective judicial protection. In that regard, the Court notes that that decision enshrines the position, as did Decision 2000/520, that the requirements of US national security, public interest and law enforcement have primacy, thus condoning interference with the fundamental rights of persons whose data are transferred to that third country. In the view of the Court, the limitations on the protection of personal data arising from the domestic law of the United States on the access and use by US public authorities of such data transferred from the European Union to that third country, which the Commission assessed in Decision 2016/1250, are not circumscribed in a way that satisfies requirements that are essentially equivalent to those required under EU law, by the principle of proportionality, in so far as the surveillance programmes based on those provisions are not limited to what is strictly necessary. On the basis of the findings made in that decision, the Court pointed out that, in respect of certain surveillance programmes, those provisions do not indicate any limitations on the power they confer to implement those programmes, or the existence of guarantees for potentially targeted non-US persons. The Court adds that, although those provisions lay down requirements with which the US authorities must comply when implementing the surveillance programmes in question, the provisions do not grant data subjects actionable rights before the courts against the US authorities.'[8]

It continues that:

> 'As regards the requirement of judicial protection, the Court holds that, contrary to the view taken by the Commission in Decision 2016/1250, the Ombudsperson mechanism referred to in that decision does not provide data subjects with any cause of action before a body which offers guarantees substantially equivalent to those required by EU law, such as to ensure

---

6   *Schrems I*, Case C-3662/14, EU:C:2015:650.
7   Commission Implementing Decision (EU) 2016/1250 of 12 July 2016 pursuant to Directive 95/46 on the adequacy of the protection provided by the EU–US Privacy Shield (OJ 2016 L 207, p 1).
8   'The Court of Justice invalidates Decision 2016/1250 on the adequacy of the protection provided by the EU–US Data Protection Shield. However, it considers that Commission Decision 2010/87 on standard contractual clauses for the transfer of personal data to processors established in third countries is valid,' Court of Justice of the European Union, press release No 91/20, 16 July 2020.

both the independence of the Ombudsperson provided for by that mechanism and the existence of rules empowering the Ombudsperson to adopt decisions that are binding on the US intelligence services. On all those grounds, the Court declares Decision 2016/1250 invalid.'[9]

The court decision at para 5 (p 44) finds that:

'Commission Implementing Decision (EU) 2016/1250 of 12 July 2016 pursuant to directive 95/46/EC of the European Parliament and of the Council on the adequacy of the protection provided by the EU – US Privacy Shield is invalid.'

In *Schrems II* the court held:

'On those grounds, the Court (Grand Chamber) hereby rules:

1. Article 2(1) and (2) of Regulation (EU) 2016/679 of the European Parliament and of the Council of 27 April 2016 on the protection of natural persons with regard to the processing of personal data and on the free movement of such data, and repealing Directive 95/46/EC (General Data Protection Regulation), must be interpreted as meaning that that regulation applies to the transfer of personal data for commercial purposes by an economic operator established in a Member State to another economic operator established in a third country, irrespective of whether, at the time of that transfer or thereafter, that data is liable to be processed by the authorities of the third country in question for the purposes of public security, defence and State security.

2. Article 46(1) and Article 46(2)(c) of Regulation 2016/679 must be interpreted as meaning that the appropriate safeguards, enforceable rights and effective legal remedies required by those provisions must ensure that data subjects whose personal data are transferred to a third country pursuant to standard data protection clauses are afforded a level of protection essentially equivalent to that guaranteed within the European Union by that regulation, read in the light of the Charter of Fundamental Rights of the European Union. To that end, the assessment of the level of protection afforded in the context of such a transfer must, in particular, take into consideration both the contractual clauses agreed between the controller or processor established in the European Union and the recipient of the transfer established in the third country concerned and, as regards any access by the public authorities of that third country to the personal data transferred, the relevant aspects of the legal system of that third country, in particular those set out, in a non-exhaustive manner, in Article 45(2) of that regulation.

3. Article 58(2)(f) and (j) of Regulation 2016/679 must be interpreted as meaning that, unless there is a valid European Commission adequacy decision, the competent supervisory authority is required to suspend or prohibit a transfer of data to a third country pursuant to standard data protection clauses adopted by the Commission, if, in the view of that supervisory authority and in the light of all the circumstances of that transfer, those clauses are not or cannot be complied with in that third country and the protection of the data transferred that is required by EU law, in particular by Articles 45 and 46 of that regulation and by the Charter of Fundamental Rights, cannot be ensured by other means, where the controller or a processor has not itself suspended or put an end to the transfer.

4. Examination of Commission Decision 2010/87/EU of 5 February 2010 on standard contractual clauses for the transfer of personal data to processors established in third countries under Directive 95/46/EU of the European Parliament and of the Council, as amended by Commission Implementing Decision (EU) 2016/2297 of 16 December 2016 in the light of Articles 7, 8 and 47 of the Charter of Fundamental Rights has disclosed nothing to affect the validity of that decision.

5. Commission Implementing Decision (EU) 2016/1250 of 12 July 2016 pursuant to Directive 95/46/EC of the European Parliament and of the Council on the adequacy of the protection provided by the EU-US Privacy Shield is invalid.'

---

9   Ibid.

Implications

32.05   The immediate impact is that companies seeking to rely on these mechanisms as the lawful mechanism for the transfer of data to the US can no longer rely on it.

New companies seeking to legitimise data transfer from the EU to the US had to identify a Plan B given that the often preferred Plan A is now invalidated.

US companies may need, therefore, to engage with their EU partners to identify alternative legal routes where available. This may mean consideration of the standard contractual clauses route which has been recognised as legally valid by the court.

Invalidating the Privacy Shield has resulted in lots of headaches and complexity for companies, and for politicians. While a new arrangement has been put in place, known as the Privacy Framework, it shows that even small and ill resourced entities can have a large impact in the practice of data protection.

Brexit

32.06   One Brexit-related impact is that a number of commentators have been speculating on the current and proposed changes to the UK data protection regime and whether such changes will venture so far as to encourage some entity or entities to challenge transfers of data to the UK and or to challenge the EU–UK Adequacy Decision. The potential is that some of the practical headaches which arose in the EU challenges cannot be ruled out for the UK, but only time will tell.

Further considerations arise in terms of ascertaining the type of company or indeed industry sector involved, as certain companies may be treated differently for the purposes of US law and US law safeguards.

As is pointed out elsewhere in this edition, there are significant issues facing UK politicians in terms of assuring businesses that announced or intended post-Brexit law changes will no create unnecessary speedbumps with the EU. There would certainly be adverse consequences if, for example, UK business could not continue to trade as normal and receive EU data as part of its normal activities due to some new law changes. There is still a worry that post-Brexit UK law changes will be deemed to be too divergent from the EU GDPR (and wider corpus of EU data protection relevant laws), to result in legal challenges and ultimately resulting in the default data transfer ban kicking in. There is also a worry that too many UK law changes could undermine the UK Adequacy Decision received from the EU.

While applying for, processing and receiving an EU Adequacy Decision is time-consuming and complex, some commentators are suggesting after *Schrems II* that the UK will not at all be successful in obtaining an Adequacy Decision.

Mr Schrems, while deliberately avoiding a detailed view on Brexit, does state that after the decision there 'may be a huge problem for UK adequacy'.[10]

In that scenario, and even with a Brexit lens, firms regularly look to consider standard contracts as their means to legally continue to have data interactions with EU countries, or as a back up means in the event or problems arising a s a result of challenge issues. *Schrems II* offers assurance in this regard that this is a viable route – even if the complexity and level of detail required is now much more onerous.

Perhaps the lesson is that while a successful Adequacy Decision is aspired to, one cannot hold one's breath waiting on uncertain political and administrative processes. The standard contracts become a matter of primary practical importance. (Note also that for certain large organisations the additional route for inter-group international data transfers may lead towards the Binding Corporate Rules (BCRs) transfer mechanism for certain transfers.)

10   Interview with IAPP, 17 July 2019.

Conclusion

32.07   There are also other issues disclosed in the decision, such as the ability of national data protection regulators, to regulate data transfer. The decision suggests that there may indeed be positive obligations on such authorities to be proactive in policing data transfers which may not be adhering to or be permitted under the data protection regime.

However, the decision issues referred to above will require to be carefully monitored for further official guidance and potential official decisions on data transfers. At the same time, those proposing to engage in data transfers will need to examine the feasibility of contract mechanisms (and also BCC mechanisms) as appropriate. In addition, those with pre-existing executed standard contracts arrangements would be prudent to review their existing documentation. It may be that contracts or practice documentation might be enhanced further.

Vice-President Jourová states that '[w]hen personal data travels abroad from Europe, it must remain safe', but acknowledges that 'it is essential to have a broad toolbox for international transfers while ensuring a high level of protection for personal data'.[11]

The EU and US authorities are already in contact and will discuss the avenues available. It may, for example, be possible to consider a Privacy Shield 2.0 or other updated arrangement.

Commissioner Reynders adds that:

> 'In the meantime, transatlantic data flows between companies can continue using other mechanisms for international transfers of personal data available under the GDPR.

> 'We will work together with the national data protection to ensure a swift and coordinate response to the judgement. This is essential to provide European citizens and businesses with legal certainty.'[12]

The Vice President sets out priorities for considering and future replacement, namely:

- guaranteeing the protection of personal data transferred across the Atlantic;
- working constructively with our American counterparts with an aim of ensuring safe transatlantic data flows;
- working with the European Data Protection Board and national data protection authorities to ensure our international data transfer toolbox is fit for purpose.[13]

In addition, the Commission is already 'working intensively to ensure that this toolbox is fit for purpose, including the modernisation of the Standard Contractual Clauses'.[14] So we can also expect that new more enhanced clauses will be released sometime in the future.

Just to add one note of caution, however, there is a potential sting in the tail in the judgment to the extent that the court said that the (current) '[e]xamination of ... standard contractual clauses ... has disclosed nothing to affect the validity of that decision.' That is not a guarantee of permanent immunity from a future adverse decision.

---

11   "Opening remarks by Vice-President Jourová and Commissioner Reynders at the press point following the judgment in case C-311/18 Facebook Ireland and Schrems' Statement, 16 July 2020. At https://ec.europa.eu/commission/presscorner/detail/en/statement_20_1366.
12   Ibid.
13   Ibid.
14   Ibid.

Indeed, Mr Schrems already seemed to suggest after the judgment that if the clauses were seriously challenged they may fall too.[15]

Controllers and Processors should note that current best practice never stands still. A contact or practice which was legal last year may have to be reviewed, updated or replaced today. Legal compliance is an ongoing task – and as the judgment confirms, can become more onerous over time.

This is further emphasised by the judgment's requirement that the national data protection supervisory authorities must be (more) proactive in enforcing the rules of data protection.[16] From Mr Schrems' perspective, this was the most important issue decided.

Depending on the circumstances, there may also arise situations where companies might have to consider where data already transferred to the US may have to be returned or deleted, and consideration of the documentation surrounding such a deletion.

---

15 The comment is that they 'would be splattered in pieces too if they were.' Interview with IAPP, 17 July 2019.
16 See, for example decision [3], p 44.

Chapter 33

Other Data Protection Issues

Introduction

33.01 Data protection covers many separate but important topics. Many of these are directly relevant to many organisations. Unfortunately they cannot all be adequately covered in a book such as this. However, it may assist to briefly refer to some of these issues, and to convey at least to some extent the wide scope of the data protection regime. Quite simply, data protection affects every business, organisation and individual.

New Regime

33.02 The new GDPR/UK GDPR overhauls and modernises the data protection regime. Some of the specific changes and updates for organisations are highlighted in Part 5 of the book.

The whole area of transfers of personal data outside of the EEA (TBDFs or data transfers) is regularly changing, for example, as new countries are added to a white list of permitted export countries after having been examined on behalf of the EU Commission. There are also other changes such as contractual clauses and binding corporate rules (BCR) (and noting related updates in relation to the Privacy Framework, and the debate as to whether there are knock on consequences for contractual clauses and BCRs). If an organisation needs to consider the possibility of data transfer exports to non-EEA countries, the current most up to data transfer rules should be assessed, as well as appropriate professional advice. It may be necessary to have specific legal contracts in place. These rules may also be sector specific for certain industries eg airlines flying to US from Europe. The EDPB (previously WP29) is also an important resource for organisations.

Further topical issues are regularly being analysed by the EDPB (previously WP29). These issues may be consulted at, https://ec.europa.eu/justice/data-protection/article-29/index_en.htm, and also https://edpb.europa.eu/.

The Information Commissioners Officer's website should also be consulted regularly, at https://ico.org.uk/.

AI, ChatGPT, and Chatbots

33.03 Significant legal as well as media attention is focusing on the 'release' of new artificial intelligence or AI chat bots to the public. Some of the discussion relates to the capacity for advanced computer intelligence (or otherwise) of these new technologies. Other discussion refers to concerns, or rather worries, as to how these technologies could get out of hand, meaning get away from human oversight and control. There are other concerns, however. One of these squarely relates to the issue of data protection and personal data.

As a clear indication of these concerns, the Italian data supervisory authority has banned the use of ChatGPT in Italy. The UK ICO has also voiced concerns.[1] Stephen Almond, the ICO Executive Director for Regulatory Risk, made the following statement on 3 April 2023 namely, that: 'it is important to take a step back and reflect on how personal data is being used by' these new technologies. He continues:

> 'Organisations developing or using generative AI should be considering their data protection obligations from the outset, taking a data protection by design and by default approach. This isn't optional – if you're processing personal data, it's the law.

> Data protection law still applies when the personal information that you're processing comes from publicly accessible sources. If you're developing or using generative AI that processes personal data you need to ask yourself the following questions:

>> What is your lawful basis for processing personal data? If you are processing personal data you must identify an appropriate lawful basis, such as consent or legitimate interests.

>> Are you a controller, joint controller or a processor? If you are developing generative AI using personal data, you have obligations as the data controller. If you are using or adapting models developed by others, you may be a controller, joint controller or a processor.

>> Have you prepared a Data Protection Impact Assessment (DPIA)? You must assess and mitigate any data protection risks via the DPIA process before you start processing personal data. Your DPIA should be kept up to date as the processing and its impacts evolve.

>> How will you ensure transparency? You must make information about the processing publicly accessible unless an exemption applies. If it does not take disproportionate effort, you must communicate this information directly to the individuals the data relates to.

>> How will you mitigate security risks? In addition to personal data leakage risks, you should consider and mitigate risks of model inversion and membership inference, data poisoning and other forms of adversarial attacks.

>> How will you limit unnecessary processing? You must collect only the data that is adequate to fulfil your stated purpose. The data should be relevant and limited to what is necessary.

>> How will you comply with individual rights requests? You must be able to respond to people's requests for access, rectification, erasure or other information rights.

>> Will you use generative AI to make solely automated decisions? If so – and these have legal or similarly significant effects (eg major healthcare diagnoses) – individuals have further rights under Article 22 of UK GDPR.

> As the data protection regulator, we will be asking these questions of organisations that are developing or using generative AI. We will act where organisations are not following the law and considering the impact on individuals.'

These will form some of the biggest public facing discussions in the coming years, as will issues of data ethics, referred to below.

---

1   Milmo, D, and Hern, A, 'UK Watchdog Warns Developers Over Data Protection Laws,' *Guardian*, 3 April 2023.

AI, Big Data and Data Ethics

33.04   The government agreed to a proposal from the Science and Technology Committee to establish a 'Council of Data Science Ethics'. The government is developing an 'ethical framework for government data science'. The Committee issued a report entitled 'Report: The Big Data Dilemma' in February 2016, to which the government issued a response.

In addition, the government has also indicated that it does not at present have plans to introduce criminal penalties for serious data breaches, and will consider developments, including the new GDPR. The ICO had previously called for criminal sanctions on a number of occasions.

The government also confirmed that it will not introduce compulsory data protection audits of local authorities, as there is already ongoing progress in that area.

Nicola Blackwood, MP, the Chair of the Committee stated that:

'Big Data has enormous potential to improve public services and business productivity, but there are also justified privacy concerns when personal data is used in new applications, services and research. Getting the balance between the benefits and the risks right is vital.

I am pleased therefore that the Government has accepted our call to set up a "Council of Data Science Ethics" to address the growing legal and ethical challenges associated with balancing privacy, anonymisation of data, security and public benefit.'[2]

Medical and Health Data

33.05   Medical and health data comprise one of the categories of special personal data. Hence, there are greater conditions and compliance obligations. There is also a greater need for higher data security measures. The concerns in relation to medical and health data increase once such data is held in electronic form and electronic databases. There is a need for enhanced practical and security procedures.[3]

There are various and increasing forms of recording personal health and related data regarding individuals, held in databases or biobanks.[4] One of the concerns is also the increasing possibility for profiling individuals from bio-informatic and genetic data.[5] The issue of consent in relation to bio data and biobanks is an issue of increasing concern.[6]

There is controversy in relation to the apparent transfer of sensitive medical health data relating to 1.6 million patients. This involves current, historical and live feed

---

2   'Government Agree to set up "Council of Data Ethics,"' The Science and Technology Committee, available at http://www.parliament.uk/business/committees/committees-a-z/commons-select/science-and-technology-committee/news-parliament-2015/big-data-dilemma-government-response-15-16/. The report is at http://www.publications.parliament.uk/pa/cm201516/cmselect/cmstech/468/468.pdf; the government response is at http://www.publications.parliament.uk/pa/cm201516/cmselect/cmstech/992/99202.htm. The report is officially titled *House of Commons Science and Technology Committee, The Big Data Dilemma*, Fourth Report of Session 2015–16. The government response was published on 26 April 2016.

3   I Sandea, 'Analysis of the Legal Aspects Concerning Data Protection in Electronic Medical Registry,' *Applied Medical Informatics* (2009) (25) 16–20.

4   LA Bygrave, 'The Body as Data? Biobank Regulation via the "Back door" of Data Protection Law,' *Law, Innovation & Technology* (2010) (2) 1–25.

5   IM Azmi, 'Bioinformatics and Genetic Privacy: The Impact of the Personal Data Protection Act 2010,' *Computer Law & Security Review* (2011) (27) 394–401.

6   See, for example, J Taupitz and J Weigel, 'The Necessity of Broad Consent and Complementary Regulations for the Protection of Personal Data in Biobanks: What Can We Learn from the German Case?' *Public Health Genomics* (2012) (15) 263–271.

patient data. The transfer is being made by the Royal Free NHS Trust to DeepMind and/or Google UK Limited and or a third party, the details of which are redacted in an Information Sharing Agreement signed by one party on 29 September 2015.[7] The exact details are somewhat unclear. It is clear, however, that serious questions arise as to how the arrangement could be data protection complaint based on the details currently available, including lack of transparency in particular to the patients whose special personal data are involved. There does not appear to have been any opportunity or mechanism for patients to opt-in or to opt-out before any proposed data transfers. The purpose of the transfer and the details leading up to the transfer and arrangement are also unclear, which also undermines the possibility of fair, compliant processing. Fundamentally, the entire project relates to a new secondary use in relation to the medical data in question, which requires proper consideration and data protection compliance, which is not evident from the documentation thus far available. The data referred to is also of such a nature as to appear to go beyond the purported purpose thus far disclosed. One would expect any medical data being transferred for research – in particular names, address and other non-necessary information – to be redacted and or pseudononymised prior to transfer, which does not appear to have happened and which is not required in the Information Sharing Agreement.

While Big Data health projects can have benefits, and such projects can be worth the endeavour even without a successful end-resulting health benefit, they all need to be data protection complaint. Serious questions remain in relation to this project, and thus far compliance has not been demonstrated. In fact, the information disclosed in the Data Sharing Agreement and an official NHS Q&A document raise more questions than answers. It appears that on the basis of these documents to be non-data protection compliant.

Recently the ICO has commented on issues of data protection, contact tracing, and mobile applications as they relate to Covid-19.[8]

Genome Data

33.06 A related and growing area is genomic,[9] genome research, and the implications for individuals' privacy and personal data. Individuals may be concerned with what happens with their own DNA gene sequence, information regarding predispositions to diseases, how this may affect them, and how doctors, employers, insurers, and government may access and use such personal data. One resource relating to this area is *The Governance of Genetic Information, Who Decides?* by Widdows and Mulle.[10]

Body Scanners

33.07 The introduction of body scanning technology in airports has been controversial.[11] While the prime argument in favour relates to airline security and terrorism,

---

7   'DeepMind Rapped,' *New Scientist*, 8 July 2017; Powles, Julia, and Hodson, Hal, 'Google DeepMind and Healthcare in an Age of Algorithms,' Health and Technology (2017) (7:4) 351–367.
8   ICO, 'Apple and Google Joint Initiative on COVID-19 Contact Tracing Technology,' ICO (17 April 2020).
9   L Curren et al, 'Identifiability, Genomics, and UK Data Protection Law,' *European Journal of Health Law* (2010) (17) 329–344.
10 H Widdows and C Mullen, eds, 'Frontmatter, The Governance of Genetic Information, Who Decides?' *Cambridge Law, Medicine and Ethics* (2009).
11 See, for example, O Mironenko, 'Body Scanners Versus Privacy and Data Protection,' *Computer Law & Security Review* (2011) (27) 232–244.

not everyone is convinced, and those challenged to produce evidence of successful attacks prevented, have been less forthcoming.

The main controversy centres on the ability of the body scanners to provide a complete, graphic, internal and intrusive image of a person's naked body once they walk through the scanner. There are of course different types and different settings. However, the introduction of body scanners is a perfect example of the introduction of a new technology without considering the privacy and data protection implications in advance. Later versions of body scanners have been developed which produce a line image drawing, not a biological, naked representation. They are equally capable of highlighting contraband material. Privacy designed body scanners can be equally effective. While the original versions of body scanners were problematic, the more recent versions demonstrate that technology can be much more privacy- and data protection friendly when properly designed. The further lesson is that these considerations should be incorporated at the design stage – not after the product launches on the market.

Investigation, Discovery and Evidence

33.08 The issue of electronic evidence is important and critical, whether for the organisation or the Data Subject wishing to use such evidence. It is recommended that organisations consider these issues proactively in advance rather than hoping to be able to deal with them adequately in a reactive manner.

The new data protection regime also sets higher obligations in terms of the need for more extensive record keeping. While data regulators are already looking at some of these new sets of documentation, it is only a matter of time before data plaintiffs and privacy groups focus more attention on these documents.

The *Morrisons* case record seems to suggest certain avenues where further documentation may have assisted the court.[12]

Recently, the Information Commissioner commented that '[o]ur work needs to meet the civil and criminal standards of evidence gathering and recovery of it is to be useful.'[13] Business in taking and defending claims in relation to data protection will face increasing calls to ensure appropriate diligence in the data records existing and available, and of the data gaps that may exist.

Cloud/Metaverse

33.09 The popularity of cloud computing and virtualisation services and related forecasts of a metaverse with users, enterprise and increasingly official organisations is increasing. However, there are real concerns in relation to privacy, data protection, data security,[14] continuity, discovery, liability, record keeping, etc.[15] One commentator

---

12 *Various v Morrison* (rev 1) [2017] EWHC 3113 (QB) (1 December 2017); *Various v Morrison* [2020] UKSC 12 (1 April 2020).

13 Information Commissioner, 'ICO opening remarks – The Commitee on Civil Liberties, Justice and Home Affairs (LIBE) of the European Parliament – Hearing on the Facebook/Cambridge Analytica case' (4 June 2018).

14 See for example, C Soghoian, 'Caught in the Cloud: Privacy, Encryption, and Government Back Doors in the Web 2.0 Era,' *Journal of Telecommunications & High Technology Law* (2010) (8) 359–424. Also note U Pagallo, 'Robots in the Cloud with Privacy: A new Threat to Data Protection?' *Computer Law & Security Report* (2013)(29:5) 501.

15 ICO, *Guidance on the Use of Cloud Computing*, at https://ico.org.uk; Article 29 Working Party, *Opinion 05/2012 on Cloud Computing*, WP 196, 1 July 2012; P Lanois, 'Caught in the Clouds: The Web

refers to cloud computing as 'the privacy storm on the horizon.'[16] Any organisation considering cloud services needs to carefully consider the advantages, disadvantages, assessments and contract assurances that will be required. Such organisations, as well as the service operators, also need to assure themselves as to how they ensure data protection compliance.

New Hardware Devices, New Software

33.10   The arrival of new devices, from smartphones, combined devices and even communications devices on devices (such as RFID tags), emphasise that organisations need to be much more aware and considered in their policies and risk assessments under the data protection regime. Gaming and new headset devices (eg VR) will increase and will raise many new issues, including for personal rights, consent, representations and personal data.

The software used in new facial recognitions technology is just one example of how device development and software development will continually bring new services, but also new data protection challenges. The ICO points out that facial recognition – including live facial recognition (LFR) – needs to be appreciated as containing not just personal data, but also biometric data. The ICO also reiterates that compliance with the data rules applies to law enforcement authorities as well as more commercial entities.[17]

Internet of Things

33.11   The beginning of the so called Internet of Things (IoT) or connected devices era is now well heralded. However, the full consideration of the data protection implications are yet to be fully outlined. Organisations need to appreciate the implications for employees, users and also their compliance systems. Manufacturers are assisted in identifying and reducing these risks by the new risk and assessment tools of the EU General Data Protection Regulation (GDPR).

On-Site/Off-Site

33.12   Organisations have to tackle the issues presented by employees not just working on-site, but also travelling and working at home or other locations off-site. This trend will likely increase even following the Covid-19 pandemic. This can impact, for example, the security and security risks regarding the personal data collected and

---

2.0, Cloud Computing, and Privacy?' *Northwestern Journal of Technology and Intellectual Property* (2010) (9) 29–49; FM Pinguelo and BV Muller, 'Avoid the Rainy Day: Survey of US Cloud Computing Caselaw,' *Boston College Intellectual Property & Technology Forum* (2011) 1–7; IR Kattan, 'Cloudy Privacy Protections: Why the Stored Communications Act Fails to Protect the Privacy of Communications Stored in the Cloud,' *Vandenburg Journal of Entertainment and Technology Law* (2010–2011) (13) 617–656.

16   AC DeVere, 'Cloud Computing: Privacy Storm on the Horizon?' *Albany Law Journal* (2010) (20) 365–373.

17   ICO, 'The Use of Live Facial Recognition Technology by Law Enforcement in Public Places', 31 October 2019.

processed by the organisation. It also means that devices may be taken off-site and or that third party devices may exist and which are utilised to access the organisation's systems remotely.

Note also the EDPB document:

- Guidelines 3/2019 on processing of personal data through video devices.

Online Abuse

33.13 The increasingly evident problem of online abuse such as cyberbullying, trolling, defamation, copying and utilising personal data to abuse and blackmail children, teenagers, etc, are issues which need to be considered by all organisations, as well as policymakers. Pierre Trudel, for example, notes that the risks to individuals increase from many online activities, including in relation to data protection, safety, etc.[18]

The Information Commissioner comments more generally that websites 'can be held liable for their misuse of personal data.' She adds that '[t]hese organisations have control over what happens with an individual's personal data and how it is used to filter content – they control what we see, the order in which we see it, and the algorithms that are used to determine this. Online platforms can no longer say that they are merely a platform for content; they must take responsibility for the provenance of the information that is provided to users.'[19]

'Data crimes are real crimes,' states the Information Commissioner.[20]

The final version of the much discussed Online Safety Bill will bear detailed review and consideration.

Drones

33.14 As much as there is a new GDPR data protection regime, there are also new rules and regulations being developed in relation to drones. Drones now have to be registered in more and more jurisdictions, However, the privacy and data protection implications, while being highlighted in general discussion, are not yet adequately encompassed in express privacy and data protection rules. There will be increasing calls to do so, as well as increasing examples of why such an accommodation is needed. A number of headline issues are raised by drones, including privacy and data protection, drones as transport or delivery vehicles, and the interference and malicious use of drones (such as at airports).

Note also the EDPB document:

- Guidelines 1/2020 on processing personal data in the context of connected vehicles and mobility related applications.

---

18 P Trudel, 'Privacy Protection on the Internet: Risk Management and Networked Normativity,' in S Gutwirth, Y Poullet, P de Hert, C de Terwange and S Nouwt, *Reinventing Data Protection?* (Springer, 2009) 317.

19 Information Commissioner, 'ICO opening remarks – The Committee on Civil Liberties, Justice and Home Affairs (LIBE) of the European Parliament – Hearing on the Facebook/Cambridge Analytica case' (4 June 2018).

20 Ibid.

Increasing Actions

33.15 There will be increasing enforcement and fines facing organisations when compliance goes wrong and also when data breach incidents arise. In addition to the actions of regulators such as the ICO, there will also be increasing actions from individual Data Subjects, class actions and representative organisations. While this might occur most frequently where financial data or special data are concerned, it will not be limited to these areas. For example, there are already examples of data breach and data loss in relation to Internet of Things devices and services which open up new areas of exposure.

Codes and Certification

33.16 Two of the innovations contained within the GDPR relate to the possibility of organisations demonstrating their compliance (whether in whole or in part) by use of complying with established Codes of Practice (see GDPR Article 40) and or with particular Certification mechanisms (see GDPR Article 42).

The ICO accepts inquiries and applications for the recognition of such codes and certification, and the respective bodies which would administer and operate such schemes.[21]

This is likely to be one of the growing areas of data protection compliance.

Politics

33.17 The Cambridge Analytical scandal was a shock to many, in terms of how so much private personal data could be collected without knowledge, transparency or consent, and then used for data analytical purposes with a view to political user profiling and ultimately political influence manipulation, Various actions were initiated by data regulators as well as policymakers. This Information Commissioner has indicated that the ICO's investigation was the largest data regulatory investigation thus far, and involved detailed cooperation with other data regulators internationally. The Commissioner comments that 'we have seen that the behavioural advertising ecosystem has been applied across to political campaigning to influence how we vote. I am deeply concerned that this has happened without due legal or ethical consideration of the impacts to our democratic system.'[22]

While a number of significant data fines have been issued and detailed reports have been published, one should not assume that there are not more shoes to drop, nor that further investigation and problem issues need to be dealt with.

Conclusion

33.18 Data protection compliance is never a one size fits all or a single one time policy document. The nature of what amounts to personal data and the activities to which such data can be processed for are ever changing. Those within an organisation,

---

21 ICO, 'ICO Codes of Conduct and Certification Schemes Open for Business,' ICO (28 February 2020).

22 Information Commissioner, 'ICO opening remarks – The Committee on Civil Liberties, Justice and Home Affairs (LIBE) of the European Parliament – Hearing on the Facebook/Cambridge Analytica case' (4 June 2018).

therefore, need to be constantly alert to compliance issues and changes. Organisations also need to be constantly alert to new issues and dangers generally, and also those hot button issues specific to their sector. Significantly, greater attention and resources are needed to also deal with security, data breaches and data protection compliance.

The Information Commissioner states, '[t]he spotlight is well and truly on data protection ... We need a sustained willingness by citizens to exercise their data protection rights. We need data protection authorities unafraid to use our new tools, sanctions and fining powers.' Businesses and organisations – and their advisors – need to be ready to meet this new challenge.

Appendices

Reference

Information Commissioner's Office:
https://ico.org.uk/
European Data Protection Board:
https://edpb.europa.eu/
Society of Computers and Law:
http://www.scl.org
International Journal for the Data Protection Officer, Privacy Officer and Privacy Counsel:

Legislative Links

Data Protection Act 2018:
https://www.legislation.gov.uk/ukpga/2018/12/enacted General Data Protection Regulation: http://ec.europa.eu/justice/data-protection/reform/files/regulation_oj_en.pdf

Forms and Documents Links

Notification self assessment guides:
https://ico.org.uk

Complying with Data Protection

All organisations collect and process at least some personal data as defined under the Data Protection Act 2018 (DPA 2018) and the data protection regime. Therefore, an organisation must ensure it only collects and processes personal data if complying with:

- the obligation to only collect and process personal data if in compliance with the DPA 2018;
- the updated data protection Principles;
- the updated Lawful Processing Conditions;
- the updated Special Personal Data Lawful Processing Conditions;

- the separate consideration to the processing of children's personal data;
- the security and risk conditions;
- the data breach notification conditions and incident management;
- the new Data Protection by Design and by default obligations;
- the new accountability obligations;
- data protection impact assessment and risk assessment;
- the personal data outsourcing and data processor conditions;
- the personal data transfer ban and restrictions and standards;
- the individual data subject rights, including access, deletion, right to be forgotten, etc;
- queries, audits and investigation orders from the ICO;
- the time limits for undertaking various tasks and obligations.

Objections to Marketing

Jay[1] provides the following suggestions for organisations when dealing with access requests/marketing objections, namely,

- does the objection relate to marketing or another form or processing?
- does it relate to direct marketing within the definition?
- is it in writing or sent electronically or oral?
- if it is not in writing or electronic is it appropriate to deal with it as sent or should the individual be require to put it in writing or send it by electronic means?
- at which branch or office was it received?
- on what date was the request received?
- has the individual making the request given an intelligible name and address to which the controller can respond?
- when does the period for response expire?
- what time scale has the individual specified to stop marketing processing on a notice?
- what marketing processing is affected?
- is more time needed to comply with the requirement?
- how is the marketing data held? Is it manual or automated or some of both?
- does the objection apply to manual or automated?
- has the individual described the data?
- has the individual described the processing?
- has the individual explained why unwarranted damage and distress would be caused?
- on what grounds are the data being processing?
- can one of the primary grounds be claimed?
- does the notice amount to a revocation of an existing consent?
- is it possible to comply with the objection?
- is processing about others affected?
- would compliance mean system changes?

---

1   Jay and Hamilton, *Data Protection: Law and Practice*, (London: Sweet and Maxwell, 2007), pp 436–437.

Audit Checklist

Morgan and Boardman[2] refer to the audits. Their checklists include for example:

Extent of Audit

- what parts of the organisation and its files and systems have been audits and for what reason?
- are they likely to be sufficient to give an indication of the organisation's overall data protection compliance or not?

Classes of Personal Data Audited

- computer
- email
- other letter/memo files
- internet
- intranet
- manual (relevant filing system)
- video (scanned images, CCTV, photographic, film)
- audio (contract, training, voicemail)
- biometric
- other categories of personal data (eg tachograph)
- types of Personal Data
- is there personal data or not?
- if yes, is the personal data sensitive personal data?
- or accessible personal data?
- is any of the personal data confidential? eg medical/financial? If so, what are the consequences of this and what are individuals told about this?
- is there any automatic or automated processing of personal data? If so, what are the consequences of this and what are individuals told about this?
- are there any cookies? If so, how are they used?

Types of Data Subject

- staff
- retired staff
- staff spouses or other family members
- embers of the public
- customers
- prospective customers
- business contacts, which may include,
  - sole traders or partnerships, who are identifiable individuals and so data subjects; or
  - managers or other individual office holders in those bodies the organisation has contracts with?

'Owner' of Personal Data

- who?
- any 'private' files?

---

2   Morgan, R, and Boardman, R, *Data Protection Strategy, Implementing Data Protection Compliance*, (London: Sweet and Maxwell, 2012), pp 78 onwards.

- how are private emails handled?
- what, if any, of the data is processed by a data processor?
- what personal data is received from another organisation?
- what personal data is shared with one or more other organisations?
- does the organisation process data itself on behalf of others, as a data processor?

Purposes of Processing

- how and why is the personal data collected?
- what information is given to individuals about this, how and when?
- how well does the data's use match the purposes for which it is collected?
- does the organisation carry out direct marketing? If so, how?
- does it subscribe to 'preference' service?
- what or whom ensures that the personal data are accurate?
- what are the consequences if the personal data is inaccurate?
- how long is it kept?
- what happens to it when it is no longer used?
- what are the criteria for its destruction?
- is it in fact destroyed: if so, who does this and how do they do it?

Contracts

- data processing contracts
- data sharing contracts
- contracts involving personal data outside of the EEA
- fair obtaining warranties

Security of Personal Data

- physical security
- staff security
- what standards accreditation does the organisation have?
- system security – eg passwords, firewalls, etc
- what about portable media eg Laptops, memory sticks, CDs, etc?
- procedures for sending secure faxes – and emails – for sensitive personal data?
- is there any use of wireless transmission wi-fi?
- security with data processors
- how were they selected?
- was their security checked?
- how is it guaranteed by the data processor and documented?
- is there any ongoing review processing?

Sending Outside EEA?

- files?
- emails?
- internet material?
- intranet material?

Cookies

- which?
- from where?
- how intrusive?

Noting also of course the updates and clarifications of the new EU General Data Protection Regulation (GDPR) require separate additional audit and record processes for the data protection impact and risk impact assessments.

Procedures

Morgan and Boardman[3] refer to processes and procedures in relation compliance and ongoing compliance. The queries checklist includes for example:

Procedures and Procedures

- what industry/trade association guidance is available?
- what published processed and procedures are there in respect of personal data?
- how are they brought to the attention of staff others?
- how enforced?
- how updated?
- who is responsible for this?
- how does he/she fit into the organisations structure?

Data Protection Notification/Registration

- has the organisation notified?
- if not, why does it consider itself exempt?
- is the notification consistent with the personal data identified by the audit?
- purposes?
- is the notification up to date?
- how is the notification kept up to date?

Data Subjects' Rights

- what Procedures are in place to deal with requests in connection with data subjects rights?
- how has it worked so far?
- any problems with identifying a particular individual in the personal data?
- are the Information Commissioner's Codes (eg CCTV, employment practice, data sharing) followed?

People

- who is in charge of data protection?
- what resources does he/she have?
- how is he/she supported by senior management?
- what if any disciplinary action has been taken in respect of data protection?

Information Commissioner Office (ICO)

- apart from notification/registration, has the organisation ever had any dealings with the ICO? If so, what and when and with what particular results?

Obviously in future, risk issues and risk assessments will be very important.

---

3   Morgan, R, and Boardman, R, *Data Protection Strategy, Implementing Data Protection Compliance*, (London: Sweet and Maxwell, 2012), pp 80 onwards.

Index

[all references are to paragraph number]

A

Abuse
employee monitoring, 17.07
generally, 33.13
social media, 29.10
Access right
data subject's rights, 29.27–29.30
dealing with requests, 9.07
GDPR, and, 9.06
generally, 9.05
Accuracy
overview, 1.19
Additional parties
amicus briefs, and, 32.02
Brexit, 32.06
conclusion, 32.07
decisions, 32.04–32.05
EU/UK Adequacy Decision, 32.06
EU/US mechanisms, 32.03–32.05
impact, 32.02
introduction, 32.01
meaning. 32.02
Privacy Framework, 32.03
Privacy Shield arrangement,
32.03–32.04
Safe Harbour arrangement, 32.03
Schrems decisions, 32.03–32.04
Adequate protection
transfer of personal data, 21.03
Amicus briefs
additional parties, and, 32.02
Anonymised data
transfer of personal data, 21.16
Artificial intelligence (AI)
Big Data, 33.04
Chatbots, 33.03
ChatGPT, 33.03
data ethics, 33.04
Assessment notices
destroying or falsifying information
and documents, 20.04
generally, 20.04
limitations, 20.05
restrictions, 20.05
Audits
request, 20.08
Automated calling systems
ePrivacy Directive, 22.04

B

Automated decision taking
data subject's rights
generally, 9.16, 9.29–9.30, 26.66
introduction, 9.14
right to object, 9.15, 9.29
social media, 29.22, 29.37–29.39
employee data protection regime
introduction, 15.09
object, to, 15.10
profiling, 15.11
social media
generally, 29.39
introduction, 29.22, 29.37
right to object, 29.38

B

Big data
generally, 33.04
Binding corporate rules
definition, 3.03
generally, 21.11
WP29 documents, 21.07
Biometric data
definition, 3.03
employee considerations, 16.08
Blocking
generally, 9.01
social media, 29.21
Blogs
social media, 29.15
sources of law, 2.18
Body scanners
generally, 33.07
Breaches of rules
data processing activities, 11.03
generally, 11.02
other consequences, 11.04
Brexit
additional parties, and, 32.06
background, 24.07
compliance, 24.13
conclusion, 24.19
DPA 2018, and, 24.02
EDPB guidance, 24.14
EDPS guidance, 24.14
employee monitoring and human rights,
17.14–17.15

Index

Index

Index

Index

Index

Index

Index